PROFESSIONS IN ETHICAL FOCUS

PROFESSIONS IN ETHICAL FOCUS

AN ANTHOLOGY

 *nd edition*

EDITED BY

*Fritz Allhoff, Jonathan Milgrim,
and Anand J. Vaidya*

broadview press

BROADVIEW PRESS — www.broadviewpress.com
Peterborough, Ontario, Canada

Founded in 1985, Broadview Press remains a wholly independent publishing house. Broadview's focus is on academic publishing; our titles are accessible to university and college students as well as scholars and general readers. With 800 titles in print, Broadview has become a leading international publisher in the humanities, with world-wide distribution. Broadview is committed to environmentally responsible publishing and fair business practices.

Library and Archives Canada Cataloguing in Publication

Title: Professions in ethical focus : an anthology / edited by Fritz Allhoff, Jonathan Milgrim, and
  Anand J. Vaidya.
Names: Allhoff, Fritz, editor. | Milgrim, Jonathan, editor. | Vaidya, Anand, editor.
Description: 2nd edition. | Includes bibliographical references.
Identifiers: Canadiana (print) 20200211064 | Canadiana (ebook) 20210171340 | ISBN 9781554814442
  (softcover) | ISBN 9781770488069 (PDF) | ISBN 9781460407554 (EPUB)
Subjects: LCSH: Professional ethics.
Classification: LCC BJ1725 .P764 2021 | DDC 174—dc23

Broadview Press handles its own distribution in North America:
PO Box 1243, Peterborough, Ontario K9J 7H5, Canada
555 Riverwalk Parkway, Tonawanda, NY 14150, USA
Tel: (705) 743-8990; Fax: (705) 743-8353
email: customerservice@broadviewpress.com

For all territories outside of North America, distribution is handled by Eurospan Group.

Canada

Broadview Press acknowledges the financial support of the Government of Canada for our publishing activities.

Copy edited by Tania Therien
Book design by Michel Vrana

PRINTED IN CANADA

CONTENTS

UNIT 7: PROFESSIONALISM, DIVERSITY, AND PLURALISM

UNIT 8: PROFESSIONALISM IN A GLOBAL CONTEXT

UNIT 9: CLIENT-BASED PROFESSIONS

CONTENTS, ORGANIZED BY PROFESSION

LAW

MEDICINE

MILITARY

POLICE

POLITICS/LEADERSHIP

PUBLIC RELATIONS

RELIGION

INTRODUCTION

WHY STUDY PROFESSIONAL ETHICS?

Fritz Allhoff, Jonathan Milgrim, and Anand J. Vaidya

IN THIS VOLUME, WE WILL OFFER VARIOUS READings on professional ethics: professional ethics is a branch of applied ethics which, in turn, is part of philosophical ethics (and, thereafter, philosophy) more generally. But this raises an interesting question, which is whether professional ethics are really necessary at all. For we already have general moral theory; for example, utilitarianism, which says that the right actions are the ones that maximize total aggregate happiness. If utilitarianism is correct, then a professional ethic would seem irrelevant or superfluous because we already have the tools to obligate the professional in this moral framework without invoking any further professional ethic. Perhaps, then, the lawyer should represent the needy client because so-doing would maximize happiness (let us assume that an exoneration would, in fact, do this). Similarly, the non-lawyer need not represent the client because such representation would not likely be successful and therefore not maximize happiness. In other words, we get the same results (*viz.*, obligation for the lawyer and no obligation for the non-lawyer) through our espousal of a general moral theory as we would have gotten with a role-differentiated morality: does this render the latter irrelevant or superfluous?

Some people certainly think so, and this skepticism will be apparent through some of the readings in this volume. Alternatively, some people think not, and that line of argumentation will also present itself. Or indeed we might take some intermediate stance wherein *even if* the professional ethic can be subsumed under general moral philosophy, there is still something to be gained by tending to the issues that present themselves within professional contexts; this might not give us a metaphysically independent professional ethic but nevertheless license our forthcoming investigations.

* * *

This second edition of *Professions in Ethical Focus* comprises seventy-eight readings about professional ethics, complemented by twenty case studies. Readers of the first edition will notice a substantial change. In that edition, we had grouped the readings by profession, focusing on five: accounting, engineering, journalism, law, and medicine. These professions have been the most fertile, as well as historically important, in the development of professional ethics. But the decade between the two editions has seen an explosion of interest in other professions as well.

With this in mind, we have substantially broadened the coverage in this edition to include professions not previously represented: education, military, negotiation, nursing, police, public relations, religion, scientific research, social work, and software design. This list is not meant to be comprehensive, but rather to identify core issues in professional ethics, which are instantiated in specific contexts. By studying those contexts, students will gain a greater understanding of the field of professional ethics as a whole, as well as explore particular interests they may have.

Of course, this list raises just as many questions as it answers. What, exactly, *is* a profession? Does everything on the list even count? Following the seminal treatment of Ernest Greenwood (reprinted in this volume), professions have: (1) systematic theory, (2) authority, (3) community sanction, (4) ethical codes, and (5) cultural norms. Thinking through what these criteria mean in practice will take some articulation, but it is a good list to keep in mind from the outset.

We have also reorganized the volume by theme, or ethical issue, rather than by profession. Each unit begins with broadly theoretical approaches that are then applied to particular professions. The point here is to pursue the theoretical approaches to inform what the particular applications, or professions, *have in common*, so that we don't have to figure out, from scratch, what's at stake in every profession. However, professions differ in important ways and the profession-specific readings will help elucidate those differences. We hope this approach is attractive to instructors—as well as students!—but to allow for flexibility we have also supplemented the new thematic table of contents with a profession-by-profession table of contents.

* * *

We begin the volume with readings on ethical principles and practice: while a course on professional ethics need not also be an in-depth course on ethical theory, it will be useful to get some standard views on the table from the outset. The second unit then considers the question mentioned above: what is a profession? And the third considers the complementary concept of professional responsibility: aside from what a profession *is*, what are professionals' *responsibilities*, and are they incurred merely in virtue of professionals' roles? These three units set the stage for more specific investigations.

The middle units consider, respectively, conflicts of interest (Unit 4); honesty, deception, and trust (Unit 5); and privacy and confidentiality (Unit 6). These issues show up across myriad different professions, if not in all of them.

Units 7 and 8 are completely new and represent a principal innovation with this second edition. Unit 7 is entitled "Professionalism, Diversity, and Pluralism" and considers issues arising from a more diverse professional workforce, as well as a workforce with often incompatible worldviews. On the former, we have included readings on sexual harassment and affirmative action. On the latter, we have included readings on religious toleration and LGBT+ accommodations. These contemporary issues found in the professional environment raise a host of nuanced and complicated theoretical problems. Unit 8 then extends some of these issues to the international context, recognizing that much of our professional lives may now transcend national borders. What changes in the international—it as opposed to domestic—context, if anything? How does our global connectedness inform our approaches to professional ethics?

The last two units, 9 and 10, explore *particular professions*, providing overviews of their attendant ethical issues. These units provide an opportunity for emerging (if, as yet, inchoate) fields to participate in the dialogue. These readings have been tentatively divided into "client-based" and "institution-based" professions, though the unit introductions make clear that this distinction is provisional at best—and untenable at worst. But, as a first approximation, it seems uncontroversial that some professions are constructed around clienteles (e.g., physicians, lawyers), whereas others are not (e.g., militaries, scientific researchers). The point isn't that the latter aren't beholden to anyone—at a minimum they're beholden to society at large—but rather that they are structurally different.

As previously mentioned, each unit comprises both primary-source readings and case studies. The case studies are meant to complement the more theoretical readings, often pulling recent controversies from the headlines. The case studies have discussion questions for in-class conversations. Each unit also has a unit introduction, summarizing both the issues in the unit in general and the individual selections in particular. We think that these three elements—unit introductions, readings, and case studies—provide a user-friendly format that allows students to access and understand important themes in professional ethics. Finally, as Broadview is a Canadian publisher and this volume stands to be adopted at various Canadian institutions, we have included several case studies and readings that are particularly Canadian in focus. However, we have done so without narrowing the overall focus of the book; it is still otherwise very much contemporary and global in orientation.

* * *

We would like to thank several people who have made this project possible. Sandra Borden, Michael Davis, and Michael Pritchard—three very distinguished professional ethicists—provided copious feedback on early drafts of contents. The unit-based model allowed us to assemble an excellent team of unit editors, who edited the readings assigned to their units—for concision, thematic coherence, and so on—as well as wrote unit introductions. For their efforts, we thank: Anna Bates, T.J. Broy, Jill Gatfield, Luke Golemon, Alexander Hoffmann, Erika Versalovic, and Kyle Yrigoyen. Jill also used the first edition of the book, and provided important feedback through developmental reviews of the second edition's contents. Several of the case studies were co-developed with *Business Cases in Ethical Focus*—a text consisting wholly of case studies—and we thank that text's co-editor, Alex Sager, for his collaboration. Also, we thank our editor at Broadview, Stephen Latta, for commissioning this project and providing excellent feedback along the way. Penultimately, we thank the production staff at Broadview for clearing copyrights, copy-editing the manuscript, and assembling it into its final form. Finally, we thank you, the readers of this volume, and wish you the best in your studies of professional ethics.

ETHICAL PRINCIPLES AND PRACTICE

Jonathan Milgrim

1. INTRODUCTION

AN IMPORTANT FIRST STEP IN EXPLORING PROFES-sional ethics is to understand what is meant by ethics in general. It is quick and easy to explain ethics as the study of morality, or the determination of what constitutes right versus wrong. The more interesting, and much more difficult line of inquiry is determining how we decide what constitutes a right action or what makes something wrong. There might be the intuition to equate ethical behavior with what is legal. That intuition quickly falls apart under scrutiny. For example, we generally think that infidelity is wrong, but not illegal. Or, we may associate right and wrong with what we learned from our parents (a form of ethical theory called cultural relativism), but this also falls apart when we consider that not all parents teach their kids the same lessons. Trying to answer these questions about what makes something right or wrong, good or bad, moral or immoral, falls into the realm of ethical theories.

It is important to note that "theories" is plural, because there is no one, agreed-upon answer to these questions. Some ethical theories are complementary, while others seem to stand in opposition to each other. How then, are we to decide what actions are morally permissible? The answer is both depressing and hopeful. On one hand, there are questions about which there are widespread disagreements. However, most theories find workable levels of concession about what is right

or wrong, despite their internal disagreements. For example, if I steal my neighbor's television simply because it is better than mine and I want it, every serious ethical theory would condemn my actions. They may arrive at the answer by a different method, but the answer would be the same. This is often due to shared ethical principles.

Ethical principles are generalized ideals. Some common examples are respect for human life, respect for autonomy, beneficence, nonmaleficence, and justice. While there is some disagreement about what is meant by some principles, in general there is enough agreement that these principles can be seen as ideals that cross theoretical boundaries. Although, they may be, and often are, prioritized quite differently. As we explore the various issues related to professional ethics, we will see that it is the ethical principles that are addressed, while ethical theories remain primarily in the background. However, it remains important to have a minimal level of understanding regarding the various ethical theories, as they motivate ethical principles and help explain the different priorities placed on them. With that in mind, the first unit attempts to give a brief survey of ethical theories as a foundation for the units that follow.

2. CONTENTS

The first article of the unit, "Some Approaches to Determining Ethical Obligations" by Robert Audi, provides an overview of the major ethical theories in Western thought. This article was written with the business professional as the target audience, but it works well for professional ethics as a whole. This is followed by excerpts from what are arguably the two most famous and influential works in ethics, *Groundwork for the Metaphysics of Morals* by Immanuel Kant and *Utilitarianism* by John Stuart Mill. These excerpts are by no means comprehensive, but when paired with the summary by Audi they should give the reader a basic understanding of the two most influential ethical theories.

A few short decades ago, the discussion of ethical theories could have ended after John Stuart Mill. However, there is now a recognition that discussions dominated by male and Western thought are missing something important. The next reading in the unit, "The Ethics of Care as Moral Theory" by Virginia Held, addresses this by first critiquing the more individualistic theories and then arguing for a more interdependent understanding of the human experience. This is followed by "What Can Eastern Philosophy Teach Us about Business Ethics?" by Daryl Koehn and

"Toward an African Moral Theory" by Thaddeus Metz. These readings help introduce a non-Western perspective—a necessary perspective as professions become more global than ever before.

The unit readings conclude with "Reflective Equilibrium" by Yuri Cath and "Sophie's Choice" by John P. Anderson. In "Reflective Equilibrium," Cath lays out the process by which we poll our intuitions and develop ethical principles that was first articulated by John Rawls. The final article by Anderson serves to demonstrate how we use ethical theories and principles to determine the right course of action in situations where all the choices seem bad. For his purposes, he used the famous story of Sophie having to choose between her children when given an ultimatum by a Nazi doctor in the book *Sophie's Choice* by William Styron.

The unit is rounded out with two famous case studies, "The Trolley Problem," based on Judith Jarvis Thomson's work, and the "Alligator River Story." Both cases provide an opportunity to check intuitions and to compare how the decisions might be different depending on which ethical theory or principle is prioritized.

—1—

SOME APPROACHES TO DETERMINING ETHICAL OBLIGATIONS

Robert Audi

UTILITARIANISM

FOR JOHN STUART MILL (THE GREATEST NINE-teenth-century English philosopher), the master utilitarian principle is roughly this: choose that act from among your options which is best from the twin points of view of increasing human happiness and reducing human suffering:

> The creed which accepts as the foundation of morals "utility" ... holds that actions are right in proportion as they tend to promote happiness, wrong as they tend to produce the reverse of happiness. By happiness is intended pleasure, and the absence of pain.[1]

This formula does not tell us when an act is right, period; but the idea is that right acts contribute at least as favorably to the "proportion" of happiness to unhappiness (in the relevant population) as any alternative the agent has. Thus, if one act produces more happiness than another, it is preferable, other things equal. If the first also produces suffering, other things are not equal. We have to weigh good consequences of our projected acts against any bad consequences and, in appraising a prospective act, subtract its negative value from its positive value.

Utilitarianism calls for maximization. To see why producing even a *lot* of good may not be not ethically sufficient, consider two points: (1) the more we have of what is good—good in itself, *basically* good—the better; (2) it is a mistake to produce less good than we can or, correspondingly, to reduce what is bad less than we can. Arguably, no good person would act suboptimally if this could be avoided. Ideally, then, we would simultaneously produce pleasure and reduce pain. Often we cannot do both. A situation may be so dire that reducing pain is all we can do. For utilitarianism, although some people are better candidates to be made happy—or less unhappy—everyone matters morally.

On the plausible assumption that total happiness is best served by maintaining minimal well-being for the worst off, utilitarianism supports welfare capitalism. But it does not automatically support any highly specific position on the obligations of business. One might otherwise if one identifies utilitarianism with the idea that ethics requires our producing the "greatest good for the greatest number." One reason utilitarianism does *not* imply any such thing is that great benefits (hence much good) to some, say college students, could quantitatively outweigh even the

3

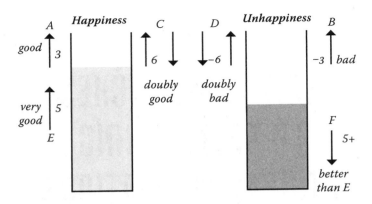

Figure 1 Utilitarianism: Six types of act scored in terms of maximizing the "'ratio" of the good (represented by the lighter shading) to the bad (represented by the darker shading). The containers represent the "quantities" of the good (happiness) and the bad (unhappiness) in the population (possibly all persons) whose well-being concerns the utilitarian. The letters represent acts considered; the length of the accompanying arrows—and the positive or negative numbers beside the acts—represent the positive or negative change in quantity of well-being the acts produce in the indicated direction. Act A is good; B is bad (hence its negative score). For acts C and D, let the left arrow represent the change produced in the [happiness] level and the right arrow represent the change produced in the unhappiness level. C, then, is doubly good, since it both increases happiness and decreases unhappiness; D is doubly bad, since it does the opposite. E is better than A, since it produces more happiness. Our obligation is to maximize the difference between the levels, favoring happiness (the lighter shading) over unhappiness (the darker shading). For a qualified utilitarian view that weights reducing unhappiness higher than increasing happiness, F might be better than E even if they produce the same net change in the ratio of the good to the bad.

greatest benefits a business or government could provide for a larger number of people, say by tax cuts for the whole population. Figure 1 makes this clear: the former, educational policy, could raise the *overall* happiness level (or lower the unhappiness level, or both) more than the latter, tax relief legislation, regardless of the smaller number of beneficiaries of the educational policy.

How utilitarianism apparently supports welfare capitalism over other economic systems needs explanation. Here is a possible account. Arguably, businesses will contribute most favorably to human happiness (roughly, to the proportion of happiness to unhappiness in the world) by simply making a profit in a fair system of competition and paying taxes at a level high enough to support effective welfare programs and low enough to preserve incentives to gain wealth. For—given the incentives this arrangement might provide for talented people—it might not only support welfare programs

but also lead to miracle drugs, fuel-efficient cars, superior fertilizers, and the like. Utilitarians may also argue that—at least if business leaders are utilitarians—then for both economic and ethical reasons, businesses operating in a welfare capitalist system will also contribute to the overall well-being of society through voluntary contributions, such as support for community projects, education, and the arts.

RIGHTS-BASED ETHICS

A very different ethical approach takes off from the idea that the main ethical demand is that we act within our rights and accord other people theirs. On this view, right action is simply action within one's rights, whereas wrong action violates rights. Rights may be negative, for instance rights *not* to be harmed or deprived of free expression, or positive, say rights to be given what is promised you,

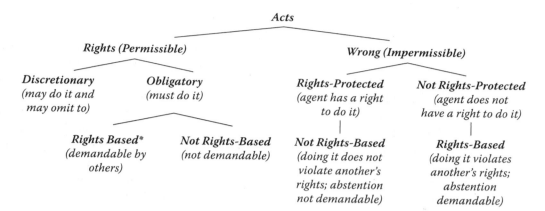

Figure 2 This figure shows an ethical classification of acts indicating how a rights-based ethics views obligation: our obligations lie *only* within others' rights against us. Most other ethical views recognize *wrongs within rights*, i.e., violations of obligations to others by acts that are *not* within their rights against us. Note that many right acts are discretionary (e.g., having coffee as opposed to tea) rather than obligatory (e.g., keeping a promise). Rights-based obligations—the *only* obligations under a rights-based ethics—lie in the starred category. Wrongs within rights are shown in the *rights-protected* category; e.g., giving nothing to charity may be wrong, though within one's rights and not *demandable* by charities. Unlike promise-keeping, it is a non-rights-based obligation and may be wrong, though within one's rights and not *demandable* by charities.

including such things as emergency medical treatment if the government has guaranteed it. *Roughly speaking*, negative rights coincide with liberties, positive rights with entitlements to benefits.

From this perspective we can see how someone might ask: Why should businesses *have* to contribute to the well-being of society by doing anything positive for society? What right does government have to force taxation for this purpose, as opposed to police and military protection? Granted, our property rights are limited by obligations to support some government programs, most notably policing and defense, but once businesses pay their fair share of taxes for these, why should they do more?

To this view, utilitarians and other *good-based* theorists may reply that even if businesses have a *right* not to do more, in the sense that their freedom not to do more should not be abridged by *compulsion*, they *ought* to do more. The plausible ethical point here is that a rights-based morality is unduly narrow. It takes what we ought (morally) to do to be only what we have no right not to do—presumably because someone else has a

right to demand our doing it, in the sense that our not doing it violates that person's rights. All else is discretionary, as shown in Figure 2. In reality, however, we can and do distinguish between what we ought and ought not to do even *within* the sphere of our rights. Take a simple example: relations with coworkers. Our coworkers have a right to some consideration, say to being given at least minimal cooperation, but we *ought* to do more to support them than the minimum they can claim as their right.

It is not just utilitarians who think that ethics calls on us to do things we have a right not to do. This will be apparent from an outline of two other plausible and widely held ethical views: Kantianism and virtue ethics.

KANTIAN ETHICS

The great eighteenth-century German philosopher Immanuel Kant held that we should always act in such a way that we can rationally will the principle we are acting on to be a universal law:

So act as if the maxim of your action [that is, the principle of conduct underlying the action] were to become through your will a universal law of nature.

This "Categorical Imperative" implies that I should not leave someone to bleed to death on the roadside if I could not rationally will the universality of the practice—say, even where *I* am the victim. We would not want to universalize, and thus live by, the callous principle: one should stop for someone bleeding to death provided it requires no self-sacrifice. Similarly, I should not make a lying promise to repay borrowed money if I could not rationally universalize my underlying principle, say that when I can get money only by making a lying promise, I will do this. One way to see why the Imperative apparently disallows this is to note that we *count on* promises from others and cannot rationally endorse the universality of a deceitful promissory practice that would victimize us.

Kant also gave a less abstract formulation of the Categorical Imperative:

Act so that you use humanity, as much in your own person as in the person of every other, always at the same time as an end and never merely as a means.

The idea is roughly that we must treat people as valuable in themselves, never merely as means to some end of ours. We are never to *use* people—including low-level, readily replaceable employees—as in manipulatively lying to them. Treating people as ends clearly requires caring about their good. They matter as persons, and we must at times and to some extent act for *their sake*, whether or not we benefit from it.

VIRTUE ETHICS

Virtue ethics differs from both utilitarianism and Kantianism in not being *rule centered*. Instead of proposing rules of conduct, it demands that we concentrate on being good as persons. Be honest,

just, kind, and honorable, for instance. Thus, the ancient Greek philosopher Aristotle described just acts as the kind that a just person would perform. He did not define a just person as one who performs just acts, nor as one who follows certain rules. He apparently considered moral traits of character ethically more basic than moral acts and moral rules. He said, regarding the types of acts that are right: "Actions are called just or temperate when they are the sort that a just or temperate person would do." Similar virtue-ethical ideas are also found in non-Western traditions, such as Confucian ethics, especially as represented by the ancient Chinese philosopher Mencius.

For a virtue ethics, then, agents and their traits, as opposed to rules of action, are morally basic. Virtue ethics would have us ask both what kind of person we want to be and how we want to be seen by those we care about, say friends and family. Who wants to be (correctly) seen as cheap, insensitive, or even just indifferent to others' suffering? Who does not want to be seen as generous, caring, and fair?

One could say that virtue ethics endorses *be-rules* (be just, be honest, be kind) in contrast with *do-rules* (keep your promises). But, suggestive as it is, this contrast is misleading since be-rules do not make clear reference to *how* to fulfill their demands. We cannot fulfill be-rules without some prior knowledge of what to *do*. (It is because this point is understood that virtue ethics is often seen to require a good upbringing with definite kinds of acts prescribed for children.) The positive idea underlying virtue ethics is that we are to understand what it is to behave justly through studying the nature and tendencies of the just person, not the other way around. We do not, for instance, define just deeds as those that, say, treat people equally, and then define a just person as one who characteristically does such deeds.

Thus, for adults as well as for children, and in ordinary life as in business, *role models* are absolutely crucial for moral learning. Virtue ethics is indeed a kind of ethics of role modeling: good role models are *sources*, as well as potential teachers, of ethical standards. Rules of action can be formulated by generalizing from observations of virtuous agents, such as team leaders in a sales division; but the basic ethical standard is character rather than rules of action.

One value of the virtue approach to business ethics is that leadership in business is partly a role-modeling function. To call for conduct of any kind—but especially ethical conduct—when we do not exhibit it ourselves is at best unlikely to succeed and often hypocritical too. Good role modeling, as any major ethical view can stress, is both instructive and motivating.

COMMON-SENSE ETHICAL PLURALISM

Many readers will find something plausible in each of the approaches just sketched. Might a less abstract, more definite view capture much of the best in each? Utilitarianism above all requires good deeds; rights-based views stress respecting freedom, keeping commitments, and protecting property; Kantianism demands respecting others and acting on principles that accord with this respect; and virtue ethics demands such ethical decisions as are made by people who are, say, just, honest, and beneficent. There are many standards here, but they are not too numerous to be reflected in ordinary principles that morally decent people teach their children and generally follow.

These ordinary ethical principles (1) prohibit injustice, harming others, lying, and breaking promises and (2) positively, call for doing good deeds toward others and for efforts toward self-improvement. They do not require *maximizing* good consequences, but do require at least certain good deeds we can do without great self-sacrifice. Thus, fraudulent accounting, as lying, is prohibited; providing for employees' healthcare, up to some reasonable point, is, as doing good deeds, an obligation of most companies.

Most people find these principles intuitively plausible, and the view that such principles are directly knowable on the basis of reflection on their content—intuitively knowable—is called *ethical intuitionism*. It is considered a common-sense view because these and a few other principles seem to be a commonsensical core toward which the best ethical theories converge....

Many who reflect on ethics find something of value in all the approaches just described, especially virtue ethics, Kantianism, and utilitarianism. Might a single wide principle include much of their content and encompass much of the common-sense plurality of obligations just indicated? There are apparently at least three conceptually independent factors that a sound ethical view should take into account: happiness, which we may think of as welfare conceived in terms of pleasure, pain, and suffering; justice, conceived largely as requiring equal treatment of persons; and freedom. On this approach—call it *pluralist universalism*—our broadest moral principle would require standards of conduct that optimize happiness as far as possible without producing injustice or curtailing freedom (including one's own). This principle is to be *internalized*—roughly, automatically presupposed and normally also strongly motivating—in a way that yields moral virtue.... Each value (happiness, justice, and freedom) becomes, then, a guiding standard, and mature moral agents will develop a sense of how to act (or at least how to reach a decision to act) when the values pull in different directions.

Pluralist universalism is triple-barreled. It implies that no specific, single standard can be our sole moral guide. This is especially so in the case of principles (like this one) that appeal to different and potentially conflicting elements. How should we balance these in the triple-barreled principle? A priority rule for achieving a balance among the three values—and among the common-sense principles that pluralist universalism helps to unify—is this: Considerations of justice and freedom take priority (at least normally) over considerations of happiness; justice and freedom do not conflict because justice requires the highest level of freedom possible within the limits of peaceful coexistence, and this is as much freedom as any reasonable ideal of liberty demands. Thus, public sale of a drug that gives people pleasure but reduces their freedom would be prohibited by the triple-barreled principle (apart from, say, special medical uses); a social policy (say, draft exemptions for all who have a high-school education) that makes most citizens happy but causes great suffering for a minority (who must go to war) would be rejected as unjust. Moreover, although one may voluntarily devote one's life to enhancing human happiness (if only by reducing human suffering), this is not obligatory. Thus, coercive force may not be used to produce even such highly desirable beneficence.

NOTE

1   John Stuart Mill, *Utilitarianism*, Oscar Priest, ed. CNY: Macmillan, 1957, p. 10.

—2—

GROUNDWORK FOR THE METAPHYSICS OF MORALS

Immanuel Kant

NOTHING CAN POSSIBLY BE CONCEIVED IN THE world, or even out of it, which can be called good without qualification, except a *good will*....

We have then to develop the concept of a will which deserves to be highly esteemed for itself, and is good without a view to anything further, a concept which exists already in the sound natural understanding, requiring rather to be clarified than to be taught, and which in estimating the value of our actions always takes the first place and constitutes the condition of all the rest. In order to do this, we will take the concept of duty, which includes that of a good will, although implying certain subjective limitations and hindrances. These, however, far from concealing it or rendering it unrecognizable, rather bring it out by contrast and make it shine forth so much the brighter....

The second proposition is: That an action done from duty derives its moral worth, *not from the purpose* which is to be attained by it, but from the maxim by which it is determined, and therefore does not depend on the realization of the object of the action, but merely on the *principle of volition* by which the action has taken place, without regard to any object of desire. It is clear from what precedes that the purposes which we may have in view in our action, or their effects regarded as ends and incentives of the will, cannot give to actions any unconditional or moral worth. In what, then, can their worth lie if it is not to consist in the will in reference to its expected effect? It

cannot lie anywhere but in the *principle of the will* without regard to the ends which can be attained by the action. For the will stands between its *a priori* principle, which is formal, and its *a posteriori* incentive, which is material, as between two roads, and as it must be determined by something, it follows that it must be determined by the formal principle of volition when an action is done from duty, in which case every material principle has been withdrawn from it.

The third proposition, which is a consequence of the two preceding, I would express thus: *Duty is the necessity of acting from respect for the law*. I may have *inclination* for an object as the effect of my proposed action, but *never respect* for it, just because it is an effect and not an activity of will. Similarly, I cannot have respect for inclination, whether my own or another's; I can at most, if my own, approve it; if another's, sometimes even love it, that is, look on it as favorable to my own interest. It is only what is connected with my will as a principle, by no means as an effect—what does not serve my inclination, but outweighs it, or at least in case of choice excludes it from its calculation—in other words, simply the law of itself, which can be an object of respect, and hence a command. Now an action done from duty must wholly exclude the influence of inclination, and with it every object of the will, so that nothing remains which can determine the will except objectively the *law*, and subjectively *pure respect* for this practical law, and consequently the maxim that I should follow this law even to the thwarting of all my inclinations.

Thus the moral worth of an action does not lie in the effect expected from it, nor in any principle of action which needs to borrow its motive from this expected effect. For all these effects—agreeableness of one's condition, and even the promotion of the happiness of others—could have been also brought about by other causes, so that for this there would have been no need of the will of a rational being; whereas it is in this alone that the supreme and unconditional good can be found. The pre-eminent good which we call moral can therefore consist in nothing else than *the representation of the law* in itself, *which certainly is only possible in a rational being*, insofar as this representation, and not the expected effect, determines the will. This is a good which is already present in the person who acts accordingly, and we need not wait for it to appear first in the result.

But what sort of law can that be, the conception of which must determine the will, even without paying any regard to the effect experienced from it, in order that this will may be called good absolutely and without qualification? As I have deprived the will of every impulse which could arise for it from obedience to any particular law, there remains nothing but the universal conformity of its actions to law in general, which alone is to serve the will as a principle, that is, I am never to act otherwise than so *that I could also will that my maxim should become a universal law*. Here, now, it is the simple lawfulness in general, without assuming any particular law applicable to certain actions, that serves the will as its principle, and must so serve it if duty is not to be a vain delusion and a chimerical notion. The common reason of human beings in its practical judgments perfectly coincides with this, and always has in view the principle here suggested.

—3—

UTILITARIANISM

John Stuart Mill

CHAPTER 1: GENERAL REMARKS

THERE ARE FEW CIRCUMSTANCES AMONG THOSE which make up the present condition of human knowledge, more unlike what might have been expected, or more significant of the backward state in which speculation on the most important subjects still lingers, than the little progress which has been made in the decision of the controversy respecting the criterion of right and wrong. From the dawn of philosophy, the question concerning the *summum bonum*, or, what is the same thing, concerning the foundation of morality, has been accounted the main problem in speculative thought, has occupied the most gifted intellects, and divided them into sects and schools, carrying on a vigorous warfare against one another. And after more than two thousand years the same discussions continue, philosophers are still ranged under the same contending banners, and neither thinkers nor mankind at large seem nearer to being unanimous on the subject, than when the youth Socrates listened to the old Protagoras, and asserted (if Plato's dialogue be grounded on a real conversation) the theory of utilitarianism against the popular morality of the so-called sophist.

All action is for the sake of some end, and rules of action, it seems natural to suppose, must take their whole character and colour from the end to which they are subservient. When we engage in a pursuit, a clear and precise conception of what we are pursuing would seem to be the first thing we need, instead of the last we are to look forward to. A test of right and wrong must be the means, one would think, of ascertaining what is right or wrong, and not a consequence of having already ascertained it.

CHAPTER 2: WHAT UTILITARIANISM IS

The creed which accepts as the foundation of morals, Utility, or the Greatest Happiness Principle, holds that actions are right in proportion as they tend to promote happiness, wrong as they tend to produce the reverse of happiness. By happiness is intended pleasure, and the absence of pain; by unhappiness, pain, and the privation of pleasure. To give a clear view of the moral standard set up by the theory, much more requires to be said; in particular, what things it includes in the ideas of pain and pleasure; and to what extent this is left an open question. But these supplementary explanations do not affect the theory of life on which this theory of morality is grounded—namely, that pleasure, and freedom from pain, are the only things desirable as ends; and that all desirable things (which are as numerous in the utilitarian as in any other scheme) are desirable either for the pleasure inherent in themselves, or as means to the promotion of pleasure and the prevention of pain.

I have dwelt on this point, as being a necessary part of a perfectly just conception of Utility or Happiness, considered as the directive rule of human conduct. But it is by no means an indispensable condition to the acceptance of the utilitarian standard; for that standard is not the agent's own greatest happiness, but the greatest amount of happiness altogether; and if it may possibly be doubted whether a noble character is always the happier for its nobleness, there can be no doubt that it makes other people happier, and that the world in general is immensely a gainer by it. Utilitarianism, therefore, could only attain its end by the general cultivation of nobleness of character, even if each individual were only benefited by the nobleness of others, and his own, so far as happiness is concerned, were a sheer deduction from the benefit. But the bare enunciation of such an absurdity as this last, renders refutation superfluous.

According to the Greatest Happiness Principle, as above explained, the ultimate end, with reference to and for the sake of which all other things are desirable (whether we are considering our own good or that of other people), is an existence exempt as far as possible from pain, and as rich as possible in enjoyments, both in point of quantity and quality; the test of quality, and the rule for measuring it against quantity, being the preference felt by those who in their opportunities of experience, to which must be added their habits of self-consciousness and self-observation, are best furnished with the means of comparison. This, being, according to the utilitarian opinion, the end of human action, is necessarily also the standard of morality; which may accordingly be defined,

the rules and precepts for human conduct, by the observance of which an existence such as has been described might be, to the greatest extent possible, secured to all mankind; and not to them only, but, so far as the nature of things admits, to the whole sentient creation.

Again, defenders of utility often find themselves called upon to reply to such objections as this—that there is not time, previous to action, for calculating and weighing the effects of any line of conduct on the general happiness. This is exactly as if any one were to say that it is impossible to guide our conduct by Christianity, because there is not time, on every occasion on which anything has to be done, to read through the Old and New Testaments. The answer to the objection is, that there has been ample time, namely, the whole past duration of the human species. During all that time, mankind have been learning by experience the tendencies of actions; on which experience all the prudence, as well as all the morality of life, are dependent. People talk as if the commencement of this course of experience had hitherto been put off, and as if, at the moment when some man feels tempted to meddle with the property or life of another, he had to begin considering for the first time whether murder and theft are injurious to human happiness. Even then I do not think that he would find the question very puzzling; but, at all events, the matter is now done to his hand.

—4—

THE ETHICS OF CARE AS MORAL THEORY

Virginia Held

THE ETHICS OF CARE IS ONLY A FEW DECADES old.[1] Some theorists do not like the term 'care' to designate this approach to moral issues and have tried substituting 'the ethic of love,' or 'relational ethics,' but the discourse keeps returning to 'care' as the so far more satisfactory of the terms considered, though dissatisfactions with it remain. The concept of care has the advantage of not losing sight of the work involved in caring for people and of not lending itself to the interpretation of morality as ideal but impractical to which advocates of the ethics of care often object. Care is both value and practice....

The ethics of care is sometimes seen as a potential moral theory to be substituted for such dominant moral theories as Kantian ethics, utilitarianism, or Aristotelian virtue ethics. It is sometimes seen as a form of virtue ethics. It is almost always developed as emphasizing neglected moral considerations of at least as much importance as the considerations central to moralities of justice and rights or of utility and preference satisfaction. And many who contribute to the understanding of the ethics of care seek to integrate the moral considerations, such as justice, which other moral theories have clarified, satisfactorily with those of care, though they often see the need to reconceptualize these considerations.

FEATURES OF THE ETHICS OF CARE

... First, the central focus of the ethics of care is on the compelling moral salience of attending to and meeting the needs of the particular others for whom we take responsibility. Caring for one's child, for instance, may well and defensibly be at the forefront of a person's moral concerns. The ethics of care recognizes that human beings are dependent for many years of their lives, that the moral claim of those dependent on us for the care they need is pressing, and that there are highly important moral aspects in developing the relations of caring that enable human beings to live and progress. All persons need care for at least their early years. Prospects for human progress and flourishing hinge fundamentally on the care that those needing it receive, and the ethics of care stresses the moral force of the responsibility to respond to the needs of the dependent. Many persons will become ill and dependent for some periods of their later lives, including in frail old age, and some who are permanently disabled will need care the whole of their lives. Moralities built on the image of the independent, autonomous, rational individual largely overlook the reality of human dependence and the morality for which it calls. The ethics of care attends to this central concern of human life and delineates the moral values involved. It refuses to relegate care to a realm "outside morality." How caring for particular others should be reconciled with the claims of, for instance, universal justice is an issue that needs to be addressed. But the ethics of care starts with the moral claims of particular others, for instance, of one's child, whose claims can be compelling regardless of universal principles.

Second, in the epistemological process of trying to understand what morality would recommend and what it would be morally best for us to do and to be, the ethics of care values emotion rather than rejects it. Not all emotion is valued, of course, but in contrast with the dominant rationalist approaches, such emotions as sympathy, empathy, sensitivity, and responsiveness are seen as the kind of moral emotions that need to be cultivated not only to help in the implementation of the dictates of reason but to better ascertain what morality recommends.[2] Even anger may be a component of the moral indignation that should be felt when people are treated unjustly or inhumanely, and it may contribute to (rather than interfere with) an appropriate interpretation of the moral wrong. This is not to say that raw emotion can be a guide to morality; feelings need to be reflected on and educated. But from the care perspective, moral inquiries that rely entirely on reason and rationalistic deductions or calculations are seen as deficient.

The emotions that are typically considered and rejected in rationalistic moral theories are the egoistic feelings that undermine universal moral norms, the favoritism that interferes with impartiality, and the aggressive and vengeful impulses for which morality is to provide restraints. The ethics of care, in contrast, typically appreciates the emotions and relational capabilities that enable morally concerned persons in actual interpersonal contexts to understand what would be best. Since even the helpful emotions can often become misguided or worse—as when excessive empathy with others leads to a wrongful degree of self-denial or when benevolent concern crosses over into controlling domination—we need an *ethics* of care, not just care itself. The various aspects and expressions of care and caring relations need to be subjected to moral scrutiny and *evaluated*, not just observed and described.

Third, the ethics of care rejects the view of the dominant moral theories that the more abstract the reasoning about a moral problem the better because the more likely to avoid bias and arbitrariness, the more nearly to achieve impartiality. The ethics of care respects rather than removes itself from the claims of particular others with whom we share actual relationships.[3] It calls into question the universalistic and abstract rules of the dominant theories. When the latter consider such actual relations as between a parent and child, if they say anything about them at all, they may see them as permitted and cultivating them a preference that a person may have. Or they may recognize a universal obligation for all parents to care for their children. But they do not permit actual relations ever to take priority over the requirements of impartiality. As Brian Barry expresses this view, there can be universal rules permitting people to favor their friends in certain contexts, such as deciding to whom to give holiday gifts, but the latter partiality is morally acceptable only because universal rules have already so judged it.[4] The ethics of care, in contrast, is skeptical of such abstraction and reliance on universal rules and questions the priority given to them....

Annette Baier considers how a feminist approach to morality differs from a Kantian one and Kant's claim that women are incapable of being fully moral because of their reliance on emotion rather than reason. She writes, "Where Kant concludes 'so much the worse for women,' we can conclude 'so much the worse for the male fixation on the special skill of drafting legislation, for the bureaucratic mentality of rule worship, and for the male exaggeration of the importance of independence over mutual interdependence.'"[5]

Margaret Walker contrasts what she sees as feminist "moral understanding" with what has traditionally been thought of as moral "knowledge." She sees the moral understanding she advocates as involving "attention, contextual and narrative appreciation, and communication in the event of moral deliberation." This alternative moral epistemology holds that "the adequacy of moral understanding decreases as its form approaches generality through abstraction."[6]

The ethics of care may seek to limit the applicability of universal rules to certain domains where they are more appropriate, like the domain of law, and resist their extension to other domains. Such rules may simply be inappropriate in, for instance, the contexts of family and friendship, yet relations in these domains should certainly be *evaluated*, not merely described, hence morality should not be limited to abstract rules. We should be able to give moral guidance concerning actual relations that are trusting, considerate, and caring and concerning those that are not.

Dominant moral theories tend to interpret moral problems as if they were conflicts between egoistic individual interests on the one hand, and universal moral principles on the other. The extremes of "selfish individual" and "humanity" are recognized, but what lies between these is often overlooked. The ethics of care, in contrast, focuses especially on the area between these extremes. Those who conscientiously care for others are not seeking primarily to further their own *individual* interests; their interests are intertwined with the persons they care for. Neither are they acting for the sake of *all others* or *humanity in general*; they seek instead to preserve or promote an actual human relation between themselves and *particular others*. Persons in caring relations are acting for self-and-other together. Their characteristic stance is neither egoistic nor altruistic; these are the options in a conflictual situation, but the well-being of a caring relation involves the cooperative well-being of those in the relation and the well-being of the relation itself.

In trying to overcome the attitudes and problems of tribalism and religious intolerance, dominant moralities have tended to assimilate the domains of family and friendship to the tribal, or to a source of the unfair favoring of one's own. Or they have seen the attachments people have in these areas as among the nonmoral private preferences people are permitted to pursue if restrained by impartial moral norms. The ethics of care recognizes the *moral* value and importance of relations of family and friendship and the need for *moral* guidance in these domains to understand how existing relations should often be changed and new ones developed. Having grasped the value of caring relations in such contexts as these more personal ones, the ethics of care then often examines social and political arrangements in the light of these values. In its more developed forms, the ethics of care as a feminist ethic offers suggestions for the radical transformation of society. It demands not just equality for women in existing structures of society but equal consideration for the experience that reveals the values, importance, and moral significance, of caring.

A fourth characteristic of the ethics of care is that like much feminist thought in many areas, it reconceptualizes traditional notions about the public and the private. The traditional view, built into the dominant moral theories, is that the household is a private sphere beyond politics into which government, based on consent, should not intrude. Feminists have shown how the greater social, political, economic, and cultural power of men has structured this "private" sphere to the disadvantage of women and children, rendering them vulnerable to domestic violence without outside interference, often leaving women economically dependent on men and subject to a highly inequitable division of labor in the family. The law has not hesitated to intervene into women's private decisions concerning reproduction but has been highly reluctant to intrude on men's exercise of coercive power within the "castles" of their homes.

Dominant moral theories have seen "public" life as relevant to morality while missing the moral significance of the "private" domains of family and friendship. Thus the dominant theories have assumed that morality should be sought for unrelated, independent, and mutually indifferent individuals assumed to be equal. They have posited an abstract, fully rational "agent as such" from which to construct morality,[7] while missing the moral issues that arise between interconnected persons in the contexts of family, friendship, and social groups. In the context of the family, it is typical for relations to be between persons with highly unequal power who did not choose the ties and obligations in which they find themselves enmeshed. For instance, no child can choose her parents yet she may well have obligations to care for them. Relations of this kind are standardly noncontractual, and conceptualizing them as contractual would often undermine or at least obscure the trust on which their worth depends. The ethics of care addresses rather than neglects moral issues arising in relations among the unequal and dependent, relations that are often laden with emotion and involuntary, and then notices how often these attributes apply not only in the household but in the wider society as well. For instance, persons do not choose which gender, racial, class, ethnic, religious, national, or cultural groups to be brought up in, yet these sorts of ties may be important aspects of who they are and how their experience can contribute to moral understanding.

A fifth characteristic of the ethics of care is the conception of persons with which it begins....

THE CRITIQUE OF
LIBERAL INDIVIDUALISM

The ethics of care usually works with a conception of persons as relational, rather than as the self-sufficient independent individuals of the dominant moral theories. The dominant theories can be interpreted as importing into moral theory a concept of the person developed primarily for liberal political and economic theory, seeing the person as a rational, autonomous agent, or a self-interested individual. On this view, society is made up of "independent, autonomous units who cooperate only when the terms of cooperation are such as to make it further the ends of each of the parties," in Brian Barry's words.[8] Or, if they are Kantians, they refrain from actions that they could not will to be universal laws to which all fully rational and autonomous individual agents could agree. What

such views hold, in Michael Sandel's critique of them, is that "what separates us is in some important sense prior to what connects us—epistemologically prior as well as morally prior. We are distinct individuals first and then we form relationships."[9] In Martha Nussbaum's liberal feminist morality, "the flourishing of human beings taken one by one is both analytically and normatively prior to the flourishing" of any group.[10]

The ethics of care, in contrast, characteristically sees persons as relational and interdependent, morally and epistemologically. Every person starts out as a child dependent on those providing us care, and we remain interdependent with others in thoroughly fundamental ways throughout our lives. That we can think and act as if we were independent depends on a network of social relations making it possible for us to do so. And our relations are part of what constitute our identity. This is not to say that we cannot become autonomous; feminists have done much interesting work developing an alternative conception of autonomy in place of the liberal individualist one.[11] Feminists have much experience rejecting or reconstituting relational ties that are oppressive. But it means that from the perspective of an ethics of care, to construct morality *as if* we were Robinson Crusoes, or, to use Hobbes's image, mushrooms sprung from nowhere, is misleading.[12] As Eva Kittay writes, this conception fosters the illusion that society is composed of free, equal, and independent individuals who can choose to associate with one another or not. It obscures the very real facts of dependency for everyone when they are young, for most people at various periods in their lives when they are ill or old and infirm, for some who are disabled, and for all those engaged in unpaid "dependency work."[13] And it obscures the innumerable ways persons and groups are interdependent in the modern world....

The conception of the person adopted by the dominant moral theories provides moralities at best suitable for legal, political, and economic interactions between relative strangers, once adequate trust exists for them to form a political entity.[14] The ethics of care is, instead, hospitable to the relatedness of persons. It sees many of our responsibilities as not freely entered into but presented to us by the accidents of our embeddedness in familial and social and historical contexts. It often calls on us to *take* responsibility, while liberal individualist morality focuses on how we should leave each other alone. The view of persons as embedded and encumbered seems fundamental to much feminist thinking about morality and especially to the ethics of care....

The ethics of care builds concern and mutual responsiveness to need on both the personal and the wider social level. Within social relations in which we care enough about each other to form a social entity, we may agree for limited purposes to imagine each other as liberal individuals and to adopt liberal policies to maximize individual benefits. But we should not lose sight of the restricted and artificial aspects of such conceptions. The ethics of care offers a view of both the more immediate and the more distant human relations on which satisfactory societies can be built. It provides new theory with which to develop new practices and can perhaps offer greater potential for moral progress than is contained in the views of traditional moral theory.

NOTES

1 I use the term 'ethics' to suggest that there are multiple versions of this ethic, though they all have much in common, making it understandable that some prefer 'the ethic of care.' I use 'the ethics of care' as a collective and singular noun. Some moral philosophers have tried to establish a definitional distinction between 'ethics' and 'morality'; I think such efforts fail, and I use the terms more or less interchangeably, though I certainly distinguish between the moral or ethical beliefs groups of people in fact have and moral or ethical recommendations that are justifiable or admirable.

2 See, for example, Annette C. Baier, *Moral Prejudices* (Cambridge, Mass: Harvard University Press, 1994); Virginia Held, *Feminist Morality:*

Transforming Culture, Society, and Politics (Chicago: University of Chicago Press, 1993); Diana Tietjens Meyers, *Subjection and Subjectivity* (New York: Routledge, 1994); and Margaret Urban Walker, *Moral Understandings: A Feminist Study in Ethics* (New York: Routledge, 1998).

3 See, for example, Seyla Benhabib, *Situating the Self: Gender, Community, and Postmodernism in Contemporary Ethics* (New York: Routledge, 1992); Marilyn Friedman, *What Are Friends For? Feminist Perspectives on Personal Relationships* (Ithaca, N.Y.: Cornell University Press, 1993); Held, *Feminist Morality*; and Eva Feder Kittay, *Love's Labor: Essays on Women, Equality, and Dependency* (New York: Routledge, 1999).

4 See Brian Barry, *Justice as Impartiality* (Oxford: Oxford University Press, 1995); Diemut Bubeck, *Care, Gender, and Justice* (Oxford: Oxford University Press, 1995), 239–40; and Susan Mendus, *Impartiality in Moral and Political Philosophy* (Oxford: Oxford University Press, 2002). See also chapters 5 and 6 [of Virginia Held, *The Ethics of Care: Personal, Political, and Global* (Oxford: Oxford University Press, 2006)].

5 Baier, *Moral Prejudices*, 26.

6 Margaret Urban Walker, "Moral Understandings: Alternative 'Epistemology' for a Feminist Ethics," *Hypatia* 4 (summer 1989): 15–28, 19–20.

7 Good examples are Stephen L. Darwall, *Impartial Reason* (Ithaca, N.Y.: Cornell University Press, 1983), and David Gauthier, *Morals by Agreement* (Oxford: Oxford University Press, 1986).

8 Brian Barry, *The Liberal Theory of Justice* (London: Oxford University Press, 1973), 166.

9 Michael Sandel, *Liberalism and the Limits of Justice* (Cambridge: Cambridge University Press, 1982), 133. Other examples of the communitarian critique that ran parallel to the feminist one are Alasdair MacIntyre, *After Virtue: A Study in Moral Theory* (Notre Dame, Ind.: University of Notre Dame Press, 1981), and *Whose Justice? Which Rationality?* (Notre Dame, Ind.: University of Notre Dame Press, 1988); Charles Taylor, *Hegel and Modern Society* (Cambridge: Cambridge University Press, 1979);

and Roberto Mangabeire Unger, *Knowledge and Politics* (New York: Free Press, 1975).

10   Martha Nussbaum, *Sex and Social Justice* (New York: Oxford University Press, 1999), 62.

11   See, for example, Diana T. Meyers, *Self, Society, and Personal Choice* (New York: Columbia University Press, 1989); Grace Clement, *Care, Autonomy, and Justice* (Boulder, Colo.: Westview Press, 1996); Diana T. Meyers, ed., *Feminists Rethink the Self* (Boulder, Colo.: Westview Press, 1997); and Catriona MacKenzie and Natalie Stoljar, eds., *Relational Autonomy: Feminist Perspectives on Autonomy, Agency, and the Social Self* (New York:

Oxford University Press, 2000). See also Marina Oshana, "Personal Autonomy and Society," *Journal of Social Philosophy* 29(1) (spring 1998): 81–102.

12   This image is in Thomas Hobbes's *The Citizen: Philosophical Rudiments Concerning Government and Society*, ed. B. Gert (Garden City, N.Y.: Doubleday,1972), 205. For a contrasting view, see Sibyl Schwarzenbach, "On Civic Friendship," *Ethics* 107(1) (1996): 97–128.

13   Kittay, *Love's Labor.*

14   See Virginia Held, *Rights and Goods: Justifying Social Action* (Chicago: University of Chicago Press, 1989), chap. 5, "The Grounds for Social Trust...."

—5—

WHAT CAN EASTERN PHILOSOPHY TEACH US ABOUT BUSINESS ETHICS?

Daryl Koehn

AS ASIAN MARKETS HAVE GROWN, THERE HAS been a corresponding increase in interest among businesspeople and philosophers in so-called "Asian Values." Knowledge of the values and ethical systems of Asians is touted as necessary if Western businesses are to successfully negotiate the opening of markets in Japan, South Korea and China and to sell their products to the citizens of these countries. *Real politik* has played an important role as well in generating interest in Asian Values. With the increased wealth of these developing countries has come a greater say in international affairs.[1] Westerners now feel compelled to take note of Asians and to understand them as well as possible. Moreover, as Asian markets have become more lucrative, the power of Southeast Asian governments has increased simply by virtue of the fact that they control which businesses get access to their people and on what terms. The power of voice, coupled with this power to regulate access, has gotten the West's attention....

PART ONE: THE RHETORIC OF "ASIAN VALUES"

It is questionable whether Asian Values do exist or ever could do so. The term "Asia" refers to an enormous geographical area. China, Japan, India and the rest of the Southeast and East Asian countries fall under the rubric. The former U.S.S.R., too, historically has been considered part of Asia by Europeans. The same is true of what we now term the Mideast. The Greek historian Herodotus, for example, consistently treats Persia and Phoenicia as Asian empires.[2] As one would expect, given the vastness of Asia, the cultures therein vary tremendously, reflecting just about every world religion— Buddhism (in numerous varieties), Shintoism, Confucianism, Islam, Christianity, etc. While we can carve out a certain region of the globe and label it "Asia," it is very hard to ascertain what values all of these different cultures might share.

Identifying a "core" set of Asian Values is not the only problem. Even if there were some widely shared values within this region, these values would not be static. Asian Values would be just as subject as Western ones to the transforming effect of political and economic factors.[3] The contrast between Western and Asian Values has the unfortunate effect of making it seem as though the two are eternally opposed to each other. For example, one common variant of this distinction opposes Western individualism to Asian collectivism and deference to authority.[4] Yet, as Kawato rightly notes, the West has not always been as committed to individualism as it now is.[5]

Europeans in the Middle Ages were much more clannish than they are today. Aristotle argues that the Greek polis evolved out of tribal arrangements in which there was one dominant leader to whom all tribe members deferred.[6] Asia might become more "individualistic" or the West more "tribal" or "group-centered" as the years unfold.[7] No culture is hermetically sealed and, as Midgely argues, to think that a culture is a closed system grossly misunderstands cultures and their evolution, an evolution stimulated and influenced by contact with other cultures.[8] In other words, "Asian Values" might once have been "Western Values" (or vice versa) and could become so again. So, even if there were a core set of distinct Asian Values, it would be simple-minded to treat these values in a completely ahistorical fashion....

To summarize: The contrast between Asian and Western values is misleading because it seems very unlikely that there is some monolithic static set of Asian (or, for that matter, Western) values. Positing an incommensurable gap between the two prevents us from trying to ascertain where there might be common ground. While the assertion of Asian Values is often meant to gain a hearing for previously silenced voices, the polarizing strategy of opposing the values of the East to the West paradoxically may lead to a further silencing. After all, if these values are completely distinct and incommensurable, why bother listening to what the other has to say? There is nothing that can be learned from another whose values are so different from ours as to make it impossible for either of us to intelligibly compare our respective positions.

PART TWO: LEARNING FROM WATSUJI TETSURO AND CONFUCIUS

At one level, then, "Eastern ethics" has nothing to teach us about business ethics since such ethics may not even exist. If we take the expression "Eastern ethics" in a more limited sense, however, and think of it as applying to the ethics of particular individuals living within China or Japan or India, then business can learn something from Eastern ethics. While there may not be a single ethic of the Japanese or Chinese, individual thinkers such as Confucius and Watsuji Tetsuro have unquestionably both captured and influenced some dimensions of the ways in which their fellow citizens think about what is morally right. In the remainder of this paper, I draw upon these two thinkers to examine three larger themes:

1. the meaning of trust;
2. relations for life;
3. ethics beyond rights.

The Meaning of Trust

... For Watsuji, human social relations are not grounded in trust. Rather trust is based in human being or *ningen sonzai*. Society cannot be the result of a voluntary decision by citizens to come together and to agree to show each other mutual good will. Trust exists because we are all always already related to each other in a variety of ways— as parents of children and children of parents; as spouses, clients, employees, supervisors, subordinates, etc. We move within these relations conforming to expectations we did not form. Even to deny these expectations is indirectly to confirm them. Over time such role expectations change as the result of individual rebellion, but they do not disappear. Another set of role expectations emerges to take the place of the prior set.

Trusting others is nothing other than living and acting within this social matrix. Sometimes people betray us, but betrayals do not destroy trust. There is no betrayal where there is no trust; and trust exists wherever there are human beings—i.e., activities in accordance with relations. In fact, most betrayals are parasitic upon trust. To take Watsuji's example: The pickpocket can operate only as long as people are not excessively guarded when shopping, going to movies or, more generally, moving within the public space. A theft does not destroy this trust. It might make the individual more cautious but that individual will still be trusting in most dimensions of his or her life. Our trust is never the result of some cost-benefit calculation. Nor is it something we repose in another on the strength of evidence. Anyone who is human trusts simply by virtue of being human....

Truth also takes on a different meaning within this scheme. Trust cannot be built up by speaking the truth—i.e., by making one's words and deeds correspond with the fact of the matter. Truth depends upon trust. A "true" friend is not one who gives us the facts. Rather true friends speak in the way our friendship with them merits. Similarly businesses will not earn our trust by pursuing a strategy of "truth in advertising." Instead business-people should speak in accordance with a con-sciousness of what it means to be a businessperson in society, a businessperson who is already trusted by customers, government officials, suppliers, etc. Truth should not emerge as the result of a strategic calculation but out of the businessperson's strong sense of himself or herself as a human being in that role which is but one among many.

Truth and trust have the same structure wherever they exist. Watsuji would thus agree in spirit with the powerful statement of Aaron Feuerstein, the CEO whose family rebuilt Malden Mills after a devastating fire: "God is one. There is no god of the family, god of the marketplace, god of the temple. God is one and is present every-where." For Feuerstein, there never was a possibil-ity of not rebuilding the family-owned business. He was a human being in a community of people who had built their lives around the mill. He thus spoke as a true CEO when he rejected out of hand suggestions that he rebuilt because doing so was a shrewd way of making money.

Relations Are for Life

Both Watsuji and Confucius reject the radi-cal, atomistic understanding of human beings. To be human is always already to be in rela-tion—or, more precisely, in a matrix of inter-re-lated highly determinate relations (e.g., par-ent-child; older-younger sibling; teacher-student;

superior-subordinate, etc.). These relations are for life. Certain problems which plague Western thought simply do not arise in this alternative worldview. For example, if the person is an indi-vidual and if an individual is identified with the capacity for rational thought, then a comatose person suffering extensive brain damage may not be a person at all within this Western framework. This problem does not arise in a Watsujian or Confucian framework. The comatose daughter does not cease to be the daughter of the mother. She is and forever will be that mother's child. Should she die, she remains the mother's "dead daughter." Nor does the next daughter in line become the eldest daughter upon her sister's death. She, too, remains the second daughter for life.

Since relations are for life, the person of *jen* or humanity does not form new relations lightly. Friendships, for example, require both parties to show good will to each other as long as each is alive. The sense of obligation to the friend may extend beyond death. For example, the friend may feel it is necessary to help the child of a dead friend to get a college education. The Chinese were shocked and offended when Nixon declared himself a friend to China because America and China would each get something out of the rela-tion.[9] This attitude of expediency is utterly foreign to the way the person of *jen* or person with a true heart (*makoto*) thinks about friendship. Showing good will, not getting advantage, is the mark of the true friend.

From the Watsujian and Confucian perspec-tives, commercial relations are longterm as well. An action or choice is not good simply because it has taken into account the interests of stockhold-ers or many stakeholders. It goes without saying that the effect of one's actions on the larger social matrix of relations must always be considered. It is also necessary for the actor to consider the longterm effect of her actions on relations. Each generation of agents shows such regard; and that accounts for why many commercial relations in Japan and China (Taiwan, Hong Kong, etc.) go back many generations.

Businesses are not, therefore, selling products or marketing their reputation. They are establishing a relation or, in the catchy phrase of one modern author, developing a customer for life.[10] Customers in Japan historically have not been especially price-conscious;[11] they stick with those they know. Habits have changed somewhat as the Japanese travelled abroad and came to see how much more costly some items were in Japan than in America or Europe.[12] Yet customers still expect that those who sell them a product will stand behind that product for years and will prove solicitous in their service to the buyer....

There are numerous problems with such a system. It is difficult to dump a distributor or supplier who fails to do a good job. These longterm relations may limit competition. Newcomers cannot simply buy marketshare by offering loss leaders in a system where customers remain exceptionally loyal to brandnames. On the other hand, there is an important lesson here for both businesspeople and business ethicists—namely, that business transactions do not occur in a void or in some separate discrete "economic" sphere completely cut off from the rest of social life. The habits acquired in one sphere carry over into others. If we want our citizenry to know what it means to be a good parent and a true friend, then we need to think about the form and bases of our economic transactions as well. Encouraging people to respond only to price signals may develop an deeply rooted worldview in which everything is valued using a standard of expediency alone.

Ethics beyond Rights

A third important strand common to Watsuji and Confucius is their emphasis on what we owe to each other. It is tempting to say that their systems and, for that matter, the Japanese and Chinese cultures are duty-based while Western cultures are rights-based. This distinction, while nice and tidy, simplifies too much. If the ethics of the Japanese and Chinese have no idea of rights, they equally have no idea of duty. Duties are the correlatives of

rights. There cannot be one without the other. Both duties and rights are enforceable claims. Citizens have the right to demand that elected officers fulfill their responsibilities—i.e., the duties of their office. If the officers fail to do so, the citizens have a right to impeach them, sue, vote them out of office, etc. But the duties Watsuji and Confucius are describing are not enforceable. Quite the contrary. As the noted Japanese legal theorist Kawashima Takeyoshi has observed, it is ethically "improper for the other party (beneficiary) of an obligation to demand or claim that the obligated person fulfill his obligation. An obligation is considered valueless, if, although it is fulfilled by the obligated person, he does not fulfill it in addition with a special friendliness or favor toward the other party.

In other words, the actual value of social obligations depends upon the good will and favor of the obligated person, and there is no place for the existence of the notion of right ..." (Kawashima, 1967).

So an obligation does not derive ethical value from the fact that a rational being would make this demand and want to enforce it. Whatever ethical worth it has comes from the agent's perception or intuitive understanding of her place in the whole of human relations. This understanding will lead her to act with *makoto* or a true-heartedness or *jen*—i.e., humanity. Acts of *makoto* or *jen* are ethically good. An act which honored another's "rights" but which was not done voluntarily or in the spirit of *jen* would not be ethically (or politically) good.

This point of view subordinates the law to moral considerations. Mere adherence to a statute (or, for that matter, a principle such as the categorical imperative) cannot be ethically good. Simple conformity does not exhibit *makoto* or *jen*. In addition, always obeying the law will lead one into a mechanical life. Laws by definition are general. They are not necessarily suited to the circumstances of the particular case or the specific relation. They may therefore be hostile to our true-hearted efforts to honor the requirements of particular human relations. It is better not to try to legislate too much.

What laws do exist should be enforced in a spirit of equity (Kawashima, 1967) or *jen*.

This more flexible approach can be dangerous. Those who enforce the law are given a tremendous amount of discretion. If the judges are people of *makoto*, then perhaps the decisions will prove just and appropriate. But such people are not always at the helm of the ship of state. If the judge hands down a bad decision, those affected by the decision have traditionally had few, if any, rights to which they can appeal in order to protest the decision.

The approach does have certain strengths, though, that are relevant to business practice. Managers and employees avoid asserting mutually incompatible rights. While there sometimes are strikes in Japan, these strikes usually occur after a settlement has been reached. They last for one day and are intended more as a PR device for making a statement than a mechanism of confrontation designed to force management's hand.[13] (Strikes also occur with some frequency in South Korea, a supposedly Confucian country. This difference may be due to the greater impact the rights-oriented United States has had on the Korean subcontinent where it has maintained a military presence since [1950], a presence on which the S. Koreans rely in order to preserve their democracy.)

…

Finally, this more flexible approach changes what it means for a business to be socially responsible. In the West, we tend to say, "Business has a right to make a profit, but they must do so in a socially responsible way." This formulation makes it hard to assess social responsibility. How much profit does business have a right to make? And might not the largely unfettered pursuit by private institutions of maximum profit lead to the greatest social good? If so, then it would be better to just let business go its own way without interference by the government or any other social institution. In other words, having granted business the right to make a profit, the problem becomes one of fitting business back into society. The Watsujian and Confucian approaches, by contrast, treat business as just one of many institutions thoroughly embedded within the social matrix. It is not entitled to make absolute claims for itself. The question for the businessperson, as for every human being in the society, is: What is the good of the larger whole and how can I behave in such a way as to contribute to that whole? The first responsibility of an agent is to consider the whole. Only after having done so is the agent able to be true to the specific human relation in which he or she is operating.

On this second view, the business ethicist should be less concerned with whether multinational corporations or their local subsidiaries are honoring workers' rights to a safe environment or a living wage and more concerned with the larger questions of what contributions business is making to China or Japan. As Henry Rosemont, a Sinologist, has put it, we should be asking what a person of good will would wish for the Chinese at this point in their moral development (Rosemont). When we ask that question, we are driven to admit that it is not at all clear that the Chinese will be well-served if American and European countries sell them hundreds of thousands of cars. The Chinese already have severe pollution problems and do not have the road infrastructure to support a huge increase in automobile transportation. The loss of life may be huge just as it was in Nigeria when Western automobiles arrived before eye glasses. Focussing on the rights questions obscures these larger questions, questions which require Westerners to look at their own business practices and controlling values more closely instead of demonizing the Chinese or other developing countries in Asia.

CONCLUSION

Adopting the perspective of Watsuji or Confucius is certainly not a panacea for all that ails the West. However, taking this tradition seriously will help us to identify our own prejudices regarding business practice as well as to learn about some alternative conceptions of key business ideas such as trust. We may not want to accept these ideas but at least we will be in a better position to make an informed argument for why they should be rejected and to understand the criticisms some Chinese or Japanese businesspeople and philosophers may make regarding our own tradition.

NOTES

1 APEC (Asia Pacific Economic Cooperation) is now the most important regional economic organization in the world, with its members constituting 53% of the world economy. Kiyohiko Fukushima, Book review of *Asia Pacific Fusion: Japan's Role in APEC* in *SAIS Review*, vol. 16, no. 2 (1996), pp. 205–207.

2 Herodotus, *The Persian Wars*, trans. A.D. Godley (Cambridge: Harvard University Press, 1975).

3 And, of course, the "West" affects the "East" and vice versa. The Chinese dissident Liu Binyan has argued that "though Confucianism is gradually coming back to China, it cannot be compared to the increasingly forceful influence of Western culture on the Chinese people in the last twenty years." Binyan quoted in Stein Tonnesson, "Orientalism, Occidentalism, and Knowing about Others," in *NIASnytt*, no. 2 (April, 1994) at http://nias.ku.dk./Nytt/Thematic/Orientalism/orientalism.html.

4 Thi Lam, "The Notion of Asian Values Is a Myth" at http://www.viet.net/vietmag/507.

5 Akio Kawato, "Beyond the Myth of Asian Values," first published in *Chuokoron*, December 1995 at http://ifrm.glocom.jp/DOC.

6 Aristotle, *Politics*, 1252b.

7 Even the West is far from a monolith of liberal democracies. It might prove very interesting to compare "Western" countries such as Albania or Serbia with Malaysia or the Philippines.

8 Mary Midgley, *Can't We Make Moral Judgments?* (NY: St. Martin's Press, 1993), pp. 87–96. Many tend to forget that the U.S. has played an enormous role in shaping modern Japan. "The differences between Japan before and after 1945 are dramatic. In the years of occupation following the war, the U.S.A. refashioned all of Japan's political and social institutions. During the war, for example, Japan was dominated by the military caste. Afterwards, the U.S. written constitution officially defined Japan as a pacifist state." Daniel Nassim, "Shaming the Japanese," in *Living Marxism*, no. 81 (July/August 1995) at www.junius.co.uk/LM/LM81/LM81_Books.html.

9 Huang Quanyu, Richard S. Andrulis, and Chen Tong, *A Guide to Successful Business Relations with the Chinese* (NY: The Haworth Press, 1994), pp. 119–120.

10 Carl Sewell and Paul B. Brown, *Customers for Life: How to Turn That One-Time Buyer into a Lifetime Customer* (NY: Doubleday Currency, 1990).

11 Boye Lafayette De Mente, *How to Do Business with the Japanese* (Lincolnwood, IL: NTC Publishing, 1994), p. 211.

12 Mente, p. 217.

13 Mente, p. 170.

—6—

TOWARD AN AFRICAN MORAL THEORY

Thaddeus Metz

IN THE LITERATURE ON AFRICAN ETHICS, ONE finds relatively little that consists of normative theorization with regard to right action, that is, the articulation and justification of a comprehensive, basic norm that is intended to account for what all permissible acts have in common as distinct from impermissible ones.[1] By "African ethics" I mean values associated with the largely black and Bantu-speaking peoples residing in the sub-Saharan part of the continent, thereby excluding Islamic Arabs in North Africa and white Afrikaners in South Africa, among others....

I. CLARIFICATION OF THE PROJECT

In seeking to construct an African theory of right action, my aim is to develop a principle that sub-Saharan Africans ought to believe, given adherence to claims they typically deem to be less controversial than it. Hence, this largely epistemic project is neither simply moral anthropology nor even straightforwardly normative ethics....

To obtain focus in the search for an attractive African normative principle, I address the (English-speaking) literature that comes closest to my project. Most of this literature analyzes the values associated with the term *"ubuntu"* and related terms in sub-Saharan Africa and draws out their practical implications for political power, workplace organization and the like. *"Ubuntu"* is a word used by the Zulu people of South Africa,[2] and is difficult to translate into English because it has many different connotations associated with it.[3] Roughly, it means humanness, and it often figures into the maxim that "a person is a person through other persons." This maxim has descriptive senses to the effect that one's identity as a human being causally and even metaphysically depends on a community. It also has prescriptive senses to the effect that one ought to be a *mensch*, in other words, morally should support the community in certain ways. Desmond Tutu, the Nobel Peace Prize winner renowned for supervising the South African Truth and Reconciliation Committee (TRC), provides a rough gloss of the normative connotations of *"ubuntu"*:

> When we want to give high praise to someone we say, *"Yu, u nobuntu"*; "Hey, so-and-so has *ubuntu*." Then you are generous, you are hospitable, you are friendly and caring and compassionate. You share what you have. It is to say, "My humanity is caught up, is inextricably bound up in yours."[4]

In this article, I critically discuss the ways that the literature construes *ubuntu* as grounding a normative ethical theory of right action (or at least brings to mind such a construal), analytically setting aside *ubuntu* as a comprehensive worldview or a description of a way of life as a whole.

To give the reader more of a sense of what the morality of *ubuntu* involves, and to present some criteria for an adequate moral theory, I here review some intuitions that most friends of *ubuntu* firmly hold. More specifically, it will be revealing to distinguish between two groups of such intuitions, those held by Westerners and Africans to roughly the same extent, and those more often held by Africans than by Westerners. I seek a theory inspired by *ubuntu* that best accounts for both groups of intuitions.

First, consider moral judgments that are commonly accepted by both adherents of *ubuntu* and Western people in modern, industrialized, constitutional democracies. For both groups, it is by and large uncontroversially *pro tanto* immoral:

A. to kill innocent people for money.
B. to have sex with someone without her consent.
C. to deceive people, at least when not done in self- or other-defence.
D. to steal (that is, to take from their rightful owner) unnecessary goods.
E. to violate trust, for example, break a promise, for marginal personal gain.
F. to discriminate on a racial basis when allocating opportunities.

I take it these judgments are self-explanatory, needing no elaboration.

Before sketching the intuitions that I maintain Africans hold more often than Westerners, I warn the reader that I do not mean to suggest that all sub-Saharan societies, let alone all individuals in them, hold them. What I claim are moral judgments more common among Africans than Westerners are values that are more widespread in the sub-Saharan part of the continent than in Europe, North America or Australasia. They are values that are more often found across not only a certain wide array of space, from Ghana to South Africa, but also a long span of time in that space, from traditional societies to contemporary African intellectuals.... More often for Africans

than for Westerners, then, it is uncontroversially *pro tanto* immoral:

G. to make policy decisions in the face of dissent, as opposed to seeking consensus.

In the political realm, unanimity is prized, and majoritarianism is typically seen as a morally inadequate way to resolve conflicts of interest or to determine law. In many small-scale African communities, discussion continues until a compromise is found and all in the discussion agree with the outcome.[5] ...

H. to make retribution a fundamental and central aim of criminal justice, as opposed to seeking reconciliation.

By "retribution" I mean any consideration that could be invoked to justify punishing a lawbreaker fundamentally for, and in proportion to, wrongdoing. For example, one retributive reason to punish an offender could be the bare fact that he justly deserves condemnation because of, and to the same degree as, his having done wrong in the past. In contrast to such a backward-looking rationale for punishment, many African communities believe it appropriate to respond to crime with the expectation of a good result of some sort, whether to appease angry ancestors and thereby protect the community from their wrath, or to mend a broken relationship between the offender, his victim and the community.[6] ...

I. to create wealth largely on a competitive basis, as opposed to a cooperative one.

In many traditional African societies land is ultimately owned in common and it is held that labour should be undertaken for the sake of the community, neither in order to make a profit in light of demand nor simply to care for one's immediate family.[7] The "empire building" of a Warren Buffet is anathema here, where the point of work should not be to amass wealth for oneself or for its own sake, but rather to benefit others....

J. to distribute wealth largely on the basis of individual rights, as opposed to need.

The requirements of an individual to help others are typically deemed heavier in African morality than in Western.... Illustrative is the parable of the cow (and similar widespread sayings): "if you have two cows and the milk of the first cow is sufficient for your own consumption, *Ubuntu* expects you to donate the milk of the second cow to your underprivileged brothers and sisters."[8] Conversely, more Africans than Westerners think that it is permissible to take goods such as food without others' consent, so long as one does not overdo it.[9]

K. to ignore others and violate communal norms, as opposed to acknowledging others, upholding tradition and partaking in rituals.

A nice illustration of this point is a study recounted by Augustine Shutte in his book devoted to *ubuntu*.[10] He notes a survey that was taken of two groups of nuns at a convent. After the obligatory chores and praying were done, the study found that the German nuns often continued to work by knitting or sewing, while the African nuns did not and instead spent time in conversation. The study noted that each group of sisters deemed the other morally lacking; the Germans judged the Africans insufficiently diligent, while the Africans considered the Germans to objectionably care more about practical matters than about people....

L. to fail to marry and procreate, as opposed to creating a family.

Many African people think there is some strong moral reason to extend familial relationships by finding a (heterosexual) spouse and having children. Polygamy is often permitted, and indeed welcomed, because of its effectiveness at generating more children than monogamy would.[11] ...

We now have twelve firm moral intuitions, six both Western and African and six more African than Western, by which to evaluate moral theories in the rest of this article. I seek to discover a principle that both entails and well explains all twelve....

II. *UBUNTU* AS A MORAL THEORY

In this section, I point out that there are six competing theoretical interpretations of *ubuntu* to be found in the literature. I distinguish between them, and argue that one promises to do much better than the other five at accounting for all twelve of the intuitions canvassed in the previous section. Here is the first account of *ubuntu* as a moral theory:

U1: *An action is right just insofar as it respects a person's dignity; an act is wrong to the extent that it degrades humanity.*

This principled rendition of *ubuntu* states that there is value intrinsic to something about human nature that demands honouring. It is inspired by some remarks of members of the South African Constitutional Court, which has on occasion appealed to the value of *ubuntu* when making legal decisions. For instance, Justice Yvonne Mokgoro remarks: "(H)uman rights derive from the inherent dignity of the human person. This, in my view, is not different from what the spirit of *ubuntu* embraces."[12] ...

The principle of respect for life ... fails to account for a number of core values associated with *ubuntu*, leading me to consider another principle.

U2: *An action is right just insofar as it promotes the well-being of others; an act is wrong to the extent that it fails to enhance the welfare of one's fellows.*

As opposed to the respect-based understanding of *ubuntu* in U1, U2 is a more utilitarian one....

The problem facing this construal of *ubuntu* is the problem facing any utilitarianism: an exclusively consequentialist focus on human well-being has notorious difficulties grounding constraints, for example, against stealing (D) or discriminating (F) as means to the greater good. To avoid this problem, consider a theory that includes such constraints at a fundamental level.

U3: An action is right just insofar as it promotes the well-being of others without violating their rights; an act is wrong to the extent that it either violates rights or fails to enhance the welfare of one's fellows without violating rights....

Different interpretations of the view will have different accounts of the relevant rights and of what counts as their violation.

We need not specify which rights there are and what it is to violate them, in order to know that this theory has difficulty accounting for all the intuitions at stake. In particular, consensus (G), cooperation (I), and tradition (K), which are *pro tanto* morally desirable from many an African perspective, can be inefficient as ways to promote human welfare....

U4: An action is right just insofar as it positively relates to others and thereby realizes oneself; an act is wrong to the extent that it does not perfect one's valuable nature as a social being.

This is probably the dominant interpretation of African ethics in the literature.[13] Many thinkers take the maxim "a person is a person through other persons" to be a call for an agent to develop her personhood. Shutte, whose book I mentioned above, captures *ubuntu* this way:

> (T)he moral life is seen as a process of personal growth.... Our deepest moral obligation is to become more fully human. And this means entering more and more deeply into community with others. So although the goal is personal fulfilment, selfishness is excluded.[14]

And Mogobe Ramose, author of another useful book on *ubuntu*, says that "to be a human being is to affirm one's humanity by recognizing the humanity of others and, on that basis, establish human relations with them.... One is enjoined, yes, commanded as it were, to actually become a human being."[15] Instead of others' welfare being the relevant good for a moral agent to promote, here it is the realization of one's distinctively human and valuable nature, specifically, one's special ability to engage in communal relationship. One is reminded of the young Marx's views[16] and, of course, ultimately of Aristotle's.

This theory will vary depending on how our social nature or capacity for community gets cashed out. As with the previous theory, however, we do not need to specify the present one in order to become aware of serious problems. I submit that its fundamental emphasis on self-realization has counter-intuitive implications. Suppose that you need a new kidney to survive and that no one will give one to you. Then, to maximize your self-realization, you would need to kill another innocent person so as to acquire his organs. Of course, in killing you would not be realizing yourself, for the theory says that to realize yourself you must do so by positively supporting other persons in some way. However, since you can positively support other persons *in the long-term* only by remaining alive, which in this case requires killing another person, the theory counter-intuitively seems to permit murder for one's own benefit (A)....

Before turning to the remaining two accounts of *ubuntu* as a moral theory, notice that the above four ground morality in something internal to the individual, whether it be her life (U1), well-being (U2), rights (U3), or self-realization (U4). A different understanding of the morality of *ubuntu* includes the idea that moral value fundamentally lies not in the individual, but rather in a *relationship* between individuals. The distinction here is analogous to that between individualism and holism in environmental ethics.... Let us now consider some properly communitarian renditions of *ubuntu*.

U5: *An action is right just insofar as it is in solidarity with groups whose survival is threatened; an act is wrong to the extent that it fails to support a vulnerable community.*

One of the first and most cited books on *ubuntu* advocates this understanding of the basic idea. Its authors say, "Ubuntu is ... a concept of brotherhood and collective unity for survival among the poor in every society."[17] ...

    This understanding of *ubuntu* is obviously too narrow to be an acceptable moral theory. For one, it prescribes actions only to certain agents, the destitute, and not to others. And even if it were broadened to include all agents (which U5 does), it would still be too limited for ascribing the single end of survival, or, again more broadly, flourishing.... What is needed is a broader notion of the sort of relationships that morally matter.

U6: *An action is right just insofar as it produces harmony and reduces discord; an act is wrong to the extent that it fails to develop community.*

This, I submit, is the most promising theoretical formulation of an African ethic to be found in the literature. Tutu expresses it in the following characterization of *ubuntu*:

> Harmony, friendliness, community are great goods. Social harmony is for us the summum bonum—the greatest good. Anything that subverts or undermines this sought-after good is to be avoided like the plague. Anger, resentment, lust for revenge, even success through aggressive competitiveness, are corrosive of this good.[18]

As opposed to well-being or self-realization, this account of *ubuntu* posits certain relationships as constitutive of the good that a moral agent ought to promote. "What is right is what connects people together; what separates people is wrong."[19]

    This account of *ubuntu* has the potential to account for all the intuitions addressed here, but not particularly well as it stands, for it is too

vague.... In the following section, I seek to make the metaphors less metaphorical. After doing so, I return to the intuitions and illustrate how well this theory does at accounting for them, at least relative to the rivals rejected above.

III. DEVELOPING THE FAVOURED ACCOUNT

In this section, I aim to answer the question of what harmony or togetherness is, so that the prescription to promote it is better understood....

H1: *Shared Identity.*

One thing "harmony" and "togetherness" might essentially involve is a common sense of self, which includes at least the following distinct conditions.[20] First, a given individual conceives of herself as part of a group. You refer to yourself in the first person plural, including yourself in a "we."

    Second, the group that you consider yourself a member of also considers you to be a member of it. So, others in the "we" you refer to also include you in their "we." You can hardly claim to share identity with the Zulu people merely on the basis of saying things like, "We Zulus need to stick together." Self-described Zulus must also consider you Zulu.

    Third, people share identity when they have common ends, if not also the same motives or reasons that underlie them. It is logically possible to be part of a group that does not do anything, but the relevant sort of group under consideration here is one that has some projects.

    Fourth and finally, shared identity consists of people in the group coordinating their activities in order to realize their ends, even if they do not use the same means or make the same amount of effort....

    While a shared identity might ground some duties of loyalty, it is hard to see how it could be very morally important in itself. After all, members of the former South African Nationalist Party that enforced apartheid had a common sense of self. One surely has no duty to promote such a group if one is not a member. And if one is a member, though one might owe some fidelity to other members, there is in all likelihood a much stronger duty to try to dissolve the group (and not merely because the group fails to promote the shared identity of others outside the group). Therefore, let us consider a different sort of harmony, one more worth promoting from a moral point of view.

H2: Good-Will.

Another thing that "harmony" might mean is a certain caring or supportive relationship.[21] One has a relationship of good-will insofar as one: wishes another person well (conation); believes that another person is worthy of help (cognition); aims to help another person (intention); acts so as to help another person (volition); acts for the other's sake (motivation); and, finally, feels good upon the knowledge that another person has benefited and feels bad upon learning she has been harmed (affection). In the model case, there are certain causal relationships that obtain among these pro-attitudes, for example, the intention is partially responsible for bringing about the volition....

Good-will and shared identity are logically distinct types of relationship. First off, there are cases of shared identity without good-will. Think about the relationship between management and workers in a firm. There is little or no good-will there—workers don't typically work for the sake of management, after all—but both sides would readily think of themselves as part of a larger group that is involved in joint projects ("We're MTN").

Conversely, there can be cases of good-will without shared identity....

Good-will without shared identity has more moral value on the face of it than does shared identity without good-will. If we had to choose between promoting relationships of solidarity or identity, solidarity would usually win. However, we often need not choose between them, and the most attractive sort of harmonious relationship to promote is surely one that includes both.

H3: The Combination of Shared Identity and Good-Will.

While good-will without shared identity is morally more valuable than the converse, it is better still with shared identity. A condition in which individuals anonymously help each other is less desirable than mutually recognizing members of a group who care for one another. Such a communal relationship is perhaps what Mokgoro has in mind when she says of *ubuntu* that "harmony is achieved through close and sympathetic social relations within the group"[22] and when Segun Gbadegesin says, "Every member is expected to consider him/herself an integral part of the whole and to play an appropriate role towards achieving the good of all."[23] To be close or part of the whole is reasonably understood as sharing an identity, whereas to be sympathetic or realize the well-being of others is to have good-will. The combination of the two conditions is what I deem to be the most attractive conception of harmony—or a broad sense of "love." A loving relationship is a *prima facie* attractive moral value and is the good that, I show below, best accounts for the relatively uncontroversial intuitions.

Analogies are often drawn between the sort of society many Africans value and an extended family. Now, the attractive sort of family is one in which people are loving, that is, they have a common sense of self and act for one another's sake. Conceiving of harmony in terms of love therefore makes good sense of the analogy. In addition, although the requirement to promote harmony has a basic teleological structure that is familiar in Western ethics, its holistic conception of the good to be promoted differs from what is predominant there, typically either pleasure, preference satisfaction, need fulfilment, autonomy or self-development. As noted above, African thought is often characterized as "communitarian," which the present theory captures markedly better than its rivals. Placing basic moral status in a loving relationship between people is more holistic than putting it in an individual's life (U1), well-being (U2), rights (U3), or self-realization (U4), even if these latter views entail that individuals ought to sacrifice much for the sake of others. Note that the moral injunction to produce harmony *qua* the combination of identity and solidarity is relational in a way that differs from the most influential forms of holism in contemporary Western ethics. It is less relativist than, say, the views of those communitarians who think that the norms of a particular community are binding on those who are born into it,[24] and it is more impartial than the views of certain care ethicists who believe that one's extant relationships alone have moral status.[25]

I am now in a position to enrich U6, the terse statement that directs agents to produce harmony: *An action is right just insofar as it promotes shared identity among people grounded on good-will; an act is wrong to the extent that it fails to do so and tends to encourage the opposites of division and ill-will.* While this principle still needs clarification and refinement in many respects... it is less vague and metaphorical than the initial statement. Furthermore, I submit that it is intelligible enough to see that, of the six theoretical accounts of *ubuntu* discussed in section II, this one best accounts for the twelve intuitions from section I....

NOTES

1   One more often finds something closer to moral anthropology or cultural studies, i.e., discussion recounting the ethical practices or norms of a certain African people. For representative examples, see Anthony Kirk-Greene, "'Mutumin Kirki': the concept of the good man in Hausa," *African Philosophy: An Anthology*, ed. Emmanuel Chukwudi Eze (Oxford: Blackwell, 1998), pp. 121–29; and John Ayotunde Isola Bewaji, "Ethics and morality in Yoruba culture," *A Companion to African Philosophy*, ed. Kwasi Wiredu (Oxford: Blackwell, 2004), pp. 396–403. I do not mean

to disparage these discussions; I aim merely to distinguish them from this one.

2   There are cognate terms and ideas associated with them in at least all the other Bantu languages of sub-Saharan Africa, e.g., "*Nunhu*" in Shona (Zimbabwe) and "*Utu*" in Swahili (Kenya), on which see Johann Broodryk, *Ubuntu: Life Lessons from Africa* (Pretoria: Ubuntu School of Philosophy, 2002), p. 14.

3   For discussion of the etymology of "*ubuntu*," see Mogobe Ramose, *African Philosophy Through Ubuntu* (Harare: Mond Books, 1999), pp. 49–53, and Mogobe Ramose, "The ethics of *Ubuntu*," *Philosophy from Africa*, 2nd edn, ed. P.H. Coetzee and A.P.J. Roux (Oxford: Oxford University Press, 2003), pp. 324–30 at pp. 324–28.

4   Desmond Tutu, *No Future Without Forgiveness* (New York: Random House, 1999), p. 31.

5   For an anthropological overview of traditional African politics and the role of consensus in it, see the classic text, Meyer Fortes and Edward Evans-Pritchard, eds., *African Political Systems* (London: Kegan Paul, 1994, originally published 1940).

6   See Kwasi Wiredu, *Cultural Universals and Particulars: An African Perspective* (Bloomington: Indiana University Press, 1996), pt. 4. See also Ramose, *African Philosophy Through Ubuntu*, pp. 135–53.

7   See, e.g., Leo Marquard and T.G. Standing, *The Southern Bantu* (London: Oxford University Press, 1939), esp. pp. 20–32; Stanlake Samkange and Tommie Marie Samkange, *Hunhuism or Ubuntuism: A Zimbabwean Indigenous Political Philosophy* (Harare: Graham Publishing Company, 1980), esp. pp. 80–87; and Segun Gbadegesin, "Yoruba philosophy: individuality, community, and moral order," *African Philosophy: An Anthology*, ed. Emmanuel Chukwudi Eze, pp. 130–41 at pp. 132–33.

8   Walter Sisulu quoted in Broodryk, *Ubuntu*, pp. vii; see also pp. 1, 36–39.

9   Tangwa, "The HIV/AIDS pandemic, African traditional values and the search for a vaccine in Africa," p. 180; and Heidi Verhoef and Claudine Michel, "Studying morality within the African context," *Journal of Moral Education*, 26 (1997),

389–407 at p. 399. Note that such taking would not count as "stealing" since the person in possession of the item is presumably not its rightful owner in light of the other's need for it.

10 Augustine Shutte, *Ubuntu: An Ethic for the New South Africa* (Cape Town: Cluster Publications, 2001), pp. 27–28.

11 Ramose, "The ethics of *Ubuntu*," p. 329.

12 Justice Yvonne Mokgoro of the Constitutional Court of South Africa, *The State versus T Makwanyane and M Mchunu*, para. 309. See also the remarks of Justice Langa in the same case, para. 225.

13 In addition to quotations in the text from Shutte and Ramose, see [Kwame] Gyekye, *An Essay on African Philosophical Thought* [(Cambridge: Cambridge University Press, 1987)], pp. 156–57; [Yvonne] Mokgoro, "*Ubuntu* and the law in South Africa," [*Potchefstroom Electronic Law Journal*, 1 (1998),] p. 3; Drucilla Cornell and Karin van Marle, "Exploring *ubuntu*: tentative reflections," *African Human Rights Law Journal*, 5 (2005), 195–220 at p. 206; and perhaps Bujo, *Foundations of an African Ethic*, pp. 87–94.

14 Shutte, *Ubuntu*, p. 30.

15 Ramose, *African Philosophy Through Ubuntu*, p. 52.

16 See especially the infrequently read fragment, "On James Mill," *Karl Marx: Selected Writings*, ed. David McLellan (Oxford: Oxford University Press, 1977), pp. 114–22.

17 Lovemore Mbigi and Jenny Maree, *Ubuntu. The Spirit of African Transformation Management* (Randburg: Knowledge Resources, 1995), pp. 1, 58.

18 Tutu, *No Future Without Forgiveness*, p. 35.

19 Verhoef and Michel, referring to the work of John Mbiti, in "Studying morality within the African context," p. 397. Commenting on the practices of the G/wi people of Botswana, George Silberbauer says, "(T)here was another value being pursued, namely the establishing and maintaining of harmonious relationships. Again and again in discussion and in general conversation this stood out as a desired and enjoyed end in itself, often as the ultimate rationale for action." See his "Ethics in Small-Scale Societies," *A Companion to Ethics*, ed. Peter Singer (Oxford: Basil Blackwell, 1991), pp. 14–28.

20 This interpretation of harmony is inspired by some of Gyekye's remarks about what counts as a community in "Person and community in African thought," p. 320.

21 This understanding of community comes to mind from Wiredu's discussion of the "empathetic harmonization of human interests" ("Custom and morality," p. 64), which, *contra* Tutu, he does not take to have final moral value.

22 Mokgoro, "*Ubuntu* and the law in South Africa," p. 3.

23 Gbadegesin, "Yoruba philosophy," p. 131.

24 See, e.g., Michael Sandel's notion of "encumbered selves" in *Liberalism and the Limits of Justice* (New York: Cambridge University Press, 1982).

25 For instance, Nel Noddings thinks that there is "no command to love" and hence no duty to aid strangers since one lacks any caring relationship with them. See *Caring: A Feminine Approach to Ethics and Moral Education* (Berkeley: University of California Press, 1984).

—7—

REFLECTIVE EQUILIBRIUM

Yuri Cath

1. INTRODUCTION

THE METHOD OF REFLECTIVE EQUILIBRIUM IS A method for figuring out what to believe about some target domain of philosophical interest like, say, justice, morality, or knowledge. This method is most closely associated with John Rawls who introduced the term 'reflective equilibrium' into the philosophical lexicon in *A Theory of Justice* (1971), where he appealed to this method in arguing for his famous theory of justice as fairness. However, Rawls had already advocated essentially the same method (without calling it 'reflective equilibrium') in an earlier paper (Rawls 1951), and Goodman (1954) is widely identified (including by Rawls himself) as being the first clear advocate of this kind of method, albeit with respect to a different normative domain, namely, logic.

Due to Rawls' influence, there has been a great deal of discussion of reflective equilibrium (or 'RE') in moral philosophy, and many philosophers have suggested that this method is uniquely suited to theorizing about morality or normativity more generally....

As well as different views of the scope and status of this method, there are also different views of what the method is, to the point where it can be misleading to talk (as is standard) of *the* method of RE....

2. AN INITIAL SKETCH

The aim of this section is to offer an initial sketch of the method of RE which will serve as a useful basis for our discussion. Following Scanlon (2003) and others, the method of RE can be usefully conceptualized as involving three distinct stages:

Stage 1: In this stage one identifies a relevant set of one's initial beliefs (or judgements or intuitions) about the relevant domain. These initial beliefs are often characterized as concerning particular rather than general features of the relevant domain. For example, if the domain is justice then one's set of initial beliefs might include the belief that a particular action was just, or if the domain is logic it might include the belief that a particular token inference was invalid, or if the domain is knowledge it might include the belief that a particular subject possesses knowledge, and so on. However, proponents of the method of RE often allow that the set of initial beliefs can also include beliefs about more general features of the relevant domain, including abstract general principles (see e.g., Rawls 1974, p. 8).

Stage 2: In the second stage one tries to come up with an initial set of theoretical principles that would systematize or account for the initial beliefs identified at the first stage. Scanlon (2003, pp. 140–1), in describing Rawls' version of the method of RE, writes that one is trying to come up with principles such that "had one simply been trying to apply them rather than trying to decide what seemed to be the case as far as justice is concerned, one would have been led to this same set of [initial] judgments."[1]

Stage 3: There are likely to be conflicts between one's initial beliefs and one's initial principles that aim to account for those beliefs. Furthermore, there are also likely to be conflicts between the members of one's initial set of beliefs, and perhaps even between the members of one's initial set of theoretical principles. These conflicts lead to the need for a third stage in which one engages in a reflective process of moving back and forth between these two sets and eliminating, adding to, or revising the members of either set until one ends up with a final set of beliefs and principles which cohere with each other. This final state is called a state of reflective equilibrium.

One point worth clarifying is that what the theoretical principles are meant to account for, and be in equilibrium with, is not the psychological fact that one has certain initial beliefs. This point is often obscured because: (i) descriptions of this method typically just speak of 'accounting for our beliefs,' or 'bringing our beliefs into equilibrium'; and (ii) such descriptions are ambiguous, given that propositional attitude terms like 'belief' can pick out both the psychological state of belie*ving* and the proposition that is belie*ved* to be true (as is the case for 'intuition' and 'judgement'). However, on close inspection, it is almost always clear that such descriptions should be interpreted in a non-psychologistic way. That is, when proponents of RE talk of theories 'accounting for our initial beliefs,' they should be interpreted as making a claim equivalent to something like 'accounting for the assumed truth of the contents of our initial beliefs,' as opposed to 'accounting for the fact that we have certain initial beliefs.'[2] Similarly, when proponents of RE talk of 'our beliefs being in a state of equilibrium,' such claims are best interpreted as being equivalent to something like 'the contents of our beliefs being in a state of equilibrium' or 'our beliefs being in a state of equilibrium in virtue of their contents being in a state of equilibrium.' Some proponents of the method of RE do explicitly clarify this interpretative point,[3] but often it is left merely implicit, which can lead to unnecessary confusion and to misplaced criticisms.

With that clarification in mind, we can explain how this method is meant to be one of figuring out what to believe about the target domain. The idea is that the process of bringing the contents of one's beliefs and one's theoretical principles into a state of equilibrium is one that should be mirrored by corresponding changes in one's belief states, so that by the end of this process the contents of one's resulting beliefs about the relevant domain should be captured by the final coherent set of propositions that one reaches in stage 3.

Importantly, proponents of this method usually add the qualification that this state of equilibrium is an ideal that we should strive towards but will perhaps never achieve. For this reason, RE is best viewed as a method that one is meant to continuously return to and reapply, rather than as a method that one would apply once and then set aside.

3. INTERPRETING THE SKETCH

To help fill in our initial sketch it will be useful to now consider a series of questions about how to interpret it.

What is meant to recommend this method of forming beliefs about the target domain? Proponents of this method hold that, when applied correctly, it will lead to beliefs that enjoy some positive normative status, where the most common suggestion is that these beliefs will be *justified* (or, at least, that one will have a justification to so believe). And proponents of this method often go further and suggest that it is the *best* and perhaps even the *only* method by which we can form justified beliefs about the relevant domain. For example, Scanlon (2003, p. 149) endorses both these claims with respect to morality and other (non-specified) subjects:

[I]t seems to me that this method, properly understood, is in fact the best way of making up one's mind about moral matters and about many other subjects. Indeed, it is the only defensible method: apparent alternatives to it are illusory.

Why think that the beliefs formed by this method would be justified? The method of RE is standardly interpreted as relying on a coherentist theory of justification and, indeed, is often referred to as simply being a 'coherence method.' This coherentist interpretation of the method of RE is sometimes disputed.... But for now it will suffice to point out how this standard interpretation, if correct, provides a straightforward answer to the justification question, namely, that any belief formed by this method will be justified simply in virtue of it being a member of a system of beliefs that cohere with each other. On this interpretation then, the method of RE is minimally committed to the claim that a belief's being part of a coherent system of beliefs is a *sufficient* condition for it being a justified belief.[4] And when proponents of RE suggest that this method is the *only* way of reaching justified beliefs about some relevant domain, they appear to commit themselves to the idea that it is a *necessary* condition of a belief's being justified (at least for beliefs about the relevant domain) that it be a part of a system of beliefs that is coherent to some degree.[5]

What exactly does it mean to say that the beliefs one reaches at step 3 'cohere' with each other or are in a state of 'equilibrium'? Proponents of RE often do not provide much in the way of detailed answers to this question. One can find more detailed answers in the coherentism literature but there is no consensus account of what coherence is, and it is widely acknowledged that existing accounts are inadequate in different ways.[6] However, for our purposes, it will suffice to note that common to almost all accounts of coherence (in both the coherentist and RE literatures) is the very general thought that increasing the coherence of one's belief system is (at least partly) a matter of minimizing conflicts between the contents of one's beliefs, and maximizing certain relations of support between those contents. These notions of conflict and support are then analysed in a variety of ways by appealing to some mixture of deductive, probabilistic, evidential, or explanatory, relations between the contents of one's beliefs.[7]

What constraints, if any, are placed on the initial set of beliefs one identifies at stage 1? Some prominent proponents of this method—like Goodman (1953) and Lewis (1983)—place very few, if any, constraints on this set of initial beliefs. On the other hand, Rawls placed very specific constraints on the judgements that are the initial inputs into his version of the method of RE. According to Rawls, we should begin with only our "considered judgments," where he uses this as a technical term for those judgements which satisfy a range of constraints aimed at eliminating "judgments [that] are likely to be erroneous or to be influenced by excessive attention to our own interests" (Rawls 1971, p. 42). Rawls' version of RE can be thought of as one on which there is an intermediate step between stages 1 and 2 where one checks one's initial set of gathered judgements and filters out any that do not meet his constraints. These include the constraints that these judgements should not be ones made when one is upset or frightened, or where one's self-interests could be impacted by what the answer is to the relevant question. Rawls also requires that we only include those judgements in which we are confident, and which will be held stably over time. Another restriction that is sometimes placed on the initial inputs identified at stage 1 is that they have to be *intuitive* judgements or beliefs, and sometimes these inputs are described as simply being intuitions. Rawls (1951, p. 183) endorses a restriction of this kind, but it is worth noting that he has a very minimal sense of this restriction in which an intuitive judgement is simply one that is not "guided by a conscious application of principles so far as this may be evidenced by introspection." ...

NOTES

1   Sometime the method of RE is described in ways that do not fit so well with the characterization I have given of this second stage. For example, I said that in the second stage one tries to 'come up with' theoretical principles that would account for one's initial beliefs, which suggests that one need not

have believed these principles to be true prior to engaging in this reflective process. But sometimes the method is described so that the theoretical principles one identifies are just further things that one already believed to be the case before applying this method.

2   To see this point, it is useful to consider examples of the kinds of conflicts between our initial beliefs or intuitions and our initial theories that are meant to be resolved by the method of RE. Consider a familiar case from epistemology, namely, the conflict between the justified true belief ('JTB') analysis of knowledge and our intuition that the Gettier subject has non-knowledgeable justified true belief ('NKJTB'). This is a paradigm example of the kind of conflict between 'intuition' and 'theory' that the method of RE is meant to address. But, as Williamson (2007, p. 245–6) points out, it makes no sense if we interpret this conflict as one between the JTB analysis and the psychological fact that we believe or intuit that the Gettier subject has NKJTB because the assumed truth of the JTB analysis is consistent with that psychological fact.

3   For example, Sayre-McCord (1996) makes this point clear when he writes: "The relative coherence of a set of beliefs is a matter of whether, and to what degree, the set exhibits (what I will call) *evidential consistency, connectedness, and comprehensiveness....* Each ... is a property of a set of beliefs, if it is at all, only in virtue of the evidential relations that hold among the *contents* of the beliefs in the set" (p. 166 bold emphasis added).

4   Or, alternatively, instead of appealing to this idea that it is sufficient for one's belief being doxastically justified, one might merely appeal to the weaker claim that it is a sufficient condition for having propositional justification to so believe.

5   I say 'to some degree' in relation to the fact that, as noted earlier, the state of reflective equilibrium is usually thought of as an ideal that we should aim for but may never reach. But proponents of the method of RE will obviously want to say that we can still justify our beliefs (at least to some degree) by making steps towards this ideal.

6   For example, Bonjour (1985) offered one of the most prominent and detailed accounts of the nature of coherence, but even he saw his account as "a long way from being as definitive as desirable" (1985, p. 101).

7   How exactly should one bring one's beliefs into a state where they cohere with each other? For example, suppose that one's initial set of moral beliefs includes the belief that it would be morally impermissible for a surgeon to save the lives of five of their patients by giving them the organs of one of their other patients against the wishes of that patient (Foot 1967, Thomson 1976). Furthermore, suppose that one's initial set of moral principles include some simple act-consequentialist principle that, if correct, would classify this action as being morally obligatory. How should one resolve this conflict? Should one reject the initial belief or the theoretical principle or both? Again, proponents of the method of RE do not say as much about this kind of issue as one might like. But one idea that is present in many statements of the method of RE is that decisions about how to resolve such questions should be sensitive to the *strength* of one's initial beliefs, as well as the *power* of the theoretical principles. See DePaul (1998, p. 295) for a nice discussion of these ideas....

REFERENCES

BonJour, L. (1985). *The Structure of Empirical Knowledge.* Cambridge, MA: Harvard University Press

DePaul, M. (1998). "Why Bother With Reflective Equilibrium?" In Michael DePaul and William Ramsey (eds.) *Rethinking Intuition.* Lanham, MD: Rowman and Littlefield: 293–309.

Foot, P. (1967). "The Problem of Abortion and the Doctrine of Double Effect." *Oxford Review* 5:5–15.

Goodman, N. (1954). "The New Riddle of Induction." In his *Fact, Fiction, and Forecast.* Cambridge MA: Harvard University Press: 59–83.

Lewis, D. (1983). *Philosophical Papers, Volume I.* Oxford: Oxford University Press.

Rawls, J. (1951). "Outline of a Decision Procedure for Ethics." *Philosophical Review* 60: 2:177–97. Reprinted in Rawls (1999): 1–19.

Rawls, J. (1971). *A Theory of Justice*, 2nd edition 1999. Cambridge MA: Harvard University Press.

Rawls, J. (1974). "The Independence of Moral Theory." *Proceedings and Addresses of the American Philosophical Association* 47: 5–22. Reprinted in Rawls (1999): 286–302. Page references are to the reprinted version.

Rawls, J. (1999). *Collected Papers*, Sam Freeman, (ed.). Cambridge MA: Harvard University Press.

Sayre-McCord, G. (1996). "Coherentist Epistemology and Moral Theory." In Sinnott-Armstrong, W. and Timmons, M. (eds.), *Moral Knowledge? New Readings in Moral Epistemology*. New York: Oxford University Press: 137–89.

Scanlon, T.M. (2003). "Rawls on Justification." In Samuel Freeman (ed.), *The Cambridge Companion to Rawls*. New York: Cambridge University Press: 139–67.

Thomson, J.J. (1976). "Killing, Letting Die, and the Trolley Problem." *The Monist* 59 (2): 204–17.

Williamson, T. (2007). *The Philosophy of Philosophy*. Oxford: Blackwell Publishing

—8—

SOPHIE'S CHOICE

John P. Anderson

Sophie stood with her young daughter and son before the Nazi doctor on the railway platform at Auschwitz:

... the doctor said, "You may keep one of your children"

"Bitte!" said Sophie.

"You may keep one of your children," he repeated. "The other one will have to go. Which will you keep?"

"You mean I have to choose?"

... Her thought process dwindled, ceased. Then she felt her legs crumple. "I can't choose! I can't choose!" She began to scream....

Tormented angels never screeched so loudly above hell's pandemonium. "Ich kann nicht wahlen!" she screamed.

The doctor was aware of unwanted attention. "Shut up!" he ordered. "Hurry now and choose. Choose goddamnit, or I'll send them both over there. Quick!"

... "Don't make me choose," she heard herself plead in a whisper, "I can't choose."

"Send them both over there, then," The doctor said to the aide, "nach links."

"Mama!" She heard Eva's thin but soaring cry at the instant that she thrust the child away from her and rose from the concrete with a clumsy stumbling motion. "Take the baby!" she called out. "Take my little girl!"

William Styron
Sophie's Choice[1]

THAT AN UNSPEAKABLE EVIL IS DONE HERE IS clear. That the Nazi doctor ought to be blamed as an architect and executor of this evil is also indisputable. The question is whether Sophie's choice was morally impermissible, whether she had reason to torment herself with guilt, as she did, over the role she played in what happened that day on the platform at Auschwitz. It would seem Sophie's knowingly and voluntarily handing her innocent daughter over to certain death in the manner she did would be recognized as morally impermissible on myriad related and not so related standards of moral evaluation: e.g., as a violation of Kant's categorical imperative, as a violation of the doctrine of double effect, and perhaps even as showing a lack of integrity qua mother. I will argue, however, that Sophie's guilt was groundless, that what she did in giving her daughter to the Nazi doctor was on any reasonable account of conditions for moral permissibility either moral or amoral, but clearly *not* immoral.

One may object that any "cool" moral evaluation of such an emotionally charged decision must somehow oversimplify and consequently fail to fully address the profundity of the experience Sophie was forced to endure. I am not, however, impressed by this as an objection. *Sophie's Choice* is in many ways a novel about exploring and reconciling oneself to the moral reactive attitudes (both first-personal and third-personal) associated with one's past decisions and one's moral inheritance. Any exploration, reconciliation, or perhaps even overcoming, of a moral reactive attitude (e.g., that of guilt) will make a crucial appeal to the reasons lying behind and supporting that attitude. If Sophie could have seen that the reasons lying behind her guilt failed to justify that sentiment, or at least that there is a description of her choice under which she was not morally blameworthy for it, then this might have provided her with the groundwork for a possible reconciliation with her decision, and an overcoming of her past. My object here is an apology for Sophie, one that I hope, had she read it, might have spoken to some of her doubts and alleviated some of her pain.

If one is going to argue that Sophie's choice was morally impermissible, it will most likely be via an appeal to what Samuel Scheffler has labeled "agent-centered restrictions." We can think of a moral restriction as *agent-centered* where it is at least *sometimes* (allowing for threshold theories) not permissible to violate that restriction when such a violation would be certain to prevent one or more equally impermissible violation(s), there being no other morally relevant factors.[2] Such restrictions are *agent-centered* insofar as they are restrictions only on what an agent can do *herself*, and not on what an agent can knowingly allow *others* to do. I take it the critic would say that Sophie violated an agent-centered restriction by voluntarily handing her child over to a man whom she knows will certainly put that child to death; i.e., she willingly took part in some terrible evil that morality requires one under no circumstances willingly take part in. In defending Sophie, I will first attack the idea of agent-centered restrictions.

The debate over the legitimacy of agent-centered restrictions has been traditionally understood as engaging the opposing forces of commonsense morality (pro) and consequentialism (con), where central premises of each (e.g., respectively, the inviolability of persons and maximizing rationality) clash, and the weakness of one is considered a strength of the other. Thus, rejecting agent-centered restrictions has usually meant (at least indirectly) defending consequentialism. The argument I present here, however, rejects the idea of agent-centered restrictions independently of any consequentialist suppositions by appealing to nothing more than a clear moral symmetry between commissions and omissions in special choice situations like Sophie's. So while my argument *will* undermine agent-centered restrictions it will do this while remaining neutral with respect to the broader debate between commonsense morality and consequentialism.

An omission by Sophie (refusing to choose a child) would have meant allowing the Nazi doctor to put *both* of her children to death. Her commission meant selecting one of her children to be put to death, leaving the other by her side. I will argue the question of whether Sophie did something morally impermissible in choosing the commission can be decided by the question of whether we take omissions qua omissions to be intrinsically *asymmetric* or *symmetric* to commissions with respect to their moral permissibility in unfortunate choice situations like Sophie's, i.e., whether even where the consequences of the commission and omission are certain to be *the same* (say, only one child dies either way), the commission will always be *more* morally impermissible than the omission. Depending on how this question is settled, we might anticipate (roughly) four possible interpretations of the status of agent-centered restrictions and their role in morally evaluating these choice situations.

Regarding the first two interpretations, if we hold that, where the same evil consequences are certain to result from the commission and the omission in some choice situation, the commission will *always* be more impermissible than the omission, then we can conclude that commissions are intrinsically more morally impermissible than omissions in such cases. I will refer to this as the *asymmetry thesis*. With the asymmetry thesis in hand, we might turn to cases like Sophie's, where arguably it is *not* certain the evil consequences will be the same for the omission (where two children die) and the commission (where one child dies), and say one of the two following statements will hold true—depending on the further question of whether we take the *number* of those affected to be of moral importance:

(AS1) The morally objectionable property of killing innocents (however one defines it) is *additive* (i.e., a state of affairs in which one innocent is killed is ceterus paribus viewed as better from the moral point of view than a state of affairs wherein two innocents are killed). Maximizing rationality applies in Sophie's case, but its force could be *outweighed* by the extra importance of her not actively participating in the act of killing by choosing and giving a child to the killer *herself*.

(AS2) The morally objectionable property of killing innocents is *not* additive in nature; maximizing rationality does *not* apply, and it is *never* permissible to commit an act of the type Sophie commits.

Accepting the asymmetry thesis under the conditions outlined in (AS1) leaves room for the claim that it will at least *sometimes* be impermissible to prevent an evil act, e.g., the killing of innocents, by a single performance of this very same act-type, and that agent-centered restrictions *can* therefore be justified. Whether such a restriction would hold in Sophie's case given (AS1) will depend on whether *one* thinks the extra killing of one innocent would be enough to outweigh the asymmetry thesis' presumption against Sophie's killing an innocent *herself*. Accepting the asymmetry thesis on the terms outlined by (AS2), however, forces one to admit agent-centered restrictions are *absolute*.

If, on the other hand, we hold that a commission and an omission will be *equally* impermissible (if impermissible at all) where the consequences of each are certain to be the same—I will refer to this as the *symmetry thesis*—then we might say one of the following alternatives will hold true in evaluating Sophie's choice:

(S1) The morally objectionable property of killing innocents is additive in value; maximizing rationality applies, and it would *not* therefore be morally impermissible for Sophie to seek to minimize the killing of innocents by choosing one child to die.

(S2) The morally objectionable property of killing innocents is *not* additive; maximizing rationality does *not* apply, and Sophie is left with options that cannot be distinguished with respect to their moral permissibility.

If we take these four alternatives to be reasonably exhaustive, we can see that, if the symmetry thesis is adopted, agent-centered restrictions are rejected *regardless* of whether we accept the moral relevance of maximizing rationality.[3] Thus, the fate of agent-centered restrictions seems to depend on that of the asymmetry thesis....

In "Autonomy and Deontology,"[4] Thomas Nagel addresses this issue: "How can what we *do* in this narrow sense be so important?"[5] Nagel argues that agent-centered restrictions are in place because "deontological reasons" tell us nothing more than not to *aim* at what is evil. When one aims at something, one's actions are guided by that thing, following it if it should change its course. By contrast, when one is merely knowingly allowing something to happen, but is not striving to produce it, one's actions are not guided by that thing. If the thing in question is evil, by aiming at it, one's actions will be directed by it and one will be "swimming head-on against the normative current,"[6] flying in the face of what "deontological reasons" tell us.

Nagel considers a case in which one might save lives by twisting a young child's arm.[7] He argues that if one seeks this good end by these evil means, one must in fact aim at the evil of the child's pain, and allow one's actions to be guided by it. If the child is not screaming loud enough, one must twist harder. In this case, at "every point, the intentional function is simply the normative function reversed, and from the point of view of the agent, this produces an acute sense of moral dislocation."[8] Thus, it is the inherent wrongness of striving against our moral goal by aiming at evil in an act that, for Nagel, motivates and justifies agent-centered restrictions.

... [L]et us return to Sophie and consider how her choice might be evaluated in light of the symmetry thesis. If the symmetry thesis is adopted, then (as was pointed out above) it seems clear either

(S1) The morally objectionable property of killing innocents is additive in value; maximizing rationality applies, and it was *not* impermissible for Sophie to seek to minimize the number of killings of innocents by choosing one child to die.

or

(S2) The morally objectionable property of killing innocents is *not* additive; maximizing rationality does *not* apply, and Sophie's options (the commission and omission) cannot be distinguished with respect to their moral permissibility.

must hold true, and agent-centered restrictions play no part in either. If we adopt (S1), we might say that not only did Sophie do what was morally *permissible*, she did what was morally *required* of her; we can say Sophie's choice was a *moral* one. What, however, can we say if we adopt (S2)?

I see two possible interpretations of the moral ramifications of adopting (S2): Under the first, one might say Sophie just had bad moral luck and no matter what she did she would have acted equally immorally. But not only does this seem too hard an evaluation of Sophie's action in the situation we know her to have been in, it also makes little sense. It seems to be a sound moral principle that for an act to be correctly described as morally impermissible it must stand alongside other options that bear disparate moral weights. If x and y exhaust an agent's alternatives in action (using the term "action" to cover both commissions and omissions), and both x and y bear precisely the same moral weights (whether those weights be insignificant or great), there will be no way to distinguish between x and y with respect to their moral permissibility, and there will therefore be no available criterion for judging that agent's action, whether it be x or y, as right or wrong—as moral or immoral. Thus, given (S2), insofar as there is just no sense in which Sophie *could* have chosen to act morally, it is incoherent to say she acted *immorally*.[9]

The second interpretation of (S2) is at once more interesting and more plausible than the first: We might say there was just no way for Sophie to distinguish between her two options with respect to their moral permissibility, so her choice was not within the moral realm at all. It might be argued that *any* reason Sophie gave (keeping in mind she did not want to harm either of her children) for choosing one over the other would have been morally acceptable in the sense that it would have been morally *irrelevant*. Again, I am arguing moral permissibility and responsibility are intimately related to an agent's having a *real choice* between acts with *different* moral worths. If one accepts (S2) as the consequence of adopting the symmetry thesis, there is no such morally interesting choice to be made in Sophie's case; at least with respect to moral permissibility, her options were identical. Thus, on this second interpretation of (S2) there is no sense in which we can call Sophie's choice either immoral *or* moral, but only *amoral*. In short, (S2) allows us to license Sophie's choice without forcing us to recommend it—it allows us to countenance it without judging it to be either *right* or *wrong*. This seems to me just what we want to say about it.

Thus, given the success of the symmetry thesis, we are left with either (S1) or (S2) to choose between in evaluating Sophie's conduct on the railway platform at Auschwitz. And while I think (S2) provides the most satisfying moral account of what happened, neither (S1) nor (S2) finds any room for moral censure in what *she* did. Sophie's choice was an awful one. But what made it awful had nothing to do with Sophie and everything to do with the gray-black moral landscape of Auschwitz. Evil is sometimes manifest as an ineluctable force, a juggernaut that cannot be fought, only endured.[10]

NOTES

1   William Styron, *Sophie's Choice* (New York: Random House, 1976), 483–484.

2   Samuel Scheffler, *The Rejection of Consequentialism* (Oxford: Oxford University Press, 1982), and "Agent Centered Restrictions, Rationality and the Virtues" in *Consequentialism and Its Critics*, ed. Samuel Scheffler (Oxford: Oxford University Press, 1988). Scheffler defines an agent-centered restriction differently as "a restriction which it is at least sometimes impermissible to violate in circumstances where a violation would minimize total overall violations of the very same restriction, and would have no other morally relevant consequences" (Scheffler, *Consequentialism and Its Critics*, 243). Our definitions differ on one main point: I leave out the "where a violation would minimize total overall violations" because it seems clear that the agent-centered nature of the restriction would still hold where a *single* violation could prevent another *single* violation.

3   One may object that (S2) *does* leave room for agent-centered restrictions. For, even if (S2) is admitted, it might still be the case that Sophie's omission would be impermissible; it might just be that the omission and commission in her case would be *equally* impermissible or immoral. I think this position is incoherent and I will explain why when I return to an evaluation of (S2) after having defended the symmetry thesis.

4   Thomas Nagel, "Autonomy and Deontology," in *Consequentialism and Its Critics*, ed. Samuel Scheffler (Oxford: Oxford University Press, 1988), 142–172.

5   Nagel, "Autonomy and Deontology," 163.

6   Nagel, "Autonomy and Deontology," 163.

7   Nagel, "Autonomy and Deontology." Nagel's scenario differs from the kind we are focusing on, in that his choice situation is not between two identical morally objectionable act-types. To make our discussions truly parallel, he would have to compare my twisting a young child's arm to being in a position to stop you from doing the same thing. The difference here does not, however, affect the relevancy of Nagel's argument to our discussion; for, I assume, his argument would be the same in either scenario.

8   Nagel, "Autonomy and Deontology," 164.

9   Say *x* and *y* are exhaustive alternatives for *A* and stand for acts that would respectively fulfill mutually exclusive promises *A* has made (*p1* and *p2*) which bear equal moral weight. One might object that, given my account of moral evaluation as comparative, I am committed to the claim that *A* can do no wrong here. And indeed I am, but I fail to see how this conclusion is in any way problematic: If *A* made *p2* knowing full well that he was already committed to *p1*, then he committed the wrong *there*. In such a case our moral evaluation of *A* would not be at the level of the decision between fulfilling *p1* or *p2* by performing *x* or *y*—that decision *would* be morally neutral—it would be at the level of *A*'s knowingly placing himself in such a dilemma.

10   I would like to thank John Marshall for his many helpful comments on this paper.

THE TROLLEY PROBLEM

Anna M. Kietzerow

1. BACKGROUND

IMAGINE: YOU ARE AN INNOCENT BYSTANDER simply standing by some trolley tracks. Beside you is a lever, which you know, if you were to pull it, you could change the tracks for which the trolley would be traveling down. Suddenly you see a run-away trolley thundering down the track. The driver of the trolley tries to pull the break, but it is not working. If the trolley continues on its current path, it will hit and kill five innocent people. If you were to pull the lever beside you and divert the trolley onto a different set of tracks you would save the lives of the five innocent people. If you pull the lever, however, and change the tracks, you will cause the trolley to hit and kill one innocent person. Is it okay for you to pull the lever?

Imagine: You are a remarkably successful transplant surgeon; every transplant surgery that you perform is perfect and there is no rejection of the transplanted organ. You currently have five patients in the hospital, all of whom are the same blood type and all in desperate need of different organs. Unfortunately, you have not been able to find a donor for any of them. Luckily, there is a patient who came into the hospital for a check-up who is the same blood type for all your patients. When you approach the patient to ask him if it is okay for you operate on him to take his organs, the patient politely declines. Is it still okay for the surgeon to operate on the patient to save the lives of his five patients?

While most do agree that it is okay for one to pull the lever to save the lives of five different people, most do not agree that it is okay for a

surgeon to kill a person in order to save the lives of five different people who need organs. Why is it okay for the bystander to kill one person in order to save five, and why is it not okay for the surgeon to kill one person in order to save five? While this ethical dilemma was originally presented by British philosopher Philippa Foot, it has since been coined "The Trolley Problem" because this is how Judith Jarvis Thomson referred to it in her 1985 analysis of dilemma. Since Thomson's analysis, however, the Trolley Problem has become an integral part of teaching ethics. While the two scenarios presented above are at the heart of the Trolley Problem, there are several different variations on it. Another one which Thomson presents is "Fat Man," where to stop the trolley and save the lives of five people you must push a fat man into the trolley's path. Regardless of which variation of the Trolley Problem is used, it's a way to assess one's moral intuitions about what one should do in cases where there is no straight-forward answer.

2. ANALYSIS

There are many different ways one can approach answering the Trolley Problem. One of the ways is to adopt the perspective that it is better to kill one person than let five people die. This is because we recognize that five lives are better than one life. While it is not that one life is not important, it is simply because the weight of five lives outweighs that of one life, because five lives will result in more happiness collectively, than one individual life on its own. Because we value happiness, we should want to increase how much happiness is in the world. In this case, one would always pull the lever to move the trolley in order to save the lives of five people.

Another way to look at answering this problem is that it is worse to kill one person than to let five people die. In pulling the lever, one is actively killing one innocent person whose life was not being threatened, rather than letting the five people die who were being threatened by the trolley. When the lever is pulled one person who was not at risk of being killed by the trolley will be killed. The one person's life would not have been threatened if the lever had not been pulled and they would not have been killed. It is not because the lives of the five people who would have died are not important; it is because the one life is also important.

Another way one can approach the Trolley Problem is that, while one person may be killed when the lever is pulled, it was not the intent to kill that person, rather the intent was to save the lives of the five people who were being threatened by the trolley. Because the intent is not to kill someone, but to save people, it is okay to pull the lever. Since we value human life, ideally, we should avoid taking someone's life from them when possible. That being said, because we do value human life, we also want to save human life when possible, and pulling the lever will allow human lives to be saved, even if the cost is killing one person.

These three ways of approaching the Trolley Problem are certainly not the only ways to approach it. While the traditional Trolley Problem has faceless persons in it, there are different variations that describe the people being threatened by the trolley. For example, the five individuals could be children and the one person could be an adult, or the one person could be a child, and the five people could be adults. This may impact how one would ethically approach answering the Trolley Problem.

DISCUSSION QUESTIONS

1. Is there a significant moral difference between "killing" and "letting die"? If there is, does it matter? If there is not, does it still matter? If the difference does not matter, why does it not matter?

2. How important is intention when approaching the Trolley Problem? Does it matter that the intent may not be to kill the one person, even if the one person still ends up being killed? Why or why not?

3. In real-world application, the Trolley Problem, and its many variations, is currently being used by engineers to teach self-driving cars how to make decisions on the road, by teaching it who to prioritize in an accident. Is this an ethical way to use the Trolley Problem in the real world? What are some potential problems you see with using the Trolley Problem in this way? Can an artificial intelligence system adapt enough to all the variables surrounding it to truly make a moral decision?

4. Come up with a variation of the Trolley Problem that would make you do the opposite of what you would normally do in the standard Trolley Problem. What is morally significant about this variation that changes how you approach the Trolley Problem? If you cannot come up with a variation that makes you do the opposite, why is that?

ALLIGATOR RIVER STORY

Rebecca Cobern Kates

1. BACKGROUND

IN A KINGDOM FAR AWAY, THERE LIVED TWO star-crossed lovers, Abigail and Gregory. Abigail and Gregory lived on different sides of a river filled with ferocious, man-eating alligators. One tragic day, a flood washed out the only accessible bridge that enabled Gregory and Abigail to visit one another.

After a painful period of separation, Abigail tries to find another way to reach her beloved Gregory. Abigail approaches Sinbad, a riverboat captain, begging that he take her across the river to see Gregory. Sinbad, spying an opportunity, happily agrees but only on the condition that she sleep with him that night. Outraged and not wanting to be unfaithful to Gregory, Abigail promptly refuses and seeks out help from another friend named Ivan.

Ivan impatiently listens to Abigail's plight, including Sinbad's demands. Not wanting to be bothered, Ivan refuses to help. In despair, and longing to see Gregory, Abigail reluctantly decides that she must accept Sinbad's offer and goes to bed with him.

The next day, using Sinbad's boat, Abigail blissfully reunites with Gregory. After their joyful reunion and feeling distressed by her experience with Sinbad, Abigail is honest with Gregory and confides in him the sacrifice she made to be with him. Gregory is unsympathetic and furiously spurns Abigail for her unfaithfulness. Telling her that he never wishes to see her again, Gregory forces Abigail to leave at once.

Heartbroken, Abigail leaves and tells her friend Slug of her misfortune. Slug, moved with compassion and anger by Abigail's distress, asks that Abigail lead him to Gregory so that he might confront him. Abigail leads Slug to Gregory who then beats him as Abigail looks on and laughs, satisfied that Gregory experienced pain in return for the immense suffering he had caused her.

When the king of the land hears of these incidents, he decides that all five had acted immorally and orders his royal guard to punish them. The king commands that a consequence be administered to each, with severity commensurate to the immorality of the offence.

2. ANALYSIS

One could rank the characters in various ways. Some possibilities include, but are not limited to, a consequentialist, a deontological, or an aretaic approach.

First, a consequentialist looks at the results of an action to determine whether the action was morally right or wrong; a person's action could be morally right if it maximizes the most good for the most people.

Abigail uses this approach when she concedes to Sinbad's demands, reasoning that the good of being reunited with Gregory will outweigh the bad of being unfaithful (or of any distress she will experience by sleeping with Sinbad). It is necessary with this approach, however, to define what the good for the most people is. Sinbad uses a consequentialist approach to rationalize his decision to take advantage of Abigail: he will provide himself pleasure and help Abigail reach her lover. While he did benefit from momentary personal pleasure, the consequences wreaked havoc on Abigail and Gregory's relationship and violated Abigail's dignity.

Using the consequentialist approach, how far down a chain of events is a person responsible? Ivan is at fault for being uncaring towards Abigail when he possibly could have helped, but is he responsible for all the subsequent events after his decision not to be involved? If we do not think he is responsible and those consequences are not a result of his initial inaction, we might consider other approaches to determine if he acted immorally.

We could take the deontological approach, looking at whether an act is right or wrong based on whether it conforms to a moral norm, regardless of the action's consequences. For instance, Gregory uses this approach when he rejects Abigail for sleeping with Sinbad, regardless of the benefit of being reunited.

To conceptualize how an action may violate a moral norm is to use Immanuel Kant's Categorical Imperative, which proposes that we act in such a way that the principle of our conduct could acceptably become a universal law of nature for all rational beings. For instance, Slug acted immorally by beating Gregory because we would not want to universalize his conduct such that we should beat people whenever they anger us. Sinbad's actions are also morally reprehensible because we should not universalize his conduct; sexually exploiting someone is never appropriate for personal gain. But there are certainly circumstances where it is permissible to refuse to help someone. If Ivan had other reasons besides a general lack of care about Abigail's situation, then it would be less obvious his inaction was wrong.

A third approach is the aretaic approach, also known as virtue ethics, which is based on what makes a good person. This approach more clearly illuminates what we instinctively feel is so wrong with the responses of Gregory and Ivan to Abigail's plight. Perhaps Ivan and Gregory have the right to respond as they did, but we may think a kind and compassionate person should respond differently.

All these approaches may find the same actions to be morally right or wrong but for different reasons and to varying degrees. For instance, an aretaic approach may not find infidelity universally wrong where a deontological approach might, but an aretaic approach may fault Abigail for lacking wisdom in accepting Sinbad's terms.

DISCUSSION QUESTIONS

1. If the king asked you for a ranking of the five characters from most to least morally reprehensible, what ranking would you assign to them? Why?

2. There are a number of reasons why the characters might be ranked in one order or another. Why is it is difficult to rank them?

3. Try ranking the characters from most to least morally reprehensible using the three different approaches in the discussion: consequentialist, deontological, aretaic. Which approach do you think is best?

4. Is there a single moral approach that can act as the sole guide in complex moral situations? Why or why not?

PROFESSIONS AND PROFESSIONAL ETHICS

Jonathan Milgrim

1. INTRODUCTION

WHAT DOES IT MEAN TO BE PROFESSIONAL? IT can mean that you have a specific skill set, or a specific sort of training. It might mean that you belong to a certain group. It might also mean that there are certain things expected of you that are not expected of other workers. Consider the following story: on September 25, 2013 Carlos Gomez of Major League Baseball's Milwaukee Brewers hit a towering home run off Paul Maholm of the Atlanta Braves. He stood for a few moments and watched the ball fly over the outfield fence, before slowly trotting around the bases. As he rounded the bases various Atlanta players could be seen yelling at him. Before he could reach home plate, a visibly angry Brian McCann, then the Atlanta Braves catcher, blocked his way. The benches cleared and it was several minutes before order was restored and the game resumed. The game itself was nearly meaningless, with the Braves well ahead of all others in their division, and the Brewers near last place in their division with the season nearing an end. So what infraction had Gomez committed? The answer: he stood and watched his home run, instead of immediately running the bases. While he did not break a rule in the rulebook, he was perceived to have acted unprofessionally.[1]

This story serves to highlight an important aspect of being a professional. While it is certainly the case that professionals have attributes that may not be present in other forms of employment, what truly sets professionals apart are the additional ethical obligations that they carry with them as a result of belonging to their profession. However, these obligations do not exist in a vacuum.

The additional obligations carried by a profession exist alongside a heightened level of trust and respect that is afforded most professionals. We expect more from our doctors and our lawyers, but we are also willing to trust them with our lives and our livelihoods, something that is likely not said of the non-professional. This brings up an important question. How do we decide which groups of workers are simultaneously afforded this respect while also having additional obligations expected of them? What distinguishes the lawyer from the farmer or the engineer from the factory laborer? It seems to be more than just additional training. Some factory occupations require extensive training. Meanwhile, there are many farmers with advanced degrees in agriculture, as well as those that have spent a lifetime learning in order to be successful. There must be something more; the question is what. These are the questions that this unit strives to answer.

2. CONTENTS

This unit comprises six articles and two case studies. The articles start with "Attributes of a Profession" by Ernest Greenwood. In this article, Greenwood attempts to answer the questions above by identifying five attributes that every group must possess in order to be considered a profession. This is followed by "Just Another Day at the Office: The Ordinariness of Professional Ethics" by Don Welch. Welch counters the assumption that there are additional obligations for professionals, because everyone faces moral choices and to separate out a special subset that only applies to professionals only conflates the issue.

The next two articles deal with what is considered an integral part of professional ethics, that is, rules that are specific to professions. First, "Honor Among Thieves: Some Reflections on Professional Codes of Ethics" by John T. Sanders, explores the uniqueness of the rules for each profession. He compares the rules, and how professionals identify themselves with these rules, to the rules followed by the Garduna of sixteenth-century Spain. The next article, "Professional Responsibility: Just Following the Rules?" by Michael Davis, explores the ways in which rule following can be problematic or even unethical. Examples of the latter include someone strictly interpreting a rule in order to hurt someone else, or someone using a rule to defend their own unethical behavior.

Building on this last theme, Avery Kolers examines what it means to break a rule when it violates a personal moral code in "Am I my Profession's Keeper?" This explores the contentious pull between being a good professional and being a good person. Can doctors refuse to perform a certain medical procedure if their personal moral codes forbid it? The final article in the unit, "Against Professional Ethics" by Bob Brecher, explores professional codes of ethics, and whether they are helpful or harmful to professionals in doing the right thing.

The unit concludes with two case studies. The first involves an engineer who criticized the duration of amber lights, or the time between a traffic light being green and turning red. The case study highlights some potential issues with professional codes of ethics that prohibit professionals from engaging in certain profession-related criticisms outside designated channels. The second case study explores the issues faced by nurses and other medical personnel who must balance the well-being of their patients with their own health and compensation.

NOTE

1   The video of the play can be seen here: https://www.youtube.com/watch?v=rAxJunWPDdg.

—9—

ATTRIBUTES OF A PROFESSION

Ernest Greenwood

THE PROFESSIONS OCCUPY A POSITION OF GREAT importance on the American scene.[1] In a society such as ours, characterized by minute division of labor based upon technical specializations, many important features of social organization are dependent upon professional functions. Professional activity is coming to play a predominant role in the life patterns of increasing numbers of individuals of both sexes, occupying much of their waking moments, providing life goals, determining behavior, and shaping personality. It is no wonder, therefore, that the phenomenon of professionalism has become an object of observation by sociologists.[2] The sociological approach to professionalism is one that views a profession as an organized group which is constantly interacting with the society that forms its matrix, which performs its social functions through a network of formal and informal relationships, and which creates its own sub-culture requiring adjustments to it as a prerequisite for career success.[3]

Within the professional category of its occupational classification the United States Census Bureau includes, among others, the following: accountant, architect, artist, attorney, clergyman, college professor, dentist, engineer, journalist, judge, librarian, natural scientist, optometrist, pharmacist, physician, social scientist, social worker, surgeon, and teacher.[4]

What common attributes do these professional occupations possess which distinguish them from the nonprofessional ones? After a careful canvass of the sociological literature on occupations, this writer has been able to distill five elements, upon which there appears to be consensus among the students of the subject, as constituting the distinguishing attributes of a profession.[5] Succinctly put, all professions seem to possess: (1) systematic theory, (2) authority, (3) community sanction, (4) ethical codes, and (5) a culture. The purpose of this article is to describe fully these attributes.

Before launching into our description, a preliminary word of caution is due. With respect to each of the above attributes, the true difference between a professional and a nonprofessional occupation is not a qualitative but a quantitative one. Strictly speaking, these attributes are not the exclusive monopoly of the professions; nonprofessional occupations also possess them, but to a lesser degree. As is true of most social phenomena, the phenomenon of professionalism cannot be structured in terms of clear-cut classes. Rather, we must think of the occupations in a society as distributing themselves along a continuum.[6] At one end of this continuum are bunched the well-recognized and undisputed professions (*e.g.*, physician, attorney, professor, scientist); at the opposite end are bunched the least skilled and least attractive occupations (*e.g.*, watchman, truckloader, farm laborer, scrubwoman, bus boy). The remaining occupations, less skilled and less prestigeful than the former, but more so than the latter, are distributed between these two poles. The occupations bunched at the professional pole of the continuum possess to a maximum degree the attributes about to be described. As we move away from this pole, the occupations possess these attributes to a decreasing degree....

SYSTEMATIC BODY OF THEORY[7]

It is often contended that the chief difference between a professional and a nonprofessional occupation lies in the element of superior skill. The performance of a professional service presumably involves a series of unusually complicated operations, mastery of which requires lengthy training. The models referred to in this connection are the performances of a surgeon, a concert pianist, or a research physicist. However, some nonprofessional occupations actually involve a higher order of skill than many professional ones. For example, tool-and-die making, diamond-cutting, monument-engraving, or cabinet-making involve more intricate operations than schoolteaching, nursing, or social work. Therefore, to focus on the element of skill per se in describing the professions is to miss the kernel of their uniqueness.

The crucial distinction is this: the skills that characterize a profession flow from and are supported by a fund of knowledge that has been organized into an internally consistent system, called a *body of theory*. A profession's underlying body of theory is a system of abstract propositions that describe in general terms the classes of phenomena comprising the profession's focus of interest. Theory serves as a base in terms of which the professional rationalizes his operations in concrete situations. Acquisition of the professional skill requires a prior or simultaneous mastery of the theory underlying that skill. Preparation for a profession, therefore, involves considerable preoccupation with systematic theory, a feature virtually absent in the training of the nonprofessional. And so treatises are written on legal theory, musical theory, social work theory, the theory of the drama, and so on, but no books appear on the theory of punch-pressing or pipe-fitting or bricklaying.

Because understanding of theory is so important to professional skill, preparation for a profession must be an intellectual as well as a practical experience. On-the-job training through apprenticeship, which suffices for a nonprofessional occupation, becomes inadequate for a profession.

Orientation in theory can be achieved best through formal education in an academic setting. Hence the appearance of the professional school, more often than not university affiliated, wherein the milieu is a contrast to that of the trade school. Theoretical knowledge is more difficult to master than operational procedures; it is easier to learn to repair an automobile than to learn the principles of the internal combustion engine. There are, of course, a number of free-lance professional pursuits (*e.g.*, acting, painting, writing, composing, and the like) wherein academic preparation is not mandatory. Nevertheless, even in these fields various "schools" and "institutes" are appearing, although they may not be run along traditional academic lines. We can generalize that as an occupation moves toward professional status, apprenticeship training yields to formalized education, because the function of theory as a groundwork for practice acquires increasing importance....

PROFESSIONAL AUTHORITY

Extensive education in the systematic theory of his discipline imparts to the professional a type of knowledge that highlights the layman's comparative ignorance. This fact is the basis for the professional's authority, which has some interesting features.

A nonprofessional occupation has customers; a professional occupation has clients. What is the difference? A customer determines what services and/or commodities he wants, and he shops around until he finds them. His freedom of decision rests upon the premise that he has the capacity to appraise his own needs and to judge the potential of the service or of the commodity to satisfy them. The infallibility of his decisions is epitomized in the slogan: "The customer is always right!" In a professional relationship, however, the professional dictates what is good or evil for the client, who has no choice but to accede to professional judgment. Here the premise is that, because he lacks the requisite theoretical background, the client cannot diagnose his own needs or discriminate among the range of possibilities for meeting them. Nor is the client considered able to evaluate the caliber of the professional service he receives. In a nonprofessional occupation the customer can criticize the quality of the commodity he has purchased, and even demand a refund. The client lacks this same prerogative, having surrendered it to professional authority. This element of authority is one, although not the sole, reason why a profession frowns on advertising. If a profession were to advertise, it would, in effect, impute to the potential client the discriminating capacity to select from competing forms of service. The client's subordination to professional authority invests the professional with a monopoly of judgment. When an occupation strives toward professionalization, one of its aspirations is to acquire this monopoly....

Thus far we have discussed that phase of professional authority which expresses itself in the client-professional relationship. Professional authority, however, has professional-community ramifications. To these we now turn.

SANCTION OF THE COMMUNITY

Every profession strives to persuade the community to sanction its authority within certain spheres by conferring upon the profession a series of powers and privileges. Community approval of these powers and privileges may be either informal or formal; formal approval is that reinforced by the community's police power.

Among its powers is the profession's control over its training centers. This is achieved through an accrediting process exercised by one of the associations within the profession. By granting or withholding accreditation, a profession can, ideally, regulate its schools as to their number, location, curriculum content, and caliber of instruction. Comparable control is not to be found in a nonprofessional occupation.[8] ...

Among the professional privileges, one of the most important is that of confidentiality. To facilitate efficient performance, the professional encourages the client to volunteer information he otherwise would not divulge. The community regards this as privileged communication, shared solely between client and professional, and protects the latter legally from encroachments upon such confidentiality. To be sure, only a select few of the professions, notably medicine and law, enjoy this immunity. Its very rarity makes it the ultimate in professionalization. Another one of the professional privileges is a relative immunity from community judgment on technical matters. Standards for professional performance are reached by consensus within the profession and are based on the existing body of theory. The lay community is presumed incapable of comprehending these standards and, hence, of using them to identify malpractice. It is generally conceded that a professional's performance can be evaluated only by his peers.

The powers and privileges described above constitute a monopoly granted by the community to the professional group. Therefore, when an occupation strives toward professional status, one of its prime objectives is to acquire this monopoly.... Specifically the profession seeks to prove: that the performance of the occupational skill requires specialized education; that those who possess this education, in contrast to those who do not, deliver a superior service; and that the human need being served is of sufficient social importance to justify the superior performance.

REGULATIVE CODE OF ETHICS

The monopoly enjoyed by a profession vis-à-vis clients and community is fraught with hazards. A monopoly can be abused; powers and privileges can be used to protect vested interests against the public weal.[9] The professional group could peg the price of its services at an unreasonably high level; it could restrict the numbers entering the occupation to create a scarcity of personnel; it could dilute the caliber of its performance without community awareness; and it could frustrate forces within the occupation pushing for socially beneficial changes in practices.[10] Were such abuses to become conspicuous, widespread, and permanent, the community would, of course, revoke the profession's monopoly. This extreme measure is normally unnecessary, because every profession has a built-in regulative code which compels ethical behavior on the part of its members.

The profession's ethical code is part formal and part informal. The formal is the written code to which the professional usually swears upon being admitted to practice; this is best exemplified by the Hippocratic Oath of the medical profession. The informal is the unwritten code, which nonetheless carries the weight of formal prescriptions. Through its ethical code the profession's commitment to the social welfare becomes a matter of public record, thereby insuring for itself the continued confidence of the community. Without such confidence the profession could not retain its monopoly. To be sure, self-regulative codes are characteristic of all occupations, nonprofessional as well as professional. However, a professional code is perhaps more explicit, systematic, and binding; it certainly possesses more altruistic overtones and is more public service-oriented.[11] These account for the frequent synonymous use of the terms "professional" and "ethical" when applied to occupational behavior....

The ways and means whereby a profession enforces the observance of its ethical code constitute a case study in social control. Self-discipline is achieved informally and formally.

Informal discipline consists of the subtle and the not-so-subtle pressures that colleagues exert upon one another. An example in this connection is the phenomenon of consultation and referral.[12] Consultation is the practice of inviting a colleague to participate in the appraisal of the client's need and/or in the planning of the service to be rendered. Referral is the practice of affording colleagues access to a client or an appointment. Thus, one colleague may refer his client to another, because lack of time or skill prevents his rendering the needed service; or he may recommend another for appointment by a prospective employer. Since professional ethics precludes aggressive

competition and advertising, consultation and referral constitute the principal source of work to a professional. The consultation-referral custom involves professional colleagues in a system of reciprocity which fosters mutual interdependence. Interdependence facilitates social control; chronic violation of professional etiquette arouses colleague resentment, resulting in the cessation of consultation requests and referrals.

A more formal discipline is exercised by the professional associations, which possess the power to criticize or to censure, and in extreme cases to bar recalcitrants. Since membership in good standing in the professional associations is a *sine qua non* of professional success, the prospect of formal disciplinary action operates as a potent force toward conformity.

THE PROFESSIONAL CULTURE

Every profession operates through a network of formal and informal groups. Among the formal groups, first there are the organizations through which the profession performs its services; these provide the institutionalized setting where professional and client meet. Examples of such organizations are hospital, clinic, university, law office, engineering firm, or social agency. Secondly, there are the organizations whose functions are to replenish the profession's supply of talent and to expand its fund of knowledge. These include the educational and the research centers. Third among the formal groups are the organizations which emerge as an expression of the growing consciousness-of-kind on the part of the profession's members, and which promote so-called group interests and aims. These are the professional associations. Within and around these formal organizations extends a filigree of informal groupings: the multitude of small, closely knit clusters of colleagues. Membership in these cliques is based on a variety of affinities: specialties within the profession; affiliations with select professional societies; residential and work propinquity; family, religious, or ethnic background; and personality attractions.

The interactions of social roles required by these formal and informal groups generate a social configuration unique to the profession, *viz.*, a professional culture. All occupations are characterized by formal and informal groupings; in this respect the professions are not unique. What is unique is the culture thus begotten. If one were to single out the attribute that most effectively differentiates the professions from other occupations, this is it. Thus we can talk of a professional culture as distinct from a nonprofessional culture. Within the professions as a logical class each profession develops its own sub-culture, a variant of the professional culture; the engineering subculture, for example, differs from the subcultures of medicine and social work. In the subsequent discussion, however, we will treat the culture of the professions as a generic phenomenon. The culture of a profession consists of its *values, norms,* and *symbols.*

The social values of a professional group are its basic and fundamental beliefs, the unquestioned premises upon which its very existence rests. Foremost among these values is the essential worth of the service which the professional group extends to the community. The profession considers that the service is a social good and that community welfare would be immeasurably impaired by its absence. The twin concepts of professional authority and monopoly also possess the force of a group value. Thus, the proposition that in all service-related matters the professional group is infinitely wiser than the laity is regarded as beyond argument. Likewise nonarguable is the proposition that acquisition by the professional group of a service monopoly would inevitably produce social progress. And then there is the value of rationality; that is, the commitment to objectivity in the realm of theory and technique. By virtue of this orientation, nothing of a theoretical or technical nature is regarded as sacred and unchallengeable simply because it has a history of acceptance and use.

The norms of a professional group are the guides to behavior in social situations. Every profession develops an elaborate system of these role definitions. There is a range of appropriate behaviors for seeking admittance into the profession, for gaining entry into its formal and informal groups, and for progressing within the occupation's hierarchy. There are appropriate modes of securing appointments, of conducting referrals, and of handling consultation. There are proper ways of acquiring clients, of receiving and dismissing them, of questioning and treating them, of accepting and rejecting them. There are correct ways of grooming a protégé, of recompensing a sponsor, and of relating to peers, superiors, or subordinates. There are even group-approved ways of challenging an outmoded theory, of introducing a new technique, and of conducting an intraprofessional controversy. In short, there is a behavior norm covering every standard interpersonal situation likely to recur in professional life.

The symbols of a profession are its meaning-laden items. These may include such things as: its insignias, emblems, and distinctive dress; its history, folklore, and argot; its heroes and its villains; and its stereotypes of the professional, the client, and the layman.

Comparatively clear and controlling group values, behavior norms, and symbols, which characterize the professions, are not to be encountered in nonprofessional occupations....

NOTES

1   Talcott Parsons, "The Professions and Social Structure," *Social Forces*, Vol. 17 (May 1939), 457–67.
2   Theodore Caplow, *The Sociology of Work* (Minneapolis: University of Minnesota Press, 1954).
3   Oswald Hall, "The Stages of a Medical Career," *American Journal of Sociology*, Vol. 51 (March 1948), 327–36; "Types of Medical Careers," *American Journal of Sociology*, Vol. 55 (November 1949), 243–53; "Sociological Research in the Field of Medicine: Progress and Prospects," *American Sociological Review*, Vol. 16 (October 1951), 639–44.
4   US Bureau of the Census, *1950 Census of Population: Classified Index of Occupations and*

Industries (Washington, DC: Government Printing Office, 1950).

5   The writer acknowledges his debt to his former students at the School of Social Welfare, University of California, Berkeley, who, as members of his research seminars, assisted him in identifying and abstracting the sociological literature on occupations. Their conscientious assistance made possible the formulation presented in this paper.

6   The occupational classification employed by the US Census Bureau is precisely such a continuum. The categories of this classification are: (a) professionals and semiprofessional technical workers; (b) proprietors and managers, both farm and non-farm, and officials; (c) clerical, sales, and kindred workers: (d) craftsmen, skilled workers, and foremen; (e) operatives and semiskilled workers; and (e) laborers, unskilled, service, and domestic workers (US Bureau of the Census, *op. cit.*).

7   The sequence in which the five attributes are discussed in this paper does not reflect upon their relative importance. The order selected has been dictated by logical considerations.

8   To set up and run a school for floral decorating requires no approval from the national florists' association, but no school of social work could operate long without approval of the Council on Social Work Education.

9   Abraham Flexner, "Is Social Work a Profession?" in *Proceedings of the National Conference of Charities and Corrections* (Chicago: 1915), 576–90; Robert K. Merton, "Bureaucratic Structure and Personality," in Alvin Gouldner, ed., *Studies in Leadership* (New York: Harper & Brothers, 1950), 67–79.

10   Merton, *op. cit.*

11   Flexner, *op. cit*; Parsons, *op. cit.*

12   Hall, *op. cit.*

—10—

JUST ANOTHER DAY AT THE OFFICE

The Ordinariness of Professional Ethics

Don Welch

MUCH OF THE WORK IN PROFESSIONAL ETHICS IN recent years has focused on the distinctiveness of the ethics of the professions. Alan Goldman has described the view that professional duties must override what would otherwise be moral obligations because special norms and principles should guide a professional's conduct.[1] We've been told that professionalism embodies a standard of good conduct that is not the same as the norms of morality that ordinarily govern relations among persons.[2] Often the claim is not that professionals must meet the same moral standards as the rest of us and then go beyond those, but that their distinctive moral standards may conflict with the requirements of "ordinary morality."[3]

A prevailing assumption among many professionals is that they are called on to conform to ethical standards that are "higher" than those that apply to ordinary people.[4] Professional morality places its values "at a higher position in the ethical hierarchy. It gives them greater ethical importance than does ordinary morality."[5] On reflection, however, it is not at all clear what "higher" means. Consider one statement of the ethical meaning of professionalism:

In ethical terms, to be a professional is to be dedicated to a distinctive set of ideals and standards of conduct. It is to lead a certain kind of life defined by special virtues and norms of character. And it is to enter into a subcommunity with a characteristic moral ethos and outlook.[6]

Because of these presumably distinctive ideals and standards, it is argued, professional ethics may sometimes justify, even require, a practitioner to do something different than what would otherwise be morally obligatory. This is an approach that "implies that the rules which decide what is ethical for ordinary people do not apply equally, if at all, to those with social responsibility."[7] These standards clearly establish a certain immunity for professionals from the moral requirements placed on "laypeople"; we shall return to the question of whether they are "higher."

The standards that are to govern the work of professionals are often written into canons or codes of professional ethics, which Michael Davis describes as conventions among professionals that are produced when an occupation becomes a profession. "What conscience would tell us to do *absent* a certain convention is not necessarily what conscience would tell us to do *given* that convention."[8] The existence of such professional codes, as well as conventions that take other forms, means that professionals are not permitted to engage in the weighing of the kinds of interests and factors that is allowed by ordinary morality.[9] Therefore, they are, to an extent, exempt from judgment based on moral standards outside the particular subcommunity that has its own distinctive moral ethos.

Given this heightened status that is accorded to professional ethics, it is understandable that entry into the club of professionalism is quite desirable. To the long-accepted entries of such occupations as law and medicine have been added such areas as engineering, accounting, nursing, social work, journalism, management, education, policy analysis and scientific research. The insistence of many occupational groups that they too be recognized as "professionals" has led one commentator to fear that the label "professional" is being threatened with evacuation of part of its meaning.[10]

Those who have been writing about the unique qualities and characteristics of professional ethics are themselves professionals. It is not surprising that, writing from their particular standpoints, they view their own moral dilemmas to be more noteworthy and different in kind from those faced by the masses. The sense one gets from reading much of the professional ethics literature is that, compared to the world of ordinary ethics, the demands placed on professionals are more compelling, the reasoning required of them is more sophisticated, and the compromises they make are morally superior. I am convinced, for the reasons stated below, that the distinctions are overdrawn.

Stephen F. Barker has attempted to establish the distinctiveness of professional ethics while avoiding the idea that professional obligations are more demanding and harder to comply with than those of nonprofessional occupations.[11] He identifies three features that distinguish the ethical ideology of a profession from nonprofessional ideology: (1) the ethical ideology of a profession does not stem merely from a business contract between employer and employee; (2) this professional ethical ideology involves requirements that those in the occupation have largely agreed to impose on themselves; and (3) this ideology includes an ethical ideal of service to society.[12] ...

We need to avoid taking the position that professionals impose upon themselves obligations to serve society in ways that nonprofessionals do not because the only ethical obligations nonprofessionals have is to adhere to the employee contract. Confining the moral obligations of non-professionals to those embodied in such a contract is overly restrictive. Certainly there are firefighters, cafeteria workers, construction workers, secretaries, and a host of other nonprofessionals who, as members of those groups, have felt that they should respond to moral expectations that were not a part of a business contract.

Professionals do not have a monopoly on responding to the ideal of service to society. As Barker points out, many nonprofessionals are indeed called into service to society. Nor are professionals immune from employment arrangements that override a duty they have to service a larger community good. For example, physicians reject "bedside rationing" of scarce services for the good of society because of their obligation to the single patient before them; attorneys reject being drawn into seeking justice for the good of society because of their obligation to the single client before them....

My point is that any claim for a stronger ethical content and a substantially different ethical structure for professional ethics is dubious. All of us, professionals and nonprofessionals, experience and respond to ethical problems in fundamentally the same way. The efforts to identify special concepts of morality for professionals create distracting distinctions that separate out pieces of the moral life that can be better understood as integral parts of a whole. I am not arguing that professionals do not have to respond to particular expectations that make a difference in the moral choices they make. Particular contexts do require particular kinds of ethical attention. My argument, rather, is that everyone is continuously engaged in exactly the same kind of process of moral deliberation....

Most lists of features of the professions include something like the criteria mentioned earlier. One such feature is providing services that are important to society. In recent years we have seen many examples in other countries of people starving to death because of a lack of a food distribution system. Truck drivers provide this important service to society. Airplane mechanics, firefighters and farmers, to mention only a few others, also feel that they provide important services but find themselves on few lists of professionals. Even if service to society does provide a basis for separating the professions from other occupational pursuits, it seems that that feature would argue for less moral insularity, not more. The more crucial a service is to a community, the greater the community's stake is in seeing that the service is rendered in ways that are morally appropriate in light of prevailing societal standards.

Not unrelated to this first feature of the professions is a second characteristic: professionals are committed to some good larger than their own self-interest, e.g., the welfare of society. Accordingly, we expect morally superior behavior from those engaged in a profession. But it may well be that this self-proclaimed adoption of a higher calling was rooted in economic self-interest and a desire for social status, and a gap often exists between this vision and actual professional practice. Indeed, the adoption of some ethical codes can be seen as ways of protecting professionals' self-interests by exempting them from the moral claims placed on the rest of us, rather than obligating them to higher moral aspirations in the service of the common good. And, since we're seeking distinctive features of the professions, it should be noted that we expect many others to be committed to some good larger than their own self-interest: mothers and fathers, United Way volunteers, scout masters and lay religious leaders, to name a few.

A third kind of feature often associated with the professions is the fact that they are often granted a degree of autonomy by society, sometimes including a societally granted monopoly for the services they render. This autonomy usually entails a judgment by peers, a certain insulation

from lay judgment and control. Rather than providing grounds for the claimed moral distinctiveness, this feature seems to be a result of having found such distinctiveness. A measure of autonomy is granted because of a recognition that there is something distinctive about a profession that warrants this special treatment. The issue in this inquiry is not whether this degree of moral autonomy and insulation exists, nor whether additional responsibilities are generated by such a grant of autonomy; rather, the issue is why it is appropriate to separate out certain professions in this way.

A fourth feature of the professions also gives a basis for arguing for this autonomy and thus for moral distinctiveness: the nature of professional services requires skills and knowledge not possessed by the population at large. Professions entail extensive training with a significant intellectual component. The problems and moral dilemmas encountered by professionals simply cannot be accurately assessed by laypeople....

If I want to emphasize the continuities rather than the discontinuities, it is obviously important to identify what the truck driver has in common with the doctors and lawyers. In fact, at this point, I want to enlarge the conversation to address the continuities between the ethics of the professionals and those of every other person who plays a distinctive role in our community—which is all of us. So the discussion includes not only those driving trucks and engaged in other occupations, but also mothers and fathers, participants in political parties and neighborhood organizations, citizens, members of churches and synagogues. Davis is right that the conventions that exist among us affect our moral choices. We face such conventions, however, in every role we play.

In this regard, we should look at one other feature that is sometimes mentioned as being characteristic of the professions. Individuals incur certain obligations as they enter into a profession. They pledge to abide by a code of ethics, their covenant with others to uphold the standards of that profession, they agree to act in accordance with professional expectations. This kind of contracting among members of a profession creates limits on the extent to which one can act as an individual agent. Of course, our truck driver may have certain kinds of contractual obligations—to a company from which she leases the trailer or the bank that holds a note on the cab or the shipper who relies on a delivery. But it is important to look beyond these kinds of obligations that flow from normal arrangements. Agreements like bank loans and official codes of ethics are not the only sources for moral decision-making. Many of the professional conventions are matters of less formal expectations than those codified in rules and officially adopted standards. We are also subject to the conventions and expectations of family, friends and members of nonvocational groups, i.e., the expectations of ordinary morality.

The common thread, the source of the "ordinariness of professional ethics," is that all of us, in all aspects of our lives, are subject to moral claims inherent in the roles we play. The term "positional obligation" refers to the concept that holding a particular position or filling a particular role carries with it obligations that that person would not otherwise have. This feature of role morality is not, of course, a new thought. But the well-established insights of role morality render unremarkable the weaker claims of professional ethics—that professional roles entail obligations. Further, the insights of role morality cast doubt upon the stronger claims—that professional ethics require resort to moral norms and forms of moral reasoning that are different from that required by "ordinary" roles. Professional ethics conventions—in codes and in other forms—do create prima facie duties. We can only think about the ethical issues a professional confronts in the context of the conventions of that particular profession. But this insight applies to the conventions associated with all aspects of our lives. All of the other relationships that we establish create prima facie duties as well. The difficult questions arise when we find ourselves subject to contradictory prima facie duties....

The moral dilemmas faced by professionals are fundamentally the same as those we face in all arenas of life. The challenge raised by conflicting expectations in the professions is similar to the challenge raised in everyday life. How do we balance incompatible demands? How do we weigh competing priorities? How do we determine the appropriate answer to the question, "What ought I to do?" I do not believe that the external demands of "ordinary morality" are always of secondary importance to the expectations that are generated by professional conventions. I cannot accept a moral system that asserts that professional duty always overrides other duties such as the obligations accompanying one's role as a father or as a citizen. Unless one is willing to make such a claim of unqualified preeminence for professional obligations, those obligations are recognized to be one set of moral expectations alongside others, to be responded to in the same way that we respond to ordinary moral expectations.

It does not follow that there is no such thing as professional ethics. We can recognize a particular ethic to be professional because it is marked by the realities of the relationships that exist in what we consider to be a professional setting—not by some distinctive structures for ethical reasoning. There is such a thing as professional ethics. There are also such things as parental ethics, political ethics, business ethics and religious ethics. In each case the distinctive character of the enterprise derives from the particular relationships and the content associated with particular contexts. These kinds of ethics do not call for different kinds of ethical reasoning than that called for by ordinary ethics. Rather, it is in ordinary ethics that we find the understandings of moral obligation that are common to all of these more particularized forms of ethics.

NOTES

1 Alan Goldman, *The Moral Foundations of Professional Ethics* (Totowa, NJ: Rowman and Littlefield, 1980). Goldman himself finds these assertions unconvincing in most cases.

2 Albert Flores, *Professional Ideals* (Belmont, CA: Wadsworth, 1988), 1.

3   Rob Atkinson has described the distinction, "firmly ensconced in the literature," between legal professional morality and ordinary morality in "Beyond the New Role Morality for Lawyers," *Maryland Law Review* 51 (1992): 855–60.

4   Gerald J. Postema, "Moral Responsibility in Professional Ethics," *New York University Law Review* 55 (1980): 63.

5   Benjamin Freedman, "A Meta-Ethics for Professional Morality," *Ethics* 89 (1978): 10.

6   Bruce Jennings, Callahan and Wolf, "The Professions: Public Interest and Common Good," in "The Public Duties of the Professions," Special Supp, *Hastings Center Report* 17, No. 1 (1987): 5.

7   Peter F. Drucker, "What Is 'Business Ethics'?" *The Public Interest* No. 63 (Spring 1981): 24.

8   Michael Davis, "Thinking Like an Engineer: The Place of a Code of Ethics in the Practice of a Profession," *Philosophy and Public Affairs* 20, No. 2 (1991): 154–55.

9   Ibid., 162.

10   Paul F. Camenisch, *Grounding Professional Ethics in a Pluralistic Society* (New York: Haven Publications, 1983), 4.

11   Barker, "What Is a Profession?" *Professional Ethics* 1 (Spring/Summer 1992): 73–99.

12   Ibid., 88–89.

—11—

HONOR AMONG THIEVES

Some Reflections on Professional Codes of Ethics[1]

John T. Sanders

AS COMPLICATED AN AFFAIR AS IT MAY BE TO give a fully acceptable general characterization of professional codes of ethics that will capture every nuance, one theme that has attracted widespread attention portrays them as contrivances whose primary function is to secure certain obligations of professionals to clients, or to the external community.[2] In contrast to such an "externalist" characterization of professional codes, it has occasionally been contended that, first and foremost, they should be understood as *internal conventions*, adopted among professionals as a device for securing the "interests" of the professionals themselves.[3]

In what follows, I will argue that both of these lines are incomplete. As important as service to the community and the interests of professionals may be in the full understanding of the multiple role that "codes of ethics" play in many professions, it is equally important to see them as expressive of the romance of a profession. Professional codes should be understood not only in terms of their utility to the community, or in terms of their utility to practitioners, but as expressions of callings....

I. "PROFESSIONAL" AND ITS COGNATES

In addressing these issues, it is important to acknowledge the squishiness of the conceptual terrain. When we speak of "professionals," we may mean to indicate different, even conflicting things in different contexts. In calling a person

a "professional," for example, we may mean to indicate no more than that the person has a certain competence in a certain demanding task, or we may mean no more than that the person has completed a certain course of training, or has a certain occupation (whether or not any particular competence is possessed). We may mean something praiseworthy, or something condemnatory, depending upon context. Our standards for tightness in the definition of the term will similarly vary with context.

Deploying the term in some ways makes it conceptually impossible for a person to be a professional without ever having received monetary compensation for working in the field in question. If I have been working as a waiter for the last twenty years, and have never found a position as an attorney, it might seem disingenuous for me to tell people that I am a professional lawyer, even though I might have all the certification of competence I need to prove it. Yet it would not be at all out of order for a legal periodical to note the fact that, perhaps due to hard economic times, many professionals have not been able to find work in the field.

Sometimes the difference between professional and amateur practitioners seems to betoken different competencies, sometimes nothing more than a difference between getting paid for what is done as opposed to doing it for free. Everything hangs on context....

The adjectival use of the term "professional" does not always work precisely in the way that the substantive usage does. And similar subtle differences are to be found in the various usages of terms like "profession" and "professionalism," and in the relations between these several cognates....

Nevertheless, it seems to me that some success can be gleaned if one steps back to a suitable level of generality. It appears that a common thread that runs through nearly all deployments of the cognates of the term "professional" is the idea of *competence* at a relatively *difficult* task. Where sometimes it seems that competence is *not* involved—for example, where we may wish to say that some members of the medical profession are not competent at all—it is often because of an intervening social/linguistic factor that somehow itself involves issues of competence. In the example of "incompetent doctors," we are talking about people who have successfully met what are deemed to be the standards of competence set for physicians (that's what allows us to identify them as doctors), but who aren't really competent after all.[4] ...

II. "PLATONIC" VERSUS "SOCIAL" STANDARDS OF COMPETENCY

Interesting complications—ones that serve to explain many conflicting judgments about the nature of professional *codes* of ethics—arise when one focuses attention on the fact that the notion of "competence at a difficult task" involves two evaluational terms whose satisfaction criteria are controversial. Which tasks are difficult? What are the standards of competence that are to be applied? Differences about these matters will yield differences in judgments about the propriety of describing particular kinds of activity as "professions" and particular individuals as "professionals."

An especially important area of controversy, at least for the purposes of the present paper, involves perspectival factors that come into play in deciding that a particular activity is performed "competently." One interesting way of distinguishing among evaluational perspectives involves the difference between standards that are *internal* to the task, on the one hand, and standards that are *external*, on the other. A professional athlete, for example, might become completely caught up in details of her sport that completely ignore whatever values *the fan* may wish to apply. Nevertheless, such an athlete may very well be among those most appreciated by fans. The question arises: how much should the *fans* (or any other non-professional's) criteria of "competence" affect the standards of professionalism used by the athlete? To what extent is *professionalism proper* (as opposed to social value) a function of contributions made to those *outside* the profession?...

Because the terms "internal" and "external" are used elsewhere in this paper to indicate differences between how things look from perspectives within and outside of particular professional groups, and because this is not *precisely* what I am getting at in this section, it will be desirable to find better terms. What I wish to highlight is the difference between what I call "Platonic" standards of competence and what may be called "social" standards.

In the first book of Plato's *Republic*, there is a discussion about the nature of various professions, which arises in the course of Socrates' attempt to refute the contention of Thrasymachus that "justice is the interest of the stronger."[5] There, the general contention of Socrates is that the nature of any profession—and the nature of proper professional behavior—may largely be determined through an analysis of the particular activity engaged in by the professional in question. Thus a doctor's interest is in health, a ship's captain's proper interest is in getting the ship safely from one place to another, and the ruler's interest is in running the city-state well.

Complications arise, though, depending upon how one describes a person's profession. While a doctor's job may be to heal patients, a heart specialist's job may be to fix hearts. Some things that are necessarily a part of the business of doing everything possible to fix a heart might imperil other aspects of a patient's health. So what determines one's professional responsibility? While this particular potential conflict may seem relatively easy to resolve, others won't be. Much depends on how one sees the profession....

Social criteria of competency are not the same. One might become as competent as you please at some odd task or another, and this task might be very difficult, involving skills of a high order and, even, considerable training; one will not thereby have established any *social* value. And where people other than the professional have any interest at all in what that professional does, there arises at least the possibility of conflict over criteria of competency in that profession. For any activity at all, whether legitimately to be described as a "profession" or not, the same distinction can be made: Platonic criteria of competency measure how well the activity is performed, given the internal logic of that activity; social criteria of competency measure how well the activity is performed, given various external goals and values.

Finally, the issue comes to a head when conflict arises, as it often does, over how the Platonic and social criteria of competency may best be measured against one another. Especially interesting, in this regard, are the contentions of some professionals that the best way to serve general *social* goals may be to ignore them, in the short term, and to favor, instead, Platonic goals....

III. SOLIDARITY AMONG PROFESSIONALS

So far I have briefly sketched some reasons for doubting that the idea of external service must be involved in the definition of "profession" or any of its cognates. A bit more tentatively, I have suggested that whether such considerations are central to the nature of professional codes of ethics is debatable. By way of moving toward consideration of some non-standard professions, and thereby to a consideration of a central element within professional codes of ethics that is too frequently missed or underestimated, it is useful to say a word or two about the thesis that the idea of *solidarity among professionals* is somehow central to the

very concept of a profession, and plays a necessary role in the design of professional codes of ethics.

Some of the problems that I will address are identified in a valuable recent article by Michael Davis, where he writes:

> ... a code of ethics is primarily a *convention between professionals*. According to this explanation, a profession is a group of persons who want to cooperate in serving the same ideal better than they could if they did not cooperate. Engineers, for example, might be thought to serve the ideal of efficient design, construction, and maintenance of safe and useful objects. A code of ethics would then prescribe how professionals are to pursue their common ideal so that each may do the best she can at minimal cost to herself and those she cares about (including the public, if looking after the public is part of what she cares about). The code is to protect each professional from certain pressures (for example, the pressure to cut corners to save money) by making it reasonably likely (and more likely than otherwise) that most other members of the profession will *not* take advantage of her good conduct. A code protects members of a profession from certain consequences of competition. A code is a solution to a coordination problem.[6]

Davis clearly describes a code of ethics as being fundamentally conventional. Such a reading is bound to meet with resistance among professionals who think of their codes as getting at something objective about the profession, or who aspire to capturing the real character of their profession in their code.[7] ...

If the interests of professionals were central to their codes of ethics, and if concern for outsiders were only peripheral and contingent upon the interests of the professionals, why would honesty or fair dealing to outsiders play such a fundamental role in many of them?[8] I certainly admit that honesty and fair dealing can be defended on grounds of self-interest—this is the claim, anyway, of ethical eudaemonists and egoists from Plato to Rand—but is that why they appear in professional codes? Or is this phenomenon better understood as more directly founded on considerations of professional pride and personal self-respect, whether these latter are themselves to be defended egoistically or not? Is it solely because professional groups hope to gain respectability in the broader community that it promotes such values? Is this just public relations?

Where does any sense of duty or obligation enter into Davis's analysis of professional codes of ethics? And wherever such consideration does enter the analysis—if at all—to whom or what are the several obligations owed? Must the obligations all be directed toward the community? Or toward other professionals? How about toward certain standards that themselves appear to professionals to be intrinsic to the very idea of their particular professions? Like accuracy in the case of accountants? Or like healing in the case of physicians? Surely it is reasonable to expect that professional codes of ethics will contain explicit or implicit references not only to rights and interests, but to obligations of these and other kinds, not all directed to one overarching behavioral or moral end, but directed in every which way. Indeed, it seems likely that codes of ethics are deemed valuable—or even necessary, sometimes—because of a need to establish some balance among rights, interests and obligations that point in several different directions at once.[9] ...

IV. HONOR AMONG THIEVES— ROMANCING THE CODE

... Professionals, both traditionally and in modern life, frequently identify themselves in a certain way with certain of their activities. Professional codes of ethics often strive to capture the essence of the character and style that animates the self-image common among practitioners.[10] Professions, and their codes, mean something to practitioners that is not shared with outsiders.

With this general theme in mind, I offer as an exemplar not engineering and not medicine—professions whose importance to the public makes it hard to see them purely as professions, rather than as service organizations—but professional crime.[11]

If the mark of a professional is competency at some difficult task, then not any or every criminal (i.e., breaker of the law) could be understood as a professional. But there is no reason to suppose that undesirable or illegal activity is in any way *excluded* from the domain of professionalism. Indeed, there is a considerable body of romantic fiction that focuses on criminals who are really quite good at accomplishing the most remarkable criminal feats. Our attitude toward them is characteristically torn: we are (for the most part) critical of their dirty deeds, but we admire their skill and, perhaps, their panache. It is not at all hard to understand the claim that they are real professionals, even though we are not pleased with their activities and even though they may be acting quite alone. It is not at all unheard of that such professionals can band together, and even establish codes of ethics. For the most vivid example of such a phenomenon, one need only turn to what is widely known as the realm of "organized crime."

Modern criminal brotherhoods—like the Mafia, the Cosa Nostra, or the Unione Corse—all seem to have descended from the Garduna of fifteenth-century Spain. The descent is in almost every case quite straightforward: a cadre sent out by a parent organization into new territory collaborates with native criminals to form a new society, organized along structural lines set out by the old one.[12] The parallel with political colonization is quite interesting, especially in the subsequent development of the new societies: sometimes the new organizations remain loyal to the parent, sometimes they rebel....

In order to further clarify the nature of the professional society we are talking about, it is important to realize that these were not political or religious organizations that had turned to crime to support other, more commonly accepted undertakings. As David Chandler has explained, the character of the Garduna was historically unique:

> Nothing like the brotherhood existed prior to the fifteenth century....
>
> Their conceptual innovation was to provide their services for church, state, criminals, or virtually any client with the required fee. They conducted themselves as a business, investing some of their revenues in police and political protection, setting some aside for pensions, and sharing the rest as profit. A rigorous code of conduct was imposed and secrecy and discipline were strict.
>
> Their most inflexible law was the application of the death penalty for those who violated either secrecy or discipline. The brotherhood's adherence to that law has subsequently caused a relative absence of historical treatment.[13]

... But it is just as easy to imagine that members of the society were frequently enough placed in just the kind of life-threatening situations that make it difficult to see why they would have remained silent. Is it really in one's interest to avoid death at the hands of the brotherhood by allowing oneself to be drawn and quartered?

While it is possible to imagine that the vows of secrecy and the like that were part of the Garduna code were further enforced by threats to family and loved ones, surely one ingredient is missing from this picture: honor and self-respect. For whatever reason, members of Garduna were encouraged to think of themselves as part of a special society, with special requirements. Those who violated the code were dishonored, were outcasts.

This theme is to be found, of course, in professional societies, guilds, and leagues throughout the Middle Ages....

V. CONCLUSION—ROMANCING THE PROFESSIONS

Among the consequences of this understanding of professional codes of ethics are these: where they are not simply imposed from the outside that is, where they grow from internal need within the profession—they may be expected to have considerable force. While part of this force involves threats made against non-compliance, a large part may be expected to be the result of the identification of the professional with her colleagues. Thus they may serve as ideals, evocations of the romance of the profession, and as expressions of certain general characteristics and modes of behavior deemed within the profession to be the mark of the professional.

Where they are well crafted, they have the support of the individuals who think of themselves as professionals within that field. They will not be seen as burdens, but as badges or banners. They are not rules that must slavishly be followed on threat of disbarment or other similar penalty, but proclamations of the line drawn between professionals and non-professionals, between us and them.

Thus, where they are well crafted, professional codes of ethics have great personal force in the lives of professionals. If this comes as a surprise, it is probably because contemporary examples of codes of ethics are frequently not well crafted. They do not manage to evoke the self-images of the professions. They seem to speak to the professions from outside, offering threats and compulsion rather than ideals and solidarity. Thus they do not have the force that they might have.[14] That force is reserved for the not-so-public shared commitment to ideals that are part of the "common law" among engineers, doctors, lawyers, or whomever. And where some small part of that common law actually does survive in contemporary professional codes of ethics, so does that force....

It might be best simply to leave the professional codes entirely to the professionals. Where some profession's code bothers us, let us take this up in the appropriate public forum, and let us make illegal what we cannot allow. But let *us* do that. Let us not expect professional codes of ethics to do the work of law. And let us be more tolerant and respectful of the human needs and aspirations that lead to professionalism in the first place. We stand to gain a great deal if we can do *anything* that encourages people to bring ethical standards back in out of the cold, to a position closer to the heart.

NOTES

1   This paper was read and discussed at the 138th Semiannual Meeting of the Creighton Club (The New York State Philosophical Association), held at Hobart and William Smith Colleges in Geneva, New York, in April of 1993. I am grateful to Steven Lee, Scott Brophy, and the participants in the discussion for their stimulating commentary. I must also thank Wade Robison and Victoria Varga, along with the editor and referees of *Professional Ethics*, for various helpful suggestions and references.

2   See, for example, Karen Lebacqz, *Professional Ethics* (Nashville: Abingdon Press, 1985), as well as sources she refers to, especially A.M. Carr-Saunders and P.A. Wilson, *The Professions* (Oxford: Clarendon Press, 1933) and Carnegie Samuel Calian, *Today's Pastor in Tomorrow's World* (New York: Hawthorne Books, 1977). While Lebacqz orients her careful discussion of professional ethics to issues that especially confront the ministry, the impact of her argument about professional ethics is in no way restricted to that profession alone. Nevertheless, this focus does tend to highlight features of professionalism that, while shared by a number of professions, are not fully universal. Lebacqz ultimately argues for an understanding of professional ethics which emphasizes injunctions about character, rather than about action, and the emphasis is on *other-regarding* character traits. For a more explicitly general attempt to link other-regarding injunctions with the very idea of a profession, see Stephen F. Barker, "What Is a Profession?" *Professional Ethics*, vol. I (1 & 2): 73–99.

3   June Goodfield, for example, warns that professional codes of ethics may be misnamed, since they so frequently emphasize issues that are better understood as matters of etiquette among professionals, "Reflections on the Hippocratic Oaths," *The Hastings Center Studies*, 1(2): 90. Similarly, Lisa Newton has contended that a professional code can become no more than "a code of Professional Manners oriented toward a Professional Image for the protection of Professional Compensation." See Newton, "A Professional Ethic: A Proposal in Context," John E. Thomas (ed.), *Matters of Life and Death* (Toronto: Samuel Stevens, 1978), 264. Just as is true of the more "externalist" characterization of professional codes, this "internalist" picture can be supported with empirical evidence taken from actual codes representing a wide variety of disciplines. But, as will be contended in what follows, to adopt either of these views of codes involves the underemphasis of crucial features of professional codes of ethics that have nothing at all to do with *anyone's* "interests," whether professional, client, or third party.

4   It is quite common for terms to shift meaning in this way over time as they become institutionally co-opted. For a thorough discussion of another example of this phenomenon, see John T. Sanders, "Political Authority," *The Monist*, 66(4): 545–56.

5   I am indebted to Steven Lee for reminding me of the relevance of this passage to my argument.

6   Michael Davis, "Thinking Like an Engineer: The Place of a Code of Ethics in the Practice of a Profession," *Philosophy and Public Affairs*, 20(2): 150–67.

7   Davis acknowledges that thinking of professional codes as "conventions between professionals" has the potential of being misleading. He tries to avoid the problems he sees by urging that the conventions he has in mind are not *contracts*. Instead, they are more like "quasi-contracts" (Davis, *op. cit.*, 156). This move, however, does not succeed in allaying the concerns that I am outlining here.

8   I hope it is clear, by now, that I am objecting as much to the universal *omission* of provisions about service to the community as to the universal *inclusion* of such provisions. An adequate understanding of professionalism, taken generally, ought to accommodate the fact that the inclusion of such provisions will vary from profession

to profession, not as a function of professional convention, but as a function of the internal logic of what the various professionals *do*. I will thus be arguing, in what follows, for the primacy of Platonic criteria of competency over social criteria in the analysis of professional codes of ethics.

9   There are individual self-interests, obligations to other professionals and *their* interests, obligations to clients and to the community at large, and obligations that may best be understood as being owed to the very idea of the profession. *All* of these—and many more—may come to play roles in the construction of professional codes of ethics, and all may tug in different directions. The play among the different interests, rights, and obligations may pull the code in different directions at different times during its development. And, of course, different professions will accommodate themselves differently to the sundry demands placed upon them. But as professional codes get pulled away from expression of fundamental ideals and virtues respected by the professionals themselves, they will necessarily play an increasingly less important role in their actual lives and work. Such an eventuality is in *no one's* interest.

10 For a thorough discussion of such factors, see Lebacqz, *op. cit.*

11 One subgroup among professional criminals is, of course, frequently referred to as "the oldest profession." That modern prostitutes continue to have a professional self-image of themselves is indicated clearly in a 1992 *New York Times* article, in which it was reported that prostitution in the New York City area had begun to move across the river to New Jersey because of a crack epidemic in the city. As one prostitute who made the move explained, "You could say the crack addicts ruined everything ... Here it's more professional" (quoted in Evelyn Nieves, "For Better Business, Prostitutes Leave Manhattan for Jersey City," *New York Times*, 22 September 1992, sections B1 and B6). Outsiders may not take such self-perceptions seriously, but insiders certainly do.

12 For an extraordinarily compelling history of the criminal societies, see David Leon Chandler, *Brothers in Blood: The Rise of the Criminal Brotherhoods* (New York: E.P. Dutton, 1975).

13 Chandler, *op. cit.*, 2.

14 The journal *Chemical Engineering*, for example, after conducting a survey concerning what engineers would do in a collection of hypothetical "ethical" cases, found that "Although the American Institute of Chemical Engineers, the professional society of many of our US readers, has a code of ethics, this was almost universally ignored in determining the solutions to our survey problems. Fewer than a half-dozen [out of 4318] respondents even mentioned a code of ethics at all." See Roy V. Hughson and Philip M. Kohn, "Ethics," *Chemical Engineering*, 87(19): 132.

—12—

PROFESSIONAL RESPONSIBILITY

Just Following the Rules?

Michael Davis

MY SUBJECT IS A CRITICISM OF CONDUCT SOME-thing like this: "That's not acting responsibly, that's just following the rules." The criticism appears as an attack on "legalism" in both business and professional ethics. While my focus here will be on professional ethics, everything I say should, with minor changes, apply equally well to following corporate or other business codes of ethics.

Legalism (it is said) reduces professional responsibility to doing as the profession's code of ethics requires; professional responsibility, like moral responsibility generally, is more open-ended, including (among other things) certain virtues. My subject thus overlaps the larger debate in moral theory between "principle ethics" and "virtue ethics." I shall draw some conclusions relevant to that debate.

My thesis is that following "the rules," while not all there is to professional ethics, is generally enough for responsible conduct (or, at least, is so when the profession's code of ethics is reasonably well written, as most are). Rules set the standard of professional conduct; just following those rules, in a relatively robust but not unusual sense of "following those rules," is acting as a responsible professional....

II. FOLLOWING RULES BLINDLY OR STRICTLY

Mere rule following is doing what the rule says without concern for context or consequence, a "mechanical" or "blind" obedience. Finding a clear example of such obedience is hard. Here is the best I have (blind obedience, though not exactly to a rule): One day, at age two, my son was having trouble opening a cabinet door because of a safety latch. Instead of opening the door for him, I advised him to "use his head." He imme-diately obeyed, giving the door a hard rap with his forehead, apparently without thought to any alternative interpretation of my advice or even to past experience of banging his head against a hard surface. He has not given me such blind obedi-ence since.

Though rational in some contexts, strict obedience does not seem rational as a general way to practice a profession. Strict obedience makes sense where judgment is justifiably separated from performance (for example, where some "higher" authority is in the best position to "reason why" and others, subordinates, to "do or die"). The general name for the separation of judgment from performance is "hierarchy." Since hierarchy tends to ignore what subordinates think, however well-informed and judicious the subordinates may be, any justification of strict obedience must iden-tify a compensating advantage. On the battlefield, the compensating advantage is pretty clear. The coordination of large masses in movement is dif-ficult under the best of conditions. In battle, with the noise and confusion, there is little opportunity for joint deliberation even in a unit as small as a platoon or squad. The alternative to obeying the order of a superior is disorder or delay, potentially disastrous when coordination and speed matter.

Few, if any, professions demand strict obedience to an ethical authority. But even if they all did, the result would not be relevant to our subject. Where one has rendered strict obedience to an ethical authority, the proper description is "I was just obeying orders" or "I was just following controlling precedent" rather than "I was just following the rules."

III. MALICIOUS OBEDIENCE

Sometimes the description, "I was just following the rules," occurs in defense of conduct. To have acted according to the rules, however bad the outcome and however foolish the rules, is to have acted in a way insulating one from (full) responsibility. The most common use of "just following rules" in this sense, or at least the most visible, is when employees "strike" their employer by "working to rule" or "going by the book." This form of strike is particularly satisfying to employees and maddening for the employer. The employees continue to be paid, though they are costing their employer money, time, and grief. The employer cannot complain without admitting that "the book" is wrong. For many employers, the point of having "the book" is to have a basis for disciplining employees when they fail to do as they should. So, working to rule catches the employer in his own trap. One way or another, the employer must "eat his words." Think, for example, how the police can bring traffic to a halt on a busy highway simply by ticketing every traffic violation they observe—as many police manuals require.

What does working to rule leave out? Another name for working to rule, "malicious obedience," suggests an answer. What working to rule leaves out is the good will employees otherwise give their employer. Ordinarily, employees interpret the rules to take into account the inability of general language to anticipate special cases; they try to understand what the employer is trying to achieve by laying down such rules; they use "common sense"....

We may distinguish a weak sense and a strong sense of malicious obedience. In the weak sense, malicious obedience is the malicious adoption of an interpretative strategy that is not itself malicious. For example, the principle "Be literal" might be adopted for reasons other than malice. But, in working to rule, it is adopted maliciously, that is, with the intent, expectation or hope that literalness will make trouble for the employer. Malicious obedience in the strong sense carries malice one step further. Not only is the interpretative strategy adopted maliciously but what is adopted also has malice built into it, for example, "Choose the most damaging interpretation the language allows."

What do these two forms of working to rule have to do with just following a code of professional ethics? For most of these codes, the answer must be: little. The codes themselves contain rules of interpretation. Often gathered at the front under the heading "preamble," "principles," or "canons" to distinguish them from less general directives, these rules of interpretation effectively rule out malicious obedience. For example, the NSPE's "Code of Ethics for Engineers" includes at least two "Fundamental Canons" that seem to rule out malice:

Engineers, in the fulfilment of their professional duties, shall:

1. Hold paramount the safety, health, and welfare of the public in the performance of their professional duties, [and]

2. Act in professional matters for each employer or client as faithful agents or trustees. Specific rules of practice must then be read to protect the public welfare and to serve the employer as a faithful agent or trustee. An engineer cannot simply work to rule.

I do not claim that such general principles of interpretation make following the rules easy. On the contrary, I admit they make following the rules hard. My point is that, as they do that, they also rule out most, perhaps all, the malicious interpretations of rules necessary for malicious obedience....

IV. NEGLIGENT AND ACCIDENTAL OBEDIENCE

Some writers have recently taken to contrasting the law's "malpractice" or "negligence" standard of tort liability with the "due care" (or "reasonable care") standard of true professionalism. Until I read these writers, I had supposed that negligence was a relatively clear concept. I now see that it is not. So, to avoid misunderstanding, let me explain what I once supposed obvious.

In the common law, both American and English, negligence is, almost by definition, a failure to exercise due care in our relations with others. In negligence law, the interesting question is not whether anyone, especially a professional, should be held to the due-care standard. Due care is the minimum standard even for a child or a madman. The interesting question is what due care requires. For example, Prosser, the leading authority on torts, understands a failure of due care as "[conduct] which should be recognized as involving unreasonable danger to others."[1]

Any distinction between what one's profession requires and what is merely legally required cannot be made in terms of "due care"—or, at least, cannot be so made without inviting confusion. A profession does not need a code of ethics to be held to the standard of due care. The law already does that; any malpractice suit (for negligence) will allege a failure of due care. What a code of professional ethics does, if it does anything beyond restating existing legal obligations is to set a new standard of care, one higher than existed before. That new standard can, in virtue of the code, become what may reasonably be expected of members of the profession; it is reasonable to expect members of a profession to do what they commit themselves to doing. Some dangers that had been reasonable before would then become unreasonable, raising the legal minimum for members of the profession and thereby turning into malpractice conduct previously allowed to the profession (and still allowed to others). A profession's code of ethics helps define what care is due from members of that profession and, in doing that, to set the standard of malpractice for them. But, whatever the standard, anything less than good practice is malpractice.[2]

Negligent obedience is, then, a failure to exercise due care in following the relevant rules, whether the failure unreasonably risks harm to others or is in some other way faulty. Negligent obedience differs from (what we shall call) stupid obedience in that the failure need not arise from an inability to act as one should. Stupid obedience is a matter of competence; negligent obedience is not (or, at least, need not be)....

V. STUPID OBEDIENCE

Those who obey stupidly resemble the negligent in unconsciously failing to exercise due care in interpreting the relevant rules. They differ from the negligent only in the cause of failure. Unlike the negligent, the stupid fail because they do not know better. The cause of not knowing better may be original, that is, a lack of native wit, or educational, for example, never having been taught how to interpret the rule in question. In law, the most common form of stupid obedience is the layman's trying to follow a statute without considering how case law may have made the statute's simple language treacherous. In professional ethics, the most common form of stupid obedience is, I think, reading a code of ethics as if each rule were independent of the others....

Perhaps many of those professionals who seek to excuse themselves for misconduct with the answer, "I was just following the rules," are pleading stupidity. It is therefore worth pointing out that whenever this plea is necessary, the professional in question was not in fact following the rules (even if she was doing her best to follow them). In this respect, stupid obedience resembles the other forms of "just following the rules" discussed so far. It is a failure to follow the rules.

VI. INTERPRETATIVE OBEDIENCE

Except for blind obedience, all the forms of rule following discussed so far acknowledged, however implicitly, that rules must be interpreted. In strict obedience, the interpretation is largely left to others ("higher authority"). In malicious obedience, interpretation is deliberately abused; in negligent or accidental obedience, interpretation is not given the attention it deserves; and in stupid obedience, interpretation is not done skillfully enough, whether from lack of wit or learning. This list of ways in which one can fail to follow the rules suggests that just following the rules is not simple. We must now consider just how complicated it can be.

In law, there are many methods of interpreting a rule. They are not exclusive, though some are likely to be more important in one area of the law and others in another. When interpreting a particular rule, one important question is always how that rule fits with the others in the particular document in which it appears. All else equal, a particular will, contract, statute, or other document should, if possible, be interpreted so that each term keeps the same meaning throughout, none of its rules is inconsistent with any other, and all serve the document's avowed purpose (or at least that none works against it). This "internalist" approach may yield one defensible interpretation but more often yields several. Where there are several internally defensible interpretations, there may be no way to choose except to go outside the document.

There may, in any case, be other reasons to go outside the document. For example, the internalist interpretation may have yielded an immoral or irrational result, or violated the intentions of those who composed the document (intentions indicated by evidence outside the document itself)....

What must we teach students in order to teach them how to follow the code of ethics of their hoped-for profession? We must, of course, teach them the context in which the code is to be applied, that is, something of the history of the profession, of the organizations in which members of the profession work, of the expectations other members of the profession will have of their colleagues, and of what members do (and the effect what they do can have on others). We must also teach something about the purpose of the rules, the structure of the code (the relation of one rule to another), the interpretative strategies considered appropriate, and the consequences of certain mistakes in interpretation. We should help students to see their profession's code of ethics as the work of human beings much like themselves, human beings who have specific purposes in developing such rules and should therefore be open to revising them, or standing interpretations of them, as new information comes in. Last, and perhaps most important, we should give practice in following the rules, that is, in analyzing specific "fact situations," applying the rules to those facts, reaching conclusions about what is required, allowed, or forbidden, making arguments in defense of the conclusions, and inventing ways to do as the rules so interpreted say. One does not know how to follow a rule unless one knows how to develop, state, defend, and carry out workable courses of action in accord with the rule in contexts in which the rule ordinarily applies.

VII. WHAT IS LEFT OUT?

This (interpretative) way of understanding "just following the rules" leaves us with the question with which we began: what does just following the rules leave out? What I have argued so far is that the rules of professional ethics themselves exclude certain forms of "just following the rules" (malicious, negligent, accidental, and stupid obedience); other forms (blind and strict obedience) are not following the rules at all. Only one interpretation of just following the rules of professional ethics, the interpretative, seems robust enough to count as just following the rules (without some apologetic qualification). That interpretation seems to leave nothing important out.

My argument, even admitting its soundness, may seem to miss what underlay the objection to "*just* following the rules" with which we began, the idea (introduced by "just") of trying to get by with the minimum, a failure to make room for the "spirit" of the rules as well as the "letter"....

But, surely (it may be asked), is there not something wrong with a professional trying to get by with the minimum required? This question may be understood as raising one of two objections. If we emphasize "trying" (an attitude), we get an objection to a certain interpretative strategy one to which few, if any, professional codes allow. Consider again the preamble of the NSPE code. Does it not point the faithful interpreter toward "the highest principles" rather than "the minimum"? How can an engineer follow that code and try to do the minimum?

If, instead of emphasizing the trying, we emphasize the outcome ("the minimum required"), we get an objection to doing only what the code in fact requires. The point of the objection so interpreted escapes me. Why would a professional not be acting responsibly if she did only what her profession code of ethics required? The attack on legalism (the call to "go beyond" the rules) may be a confused way of proposing reforms—in the rules themselves or in their interpretation. If so, the professional responsibilities put forward are beyond the rules—the rules as written if not the rules as they could be written—will, upon examination, turn out to be controversial.[3]

NOTES

1 "The almost universal use of the phrase 'due care' to describe conduct that is not negligent, should not be permitted to obscure the fact that the real basis of negligence is ... behavior which should be recognized as involving an unreasonable danger to others." William L. Prosser, *Law of Torts, 4th Ed.* (St. Paul, MN: West Publishing, 1971), 145.

2 Or, to be more exact, it is malpractice if the other conditions of negligence are also present (an unreasonable risk to others, a resulting harm, measurable loss, and so on).

3 Lest my own words in *Thinking Like an Engineer* (New York: Oxford University Press, 1998), 59, be quoted against me, I should point out that I am not here speaking (as I was there) of tasks professionals have "good reason" to take on or assign, but of tasks they have taken on already in virtue of membership in a profession having a certain code of ethics and are therefore required of them.

—13—

AM I MY PROFESSION'S KEEPER?

Avery Kolers

1. INTRODUCTION

'CONSCIENTIOUS REFUSAL' OR 'CONSCIENTIOUS objection' occurs when a professional recognizes a *pro tanto* role obligation to do some act *A*, but asserts that her sincere belief that *A* is seriously immoral overrides this obligation. That is, the objector recognizes the obligation as authoritative and (normally) binding, but believes that *in this case* it is overridden....

Given this normative structure, an account of the ethics of conscientious refusal may proceed in either of two ways. First, it might address the *content* of the judgment of conscience: whether the moral belief in question is *true*, whether the refusal genuinely springs from moral reasons, whether the facts of the case are as the objector believes them to be. The problem with addressing content in this way is that it grants the essentially anarchist thesis that no one has any professional or institutional obligations except insofar as the institution's directives comply with his or her own conscience. As a policy, Anarchism or 'Conscience Absolutism'[1] just bumps the problem up a level: notwithstanding any formal guarantee of the objector's impunity, his supervisor can conscientiously affirm that such behavior must be punished, and on that basis assert a right of conscience to impose sanctions on that employee. More abstractly, Anarchism is incompatible with the very idea of a profession.[2] If anyone whose job it is to implement a given policy can simply refuse to carry it out, there is no policy.

Since content assessment fails, the second strategy addresses the moral force of the *provenance*: the justification of professional or institutional authority over the agent such that individual conscience is overridden. That is, provenancial assessment requires an account of professional obligations that can explain the nature of the *pro tanto* role obligations to which the agent objects, and concomitantly, the relationship between the agent and the institution or office from which these requirements flow.[3]

Yet although conscience may be overridden, it cannot be completely flattened. The shift to provenance must not morph into the essentially totalitarian thesis that *just any* directive must be obeyed provided the institution that commands it is justified....

2. PROFESSIONAL OBLIGATIONS AND THE CONSENT CRITERION

A standard view of professional obligations holds that our free choice of occupation—our voluntary acceptance of a professional role—is what binds us to the requirements of that role. This is the *Consent* model.[4] Suppose a pharmacist refuses to fill a prescription for contraceptives. Here the pharmacist objects to the content of the act in question—dispensing these particular pills for that particular reason in this particular case. But on Consent, a moral objection to the content of the act becomes irrelevant. Typically, professionals have freely consented to perform the full panoply of services provided by their profession: taken all the required courses, enrolled in and completed professional training, secured their license, and hung out their shingles or accepted offers of employment. Each of these acts was voluntary, or so we may assume; and in voluntarily performing these acts, the agents knew themselves to be incurring obligations.[5] Thus the Consent model seems to justify deference to institutional directives beyond conscience. It is, we might say, too late to refuse. What obligates the professional now is not the content of the directive, but its provenance....

Consent faces two basic problems. First, its account of provenance is prudential rather than moral; second, it cannot specify the counterpart of the putative agreement. Consent uses the wrong tool to do the wrong job. Take these objections in order.

Crucial to the Consent model's shift from content to provenance is the moral power of the act of consent itself. Yet consent has the wrong sort of moral power for the job—or perhaps more accurately, consent does not have *enough* moral power for the job. If some act *A*, though lucrative, is morally impermissible, an agent cannot incur a moral obligation to *A* by consenting to do it; that would be a pernicious 'loophole in morality': a case 'where a [moral] code is *counterproductive* by giving *incentives* toward conduct that is *regrettable* by the code's own lights.'[6] If consent could override moral objections, then the Consent model would open a major loophole in moral restrictions on means of promoting self-interest.

Consent can thus defeat only *prudential* objections, not *moral* ones. But conscientious objection purports to be *moral* objection. Consent can obligate a conscientious objector, then, only if the objector's moral qualms are incorrect or indecisive. But if we switch to debating the validity of the objector's moral qualms we have then switched back from provenance to content, and the act of consent is morally inert: we have accepted the anarchist position that agents are obligated only if personal conscience assents in this particular instance....

The Consent model perceives compliance with professional norms as a type of instrumentally rational choice, whereas professional jobs have their special status in part because of the way that individual instrumental reasoning fades into the background. Oaths or agreements may be means of signaling one's commitment to professional norms—one's willingness to put aside instrumental reasoning and protect the patient from one's self-interest. And consent is typically essential to *causal* explanations of why professional norms apply to a particular person. But oaths and agreements do not actually account for these norms or justify adherence to them.

3. PROFESSIONAL RESPONSIBILITIES

The Consent model purports to ground professional responsibilities in the autonomy of the professional—she is obligated to *A* because she freely agreed to do so. Yet the professional context involves not one autonomous agent struggling to maintain some self-determination under the command of a sovereign, but *multiple* autonomous agents who come together under a system of rules to achieve morally important results that none of them could achieve by flouting those rules or by acting on their own or in a different context. The collaboration catalyzes their autonomy.[7] Among the morally important results are the livelihoods of the professionals who do this work, the societal goods at which the profession aims, and, most acutely, the interests of especially vulnerable persons whose autonomy may specifically need to be fostered rather than merely respected.

The autonomy of each player in the institution comes to fruition through the exercise of the autonomy of others, and the institution can achieve its distinctive good only because of this confluence of aims. The institution and the patient must therefore recognize that their aims depend on particular persons who should not be steamrolled into doing what they think is wrong; but on the other hand, the objector must accept that he is only one of many persons in an organization that has a legitimate purpose, and that individual agency—be it putatively conscience-driven or otherwise—cannot be unaccountable, and cannot be allowed to subvert the organization's agenda or throw it into disarray....

Part of what it means to identify with professional norms is to defer to those norms in interpreting one's own personal moral duties. One determines what one ought to do, and what constitutes having done it, partly by discerning what is expected and how one fits into the context. Whereas, on the Consent model, each person must be the 'guardian of her own consent,'[8] on a professional model no one is sole proprietor of her own moral agency. Identification with professional norms means that both one's moral commitments themselves, and one's interpretation of those commitments, are shaped by the institution.[9]

We avoid anarchism, then, by denying that individual autonomy has free play. Relational autonomy is achieved through the partial intertwining of individual aims with shared ones. In a just society, identification with the profession will enable persons to achieve important goods at acceptable cost: professionals typically maintain material comfort by performing socially valuable work that genuinely helps people who freely request their help. And identification with the norms of the profession is normally a necessary condition of this.

But such a happy confluence of ends is not guaranteed, and hence we avoid anarchism only by risking totalitarianism. For if institutional norms demand assistance with torture, or the needs of the institution include genocide, then the fact that 'professionals' identify with that institution will enable great evil.

The standard response to this kind of worry is to hold that role obligations are binding only if they flow from just institutions. The *locus classicus* of this 'justice-only' view is John Rawls's argument against excessive desert claims lodged by the wealthy. Rawls's reply is that only just institutions generate legitimate expectations, so the desert claims are unfounded.[10] But even Michael Hardimon, who is more skeptical of individualist liberalism, denies that role obligations can flow from unjust institutions. He writes, 'we are assuming that role obligations deriving from unjust institutions are void *ab initio.*'[11]

As a bulwark against totalitarianism, however, the justice-only view fails. It makes good sense when we don the veil of ignorance to try to discern whether our current institutions match up with ideal theory: sons have no legitimate expectation that a kinship system favor male children; physicians have no legitimate expectation of receiving undue epistemic deference from patients or nurses.[12] But these inferences are not straightforwardly applicable to our lived obligations. First, the justice-only view cannot track the crucial difference between victims of mistreatment and innocent beneficiaries (or indeed, even perpetrators). It makes sense for the victim of injustice to deny that his attacker can put him under an obligation.

But it is essential that the victim's hard-won gains be respected, even when inadequate. A *beneficiary* of injustice surely may not repudiate his obligations on grounds that his gains are ill-gotten and hence others' expectations void. Yet the justice-only view cannot see the difference....

The 'mere' injustice of an institution is compatible with the survival of institutional obligations. But it obviously does not follow that such obligations survive despite just any degree or kind of injustice. Sometimes we are within our rights to leave people in the lurch, to treat obligations to them as void. In particular, the victim of what may be generally referred to as abuse has a right, and perhaps a self-regarding duty, to escape whenever possible; so does the person who is asked to witness or participate in abuse, provided her escaping does not itself constitute or exacerbate abuse—one does not get to wash one's hands of another's misfortune.

I shall therefore use 'abuse' to name the special degree or kind of mistreatment that does indeed void our role obligations. We may define abuse as follows.

An institution and its norms perpetrate *abuse* when their normal operation does serious and unmitigated (or inadequately mitigated) violence to at least one of the three core normative contexts that are at stake in institutions—the personal lives of participants, the special vulnerability of patients or clients, and the societal goods achieved by the institution.

Key aspects of this formula—'normal,' 'serious,' 'inadequately'—remain vague. And obviously, more needs to be said in its defense. Thus the line between mere injustice and abuse requires theoretic elaboration and contextual application that go beyond what can be developed here....

... [U]nlike the justice-only view, the abuse view allows us to track the distinct institutional locations of abusers, beneficiaries, and victims, and calibrate responsibilities accordingly. If a professional refuses a role obligation *in a manner that itself constitutes or exacerbates abuse*, then that refusal is impermissible.

Let us take stock. Professionalism is built on the recognition that professions typically promote three overlapping morally significant goods: the personal lives of the participants, the special needs of the patient or client, and the societal aims that give the profession or institution its point. What is at stake here is not the autonomy of the agent alone—or for that matter, the autonomy and well-being of the client alone—but the autonomy and well-being of numerous persons, coordinated for the sake of benefiting people in general by helping particular vulnerable persons. Each institution is, on this account, a miniature republic or kingdom of ends; what generates institutional obligations is not consent but the coordination of ends and the reliance of each person on numerous others.

Even under the best circumstances, however, it is difficult to achieve this level of coordination without stepping on any toes; most institutions are fated to forever be inadequate approximations of just institutions, or jerry-rigged and path-dependent machines that nonetheless achieve important results through the dedicated labor of people acting in good faith. In light of this fact, the idea that injustice alone would void role obligations within an institution is absurd. Nonetheless, we are well within our rights to insist that institutions not be abusive, and to refuse to participate in their abusive aspects, provided we can do so without causing further abuse.

When supplemented by the abuse view, Professionalism can navigate between anarchism and totalitarianism. Unjust institutions continue to obligate those who participate in them, but abusive institutions do not. In between, however, an institution ought to license dissenters to refuse to participate when it can do so without exacerbating injustice or causing abuse. Such licenses might be granted on purely formal grounds, such as the institution's capacity to redeploy resources to accommodate an objector;[13] on purely substantive grounds, such as the institution's demanding and receiving evidence, from the objector, of the genuineness and significance of the moral judgments in question or the factual accuracy of their empirical underpinnings; or on a mix of formal and substantive grounds.[14] But refusal, on this view, is itself a privilege or indulgence rather than an entitlement. In contrast, a professional who is the victim of abuse, or who needs to blow the whistle on abuse, may repudiate her putative obligations and escape the abusive institution altogether.

Let us test this solution by applying it to a range of cases, including that of pharmacists refusing emergency contraception and that of physicians refusing to perform abortions. What is at stake here is not only injustice but disagreement over who is the victim of injustice, and over whether the embryo or fetus in particular is harmed or wronged. In the most straightforward case, where the life of the woman carrying the embryo or fetus is genuinely at stake, or if carrying it to term constitutes a significant risk to her health, then preventing her from gaining access to a feasible procedure that would save her life constitutes abuse. To refuse is, then, permissible only with a license, and if a request for such license is denied then professionals are required to participate even if they believe they are being made to participate in a murder. Similarly, emergency contraception does not constitute abuse because it does not single out a particular embryo for humiliation—nothing can be known about the embryo, including whether it even exists or, if so, how many there are or might be two weeks hence.[15] Thus emergency contraception is not abuse.

At the other end of the spectrum would seem to be the case of sex-selective or otherwise discriminatory abortions. Fetuses can be singled out for ill-treatment, and if abortion is used as a means of discriminating on the basis of sex, race, ethnicity, or ability, abortion can be abusive of target populations, as well. In all these respects there is potential for abortion to constitute abuse. When it does, the current theory would endorse the physician's refusal to participate, provided that refusal did not itself constitute or exacerbate abuse.

Nonetheless, routine abortions are not abusive and thus exemption from participation must be licensed. I grant that, unlike embryos, fetuses can be harmed insofar as they can feel pain or are sentient in other ways. Moreover, we may grant that fetuses are persons or have rights to life, and hence, that abortion is normally unjust inasmuch as it wrongs someone. Nonetheless, fetuses—at least early on and perhaps throughout gestation—do not have an interest *in continued life*.[16] So the loss of continued life does not harm them and hence does not, by itself, constitute abuse. Professionals who are asked to perform routine abortions for nondiscriminatory reasons, or who are asked for emergency contraception, may request an exemption, but have no right to exempt themselves unilaterally if the license is denied.

4. CONCLUSION

One striking feature of the recent upsurge of 'conscience clauses' and claims of conscientious objection is the anarchist assumption that a professional has no responsibilities to anyone or anything other than his own conscience. As we noted at the outset, this view is patently absurd.

And yet for all its absurdity it is ultimately hard to refute. Why should we not take a stand on 'conscience' whenever it seems right to us? How could it be that we are *morally obligated* to meet professional obligations and hence *morally forbidden to follow conscience*?

I have argued that the reason is found in the normative force of the professional obligations that such a stand would repudiate: the confluence of goods achieved by even unjust institutions, and the importance to a professional of deferring to the interests of clients. Thus it is impossible to get a handle on 'conscientious refusal' unless we understand the normative nature of professional obligations. If anarchism is to be rejected, it must be either because conscience itself is not a solid foundation for action, or because the norms that the objector wishes to override are at least sometimes stronger than conscience. This can be so only if the provenance of obligations is sometimes more significant and compelling than their content. Both the Consent model and the Professionalism model accept this shift away from content, but the Consent model aims at the wrong aspect of provenance—the causal origin of a particular agent's being obligated, rather than the moral significance of the institutions in which the agent participates. Consequently, the Consent model overcomes only prudential objections, not moral ones. In contrast, Professionalism explains professional obligations by appeal to the normative structure of professions and the confluence of morally valuable aims that professions normally achieve for practitioners, clients, and societies.

A profession that genuinely serves the public good, stoutly prevents itself from exploiting the vulnerability of clients, respects and fosters clients' autonomy, and provides expert service, all while offering practitioners a decent standard of living, is a fragile and hard-won achievement worthy of our support and identification. Preserving and enhancing such achievements is the responsibility of all who practice a profession. It is for this reason, ultimately, that conscience is not decisive in professional contexts: each of us is our profession's keeper....

NOTES

1   M. Wicclair. 2011. *Conscientious Objection in Medicine.* New York: Cambridge University Press: 34.

2   E. LaFollette & H. LaFollette. Private Conscience, Public Acts. *J Med Ethics* 2007; 33: 249–254.

3   I follow Michael Hardimon's understanding of 'role obligations' and of obligations 'flowing from' roles. See M. Hardimon. Role Obligations. *J Philos* 1994; 91: 333–363.

4   For explicit defense of this view in the healthcare context, see J.K. Alexander, Promising, Professional Obligations, and the Refusal to Provide Service. *HEC Forum* 2005; 17: 178–195. More generally see A.J. Simmons. External Justifications and Institutional Roles. *J Philos* 1996; 93: 28–36. Hardimon *op. cit.* note 3, refers to a contractual view as the 'standard' view.

5   Consent would thus make an exception for military conscripts who have not consented, and hence whose capacity to refuse unconscionable orders remains an essential bulwark of their autonomy.

6   T. Pogge. 2002. Loopholes in Moralities. In T. Pogge, *World Poverty and Human Rights.* Cambridge, MA: Polity Press: 71–90: 72 (emphases in original).

7   For discussion see C. MacDonald. Relational Professional Autonomy. *Camb Q Healthc Ethics* 2002; 11: 282–289.

8   C. Pateman. 1989. Women and Consent. In C. Pateman. *The Disorder of Women.* Stanford: Stanford University Press: 71–89, 82.

9   For discussion see K. Graham. 2002. *Practical Reasoning in a Social World.* Cambridge: Cambridge University Press. See also A. Kolers. Dynamics of Solidarity. *J Polit Philos* 2012; 20: 365–383.

10 See J. Rawls. 1999. *A Theory of Justice*, revised edn. Cambridge, MA: Belknap Press: 275.

11 Hardimon, *op. cit.* note 3: 350.

12 On undue epistemic deference see A. Buchanan. Political Liberalism and Social Epistemology. *Philos Pub Aff* 2004; 32: 95–130.

13 LaFollette and LaFollette, *op. cit.* note 2.

14 Wicclair, *op. cit.* note 1.

15 Mary Warnock defends the fourteen-day rule for manipulation of embryos on grounds that before then, the embryo is capable of splitting and so remains numerically nonidentical to any infant who might be born from it. See M. Warnock. 2003. *Making Babies.* New York: Oxford University Press.

16 Don Marquis famously argued that fetuses do, in fact, have an interest in 'a future like ours,' and if so then abortion would harm them. While I personally disagree, the view defended here—that fetuses are not abused by routine abortions—is compatible with Marquis's thesis, provided that the harm done through abortion does not constitute abuse, or that when abortion is legal, abandoning the patient *also* constitutes abuse, and hence refusal requires a license. See D. Marquis. Why Abortion Is Immoral. *J Philos* 1989; 86: 183–202.

—14—

AGAINST PROFESSIONAL ETHICS

Bob Brecher

... THE CENTRAL PHILOSOPHICAL QUESTION about professional ethics ... is this: do they serve or hinder their respective professions? Certainly the development of professional codes of ethics has been an integral part of the process of professionalisation. On the one hand, of course, that is welcome: that the conduct of doctors or engineers be regulated by a set of ethical considerations seems self-evidently something to be welcomed. What could be wrong with regulating professional activities and, more specifically, with any regulation having an ethical framework? Accepting the political need in the current climate to defend the professions—and assuming that my hesitation about the very idea of professions is indeed unjustified—there nevertheless remains an immanent set of objections about professional ethics quite independent of any objections one might raise against the notion of a profession *per se*:

- First, the extent to which professional ethics promote conduct which is in fact self-serving rather than ethical;
- Second, the extent to which professional ethics prevents rather than encourages moral thought and moral action;
- Third, the role of professional ethics in preventing certain sorts of issue from being understood as moral matters; and,
- Fourth, the efficacy of the ethical codes concerned in preventing moral abuses.

3. PROFESSIONAL ETHICS

My first objection—that professional ethics are all too easily self-serving—is in fact no less a critical than an immanent one. For actually existing professions are of course at least to some extent self-serving, and their embrace of ethics is indeed an integral part of that function; and if the notion of a professional is to be defended, then it has to be distinguished from its various and all-too common deformations. As an example, consider the United Kingdom's General Medical Council's 1995 collection of teaching materials for ethics courses,[1] which are in fact driven wholly by legal, and not by ethical, considerations. Certainly, the GMC's notion of 'professional' ethics is one that sees defence of the profession as primary. The sections on 'Professional relationships with patients,' 'Confidentiality,' 'Abuse of your professional position,' 'Your duty to protect all patients' and 'If your health may put patients at risk' take up four pages: the rest of the thirteen (e.g., 'Keeping up to date,' 'Teaching,' 'Working in teams,' 'Arranging cover,' 'Financial and commercial dealings') are all directly concerned with matters 'internal' to the profession. Nor has this balance substantially altered in the last ten years.

That the GMC attaches primacy to protecting the profession is, in itself, neither surprising nor regrettable. What ought to be surprising, however, is that such material is being used in medical schools to teach ethics; for to conflate ethical with legal concerns to the extent that this material does is fundamentally dishonest. Of course medical students—and indeed all healthcare students—need to be taught what the law requires and forbids; and to be taught about the need to defend themselves against the various exigencies of their chosen professional practice. Any professionals who have close personal contact with people need that; they need the protection of the law—not as much as the public does, but nonetheless they need it. But it will not do to confuse a necessary, and necessarily largely defensive, legal framework with morality. And so it certainly will not do to teach law under the guise of teaching ethics—let alone as a substitute for ethics. For that is to abuse both students and ethics. It is to inculcate a fundamentally non-moral, or even anti-moral, view of their practice, namely that it—and thus its defence—is in fact primary, and that patients, let alone the public, are secondary. The problem is not limited to the medical and related professions. How much of what is pursued in the name of ethics in education, business and the law itself in fact answers to legal, rather than to moral, concerns? But perhaps this is a deformation which could be remedied, rather than a more deep-seated problem about the very idea of professional ethics; a concern, that is to say, about what might be seen as a misuse of 'professional ethics.'

My second objection, however, is more fundamental: that professional ethics—and in particular codes of (professional) ethics—all too easily prevent rather than encourage moral thought and moral action. A code is a set of rules; some may take the form of advice rather than direction, but nonetheless, their form is that of rules. And that is a problem. Rules are formulae, algorithms; and to follow rules as a means of making the right decision is a matter of looking up the appropriate rule in the relevant handbook. But is looking up the rules a good way of making moral decisions? Or are rules rather a sort of moral backdrop, for use as reminders when we need them? Following Kant, to the extent that making a moral decision, and thus acting morally, is a rational matter, to that extent it is a matter of exercising one's rational capacity. Children learn to act morally by being

told what to do, by imitating their elders—that is to say, by learning to follow rules. But actually acting morally comes later, when children are no longer (just) children, when they are able to think for themselves. Of course, they—and we—might still act in accordance with a rule; but that is quite different from merely following it, merely looking up what to do and doing it. One way of putting this is that moral decision making and moral action have to be internalised in order to constitute moral decision and action; another is to remind ourselves of Kant's insistence that an action not done for the right reason—that is to say, for a moral reason—is not a moral action at all, however morally desirable its consequences may be. Only when one's action consists in rational appraisal, judgement and action is it a moral, rather than some other sort of, action. The difference is that between a genuine morality (assuming here that there is some such) and the notion of morality as the 'club rules' of a society, that is to say of those in power—the notion of 'morality' as a fundamental ideological tool of the ruling class, as Marx, pre-eminently, reminds us.[2]

There is a further and related problem about professional ethics as enshrined in a code, namely the moral status of the code itself and of the rules it contains. Who is to question these, and on what basis? Again, professional ethics have here to be subjected to ethical analysis *tout court*. Consider in this context, for example, the work of Nazi doctors and nurses in the German eugenics programme of the 1930s. It is all too easy to suppose that if the rules do not explicitly forbid something, then it is permissible. Furthermore, the content, and specifically the referents, of the rules themselves can always be redescribed, as I outlined earlier. If these people are not 'patients,' but 'subjects,' or if those are not 'people' but 'degenerates' or 'defectives,' then the rules do not apply to them. 'Professional ethics' all too easily prevent the rules in which they consist being subjected to moral critique by being presented and understood as given. Nor is this just a practical difficulty. A code cannot but be something given if it is to function as a code at all. Thus if an ethical code is to be subjected to moral critique, the problem arises as to the status and applicability of the latter: either the moral critique fails to apply, just because it countermands what is in the code; or, if not, then the code is redundant.

The problem is that in relying on a code of ethics, people can think that the moral work has been done for them. The mundane but nonetheless significant practice in the area of healthcare of patients 'being consented' by someone before an operation or some other intervention—rather than the patient's giving informed consent—sums up the difficulty. Going through the procedures of making sure the patient has signed a consent form is quite different from the patient's actually giving their informed consent; indeed, one might well suppose that consent obtained mechanically, as a matter of routine, entirely undermines the moral purpose of obtaining it at all.

My third objection is that professional codes of ethics all-too easily serve to prevent certain sorts of issue from being understood as moral matters at all. Again, the clearest examples are perhaps those of healthcare. What I have in mind, to take just a few examples, are issues of resource allocation and rationing, geographical inequities such as 'postcode prescribing,'[3] the responsibilities of patients, issues of public health, the question of who becomes and who does not become a patient, and, of course, the issue of private medicine. That is in part because the content of codes depends on what their authors think relevant—and that can never be an adequate criterion, for not only does the world change, but so does the range of issues over which 'morality' ranges. Of course, this problem can be obviated by frequent re-appraisal and revision of the code—consider the regular recasting of the Helsinki Declaration, for example—but that, necessary though it is, raises yet another difficulty. The authors of codes, however well-intentioned and however able to think disinterestedly, cannot but bring to their work their own particular views; and however much individual views are balanced out against those of others, nonetheless,

a code remains just that—a specific document expressing the moral views of a specific group. Morality, however, must aim at universality if it is not to be, or to degenerate into, the sort of ideological weapon mentioned above, and rightly rejected by Marx. Codes, in contrast, are necessarily local rather than universal: a 'universal' code, lacking borders or limits, would not be a code at all, but something far more authoritative, a necessary condition of codes rather than a code. The rules of deductive logic, for example, are not codes, but a necessary condition of the thought that makes codes (and not just codes, of course) possible. It is in that that their universal validity lies.

My final objection to professional codes of ethics is that their efficacy in preventing moral abuses is very doubtful. The recent case of Harold Shipman, the General Practitioner (family doctor) who murdered, at the latest count, over 200 of his patients, comes to mind here. The example is of course an extreme one: nobody suggests that the fundamental problem with Shipman was that he did not follow his professional ethical code. But the bigger difficulty lies precisely in less spectacular examples: any ethical code, or any part of it, can be by-passed or overridden. Indeed, I have already suggested that on occasion it needs to be overridden in the name of morality. The limited nature of ethical codes, however, also allows them to be overridden for a whole range of reasons and in the name of all sorts of interests—and it is morality *per se* which needs to determine when this is morally justified and when not. But again, it is then morality itself which is the focus and to which one has to turn. Professional ethics are once again beside the point.

At best, professional ethics—encapsulated in professional ethical codes—might constitute a backstop for internal policing. But then, it is their 'internal' character that constitutes a problem which itself requires moral judgement and action. An 'internal' approach is doubtless appropriate for matters of professional expertise—but not in the case of those that require the 'external' attentions of morality. But why, it might be objected, can professional codes of ethics not encapsulate those elements of a broader morality which are necessary—a sort of set of very general clauses, perhaps, against which any more specific rules are always to be measured? The thought, while understandable and even laudable, is, however, counterproductive. What would these broader features be, which by definition could not be overturned by any more particular considerations? What would be needed would be not some sort of code at all, but a set of moral certainties paralleling those of, say, deductive logic. On the assumption that something like this is even possible, it again remains the case that anything sufficiently code-like becomes redundant. To the extent that there are some such moral certainties, to that extent we have no need of any professional code to tell us what we already know as moral agents—that gratuitous cruelty is wrong, perhaps, or that people ought not to treat others merely as a means to their own ends.

CONCLUSION

There are of course arguments on both sides; my focus so far has been on objections to professional ethics. Perhaps the strongest argument in their favour, and perforce of their encoding, is the thought that professionals have quite enough to do without also having to attempt to solve moral problems, let alone moral dilemmas. The expertise of the physician, nurse, manager or teacher is one thing—their morality another. After all, no one expects train drivers, refuse collectors or shop assistants to wrestle with moral problems as part of their everyday work; and to the extent that being a professional is in part marked by one's work having, or being considered to have, a greater import than 'mere' work, and so is more likely to raise moral issues, then a code of professional ethics is a reasonable solution. At least keep the moral considerations within professional boundaries, and limit the scope of professionals' moral responsibilities to those directly engendered by their practice, rather than trying to insist that they have a responsibility different from that of others

to attend to general moral matters. They might do that *qua* citizen, but not *qua* nurse or engineer.

Two issues arise here. What are the relations between our moral responsibilities as citizens—as people—and our moral responsibilities as, for example, managers or doctors? Can one make a viable distinction between two classes of moral responsibility? Even more pertinently, what happens when my moral responsibility as an academic—say, to colleagues—conflicts with my moral (or political) duty as citizen?[4] My worry is that professional ethics is a way of avoiding these issues rather than facing them. In short, it can excuse 'ordinary' immorality by making ethics one consideration among others, one factor which a professional has to consider against others such as efficiency, preferment and all the rest. But the domain of morality is universal: moral considerations cannot be measured against others, since they are just those considerations which trump all others. That is what makes them moral considerations.

In conclusion, I outline briefly a universalist approach which might well guide all moral interaction, general (*qua* citizen) as well as specific (*qua* professional).

One does not have to be a Kantian to agree with Kant that there is something profoundly wrong in treating another person not as an end in themselves, but solely as a means. And that principle of Kant's—'So act that you use humanity, whether in your own person or in the person of any other, always at the same time as an end, never merely as a means'[5]—is my starting-point. Of course it is open to a range of interpretations: in particular, it is not clear just how 'humanity ... in (someone's) ... person' is supposed to relate to actual, living, people.[6] But still, the underlying thought is surely clear: there is something no less obviously than fundamentally wrong with treating people merely as a means to an end. It is fine to treat the shop assistant as a shop assistant, as a means to one's end of buying whatever it is; but wrong to treat them merely as such. Shop assistants are not merely shop assistants, one might say, but—like everyone else—they are also people. So if circumstances, say, of danger arise—a fire breaks out in the shop—one stops using the shop assistant as a means to one's end, just as one does outside the shop. People should never treat others merely as a means to their own ends.

That said, what else is there for professional ethics to add?[7]

NOTES

1   General Medical Council *Duties of a doctor: guidance from the GMC* GMC, London 1995.

2   There is of course a major issue concerning whether or not the notion of morality as (merely) bourgeois ideology was Marx's *sole* conception of morality; and behind this lurks the very large question of whether or not 'morality' names or describes anything which is in any sense real.

3   Postcode prescribing is the UK practice whereby decisions on the allocation of resources for particular purposes are made by local Trusts responsible for the provision of healthcare. Whether or not you get such-and-such a treatment, therefore, depends on where you live. For example, an expensive drug might be prescribed by a doctor in, say, Oxford, but be unavailable for prescription by a doctor in, say, Gateshead.

4   I address the issue of academics' responsibilities in 'Do Intellectuals Have a Public Responsibility?' forthcoming in Aiken W and Haldane J (eds) *Philosophy and its Public Role* (St Andrews Studies in Philosophy and Public Affairs) Imprints Academic, Exeter.

5   [Kant, *Groundwork of the Metaphysics of Morals* 4: 429.]

6   An excellent discussion is Michael Neumann 'Did Kant Respect Persons?' *Res Publica* 6 (2000) pp. 285–299.

7   This paper has its origins in a number of talks on this and related issues at the Universities of Birmingham, Brighton and Royal Holloway, London, and at an Ethics Workshop at the Royal College of Nurses. I am grateful to all who took part for their comments; and to Nigel Laurie for suggesting a number of improvements to the final text.

DETERMINING PROFESSIONAL AUTHORITY

The Canadian Amber Light Case

Jonathan Milgrim

1. BACKGROUND

IN 2015, JAMES AISAICAN-CHASE RAN A RED LIGHT in Winnipeg, Canada. After receiving a ticket for the infraction, Aisaican-Chase chose to dispute the citation in court. His claim was not that he did not run the red light; he stipulated that he did indeed commit the infraction. Instead, he disputed the ticket because he considered the amber light duration to be far too short for him to safely stop (a four-second duration with a posted speed of 80 km/h). There was some reasonable support for his claim. First, Winnipeg is one of the only cities in Canada that does not offer extended amber light durations for intersections with higher speeds. More interesting, Aisaican-Chase had expert testimony that stated it would have been unsafe for him to attempt to stop.[1] James Aisaican-Chase, who was terminally ill, lost his initial case and appealed the decision to multiple courts before passing away in 2018 without a resolution. However, for his expert witness, David Grant, the fight is not over, though the fight is not with the traffic court system but with Engineers Geoscientists Manitoba (EGM), a professional body that licenses and regulates members of the Manitoba engineering profession.

In addition to testifying in court, Grant gave several interviews to local news stations. Each of these instances involved him providing expert opinion that the four-second amber-light duration is only adequate at lower speeds, or else in perfect conditions. For higher speed intersections, such as the one in question, less than perfect conditions would result in an inability to safely stop at the light in time. For his efforts, EGM charged Grant with professional misconduct. The regulatory body's filing accuses grant of practicing engineering while retired, offering unqualified expert testimony, and bringing the profession of engineering into "ill repute."[2] In short, EGM argues that Grant had no right to make the claims that he made under the auspices of a professional engineer. Those claims should have been restricted to the courtroom only, been made by an expert in traffic control (which Grant was not), and been made by someone still active in the profession. If the regulatory body finds Grant guilty, he could be stripped of his engineering credentials and fined up to CAD 30,000.

Grant points to his years as an engineer for Manitoba Hydro, as well as work with Formula 1 and IndyCar races as a safety consultant as proof of his expertise. Outside his first hearing he stated, "They allege that I am not qualified to comment on traffic. I've been facing yellow lights for 55 years or so. I know how they work."[3]

2. ANALYSIS

This case serves to highlight two issues within the professions. First is the role and authority of the professional regulatory bodies. Second is the manner in which a professional's obligations (those obligations that potentially extend beyond that of the non-professional) may affect how and when they are able to use the skills associated with their profession. Of course, these two issues are interconnected in that a failure of a professional to satisfy professional obligations, even outside the profession, might trigger the first issue regarding the regulatory body.

Every professional must abide by a professional code of ethics, some of which are informal and others that are formal and enforced by the relevant professional organization. According to Ernest Greenwood in "Attributes of a Profession," the enforcement of these rules is important because they are integral for community sanction and the authority professionals possess as a result of their professional status.[4] If a profession is seen as irresponsible for whatever reason, including offering testimony outside the bounds of expertise, then the profession as a whole suffers. Professional regulatory bodies must be diligent to protect this authority and the related community sanction. The key to the above case is whether Grant was operating outside his authority, and whether EGM was correct in attempting to sanction him.

Part of the answer to this question depends on how we understand the obligations of a professional in relation to the obligations of the regulatory body. Bob Brecher, in his article titled "Against Professional Ethics," argues that we should be worried about the perceived obligations owed the profession.[5] On one hand regulatory bodies seem to provide a valuable service. They stop rogue professionals from doing great harm and ensure that when someone claims to be a professional, they do indeed have the training and qualifications to make such a claim (one issue in the case above). However, there is also the worry that such regulatory agencies may, at best, prevent a professional from engaging due to worries of sanction, and at worst may attempt to thwart the public good in order to preserve and protect the profession itself. How we view the tension between professional obligations and regulatory authority will likely decide how we view the case above.

NOTES

1   Jacques Marcoux, "I'm Motivated to Fight It: Terminally ill red-light running senior loses ticket challenge, will appeal," *CBC News*, 4 May 2018, https://www.cbc.ca/news/canada/manitoba/red-light-ticket-senior-winnipeg-1.4648473.

2   Bartley Kives, "Retired Engineer Faces Disciplinary Hearing for Speaking Out about Amber Lights," *CBC News*, 11 July 2018, https://www.cbc.ca/news/canada/manitoba/engineers-pursue-disciplinary-action-traffic-lights-1.4741623.

3   Laura Glowacki, "Retired Engineer Faces Colleagues at Disciplinary Hearing in Amber Light Dispute," *CBC News*, 26 July 2018, https://www.cbc.ca/news/canada/manitoba/amber-yellow-lights-discipline-engineer-1.4763031.

4   Ernest Greenwood, "Attributes of a Profession," this volume.

5   Bob Brecher, "Against Professional Ethics," this volume.

DISCUSSION QUESTIONS

1. How would you answer the case above? Did Grant overstep his professional authority or is the potential sanction by EGM unreasonable? Consider similar cases. What about an unqualified doctor who performs surgery?

2. Would your answer have changed if Grant only spoke in the courtroom and not to reporters outside the courtroom? What place does "public testimony" have in relation to "bringing the profession into ill repute"?

3. Consider the worry by Brecher that professions may place regulations with an aim of protecting the profession at the expense

of other ethical obligations. Is this worry legitimate? Why or why not?

4. Consider the worry in the previous question. Should there be another level of regulatory agencies (governmental perhaps) that watch over the professional bodies? I.e., Who is watching the watchers?

REFUSING TO WORK

Weighing Patient Safety against Long Hours

Jonathan Milgrim

1. BACKGROUND

A 2014 STORY PENNED UNDER THE NAME DENNIS Tong relays an all-too-often-told tale in the medical field.[1] Nurses at an undisclosed urban emergency department faced the pressure of needing to see more patients in less time because labor shortages meant that the ratio of nurses to patients was inadequate. This caused nurses to adopt an "assembly line approach" and find ways to reduce the amount of time spent with each patient. Attempting to quickly do a job that requires careful attention invariably leads to mistakes, mistakes that could risk the health of patients. The other option was to cut types of care provided, and one of the first things reduced was the time spent explaining after-care and discharge instructions. However, nurses view this as one of the most important parts of their job, integral to the health and well-being of patients after returning home.

The nurses of the emergency department signed a petition explaining their concerns to the hospital administration in hopes they would hire more nurses. In response to the petition, the hospital instead removed all overtime restrictions as a "temporary" measure. This resulted in nurses routinely working long hours, which led to fatigue and concerns of fatigue-related mistakes. Other occupations, such as truck drivers, have their hours strictly limited out of safety concerns, but there are virtually no corresponding regulations in the medical professions.[2] After three years of complaints, negotiations, and petitions, the emergency department nurses decided to organize a boycott of overtime hours. The decision to boycott was not taken lightly, since the emergency room would be woefully understaffed, potentially endangering patients.

In total, 150 nurses participated in the boycott and refused to sign up for voluntary overtime. The result was better than they expected. Over 20 elective surgeries were rescheduled, and an entire wing was closed as nurses were pulled from other parts of the hospital. Inbound emergencies had to be rerouted to nearby private hospitals as doctors, residents, and medical students sat around, unable to perform their duties and rounds due to the nurse shortage. The hospital administration quickly capitulated and agreed to hire more nurses. By the following year the hospital had increased its emergency nursing staff by eight nurses and negotiations continued regarding overtime and extended work hours. However, staffing and the length of work shifts remains a concern.

2. ANALYSIS

The key consideration in this case is the division between what an employee owes their employer, versus what an employee owes the consumer. In most occupations, the employee's obligations to the consumer are dictated by the employer and by standard ethical principles. For example, a store clerk should rightly refuse to cheat customers at the behest of store management, but they owe the customer nothing as it relates to their own benefits, work hours, or time off. Other than honesty, respect, and perhaps a few other related principles, they owe the customer nothing. However, in those occupations that fall into the category of a profession, there is a larger set of obligations that many believe are owed to the customer or society at large.

In the case above, one of the problematic elements is that the nurses appear to have an obligation to their patients that is beyond what is owed to their employer. This creates situations in which they are forced to work longer hours than they would like, and cases where they are expected to risk their jobs to force change for the benefit of the patient. In his article titled "Am I My Profession's Keeper?" Avery Kolers examines how it might be that we expect this extra responsibility from professionals.[3] On the other hand, Don Welch, in his article "Just Another Day at the Office," argues that no such obligation exists beyond what is expected of every person acting morally as a rational agent.[4]

NOTES

1 Dennis Tong, "Pushed to the Wall, Nurses Refused Overtime," *LaborNotes*, 15 July 2014, https://labornotes.org/2014/07/pushed-wall-nurses-refused-overtime.

2 Ryan Park, "Why So Many Young Doctors Work Such Awful Hours," *The Atlantic*, 21 February 2017, https://www.theatlantic.com/business/archive/2017/02/doctors-long-hours-schedules/516639/.

3 Avery Kolers, "Am I My Profession's Keeper?" this volume.

4 Don Welch, "Just Another Day at the Office: The Ordinariness of Professional Ethics," this volume.

DISCUSSION QUESTIONS

1. Consider the case above: did the nurses have an obligation to boycott and demand fewer hours to potentially save the lives of patients?

2. Is there an obligation as a professional that extends past those obligations for a non-professional worker? Or, as Welch suggests, does this all fall under the normal obligations everyone carries as a rational moral agent?

3. Imagine that during the boycott detailed above a patient dies. Who is responsible for this death? Are the nurses responsible for not working the extra shifts? Is the hospital administration responsible for failing to hire additional workers? What would have to change for you to change your answer?

4. Some workers are considered "essential" and work in professions in which they are not allowed, by law, to boycott or strike. Should nurses and doctors in an emergency department be considered such a field? If so, what worker protections would need to be in place to protect them?

PROFESSIONAL RESPONSIBILITY

Jonathan Milgrim and Fritz Allhoff

1. INTRODUCTION

THE PREVIOUS UNITS DISCUSSED ETHICAL THEO-ries and ethical behavior within the professions. These discussions generally involve critiques of behavior that ought to be avoided or actions in which we ought to be engaged. In one sense, professional responsibility might rightly be viewed as an ethical obligation, plus something else. Michael Pritchard evokes the image of Calvin from the comic strip *Calvin and Hobbes*. He states:

> Six-year-old Calvin has finally made his bed. His pal, Hobbes the stuffed tiger, says, "Gee, your mom sure was impressed when you made your bed." Calvin replies, "Right. That's how I like it—to impress her by fulfilling the *least* of my obligations."[1] We can think of Calvin as occupying one end of a spectrum of responsibility that ranges from the minimal to the supererogatory ("above and beyond the call of duty").[2]

Following this line of thought, individual ethical requirements might be the least of our obligations, while professional responsibility exists further along the spectrum toward the supererogatory. However, it would be overly simplistic to view professional responsibility as existing only as a stricter set of ethical obligations.

The reality of professional responsibility is much more complex. Professional responsibility considers what actions might be prohibited or required for a professional that might not be the case for the individual. For example, it might be part of a professional's responsibility to put the needs and desires of their client ahead of their own, whereas the individual might bear no such responsibility. This is seen in the legal profession, where a lawyer's personal moral code is, to some degree, secondary to the needs of the client.[3] This tension between the needs of the professional and that of the client is even more complicated in some cases, such as whistleblowing, where the professional also has to weigh the needs of society and an employer.

When viewed in this manner, this responsibility points to an important part of being a professional. The respect and standing that is afforded professionals, from the engineer, to the doctor, to the law enforcement officer, is an acknowledgement that we lay additional duties and obligations on the shoulders of the professional that other workers are not expected to bear. This unit serves to further explore the themes from above in determining what exactly it means to be responsible as a professional, both as a general concept and for individual professions.

2. CONTENTS

The unit begins with four articles aimed at understanding professional responsibility from a general perspective. The first article, "The Parable of the Sadhu," relates the story of a group of climbers attempting to travers a high ridge in the Himalayas while on a journey around Nepal. They discover a Sadhu, an Indian holy man, who is struggling and wholly unprepared for the weather and altitude. They clothe and feed him, but fearful of missing the second half of their trip, they continue on after pointing him in the direction of a village lower down the mountain. The author then wonders what more they should have done. What further responsibilities did they have beyond the efforts they made? The struggle the author faces is an appropriate analogy for struggles faced by professionals when attempting to satisfy responsibilities that fall beyond those of the individual.

The second article, titled "Social Responsibility and Ethics: Clarifying the Concepts," explores responsibility between the professional and society at large. While themes such as forgoing profit in order to benefit society are explored in the context of business, the principles apply to the professions and to professionals as well. This article is followed by "The Nature of Responsibility in a Professional Setting," which explores the concept of responsibility in greater depth, attempting to answer what is actually meant when we use the term "responsibility." The last general article, "Whistleblowing and Leaks," explores the complexity of being a whistleblower as a professional, because it requires violating the very codes that professionals are supposed to uphold (confidentiality, loyalty, etc.).

The general articles are followed by a selection of four articles that explore professional responsibility within specific professions. These articles target journalism, engineering, law, and public relations in particular, but many of the issues covered here also apply to numerous other professions.

The fifth article in the unit, "Objectivity Precludes Responsibility" examines what is meant by "objectivity" within journalism, and why objectivity is such a motivator for professional responsibility. This is followed by "Responsible Engineering: The Importance of Character and Imagination," which explores what tools are needed for the engineer (and potentially other professionals) to act in a responsible manner. The final two articles, "Ethics and the Professional Responsibility of Lawyers," followed by "Toward a Professional Responsibility Theory of Public Relations Ethics," investigate what is required to be responsible in the professions of law and public relations in turn.

The unit concludes with two cases studies. The first, "The West Gate Bridge: Who Was Responsible?" examines the events that lead to the collapse of a section of the West Gate Bridge while it was being built in Melbourne, Australia. While primarily used to highlight failures in engineering responsibility, the case serves to highlight the problems with determining responsibility when multiple parties and professions are involved. The unit concludes with "Snowden, Security, and Civil Liberties: The Ethics of Whistleblowing," which covers the events surrounding Edward Snowden's leaking of information collected and stored by government entities. This case serves to display the complexity and difficulty of determining when professional responsibility has been met or violated in whistleblowing cases.

NOTES

1   Bill Watterson, *Calvin and Hobbes*, (1990), quoted in Michael Pritchard, "Responsible Engineering: The Importance of Character and Imagination," this volume.

2   See Michael Pritchard, "Responsible Engineering: The Importance of Character and Imagination," this volume.

3   See, for example, Kenneth Kipnis, "Ethics and the Professional Responsibility of Lawyers," this volume.

—15—

THE PARABLE OF THE SADHU

Bowen H. McCoy

LAST YEAR, AS THE FIRST PARTICIPANT IN THE new six-month sabbatical program that Morgan Stanley has adopted, I enjoyed a rare opportunity to collect my thoughts as well as do some traveling. I spent the first three months in Nepal, walking 600 miles through 200 villages in the Himalayas and climbing some 120,000 vertical feet. On the trip my sole Western companion was an anthropologist who shed light on the cultural patterns of the villages we passed through.

During the Nepal hike, something occurred that has had a powerful impact on my thinking about corporate ethics. Although some might argue that the experience has no relevance to business, it was a situation in which a basic ethical dilemma suddenly intruded into the lives of a group of individuals. How the group responded I think holds a lesson for all organizations no matter how defined.

THE SADHU

The Nepal experience was more rugged and adventuresome than I had anticipated. Most commercial treks last two or three weeks and cover a quarter of the distance we traveled.

My friend Stephen, the anthropologist, and I were halfway through the 60-day Himalayan part of the trip when we reached the high point, an 18,000-foot pass over a crest that we'd have to traverse to reach the village of Muktinath, an ancient holy place for pilgrims.

Six years earlier I had suffered pulmonary edema, an acute form of altitude sickness, at 16,500

feet in the vicinity of Everest base camp, so we were understandably concerned about what would happen at 18,000 feet. Moreover, the Himalayas were having their wettest spring in 20 years; hip-deep powder and ice had already driven us off one ridge. If we failed to cross the pass, I feared that the last half of our "once in a lifetime" trip would be ruined.

During the late afternoon, four backpackers from New Zealand joined us, and we spent most of the night awake anticipating the climb. Below we could see the fires of two other parties, which turned out to be two Swiss couples and a Japanese hiking club.

To get over the steep part of the climb before the sun melted the steps cut in the ice, we departed at 3:30 a.m. The New Zealanders left first, followed by Stephen and myself, our ports and Sherpas, and then the Swiss. The Japanese lingered in their camp. The sky was clear, and we were confident that no spring storm would erupt that day to close the pass.

At 15,500 feet, it looked to me as if Stephen were shuffling and staggering a bit, which are symptoms of altitude sickness. (The initial stage of altitude sickness brings a headache and nausea. As the condition worsens, a climber may encounter difficult breathing, disorientation, aphasia, and paralysis.) I felt strong, my adrenaline was flowing, but I was very concerned about my ultimate ability to get across. A couple of our porters were also suffering from the height and Pasang, our Sherpa sirdar (leader), was worried.

Just after daybreak, while we rested at 15,000 feet, one of the New Zealanders, who had gone ahead, came staggering down toward us with a body slung across his shoulders. He dumped the almost naked, barefoot body of an Indian holy man—a Sadhu—at my feet. He had found the pilgrim lying on the ice, shivering and suffering from hypothermia. I cradled the Sadhu's head and laid him out on the rocks. The New Zealander was angry. He wanted to get across the pass before the bright sun melted the snow. He said "Look, I've done what I can. You have porters and Sherpa guides. You care for him. We're going on!" He turned and went back up the mountain to join his friends.

I took a carotid pulse and found that the Sadhu was still alive. We figured he had probably visited the holy shrines at Muktinath and was on his way home. It was fruitless to question why he had chosen this desperately high route instead of the safe, heavily traveled caravan route through the Kali Gandaki gorge. Or why he was almost naked and with no shoes, or how long he had been lying in the pass. The answers weren't going to solve our problem.

Stephen and the four Swiss began stripping off outer clothing and opening their packs. The Sadhu was soon clothed from head to foot. He was not able to walk, but he was very much alive. I looked down the mountain and spotted below the Japanese climbers marching up with a horse.

Without a great deal of thought, I told Stephen and Pasang that I was concerned about withstanding the heights to come and wanted to get over the pass. I took off after several of our porters who had gone ahead.

On the steep part of the ascent where, if the ice steps had given way, I would have slid down about 3,000 feet, I felt vertigo. I stopped for a breather, allowing the Swiss to catch up with me. I inquired about the Sadhu and Stephen. They said the Sadhu was fine and that Stephen was just behind. I set off again for the summit.

Stephen arrived at the summit an hour after I did.

Still exhilarated by victory, I ran down the snow slope to congratulate him. He was suffering from altitude sickness, walking 15 steps, then stopping, walking 15 steps, then stopping. Pasang accompanied him all the way up. When I reached them, Stephen glared at me and said: "How do you feel about contributing to the death of a fellow man?"

I did not fully comprehend what he meant. "Is the Sadhu dead?" I inquired.

"No," replied Stephen, "but he surely will be!"

After I had gone, and the Swiss had departed not long after, Stephen had remained with the Sadhu. When the Japanese had arrived, Stephen asked to use their horse to transport the Sadhu down to the hut. They had refused. He had then asked Pasang to have a group of our porters carry the Sadhu. Pasang had resisted the idea, saying that the porters would have to exert all their energy to get themselves over the pass. He had thought they could not carry a man down 1,000 feet to the hut, reclimb the slope, and get across safely before the snow melted. Pasang had pressed Stephen not to delay any longer.

The Sherpas had carried the Sadhu down to a rock in the sun at about 15,000 feet and had pointed out the hut another 500 feet below. The Japanese had given him food and drink. When they had last seen him he was listlessly throwing rocks at the Japanese party's dog, which had frightened him.

We do not know if the Sadhu lived or died.

For many of the following days and evenings Stephen and I discussed and debated our behavior toward the Sadhu. Stephen is a committed Quaker with deep moral vision. He said "I feel that what happened with the Sadhu is a good example of the breakdown between the individual ethic and the corporate ethic. No one person was willing to assume ultimate responsibility for the Sadhu. Each was willing to do his bit just so long as it was not too inconvenient. When it got to be a bother, everyone just passed the buck to someone else and took off."

I defended the larger group saying "Look, we all cared. We all stopped and gave aid and comfort. Everyone did his bit. The New Zealander carried him down below the snow line. I took his pulse and suggested we treat him for hypothermia. You and the Swiss gave him clothing and got him warmed up. The Japanese gave him food and water. The Sherpas carried him down to the sun and pointed out the easy trail toward the hut. He was well enough to throw rocks at a dog. What more could we do?"

"You have just described the typical affluent Westerner's response to a problem. Throwing money—in this case food and sweaters—at it, but not solving the fundamentals!" Stephen retorted.

"What would satisfy you?" I said. "Here we are, a group of New Zealanders, Swiss, Americans, and Japanese who have never met before and who are at the apex of one of the most powerful experiences of our lives. Some years the pass is so bad no one gets over it. What right does an almost naked pilgrim who chooses the wrong trail have to disrupt our lives? Even the Sherpas had no interest in risking the trip to help him beyond a certain point."

Stephen calmly rebutted, "I wonder what the Sherpas would have done if the Sadhu had been a well-dressed Nepali, or what the Japanese would have done if the Sadhu had been a well-dressed Asian, or what you would have done, Buzz, if the Sadhu had been a well-dressed Western woman?"

"Where, in your opinion," I asked instead, "is the limit of our responsibility in a situation like this? We had our own well-being to worry about. Our Sherpa guides were unwilling to jeopardize us or the porters for the Sadhu. No one else on the mountain was willing to commit himself beyond certain self-imposed limits."

Stephen said, "As people with a Western ethical tradition, we can fulfill our obligations in such a situation only if (1) the Sadhu dies in our care, (2) the Sadhu demonstrates to us that he could undertake the two-day walk down to the village, or (3) we carry the Sadhu for two days down to the village and convince someone there to care for him."

"Leaving the Sadhu in the sun with food and clothing, while he demonstrated hand-eye coordination by throwing a rock at a dog, comes close to fulfilling items one and two," I answered. "And it wouldn't have made sense to take him to the village where the people appeared to be far less caring than the Sherpas, so the third condition is impractical. Are you really saying that, no matter what the implications, we should, at the drop of a hat, have changed our entire plan?"

THE INDIVIDUAL VERSUS THE GROUP ETHIC

Despite my arguments, I felt and continue to feel guilt about the sadhu. I had literally walked through a classic moral dilemma without fully thinking through the consequences. My excuses for my actions include a high adrenaline flow, a superordinate goal, and a once-in-a-lifetime opportunity—common factors in corporate situations, especially stressful ones.

Real moral dilemmas are ambiguous, and many of us hike right through them, unaware that they exist. When, usually after the fact, someone makes an issue of one, we tend to resent his or her bringing it up. Often, when the full import of what we have done (or not done) hits us, we dig into a defensive position from which it is very difficult to emerge....

Among the many questions that occur to me when I ponder my experience with the sadhu are: What are the practical limits of moral imagination and vision? Is there a collective or institutional ethics that differs from the ethics of the individual? At what level of effort or commitment can one discharge one's ethical responsibilities?...

—16—

SOCIAL RESPONSIBILITY AND ETHICS

Clarifying the Concepts

Josie Fisher

... THE CONCEPT OF SOCIAL RESPONSIBILITY IS ambiguous. De George (1999) has identified four different ways the term is used: First, when a corporation is described as being socially responsible this can mean simply that it meets its legal obligations. Second, when a corporation is described as being socially responsible it sometimes means that, in addition to meeting its legal obligations, the organisation also fulfils its social obligations. The important point about these two uses of the term is that they refer to the level of commitment that particular organisations do, in fact, demonstrate, thus these uses are descriptive.

The possible levels of commitment have been represented in management texts as a continuum that, at one extreme, identifies resistance to social demands, then a defensive or social obligation approach (the organisation meets its economic and legal responsibilities), followed by accommodation or a social response approach (in addition to meeting its economic and legal responsibilities, the organisation also fulfils society's ethical expectations) and, at the other extreme, a proactive, social contribution approach (see, for example, Davidson and Griffin, 2000 and Schermerhorn, 2002 ... and Samson and Daft, 2003)....

The term *social responsibility* is also used to stand for the obligations themselves—either those imposed by society, or those assumed by a particular organisation (whether or not these reflect society's concerns). These are the third and fourth uses identified by De George (1999). Since these are obligations that ought to be fulfilled (according to society or the particular organisation) this indicates a normative use of the term....

A major reason for there being no consensus about the social responsibilities of business is that there is no general agreement about the purpose of business nor who has legitimate claims on it. One way the debate about the requirements of social responsibility has been framed is in terms of two competing views of the role of business in society: the classical (or free market view, or narrow view) and the socioeconomic view (or broader view) (see, for example, Kitson and Campbell, 1996; Robbins et al., 2000; Schermerhorn, 2002). According to the former view, attributed to Friedman and Levitt, the only social responsibility of business is to maximise profits.... [H]owever, ... this is a misrepresentation. Profit maximisation is constrained by the "rules of the game," which require compliance with the law and other social norms. Thus, the "rules of the game" identify the social responsibilities of business. According to Friedman (2000) these are to engage in open and free competition without deception and fraud, and to conform with the norms of society. Levitt is less specific, however; he identifies the responsibility of business to act honestly, in good faith "and so on" (cited in Shaw and Barry, 2001, p. 204). This view might more accurately be identified as the minimalist approach to social responsibility. Business has a social responsibility to do what is demanded by society and no more.

The socioeconomic view offers a broader account of social responsibility. According to this view, business has obligations that go beyond pursuing profits and include protecting and improving society (see, for example, Robbins et al., 2000; Shaw and Barry, 2001). "The concept of corporate social responsibility is often expressed as the voluntary assumption of responsibilities that go beyond the purely economic and legal responsibilities of business firms" (Boatright, 2000, p. 340). Boatright goes on to say that by implication businesses must be willing "... to forgo a certain measure of profit in order to achieve noneconomic ends" (p. 340). According to Ferrell et al. (2000) a business that is socially responsible will maximise the positive effects it has on society and minimise the negative effects. Writing in 1975, Backman identified some examples of corporate social responsibility: "Employment of minority groups, reduction in pollution, greater participation in programs to improve the community, improved medical care, improved industrial health and safety" (cited in Carroll, 1999, p. 279).

What level of social responsibility is expected? Sethi claims that social responsibility can be defined as "... bringing corporate behaviour up to a level where it is congruent with the prevailing social norms, values, and expectations" (quoted in Boatright, 2000, p. 340). Social responsibility encompasses those expectations society has of organisations (economic, legal, ethical and discretionary) at a given point in time. They are "... the behaviours and norms that society expects

business to follow (Carroll, 1999, p. 283)." Society expects businesses to make a profit and obey the law and, in addition, to behave in certain ways and conform to the ethical norms of society. These behaviours and practices go beyond the requirements of the law, and seem to be constantly expanding (Carroll, 1999). The focus of the socioeconomic view is on how society believes business ought to behave, therefore it is a normative view. Society identifies what business firms are expected to do beyond making a profit, and this varies over time and is becoming more demanding (De George's third use of the term). De George (1999, p. 208) sounds a warning about the level of social responsibility business can reasonably be expected to bear:

> If as a society we decide that corporations should be forced to rebuild the inner city, should not be allowed to close down unprofitable plants, or should be made to train the hard-core unemployed, these demands should be thought through, discussed in the political forum, and then clearly legislated. They are controversial social demands and should not be confused with what is morally required.

The reason society can make demands on business is because business functions by public consent and its purpose is to serve society (see for, example, Carroll, 1999; Grace and Cohen, 1998; Robbins et al., 2000).... Since society does expect business firms to demonstrate genuine social responsibility, and stakeholder expectations receive a lot of public attention, there are prudential reasons for businesses to take seriously their social responsibility.

Since the 1960s it has been claimed that social responsibility and long-term profits are not incompatible, however, it was Drucker writing in 1984 who claimed he was proposing a "new idea"—that being socially responsible could be converted into business opportunities (Carroll, 1999). Studies on the relationship between social responsibility and financial performance are, however, ambiguous (Robbins et al., 2000). In examples where there is both good financial and social performance it is unclear whether good social performance leads to increased financial performance, or if good financial performance provides the resources to fund good social performance. In contrast, there is evidence that there is a link between social irresponsibility and negative stock market returns (Trevino and Nelson, 1999).

According to an alternative view,

> [t]o qualify as socially responsible corporate action, a business expenditure or activity must be one for which the marginal returns to the corporation are less than the returns available from some alternative expenditure, must be purely voluntary, and must be an actual corporate expenditure rather than a conduit for individual largesse. (Carroll, 1999, p. 276)

This is consistent with Boatright's (2000) claim, identified above, that a business should be prepared to sacrifice some profit in order to promote noneconomic goals. Of course, this view does not rule out the possibility of good financial performance, rather it claims that maximum economic returns have not been achieved because of the focus on social performance....

The above discussion draws attention to the various ways—descriptive and normative—the term *social responsibility* is employed in the literature. It is easy to see how these different uses can cause readers unfamiliar with these various concepts to become confused....

REFERENCES

Boatright, J.R.: 2000, *Ethics and the Conduct of Business*, 3rd Edition (Prentice Hall, Upper Saddle River, NJ).

Carroll, A.J.: 1999, 'Corporate Social Responsibility: Evolution of a Definitional Construct,' *Business and Society* 38(3), 268–295.

Davidson, P. and R.W. Griffin: 2000, *Management: Australia in a Global Context* (Wiley, Brisbane).

De George, R.T.: 1999, *Business Ethics*, 5th Edition (Prentice Hall, Upper Saddle River, NJ).

DesJardins, J.R. and J.J. McCall: 2000, *Contemporary Issues in Business Ethics* (Wadsworth, Belmont, CA).

Ferrell, O.C., J. Fraedrich and L. Ferrell: 2000, *Business Ethics*, 4th Edition (Houghton Mifflin, Boston).

Friedman, M.: 2000, 'The Social Responsibility of Business Is to Increase Its Profits,' in DesJardins, J.R. and J.J. McCall (eds.), *Contemporary Issues in Business Ethics* (Wadsworth, Belmont, CA), 8–12.

Grace, D. and S. Cohen: 1998, *Business Ethics: Australian Problems and Cases*, 2nd Edition (Oxford University Press, Melbourne).

Kitson, A. and R. Campbell: 1996, *The Ethical Organisation* (Macmillan, Houndmills).

Robbins, S.P., R. Bergman, I. Stagg and M. Coulter: 2000, *Management*, 2nd Edition (Prentice Hall, Sydney).

Samson, D. and R.L. Daft: 2003, *Management: Pacific Rim Edition* (Thomson, Southbank, Victoria).

Schermerhorn, J.R.: 2002, *Management*, 7th edition (Wiley, New York).

Shaw, W.H. and V. Barry: 2001, *Moral Issues in Business*, 8th Edition (Wadsworth, Belmont, CA).

Trevino, L.K. and D.A. Nelson: 1999, *Managing Business Ethics*, 2nd Edition (Wiley, New York).

—17—

THE NATURE OF RESPONSIBILITY IN A PROFESSIONAL SETTING

Simon Robinson

... Responsibility: A detachable burden easily shifted to the shoulders of God, Fate, Fortune, Luck or ones neighbour. In the days of astrology it was customary to unload it upon a star. (Bierce, 2003)

Everyone is really responsible for all men, for all men and for everything. (Markel in Dostoevsky's *Grand Inquisitor*, 1993, p. 41)

IN THIS PAPER I WILL FIRST LOOK AT THE NATURE of responsibility, suggesting that this is a complex but dynamic concept, at the base of which is a view of universal responsibility. I will then examine some implications of this view of responsibility for the professions. I will suggest that shared responsibility is expressed in the critical dialogue between the responsibilities of different roles, that it demands moral leadership from the professions and that this is based in integrity and critical dialogue.

RESPONSIBILITY

Schweiker (1995) sums up three interconnected modes of responsibility, the first two of which originate in Aristotle's thinking (Alexander, 2008):

1. *Imputability*. Actions can be attributed to a person. Hence, the person can be seen to have been responsible for those actions and the decisions that led to them.
2. *Accountability*. The person is responsible or answerable to someone.
3. *Liability*. The person is responsible for something or someone.

Imputability

There are strong and weak views of imputability. The weak views (McKenny, 2005, p. 242) simply refer to the causal connection between the person and any action. This shows that the action can be attributed to the person. Such a view does not help in determining just how much the person is actually involved in and therefore fully responsible for the action. A stronger view suggests that responsibility involves a rational decision-making process that enables the person to fully own the action that arises from the decision. Taylor (1989) argues that this decision-making constitutes a strong valuation that connects action to deep decision making, and is what constitutes the moral identity of the person. In order to be fully responsible the person would have to be aware of his or her social context, the significant relationships, the mutual effect of those relationships and so on.

Accountability

The second mode of responsibility is accountability. This is based on contract relationships, formal or informal. The contract sets up a series of mutual expectations. At one level, these are about discernible targets that form the basis of any project, and without which the competence of the person cannot be assessed. At another level, there will be broader moral expectations of how one should behave in any contract or any membership of a group such as a profession. This would include the importance of openness and transparency in relationships and other such behaviours that provide the basis for trust.

Liability

Liability (as distinguished from legal liability) goes beyond accountability, into the idea of caring for others, of sense of wider liability for certain projects or people. Each person or profession has to work these out in context, without an explicit contract. Working that out demands an awareness of the limitations of the person or organisation, avoiding taking too much responsibility and a capacity to work together with others and to negotiate and share responsibility. This is responsibility *for* people and projects in the past, present and future. This can have a strictly legal sense or a wider moral one that encompasses the broadest possible view of stakeholders, from those directly affected by any business or project to the social and natural environment in which these operate.

For any profession the first of these modes demands the development of systematic reflection around a view and practice of its responsibilities. This requires, firstly, the articulation of purpose, usually as part of any mission statement. Secondly, there should be some planning and process outlining how that responsibility is worked through in practice. Finally, there should be a means of reflecting on and developing best practice. The second mode demands that the professional carefully work through contracts of accountability, ranging from legal obligations to responsibilities to the work force and beyond. The third has less clear guidance, and demands working through responsibilities that the business shares with others.

The concept of responsibility is not a substantive moral principle (McKenny, 2005). It does not tell the person or the profession what they should do. It does, however, have the force of an imperative that urges the person or profession to work out how it should relate to its environment and then to respond to that environment. To that degree, Friedman (1983) and Sternberg (2000) are right. They are concerned for the freedom of the executive to work out how the firm should respond. The problem with their perspective, however, is precisely what they mean by freedom. They define freedom in negative terms. Negative freedom (Berlin, 1969) is defined as 'freedom from' any form of coercion. Berlin contrasts this with positive freedom, 'freedom to' develop or create. Such a freedom requires conditions or resources, and thus leads to positive means of providing these, requiring equality of education and so on. However, neither of these views of freedom are adequate for the modes of responsibility noted above. Novak (1990) suggests instead the idea of 'moral freedom', the freedom to fulfil one's duty. Such freedom is based in the development of virtues that enable one to make rational decisions, and to control the emotions. This lies at the base of imputability, but does not address the other modes of responsibility. These point to the responsive or relational view of freedom (Tawney, 1930), which acknowledges that any freedom operates within society and affects any other person's or group's freedom. Hence, freedom has to be worked out in relationships, requiring appropriate response to others.

Each of these views of freedom is in turn based in an anthropology. In the case of Friedman and Sternberg this views humanity as individualistic. In the case of Novak and more especially Tawney humanity is seen as interactive and interdependent. The individualist view in turn tries to restrict any view of responsibility, such that it can be clearly defined and limited. The interactive view sees responsibility as something that can only be worked out in context, in response to one's social and physical environment, and therefore cannot be predetermined.

The idea that responsibility cannot be predetermined leads some to argue that the only acceptable form of responsibility is universal.

UNIVERSAL RESPONSIBILITY

For some this takes liability on to a much more profound level, the idea that one is responsible, in some sense, for everything. Professions will, of course, demur at this prospect. It is one thing to claim this in a Dostoevsky novel (*Grand Inquisitor*, 1993), but how can a person or a profession be responsible for everything or everyone? However, it is worth exploring this idea.

First, theologians of the Abrahamic faiths share the view that responsibility is based in creation theology (Carroll, 2007; Robinson, 2008b; Sacks, 2005). Creation theology sees God as the prime creator who gives responsibility to humankind for maintaining and developing that creation. In this view, every human being is accountable to God for creation. We become stewards or vicegerents of that creation. In one Islamic view (Carroll, 2007) this means constantly serving God in action (*hizmet*). The call to be responsible is a call to action. The same theme is there in Judaism, with the concept of *hesed*, or love in action (Sacks, 2005), and in Christianity with *agape* (Robinson, 2007b). Importantly, this is a response to the plurality of creation. God made everything and everyone different (Sacks, 2005). Hence, this would call the person or profession to be aware of and to appreciate the particularity of the social and physical environment. Theology then looks to a responsibility that is based in transcendence, and thus impels one to go beyond simply the consideration of interests. This also provides a strong motivation for responsibility. Such theological accounts of responsibility are very much part of the public

debate, not least because they are practice centred, and thus look to see what difference can be made. They also reinforce the need to provide an adequate world view on which to base concept and practice, and thus provide motivation. They do not demand a univocal world view, but do demand shared responsibility for working out response.

Jonas (1984) provides an equivalent world view that rests in 'creation' rather than creator, but equally looks to an existential response to the 'other'.

Operating as a philosopher from a Jewish background Jonas looks to provide an ontological rather than theological justification for responsibility for the whole global environment. Nonetheless, as Vogel (2006, p. 215) notes, his ontological grounding of this is an analogue of Jewish creation theology. He argues, firstly, that living nature is good in itself, attested to by matter's capacity to organise itself for life (the analogue of God attesting to the goodness of his creation). Secondly, he argues that the creation of humankind is an event of the highest importance, establishing a reflective stewardship responsibility for nature (the analogue of man created in God's image). Thirdly, he argues that the imperative to be responsible is answered by the capacity of humankind to feel responsible for the whole (the analogue of God writing in man's heart the consciousness of the good). Responsibility in this is based on an identification with the environment and an acute awareness of man's role in relation to the environment. For Jonas this also tends to see liability as to do with responsibility for the consequences or potential consequences of human actions.

If these provide a positive basis for response, then Bauman (1989) provides a negative foundation. Building on the philosophy of Levinas, Bauman argues that the Holocaust demonstrated decisively that humankind must take responsibility for everything and everyone. The Holocaust was built explicitly around limiting responsibility to a particular group, the Aryan Race, and this led to a denial of responsibility for any outside that sphere. Where the identity of the core group was then built on response to the threat of the other then ethnic cleansing became acceptable. Hence, Bauman argues the importance of a responsibility that is limitless. This fits exactly with the moral imperative in the Christian gospels where Jesus exhorts his followers not to restrict forgiveness to a prescribed 7 or even 70 times 7 (Matthew 18:22). The point of this saying is that, once you have exhausted the rule to forgive seven times, you still have to be responsible for the other. Responsibility takes one beyond the safety of rules or codes, which tell you where you can stop. Hence, with Bauman there is a strong sense of the suffering that goes with an awareness of universal responsibility. For Bauman "the moral self is always haunted by the suspicion that it is not moral enough" (1989). No response can completely fulfil the call of the other, and thus the person can never be satisfied.

Despite these attempts to justify the widest possible responsibility, any profession would think twice before signing up to it. No one can begin to accept such responsibility. It would be impossible to fulfil. This, however, is to misunderstand the logic of the term. Responsibility in this light is about attitude, awareness and responsiveness as part of the make-up of the profession, rather than precise descriptions of accountability or liability. One begins with the acceptance of responsibility for the other and then works through to how that might be achieved in the particular situation, requiring the exercise of related virtues.

This calls for three important elements: awareness, negotiation and creativity. Awareness of the other is often thought of as a matter of value-neutral consciousness. However, awareness of the social and physical environment is in fact value centred. We choose to be aware of our environment based upon what we value. Hence, the Christian parable of the rich man ignoring the poor man at his gate shows how the poor man did not exist for him (Robinson, 2007a). Universal responsibility requires an awareness of the equal value of all, with all potentially requiring a shared response, that we might or might not be a part of. Negotiation of responsibility accepts that all are responsible for the social and physical environment. It then involves working out how that can be fulfilled together. This demands an analysis of the shared resources and how they can best be used. As part of that there has to be a consideration of the strengths and limitations of the profession, what they can and cannot contribute. As Finch and Mason (1993) note in their work on responsibility in families, such negotiation is commonly used in decision making, rather than recourse to ethical principles, and it provides the basis for working out ethical identity. The third element, creativity, picks up the imperative to respond. This requires the profession to look always for the most creative shared response. Part of this can be looked at in terms of targets, such as emission levels. Creativity, however, can only be fully understood in terms of narrative, showing how groups work together to fulfil responsibility (Robinson, 2008a).

There are increasing examples of business, professions, NGOs and local and national government developing such creativity, focussed in shared responsibility for local or global issues, not least in post-conflict societies (Robinson and Hussein, 2009)....

REFERENCES

Alexander, J.: 2008, *Capabilities and Social Justice* (Ashgate, Aldershot).

Bauman, Z.: 1989, *Modernity and the Holocaust* (Polity, London).

Berlin, I.: 1969, 'Two Concepts of Liberty,' in A. Quinton (ed.), *Political Philosophy* (Penguin, London), pp. 141–153.

Bierce, A.: 2003, *The Devil's Dictionary* (Folio Society, London).

Carroll, B.: 2007, *A Dialogue of Civilizations* (The Gulen Institute, Istanbul).

Dostoevsky, F.: 1993, *The Grand Inquisitor* (Hackett, Indianapolis).

Finch, J. and J. Mason: 1993, *Negotiating Family Responsibilities* (Routledge, London).

Friedman, M.: 1983, 'The Social Responsibility of Business Is to Increase Its Profits,' in T. Donaldson and P. Weherne (eds.), *Ethical Issues in Business* (Prentice Hall, New York), pp. 239–243.

Jonas, H.: 1984, *The Imperative of Responsibility* (Chicago University Press, Chicago).

McKenny, G.: 2005, 'Responsibility,' in G. Meilander and W. Werpehowski (eds.), *Theological Ethics* (Oxford University Press, Oxford), pp. 237–253.

Milgram, S.: 2005, *Obedience to Authority* (Pinter and Martin, New York).

Novak, M.: 1990, *Morality, Capitalism and Democracy* (IEA, London).

Robinson, S.: 2007a, 'Spirituality, Sport and Virtues,' in J. Parry, S. Robinson, N. Watson and M. Nesti (eds.), *Sport and Spirituality* (Routledge, London), pp. 173–185.

Robinson, S.: 2007b, *Spirituality, Ethics and Care* (Jessica Kingsley, London).

Robinson, S.: 2008a, 'Can the Marketplace Be Ethical?' in P. Wetherly and D. Otter (eds.), *The Business Environment* (Oxford University Press, Oxford), pp. 187–212.

Robinson, S.: 2008b, Creation Theology and Responsibility. Conference Paper in Georgetown University Conference 'The Theology of Gulen,' November, 12–13.

Robinson, S. and Z. Hussein: 2009, *Tales of the GRLI* (Emerald, Bingley) (in press).

Sacks, J.: 2005, *To Heal a Fractured World: The Ethics of Responsibility* (Continuum, London).

Schweiker, W.: 1995, *Responsibility and Christian Ethics* (Cambridge University Press, Cambridge).

Sternberg, E.: 2000, *Just Business* (Oxford University Press, Oxford).

Tawney, R.H.: 1930, *Equality* (Allen and Unwin, London).

Taylor, C.: 1989, *Sources of the Self* (Cambridge University Press, Cambridge).

Vogel, L.: 2006, 'Natural Law Judaism? The Genesis of Bioethics in Hans Jonas, Leo Strauss, and Leon Kass,' in W. Schweiker, M. Johnson and K. Jung (eds.), *Humanity before God* (Augsburg, Minneapolis), pp. 209–237.

—18—
WHISTLEBLOWING AND LEAKS

Sissela Bok

REVELATION FROM WITHIN

All that pollution up at Mølledal—all that reeking waste from the mill—it's seeped into the pipes feeding from the pump-room; and the same damn poisonous slop's been draining out on the beach as well. I've investigated the facts as scrupulously as possible. There's irrefutable proof of the presence of decayed organic matter in the water—millions of bacteria. It's positively injurious to health, for either internal or external use. Ah, what a blessing it is to feel that you've done some service for your home town and your fellow citizens.

Dr. Thomas Stockman, in HENRIK IBSEN, *An Enemy of the People*, Act I

SUCH WAS DR. STOCKMAN'S ELATION, IN IBSEN'S play, after having written a report on the contamination of the town's newly installed mineral baths. As the spa's medical director, he took it for granted that everyone would be eager to learn why so many who had come to the baths for health purposes the previous summer had been taken ill; and he assumed that the board of directors and the taxpayers would gladly pay for the extensive repairs that he recommended. By the fifth act of the play, he had been labeled an "enemy of the people" at a public meeting, lost his position as the spa's medical director, and suffered through the stoning of his house by an angry crowd. But he held his ground: "Should I let myself be whipped from the field by public opinion and the solid majority and other such barbarities? No thank you!"[1]

"Whistleblower" is a recent label for those who, like Dr. Stockman, make revelations meant to call attention to negligence, abuses, or dangers that threaten the public interest. They sound an alarm based on their expertise or inside knowledge, often from within the very organization in which they work. With as much resonance as they can muster, they strive to breach secrecy, or else arouse an apathetic public to dangers everyone knows about but does not fully acknowledge.[2]

Few whistleblowers, however, share Dr. Stockman's initial belief that it will be enough to make their message public, and that people who learn of the danger will hasten to counter it. Most know, rather, that their alarms pose a threat to anyone who benefits from the ongoing practice and that their own careers and livelihood may be at risk. The lawyer who breaches confidentiality in reporting bribery by corporate clients knows the risk, as does the nurse who reports on slovenly patient care in a hospital, the engineer who discloses safety defects in the braking systems of a fleet of new rapid-transit vehicles, or the industrial worker who speaks out about hazardous chemicals seeping into a playground near the factory dump....

Blowing the Whistle

The alarm of the whistleblower is meant to disrupt the status quo: to pierce the background noise, perhaps the false harmony, or the imposed silence of "business as usual." Three elements, each jarring, and triply jarring when conjoined, lend acts of whistleblowing special urgency and bitterness: dissent, breach of loyalty, and accusation.*

Like all *dissent*, first of all, whistleblowing makes public a disagreement with an authority or a majority view. But whereas dissent can arise from all forms of disagreement with, say, religious dogma or government policy or court decisions, whistleblowing has the narrower aim of casting light on negligence or abuse, of alerting the public to a risk and of assigning responsibility for that risk.

It is important, in this respect, to see the shadings between the revelations of neglect and abuse which are central to whistleblowing, and dissent on grounds of policy. In practice, however, the two often come together. Coercive regimes or employers may regard dissent of any form as evidence of abuse or of corruption that calls for public exposure. And in all societies, persons may blow the whistle on abuses in order to signal policy dissent. Thus Daniel Ellsberg, in making his revelations about government deceit and manipulation in the Pentagon Papers, obviously aimed not only to expose misconduct and assign responsibility but also to influence the nation's policy toward Southeast Asia.

In the second place, the message of the whistleblower is seen as a *breach of loyalty* because it comes from within. The whistleblower, though he is neither referee nor coach, blows the whistle on his own team. His insider's position carries with it certain obligations to colleagues and clients. He may have signed a promise of confidentiality or a loyalty oath. When he steps out of routine channels to level accusations, he is going against these obligations. Loyalty to colleagues and to clients comes to be pitted against concern for the public interest and for these who may be injured unless someone speaks out. Because the whistleblower criticizes from within, his act differs from muckraking and other forms of exposure by outsiders. Their acts may arouse anger, but not the sense of betrayal that whistleblowers so often encounter.

The conflict is strongest for those who take their responsibilities to the public seriously, yet have close bonds of collegiality and of duty to clients as well. They know the price of betrayal. They know, too, how organizations protect and enlarge the area of what is concealed, as failures multiply and vested interests encroach. And they are aware that they violate, by speaking out, not only loyalty but usually hierarchy as well.

It is the third element of *accusation*, of calling a "foul" from within, that arouses the strongest reactions on the part of the hierarchy. The charge may be one of unethical or unlawful conduct on the part of colleagues or superiors. Explicitly or implicitly, it singles out specific groups or persons as responsible: as those who knew or should have known what was wrong and what the dangers were, and who had the capacity to make different choices. If no one could be held thus responsible—as in the case of an impending avalanche or a volcanic eruption—the warning would not constitute whistleblowing. At times the whistleblower's greatest effort is expended on trying to show that someone *is* responsible for danger or suffering: that the collapse of a building, the derailment of a train, or a famine that the public may have attributed to bad

---

* Consider the differences and the overlap between whistleblowing and civil disobedience with respect to these three elements. First, whistleblowing resembles civil disobedience in its openness and its intent to act in the public interest. But the dissent in whistleblowing, unlike that in civil disobedience, usually does not represent a breach of law; it is, on the contrary, protected by the right of free speech and often encouraged in codes of ethics and other statements of principle. Second, whistleblowing violates loyalty, since it dissents from within and breaches secrecy, whereas civil disobedience need not and can as easily challenge from without. Whistleblowing, finally, accuses specific Individuals, whereas civil disobedience need not. A combination of the two occurs, for instance, when former CIA agents publish books to alert the public about what they regard as unlawful and dangerous practices, and in so doing openly violate, and thereby test, the oath of secrecy that they have sworn.

luck or natural causes was in reality brought about by specific individuals, and that they can be held responsible, perhaps made to repair the damage or at least to avoid compounding it....

Individual Moral Choice

What questions might individuals consider, as they wonder whether to sound an alarm? How might they articulate the problem they see, and weigh its seriousness before deciding whether or not to reveal it? Can they make sure that their choice is the right one? And what about the choices confronting journalists or others asked to serve as intermediaries?

In thinking about these questions, it helps to keep in mind the three elements mentioned earlier: dissent, breach of loyalty, and accusation. They impose certain requirements: of judgment and accuracy in dissent, of exploring alternative ways to cope with improprieties that minimize the breach of loyalty, and of fairness in accusation. The judgment expressed by whistleblowers concerns a problem that should matter to the public. Certain outrages are so blatant, and certain dangers so great, that all who are in a position to warn of them have a *prima facie* obligation to do so. Conversely, other problems are so minor that to blow the whistle would be a disproportionate response. And still others are so hard to pin down that whistleblowing is premature. In between lie a great many of the problems troubling whistleblowers. Consider, for example, the following situation:

An attorney for a large company manufacturing medical supplies begins to suspect that some of the machinery sold by the company to hospitals for use in kidney dialysis is unsafe, and that management has made attempts to influence federal regulatory personnel to overlook these deficiencies.

The attorney brings these matters up with a junior executive, who assures her that he will look into the matter, and convey them to the chief executive if necessary. When she questions him a few weeks later, however, he tells her that all the problems have been taken care of, but offers no

evidence, and seems irritated at her desire to learn exactly where the issues stand. She does not know how much further she can press her concern without jeopardizing her position in the firm.

The lawyer in this case has reason to be troubled, but does not yet possess sufficient evidence to blow the whistle. She is far from being as sure of her case as was Ibsen's Dr. Stockman, who had received laboratory analyses of the water used in the town spa, or as the engineers in the BART case, whose professional expertise allowed them to evaluate the risks of the faulty braking system. Dr. Stockman and the engineers would be justified in assuming that they had an obligation to draw attention to the dangers they saw, and that anyone who shared their knowledge would be wrong to remain silent or to suppress evidence of the danger. But if the attorney blew the whistle about her company's sales of machinery to hospitals merely on the basis of her suspicions, she would be doing so prematurely. At the same time, the risks to hospital patients from the machinery, should she prove correct in her suspicions, are sufficiently great so that she has good reason to seek help in looking into the problem, to feel complicitous if she chooses to do nothing, and to take action if she verifies her suspicions.

Her difficulty is shared by many who suspect, without being sure, that their companies are concealing the defective or dangerous nature of their products—automobiles that are firetraps, for instance, or canned foods with carcinogenic additives. They may sense that merely to acknowledge that they don't know for sure is too often a weak excuse for inaction, but recognize also that the destructive power of adverse publicity can be great. If the warning turns out to have been inaccurate, it may take a long time to undo the damage to individuals and organizations. As a result, potential whistleblowers must first try to specify the degree to which there is genuine impropriety, and consider how imminent and how serious the threat is which they perceive.

If the facts turn out to warrant disclosure, and if the would-be whistleblower has decided to act upon them in spite of the possibilities of reprisal, then how can the second element—breach of loyalty—be overcome or minimized? Here, as in the Pentagon Papers case, the problem is one of which set of loyalties to uphold. Several professional codes of ethics, such as those of engineers and public servants, facilitate such a choice at least in theory, by requiring that loyalty to the public interest should override allegiance to colleagues, employers, or clients whenever there is a genuine conflict. Accordingly, those who have assumed a professional responsibility to serve the public interest—as had both Dr. Stockman in Ibsen's play and the engineers in the BART case—have a special obligation not to remain silent about dangers to the public.

Before deciding whether to speak out publicly, however, it is important for them to consider whether the existing avenues for change within the organization have been sufficiently explored. By turning first to insiders for help, one can often uphold both sets of loyalties and settle the problem without going outside the organization. The engineers in the BART case clearly tried to resolve the problem they saw in this manner, and only reluctantly allowed it to come to public attention as a last resort. Dr. Stockman, on the other hand, acted much more impetuously and with little concern for discretion. Before the directors of the mineral baths had even received his report, he talked freely about it, and welcomed a journalist's request to publicize the matter. While he had every reason to try to remedy the danger he had discovered, he was not justified in the methods he chose; on the contrary, they were singularly unlikely to bring about corrective action.

It *is* disloyal to colleagues and employers, as well as a waste of time for the public, to sound the loudest alarm first. Whistleblowing has to remain a last alternative because of its destructive side effects. It must be chosen only when other alternatives have been considered and rejected. They may be rejected if they simply do not apply to the problem at hand, or when there is not time to go through routine channels, or when the institution is so corrupt or coercive that steps will be taken to silence the whistleblower should he try the regular channels first.

What weight should an oath or a promise of silence have in the conflict of loyalties? There is no doubt that one sworn to silence is under a stronger obligation because of the oath he has taken, unless it was obtained under duress or through deceit, or else binds him to something in itself wrong or unlawful. In taking an oath, one assumes specific obligations beyond those assumed in accepting employment. But even such an oath can be overridden when the public interest at issue is sufficiently strong. The fact that one has promised silence is no excuse for complicity in covering up a crime or violating the public trust.

The third element in whistleblowing—accusation—is strongest whenever efforts to correct a problem without going outside the organization have failed, or seem likely to fail. Such an outcome is especially likely whenever those in charge take part in the questionable practices, or have too much at stake in maintaining them. The following story relates the difficulties one government employee experienced in trying to decide whether to go public with accusations against superiors in his agency:

As a construction inspector for a federal agency, John Samuels (not his real name) had personal knowledge of shoddy and deficient construction practices by private contractors. He knew his superiors received free vacations and entertainment, had their homes remodeled, found jobs for their relatives—all courtesy of a private contractor. These superiors later approved a multimillion no-bid contract with the same "generous" firm.

Samuels also had evidence that other firms were hiring nonunion laborers at a low wage while receiving substantially higher payments from the government for labor costs. A former superior, unaware of an office dictaphone, had incautiously instructed Samuels on how to accept bribes for overlooking sub-par performance.

As he prepared to volunteer this information to various members of Congress, he became tense and uneasy. His family was scared and the fears were valid. It might cost Samuels thousands of dollars to protect his job. Those who had freely provided him with information would probably recant or withdraw their friendship. A number of people might object to his using a dictaphone to gather information. His agency would start covering up and vent its collective wrath upon him. As for reporters and writers, they would gather for a few days, then move on to the next story. He would be left without a job, with fewer friends, with massive battles looming, and without the financial means of fighting them. Samuels decided to remain silent.[3]

Samuels could be sure of his facts, and fairly sure that it would not help to explore avenues within the agency in trying to remedy the situation. But was the method he envisaged—of volunteering his information to members of Congress and to the press—the one most likely to do so, and to provide a fair hearing for those he was charging with corruption and crime? Could he have gone first to the police? If he had been concerned to proceed in the fairest possible manner, he should at least have considered alternative methods of investigating and reporting the abuses he had witnessed.

These abuses were clearly such as to warrant attention. At other times, potential whistleblowers must also ask themselves whether their message, however accurate, is one to which the public is entitled in the first place or whether it infringes on personal and private matters that no one should invade. Here, the very notion of what is in the public interest is at issue: allegations regarding an official's unusual sexual or religious practices may well appeal to the public's interest without therefore being relevant to "the public interest." Those who regard such private matters as threats to the public voice their own religious and political prejudices in the language of accusation. Such a danger is never stronger than when the accusation is delivered surreptitiously; the anonymous allegations made during the McCarthy period regarding political beliefs and associations often

injured persons who did not even know their accusers or the exact nature of the charges.

In fairness to those criticized, openly accepted responsibility for blowing the whistle should therefore be preferred to the secret denunciation or the leaked rumor—the more so, the more derogatory and accusatory the information. What is openly stated can be more easily checked, its source's motives challenged, and the underlying information examined. Those under attack may otherwise be hard put to it to defend themselves against nameless adversaries. Often they do not even know that they are threatened until it is too late to respond.

The choice between open and surreptitious revelation from within is admittedly less easy for the persons who intend to make them. Leaking information anonymously is safer, and can be kept up indefinitely; the whistleblower, on the contrary, shoots his bolt by going public. At the same time, those who leak know that their message may be taken less seriously, precisely because its source remains concealed. And because these messages go through several intermediaries before they appear in print, they may undergo changes along the way. At times, they are so adulterated that they lose their point altogether.

Journalists and other intermediaries must make choices of their own with respect to a leaked message. Should they use it at all, even if they doubt its accuracy? Should they pass it on verbatim or interpret it? Or should they seek to "plug" the leak? Newspaper and television bureaus receive innumerable leaks but act on only some of them. Unless the information is accompanied by indications of how the evidence can be checked, the source's anonymity, however safe, diminishes the value of the message.

In order to assure transmission of their message, yet be safe from retaliation, leakers often resort to a compromise: by making themselves known to a journalist or other intermediary, they make it possible to verify their credibility; by asking that their identity be concealed, they still protect themselves from the consequences they fear.

If anonymous sources can point to independent evidence of genuine risk or wrongdoing, the need for them to step forward is reduced and their motives are less important. For this reason, the toll-free numbers that citizens can use to report on government fraud, tax evasion, or police abuse serve an important purpose in protecting critics both from inside and from outside an organization. Without such evidence, accusations openly made by identifiable persons are preferable. The open charge is fairer to the accused, and allows listeners to weigh the motives and the trustworthiness of the whistleblowers.

Must the whistleblower who speaks out openly also resign? Only if staying on means being forced to participate in the objectionable activity, and thus to take on partial responsibility for its consequences. Otherwise, there should be no burden on whistleblowers to resign in voicing their alarm. In principle, at least, it is often their duty to speak out, and their positions ought not thereby to be at issue. In practice, however, they know that retaliation, forced departure, perhaps blacklisting, may be sufficient risks at times so that it may be wise to resign before sounding the alarm: to resign in protest, or to leave quietly, secure another post, and only then blow the whistle.[4] In each case, those who speak out can then do so with the authority and knowledge of insiders, but without their vulnerability.

It is not easy to weigh all these factors, nor to compensate for the degree of bias, rationalization, and denial that inevitably influences one's judgment. By speaking out, whistleblowers may spark a re-examination of these forces among colleagues and others who had ignored or learned to live with shoddy or corrupt practices. Because they have this power to dramatize moral conflict, would-be whistleblowers have a special responsibility to

ask themselves about biases in deciding whether or not to speak out: a desire for self-defense in a difficult bureaucratic situation perhaps, or unrealistic expectations regarding the likely effects of speaking out.[†]

As they weigh the reasons for sounding the alarm, or on the contrary for remaining silent, they may find it helpful to ask about the legitimacy of the rationale for collective secrecy in the particular problem they face. If they are wondering whether or not to blow the whistle on the unnecessary surgery they have witnessed, for example, or on the manufacture of unsafe machinery, what weight should they place on claims to professional confidentiality or corporate secrecy?

Reducing bias and error in moral choice often requires consultation, even open debate; such methods force us to articulate the arguments at stake and to challenge privately held assumptions. But choices about whether or not to blow the whistle present special problems for such consultation. On the one hand, once whistleblowers sound their alarm publicly, their judgment will be subjected to open scrutiny; they will have to articulate their reasons for speaking out and substantiate their charges. On the other hand, it will then be too late to retract their charges should they turn out to have been unfounded.

For those who are concerned about a situation within their organization, it is therefore preferable to seek advice *before* deciding either to go public or to remain silent. But the more corrupt the circumstances, the more dangerous it may be to consult colleagues, and the more likely it is that those responsible for the abuse or neglect will destroy the evidence linking them to it. And yet, with no one to consult, the would-be whistleblowers themselves may have a biased view of the state of affairs; they may see corruption and conspiracy where

---

† If, for example, a government employee stands to make large profits from a book exposing the iniquities in his agency, there is danger that he might slant his report in order to cause more of a sensation. Sometimes a warning is so clearly justifiable and substantiated that it carries weight no matter what the motives of the speaker. But scandal can pay; and the whistleblower's motives ought ideally to be above suspicion, for his own sake as well as for the sake of the respect he desires for his warning. Personal gain from speaking out increases the need to check the accuracy of the speaker.

none exists, and choose not to consult others when in fact it would have been not only safe but advantageous to do so....

NOTES

1   Henrik Ibsen, *An Enemy of the People*, (1882), in *Henrik Ibsen: The Complete Major Prose Plays*, trans. and ed. Rolf Fjelde (New York: New American Library, 1965), pp. 281–386; passage quoted on p. 384.

2   I draw, for this chapter, on my earlier essays on whistleblowing: "Whistleblowing and Professional Responsibilities," in Daniel Callahan and Sissela Bok, eds., *Ethics Teaching in Higher Education* (New York: Plenum Press, 1980), pp. 277–95 (reprinted, slightly altered, in *New York University Education Quarterly* II (Summer 1980):2–10; "Blowing the Whistle," in Joel Fleishman, Lance Liebman, and Mark Moore, eds., *Public Duties: The Moral Obligations of Officials* (Cambridge, Mass.: Harvard University Press, 1981), pp. 204–21.

3   This case is adapted from [Louis Clark, "The Sound of Professional Suicide," *The Barrister* 5 (Summer 1978):10.]

4   On resignation in protest, see Albert Hirschman, *Exit, Voice, and Loyalty* (Cambridge, Mass.: Harvard University Press, 1970); Brian Barry, in a review of Hirschman's book in *British Journal of Political Science* 4 (1974):79–104, has pointed out that "exit" and "voice" are not alternatives but independent variations that may occur separately or together. Both leaking and whistleblowing represent "voice." They can be undertaken while staying on at work, or before one's voluntary exit, or simultaneously with it, or after it; they can also have the consequence of involuntary or forced "exit" through dismissal or being "frozen out" even though retained at work. See also Edward Weisband and Thomas M. Franck, *Resignation in Protest* (New York: Viking Press, 1975); James Thomson, "Getting Out and Speaking Out," *Foreign Policy*, no. 13 (Winter 1973–1974), pp. 49–69; Joel L. Fleishman and Bruce L. Payne, *Ethical Dilemmas and the Education of Policymakers* (Hastings-on-Hudson, N.Y.: Hastings Center, 1980).

—19—

OBJECTIVITY PRECLUDES RESPONSIBILITY

Theodore L. Glasser

BY OBJECTIVITY I MEAN A PARTICULAR VIEW OF journalism and the press, a frame of reference used by journalists to orient themselves in the newsroom and in the community. By objectivity I mean, to a degree, ideology; where ideology is defined as a set of beliefs that function as the journalist's "claim to action." As a set of beliefs, objectivity appears to be rooted in a positivist view of the world, an enduring commitment to the supremacy of observable and retrievable facts. This commitment in turn, impinges on news organizations' principal commodity—the day's news. Thus my argument, in part, is this: Today's news is indeed biased—as it must inevitably be—and this bias can be best understood by understanding the concept, the conventions, and the ethic of objectivity.

Specifically, objectivity in Journalism accounts for—or at least helps us understand—three principal developments in American journalism; each of these developments contributes to the bias or ideology of news. First, objective reporting is biased against what the press typically defines as its role in a democracy—that of a Fourth Estate, the watchdog role, an adversary press.

Indeed, objectivity in journalism is biased in favor of the status quo; it is inherently conservative to the extent that it encourages reporters to rely on what sociologist Alvin Gouldner so appropriately describes as the "managers of the status quo"—the prominent and the elite. Second,

objective reporting is biased against independent thinking; it emasculates the intellect by treating it as a disinterested spectator. Finally, objective reporting is biased against the very idea of responsibility; the day's news is viewed as something journalists are compelled to report, not something they are responsible for creating.

This last point, I think, is most important. Despite a renewed interest in professional ethics, the discussion continues to evade questions of morality and responsibility. Of course, this doesn't mean that journalists are immoral.

Rather, it means that journalists today are largely amoral. Objectivity in journalism effectively erodes the very foundation on which rests a responsible press.

By most any of the many accounts of the history of objectivity in journalism, objective reporting began more as a commercial imperative than as a standard of responsible reporting. With the emergence of a truly popular press in the mid-1800s—the penny press—a press tied neither to the political parties nor the business elite, objectivity provided a presumably disinterested view of the world.

But the penny press was only one of many social, economic, political, and technological forces that converged in the mid- and late-1800s to bring about fundamental and lasting changes in American journalism. There was the advent of the telegraph, which for the first time separated communication from transportation. There were radical changes in printing technology, including the steam-powered press and later the rotary press. There was the formation of the Associated Press, an early effort by publishers to monopolize a new technology—in this case the telegraph. There was, finally, the demise of community and the rise of society; there were now cities, "human settlements" where "strangers are likely to meet."

These are some of the many conditions that created the climate for objective reporting, a climate best understood in terms of the emergence of a new mass medium and the need for that medium to operate efficiently in the marketplace.

Efficiency is the key term here, for efficiency is the central meaning of objective reporting. It was efficient for the Associated Press to distribute only the "bare facts," and leave the opportunity for interpretation to individual members of the cooperative. It was efficient for newspapers not to offend readers and advertisers with partisan prose. It was efficient—perhaps expedient—for reporters to distance themselves from the sense and substance of what they reported.

To survive in the marketplace, and to enhance their status as a new and more democratic press, journalists principally publishers, who were becoming more and more removed from the editing and writing process—began to transform efficiency into a standard of professional competence, a standard later—several decades later—described as objectivity. This transformation was aided by two important developments in the early twentieth century: first, Oliver Wendell Holmes's effort to employ a marketplace metaphor to define the meaning of the First Amendment; and second, the growing popularity of the scientific method as the proper tool with which to discover and understand an increasingly alien reality.

In a dissenting opinion in 1919, Holmes popularized "the marketplace of ideas," a metaphor introduced by John Milton several centuries earlier. Metaphor or not, publishers took it quite literally. They argued—and continue with essentially the same argument today—that their

opportunity to compete and ultimately survive in the marketplace is their First Amendment right, a Constitutional privilege. The American Newspaper Publishers Association, organized in 1887, led the cause of a free press. In the name of freedom of the press, the ANPA fought the Pure Food and Drug Act of 1906 on behalf of its advertisers; it fought the Post Office Act of 1912, which compelled sworn statements of ownership and circulation and thus threatened to reveal too much to advertisers; it fought efforts to regulate child labor, which would interfere with the control and exploitation of paper boys; it fought the collective bargaining provisions of the National Recovery Act in the mid-1930s; for similar reasons, it stood opposed to the American Newspaper Guild, the reporters' union; it tried—unsuccessfully—to prevent wire services from selling news to radio stations until after publication in the nearby newspaper.

Beyond using the First Amendment to shield and protect their economic interests in the marketplace, publishers were also able to use the canons of science to justify—indeed, legitimize—the canons of objective reporting. Here publishers were comforted by Walter Lippmann's writings in the early 1920s, particularly his plea for a new scientific journalism, a new realism; a call for journalists to remain "clear and free" of their irrational, their unexamined, their unacknowledged prejudgments.

By the early 1900s objectivity had become the acceptable way of doing reporting—or at least the respectable way. It was respectable because it was reliable, and it was reliable because it was standardized. In practice, this meant a preoccupation with how the news was presented, whether its form was reliable. And this concern for reliability quickly overshadowed any concern for the validity of the realities the journalists presented.

Thus emerged the conventions of objective reporting, a set of routine procedures journalists use to objectify their news stories. These are the conventions sociologist Gaye Tuchman describes as a kind of strategy journalists use to deflect criticism, the same kind of strategy social scientists use to defend the quality of their work. For the journalist, this means interviews with sources; and it ordinarily means official sources with impeccable credentials. It means juxtaposing conflicting truth-claims, where truth-claims are reported as "fact" regardless of their validity. It means making a judgment about the news value of a truth-claim even if that judgment serves only to lend authority to what is known to be false or misleading.

As early as 1924 objectivity appeared as an ethic, an ideal subordinate only to truth itself. In his study of the Ethics of Journalism, Nelson Crawford devoted three full chapters to the principles of objectivity. Thirty years later, in 1954, Louis Lyons, then curator for the Nieman Fellowship program at Harvard, was describing objectivity as a "rock-bottom" imperative. Apparently unfazed by Wisconsin's Senator Joseph McCarthy, Lyons portrayed objectivity as the ultimate discipline of journalism. "It is at the bottom of all sound reporting indispensable as the core of the writer's capacity." More recently, in 1973, the Society of Professional Journalists, Sigma Delta Chi formally enshrined the idea of objectivity when it adopted as part of its Code of Ethics a paragraph characterizing objective reporting as an attainable goal and a standard of performance toward which journalists should strive. "We honor those who achieve it," the Society proclaimed.

So well ingrained are the principles of objective reporting that the judiciary is beginning to acknowledge them. In a 1977 federal appellate decision, *Edwards v. National Audubon Society*, a case described by media attorney Floyd Abrams as a landmark decision in that it may prove to be the next evolutionary stage in the development of the public law of libel, a new and novel privilege emerged. It was the first time the courts explicitly recognized objective reporting as a standard of journalism worthy of First Amendment protection.

In what appeared to be an inconsequential story published in *The New York Times* in 1972— on page 33—five scientists were accused of being paid liars, men paid by the pesticide industry to lie about the use of DDT and its effect on bird life. True to the form of objective reporting, the accusation was fully attributed—to a fully identified official of the National Audubon Society. The scientists, of course, were given an opportunity to deny the accusation. Only one of the scientists, however, was quoted by name and he described the accusation as "almost libelous." What was newsworthy about the story, obviously, was the accusation; and with the exception of one short paragraph, the reporter more or less provided a forum for the National Audubon Society.

Three of the five scientists filed suit. While denying punitive damages, a jury awarded compensatory damages against the *Times* and one of the Society's officials. The *Times*, in turn, asked a federal District Court to overturn the verdict. The *Times* argued that the "actual malice" standard had not been met; since the scientists were "public figures," they were required to show that the *Times* knowingly published a falsehood or there was, on the part of the *Times*, a reckless disregard for whether the accusation was true or false. The evidence before the court clearly indicated the latter— there was indeed a reckless disregard for whether the accusation was true or false. The reporter made virtually no effort to confirm the validity of the National Audubon Society's accusations. Also the story wasn't the kind, of "hot news" (a technical term used by the courts) that required immediate dissemination; in fact ten days before the story was published the *Times* learned that two of the five scientists were not employed by the pesticide industry and thus could not have been "paid liars."

The *Times* appealed to the Second Circuit Court of Appeals, where the lower court's decision was overturned. In reversing the District Court, the Court of Appeals created a new First Amendment right, a new Constitutional defense in libel law—the privilege of "neutral reportage." "We do not believe," the Court of Appeals ruled, "that the press may be required to suppress newsworthy statements merely because it has serious doubts regarding their truth." The First Amendment, the Court said, "protects the accurate and disinterested reporting" of newsworthy accusations "regardless of the reporter's private views regarding their validity."

I mention the details of the *Edwards* case only because it illustrates so well the consequences of the ethic of objectivity. First, it illustrates a very basic tension between objectivity and responsibility. Objective reporting virtually precludes responsible reporting, if by responsible reporting we mean a willingness on the part of the reporter to be accountable for what is reported. Objectivity requires only that reporters be accountable for how they report, not what they report. The *Edwards* Court made this very clear: "The public interest in being fully informed," the Court said, demands that the press be afforded the freedom to report newsworthy accusations "without assuming responsibility for them."

Second, the *Edwards* case illustrates the unfortunate bias of objective reporting—a bias in favor of leaders and officials, the prominent and the elite. It is an unfortunate bias because it runs counter to the important democratic assumption that statements made by ordinary citizens are as valuable as statements made by the prominent and the elite. In a democracy, public debate depends on separating individuals from their powers and privileges in the larger society; otherwise debate itself becomes a source of domination. But *Edwards* reinforces prominence as a news value; it reinforces the use of official sources, official records, official channels. Tom Wicker underscored the bias of the *Edwards* case when he observed recently that "objective journalism almost always favors Establishment positions and exists not least to avoid offense to them."

Objectivity also has unfortunate consequences for the reporter, the individual journalist. Objective reporting has stripped reporters of their creativity and their imagination; it has robbed journalists of their passion and their perspective. Objective reporting has transformed journalism into something more technical than intellectual; it has turned the art of story-telling into the technique of report writing. And most unfortunate of all, objective reporting has denied journalists their citizenship; as disinterested observers, as impartial reporters, journalists are expected to be morally disengaged and politically inactive....

In his frequently cited study of Washington correspondents—a study published nearly fifty years ago—Leo Rosten found that a "pronounced majority" of the journalists he interviewed considered themselves inadequate to cope with the bewildering complexities of our nation's policies and politics. As Rosten described it, the Washington press corps was a frustrated and exasperated group of prominent journalists more or less resigned to their role as mediators, translators. "To do the job," one reporter told Rosten, "what you know or understand isn't important. You've got to know whom to ask." Even if you don't understand what's being said, Rosten was told, you just take careful notes and write it up verbatim: "Let my readers figure it out. I'm their reporter, not their teacher."

That was fifty years ago. Today, the story is pretty much the same. Two years ago another study of Washington correspondents was published, a book by Stephen Hess called *The Washington Reporters*. For the most part, Hess found, stories coming out of Washington were little more than a "mosaic of facts and quotations from sources" who were participants in an event or who had knowledge of the event. Incredibly, Hess found that for nearly three-quarters of the stories he studied, reporters relied on no documents—only interviews. And when reporters did use documents, those documents were typically press clippings—stories they had written or stories written by their colleagues.

And so what does objectivity mean? It means that sources supply the sense and substance of the day's news. Sources provide the arguments, the rebuttals, the explanations, the criticism. Sources put forth the ideas while other sources challenge those ideas. Journalists, in their role as professional communicators, merely provide a vehicle for these exchanges.

But if objectivity means that reporters must maintain a healthy distance from the world they report, the same standard does not apply to publishers. According to the SPJ/SDX Code of Ethics, "Journalists and their employers should conduct their personal lives in a manner which protects them from conflict of interest, real or apparent." Many journalists do just that—they avoid even an appearance of a conflict of interest. But certainly not their employers....

Publishers and broadcasters today are a part of a large and growing and increasingly diversified industry. Not only are many newspapers owned by corporations that own a variety of non-media properties, but their boards of directors read like a Who's Who of the powerful and the elite. A recent study of the twenty-five largest newspaper companies found that the directors of these companies tend to be linked with "powerful business organizations, not with public interest groups; with management, not with labor; with well established think tanks and charities, not their grassroots counterparts."

But publishers and broadcasters contend that these connections have no bearing on how the day's news is reported—as though the ownership of a newspaper had no bearing on the newspaper's content; as though business decisions have no effect on editorial decisions; as though it wasn't economic considerations in the first place that brought about the incentives for many of the conventions of contemporary journalism.

No doubt the press has responded to many of the more serious consequences of objective reporting. But what is significant is that the response has been to amend the conventions of objectivity, not to abandon them. The press has merely relined the canons of objective reporting; it has not dislodged them.

What remains fundamentally unchanged is the journalist's naively empirical view of the world, a belief in the separation of facts and values, a belief in the existence of a reality—the reality of empirical facts. Nowhere is this belief more evident than when news is defined as something external to—and independent of—the journalist. The very vocabulary used by journalists when they talk about news underscores their belief that news is "out there," presumably waiting to be exposed or *uncovered* or at least *gathered*.

This is the essence of objectivity, and this is precisely why it is so very difficult for journalism to consider questions of ethics and morality. Since news exists "out there"—apparently independent of the reporter—journalists can't be held responsible for it. And since they are not responsible for the news being there, how can we expect journalists to be accountable for the consequences of merely reporting it?...

—20—

RESPONSIBLE ENGINEERING

The Importance of Character and Imagination

Michael S. Pritchard

INTRODUCTION

... IN THIS PAPER I WILL EXPLORE THE ROLE THAT character and imagination might play in determining how engineers understand and deal with their responsibilities as engineers. I will offer only preliminary reflections on this relatively unexplored topic, inviting others to join in both widening and deepening the inquiry. In illustrating what I have in mind, I will limit my primary focus to the responsibilities of engineers to protect public safety, health and welfare. These are by no means the only sorts of responsibilities engineers have, but I will say little about them here. My basic thesis is that fulfilling an engineer's responsibilities to protect public safety, health, and welfare calls as much for *settled dispositions*, or *virtues*, as it does for performing this or that specific action.

My reflections take their cue from William F. May's observation that it is particularly important for professional ethics to pay attention to moral character and virtue, as these dispositions shape professionals' approach to their work.[1] He notes that professionals typically work in institutional settings, often making it difficult to determine just where things have gone wrong and who should bear the responsibility. Also, professional expertise, particularly in large organizations, is not widely shared, even by fellow professionals. So, May concludes, we need professionals to have virtues that warrant their being trusted: "Few may be in a position to

discredit [them]. The knowledge explosion is also an ignorance explosion; if knowledge is power, then ignorance is powerlessness." He adds, "One test of character and virtue is what a person does when no one else is watching. A society that rests on expertise needs more people who can pass that test."[2]

What counts as "passing" this test of character? Especially when bad consequences become apparent only after the passage of considerable time, it can be very difficult to discredit specific professionals. This suggests that, when no one is watching (which is much of the time), professionals may be able to get away with shoddy, if not deliberately wrongful, behavior. So, "passing" the test seems to require avoiding such behavior even when no one will notice. But this is essentially negative— the avoidance of behavior that would be to one's *discredit* if noticed by others. Although this is the dominant emphasis in literature on professional responsibility, we should also want to know what contributions professionals make to *desirable* outcomes when no one is looking. This can be equally difficult to notice and to assess. We typically take for granted the reliability of the work of engineers. For example, we assume that the elevator will work, that the bridge will bear the weight of traffic, that the building will not fall, and so on, even though we have little understanding of the work that is required to make this so—let alone the special engineering efforts that may have prevented failures or improved reliability.

When we shift our attention in this more positive direction, it quickly becomes apparent that what might count as responsible (as distinct from irresponsible) professional practice can vary widely. Followers of the now retired comic strip *Calvin and Hobbes* may recall the episode in which six-year-old Calvin has finally made his bed. His pal, Hobbes the stuffed tiger, says, "Gee, your mom sure was impressed when you made your bed." Calvin replies, "Right. That's how I like it—to impress her by fulfilling the *least* of my obligations."[3] We can think of Calvin as occupying one end of a spectrum of responsibility that ranges from the minimal to the supererogatory ("above and beyond the call of duty"). Somewhere between these two ends of the spectrum is where most of us spend most of our time.

It is interesting that, like the work of professionals, Calvin's bed-making requires certain skills—skills that may be well developed or poorly developed, conscientiously employed or lackadaisically employed, and so on. Of course, we would prefer the services of conscientious professionals who have well developed skills, good judgment, and the like. However, we may end up with a clever Calvin who is content to stay out of trouble and to exert the least effort necessary for "success"; and if May is right, we may not be in a good position to know just how marginal the services are. By the same token, we may not be in a good position to know just how competent and conscientious other professionals are.

Whether or not we are in a good position to determine these things, our well-being, both as individuals and as a society, is at stake. As we reflect on the extent to which our well-being is dependent on the performance of professionals whose expertise and organizational workplace we do not understand, we can see why it is not only moral dispositions such as honesty, fairmindedness, and benevolence that are important to professional ethics; equally important are those dispositions that relate to professional competence. Professional ethics calls for a level of performance, not just good moral purpose and intention.

Competence needs to be linked with commitment to ethical values that are basic in a given profession—for example, public safety, health and welfare in engineering. But commitment, like competence, can range from the minimal to the exemplary. Unfortunately, by emphasizing wrongdoing and its avoidance, most of the engineering ethics literature slights the more positive end of the responsibility spectrum. Even if falling short of the exemplary does not warrant discredit or blame, our needs exceed what merely avoiding discredit or blame provides. In what follows, I will expand May's concern about what professionals do when no one is watching to include the exemplary as well.

Although May intends his remarks to apply to all the professions, they are especially apt for engineers. Clearly, the public depends heavily on, but is not privy to, the expertise of engineers. Furthermore, from the public's perspective, the work of engineers is largely anonymous; few members of the public ever meet the engineers whose work they depend on. But even engineers who work in the same organization, or even on the same projects, may not be in a good position to check on each other's work. Insofar as engineers do not share each others' expertise, or do not have time to check up on each other, there is an important sense in which engineers are not being watched by each other either. In short, largely unwatched by those who depend on them, engineers are expected to conduct themselves responsibly. Hence the special pertinence of May's question: "What do professionals do when no one is watching?"

DEDICATION TO SAFETY

As a glance at engineering codes of ethics reveals, many of their most important provisions are stated in such a way that what might count as satisfying them is open to considerable interpretation. The National Society for Professional Engineers code of ethics, like most other engineering codes, identifies protecting public safety, health, and welfare as the engineer's paramount obligation. It is interesting to notice how little assistance the NSPE code provides in interpreting what this responsibility entails. The Preamble says that, because engineering work has a direct and vital impact on everyone's quality of life, engineers must be dedicated to the protection of the public health, safety and welfare. The first of the Fundamental Canons says that engineers shall *hold paramount* the safety, health and welfare of the public. Under Rules of Practice this same language is used. But just what does this come to? And what is implied by being *dedicated* to protecting the public?

At its best, a code of engineering ethics prescribes the highest *common* denominator for members of its society. This means that individual professionals may have higher aspirations than the code requires. Much is left for individual interpretation. For example, under the Rules of Practice, the NSPE code offers guidance for only two kinds of circumstance that have to do specifically with protecting public safety, health, and welfare: 1) an engineer should inform appropriate persons if his or her engineering judgment is overruled when the public is endangered; and 2) an engineer should approve only those engineering documents that protect the public safety, health, and welfare. Can this be all that the framers of the code had in mind in saying that the engineer's paramount responsibility is to protect public safety, health, and welfare? Clearly the answer is, no. However, this may be all that can be identified in terms of specific courses of action that are required (and even "appropriate persons" is left open to interpretation). In any case, being *dedicated* to protecting the public and *holding paramount* public safety, health, and welfare seem to be more enduring requirements; they refer to dispositions engineers are expected to have. They mark a *readiness* to take safety, health, and welfare into appropriate account. Sometimes we can see this exemplified in particular actions. But there does not seem to be any way to prescribe a certain set of required courses of action.

THE IMPORTANCE OF DISPOSITIONS

What I hope to show is that both character and imagination can assist the end of protecting the public in ways that no list of required courses of action can specify. Here there are no algorithms. Despite this, we should be able to list a number of dispositions that, by framing an engineer's approach to his or her work, can importantly contribute to protecting public safety, health, and welfare.

Several years ago, my colleague James Jaksa and I undertook a project to develop educational materials that illustrate responsible, if not exemplary engineering practice.[4] We sought stories from engineers and their managers. To give them some idea of what we were interested in, we first asked them what characteristics they would look for if they were trying to hire a highly responsible engineer. Then we asked them if they could provide illustrations of engineers who exemplified these characteristics in their engineering practice. Although hardly a scientific survey, a list of commonly mentioned dispositions emerged. Many items on the list seem to have an inherent connection with ethics and would be expected to appear in one form or another on virtually anyone's list of virtues. For example:

- integrity
- honesty (even candor)
- civic-mindedness
- courage (to speak up, to "stick to one's guns")
- willingness to make self-sacrifice (including willingness to assume some personal risk)
- not being too personally ambitious

Virtues such as these are quite generic, not only in regard to the professions, but in regard to ordinary, non-professional life as well. How they might manifest themselves in engineering practice requires special attention to the working environment of engineers.

As attention shifts to the context of engineering practice, other items show up on the list.

However, these items are less obviously connected with ethics, and several can readily be associated with undesirable behavior as well:

- competence
- ability to communicate clearly and informatively
- cooperativeness (being a good "team player")
- willingness to compromise
- perseverance
- habit of documenting work thoroughly and clearly
- commitment to objectivity
- openness to correction (admitting mistakes, acknowledging oversight)
- commitment to quality
- being imaginative
- seeing the "big picture" as well as the details of smaller domains

As with the first group of virtues, when listed abstractly, they are not engineering-specific. To understand how they might manifest themselves in the lives of engineers, they must be seen in the context of engineering practice. However, it is conceivable that an engineer could have all of the dispositions in this second group and still be dedicated to any number of morally reprehensible engineering projects.

This may suggest to some that items in this second group of dispositions should not be included in an account of the virtues of responsible engineers. Admittedly, *having* these dispositions is not sufficient for responsible engineering practice. However, *lacking* them detracts from responsible engineering practice in general, and exemplary practice in particular. Furthermore, having these dispositions is a fundamental part of what we admire in those engineers who are likely to be identified as morally commendable. It is fundamental because, without these dispositions in addition to the more obvious virtues of honesty, justice, and benevolence (to take three traditional moral virtues), there is little reason to expect even competent engineering practice. In short, having the virtues of honesty, justice, and

benevolence does not qualify one as a competent engineer. In fact, many who have these virtues might correctly conclude that they should not try to become engineers—they might be better suited for other kinds of work.

Given their fundamental role in responsible engineering practice, it is no accident that this second group of dispositions show up on the list of characteristics engineers and their managers would look for if they were trying to hire a highly responsible engineer. What still needs to be explained, however, is the specific fit these dispositions might have in engineering practice. Simply listing a set of desirable dispositions, or virtues, does not tell us how they might play themselves out in responsible engineering practice. A good place to begin is with examples that show concretely that the presence or absence of some of these dispositions can have an important impact on ethical values in engineering.

AN ILLUSTRATION

To illustrate more concretely what I have in mind regarding the role of character and imagination in responsible engineering practice, I will turn to the much celebrated story of William LeMessurier and the Citicorp Center in Manhattan.[5] This story centers around the engineer's responsibility to protect public safety. Engineer William LeMessurier designed the structural frame of the Citicorp Center, built in 1977. In 1978 he discovered a structural problem that, because of the building's unusual features, rendered the building vulnerable to 16 year storms. He knew how to correct the problem, but only at the cost of millions of dollars and at the risk of his career if he were to tell others about the problem. Nevertheless, he promptly notified lawyers, insurers, the chief architect of the building, and Citicorp executives. Corrections were made, all parties were cooperative, and LeMessurier's career was not adversely affected....

In some respects, we could say William LeMessurier was just doing his job. However, I think this understates matters a great deal. Calvin, too, was just doing his job—minimally. Engineers like LeMessurier bring something more to their work. They exemplify what it means to *dedicate* oneself fully to the protection of public safety, health, and welfare. The recognition of such dedication evokes praise from others.

Calvin thinks he deserves praise, too. He wants Santa Claus to reward him for being good: "How good do you have to be to qualify as good?" he asks. "I haven't *killed* anybody. See, that's good, right? I haven't committed any felonies. I didn't start any wars. I don't practice cannibalism. Wouldn't you say I should get lots of presents?" Pausing for a moment of reflection, Hobbes wisely replies: "But maybe good is more than the absence of bad."[6]

However, even granting that Hobbes has a point, some might question whether it actually applies to William LeMessurier's handling of the Citicorp problem. In response to a talk I once gave on this story, a member of the audience posed the following challenge. Why, he asked, should LeMessurier be lauded for his handling of the Citicorp problem? After all, once he discovered the problem, it was, as he himself acknowledges, his duty to report it to the appropriate authorities. Furthermore, the questioner continued, wasn't it just a matter of *luck* that LeMessurier made the discovery at all? An unexpected phone call from a student, a fortuitous conversation about welded joints in Pittsburgh, and so on.

My response about LeMessurier's duty to report the problem is twofold. First, although acting on his duty may not be "going above and beyond the call of duty," a reason for lauding LeMessurier is that it did take a fair amount of courage to do this. Admittedly, failure to report the problem would have been blameworthy, but doing what is right under such challenging circumstances can nevertheless merit praise. Second, *how* LeMessurier handled this duty also seems to warrant praise. He not only reported the existence of the problem, he also proposed a solution; and his ability to do so, especially in such circumstances, reflects his character and imagination as an engineer. There can be, we might say, better and worse ways of fulfilling one's duty; and LeMessurier's was exemplary.

My response to the comment about luck is that it is precisely LeMessurier's character and imagination as an engineer that explains why he made something of the crucial moments that ultimately led to his discovery of the problem. Many, perhaps most, other engineers would not have capitalized on these events in the way he did. They could not fairly be faulted for this. But LeMessurier can be praised for his perceptiveness, persistence, and imagination—and his unqualified commitment to safety and quality. Engineers like LeMessurier seem to be somehow *prepared to be lucky.* That is, because of their skills and commitment, they are prepared to pick up cues and run with them, to notice what others fail to notice, and so on.

In the end, ethical values appropriate to a profession must be joined with professional commitment, competence, and imagination in order to provide a complete picture of the virtues in professional life. It is important for professionals to be prepared to be lucky. This requires a blending of moral dispositions and professional expertise; and this is not primarily a matter of making this or that momentous, ethical decision. It is a way of (professional) life....

NOTES

1   William F. May (1988) "Professional Virtue and Self-Regulation," in Callahan, Joan (ed.) *Ethical Issues in Professional Life* (New York, NY: Oxford University Press), 408.

2   Ibid.

3   Bill Watterson (1990) *Calvin and Hobbes.*

4   For a discussion of some of the results of this project, see Michael S. Pritchard (1988) "Professional Responsibility: Focusing on the Exemplary," *Science and Engineering Ethics* Vol. 4 (2): 215–33. This was supported by National Science Foundation Grant #SBR-930257.

5   My account is based on Joseph Morgenstern's excellent, "The Fifty-Nine Story Crisis," *The New Yorker,* May 29, 1995.

6   Bill Watterson (Dec. 23, 1990) *Calvin and Hobbes.*

—21—

ETHICS AND THE PROFESSIONAL RESPONSIBILITY OF LAWYERS

Kenneth Kipnis

... THE TERM "LAWYER" DENOTES A SPECIFIC ROLE, a possible social identity. And so for lawyers to have distinctive professional responsibilities, it is necessary to conceptualize attorneys as participants in some larger complex task, a social structure with some institutional legitimacy.[1] But just as a large enough camping expedition can have a cooking crew (a complex task set within a larger one), so the legal profession (a social institution in itself) exists to provide certain essential services within a larger complex task, a more encompassing social institution: our adversarial system of adjudication.

Adjudication is one way for a community to deal with serious disputes between members, disputes where at least one of the parties believes that the bounds of tolerability have been overstepped. The idea of "rights," so much a preoccupation in the west, is the conceptual tool we have come to use to delimit those boundaries. The central task of adjudication is to resolve these cases by means of a community-backed decision, a decision that is made in such a way as to bring it about that (1) the method for reaching the decision will be procedurally just, (2) the decision itself will be substantively just (or at least not substantively unjust) and (3) both the procedure and the decision will be accepted as just by the parties to the dispute and by the community as a whole. Adjudication can be an effective method for settling disputes.

The social implementation of a system of adjudication establishes four significant permissions for community members. They are empowered (1) to submit certain types of complaint to a judge; (2) to have the other party summoned before the judge to answer the complaint; (3) to have the judge make a decision in the case; and, (4) where the judge decides in one's favor, to have the decision enforced against the other party. One permission is given up: permission to use direct action to settle disputes on one's own.

When one considers the grave defects of vendetta culture, i.e., the informal acts of vengeance that represent the main alternative to adjudication, so patent are the advantages of adjudication that comparatively little systematic work has been done in justification of it.[2] The common notions that every malefactor deserves a fair trial, that it is wrong to take justice into one's own hands, and that the use of force is the responsibility of duly constituted authorities: these ideas seem to be built into our basic understanding of ourselves as together constituting a civilized society rather than an assemblage of savages. It may be that we can generate a variety of justifications for the practices of adjudication: Hegelian, Thomisitic, rule utilitarian, Kantian, Aristotelian, libertarian, and contractualist approaches readily come to mind. But when all is said and done, I expect we will be considerably more confident that the social institution of adjudication is legitimate than we are about which foundational ethical theory is the correct one to appeal to in demonstrating that legitimacy. Perhaps all that needs to be said is that there are many good reasons, drawn from diverse perspectives, for instituting a system of adjudication [and] that adjudication is a legitimate institution in that the case for having it is far stronger than the case for not having it.

But even if we accept that a system of adjudication can be legitimate (and I believe few would question this), there is still no social role for lawyers (at least as we know them) until the system of adjudication provides for them. We do not get our legal profession until three additional steps are taken.

1. The judge is relieved of the responsibility to gather and marshall evidence relevant to the needed judicial finding.

This moves the system from an inquisitorial model, common on the Continent and in Latin America, to an adversarial one, common in Anglo-American countries. Primary responsibility for gathering and marshalling evidence and for generating candidate interpretations of the law now falls to the parties in the dispute.

2. The legal system is permitted to become "sophisticated," i.e., complicated to the point where lay persons cannot be expected to be able to understand their legal positions nor can they be expected to possess the skill required to secure that to which the law entitles them.

The gap between the levels of legal knowledge and skill commonly exhibited by lay persons and the levels needed to function in the legal system can become so great that the generality of citizens cannot be expected to be fairly treated in the judicial system if they are acting on their own behalf. They require expert counseling and representation services. But if the laity's lack of expertise makes it impossible for them to negotiate the court system on their own, it is equally impossible for the uninitiated to distinguish the masters from the pretenders. Under these circumstances, the system of justice itself can be a major source of injustice. The solution to this problem takes us to a legal profession.

3. The distribution of legal counseling services and representation services before the courts is essentially restricted to a set of publicly approved practitioners, the unauthorized practice of law becoming a criminal offense.

Collectively, it is open to us to bypass the need for a legal profession. We can adopt an inquisitorial system of adjudication within which judges and their magistrates do much of the work now done by private attorneys, or we can adopt a convivial system of adversarial adjudication, providing general legal education to all (as we now provide mathematics education to all) and, in addition, making the law simple enough so citizens of modest education can function effectively within the system. But if we fail to do either of these, a legal profession becomes a necessity.

If we reject the inquisitorial and convivial solutions and establish a sophisticated adversarial system of adjudication, then we have to fill the gap between the expertise required of participants in the judicial system and the artless innocence of the many. At a minimum, a legal profession is necessary because citizens ought to be entitled to information about what the law requires and permits (hence the need for legal counseling services), and because citizens ought to be empowered to obtain whatever protection and support the community guarantees to them as a matter of law (hence the need for legal representation services). The legal profession exists to provide counseling and representation services within sophisticated adversarial systems of adjudication.

Their exclusive monopoly on the delivery of these legal services, coupled with the frequent critical necessity of those services, places members of the bar in a position that is easily exploited. It is not for the uninitiated to judge the quality of professional services or the fairness of the price. Some assurance needs to be given that lawyers won't take advantage of their privileged positon. Legal ethics, as an area of ethical and jurisprudential inquiry, asks what principles lawyers must conform to, what ideals they must strive to achieve, and what professional review processes must be instituted in order to assure that the bar fairly discharges the two critical responsibilities it has assumed in the system of adjudication as we have created it. It is from this perspective that the attorney's duties of confidentiality and zealous advocacy need to be assessed.

As a counselor, a lawyer has a duty to educate the lay client as to the complexities of the client's legal situation. This is one of the two basic responsibilities of attorneys, a key part of the reason why we are required to maintain a legal profession in a sophisticated adversarial system. But lawyers will be unable to provide such counseling services if clients are afraid to divulge potentially damaging facts to their attorneys. For one cannot advise a client as to what to do in the client's situation if one is ignorant of the client's situation. We assume here that people cannot be expected knowingly to act in ways that are damaging to themselves. Thus, other things being equal, clients who do not trust their lawyers to keep damaging facts in confidence will not feel as free to divulge potentially damaging facts to their attorneys as clients who trust their attorneys. Thus it is reasonable to believe that lawyers who reliably promise confidentiality can be expected to provide better counseling services than lawyers who don't. If lawyers have an ethical responsibility to provide counseling services, and if the provision of such services will be impaired unless lawyers reliably promise confidentiality, then lawyers must, as a matter of professional responsibility, reliably promise confidentiality.[3]

Likewise a lawyer has a responsibility to represent, to assist, and to act on behalf of the client in carrying out certain formal tasks. In sophisticated adversarial systems, it is only through such

essential professional assistance that citizens can exercise their powers to obtain the protection and support the community guarantees to them as a matter of law. While it is conceivable that we, as a community, guarantee more protection and support than we ought to, it is not up to attorneys to disempower clients by peremptorily truncating their capacities to exercise their legal rights. On the contrary, the duty of zealous advocacy within the bounds of the law obligates lawyers to assure that those in authority (judges, juries, etc.) have the opportunity to hear that which can be said on behalf of the client, no matter how loathsome the offense. The lawyer's duty to advocate on behalf of the client must be faithfully discharged even though some escape the punishment they deserve or lose the compensation they are due.[4]

To become a good professional is, in part, to identify oneself as occupying a certain institutional role; it is to appreciate the special responsibilities that attach to that role, and to take those responsibilities very, very seriously. As children, we absorb certain ambient beliefs about the obligations each person is supposed to have. These beliefs, reflected upon, may develop into an articulated personal morality. At the same time we gradually become clearer about the values we embrace, the particular goods we want to realize in the course of our lives. But when, in the midst of all of this personal development, we undertake to enter a profession, there is no necessity that the ethics of that profession will be consistent with our personal morality. There is no necessity that the core values of that profession (what good professionals ought to care about) will be consistent with our personal values. A decision to enter a profession should be informed by an appreciation of the profession's ethical responsibilities and its core values. To live life with integrity as a professional is in part to have achieved a measure of consistency between personal values and the core values of the profession.

A profession is a collectivity that has assumed responsibility for some significant arena of social concern, as lawyers have assumed responsibility for the delivery of counseling and representation services within our sophisticated adversarial system. For a professional, ethical responsibility is wholly expressed in principles, the general adherence to which can be expected to result in the profession's discharging the collective responsibility it has assumed. In the end, it is a community's choice whether or not to have a profession; whether or not to delegate an exclusive responsibility to some discrete collective. But once the collective responsibility is delegated and assumed, once the complex task of providing services is undertaken, once individual responsibilities have precipitated out of the complex task, we may then be bound into obligations of mutual dependency. Two weeks into the camping expedition, it is no longer open to me to take MY stove (now the expedition's stove), MY matches (the expedition's matches), and MY water jug (the expedition's jug) and leave the group to go off on my own.

Critics of the professions often express concern that practitioners breach ethical standards out of self-interest or greed. But I would say that a much graver threat to the integrity of our professions can flow from the failure to distinguish between the personal moralities we bring with us into our professions and the ethical responsibilities attaching to the professional role itself (that is, the ethical responsibilities apart from the values or moral beliefs of the occupant of the role). It would appear that I owe it to the profession and to the clients I may someday serve, to ensure, before entry into the profession, that I will not have crippling moral reservations about discharging what may become my professional obligations.

A Jehovah's Witness M.D., for example, with firm convictions against giving blood transfusions, should not be the sole physician on duty in an hospital emergency room. The risk is too great that an accident victim will show up and force an impossible choice between betraying God and betraying one's patient. Since professional responsibility can require the setting aside of such moral reservations, no one should become a lawyer who is not ready to do those things they may be professionally obligated to do as an attorney.

NOTES

1   The approach to be used here—elaborating upon the social identity of the professional and deriving from it a conception of the profession's ethical responsibility—has the enormous pedagogical advantage of communicating to professionals where they live.

2   Locke's analysis of dispute resolution—in the *Second Treatise of Government*—is the *locus classicus*. But others have had useful things to say including Lon Fuller and Edmund Cahn. Anarchists have occasionally questioned instituting adjudication as a communal task. The concerns here are the subject matter of Chapter Two of [Kenneth Kipnis. *Legal Ethics*. (New Jersey: Prentice-Hall, 1986)].

3   The issue of confidentiality in criminal practice is more thoroughly explored in Chapter Four of *Legal Ethics*.

4   The issue of complicity [in] legal representation is more thoroughly explored in Chapter Five of *Legal Ethics*.

—22—

TOWARD A PROFESSIONAL RESPONSIBILITY THEORY OF PUBLIC RELATIONS ETHICS

Kathy Fitzpatrick and Candace Gauthier

"CENTRAL TO THE IMPORTANCE OF ETHICS IN American public relations is the reality that, most of the time, practitioners have the voluntary choice of whether to be ethical or not" (Wright, 1989, p. 3). This statement by public relations scholar Don Wright captures the need for the development of a philosophical foundation for ethical decision making in public relations. Practitioners need some basis on which to judge the rightness of the decisions they make everyday. They need ethical principles derived from the fundamental values that define their work as public relations professionals. They need guidance in reconciling the potentially conflicting roles of the professional advocate and the social conscience.

An important first step in developing such standards is recognition of the public relations practitioner's position as a professional. Notwithstanding the debate about whether the field's members have achieved professional status, we presume such standing. Thus, the special ethical obligations of a professional must be addressed. As Goldman (1992) observed, "[Professionals must be committed to] some overriding value that defines both expertise and service, whether it be health, salvation, the protection of legal rights, or the provision of public information, knowledge, and education" (p. 1019).

In reviewing the professions literature, four criteria emerge as the defining characteristics of a professional: membership in an occupational organization, special expertise, a service orientation, and autonomy. In writing about the professions in 1960, W.J. Goode stated what is still true today

> If one extracts from the most commonly cited definitions all the items which characterize a profession ... a commendable unanimity is disclosed, ... core characteristics are a prolonged specialized training in a body of abstract knowledge, and a collectivity or service orientation. (p. 671)

Another states

> [A] professional service requires, among other things, advanced intellectual training, mastery of technical subject matter, the exercise of skilled and responsible judgment. These attributes are beyond appraisal by the client... the client must take the professional man [sic] on faith—faith in his competence and faith in his motives. (Carey, 1957, p. 7)

Put another way, "Professionals are charged by their clients with making important decisions on their behalf, and they are compensated for assuming this decision making responsibility and bringing their knowledge to bear on the decisions" (Wolfson, Trebilcock, & Tuohy, 1980, p. 191). "A qualified professional is supposed to be an authority on his subject as a body of knowledge and an expert on the application to the solution of particular problems presented by clients" (Moore, 1970, p. 106).

> Professionalism involves the application of a general system of knowledge to the circumstances of a particular case. In treating a client's problem, this knowledge is necessary (1) to identify the precise nature of the problem (diagnosis), (2) to determine the best way of dealing with it (prescription), and (3) to provide specialized services so as to solve the problems (therapy). (Wolfson et al., 1980, p. 190–191)

The professional services provided by public relations professionals include expert counsel on matters involving institutional relationships with constituents and the management of communication between the two. Special knowledge regarding the formation of public opinion, social science research, media channels, and communication strategies and tactics is assumed.

In rendering these special services, "the professional proceeds by his own judgment and authority; he thus enjoys autonomy restrained by responsibility" (Moore, 1970, p. 6). Public relations professionals—as professionals—have obligations that extend beyond the profitability (however defined) of the organization represented. Responsibility to the public—or in the case of public relations, to multiple publics—must be balanced with responsibility to a client or employer.

Indeed, public service always has been the hallmark of the professions, which serve society by providing essential services. Carey (1957) concluded that professionals enjoy the prestige of professional status because "they are presumed to accept a special obligation to place service ahead of personal gain" (p. 7). In a recent study, Reynolds (2000) observed that "society grants professional standing to those groups which contribute to the well-being of the broader society" (p. 115).

To summarize, professionals perform an essential public service that is realized through the provision of specialized services to clients or employers who retain them because of their special expertise and trust them to represent their interests. Because of this special relationship, the professional owes the client his or her loyalty. In fact, some would go so far as to define such associations as "fiduciary" relationships to which legal liabilities attach (see *Black's Law Dictionary*, 1979, defining a "fiduciary" relationship as one in which there exists a "reposing of faith, confidence, and trust, and the placing of reliance by one upon the judgment and advice of another," p. 6).

Thus, as professionals, it would seem that public relations practitioners owe a higher duty to client organizations and employers than to these institutions' constituents. This would support the role of public relations professionals as advocates of—and voices for—institutional interests. By definition, an *advocate* is one who pleads another's cause or who speaks or writes in support of something" (*Webster's New World Dictionary*, 1979, p. 20).

Now, how does this jibe with the oft assumed function of the public relations practitioner as the institutional *social conscience*? The term suggests that one who serves in such a capacity counsels an institution regarding the social implications of decisions and actions and—as a "conscience"—advises the institution to take actions that are in the best interest of society and to avoid those that are not. The concept seems simple in language and, on its face, seems to be in line with the professional's obligation to serve the public interest. However, the vagueness of such responsibility may be the reason public relations professionals struggle with this concept.

How does an institution best serve society? This is the question that public relations professionals must resolve if they truly are to serve as the social consciences of the organizations they represent. It's a big question and, indeed, one that business leaders throughout the world have not been able to answer. Following a 10-year study in the corporate arena on issues related to corporate social responsibility, Clarkson (1995) concluded that there is "[no] general agreement about the meaning of these terms from an operational or a managerial viewpoint" (p. 92).

Scholars in public relations have reached the same conclusion. The question, as posed by public relations scholar Tom Bivins (1993), is "How can a practitioner advocating a discrete point of view serve the interest of the greater public" (p. 120)?

Bivins (1993) suggested four possible paradigms:

First, if every individual practicing public relations acts in the best interest of his or her client, then the public interest will be served.

Second, if, in addition to serving individual interests, an individual practicing public relations serves public interest causes, the public interest will be served.

Third, if a professional or professionals assure that every individual in need of or desiring its/their services receives its/their services, then the public interest will be served.

Fourth, if public relations as a profession improves the quality of debate over issues important to the public, then the public interest will be served. (p. 120)

Noting that none of three approaches provides the definitive answer, Bivins (1993) concluded that

In its dual role as mediator and advocate, public relations has the opportunity both to engage in and to encourage public debate. By doing so, it also has the opportunity, and the obligation, to lessen the obfuscation often surrounding the mere provision of information. It must develop clear guidelines and formal mechanisms by which issues important to society are clarified and presented to the public for open, democratic debate. (p. 121)

Bivins's (1993) focus on the value of ethical communication to open public debate captures the essence of public relations' social role. By providing voices for special interests, public relations contributes to the harmonization of diverse points of view, thereby promoting "mutual understanding and peaceful coexistence among individuals and institutions" (Seib & Fitzpatrick, 1995, p. 1).

To get beyond the general concepts of social responsibility or public service, however, we must focus on public relations practitioners as professionals rather than as communicators. Although, as noted earlier, we reject the idea that the attorney-adversary model is fully appropriate as a moral foundation for public relations, the professional service model employed in the legal profession may be an appropriate guide for determining the ethical—and morally justifiable—role of the public relations professional.

Lawyer jokes aside, people in and outside the legal profession recognize the value of the legal profession in the functioning of a democratic society. Attorneys represent clients to ensure that they are treated fairly in the criminal and civil justice systems, to ensure that their legal interests are protected. Lawyers serve as zealous advocates of their clients, with no special obligation to the opposing party. In other words, they serve the public's interest by serving their clients' interests. A former federal judge put it this way:

To the client [the lawyer] owes loyalty, undivided and undiluted, zeal and devotion and some additional obligations.... His object is to achieve for his client the best which is available within the law by means compatible with the canons of ethics. (As cited in Gillers & Dorsen, 1989, p. 22)

The judge went on to say that the lawyer also owes duties to the profession and to the community. "From the community, the lawyer derives his special status, special franchise, his unique accessory role" (Gillers & Dorsen, 1989, p. 22).

In applying this analogy to public relations, it can be argued that public relations professionals best serve society by serving the special interests of their clients and employers. Like other professionals, however, they must balance such service with their obligations to operate in the public interest. In public relations this means that the special interests of the institution served must be balanced with the interests of those directly affected by the institution.

Such balancing begins with the recognition that the public relations professional's greatest loyalty is to his or her client. At the same time, he or she ensures that the institution hears and considers the interests of its stakeholders. We contend that serving the public interest simply requires public relations professionals to consider the interests of all affected parties and make a committed effort to balance them to the extent possible while avoiding or minimizing harm and respecting all of the persons involved.

As such, a significant aspect of professional responsibility means responsibility to publics. In this way, we borrow from the meaning of public interest in the public policy arena:

> [P]ublic interest is part of our political language—a term we use to express concern for all interests affected by a decision and for a set of fundamental social principles. Invoking the public interest requires all parties to a discussion to make their arguments in terms of these interests and these principles, and it requires that the consequences of all proposals be shown and discussed in a public forum. (Wolfson et al., 1980, p. 84)

Thus, the views of those affected by an institution's decisions and actions should be heard before decisions are made or action is taken.

In further developing this idea, we propose that the term *social conscience* be eliminated from the public relations literature. Such terminology simply contributes to the confusion about the proper role of public relations. In addition to the fact the term appears to be indefinable, many contemporary practitioners reject the title as an accurate reflection of their work (see, e.g., Katzman, 1993). Additionally, there is some evidence that public relations is not viewed by institutional leaders as the appropriate function to serve in the capacity of a social conscience. Many organizations that have taken steps to institutionalize ethics have turned to legal or other advisors outside public relations for advice in this area (see, e.g., Fitzpatrick, 1996). At the same time, only a third of corporate Chief Executive Officers participating in a recent survey said they sought the counsel of public relations advisors on matters related to social responsibility (Fitzpatrick, 2000).

Next, we propose that the term *social conscience* be replaced with the term *public conscience*. Although the terms *social* or *society* are acceptable in reference to the groups of people affected by institutional decisions and actions, they carry a sense of the "greater society" rather than of those specifically and directly affected by or, alternately, who affect an institution in a given situation.

In the context of public relations, the term *public* is widely defined as "a specific part of the people; those people considered together because of some common interest or purpose" (*Webster's New World Dictionary*, 1979, p. 1148). Thus, the use of the term public conscience better captures the more focused obligation of public relations professionals to best serve society by balancing their clients' and employers' interests with the interests of those directly associated with their clients' decisions and actions.

A social conscience provides moral limits or checks on decision-making power within an institution that has effects (good and ill) on society, both individual members and the society as a whole. A public conscience weighs the effects of decisions and actions on specific parties, thereby serving society by serving these special interests.

A theory of public relations ethics based on responsibility to specific publics not only helps to resolve the ambiguity of such phrases as "serve the public interest" and "social responsibility." It also reflects what recent studies in the field have concluded—that "relationships ought to be at the core of public relations scholarship and practice" (Ledingham & Bruning, 2000, p. xiii). By focusing on relationships between an organization and its constituents—rather than on an organization's relationship with or obligation to serve an intangible society—scholars and public relations professionals can begin to define an organization's ethical responsibilities to its publics. Then practitioners can go further in defining standards of performance that are appropriate to the ethical practice of public relations....

REFERENCES

Black's Law Dictionary (5th ed.). (1979). St. Paul, MN: West.

Bivins, T.H. (1993). Public relations, professionalism, and the public interest. *Journal of Business Ethics*, 12, 120–121.

Carey, J.L. (1957, March). Professional ethics are a helpful tool. *Public Relations Journal* [13(3), 7-18].

Clarkson, M.B.E. (1995). A stakeholder framework for analyzing and evaluating corporate social performance. *Academy of Management Review*, 20, 92–117.

Fitzpatrick, K.R. (1996). The role of public relations in the institutionalization of ethics. *Public Relations Review*, 22(3), 249–258.

Fitzpatrick, K.R. (2000). CEO views on corporate social responsibility. *Corporate Reputation Review*, 3, 290–300.

Gillers, S., & Dorsen, N. (1989). *Regulation of lawyers: Problems of law and ethics* (2nd ed.). Boston: Little, Brown.

Goldman, A.H. (1992). Professional ethics. In C. Becker & C.B. Becker (Eds.), *Encyclopedia of Ethics* (Vol. 2), pp. 1018–1020. New York: Garland.

Katzman, J.B. (1993). What's the role of public relations? Profession searches for its identity. *Public Relations Journal*, 49(4), 11–17.

Ledingham, J., & Bruning, S. (2000). Introduction: Background and current trends in the study of relationship management. In J. Ledingham & S. Bruning (Eds.), *Public relations as relationship management: A relationship approach to the study and practice of public relations* (p. xiii). Mahwah, NJ: Lawrence Erlbaum Associates, Inc.

Moore, W. (1970). *The professions: Roles and rules.* New York: Russell Sage Foundation.

Reynolds, M.A. (2000). Professionalism, ethical codes and the internal auditor: A moral argument. *Journal of Business Ethics*, 24, 115–124.

Seib, P., & Fitzpatrick, K. (1995). *Public relations ethics.* Fort Worth, TX: Harcourt Brace.

Webster's New World Dictionary, Second College Ed. (1979). New York: William Collins.

Wolfson, A.D., Trebilcock, M.J., & Tuohy, C.J. (1980). Regulation of the professions: A theoretical framework. In S. Rotenberg (Ed.), *Occupational licensure and regulation* (pp. 180–214). Washington, DC: American Enterprise for Public Policy Research.

Wright, D.K. (1989). Ethics research in public relations. *Public Relations Review*, 15(2), 3–5.

THE WEST GATE BRIDGE

Who Was Responsible?

Joanne Lau

1. BACKGROUND

BUILT BETWEEN 1968 AND 1978, THE WEST GATE Bridge in Melbourne, Australia was to be a "masterpiece among bridges." Original in design, it is a vital link between Melbourne's city district and the industrial suburbs in the west. The bridge is over 2.5 kilometers (1.6 mi) long and carries eight lanes of traffic, 58 meters (190 ft) above the Yarra River. It is the world's largest cable-stayed girder bridge, and, at the time of its construction, it was the longest bridge in Australia. The West Gate Bridge is also the site of Australia's single worst workplace catastrophe.

Over 1,000 people were involved in the construction of the West Gate Bridge, including a host of notable designers, prime contractors, suppliers, and engineers. Two engineering firms, Maunsell and Freeman Fox Partners (FFP) were appointed as joint consultants for the design and preparation of tender documents. FFP was responsible for the structural design of the bridge. Two construction companies were awarded contracts: one for building the foundations and concrete construction, and the other for steelwork construction.

Unfortunately, relations between various groups quickly deteriorated. The construction company responsible for steelwork claimed no responsibility for the joining of the bridge sections, and this role was transferred to FFP. Several work-delaying union strikes and poor on-site supervision meant that, in its first two years of construction, the building schedule fell seven months behind.

In June 1970, a counterpart of the West Gate Bridge in Wales—also designed by FFP—collapsed during construction, killing several workmen. This news created more problems for the West Gate Bridge project. Unions wanted greater safety measures for workers, and a mass stop-work meeting was held to demand assurances that what had happened in Wales would not happen on the West Gate Bridge. A senior engineer from FFP present at the meeting unhesitatingly gave the assurance and work resumed.

It was common practice to assemble the different sections of the bridge on the ground, then hoist them into place with cranes and bolt them together. However, in August 1970, when two particular sections were brought together, it was discovered that the north section was 114 millimeters (4.5 in) higher than the south section. Rather than take the sections down for correction, engineers decided to put several 8-ton weights on the high section to bring it level with the lower.

In September 1970, there was a major buckle.[1] Work came to a halt, followed by a month of deliberation. In October, the engineers decided to unbolt the two sections on each side of the buckle, theorizing that the weight of the higher section would cause it to lower and match the level of the lower section, and then it could be rebolted. However, before the process could be completed, the buckle became greater and the 2000-ton span collapsed, killing 35 of the 68 workers and causing

AUD 10 million in damage. Several other workers were severely injured. The rebuilding cost AUD 31 million and the total cost of the bridge was three hundred million dollars, more than ten times the original estimated cost.

2. ANALYSIS

A Royal Commission was established to investigate the cause of the collapse. It found that one of the main causes was FFP's structural design. Other causes were "mistakes, miscalculations, errors of judgment, failure of communication and sheer inefficiency. In greater or less degree, the Authority itself, the designers, the contractors, even the labor engaged in the work, must all take some part of the blame."[2]

It is quite clear from the judgment that the Commission found various parties liable for the collapse. However, perhaps it is not the case that FFP should have been the *main* cause. One morally relevant issue in this case is the fact that the different parties all contributed to the end result. For example, the designers of the bridge were particularly proud of their original "box-girder" design and insisted that the engineers adhere to it, despite the fact that such a design had not been tested before. Perhaps if they had gone with a more conventional design, the risk of collapse would have been reduced, but at the cost of a lack of originality.

A related issue was how directly related to the collapse a party's action had to be to assign liability. For example, the unions held up construction with protests and stop-work meetings. Being already seven months behind, such delays in the construction probably contributed to the decision by the engineers to weigh down the section of the bridge that was too high so as to make up time, instead of demolishing and rebuilding it. Doing this would also have been an extremely costly process for the client. How much weight should *this* be given?

Perhaps each party's actions were bound together in such a way that blame should not be attributed specifically to one group (such as FFP). It seems that, but for the actions of each of the parties involved, a collapse could have been avoided. If only one party had acted irresponsibly, blame would have been much easier to attribute. However, in this case, where all the parties were connected in such a way that an action by one would irrevocably affect the others, it may simply be the case that accountability could not be separated so simply.

It could also be a question of regulation. Engineers and builders, for instance, have different codes that govern the extent of their liability, and the code for one industry is often written in isolation from the other. If the level of liability varies between different industries, perhaps this should be made uniform for all industries involved in a project. However, the different roles that each party has initially may change in the project (as it did in this case) making it difficult to predetermine the extent of each party's liability.

The Royal Commission found that almost all the parties involved were liable. Only the suppliers were deemed to be blameless. The surviving designers, contractors, and engineers were dismissed. In 2004, on the 34th anniversary of the disaster, a memorial park was opened at the site of the collapse. Thirty-five pillars were constructed, one for each worker who died.

NOTES

1 Buckling is a sign of structural failure where a column is loaded too heavily for its capacity and bends or twists sharply and noticeably.

2 Report of Royal Commission into the Failure of West Gate Bridge (1971) VPRS 2591/Po, unit 14.

DISCUSSION QUESTIONS

1. Should there be different rules and regulations for the different groups involved in a large project like building a bridge? Why or why not?

2. Imagine that you are a builder at the stop-work meeting following the collapse of the FFP-designed bridge in Wales. Would you have believed the engineer who made assurances that the West Gate Bridge was safe? Why or why not?

3. In the engineering industry, originality and visual appeal in design is important, but having a structurally sound bridge is also crucial. How should the interests of originality and design be weighed against safety and social responsibility?

4. Sometimes experts can do everything right, and something can still go wrong. In this case, engineers deliberated for at least a month to decide how to deal with the buckle, and yet disaster still ensued. Presumably they had all the best knowledge of engineering principles at the time. To what extent is the expert responsible when things go wrong?

SNOWDEN, SECURITY, AND CIVIL LIBERTIES

The Ethics of Whistleblowing

Dale Brown

1. BACKGROUND

STARTING IN JUNE OF 2013, EDWARD SNOWDEN— a former Central Intelligence Agency (CIA) employee and former United States government contractor—began leaking classified information that he had collected from a National Security Agency (NSA) facility in Hawaii. Alarmed by the sheer scale of surveillance being conducted by US and British intelligence agencies, Snowden blew the whistle, disclosing one of the biggest caches of secret government documents of all time. The initial documents were published in *The Guardian*, and the rest, as they say, is history.

Let's back up a minute, though, to account for some of this story's moving parts. After a medical discharge ended his US Special Forces candidacy in 2004, Snowden accepted a cybersecurity position with the CIA. Resigning from that agency in 2009, he went on to accept NSA subcontracting positions, first for Dell that same year, and then eventually for Booz Allen Hamilton in early 2013. It was during his tenure at Dell when he first became concerned about the seemingly unlimited reach of the government's global surveillance programs—a concern that persisted and intensified as he worked for Booz Allen.

Snowden's attention was mainly directed at two main government agencies: the NSA and its British counterpart, the Government Communications Headquarters (GCHQ). Both were tasked with collecting and analyzing information and data that contributed to foreign and domestic intelligence and counterintelligence operations for their respective governments. In short, both agencies would spy on folks in the name of national security, collecting vast quantities of personal data in the process.

Toward this end, two main factors had contributed to the NSA and the GCHQ stepping up their game in terms of data they were collecting on its citizens: the terrorist attacks of September 11, 2001 and the proliferation of Internet and cell phone usage over the past 20 to 30 years. Understandably, government actors were highly motivated to use any means at their disposal to avoid future terrorist attacks. This included partnering with telecom giants, such as Verizon, and Internet providers, such as Google, to collect data on any and all of its customers' phone bills, emails, bank accounts, and the like.

But it was Snowden's contention that the collection of this "bulk" data enabled the agencies to paint a far more detailed picture of a person's goings-on than what was allowed by Congress or the US constitution. After his expressions of concern about the surveillance program were repeatedly ignored by his co-workers and supervisors (a claim disputed by government officials), Snowden downloaded the mass of information from the

Hawaii facility and flew to Hong Kong. There he met with reporters from *The Guardian* to form a plan for making that information public.

Snowden has since fled to Russia, where he remains in exile. In late June of 2013, he was accused by US officials of violating the 1917 Espionage Act for leaking the tens of thousands of classified government documents.

2. ANALYSIS

Facing a minimum of decades in prison under the Espionage Act charges, Snowden has been seeking a presidential pardon—though, interestingly, he has said that he would be willing to face *some* jail time as a result of his actions. The argument put forth by his legal counsel is that, on balance, leaking the documents has benefitted the public. They would have us note that the law and morality are two separate decision-making spheres, both of which guide human conduct; so even though there are laws on the books which proscribe the disclosure of government secrets, it was necessary for Snowden to break the law for the sake of the public good. "The ends justify the means," they might say.

But to assess the consequences of an act of this magnitude is not such an easy task. We would need to determine who has been harmed and who has benefitted—and to what extent. Beyond appealing to the purported net public benefit of his disclosure, Snowden is also claiming that his act was the right thing to do *regardless* of any consequences. It should be noted, however, that the consequences that he might face (e.g., prison) are of a different kind than the consequences that, say, a weakened intelligence community might face—in the latter case, it might not even be possible for them to be known, at least up front.

The whistleblower, if he or she is to succeed in calling attention to a specific abuse, must navigate the legitimate interests of multiple parties with care. Defining one's role-related responsibilities might help us determine whether a specific duty has been violated and perhaps whether that violation was justified. And we might do well to remember that we all play different societal roles—each of those carrying unique duties that may or may not overlap.

Snowden, as a government employee/subcontractor—especially one with a high-level security clearance—had a duty to be loyal to his employer, as well as a duty to protect his country. But as a citizen, Snowden also tried to adhere to his duty to protect his country, which seemed to override his duty to be loyal to his employer. What's more, he expressed that he had a duty as an ethical being to stand up for what he thought was right. Still, knowing which duty to abide can, at times, be less than straightforward.

It might also be helpful to frame the debate as a matter of security vs. freedom: to keep its citizens safe, the US and the British governments have stripped citizens of some of their individual civil liberties. One of which, salient to Snowden's case, is a person's right to privacy. Here we must not only consider the degree to which this right exists, but also the degree to which it *should* exist. What price are we willing to pay, for example, in order to prevent another 9/11? Should we have the right to opt-out of having our data collected even if this makes us less safe?

DISCUSSION QUESTIONS

1. Did Snowden make the right choice, morally speaking, in disclosing the intelligence documents? Explain why or why not.
2. Not all cases of whistleblowing are as big or well-covered in the media as the present case. It might be said that Snowden blew a very loud whistle in a very large game. Are there special considerations that apply to a case of this magnitude? If so, what are they? If not, how do we reconcile the apparent differences in a Snowden-type case from a case in which I call out my co-worker for stealing printer paper?
3. Should there be special protections for whistleblowers in the workplace? Why or why not?

4. This case involves almost all of us because we are the ones from whom governments are collecting data. Yet most of us press on with our digital interactions and transactions, knowing that, at least to some degree, our data is being collected. Does this weaken Snowden's case that we have all benefitted from his disclosure? Or is it the case that there simply haven't been enough disclosures of this kind to make us to care about being surveilled, even though we should?

CONFLICTS OF INTEREST

Fritz Allhoff and Alexander Hoffmann

1. INTRODUCTION[1]

CONFLICTS OF INTEREST WERE RECOGNIZED AT least as early as the Bible: "No man can serve two masters: for either he will hate the one, and love the other; or else he will hold to the one, and despise the other."[2] In the professional context, there has been a long tradition of norms to address conflicts of interest, with law playing a particularly formative role. In 1908, the American Bar Association adopted the Canons of Professional Ethics, and Canon 6 spoke to conflicts of interest:

> It is unprofessional to represent conflicting interests, except by express consent of all concerned given after a full disclosure of the facts. Within the meaning of this canon, a lawyer represents conflicting interests while, in behalf of one client, it is his duty to contend for that which duty to another client requires him to oppose.[3]

The Canons of Professional Ethics gave way to the Model Code of Professional Responsibility in 1969, then the Model Rules of Professional Conduct in 1983. Several of the Model Rules speak to conflicts of interest, including Rule 1.7, which states that a conflict of interest exists if "the representation of one client will be directly adverse to another client" or if "there is a significant risk that the representation of one or more clients will be materially limited by the lawyer's responsibilities to another client, a former client or a third person or by a personal interest of the lawyer."[4]

But this focus on other parties—whether current clients, former clients, or other third parties—is unnecessarily narrow. A broader principle might be that a "conflict of interest exists whenever the attorney ... has interests adverse in any way to the advice or course of action which should be available to the present client."[5] And the conflict exists even if the attorney ultimately resolves it in favor of his client.[6] Rather, a conflict simply recognizes "the variety of interests which *might dilute* a lawyer's loyalty to his clients."[7] This "dilution account" allows for infringing interests of third parties, such as the lawyer's "family, friends, business associates, employer, the legal profession, and society as a whole."[8] But it also allows for the interests *of the lawyer* to trigger the conflict, such as might be manifest through "financial security, prestige, and self-esteem."[9]

While much of this thinking has been developed in the legal context, it generalizes to other professions. Medicine, for example, is another primary locus. A particularly controversial practice here involves physicians receiving compensation from pharmaceutical companies, which could comprise a conflict between the physicians' economic interests and the well-being of their patients.[10] An additional flashpoint is the use of medically trained military interrogators to develop interrogation protocols—here the conflict could be between national security or chain-of-command against the well-being of the detainees and the medical principles of both beneficence and non-malfeasance.[11]

As we will see in the second half of this introduction, these issues arise not just in the more traditional inquiries of law and medicine, but in a range of other professional contexts as well.

2. CONTENTS

While the legal context is historically important for understanding conflicts of interest, philosophers have made contributions as well. In the first article, "Conflict of Interest as a Moral Category," Neil Luebke addresses an article first published in 1982 by Michael Davis, titled "Conflict of Interest."[12] In that article, Davis offers a robust account that recognizes, as we did above, the significance of the American Bar Association in developing conflict-of-interest analysis. Davis's project is ultimately to take that analysis[13] and to *generalize* it to non-legal contexts. However, in the article that opens this unit, Luebke disagrees with Davis' conception of conflict of interest and offers his own trust-based approach. According to Luebke, the emphasis that Davis puts on the judgment of the individual who is in a conflict of interest largely ignores the ethical concerns; what matters is whether there is *trust* within the fiduciary relationship. In the following selection, "Conflict of Interest Revisited," Davis responds in turn to Luebke by advocating a definition that is contingent upon judgments and values rather than trust.

In the following reading, titled "Comparing Conflict of Interest across the Professions," Andrew Stark argues that there are many different ways to classify a conflict of interest depending on various roles and principles. By differentiating between instances, Stark shows how the umbrella term "conflict of interest" manifests itself across professions.

Narrowing our scope opens the conversation to questions of conflicts of interest that apply more directly to specific professions. To begin, Catherine Gowthorpe and Oriol Amat analyze how the interests of accountants conflict in their article titled "Creative Accounting: Some Ethical Issues of Macro- and Micro-Manipulation." Accountants have the job of presenting a picture

of the financial state of a business, but they are also a member of that same business entity as well. Naturally, an accountant can find themselves conflicted between relating an unbiased financial statement that puts them at a disadvantage and manipulating the information to suit their own interests.

Judith Lichtenberg, in "Truth, Neutrality, and Conflict of Interest," focuses on the public press and what interests journalists should favor. Of course, the job of the press is to inform the public, but how strictly does that cash out? Judging how a reporter should weigh their own interests and the interests of the public is instrumental to the profession. In "Conflict of Interest in Engineering," Neil Luebke points out that engineers feel a similar tension between the needs of the public, the client, and the employer. These tensions go beyond individual engineers and also affect professional societies, whose goals are often in conflict. This is particularly true when governing members of such organizations also have conflicts of interest. Luebke uses the case of *American Society of Mechanical Engineers v. Hydrolevel Corporation* to highlight these issues.

On the other hand, public servants, such as police officers, are expected to exude an air of impartiality in their work. The charge of bias against a police officer is often construed as an attack on her very ability to uphold the law. Stephen Coleman, in "Conflict of Interest and Police: An Unavoidable Problem," approaches this topic by illustrating how conflicts of interest arise, their effects, and how to properly deal with them.

This unit's main readings end by looking at conflicts of interest and the United States presidency. Fritz Allhoff and Jonathan Milgrim argue that even though the president is faced with decisions that often conflict with his own interests, positing regulation to prevent this would be impractical, and thus the president should be exempt from any federal law that requires the officeholder to resolve their conflicts of interest.

The ensuing case studies examine conflicts of interest using real-life examples. In the first case study, Fritz Allhoff explains the interests at play in the relationship between pharmaceutical companies offering payments to physicians in order to promote the overprescription of opioid medication. The second case study, by Alexander Hoffmann, describes the Sandusky Assault at Pennsylvania State University and the various actors whose interests conflicted.

NOTES

1   Parts of this discussion have been adapted from Fritz Allhoff and Jonathan Milgrim, "Conflicts of Interest, Emoluments, and the Presidency," *International Journal of Applied Philosophy* 31, no. 1 (2017): 45–67.

2   Matthew 6:24 (King James), quoted in Robert H. Aronson, "Conflict of Interest," *Washington Law Review* 52 (1977): 808.

3   Aronson, "Conflict of Interest," 808.

4   American Bar Association, *Model Rules of Professional Conduct* (2016), https://www.americanbar.org/groups/professional_responsibility/publications/model_rules_of_professional_conduct/

model_rules_of_professional_conduct_table_of_contents.html. See also Rules 1.8, 1.10, and 1.11.

5   Aronson, "Conflict of Interest," 809.

6   Aronson, 809.

7   Aronson, 811 (emphasis added).

8   Aronson, 811.

9   Aronson, 811. The remainder of Aronson's article is quite useful in terms of cataloging myriad ways in which conflicts of interest may arise, not all of which appear to be anticipated by the Model Rules.

10   See, for example, Fritz Allhoff, "Pharmaceutical Payments and Opioid Prescriptions," this volume. See also Ashley Wazana, "Physicians and the Pharmaceutical Industry: Is a Gift Ever Just a Gift?" *Journal of the American Medical Association* 283, no. 3 (2000): 373–80.

11   See, for example, Fritz Allhoff, "Physician Involvement in Hostile Interrogations," *Cambridge Quarterly of Healthcare Ethics* 15, no. 4 (2006): 392–402. For more general discussion of conflicts in military medicine, see Fritz Allhoff, *Physicians at War: The Dual-Loyalties Challenge* (Dordrecht: Springer, 2008).

12   Michael Davis, "Conflict of Interest," *Business and Professional Ethics* 1, no. 4 (1982): 17–27.

13   See, e.g., the discussion of Model Rule 1.7 above.

—23—

CONFLICT OF INTEREST AS A MORAL CATEGORY

Neil R. Luebke

CALLING A SITUATION A "CONFLICT OF INTEREST" is now common in media reports, findings of professional ethics committees, government codes, court decisions, and corporate employee policies. Use of the term (henceforth, usually abbreviated "CI") will likely become more common, given growth in the service area of the economy, broader governmental supervision of financial and technological matters, and increasing professionalization of the workforce. On the other hand, the widespread use of the term has been accompanied by increasing vagueness and some ambiguity. Accordingly, the purpose of this paper is to delineate the meaning of CI as a moral category.

I claim that what is morally at stake in CI cases is a potential violation of trust on the part of the party having the CI and a corresponding "situational" basis for the other party to withhold or limit reliance. What is *not* at stake, except accidentally, is the quality of judgment, the strength of affections or desires, or the uses of information. Clarity in this matter is, I think, essential to a proper understanding of certain cases in business and professional ethics....

Some confusion is probably to be expected among the uses of so recent a term as "conflict of interest." It does not appear in either the second (1959) or third (1966) edition of the *Merriam-Webster Unabridged Dictionary*, the 1962 *Funk & Wagnall's Unabridged*, or the 1971 *Oxford English Dictionary*. The 1971 unabridged *Random House*

Dictionary of the English Language does carry an entry, but one that emphasizes the governmental use of the term to the virtual exclusion of the private sector....

I can find no use of the term "conflict of interest" prior to the 1930's nor any occurrence in court decisions prior to 1949. In his 1949 decision concerning disallowance of compensation to some parties acting in a bankruptcy reorganization, District Judge John Clark Knox introduced it to describe the situation of the parties, referencing both section 249 of the Bankruptcy Act of 1898, which discusses "beneficial interests" as a disqualifying factor, and decisions in 1941 and 1946, which involved trustees or counsels representing "conflicting interests."[1] Even the term "conflicting interests" seems not to have been used in decisions prior to 1941.[2] When it does appear, "conflicting interests" usually denotes situations in which a duty of a fiduciary to a client or trust is compromised by commitments to another client or trust. Indeed, the two terms seem synonymous, with "conflicting interests" being the earlier but "conflict of interest" becoming more common during the last few decades.[3]

Antedating both terms by many decades are references to an "interest" that might disqualify a witness, counsel, or judge and to "interested" persons who have a certain relationship to court proceedings—usually civil actions. As far as I can determine, in such contexts "interest" and its cognates always signify an objective relationship to property or some tangible right and not a subjective desire or disposition. The distinction was made explicit by the Illinois Appellate Court in 1939:

> The interest which disqualifies a witness from testifying against an administrator must be an actual financial interest that will result in pecuniary gain or loss for witness, and has nothing whatever to do with witness' understanding or feeling.[4]

It is clear from the foregoing citation, as well as from many other cases, that the term "interest" means some actual share or right on the basis of which one can materially gain or lose. It does not mean an affection for some person, a feeling of sympathy for some cause, or a desire for some area of activity. In this sense I could have an interest in the Bad-News-Corporation, through a generous bequest by my rich uncle, even though I detest its corporate practices and conscientiously refuse to buy its products.

I

In this section I shall treat the topics of (1) the bearer of a CI, (2) the marks of a CI situation, and (3) moral prescriptions directly related to a CI. The latter topic includes the sub-topics of (a) having a CI, (b) actions prior to a CI, (c) actions while having a CI, and (d) actions giving the appearance of having a CI. I shall use the expression "having a CI" and "being in a CI situation" synonymously.

(1) Any person or organized group capable of deliberate judgment or action and who acts or is empowered to act in a fiduciary role can have a CI. The parties in the fiduciary relationship may be natural persons, partnerships, corporations, nations, voluntary organizations, or political constituencies, in short, any parties capable of standing in a fiduciary relationship even if it is morally but not legally recognized. Entering into or continuing in the relationship must be voluntary

for the party open to the CI. It is often voluntary for the other party or parties as well. However, it is not necessary that the trust relationship be voluntarily undertaken by all parties, as can be seen in the case of an orphaned infant placed in the care of a court-appointed guardian. I use the word "fiduciary" here in a broad sense, consistent with at least one of its meanings, to connote any party in whom trust or reliance is reposed for the purpose of advising, aiding, acting on behalf of, or protecting the interest of another party. In this sense, employees, attorneys, physicians, consultants accountants, political officeholders, real estate agents, stockbrokers, and trustees among others are regularly involved in fiduciary relationships. The more clearly defined the fiduciary relation, as in cases of contract or standard professional practice, the more generally perceptible are the instances of CI. Thus, with the growth of complex bureaucratic society, more of us have opportunities to have recognizable CI's and there are more recognizable CI's for us to have.

(2) There is a CI (or, synonymously, a CI situation) whenever the fiduciary party has an interest which is adverse or likely to become adverse to that matter or cause for which reliance was initially placed. The interest might bias advice given, might influence efforts to aid or protect, or might lead to still other results contrary to the purpose of the relationship. By "interest" I do not mean an interest in the psychological sense of a feeling or desire; an attorney who dislikes my choice of clothes and who thinks golf is a childish game has thereby no CI in negotiating on my behalf to purchase a golf course. "Interest," as I use the term, refers to some material right, benefit, asset, or share possessed by the fiduciary or by others with whom he/she is legally or closely associated (family members, business partners, employer, benefactor, client, or the like). The terms "conflict of interest" and "conflicting interests" presumably originated out of judicial proceedings in which either the lawyer's own interests or those of one of his clients was held to be adverse to the lawyer's fiduciary duty regarding another client's interest. As I have

described the CI situation, however, it is not necessary for there to be an actual clash of two opposed interests. It *is* necessary that the direct or indirect interest of the fiduciary actually or potentially threatens the fiduciary relationship.[5]

Thus, summing up to this point, a CI exists when the existence or quality of a voluntary fiduciary relationship is threatened by a fiduciary-related interest in the sense defined above. Identifying a situation as a CI requires at least two descriptive judgment calls: one concerning the specific fiduciary relation and the other concerning the putatively adverse interest. The easier these two calls happen to be, the easier the moral judgment. My physician's ownership of large tracts of land within the city would not seem adverse to his medical responsibilities toward me, but it would threaten public confidence in him as a municipal zoning board member. Yet, would his ownership of 2000 shares of a particular pharmaceutical firm constitute an interest adverse to my receiving appropriate medication? Because, on the one hand, the seriousness and character of the relationship, and, on the other, the threateningness of the interest are both matters of degree, a large number of alleged CI cases may fall into the gray area of dispute. Still, as I shall comment later, there are some types of actions that have been labeled CI's but belong to other moral categories.

(3a) Although some CI's may also be moral dilemmas, CI's are not a subclass of moral dilemmas. A CI does not always present its bearer with a choice between two duties or two evils. However, a moral dilemma and a CI do have this in common: there is nothing wrong with *having, being in* or *finding oneself in* them; the moral prescriptions concern choosing to enter or avoid them and acting consequent to being in them. With a strong desire not to overplay the simile, I hazard that being in a CI is like being pregnant: while it might be a potentially dangerous condition, there is nothing morally wrong with *being* pregnant, but it may be wrong knowingly to become pregnant, to fail to avoid pregnancy, to act in disregard of one's pregnant condition, to cause another to become

pregnant, and to refuse to inform affected parties about the pregnancy. Although being in a CI is itself not a wrong, it is, unlike pregnancy, usually an unwelcome situation, and so to remain in a CI without attempting to alter the situation merits moral suspicion.[6]

(3b) Since one seldom leaves a CI without loss or curtailment of the fiduciary relationship, it is generally wrong knowingly to enter or knowingly to fail to avoid a CI. This prescription is similar to that against promising with the intent of nonperformance; it is not only destructive of the given instance of trust but is also contributes to a milieu of distrust. Many times, of course, a CI is, in practical terms, unavoidable: a long time client may be sued by a bank for which your law firm supplies legal services, a company in which my family has majority control acquires one of the competitive suppliers to a corporation for which I act as a Purchasing Officer, and so on. But where informed avoidance is possible, entering a CI is wrong unless a greater wrong is committed by the avoidance. For example, in a sparsely settled area where the number of lawyers is limited, a normally disqualified counsel might be allowed for an indigent client who would otherwise not receive effective representation. Similarly the corporation for which I am a Purchasing Officer may so value my expertise in evaluating certain types of supplies that I am permitted to function in spite of the CI. In such cases, as in instances of acting while in a CI, disclosure to and informed consent by the affected parties should be present.

It is also generally wrong intentionally to place a party in a CI. While bribery in one form or another is perhaps the common and easily identifiable technique for creating a CI for another party, there are other modes....

(3c) When a fiduciary is in a CI, one of two courses of action are morally required: either extrication from the CI or remaining in the CI but acting to minimize the threat to the fiduciary relationship. The former is achieved (i) by withdrawal from the relationship completely, as in resigning a government office, (ii) by abandoning the material interest, as in disposing of large stock holdings, or (iii) by partial limitation of the fiduciary relationship, as in refraining to vote on matters in which one would have a CI. While often thought ideal, extrication may be inadvisable or impracticable....

(3d) A common prescription in institutional, professional, and governmental ethics codes is that to give the *appearance* of having a CI is a wrong. As I see the matter, this is a perfectly appropriate moral requirement and not an open invitation to hypocrisy. Both failing to avoid a CI and failing to minimize the threat of a CI are standardly condemned in the codes, so this additional prescription does not assert the wrong exists only if detected....

II

Of immediate concern is [Michael] Davis' ... analysis which, while explicitly derived from the ABA Code, is intentionally generalized "so that it covers all of business and professional ethics."[7] Davis gives a formal definition[8] which I here rephrase less formally, incorporating some elements from his fuller discussion:

> Anyone who is in a relationship requiring the exercise of judgment in the service of another has a CI if and only if he is subject to influences, loyalties, concerns, or emotions that might make the judgment less reliably beneficial to the other. The relationship does not depend on the other party's actual expectations of the exerciser of judgment but on what the party is justified in expecting.

There are at least three problems with this definition: the first concerns what is clearly a crucial element—the notion of judgment—and the second concerns Davis' treatment of the term "interest." There is a third problem, encountered in a sense by default, namely the lack of any basis for condemnation of giving the appearance of a CI.

How does Davis conceive of "a relationship requiring the exercise of judgment in the service of another"? "Judgment," he writes, "implies

discretion" and is to be thought of as "the capacity to make correctly decisions not as likely to be made correctly by a simple clerk with a book of rules and access to all the facts."[9] Thus, using his examples, a bank president does not exercise judgment (as president) in deciding not to embezzle but does exercise judgment in deciding to approve a loan. Hence, for Davis, a CI cannot be involved in the decision about embezzling but may be involved in the decision about loaning. The reason Davis stresses judgment in this sense is that he sees the wrongness of a CI in its potential for worsening the quality of judgment....

Even supposing Davis' distinction between two sorts of decisions makes sense (which I think unlikely) and supposing that CI candidates are always involved in decisions of the sort he calls "judgments" (which I think is common but not necessary), I still disagree that the principal moral concern regarding a CI is the threat to the *correctness* of a decision. Davis sees the interest as merely one possible cause of incorrect judgment. To my mind, the moral issue is trust, not correctness. The appropriate question a client might raise is "Can I *trust* X to give me good advice?" not "Can I trust X to give me *good* advice?" (the latter being equivalent to "Will X give me good advice?"). A client concerned with correctness might seek several opinions; a client concerned with trust examines reputation and commitments. Granted, one normally doubts the quality of service given by a party one does not trust, but that does not imply a CI is essentially a challenge to that quality in contrast to the fiduciary relationship itself. (Davis' use of the word "reliable," which he apparently intends in the sense of "correct" but is also a synonym for "trustworthy," helps to mask the contrast between our two views.) I also grant that a bank president's acting within a CI to make a bad loan to a relative is a wrong act, but making the loan would also be a wrong act (though not necessarily *morally* wrong) for any other officer of any other bank. In the president's case it would be evidence of untrustworthiness; in other cases it would be evidence of incompetence or poor judgment.

Since Davis emphasizes judgment, he explicitly downplays "interest." Apparently any psychological factor capable of misdirecting competent judgment in the service of another may be labeled an "interest." He even goes so far as to suggest that moral constraints may be an interest, as in his example of a conscience-stricken Machiavelli who refuses to advise his prince because he is no longer wholeheartedly able to seek the prince's own benefit. (Davis slips at this point in adding "He can no longer be trusted to tell his superior how not to be good.")[10] But not only is this expansion of "interest" contrary to the legal literature Davis claims to represent, but, even worse, it renders the category of CI far larger than the bounds of standard or effective usage. A parent postponing a child's needed medical attention out of a desire to take a weekend trip and a real estate salesperson failing to show a house to a prospective buyer because of an aversion to the buyer's accent might both count as CI's by Davis' definition. By contrast, "interest" as I have defined it is situational and thus objective rather than subjective—in the sense that it is open to investigation by a Senate Committee rather than by a board of psychologists. What are regarded as evidences of a CI are records of financial holdings and business dealings, not personality profiles. The degree to which the interest may subjectively affect the fiduciary is often not clear. If it can be *firmly* established that, contrary to standard assumptions, the interest has no subjective effects adverse to the fiduciary relation, then one might conclude there is no *actual* CI in the given case, although the potential could still exist and the moral prescriptions concerning a CI would be thought still appropriate. The burden of proof normally falls on the party trying to show that, in spite of some interest (in the objective sense) that would standardly be thought to compromise trust, the fiduciary in question is *actually* immune from such effects now and in the future. It is a heavy burden.

Finally, Davis says nothing about giving the appearance of a CI. As I see it, this is not a mere oversight or editorial reduction but a lack consistent with his analysis of CI. If the moral defect of a CI is its promoting bad judgment, then there would seem to be no reason to single out the *appearance* of a CI for special mention. To be in a situation that merely *appears* to affect one's judgment has not thereby *actually* injured the quality of that judgment. However, given my definition of CI as a moral category, it is clear that avoiding the appearance of a CI is essentially related to the same rationale as are the other moral prescriptions cited: the avoidance of certain situational factors that threaten *trust*....

NOTES

1   *In re* Equitable Office Bldg. Corp., D.C.N.Y., 83 F. Supp 531 at 567.

2   The 1941 decision is Woods v. City National Bank and Trust Co. of Chicago, 61 S.Ct. 493, 312 U.S. 262, 85 L.Ed. 820.

3   In its complete edition in 1951, *Words and Phrases* (St. Paul, Mn: West Publishing Co.), Vol. 8A, listed only one entry for "conflict of interest" (the Equitable Building case *infra*). In its supplementary annual pocket part for 1985 over a dozen cases are listed under "conflict of interest" or "actual conflict of interest."

4   Johnson v. Matthews, 22 N.E. 2nd 772, 301 Ill. App. 504.

5   The distinction between what I here call "material" (or objective) and "psychological" (or subjective) interest is far from unproblematic but nonetheless important. The *Oxford English Dictionary* (pp. 392–394) finds several objective meanings to be much older than the purely subjective meanings of "a feeling of concern for or curiosity about a person or thing" and a "fact or quality of mattering or being of importance" to someone. The latter usages do not precede the 19th century whereas the earlier objective ones go back to 1400. We expect people to be subjectively interested in whatever they have an objective interest—hence the concern that a CI has a motivational force in behavior—but a subjective interest alone is not sufficient to label a situation a CI. An example of such a confusion is given in the next note.

6   I say "usually unwelcome" because I can imagine situations in which a lawyer or judge might be happy to avoid having to represent a client or hear a particular case by pleading the presence of a CI. Recently in Oklahoma two public officials, a county attorney and a state attorney general both pleaded "an appearance of conflict of interest" to avoid the politically unpopular task of prosecuting, or naming a special prosecutor to handle, a case of alleged ethics law violations by the Democratic nominee for governor. The county attorney's excuse was that he had the same campaign manager as the nominee; the attorney general pointed out that he was the nominee's opponent in the bitter party runoff election a few weeks earlier. Neither attorney claimed an actual CI, only an "appearance." I fail to see the appearance of anything except personal political posturing and an interest (psychological) in avoiding a no-win situation.

7   [Michael] Davis, ["Conflict of Interest," *Business & Professional Ethics Journal* I:4 (Summer 1982),] p. 21.

8   Davis' formal version is as follows (Davis, p. 24): A person P has a conflict of interest in role R if, and only if:

a. P_1 occupies R;

b.   R requires exercise of (competent) judgment with regard to certain questions Q;

c.   A person's occupying R justifies another person relying on the occupant's judgment being exercised in the other's service with regard to Q;

d.   Person P is justified in relying on P's judgment in R with regard to Q (in part at least) because P occupies R; *and*

e. P_1 is (actually, latently, or potentially) subject to influences, loyalties, temptations, or other interests tending to make P's (competent) judgment in R with regard to Q less likely to benefit P_2 than P_1's occupying R justifies P_2 in expecting.

9   Davis, p. 22.

10   Davis, pp. 23–24.

—24—

CONFLICT OF INTEREST REVISITED

Michael Davis

JUST OVER A DECADE AGO, IN THESE PAGES, I PUB-
lished a short article entitled "Conflict of Interest."[1]
It did not claim to offer an original analysis of
conflict of interest; rather, it generalized for use in
all of business and professional ethics the analysis
then standard in legal ethics.[2] I summarized the
analysis in this way:

> A person has a conflict of interest if a) he is
> in a relationship with another requiring him
> to exercise judgment in that other's service
> and b) he has an interest tending to inter-
> fere with the proper exercise of judgment in
> that relationship.[3]

I used "judgment" to refer to that aspect of
intelligent activity requiring more than mechanical rule-following, and "interest" for any special
influence, loyalty, or other concern capable of
biasing otherwise competent judgment (under the
circumstances in question).

The analysis has since become, more or less,
standard in business and professional ethics.[4]
One sign of its success is that two learned writers
recently published sustained criticism of it.[5] Neil
Luebke has argued that my conception of interest
makes the analysis too broad. John Boatright has
argued that my emphasis on judgment makes the
analysis too narrow, excluding from the category
of conflict of interest many improper practices
businesses often forbid as "conflicts of interest."

Both argued that the analysis underrated the
moral dimension of conflict of interest (the importance of trust or obligation).[6] Their careful arguments are not feathers to bush off. If a philosopher
is to be judged by the quality of the criticism he
receives, these two have honored me.

They have also forced me to revisit my analysis—with two results. First, I have concluded that
what divides us are primarily issues of method,
important in themselves, but more or less independent of the issue of conflict of interest as such.
Second, I have concluded nonetheless that showing our division to have this source will shed light
on what a conflict of interest is. While my critics
would deserve a response even if the response did
not have this methodological dimension, because
it does it may interest some who have no interest
in conflict of interest as such.

I. LUEBKE: ETHICS AS LAW?

Luebke's article begins with a brief history of the
concept of "conflict of interest." The term is of
surprisingly recent origin. Luebke could find no
use of it before the 1930's, no use in a court case
before 1949 (though "conflicting interests" was
used as early as 1941), no reference in a dictionary
of English until 1971, and no reference in a legal
dictionary until 1979. All "early" references emphasize "governmental use of the term to the virtual
exclusion of the private sector," but by 1949 a

federal judge was using the term while considering whether to disqualify a fiduciary in a bankruptcy proceeding.[7] The term seems to combine under one heading ideas, scattered until then, about "interests" ("adverse," "pecuniary," and so on) that should disqualify an official, trustee, counsel, or other fiduciary from performing what otherwise would be sworn duties.

Luebke also investigated the history of "interest." The results were less surprising. Unlike "conflict of interest," "interest" is an old word. Until the nineteenth century, it referred only to "objective" interests. (If someone had an interest in this sense, she would have a right to or claim for property, income, or service.) Only in the last two hundred years did the "subjective" sense of "interest" appear. Only then could an interest be an emotional attachment or concern. For the law, "conflict of law" is still largely a matter of objective interests, that is, of material gain or loss, whether to oneself, one's family, or some business associate.[8]

What lesson should we draw from this history? Luebke's answer is that we should understand "conflict of interest" solely as a matter of objective interests rather than, as my analysis does, allow for subjective interests as well. Luebke offers two arguments for using "interest" in his way instead of mine.

First, since the law understands "conflict of interest" narrowly, the "expansion of 'interest' [to include subjective interest is] contrary to the legal literature Davis claims to represent."[9] My analysis is (according to Luebke) not a mere generalization of the lawyer's analysis but a radical departure from it.

Second, the subjective sense of "interest" makes "the category of [conflict of interest] far larger than the bounds of standard or effective usage."[10] For example, a father's postponing a child's needed medical attention out of a desire to take a weekend trip "might" count as a conflict of interest under my analysis because (on my analysis) the desire is an interest (a special influence on the decision). This (Luebke seems to think) is a conclusion absurd enough to discredit my use of "interest."[11]

Luebke's two arguments seem to rest on two mistakes, one concerning what the standard of standard usage is, the other concerning what its status is. While I would like to deal with these mistakes separately, they are in fact so closely related that I cannot.

What usage is standard for purposes of evaluating an analysis of conflict of interest? My analysis began not with court opinions (the "legal literature" to which Luebke refers) but with the lawyers' code of ethics. I do not regret that. Law, even judge-made law, is not necessarily appropriate to ethics, even to the ethics of lawyers. A lawyer judging herself ordinarily has access to information courts do not—for example, to her sense of her own motivation. This difference in evidence might well justify different uses of the term "interest" (and so, of "conflict of interest") in legal ethics than in law. Since other professionals, even ordinary people exercising judgment in the service of others, are, in respect of information about themselves, more often in the lawyer's position than in the judge's, it seems to me that the lawyers' analysis rather than the judges' is the proper place to start an analysis of conflict of interest suitable for business and professional ethics. Consider again the example which (according to Luebke) reveals the absurdity of my analysis.

Suppose that the decision to postpone my child's medical care is complex enough to require judgment; suppose too that I think my desire to take a weekend trip makes it hard for me to give due weight to my child's interest: my judgment, ordinarily to be trusted in making my child's health decisions, no longer looks trustworthy. If I can, I probably should give the decision to someone else—a physician or spouse. Though perhaps no court would say I had a conflict of interest, why should we not say it? Where is the absurdity? Indeed, does not so describing my situation (or, at least, using the terms specific to a conflict of interest analysis) help us to see something troubling about the situation hard to express in other terms?

What might Luebke respond? Perhaps he would object that my usage, though illuminating in some ways, is still not "standard." That objection must fail. Thanks to Luebke's own research, we know that the term "conflict of interest" goes back only sixty years, that it evolved slowly, not reaching business cases until 1949, and that even today dictionaries have not caught up. What the standard use of "conflict of interest" is is still unsettled. Indeed, its unsettled state may explain why philosophers find it interesting.

Since Luebke and I are not lexicographers, discovering the actual use of the term is, at best, preliminary to our task of finding the best (or, as Luebke puts it, "effective") way to use the term. Our disagreement is not so much about what people say (or think they should say) as about what they should say (what their standards should be). Of course, there is a close relationship between what people say and what they should say, but the relationship is certainly not identity.

That brings me to Luebke's second mistake—that concerning the status of the usage he considers standard. While arguing that "the main moral concern regarding [conflict of interest] is the destruction of the fiduciary relationship and the milieu of other current and future fiduciary relationships,"[12] Luebke never considers whether any interests that the courts refuse to recognize as creating a conflict of interest in fact raise the same moral concerns as those the courts do recognize—that is, whether the courts might be mistaken in recognizing only "objective" interests.

The courts limit "conflicts of interest" to conflicts involving "objective interests" because they worry about being able to distinguish subjective interests that do exist from subjective interests that do not. Luebke accepts this worry uncritically. We should not. Common-law courts have worried about proof of subjective states of all sorts for more than two centuries now. They have also experimented—usually successfully—with allowing more evidence of "subjective" matters, for example, of what a defendant actually believed when he shot in what he claims to be self-defense.[13] These experiments seem to be part of a wider cultural trend—represented in Luebke's history of

"interest"—toward recognizing subjective states as open to rational study, public understanding, and proof. So, by itself, the current practice of courts is hardly decisive even concerning what their practice should be.[14]

In sum, Luebke relies too heavily and too uncritically on what courts do. His arguments in fact give no reason for discussions of business and professional ethics to exclude subjective interests from interests capable of producing a conflict of interest....

For Luebke, a fiduciary is "any party [to a voluntary relationship] in whom trust or reliance is reposed for the purpose of advising, aiding, acting on behalf of, or protecting the interests of another party."[15]

Joining Luebke in talking of "fiduciary relation" (in something like this sense) has the advantage of assuring that all conflict of interest situations in my sense would be properly pigeon-holed. But the cost would be high, blurring the concept so much that we might have to count as conflict of interest many situations more helpfully described in other terms.[16] Much better, it seems, would be to drop the term "fiduciary" altogether and offer in its place a more precise analysis. That is just what I did. My analysis identifies the crucial relation as one in which one party is to exercise judgment in the other's service. This is certainly more precise than Luebke's "fiduciary." Of course, even precision can be bought at the cost of usefulness. But, as I hope I have sufficiently shown already, that is not so here.

At this point Luebke would be justified in asking how my analysis could pick out fiduciary relations when it does not mention trust?[17] My answer is: "Easily." There are more ways to get trust into a relationship than by mention—for example, by inference, either direct or aided by additional facts or principles. Here I need only point out that, if I invite you to believe that I am both competent and ready to exercise my judgment in your behalf, I have given you reason (pretty good reason, all else equal) to trust me (or, at least, to rely on me) to exercise my judgment in your behalf within the range of my competence, a trust which (being justified by that invitation) must (all else equal) impose on me a moral obligation to remain trustworthy as long as I do not withdraw the invitation and you continue to trust in it.[18]

"Okay," Luebke might respond, "I will concede that, after all, trust is implicit in your analysis of conflict of interest in the way you just indicated. I still do not understand why you want to limit talk of conflict of interest to situations in which the fiduciary is exercising judgment. Why not include, as well, other forms of action, such as advising, aiding, acting on behalf of, or protecting another?"

My answer is that, where judgment is not at issue, advising, aiding, acting on behalf of, or protecting do not seem to involve conflicts of interest in any interesting sense. If Luebke, Boatright, or anyone else thinks otherwise, let them produce a case. I am willing to change my mind.

...

"But," Luebke might break in here, "your distinction between acts involving judgment and those that do not makes no sense. There is no way to use it in practice. It's just your way of doing what I tried to do by distinguishing between objective and subjective interests, an attempt to save your analysis from a horde of counter-examples. So, any analysis which, like yours, relies on the concept of judgment must be rejected for just that reason."[19]

What is the objection here? It cannot be that a wily philosopher could come up with an example in which an act would neither clearly involve judgment nor clearly not involve it. Such an example would show only that the boundary between acts involving judgment and those not involving it is fuzzy (in other words, that some cases are open to dispute), a truth as easy to prove as it is uninteresting. Most distinctions of theory, especially those that are useful in practice, are somewhat fuzzy. Why should "judgment" be any different? The important question, the one about which Luebke is silent, is whether any alternative to my analysis is less fuzzy (without giving up something more important).

So, Luebke's objection cannot be of this theoretical sort. But it also cannot be practical. We have worked with the distinction throughout this paper without difficulty (or, at least, without any difficulty with the concept of judgment itself). That is some evidence for its practicality. There is more. For example, the distinction is an ancient workhorse of the law. Even The Restatement of Agency expressly distinguishes "acts ... which involve discretion or the agent's special skill" from "mechanical and ministerial acts."[20] I think it evident that, for most practical purposes, we have little trouble deciding whether an activity does or does [not] require judgment.

What then could be Luebke's objection? I have no idea.[21]

IV. CONCLUSION

I have so far emphasized my disagreements with Luebke and Boatright, explaining these disagreements as the result of various errors in method (for example, uncritical acceptance of ordinary usage of one sort or another). While those disagreements are important, they should not be allowed to overshadow how much we agree. We agree in rejecting analyses which attempt to understand conflict of interest as consisting merely of conflict of roles.[22] We agree too in rejecting attempts to understand conflict of interest as consisting merely of conflict between one interest and another, that is, of mere conflicting interests.[23] We even agree in trying to analyze conflict of interest as a sub-class of morally significant violations of justified expectations of another's service in one's behalf. Compared to all this, our disagreements are small. That our disagreements are so small testifies to the decade's progress in understanding conflict of interest.

...

NOTES

1   Michael Davis, "Conflict of Interest," *Business and Professional Ethics Journal* 1 (Summer 1982): 17–27; hereafter cited as "Conflict."

2   Since 1982, the American Bar Association's Model Rules of Professional Conduct has largely replaced the short-lived Model Code of Professional Responsibility, changing somewhat the state of legal ethics. Unlike the Code, the Rules are designed primarily for use in disciplinary hearings and other judicial proceedings. Its language is, accordingly, much more like other legal documents. Concerns about "independent judgment" are confined to its commentary. This change, though understandable, has made the Rules less helpful for teaching professional ethics (and reduced somewhat the value for business and professional ethics generally of lawyers' discussions of conflict of interest).

3   "Conflict," p. 21. But note the fuller statement, p. 24.

4   Note, for example, Tom L. Beauchamp, "Ethical Issues in Funding and Monitoring University Research," *Business and Professional Ethics Journal* 11 (Spring–Summer 1991): 5–16, especially pp. 9–11, where he presents my analysis (more or less), apparently without feeling the need to give any reference or defense.

5   Another sign of its success is that the article has been reprinted in two important anthologies: *Ethical Theory and Business*, 3rd., edited by Tom L. Beauchamp and Norman E. Bowie (Prentice-Hall: Englewood Cliffs, NJ, 1988), pp. 482–487 (abridged and revised); and *Ethical Issues in Engineering*, edited by Deborah Johnson (Prentice-Hall: Englewood Cliffs, NJ, 1991), pp. 317–326.

6   Neil R. Luebke, "Conflict of Interest as a Moral Category," *Business and Professional Ethics Journal* 6 (Spring 1987): 66–81; John R. Boatright, "Conflict of Interest: An Agency Analysis," in *Ethics and Agency Theory: An Introduction*, edited by Norman E. Bowie and R. Edward Freeman (Oxford University Press: New York, 1992), pp. 187–203.

7   Luebke, 67.

8   Luebke, 67–68.

9   Luebke, 74.

10 Luebke, 74

11 Boatright makes the same point, p. 192.

12 Luebke, 72.

13 Wayne R. LaFave and Austin W. Scott, Jr., *Criminal Law* (West Publishing Co.: St. Paul, Minn., 1972), pp. 393–394.

14 See, for example, Judith Lichtenberg, "Truth, Neutrality, and Conflict of Interest," *Business and Professional Ethics Journal* 9 (Spring–Summer 1990): 65–78, p. 69: "the most fundamental sources of conflicts of interest [are] personal relationships, which can exert a powerful pull at odds with professional duty." From her perspective, the objective categories of the courts seem mere stand-ins for subjective interests. The subjective interests, not the objective, explain why, for example, kinship to one with adverse interests can threaten a fiduciary relationship.

15 Luebke, 68–69. The legal definition is at least as murky as Luebke's version. Consider just one of the definitions of "fiduciary relation" in *Black's Law Dictionary* (West Publishing Co.: St Paul, Minn., 1968): "An expression including both technical fiduciary relations and those informal relations which exist whenever one man trusts or relies upon another." (*Black's*, 753). This murkiness is, I think, caused by the absence of any general theory of what the obligations of a fiduciary are and of why they have them. The absence of such a unifying theory no doubt explains why there is no Restatement of Fiduciary Law comparable to the Restatement of Agency (though there is a Restatement of Trusts).

16 Luebke succeeds in avoiding many obvious counter-examples by his (poorly motivated) restriction of "interest" to "objective interest."

17 Luebke, 73–75. Boatright seems to have a similar concern that my definition of "conflict of interest" contains no explicit reference to "obligation" (by which he seems to mean "moral obligation") but instead to "requiring" and "proper" (by which I mean only a standard of evaluation connected with the role, the morality of which needs further argument). Compare Boatright, 199–200.

18 Here, perhaps, is the place to respond to Luebke's claim that my analysis "[lacks] any basis for condemnation of giving the appearance of a

(conflict of interest)." Luebke, 72. The basis is ordinary morality (just as it is for Luebke). Here is how I explained it (in 1988): "What is wrong with merely appearing to have a conflict of interest is what is wrong with merely appearing to engage in any form of wrongdoing. It has the same effect 'real' wrongdoing has, once discovered, justifying precautions costing time, money, the ability to maintain relationships of trust, or the like. The only difference in this respect between real conflicts of interest and merely apparent ones is that the precautions adopted because of an apparent conflict are in fact unnecessary." Beauchamp and Bowie, 485.

19 Luebke, 73. Compare Boatright, 199.

20 Restatement, 198–200. There is also the mathematician's distinction between decisions for which there is an algorithm (where a computer can do the work) and those for which there is none (where a computer cannot).

21 Luebke also claims that I confuse "reliability" (or "trustworthiness") with "correctness." Luebke, 74. I don't think I do, though I do think the relation between correctness and (rational) trust is close. For example, who would trust a lawyer to write a will if he was known to get things wrong far more often than he got them right (and better lawyers were available)? Conflict of interest would not be an interesting concept did it not pick out a specific (and not otherwise clearly distinguished) way in which competent judgment could be made more likely to err. Conflict of interest endangers correctness (without guaranteeing incorrectness), endangering it in a way justifying distrust even of a well-meaning and competent fiduciary.

22 See references to "Margolis": Luebke, 72; Boatright, 190.

23 Luebke, 75–76; Boatright, 189–190.

—25—

COMPARING CONFLICT OF INTEREST ACROSS THE PROFESSIONS

Andrew Stark

...

MANY ROLES, ONE PRINCIPAL

THERE ARE ... TWO BASIC KINDS OF IN-ROLE CONflict, one that arises when a professional occupies more than one role with respect to any given principal; the other, when the professional occupies the same role with respect to many principals. Consider, to begin with, the first type, which ... is itself amenable to being divided into two classes. On the one hand, there are professions in which such multiple-role conflicts emerge because the professional simultaneously occupies a judging and an advocating role—an impartial and a partial role—in the work he does for the principal. On the other hand, conflicts inhere in a tension between the professional's diagnostic and service-provision roles, his roles as both a buyer of services for and a seller of services to the principal.

Consider first the professions that fuse a judging with an advocacy role. Many officials fall into this class. Think, for example, of legislators whose role it is to advocate aggressively for various interests held by different sections of the public while, in the final analysis, judging legislation impartially in the interest of the public as a whole. Or think of agency officials who help prepare cases which they ultimately have to participate in deciding. Primary-market financial services underwriters, too, find themselves riven between judging and advocacy roles when they assess the merits of a client I.P.O. (initial public offering) which they are, at the same time, promoting. Likewise journalists, who often combine reportorial with commentative work, or who wrestle with the need to be "objective"—to judge the hard truth of a story—and yet at the same time display "balance," by rendering "all sides of the story." Literary critics, too, find the distinction between judging and advocacy, between being an arbiter and a tribune of public taste, extremely fuzzy. The same with university teachers, who, as Jane Gallop shows, must confront a conflict posed by their having to judge their graduate students—grade and assess them—while at the same time advocating for them in the professional marketplace....

True, some of these professionals—in particular, journalists, financial underwriters, show-business agents, and officials—work in organizations which, if they are suitably structured, can largely segregate those occupying judging from those occupying advocacy roles. Commentators need not be reporters, financial analysts need not also be salespeople, show-business agents need not double as producers, and decision-making officials—administrative judges, for example—need not at the same time fill the roles of preliminary investigators. But in the remaining three professions—judging, criticism, and university teaching—the professional operates with far greater independence from whatever organizational structure surrounds her. In these three venues, whatever fusion of judging and advocacy roles arises is thus more likely to be inveterately internal to the individual and less amenable to resolution through organizational manipulation....

The second kind of intraprincipal role conflict arises when the professional occupies both a diagnostic and a service-providing role with respect to the same principal. Consider the accountant who provides an audit and then offers comptrolling or forensic services to deal with any shortcomings she discovers. Or the consulting engineer who recommends structural work which his firm can then supply as a contractor. Or the lawyer who reviews a client's estate and then suggests a complex series of trust arrangements. Or the corporate director whose engagement in a proxy fight involves, essentially, a conflict between her fiduciary obligation to ascertain a course of action that will best cure the company's ills and her position as someone who might be able to offer such a course of action. Or the broker who "churns," recommending "frequent trading of (possibly) unsuitable securities" on the secondary stock market in a situation where he is "compensated only for executing trades." Or, too, the official who identifies a social problem and then seeks the budget and staff to deal with it: the kind of conflict of interest public-choice scholars study. Or the physician who diagnoses a particular ailment and then prescribes a battery of tests to confirm, or who refers the patient to a specialist facility she co-owns for treatment.

In each of these cases, the professional is conflicted between a diagnostic and a service-provision role. As Stephen Latham puts it in discussing the physician in particular, in all such situations, the professional occupies the role of both buyer—the principal's agent for the purchase of services—and seller, the supplier of those services. What Latham says about the doctor is the case for each of these other professionals: "His conflict of interest is this: as [the principal's] purchasing agent, he has a duty to assist her in making prudent choices among [relevant professional] services; but as a purveyor of those services, he has

a pecuniary interest in advising her to make rather more extravagant purchases than a disinterested person would counsel."

For some of these professionals—in particular, accountants, doctors, secondary-market financial brokers, and lawyers, who operate according to traditional fee-for-service principles—the fusion of diagnostic and service-providing roles will, at some level become inveterate and incorrigible, unamenable to any kind of organizational remedy....

In sum, when it comes to conflicts of interest that arise when the professional occupies more than one role with respect to a particular principal, the professions fall neatly into two categories: those that feature a conflict between judging and advocacy roles and those that exhibit a conflict between diagnostic and service-provision roles. And, within each category, the conflict can be more or less inveterate and incorrigible....

MANY PRINCIPALS, ONE ROLE

"Internal" conflicts of interest—those intrinsic to the professional-principal relationship—can also arise not when the professional occupies more than one role with respect to any given principal but when he or she must deal with more than one principal within the ambit of any given professional role. If, for example, the central problem with fee-for-service medicine is that it creates conflicts between the various roles (diagnostic vs. service-provision) that the physician occupies with respect to a particular patient, the central problem with its alternative—capitation—is that it fosters conflicts between the various patients whom the doctor services in any given medical role. Capitation forces doctors to choose between allocating their limited time and resources to different principals, some of whose needs pose a far greater threat to that time and those resources than do others.

But medicine is not the only profession that features conflicts between various principals on matters that come under the rubric of the professional's role. Corporate directors must deal with competing majorities and minorities among shareholders. Lawyers often face the problem of either concurrent or serial representation of adversarial clients. As Eric Hayot and Jeff King note, graduate students such as themselves fall into competition for the university teacher's attention and assistance in much the same way as patients do for their doctor's under capitation. In financial services, as Boatright says, a "broker who manages accounts for multiple clients may be forced to choose among the interests of these different parties when he or she decides how to allocate a security in short supply"; also, interprincipal conflicts arise because the broker represents both the buyer and the seller in many transactions. In fact, as far as interprincipal conflicts go, brokerage is unique. Whereas the interests of various principals might possibly come into conflict in medicine, law, corporate directorship, and university professorship, in brokerage, they necessarily fall into conflict, because they involve buyers and sellers, principals on either side of a market exchange.

But there is another set of professions which do not seem quite so afflicted by interprincipal conflicts of this sort. Perhaps that is because in their case—journalism, literary criticism, government, judging, accounting, and engineering—the public as a whole is either the principal whom the professional is obligated to serve or else is coequal to other principals. Engineers and accountants, as Neil Luebke and Len Brooks show, fall into this latter category. One analyst, Paul L. Busch, even explicitly couples the two professions by noting that in both, the professional bears an obligation to the "public interest" and not just the "client's interest"....

When it comes to the remaining four professions for which the public is a principal—government, journalism, judging, and criticism—the public is in fact the only principal. Unlike with accounting or engineering, these four professions do not embrace private-party principals as well. That is not to say that, for example, journalists, in serving the public, owe no obligations to various private parties, such as their sources or subjects, or that those obligations will never trump the one owed to the public to report the news. But the obligations a journalist bears to those she interviews or covers are not ones of professional to principal; they are not, as Alan Goldman puts it, role-moral obligations—heightened fiduciary duties of singular commitment and devotion—but rather "ordinary-moral" obligations—minimalist or baseline duties to be fair and decent of the kind we bear toward anyone, including those with whom we have no special relationship.[1] Likewise, critics write for their public, not for the artists they analyze, which is not to say that they bear those artists no obligations of baseline fairness. As for officials, they, too, direct their professional or role-moral obligations to the public; toward particular agency clients or groups, they hold only ordinary moral obligations.[2] ...

As with the multiple-role/one-principal variety of conflict, then, so with the one-role/multiple-principal type: The professions divide themselves into two basic categories. On the one hand are those—medicine, corporate directorships, financial services, law, and university teaching—in which the private-party principals may well come into competition or conflict within the domain in which the professional is responsible. On the other hand are professions in which many individual private-party principals are replaced either wholly or partially by the public. Thus, journalists, critics, judges, and officials owe their professional responsibilities only to the public—which is not to deny that the public might sometimes fall into internal conflict on matters for which the official or judge, say, is responsible in role....

CROSS-PROFESSIONAL PATTERNS

There is, then, a pattern—depicted in table 1—to the kinds of conflicts that arise from sources internal if not external to the professional-principal relationship. It is a pattern, or more exactly a four-quadrant matrix, born of the different structures each profession displays. In the first quadrant are professions in which the professional occupies the dual roles of judge and advocate (some more integrally and others less) and the principal is the public itself: journalism, criticism, government, and the judiciary. Second come professions—accounting, engineering, government—where this time the professional occupies the dual roles of diagnostician and service provider (again, the one more integrally than the others), while the principal continues to include the public. Third, there are professions—medicine, law, corporate directorships, and financial services—in which the professional continues to occupy the dual roles of diagnostician and service provider, but in which it is only private parties, and no longer the public itself, who number among the principals. Finally, there come the professions—university teaching, financial services again, and show business—in which the professional's dual roles are once again those of judge and advocate but the principals continue to include only private parties, not the public. This last category, I note, seems to contain a bit of an odd triumvirate: What has university teaching got to do with financial services got to do with show business? The answer is that in these professions, unique among the ones considered here, the principal is actually the product being sold by the professional. University teachers judge and advocate for their students as they propel them into the academic job market. Brokers judge and advocate for their client company as they propel its IPO into the primary stock market. Show-business agents judge and advocate for their stable of stars as they propel them into the casting market. No other profession markets its principals in the same way, which is why the three belong together.

	Roles *Judging / Advocacy*		*Roles* *Diagnosis / Service-Provision*	
Principals	*Conflicts* *Less Integral*	*Conflicts* *More Integral*		*Conflicts* *Less Integral*
Public Only or Included	*Journalism* *Criticism* *Government* *Judging*		*Accounting* *Government* *Engineering*	
Private Only	*Financial Services* *Show Business*	*University Teaching*	*Medicine* *Corporate Boards* *Law* *Financial Services*	

Table 1 Conflicts, Roles, and Principals

EX POST DECISIONS AND
EX ANTE IMPAIRMENT

... The question which any conflict-of-interest situation raises, of course, is whether a professional's judgment has been impaired or compromised. In exactly half of the professions under discussion, we have available (at least in principle) a way of answering this question by looking at the decision the impaired principal actually makes and comparing it with an independent standard of correctness. So, for example, for both journalists and judges—at least in respect of part of what they do—there is an empirical reality, a fact of the matter, against which their reporting or judging can be measured to see whether it moved off course. For both doctors, concerned as they are with health, and engineers, focused as they must be on safety, certain physical realities can be used to check a particular medical or engineering decision; peers can ascertain, in many cases, whether it was faulty or not. Finally, in both accounting—with its Generally Accepted Accounting Principles—and corporate directorships—where in a transaction involving a self-interested director, "unfairness of price ... after the fact" can "be evidence of unfairness of process"—certain numerical realities exist against which any putatively impaired decision can be measured.[3]

None of this is to say that empirical reality for journalists and judges, or physical reality for doctors and engineers, or numerical reality for accountants and corporate directors, is always knowable, accessible, or beyond contestation. But because it exists in principle, and in some cases it provides an added means of assessing the existence of impaired judgment: by looking at the actual judgment *ex post* instead of examining only the extent of the impairment *ex ante*. And this is so whether the impairment originates in external interests such as stockholdings or fees or in internal interests such as a conflicting role or principal. The availability of such a supplementary measure distinguishes these professions in a key way. After all, just because her judgment was impaired *ex ante*, it does not follow that any professional—no matter what his or her

field—was unable to rise above the impairment and produce a good judgment anyway *ex post*. In these six professions, there may be means of assessing whether this in fact happened.

Such extrinsic standards are, however, unavailable for the remaining professions. In the political world of the official, the partisan world of the lawyer, the academic world of university teaching (as distinct from university research, especially in the physical sciences), in the aesthetic (or what Tyler Cowen calls the "ambiguous") world of the critic, in the speculative world of the broker bringing a stock to market for the very first time—and in the political, partisan, aesthetic, and speculative world of the show-business agent—there are generally no independent empirical, physical or numerical standards against which to assess a professional's decision. Instead, these are realms of great and inveterate contestation. Absent such standards for assessing or second-guessing the professional's judgment *ex post*, it is not surprising that these professions (or, at least, those among them that have conflict-of-interest strictures) rely not just partially but wholly on prophylactic conflict-of-interest standards, standards which control impairments *ex ante*....

CONCLUSION

Does a professional occupy multiple roles with respect to the same principal? Are these judging and advocacy roles? Diagnostic and service provision roles? Are such role fusions integral to the individual professional, or are they amenable to organizational remediation? Does the professional exercise his or her role with respect to more than one competing principal? Are such interprincipal conflicts necessary or simply possible? Do her principals include the public or not? And are there external empirical, physical, or numerical standards available against which to assess the *ex post* results of any *ex ante* impaired judgment? These are the questions that separate the professions, that array them in a rich diversity—indeed, a patterned diversity—insofar as conflicts arising from within the professional-principal relationship are concerned. Conflicts arising from without that relationship, by contrast, show no such rich or patterned set of distinctions at all....

NOTES

1 Alan H. Goldman, *The Moral Foundations of Professional Ethics* (Totowa, NJ: Rowman & Littlefield, 1980); see also Everette E. Dennis, The Press and the Public Interest: A Definitional Dilemma, 23 *De Paul L. Rev.* 945 (1974).

2 See Andrew Stark, Beyond Quid Pro Quo: What's Wrong with Private Gain from Public Office? 91 *Am. Pol. Sci. Rev.* 115–II6 (1997).

3 Melvin Aron Eisenberg, Self-Interested Transactions in Corporate Law, 13 *J. Corp. L.* 1005 (1988).

—26—

CREATIVE ACCOUNTING

Some Ethical Issues of Macro- and Micro-Manipulation

Catherine Gowthorpe and Oriol Amat

INTRODUCTION

FINANCIAL STATEMENTS PROVIDE INFORMATION that is used by interested parties to assess the performance of managers and to make economic decisions. Users may assume that the financial information they receive is reliable and fit for its purpose. Accounting regulation attempts to ensure that information is produced on a consistent basis in accordance with a set of rules that make it reliable for users. However, communications between entities and shareholders may be deliberately distorted by the activities of financial statement preparers who wish to alter the content of the messages being transmitted. This type of distortion is often referred to as "creative accounting" or "earnings management." While opinions on the acceptability of accounting manipulation vary, it is often perceived as reprehensible.

This paper aims to identify some manipulative behaviour on the part of preparers of financial statements, taking into account some important ethical concerns. To achieve this, we will broaden out the usual definition of creativity in accounting to examine two principal categories of behaviour by the preparers of financial statements:

1. *Macro-manipulation.* When preparers become aware of a proposal to alter accounting regulation in a way that they feel will be disadvantageous to them, they may engage in lobbying to attempt to prevent the change. They attempt to bring about an alternative depiction of economic reality which is more favourable to them. In this paper we identify this type of behaviour as macro-manipulation.

2. *Micro-manipulation.* Creative accounting at an individual entity level involves preparers in altering accounting disclosures so as to create the view of reality that they wish to have communicated to users of the financial statements. This type of behaviour is described in this paper as micro-manipulation.

In both cases, preparers are interested in creating the financial statements to suit their own purposes. Of course, they may genuinely feel that their view of economic reality is preferable from all points of view. However, it is also possible that they seek to distort the picture to meet their own needs or desires. This paper identifies and discusses some significant ethical issues related to these manipulations of accounting reality....

THE ACCOUNTING
REGULATORY BACKGROUND

The "Infrastructure of Financial Reporting"

Schipper (2000) identifies four elements as forming part of "the infrastructure of financial reporting":

1. The effectiveness of mechanisms for identifying and resolving interpretative questions.
2. The structure, processes, independence, expertise, incentives and resource base of the standards setting organisation.
3. Auditing and auditors.
4. Enforcement of accounting standards and the supporting regulations.

In many national systems, one or more of these elements can be found to be relatively weak (for example, UK accounting regulation was relatively weak in respect of the first and second elements until the early 1990s when the national accounting regulatory system was overhauled).

Although international accounting regulation can claim to possess the first two of Schipper's (2000) four elements, it is vulnerable in respect of enforcement mechanisms and in respect of auditing and auditors. The IASB [International Accounting Standards Board] has to rely upon national systems and these are likely to be patchy and inconsistent. Fearnley and Macve (2001) identify some of the principal weaknesses prevalent in national systems of compliance: weak support mechanisms for auditors, lack of effective sanctions against directors, and differences between the legal framework and practice. Cairns (2001), summarizing the findings of his International Accounting Standards Survey published in 2000, notes a substantial level of non-compliance with international standards amongst companies claiming to adopt them.

Current developments in accounting regulation are proceeding rapidly, and the movements towards convergence and even international standardisation are welcomed in many quarters as helping to break down the barriers that hamper the operations of the international capital markets. However, there are some structural weaknesses in accounting regulation, as we aim to show here....

CONFOUNDING THEIR POLICIES: PREPARERS VS. REGULATORS

As Zeff (1978) observed, an important factor in accounting regulation is the sheer scale of the economic impact of accounting rules. The choice of an accounting rule may have a very significant impact on, for example, reported profits. The level of profitability of a commercial entity potentially affects distributions to owners, wage and salary negotiations, levels of pensions funding, ability to borrow or to raise further risk capital, taxes paid and so on. The stakes are high, especially in the context of major national or multi-national corporations whose activities have consequential effects on the lives of many people. Regulators may attempt to take the economic consequences of their actions into account, but they are likely to be confounded in many ways. For one thing, the consequences of actions are not always predictable (this is a significant ethical problem in its own right that will be the subject of a separate paper). Another problem, however, and the one with which this paper is concerned, is that when the stakes are high there are considerable incentives for financial statement preparers to confound the work of the regulators.

There are two principal means by which the intentions of the regulators can be confounded by preparers. First, preparers may lobby against proposals for rules that will have an adverse effect upon the financial statements prepared by their entities. Second, where strict application of the rules does not produce an accounting result that meets the needs of preparers, there is an incentive to misapply or to ignore the rule. This condition can pertain only where regulation is weak and/or is inadequately enforced. Both of these means involve manipulation, but the first is at the macro level of policy, and the second at the micro level of the business entity.

The term "creative accounting" is generally applied to the type of manipulation that takes place at the level of individual business entity. However, we characterise both the macro- and micro-activities as creative processes: in both manifestations preparers are busily engaged in managing financial accounting disclosures to their own ends. In both cases preparers assert the primacy of their own views of the world and seek to dominate the reporting process with their partisan version of the truth....

DISCUSSION

... User needs are ignored in the processes of manipulation at both macro- and micro-level.... The exercise of power of the preparers is both unjust and unfair to the supposed beneficiaries of the reporting process. The fundamental objective of financial statements is deemed to be the provision of useful information for decision-making, but it appears that accounting regulation is too compromised to fulfil this purpose properly.

Macro-manipulation is ethically questionable, since preparers engage in lobbying to attempt to prevent changes in regulations that they feel will be disadvantageous to them. Perhaps little would be wrong with this if their interests were not against the legitimate rights of those who are recipients of the financial information and will be taking decisions based upon deceiving reports. It is generally accepted that regulations have to be promulgated considering the common good of the whole society and not only the interests of a particular group.

Regarding both macro- and micro-manipulation, several ethical considerations arise. First, the system of accounting regulation shares many features with a system of law. We can look to values and ideas emanating from legal systems and systems of justice. Because such systems are societal

constructs we can look behind them to fundamental moral values such as truthfulness. Lyons (1984) discusses the values that are exemplified in legal processes, and identifies respect for the law as an important ethical element. "For example, well-designed procedures might encourage respect for law, and thus obedience to law, which many believe is a good thing" (196). It may be argued that regulations that can be easily flouted, perhaps because they have been poorly drafted, or because enforcement mechanisms are inadequate, do not command respect. Lyons is discussing the rule of law, but the point applies perhaps with even more force to non-statutory regulation such as accounting regulation. If it fails to command respect from those who are called upon to apply it, then regulatory failure is likely to ensue. In the context of the macro- and micro-manipulation of financial statements that we have identified as problematic in the existing system of accounting regulation, regulation loses authority if it is open to manipulation by a powerful interested party and if it cannot, in any case, be enforced.

Second, accounting regulators ... intend that financial statements should be useful to a wide range of users. The preparers of those financial statements act as intermediaries between the regulators and the users of the statements. They therefore occupy a powerful position as interpreters of the regulations, and, given the complexity of the business world, it is hard to see how some degree of interpretation can be avoided. Some, possibly many, preparers no doubt seek to interpret the regulation fairly and do not attempt to intervene in the regulatory process. However, it is clear that some preparers will adopt any means to hand to assert their own views. This can be seen as a misuse of the authority inherent in their position.

It is generally accepted that power implies responsibility and injustice is nothing other than abuse of power, as was pointed out 25 centuries ago (Plato, 1992). Similar ideas of justice, according rights to each person or group, have been held by many other moral philosophers throughout history. According to this conception of justice and others more recent, such as Rawls' well-known theory of justice (1972), there is no doubt that the preparers of financial statements who misuse the authority inherent in their position are committing injustices.

Empirical perceptions support these notions of justice. Fischer and Rosenzweig (1995) found accounting and MBA students to be critical of manipulated transactions and the abuse of accounting rules. Merchant and Rockness (1994) found that accountants were critical of such abuses, and Naser and Pendlebury (1992) discovered similar disapproval amongst UK auditors.

Moving from the general conceptions of injustice and unfairness, we can proceed to a more personal level where individuals make business decisions that may be more or less defensible. However, business life and decisions are not exempt from considerations of morality. As Solomon (1993) points out: "We can no longer accept the amoral idea that 'business is business' (not really a tautology but an excuse for being an unfeeling bastard)" (206). Any decisions to lobby from a partisan point of view, or to dress up financial statements, are made by a group of individuals who are themselves moral agents. An Aristotelian approach to business ethics requires virtue and good character in the individual.

It is helpful to bear in mind the idea of individual responsibility for wrong actions, and the notion of good character when examining the rather amoral arguments employed to excuse accounting manipulative behaviour. A defence of creative accounting behaviour can be made which rests upon agency and positive accounting theories. Revsine (1991) discusses the "selective financial misrepresentation hypothesis." He considers the problem in relation to both managers and shareholders, and argues that each can draw benefits from loosely drafted accounting standards that permit latitude in determining the timing of income. Shareholders can benefit from the fact that managers are able to manipulate earnings to "smooth" income since this may decrease the apparent volatility of earnings and so increase the value of their shares. The fact that

this involves deliberate manipulation and deceit is to be overlooked. Shareholders in this view become unwitting accessories to manipulation, but the agency's theoretical supposition is that such behaviour is inevitable given the conflict inherent in agency relationships.

Fundamentally, however, it is reasonable to question the validity of activities involved in dressing up financial statements to present an appearance that is not fully justified by the underlying economic activity. This type of micro-level creative accounting is informed by an intention to deceive the recipients of financial statements, and can therefore be regarded as morally reprehensible.

CONCLUSION

This paper has identified some manipulative behaviour on the part of preparers of financial statements, taking into account some important ethical concerns. To achieve this, we have tried to broaden out the usual definition of creativity in accounting examining two principal categories of behaviour by the preparers of financial statements: macro-manipulation and micro-manipulation.

At the macro-manipulation level, some preparers of financial statements are willing to engage in lobbying in an attempt to sway accounting regulators to produce rules that are advantageous to the interests of preparers. In doing so, they are likely to shift the attention of regulators away from the interests of users of the financial statements.

At the micro-manipulation level, some preparers engage in manipulation at their entities in order to present a biased view of economic reality.

Both categories of behaviour are likely to result in financial statements that may suit the purposes of the preparer but which are less than satisfactory from a user's point of view. From an ethical perspective these manipulations can be regarded as morally reprehensible. They are not fair to users, they involve an unjust exercise of power, and they tend to weaken the authority of the regulators. Where regulation is breached with impunity a diminution of respect for it and its procedures is likely to ensue.

REFERENCES

Accounting Standards Review Board [New Zealand]: (2002) Press release, 19 December, <http://www.asrb.co.nz> (accessed on March 8, 2004).

Cairns, D.: (2001) "IAS Lite Is Alive and Well," *Accountancy*, May, 88–89.

Fearnley, S. and R. Macve: (2001) "Global Problems," *Accountancy*, October, 110.

Fischer, M. and K. Rosenzweig: (1995) "Attitudes of Students and Accounting Practitioners Concerning the Ethical Acceptability of Earnings Management," *Journal of Business Ethics* Vol. 14, 433–44.

Lyons, D.: (1984) *Ethics and the Rule of Law* (Cambridge: Cambridge University Press).

Merchant, K.A. and J. Rockness: (1994) "The Ethics of Managing Earnings: An Empirical Investigation," *Journal of Accounting and Public Policy* Vol. 13, 79–94.

Naser, K. and M. Pendlebury: (1992) "A Note on the Use of Creative Accounting," *British Accounting Review* Vol. 24, 111–18.

Plato: (1992) *Republic*, translated by G.M. Grube, revised by C.D. Reeve (Indianapolis, IN: Hackett Publishing).

Rawls, J.: (1972) *A Theory of Justice* (Oxford: Oxford University Press).

Revsine, L.: (1991) "The Selective Financial Misrepresentation Hypothesis," *Accounting Horizons*, December, 16–27.

Schipper, K.: (2000) "Accounting Research and the Potential Use of International Accounting Standards for Cross-Border Securities Listings," *The British Accounting Review* Vol. 32, 243–56.

Solomon, R.C.: (1993) "Corporate Roles, Personal Virtues: An Aristotelian Approach to Business Ethics," in E.R. Winkler and J.R. Coombs (eds.), *Applied Ethics: A Reader* (Oxford: Blackwell), 201–21. Originally published in *Business Ethics Quarterly* Vol. 2(3), 1992, 317–30.

Zeff, S.A.: (1978) "The Rise of 'Economic Consequences,'" *The Journal of Accountancy*, 56–63.

—27—

TRUTH, NEUTRALITY, AND CONFLICT OF INTEREST

Judith Lichtenberg

...

THE NOVELTY OF JOURNALISTIC CONFLICTS OF INTEREST

... THE CONTEMPORARY JOURNALIST WORKING FOR a major daily, a news magazine, or a television network is expected to be neutral, fair, balanced, objective, and altogether "value-free." These traits form part of the norm of objectivity, which is a cornerstone of the professional ideology of journalists in liberal democracies....

What caused this shift to the values of objectivity and neutrality in journalism? The reasons have much to do with the nature of the contemporary mass media, which, unlike their ancestors, constitute not simply voices in the public forum but the forum itself. As a result, mass media organizations have in crucial respects become public institutions. Vested with enormous power, they must maintain at least the appearance of neutrality or impartiality....

That a news article or program secures widespread and ready agreement within a society does not prove, of course, that it is objective or neutral. It may simply mirror its audience's assumptions—held so strongly and deeply they go unrecognized as assumptions capable of challenge. It takes a certain degree of reflection and self-consciousness to see that "what goes without saying" may involve premises that those from a different culture might

question, and that it is not simply irrational to challenge. Consensus does not entail neutrality. On the other hand, members of a diverse society may regard all but the most banal truths as highly charged and nonneutral.

CASE I: THE JOURNALIST AS TABULA RASA

Should journalists participate in politically controversial activities? I want to consider four arguments for the view that they shouldn't.

1. "Journalists shouldn't have opinions on controversial issues; they should be neutral." This is a bad argument. An intelligent person will inevitably form opinions about some important moral and political issues. Even if opinionlessness were possible, it is not a trait we ought to cultivate. Engaged and informed people naturally form views about issues that confront them, and journalists may be expected to do likewise.

... The argument for an affirmative answer goes something like this: The journalist's duty is to report, or at least to seek, the truth. But if the journalist holds an opinion on an issue she is covering, that will bias her, she will abuse her position to advance her own view or at least she will fail to seek the truth because she believes she already possesses it.

This argument focuses simply on the possession of an opinion, ignoring its genesis and the manner in which it is held. But this is a mistake, and one that predisposes the conclusion.

... If I have arrived at a view through a fair and careful consideration of the evidence or of the arguments on all sides, I am involved in no conflict of interest. Why not? First, I have no hidden interest pushing me to one view or the other; my aim is to discover the most rational or defensible position. Second, insofar as I proceed fairly in considering the issues, I am unlikely, even having settled on a view, simply to dismiss the other side....

We often put this difference in terms of whether a person has a "vested interest" in a position or not. The question is whether there is "something in it for him"—whether he has some motive for believing it apart from a desire to believe the truth. The most common understanding of a vested interest suggests a material or personal interest: my stocks will go up or my brother will get hired. But someone with strong ideological commitments can likewise have a vested interest in a position....

In any case, the mere holding of a belief, even one relevant to a subject one is reporting, cannot involve one in a conflict of interest. Such a criterion is too stringent, because complete agnosticism is neither possible nor desirable. We may note in addition that a piece of reporting rarely threatens one's beliefs in the direct way that the assumption of conflict of interest supposes.

2. "Any journalist who gets politically involved has beliefs too strong to allow for fair journalism." Exactly what is the claim here? Is it that people who demonstrate or who join political organizations necessarily have stronger political beliefs than those who do not? Although some psychological experiments indicate that taking action can deepen commitment, it doesn't follow that joiners are always more committed than nonjoiners. And even if joining meant a stronger commitment or belief, that in itself would not justify prohibiting political involvements. For the crucial question is not how strong a journalist's beliefs are but whether they disable him from fair and accurate reporting. Without evidence of

a connection between the two, the prohibition remains unsupported....

Presumably, part of an editor's job is to assess the extent to which reporters possess the virtues necessary to their role—not to eliminate those who hold opinions, but to purge those whose opinions prevent them from reporting fairly. But they should decide these questions by examining a reporter's work, rather than her extracurricular activities.

We must recognize, however, the limitations in this approach. First, editors, like everyone else, will have trouble recognizing biases that match their own. Second, examining a news story is rarely sufficient to expose its biases; for that we need to know not only what it contains but what it leaves out. The sins of bias are largely sins of omission. This is a deep problem for the critique of journalism.

The conclusion nonetheless remains: the prohibition on political action cannot rest on the argument that action in itself demonstrates attitudes inappropriate for journalists.

3. "Journalists' political commitments will entangle them in relationships that compromise their ability to report news stories fairly and accurately." This is a serious concern. It is not so much journalists' political beliefs themselves that create the danger of bias but rather the personal and institutional relationships that normally flow from political involvement. A reporter actively involved in a political organization will probably find it difficult to write critically about it. Members of the group are his friends, his comrades....

4. "Journalists' political involvements create the appearance of bias and conflict of interest, and ought to be prohibited on that account." According to this argument, public political commitments create the appearance of conflict of interest because the public is likely to infer that a reporter is biased and incapable of fair and accurate reporting from knowledge of her political involvements....

Furthermore, potential sources may draw the same conclusion. They may be reluctant to talk to reporters they perceive as holding political beliefs contrary to their own. Since this could prevent a reporter from doing his job well, it is understandable that news organizations would prefer that their journalists' political affiliations remain unknown.

But arguments that rest policy conclusions on the mere appearance of impropriety require special justification. They naturally arouse suspicion: where appearance and reality diverge, why should we rest policy on mere and misleading appearances? Where they coincide, why not argue directly from reality? If, as I have argued, one's political beliefs or involvements need not taint one's reporting, why should one be bound to keep them under wraps? Having asserted that neutrality is nearly impossible and in any case undesirable, isn't the noninvolvement policy hypocritical?

To answer these questions, we must distinguish two different appearance-of-impropriety arguments. According to the first, the appearance of impropriety serves as a basis for policy just because it provides good reason to suspect genuine impropriety. On this view, if noninvolvement policies are justified on grounds of the appearance of conflict of interest, that is because the belief that such involvements bias journalists is a reasonable one.

Is this belief reasonable? It depends partly on how we characterize it. Is it the belief that people in general tend to be biased by their beliefs, or that journalists are? Journalists' professional training might make them less biased by their political beliefs than the ordinary person—not for reasons of moral or intellectual superiority but because journalists possess incentives to be unbiased that the ordinary person does not.

At the same time, the belief that political commitments bias journalists seems reasonable to the extent that—as I argued in the previous section—such commitments entangle journalists in personal relationships that make detachment and fairness difficult.

This first appearance-of-impropriety argument, then, gives modest support to prohibiting journalists' political involvements. According to the second argument, although the appearance of impropriety may be misleading, it does not follow that we should ignore it. If people believe that journalists' political views distort their work, that will undermine journalism's credibility. And this is a legitimate reason for instituting policies to counteract such beliefs.

Yet sometimes it seems downright wrong to fashion policies to suit people's false or unjustified beliefs. Even though people's racist or sexist beliefs may be very powerful, we do not think policies should be shaped around them. What's the difference? At least this: racist or sexist beliefs seriously demean and degrade minorities and women. But the belief that journalists' political commitments bias them does not degrade them in the same way. There is, I conclude, nothing wrong with designing policies around people's false beliefs, if the beliefs do not seriously degrade other people and if there is little hope of changing them.

To endorse the noninvolvement policy while denying that reporters can be or should be neutral is likely to invite condemnation from both sides. For the most natural defense of the policy relies on the premise of journalistic neutrality, while opponents tend to assert that neutrality is a fiction. Let me say a bit more, then, to defend my view.

First, I do not mean to deny that reporters (like everyone else) possess biases, and that these biases may influence their reporting. No one is perfectly detached and distanced from her opinions. But having opinions is not the same as being biased by them. The idea that bias is inescapable and poisonous leaves us no way to separate better reporting from worse. If we insist that every opinion is a bias we will simply have to invent a new distinction to separate good reporting from bad.

Second, I believe it is a common fallacy to overestimate the influence of journalists' personal beliefs on their reporting. The reason is mainly that we are likely to ignore structural and institutional forces and biases which, although often more subtle than personal political commitments, are also more powerful....

My justification for the prohibition on political involvement rests, then, on the surprising view that audiences are more likely to be biased by knowing journalists' beliefs than journalists are by having them. We can, of course, imagine circumstances in which the prohibition ought to be over-ridden. In emergencies, pressing moral and political concerns—civil rights, the threat of totalitarianism—may leave the professional with no alternative. ·

The force of the foregoing arguments must be evaluated in light of several variables:

Public acts and private acts. My view that reporters should not engage in political action rests largely on the public nature of their activities. But political involvement can be more or less public. A journalist might donate money to a cause, march anonymously in a demonstration, or work behind the scenes for an organization. On the other hand, she might sign petitions published in newspapers, testify before Congress, or in some other way make her commitments known.

How visible a person's actions are depends not only on the actions but on the person. Acts that would call immediate attention to Diane Sawyer or Ted Koppel might go entirely unnoticed if done by a reporter for a small city newspaper.

The relation between a journalist's political activities and her beat. If a journalist's political activities are thought to undermine either her credibility or her ability to report fairly, it stands to reason that some connection must exist between her beat and her political interests. We might see why a reporter active in the abortion-rights movement shouldn't cover abortion, but why shouldn't a reporter involved in environmentalism cover abortion? ...

The journalist's specific role and the nature of the organization for which she works. I have defended my view primarily with an eye to the news reporter for a mass media organization. By contrast, we don't expect writers for smaller-circulation periodicals whose audiences have a specifiable point of view to be neutral in the same way....

CASE II: THE SOUND OF MONEY TALKING

Should journalists accept income derived from sources other than the news organization for which they work? Ought they to disclose the sources, and even the amounts, of their income? These are the questions raised by the Periodical Press Gallery case.

We must consider three basic policy alternatives: (1) honoraria not accepted; (2) honoraria accepted; sources (and possibly amounts) disclosed; (3) honoraria accepted; sources not disclosed.

I believe that the first policy is best, but I do not regard it as a practical possibility, because journalists as a group would refuse to accept such a sweeping limitation on their earning power (or, as they are more likely to put it, on their freedom). Clearly this claim is arguable, but let us make it nevertheless. Which of the other alternatives is preferable?

To answer this question we must explain why ideally prohibiting honoraria altogether would be best. The rationale is hardly obscure: financial interests pose genuine threats to professional duty, because those who benefit materially from a source have a strong incentive to favor information supportive of it and to ignore information damaging to it.

In accepting such a view we mark a difference between the pull of material interests and the pull of prior beliefs and values. As I have acknowledged, beliefs and values no doubt bias those who hold them to some extent. But we do not count them prejudicial in the same way as material interests. Why not?

Here are several reasons. (a) Many of people's beliefs have some rational basis; i.e., they bear some connection to truth. The strength of the connection is a matter of dispute, but we can assert at least this much: that a person believes a given proposition provides some reason for thinking it true; that a person has a material interest in the truth of a given proposition provides no reason for thinking it true. (b) The investment most people have in particular political, social, economic, and other worldly beliefs—those beliefs reflected in the news—is rarely so great as to render them immune to change of view in light of contrary evidence or argument. The exceptions we call ideologues or fanatics or true believers. (c) When money talks, most people listen.

Yet none of these reasons alone supports the weight of the conclusion, because the truth of each is qualified. Even together, we may question how well they distinguish the biases of material interests from the biases of belief. Further doubt may be cast by those who, arguing in defense of journalists, find the imputation of greed and even bribery implausible and insulting.

For the motives of most journalists, including those who accept honoraria, are probably honorable. Journalists do not sell their souls when they give speeches for money. Indeed, the typical lecture-circuit journalist probably gives essentially the same talk ... to whatever organization invites him, no matter what its political orientation. So what's the problem?

The conflict of interest arises, however, not because most journalists can be bought in the crude way. Most people do not simply abandon all their scruples for money. For them the force of material conflicts of interest derives primarily from the relationship created between donor and beneficiary. It will be difficult for the reporter to write an exposé of the lobbying group that has just paid him thousands of dollars to give a speech. He now knows some members of the group; a relationship has been established; the group has benefited him....

Returning to the practical question, if we cannot expect journalists to forego honoraria, should we at least expect them to disclose them? Yes, because, as I have been arguing, honoraria pose a genuine threat of conflict of interest. Disclosure can serve two valuable functions: first, to alert the public to the possibility of conflicts; and second, to deter journalists from undertaking relationships that breed conflicts.

Is there any inconsistency in journalists' keeping their beliefs to themselves to avoid creating an appearance of impropriety while disclosing their finances, which may create the same appearance? I don't think so. Because material interests are more biasing than prior beliefs, the appearance of conflict of interest created by disclosure of honoraria is less misleading than the appearance of conflict created by public political involvement. And there are other asymmetries between the cases as well.

First, although each policy requires sacrifice, presumably journalists would prefer the option of political involvement, while they would rather not disclose sources of income—refraining from public political commitments, unlike refusing honoraria, is already deeply embedded in journalistic norms. It does not appear to demand more of journalists than can realistically be expected. In a different culture—fifth-century Athens or the founding fathers'—where public commitment was considered essential to a full life, this demand might be unreasonable.

Second, receiving honoraria reinforces the conservative institutional biases created by the corporate interests of news organizations and journalists' dependence on official sources, since large honoraria tend to come from powerful sources. By contrast, the biases, if any, created by journalists' political views spread out more evenly along the political spectrum.

Finally, journalists have long exerted pressure on politicians and public officials to disclose their financial involvements, on the assumption that these entangle them in conflicts of interest. Journalists' lack of embarrassment at failing to practice what they preach is remarkable. Their standard response, when they bother to make one at all, is that they are not public employees and so do not bear the same duties as politicians and public officials.

But in crucial respects the contemporary mass media are public institutions. As I argued earlier, they are not simply voices in the public debate; today they constitute the forum itself, where all significant debate takes place and to which anyone who hopes to make a difference must gain access. Just the concerns that justify financial disclosure by politicians and public officials apply to reporters for mass media organizations, who remind us of their public function whenever they invoke the First Amendment. Journalists are neither more nor less susceptible to compromising conflicts than the politicians they cover. In both cases, the question is whether they have motives at odds with their professional duties.

But suppose that a journalist only gives speeches for free. Does she not, by my argument, still form some of the ties that create conflicts of interest—meeting people, developing relationships, and the like?

She does, but not, perhaps, with the same degree of indebtedness. Conflicts of interest cannot be entirely eliminated; the argument for financial disclosure is that such a measure can at least contain them....

—28—

CONFLICT OF INTEREST IN ENGINEERING

Neil R. Luebke

ON THE BASIS OF SEVERAL SORTS OF EVIDENCE, conflict of interest is an important topic of professional ethics for engineers. The codes of ethics of major U.S. engineering professional societies include provisions dealing with conflicts of interest, although the wording and the amount of specificity vary. Conflict of interest is the largest category of ethical problems to be addressed between 1958 and 1998 by the National Society of Professional Engineers' Board of Ethical Review. Then, too, virtually every major corporation that employs engineers has policies governing conflicts of interest, and engineers in military or government service usually work under statutes or administrative rules that apply to conflicts of interest....

DEFINITION AND RELATED CONSIDERATIONS

The rationale for ethical provisions regarding conflicts of interest in professional settings rests in the nature of the professions themselves and the values they implicitly represent. Although other characteristics can be noted, it is fundamental that a professional puts his or her educated abilities of skill and judgment at the service of another party or parties who, in turn, customarily entrust the professional with a measure of authority to carry out the service. Especially with regard to engineering, many would add that "the public" is also a party to be served. Thus, technical competence in the exercise of abilities and moral integrity in the service rendered to clients, employers, and the public are two principal values which together might be termed "professional reliability." Technical competence by itself is not sufficient for reliability, for we can imagine a thoroughly skillful engineer who cannot be trusted to use the skills in legitimate ways on behalf of clients. Similarly, one can imagine a person of extraordinary integrity who, at the same time, is unable to work at an appropriate level of engineering competence. Because clients employ and trust engineering professionals to act in the client's interest, usually entrusting them with information and limited authority, and the public trusts them to act in socially beneficial or at least nonharmful ways, trustworthiness is clearly a major element in professional integrity. Conflicts of interest occur when a professional's dutiful and proper service to the client, employer, or public is threatened to be compromised by certain other "interests," possibly resulting in biased judgments or willfully contrary actions. Failure to avoid or to act properly in a conflict-of-interest situation violates the professional relationship with a client/employer, erodes the trustworthiness of the professional or professional firm in the eyes of both the client and the public, and may cast a shadow on the profession generally.

Several elements in the preceding paragraph may be elaborated. First, conflicts of interest can arise only for persons who have or are given authority to act in service to, and usually on behalf of, other parties.[1] In a broad sense, then, they can arise only for a person (or firm) insofar as that person (or firm) plays a fiduciary role. Engineers and other professionals play fiduciary roles in varying degrees. A chief consulting engineer overseeing the design and specifications for a major project may be positioned to confront more conflicts of interest than a fledgling, employed engineer merely carrying out prescribed tests on manufacturing materials.

Second, the "interests" in question should be understood, in accordance with the historically older sense of the word, as "material" or "objective" interests such as financial holdings, business associations, or family relationships rather than as "psychological" or "subjective" interests such as penchants for rock music, sunny beaches, the Boston Red Sox, or champagne. On the other hand, as the biblical "where your treasure is, there your heart will be also" is probably true, the material interests are assumed to have psychological accompaniments. Hence, the material interests may operate—using a term from [Kevin C. McMunigal]—as "perverse incentives," setting up a conflict-of-interest situation.[2] Yet, when we look for evidence of conflicts of interest we examine bank accounts, stock holdings, and family ties, not the results of psychological preference tests.[3] It is disclosure of facts of the former type, not the latter, that professionals are expected to make to their clients or employers. To interpret "conflict of interest" as meaning the opposition between psychological interests of two parties makes the extension of the term so broad as to be virtually useless.[4]

Third, conflict-of-interest policies that identify the relevant moral wrong as either an act of "disloyalty" or a diminution of "quality of judgment or service" play on ambiguities in these two terms. Insofar as an engineering professional should be a "faithful agent" of a client/employer, the professional should be committed (i.e., "loyal" in one sense) in professional service to the best interests of the party, and failure to avoid or act properly in a conflict-of-interest situation could be interpreted as a violation of loyalty in this sense. On the other hand, "disloyalty" normally connotes an intentional transfer of allegiance away from a previously pledged party. To categorize all actual conflicts of interest as acts of disloyalty is to assume the acts derive from anti-client/employer motives, whereas they might result from ignorance or insensitivity. Furthermore, categorizing them as instances of disloyalty may mislead policy writers into applying the term "conflict of interest" to such acts as buying a competitor's product or voicing dissatisfaction with one's employer.

In a similar way, the claim that a failure to act appropriately in a conflict-of-interest situation is wrong because it would impair the quality of the professional's judgment or service may play on the ambiguity of "quality." Quality can be judged on the basis of technical competence or on the basis of whether the judgment provides the best service *to the client.* What is often worrisome in conflict cases is not that the professional lacks competence but that the competence might be used on behalf of a party other than the client/employer/public. Of course, favoritism may result in decisions that are indefensible on objective grounds, but the issue is not a professional's lack of technical competence but, rather, a lack of integrity.

Finally, a few words should be said about appropriate responses to a conflict-of-interest situation. Of course, if the conflict situation can be foreseen and is serious, it should be avoided in most cases. Sometimes avoidance is not possible or at least not possible given reasonable limitations of knowledge. There may also be some cases, such as dearth of professionals in a given area, in which conflict situations should be tolerated for the sake of maximal use of limited professional services. Except for situations in which avoidance should have been practiced, there is usually nothing wrong with merely finding one's self in a conflict of interest; the ethical questions usually concern the choice (and often timing) of one's response. The minimal response, which may be sufficient in many cases, is disclosure of the facts of one's situation to some or all of the possibly affected parties. A second step, assuming some amount of disclosure, is recusal or some degree of nonparticipation by which one effectively removes one's self from the conflict situation. An extreme form of this step may be resignation. An alternative response when possible, again often assuming some amount of disclosure, is divestment of the threatening interests. Stock holdings can be sold and business associations can be terminated; however, family relationships are not so easily treated....

THE ASME V. HYDROLEVEL CASE

The most notable case of conflict of interest to affect an engineering society is *American Society of Mechanical Engineers v. Hydrolevel Corporation*, settled in 1983 after an antitrust judgment by the U.S. Supreme Court in 1982.[5] Even though all parties agreed that ASME did not financially benefit by the actions that led to the case, the courts found in favor of Hydrolevel, which ultimately settled with ASME for $4.75 million. As a result, ASME made major changes in its practices and policies. These policies may serve as a worthwhile example to other professional societies that could confront conflicts of interest on the part of their volunteer officers.

The Case

Since 1915, as a result of concern with a growing number of boiler accidents and the inability of the boiler manufacturing industry to regulate itself, the ASME has developed, published, and periodically reviewed a set of rules governing the construction of boilers. Almost all states and the majority of Canadian provinces have now incorporated the ASME Boiler and Pressure Vessel (B-PV) Code into law. Although ASME neither "enforces" the code nor renders judgments regarding the conformity of specific products, the importance of the code has given ASME—and derivatively the members of its code committees

and subcommittees—considerable power over the boiler industry. As a large share of the committee members are themselves volunteers who are employed by boiler manufacturers or related firms, the possibility of conflicts of interest seem obvious. What follows is a summary of the case. More detailed versions are readily available.

Since the 1920s, McDonnell & Miller (M&M), a Chicago firm had dominated the market for low-water boiler fuel cutoffs, producing mechanical devices incorporating a bulb floating on the surface of water within a chamber attached to the boiler. As dry-firing is a cause of many boiler explosions, the B-PV Code requires the cutoff device to shut down the fuel supply when the boiler water reaches the lowest visible level of the gauge glass. In 1965 Hydrolevel began marketing an electrical probe device ("Safgard"), mounted vertically inside the boiler, that used the boiler water as a ground for an isolated circuit. To compensate for the turbulence of the boiling water causing nuisance shutoffs as the water neared its lowest permissible level, the company installed a time-delay in some of its products. Hydrolevel's devices received the approval of Underwriters' Laboratories and Factory Mutual Engineering Laboratory as well as passing independent tests by the New York Telephone Company. Presumably the Hydrolevel control was not in violation of the B-PV Code. By 1970 Hydrolevel had begun to make inroads in the market dominated by M&M.

In March 1972, two meetings were held in Chicago that set in motion the events leading to the court decision more than a decade later. Present at both meetings were Eugene Mitchell, vice president of sales for M&M, John James, vice president of research for M&M, and T.R. Hardin, vice president of Hartford Steam Boiler Inspection and Insurance Company. M&M President James Solon was present at the second meeting. Hardin and James were, respectively, chair and vice chair of the ASME subcommittee on Code Section IV Heating Boilers. The upshot of the meeting was a brief, carefully drafted letter—to be sent by Mitchell on April 12—asking the ASME whether the code requires "that the cut-off operate immediately when the boiler water level falls to the lowest visible part of the water-gauge glass, or is it permissible to incorporate a time-delay feature in the cut-off so that it will operate after the boiler water level reaches some point below the visible range of the gauge glass?"[6] This letter was referred by B-PV Committee Secretary W. B. Hoyt to subcommittee chair Hardin, who included in his response, to be sent by Hoyt on April 29, the statement: "If a time-delay feature were incorporated in a low water fuel cut-off, there would be no positive assurance that the boiler water level would not fall to a dangerous point during a time delay period."[7] Subsequently, M&M used this statement in a memo that named Hydrolevel and told M&M representatives that "A time delay of any kind in the firing device circuitry would very definitely be against the ASME Code …" and "A time delay would defeat the intent of the ASME Code and this should definitely be brought to the attention of anyone considering the device which included a time delay in the low water cut-off circuitry." Hydrolevel began to experience rejections which, after several months, were traced to the M&M memo.

Hydrolevel President Russell Rymer insisted that ASME clarify or retract the April 29, 1971, letter, and the matter was referred to the Section IV subcommittee meeting in May 1972. Hardin had resigned as chair and had been replaced by James, who recused himself from the subcommittee deliberations and vote on Rymer's request. The subcommittee voted to reissue the letter minus its trouble-causing statement. However, when the matter came before the main committee, a new letter was drafted in which James was able to effect a slight revision. This letter was sent to more than 300 people in the boiler market. Although Hydrolevel seemed to have been satisfied with the new ASME response, a few years later, in July 1974, *The Wall Street Journal* published a story critical of the ASME and especially James's role in the Hydrolevel matter.

Shortly thereafter, the ASME Professional Practice Committee investigated and concluded at the end of 1974 that James had acted properly in absenting himself from the subcommittee meeting when the Hydrolevel complaint was dealt with. However, ASME investigators had not learned of the earlier meetings in Chicago or of James's revision in the final ASME letter. These facts came out in a hearing held by the Senate Judiciary Subcommittee on Antitrust and Monopoly in March 1975. Some ASME members favored revisiting the case, but ASME was soon put on the defensive by a second *Wall Street Journal* story in April 1975 alleging both that ASME had been duped by M&M and that its own internal investigation was a sham. The ASME Professional Practice Committee began a second investigation but was halted when, on August 23, 1975, Hydrolevel brought suit against M&M (now owned by ITT Corporation), Hartford Boiler Insurance, and ASME on the grounds, among others, of conspiracy to restrain trade in violation of the Sherman Antitrust Act.

In 1978, M&M and Hartford reached an out-of-court settlement with Hydrolevel for a total of $800,000, but ASME, convinced that as a nonprofiting not-for-profit organization it should not be held liable for the actions of its volunteer members, chose to proceed with the legal case that came to a jury trial in U.S. District Court for the Eastern District of New York in January 1979. Less than two weeks later, the six-person jury found the ASME in violation of the Sherman Act and awarded Hydrolevel $3.3 million. In accordance with the provisions of antitrust law, the judge trebled the judgment after deducting the $800,000 already received in settlement, making the judgment against ASME $7.5 million. By the time of the verdict, Hydrolevel had gone out of business and had only a month earlier sold its material assets as scrap for $55,000. Rymer, hospitalized for a heart condition, suffered a fatal seizure upon hearing the jury decision.[8]

After losing appeals in both the 2nd Circuit Court of Appeals in November 1980 and the U.S. Supreme Court in May 1982 (6–3 decision, with

Justice Blackmun writing the majority opinion), the case returned to the original District Court for a retrial to settle damages. Justice Blackmun's opinion stated that when ASME "cloaks its subcommittee officials with the authority of its reputation, ASME permits those agents to affect the destinies of businesses and thus gives them power to frustrate competition in the marketplace." Prior to a final court decision on damages, ASME settled out of court in October 1983 for $4.75 million. By this date Hardin had died and James had resigned from ASME. ASME policies also underwent change. As Charles Beardsley, editor of *Mechanical Engineering* magazine, puts it, "In the wake of the Hydrolevel ruling, the Society has changed the way it handles codes and standards interpretations, beefed up its enforcement of conflict-of-interest rules, and adopted new 'sunset' review procedures for its working bodies."[9]

NOTES

1 This statement incorporates through the words "have or are given" the sound distinction Michael Davis makes between "trustee" and "agent." See Davis, "Conflict of Interest," 3 *Encyclopedia of Applied Ethics* (1997). Virtually all engineering cases of conflict of interest involve agency.

2 See "Conflict of Interest as Risk Analyses" by Kevin C. McMunigal, Chapter 3 [of Conflict of Interest in the Professions, eds. Michael Davis & Andrew Stark (Oxford: Oxford University Press, 2001).]

3 This point is in contrast to the approach by Michael Davis, "Conflict of Interest," section I.C "Interest." Davis's case of a judge having a conflict of interest when a personal friend or enemy comes before his court is plausible, to my mind, only because there is an objective, historically describable relationship between the judge and the other party, not because the judge has a particular emotion while on the bench. Should a person with whom the judge has absolutely no prior contact, direct or indirect, come before the judge and the judge feels strong emotions of attraction or revulsion toward the person, I would not say a conflict of interest existed. The judge would be expected to exercise a strictly professional approach, which includes control over personal feelings.

4 Davis, "Conflict of Interest," properly terms this situation "conflicting interests" or "conflict of interests" in contrast to "conflict of interest."

5 See Charles W. Beardsley, The Hydrolevel Case—A Retrospective, *Mechanical Engineering*, June 1984, 66–79. An earlier article by Nancy Rueth appeared in *Mechanical Engineering*, June 1975, 34–36. The case's legal citations are 456 U.S. 556, 72 L. Ed. 2d 330, 102 S. Ct.1935. The appellate court's decision is found at 635 F.2d 118 (1980). Most of the first half of Paula Wells, Hardy Jones, and Michael Davis, *Conflicts of Interest in Engineering* (CSEP Module Series), (Dubuque, IA: Kendall/Hunt, 1986) is a detailed discussion of the case. Larry May, Professional Action and the Liabilities of Professional Associations: *A.S.M.E. v. Hydrolevel Corp.*, *Bus. & Prof Ethics J.* 1–14 (Fall 1982), contains an excellent discussion of the arguments in the case. May defends the judgment of the Court. An on-line discussion is also available at Texas A&M University's website: http://ethics.tamu.edu/ethics/.

6 Quote from "Exhibit B" in the record of the Wednesday, March 19, 1975, *Hearing of U.S. Senate Subcommittee on Antitrust and Monopoly of the Committee on the Judiciary*, 94th Cong., 1st Sess., 153–214 (Hon. Senator Philip A. Hart, chair).

7 Both this statement from Hardin and the following from M&M's memo are quoted from "Exhibit C" of the Senate subcommittee.

8 Associated Press story appearing in the *Wall St. J.* Feb. 5, 1979.

9 Beardsley, note 5 *supra*, at 73.

—29—

CONFLICT OF INTEREST AND POLICE

An Unavoidable Problem

Stephen Coleman

HOW DO CONFLICTS OF INTEREST ARISE IN POLICE WORK?

CONFLICTS OF INTEREST CAN ARISE FOR POLICE IN a number of ways. A conflict of interest may arise through a relationship that a police officer has with someone who is involved in a police matter, as either the victim of crime, or as an alleged offender, or even as a witness. A conflict of interest can arise through the financial dealings of a police officer, through other employment that a police officer has outside of the police service, through volunteer work, through study commitments, or even through an officer's deeply held personal or religious beliefs.

Let me illustrate this with some examples:

A. Suppose a police officer is called to a domestic dispute that involves the officer's sister. Both parties to the dispute claim that the other has assaulted them. One aspect of the role of a police officer in such a situation is to impartially assess the claims of both parties and determine whether any charges should be laid. But there is a clear conflict of interest in this case, since the officer's existing relationship with her sister will tend to influence that officer's ability to act impartially.

B. Suppose a police officer is a financial partner in a restaurant located within the officer's patrol area. Strict parking regulations apply in the area near the restaurant, so many of the restaurant's patrons park illegally. Part of the officer's role is to issue tickets to illegally parked cars, but if patrons of the restaurant are ticketed they are unlikely to return, which may have a severe effect on the profitability of the restaurant. In this case, the officer's financial interests are the cause of a conflict of interest.

C. Suppose a police officer is engaged in secondary employment as a bartender at a pub that is well-known for its generous support of community organizations and also for exceptionally good treatment of its employees. The publican is, understandably, extremely well-liked and respected in the local community. This off-duty officer has noticed that the publican's underage son, and a number of the son's friends (all also underage), are regularly served alcohol in the main bar by the publican. In this case, the conflict of interest for the officer arises out of conflicting duties to the officer's two employers.

These examples illustrate different types of conflicts of interest that may arise for police officers in the course of their work—all involve officers exercising their judgment on behalf of another (at least in some sense), all involve an interest that will tend to interfere with the proper exercise of that judgment, and in all cases there is an inherent conflict between the exercise of judgment and the influence on that judgment.

WHAT PROBLEMS CAN CONFLICTS OF INTEREST CAUSE IN POLICE WORK?

Conflicts of interest can cause problems in policing in three main ways.

1. The exercise of good judgment is an integral part of the professional role of police, as it is for any profession. Since conflicts of interest tend to affect the judgment of those involved in the conflict, they are thus a problem for police.
2. A police officer whose judgment is clouded by a conflict of interest may be led into inappropriate or illegal conduct.
3. Even when an officer acts completely impartially, conflicts of interest tend to create the appearance of bias in an organization that ought to appear to be, (and indeed ought actually to be) strictly impartial in the discharge of its duties to the community.

Problem (3) is particularly significant, since it exists not only in all cases of actual conflict of interest, and in all cases of potential conflict of interest, but also in all cases in which there is a perceived conflict of interest, whether or not that perception is accurate. In fact, problem (3) is doubly significant, since it will apply in situations in which either (1) or (2) also applies: if an officer's judgment is actually affected due to the conflict of interest, or if an officer is led into inappropriate conduct, these things will also have the effect of creating an impression of bias (which would, in these cases, be justified).

The appearance of bias is a significant problem only for those in positions of public trust. In other situations, perception is not a significant problem. Suppose, for example, person A is not in a position of public trust, but is instead exercising judgment on behalf of another individual. This other individual, B, believes, incorrectly, that person A has a conflict of interest in dealing with a particular matter. If person B approaches A, and alleges that A had a conflict of interest in this matter, all that needs to be done to show that the judgment was not improperly influenced, is for A to demonstrate to B that there was no conflict of interest in this matter.

On the other hand, when a person is in a position of public trust, the public perception of any situation will be extremely important. It is virtually impossible to explain to all members of the public why in a particular situation in which there was a perceived conflict of interest, there was not an actual conflict of interest; thus the only realistic way to deal with perceived conflicts of interest (whether the perception is accurate or not) is to treat them as though they were actual conflicts of interest. All those within the criminal justice system are bearers of the public trust. Police are a part of the criminal justice system, and the mere appearance of bias or impropriety within this system tends to undermine public confidence in the fair administration of justice. As the old adage goes, justice must not only be done, but must be seen to be done. Thus it is important for police officers, and for all members of the criminal justice system, to learn to deal properly with conflicts of interest, whether these conflicts of interest are perceived conflicts, potential conflicts, or actual conflicts.

HOW CAN A CONFLICT OF INTEREST BE DEALT WITH?

There are three usual methods of dealing with a conflict of interest:

1. Declare the conflict of interest.

2. Remove the conflict of interest.
3. Avoid the conflict of interest.

In police work, merely declaring the conflict of interest is rarely (if ever) going to be a final solution; the usual course of affairs would involve informing a supervisory officer of the conflict of interest, and then working with that supervisory officer to ensure that the conflict of interest is dealt with through removal of the conflict or avoidance of the conflict. An example of removing the conflict of interest might be police officers divesting themselves of the financial interests that are the cause of the conflict. An example of avoiding a conflict of interest would be a police officer distancing himself or herself from the particular matter giving rise to the conflict.

Thus police officers who realize that they may have a conflict of interest due to their financial holdings in a particular enterprise in their local police district (as in example B, mentioned earlier), ought to inform their supervisory officers of this potential conflict of interest and then take steps to remove the conflict, either through such officers divesting themselves of the financial stake in that enterprise or through transferring to another district so as to remove themselves from the potential conflict of interest.

Similarly, police officers who are called to deal with particular incidents may realize that there is the potential for a conflict of interest, and take steps to distance themselves from the incidents so as to avoid the conflict of interest. Thus were a police officer to be called to deal with a domestic disturbance at an address that she recognized as being the residence of a close relative (as in example A mentioned earlier), that police officer might inform her supervisor of the potential for a conflict of interest in that situation and request that a different officer be dispatched to the scene of the domestic disturbance.

Dealing with a conflict of interest in either of these ways, through removal of the conflict or through avoidance of the conflict, addresses all three of the problems previously mentioned: the possibility of clouded judgment, the possibility that an officer may be led into corrupt conduct, and the perception of bias.

Many police departments have recognized the problems that may be caused by conflict of interest and have introduced regulations that are designed to prevent some common conflicts of interest from arising. For example, some police departments have banned police from financial involvement in businesses within their patrol area, thus ruling out the possibility of conflicts of interest of the kind outlined in example B above. Some departments have also regulated secondary employment, either through a total ban or by a ban on employment within certain industries (such as the liquor, security, and sex industries) or by requiring police to gain approval from supervisors before undertaking any secondary employment. Such measures are designed to eliminate, or at least to minimize, the types of conflict of interest mentioned in example C. I have suggested that, where possible, police need to avoid not only actual and potential conflicts of interest, but also perceived conflicts of interest, even where that perception is inaccurate. It should be noted that even in situations in which police officers are not required to exercise any judgment, and in which a conflict of interest cannot therefore possibly arise (since the exercise of judgment is an integral part of a conflict of interest), members of the public may still perceive a conflict of interest, due to their false beliefs about the situation. This is especially likely to be the case where the actions an officer is forced to take coincide with the actions that the officer would be likely to take were the officer acting under the influence of some bias.

Consider, for example, a modified version of case A. Suppose that an officer is called to a domestic dispute involving her sister, and it is absolutely clear in this particular situation that the sister has been assaulted by her spouse. Let us also suppose that in this jurisdiction, officers are required to make an arrest in all domestic violence situations in which there is evidence that an assault has occurred. The officer has no option but to place the sister's spouse under arrest. There is therefore no exercise of judgment in this situation and no actual conflict of interest. Yet I think it quite clear that the sister's spouse will perceive a conflict of interest in this situation—that it will appear that the officer's judgment in the situation is biased—and thus that the public trust will have been violated. Police policies regarding conflict of interest need to take situations like this into account; such policies need to deal with actual, potential, and perceived conflicts of interest if they are to be of any real value....

—30—

CONFLICTS OF INTEREST AND THE PRESIDENCY[1]

Fritz Allhoff and Jonathan Milgrim

1. INTRODUCTION

ON NOVEMBER 8, 2016, DONALD J. TRUMP WAS elected President of the United States.... At the time of his election, President Trump "appears to own or control more than 500 businesses in some two-dozen countries around the world."[2] His unwillingness to disclose his tax information makes the extent of his wealth unknowable, but even by conservative estimates, he is still the wealthiest president in United States history—and very likely has more inflation-adjusted wealth than all his predecessors combined.[3] Standard practice, at least for the past several presidents, has been to divest their wealth or to place it into blind trusts.[4] However, President Trump has been reluctant to do this, and it is far from clear that it would be possible even if he wanted to.

This reluctance has raised questions about whether the President has conflicts of interest between his myriad business holdings and his role as President. Trump allies, as well as many non-supporters, have argued that the President is not bound by standard conflict of interest laws.[5] In addition, the complex nature of President Trump's holdings means that he regularly receives income from businesses on foreign soil, and that foreign states routinely spend money in domestically-located businesses.[6] This international component of his profile raises questions, not just about conflicts of interest, but also about the applicability of the Emoluments Clause of the United States Constitution.[7]

In this article, we will explore the theoretical foundations and practical applications of conflicts of interest, specifically as applied to the presidency. Though we conclude that the President is statutorily immune from conflicts of interest (i.e., as a matter of law), we go on to investigate whether this conclusion can be morally justified.... While we recognize that the Trump presidency has catalyzed interest in these questions, we propose to consider the broader theoretical issues rather than specifically focusing on his holdings or on his presidency....

2. CONFLICTS OF INTEREST

... As is relevant here, the federal government has approached conflicts of interest fairly narrowly, focusing principally on economic conflicts. The Ethics in Government Act was enacted in 1962, and 18 U.S.C. § 208 specifically addressed government employees with financial interests.[8] The upshot is that government employees are generally prohibited from participating in matters in which they have financial interests.[9] And the Act goes on to characterize two tiers of penalty for violation: anyone who violates the prohibition faces up to one year imprisonment or a fine, whereas anyone who *willfully* violates the prohibition faces up to five years imprisonment or a fine.[10]

Turning now to the principal focus of this article, what ultimately matters is that the President is exempt from 18 U.S.C. § 208. The way we get there, though, is somewhat circuitous. When the Act was passed in 1962, the President would seemingly have been bound by the conflict of interest strictures. In 1972, Richard Nixon won his presidential re-election, with Spiro Agnew as his running mate. In 1973, Agnew came under investigation for various improprieties and was ultimately charged with having accepted bribes of more than $100,000 during his time as Baltimore County Executive, Governor of Maryland, and Vice President.[11] He pled no contest to having accepted undeclared income on the condition that he resign as Vice President.

Nixon then appointed House Minority Leader Gerald Ford as Vice President; when Nixon resigned after Watergate in 1974, Ford became President. Ford selected former governor of New York Nelson Rockefeller for Vice President, and conflict of interest issues surged to the fore given Rockefeller's extensive wealth and holdings. The then-Chairman of the Committee on Rules and Administration was Senator Howard Cannon (D-Nevada), who sought clarification from the Justice Department as to whether Rockefeller was bound by the conflict of interest statute—and, if so, what he would need to do in terms of divesting his assets to assume the vice presidency.

Acting Attorney General Laurence Silberman argued that Rockefeller was not so bound, and for several reasons. First, Silberman claimed that the Twenty-Fifth Amendment—which details presidential removal and succession—placed no such encumbrances on the (prospective) Vice President.[12] Second, Silberman cautions "serious doubt" against an interpretation of 18 U.S.C. § 208 that would bind the President and continued that it would seem "almost certain" that the President and Vice President should be treated alike under this statute (i.e., if the President is not bound, then neither is the Vice President).[13] Silberman points

out that neither officer is explicitly mentioned under the purview of the statute, which only speaks to an "officer or employee of the executive branch." He also points to the legislative history of §202–209, noting no evidence that these were meant to apply to "the Chief Executive and his immediate successor."[14] He also points to an influential report, maintaining that that President and the Vice President "must inevitably be treated separately from the rest of the executive branch."[15] As the House and Senate committees that formulated the Ethics in Government Act were substantially influenced by this report, Silberman thinks it implausible that a break from this edict would have been nowhere noted in committee notes.[16]

Whether Silberman's arguments were compelling or not was ultimately rendered moot when Congress revisited this issue in the Ethics Reform Act of 1989. In this legislation, Congress amended 18 U.S.C. § 202—the definitions section of the Ethics in Government Act—such that "the terms 'officer' and 'employee' [in § 208 and elsewhere] *shall not* include the President, the Vice President, a member of Congress, or a federal judge."[17] And so, statutorily, the President is exempt from the conflict of interest provision in 18 U.S.C. § 208. This is a point worth emphasizing: for all the talk about whether the President is subject to conflicts of interest, he is quite literally exempted from those requirements under federal law.[18]

3. NORMATIVE FOUNDATIONS

Whether the President *is* exempt portends a different question from whether he *should* be. In other words, it is completely fair for us to question the wisdom of the revisions to 18 U.S.C. § 202, even if such a project is merely academic. Perhaps surprisingly, there is limited discussion on the Ethics Reform Act of 1989, at least on this issue in particular.[19] But, broadly speaking, two separate answers have been given as to the justification for this exemption. The first is that the President—or any other exempted official—certainly has the ability to divest himself of conflicts of interest, regardless of a legal requirement to that end. Most recent presidents have placed their assets in blind trusts, even if they had no legal obligation to do so; these include Lyndon Johnson, Jimmy Carter, Ronald Reagan, George W. Bush, George H.W. Bush, and Bill Clinton.[20] President Obama did not, but his assets were substantially less complicated, principally comprising mutual funds and bonds.[21]

This answer strikes us as particularly weak: why make it supererogatory for elected officials to dissolve conflicts? If conflicts are ethically significant—and we think they are—then compliance with relevant requirements should hardly be optional. An analogous line of reasoning would seem to be that presidents should not commit crimes, but we will simply exempt them from all criminal liability on the theory that they will do the right thing and not commit crimes in the first place. This is just not how criminal law—or, more specifically, criminal deterrence—works. Nobody should get a free pass on some maligned activity simply on the hopes that they will not exercise that freedom. And so, this answer could factor into some broader constellation of considerations, under which, given some reason to ground the exemption, presidents nevertheless have the option of going above and beyond their legal obligations, but we still need a story as to what these broader considerations or reasons are supposed to be.

The second putative answer is that it is simply not practical to enact a conflict-of-interest regime that would both restrict the President and simultaneously allow for effective governance. In other words, we could postulate two different kinds of answers as to why the President should not be exempted from conflicts of interests; one approach would be to argue against the exemption on moral grounds, the other of which would be to argue against it on pragmatic grounds.[22] One difference between these two approaches is modal: the pragmatic arguments are contingent on various features (e.g., the structure of our government, the nature of politics, etc.), whereas moral arguments may not be (e.g., lying is at least prima facie wrong, regardless of the empirical details).

This strategy is not particularly novel. For example, in an influential article, David Luban considers arguments for and against the adversarial legal system we have in the United States, as contrasted with the inquisitorial system more popular in Europe.[23] The adversarial system has all sorts of flaws, specifically insofar as it prizes advocacy over outcomes;[24] for example, the criminal defense attorney's fiduciary role is to secure an acquittal for his client *regardless* of whether the client actually committed a crime.[25] This is not to say that the adversarial model is bankrupt. Rather, it serves other moral ends as well, such as creating trust between lawyers and clients—with their communications protected by confidentiality—thus promoting disclosure and communication.[26] But as to whether we should, say, *switch* from the adversarial model to the inquisitorial one, Luban points to transactional costs. And so even if the inquisitorial model might eradicate some of the foibles of the adversarial model, the adversarial model might end up being pragmatically justified—as opposed to morally justified—on the grounds that switching would be too onerous.

For present purposes, we are of course less concerned with the merits of this argument than the structural approach, namely in drawing a distinction between moral values and pragmatic ones. Then turning to whether the President should be exempted from conflict of interest requirements, we can explore the possibility of a pragmatic justification, as opposed to a moral one. This is ultimately what Luban does in the legal case, arguing that pragmatic justifications are weaker than more robust moral arguments, but that pragmatic justifications can be justificatory nonetheless, particularly in the absence of convincing moral arguments to the contrary. While Luban does not explain his thinking this way, we see these pragmatic arguments as functioning something like tie-breakers when the score is close. And, importantly, this does not even require the exemption to otherwise enjoy some positive moral valence; even if there are reasons against the exemption, pragmatic arguments can be countervailing. All in, they are weaker than their moral counterparts, but this is simply meant to be a heuristic insofar as some richer discussion on the metaphysics of justification would take us too far afield.

So why, then, is it so onerous for the President to resolve conflicts of interest before entering the White House? In some ways, it is not; per above, most presidents have done just that, principally through blind trusts. We therefore need to set aside a facile argument that proceeds as follows. Suppose the President-elect is reluctant to let go of his holdings in Apple, but recognizes that such holdings might bias his decision-making, or—perhaps more relevantly—raise the specter of impropriety. The resolution here is simple: by creating a blind trust and assigning an executor, the President-elect no longer knows whether he has holdings in Apple. He therefore would not have any reason to pursue policies that disproportionately favor Apple over its competitors insofar as such policies might be detrimental to his own financial interests. Rather, not knowing what his holdings are, impartiality would be the most prudent course.

But this sort of argument can only go so far. Suppose the President is faced with a certain policy conundrum, and must choose one of two resolutions. The first is pro-business, likely to benefit the market, including the preponderance of his holdings therein. The second is regulatory, likely to hurt the market, again including the preponderance of his holdings.[27] The blind trust approach does not actually help remove the conflict here because the President can be reasonably certain as to which policy will broadly promote his economic interests.

And this argument generalizes. The President makes myriad decisions, any of which might affect his interests—particularly economic ones. Even drawing a distinction between synchronic and diachronic interests fails to help. For example, we might postulate a difference between some policy decision that would *immediately* affect the President's net worth, as opposed to some policy decision that would curry favor with some sector of industry, paving the way for speeches worth hundreds of thousands of dollars after leaving office. For all intents and purposes, the latter effectuates a conflict of interest with regards to current policy (i.e., against future gains), but is completely unnavigable pragmatically. In other words, it would be wholly unreasonable to preclude the President from doing *anything* during his tenure in the White House that *might* result in lucrative remuneration after leaving office.

This is a substantial argument against wholly binding the President from conflicts of interest, simply on the grounds that such a bind would be pragmatically impossible.[28] A critic might nevertheless try to draw distinctions, saying that these sorts of diachronic worries need not get in the way with regards to synchronic conflicts. Maybe, but then all that would have to get sorted out, and it is far from obvious how the principled resolution would go. Is it really different for a President to adopt some contemporaneous policy that would benefit Apple and his associated holdings, rather than adopting that same policy in the hope that he will be invited to Apple's Cupertino corporate headquarters a handful of years later? We just do not see this as a viable distinction.

Or, to try another tack, there would be substantial transactional costs in implementing associated policy, and to what end? The speaking circuit—both literally and metaphorically—awaits regardless, and so, at best, the prospective compensation is delayed, not barred. Meanwhile, there are other things to be done, like leading the country. And resources—whether the President's or others'—diverted into conflict of interest analysis inherently distract from these other pursuits. So, given both these transactional costs and the functional impotence of such an approach, we see a compelling argument in favor of the exemption that 18 U.S.C. § 202 offers. To be sure, this is not an argument that the President *should not* resolve conflicts of interest, but simply that he should not be *required* to do so. It is also not an argument that the President is *definitionally incapable* of being conflicted. Rather, our view is far more modest than either of these more ambitious proposals, both of which we think are radically implausible....

NOTES

1   This reading is adapted from Fritz Allhoff and Jonathan Milgrim, "Conflicts of Interest, Emoluments, and the Presidency," *International Journal of Applied Philosophy* 31.1 (2017): 45–67. For present purposes, we have removed the discussion of emoluments; please refer to the full article for further details.

2   Alex Altman, Joseph Hincks, and Tara John, "Trump's Many, Many Business Deals in 1 Map," *Time*, January 10, 2017. Available at http://time.com/4629308/donald-trump-business-deals-world-map/ (accessed June 25, 2017).

3   Ethan Wolf-Mann, "Trump Has More Money than Every U.S. President Combined," *Money*, September 25, 2015. Available at http://time.com/money/4041300/donald-trump-has-more-money-than-every-u-s-president-combined/ (accessed June 25, 2017).

4   Anne VanderMey and Nicolas Rapp, "Who Needs a Blind Trust?" *Forbes*, October 22, 2012. Available at http://fortune.com/2012/10/22/who-needs-a-blind-trust/ (accessed June 25, 2017).

5   Chris Cillizza, "This Is the Single Most Dangerous Thing Donald Trump Said in His *New York Times* Interview," *The Washington Post*, November 22, 2016. Available at https://www.washingtonpost.com/news/the-fix/wp/2016/11/22/this-is-the-single-most-dangerous-thing-donald-trump-said-in-his-new-york-times-interview/?utm_term=.34f171ac8f39 (accessed June 21, 2017). See also Lauren Carroll, "Giuliani: President Trump Will Be Exempt from Conflict-of-Interest Laws," *Politifact*, November 16, 2016. Available at http://www.politifact.com/truth-o-meter/statements/2016/nov/16/rudy-giuliani/giuliani-president-trump-will-be-exempt-conflict-i/ (accessed June 21, 2017). See also Glenn Kessler and Michelle Ye Hee Lee, "Trump's Claim that 'The President Can't Have a Conflict of Interest,'"

Washington Post, November 23, 2016. Available at https://www.washingtonpost.com/news/fact-checker/wp/2016/11/23/trumps-claim-that-the-president-cant-have-a-conflict-of-interest/?utm_term=.914a98c76a44 (accessed June 21, 2017).

6   Altman et al. (2017).

7   For more discussion, see Allhoff and Milgrim (2017). See also David Fahrenthold and Jonathan O'Connell, "What Is the Emoluments Clause?: Does It Apply to President Trump?" *The Washington Post*, January 23, 2017. Available at https://www.washingtonpost.com/politics/what-is-the-emoluments-clause-does-it-apply-to-president-trump/2017/01/23/12aa7808-e185-11e6-a547-5fb9411d332c_story.html?utm_term=.fc0c54816027 (accessed June 25, 2017).

8   18 U.S.C. 208(a).

9   Scott H. Amey, "The Politics of Contracting" [Appendix F] (Washington, DC: Project of Government Oversight, 2004). Available at http://pogoarchives.org/m/gc/politics-of-contracting/AppendixF.pdf (accessed June 16, 2017).

10 18 U.S.C. § 216 (emphasis added). The fines are controlled by 18 U.S.C. § 3571 and range from $5,000 to $500,000, depending on various considerations.

11 Richard M. Cohen and Jules Whitcover, *A Heartbeat Away: The Investigation and Resignation of Spiro T. Agnew* (New York: Viking Press, 1974).

12 Laurence Silberman, "Dear Mr. Chairman," September 20, 1974 (1974b). Available at https://fas.org/irp/agency/doj/olc/092074.pdf (accessed June 21, 2017). See also U.S. Constitution, Amendment XXV.

13 Silberman (1974b), 2.

14 *Id.*

15 *Id.*, 2–3. Referencing Special Committee on the Federal Conflict of Interest Laws, Association of the Bar of the City of New York, *Conflict of Interest and Federal Service* (1960).

16 *Id.*, 3.

17 18 U.S.C. 202 (emphasis added). Available at https://www.congress.gov/bill/101st-congress/house-bill/3660/text (accessed June 21, 2017).

18 It further bears emphasis that even the liberal media agrees with this. See, for example, Carroll (2016), Cillizza (2016), and Kessler and Lee (2016).

19 More generally, see Eric J. Murdock, "Finally, Government Ethics as if People Mattered: Some Thoughts on the Ethics Reform Act of 1989," *George Washington Law Review* 58 (1989): 502–25.

20 Kessler and Lee (2016). See also VanderMey and Rapp (2012). Available at http://fortune.com/2012/10/22/who-needs-a-blind-trust/ (accessed June 25, 2017). See also Laura Lee, "What Is a Blind Trust?: And Why It May Be Donald Trump's Best Option," *Fox Business*, December 13, 2016. Available at http://www.foxbusiness.com/politics/2016/12/13/what-is-blind-trust-and-why-it-may-be-donald-trumps-best-option.html (accessed June 25, 2017).

21 VanderMey and Rapp (2012).

22 We do not take these grounds to be mutually exclusive (e.g., all else equal, expedience is a moral good), but rather to identify broadly different strategies.

23 David Luban, "The Adversary System Excuse," in *The Good Lawyer* (Totowa, NJ: Rowman and Allanheld, 1983), 83–122.

24 Elliot D. Cohen, "Pure Legal Advocates and Moral Agents: Two Concepts of a Lawyer in an Adversary System," *Criminal Justice Studies* 4.1 (1985): 38–59. Reprinted in Allhoff and Vaidya (2008), pp. 368–78.

25 Monroe H. Freedman, "Professional Responsibility of the Criminal Defense Lawyer: The Three Hardest Questions," *Michigan Law Review* 64 (1965): 1469–84. Reprinted in Allhoff and Vaidya (2008), 326–37.

26 Bruce M. Landesman, "Confidentiality and the Lawyer-Client Relationship," *Utah Law Review* 4 (1980): 765–86. Reprinted in Allhoff and Vaidya (2008), 388–404.

27 Of course, the policy implications will likely be more variegated; this is a simplified example for illustrative purposes.

28 This is particularly true with regards to President Trump; see Rivkin and Casey (2016).

PHARMACEUTICAL PAYMENTS AND OPIOID PRESCRIPTIONS

Fritz Allhoff

1. BACKGROUND

OPIOIDS KILL MORE THAN 100 AMERICANS EACH day.[1] While illegal heroin and fentanyl—and, increasingly, fentanyl-laced heroin—are substantial culprits in this epidemic, more than 40 per cent of opioid-related deaths are owing to legally prescribed opioids. The most common of these include methadone, oxycodone (e.g., OxyContin), and hydrocodone (e.g., Vicodin). Prescription overdose deaths most often afflict people aged 25–54 years and are highest among non-Hispanic whites, American Indians, and Alaska Natives. The rates are approximately 6.2 deaths per 100,000 men and 4.3 deaths per 100,000 women. Within the United States, there are geographical variations in prescription opioid deaths, with rates being the highest in West Virginia, Maryland, Maine, and Utah. While the prescription opioids can be lethal themselves, they also can lead to use of more lethal (and illegal) opioids, such as the aforementioned heroin and fentanyl. Prescription rates have generally declined nationally, but are still as much as three times those of fifteen years ago.[2]

Pharmaceutical companies are, of course, invested in the sale of their drugs. And so they market those drugs to physicians.[3] For present purposes, let us consider "non-research opioid-related payments," which include speaking fees and/or honoraria, meals, travel, consulting fees, and education. In 2014, over 25,000 physicians—approximately 7 per cent of the national total—received such payments from pharmaceutical companies, which totaled over $9,000,000.[4] Speaking fees and/or honoraria were the largest categories, accounting for over $6,000,000. The payments were generally small, with only a couple hundred physicians receiving more than $1,000 each; the median meal payment, for example, was only $13.[5]

A recent study investigated the extent to which these non-research payments correlated to the prescription rates of their beneficiaries. The key finding of this study was that physicians who did not receive opioid-related payments prescribed fewer opioids in 2015 than in 2014. However, physicians who did receive opioid-related payments prescribed more opioids in 2015 than in 2014, by 9.3 per cent. And so the upshot is that physicians who receive payments from pharmaceutical companies are more likely to prescribe opioids than physicians who do not receive those payments.

While the nation continues to wrestle with prescription practices, the Centers for Disease Control (CDC) has undertaken a range of steps. In 2016, it released prescription guidelines, the aim being to "ensure that patients have access to safer, more effective chronic pain treatment, while reducing the number of people who misuse opioids, develop opioid use disorder, or overdose."[6] This initiative was specifically aimed to target "the prescribing of opioid pain medication to patients 18 years and older in primary care settings outside of active cancer treatment, palliative care and end of life care."[7] In other words, the target demographic is the one least in need of indefinite access to opioids, and the one with the highest propensity for long-term abuse and dependency.

As of 2018, 46 states are implementing prescribing practices in accordance with the new CDC guidelines. Providers have undertaken thousands of hours of continuing education regarding these guidelines and the majority of states' Medicaid programs have also prioritized compliance with the guidelines; even the associated mobile app has been downloaded over 30,000 times.[8] The effectiveness of these educational initiatives will be evaluated as more data becomes available, but they certainly come at a critical time, with myriad public health considerations hanging in the balance.

2. ANALYSIS

For the purposes of this case study, let us set aside the opioid epidemic more generally and focus on the potential conflict-of-interest issues that attach to pharmaceutical companies' payments to physicians, and the propensity of those payments to increase opioid prescriptions. At first pass, this might look like an egregious dereliction of professional responsibility. A physician's primary obligation is to his or her patients, as is underwritten by the four core values of medical ethics: beneficence, non-malfeasance, autonomy, and justice. Over-prescribing opioids runs afoul of all these, most obviously non-malfeasance insofar as the propensity for opioid addiction is deeply harmful. But addiction also undermines autonomy, by subjugating the patients' autonomous will to the neurochemical correlates of dependence. And over-prescribing hardly *helps* anything, either (cf., beneficence); aside from the propensity of harm, *over*-prescription is, ex hypothesi, not in the patients' best interests. Justice is always a bit trickier to analyze, but suffice it to say that over-prescribing potentially lethal drugs is not a just practice—more directly, some of the geographic variations we see in opioid overdoses cut against

principles like equality if some populations are at greater risk than others.

And so we can see that over-prescribing opioids violates physicians' obligations to patients. But that alone does not make it a conflict of interest: those derelictions could simply be the result of ill will, incompetence, or a host of other factors. What makes it a conflict of interest is that they are getting paid—by the pharmaceutical companies no less—to over-prescribe. This is actually worse than other sorts of reasons that might undergird over-prescription. Incompetence, for example, can be remediated by further education or training. But the ongoing availability of money does not go away, the temptation does not go away, and the "incentives" always push against professional obligation.

This analysis, though, presupposes that physicians prescribe more opioids *because* of the availability of non-research payments. However, the Hadland et al. study cited above does not bear this out; that study is completely silent as to *why* physicians who receive the payments are more likely to prescribe the opioids. Maybe it is because of the payments, but maybe it is for some other reason altogether. More technically, the correlation between the payments and the prescription rates does not establish that those increased prescription rates are caused by the payments.

For example, the time spent with pharmaceutical representatives over a meal might well serve an educational function, alerting physicians to risks and benefits, best practices, and so on. Perhaps the physicians who did not have those meals were simply being conservative—lacking full information or resources and choosing to err their prescriptive practices on the side of caution. Or perhaps the interactions with the pharmaceutical representatives led to implicit bias: the physicians might simply be—and probably are—susceptible to marketing like any of the rest of us. And so maybe they did not consciously increase their opioid prescriptions at all, but rather were affected in other ways.

In other words, the strengths or merits of this study need not presuppose any untoward motivations on the part of the physicians. They could be bad professionals, chasing the money. Or they could be good professionals, critically engaging the pharmaceutical representatives. Or they could just be normal people, subject to all sorts of subconscious processes, none of which cuts against their professional integrity. I would certainly think that *at least some of* the correlation could be explained away by these less nefarious explanations, just as I would equally think that at least some of it could be explained by exactly these more nefarious motivations. But we cannot simply read the intentions or motivations off of the existing data.

It is also important to note what this argument is not: specifically, there is no argument here that we should not have greater oversight and regulation of prescriptive practices. Nor is there any argument that pharmaceutical representatives should have continued unfettered access to physicians, or even that non-research payments should be allowed at all (i.e., maybe they should be banned, or at least heavily restricted). Rather, the observation is far narrower, which is simply that there are a range of reasons that prescriptive practices could correlate to non-research payments. And that the professional integrity of physicians should probably be assessed on a case-by-case basis, rather than as a blanket indictment of any that receives payments from pharmaceutical representatives. There might be other reasons that no physician should accept these payments—like optics—but those reasons would be separate from ways in which professional responsibility intersects with putative conflicts of interest.

NOTES

1   Ayesha Rascoe and Scott Horsley, "Signing Opioid Law, Trump Pledges to End 'Scourge' of Drug Addiction," *NPR*, 24 October 2018, https://www.npr.org/2018/10/24/660205718/signing-opioid-law-trump-pledges-to-end-scourge-of-drug-addiction.

2   Centers for Disease Control and Prevention, "Prescription Opioid Data," (2017), https://www.cdc.gov/drugoverdose/data/prescribing.html.

3   Professional ethics has, in my view, generally overbalanced the focus on physicians against other health care providers (e.g., nurses, physician assistants, etc.)—elsewhere in this volume, we have tried to remediate that oversight. But, regarding opioid prescriptions, the focus is more appropriate since many other providers are not able to prescribe narcotics or other controlled substances.

4   Almost half of this was paid out by a single pharmaceutical company, INSYS Therapeutics, which manufactures a fentanyl-based sublingual spray, Subsys. Subsys is primarily used for pain relief in cancer patients.

5   Scott E. Hadland, Magdalena Cerdá, Yu Li, Maxwell S. Krieger, and Brandon D.L. Marshall, "Association of Pharmaceutical Industry Marketing of Opioid Products to Physicians with Subsequent Opioid Prescribing," *JAMA Internal Medicine* 178, no. 6 (2018): 861–863.

6   CDC, "Prescription Opioid Data."

7   CDC.

8   CDC.

DISCUSSION QUESTIONS

1. What should the relationship between doctors and pharmaceutical companies be? How might we formulate this relationship in order to mitigate conflicts of interest?

2. Do doctors have an obligation to inform their patients when they are receiving non-research funding from pharmaceutical companies?

3. If it was found that non-research funding did not directly cause doctors to overprescribe patients certain opioids, would other factors, like representatives meeting with physicians or marketing exposure, still merit cause for concern? If yes, then what limits should be imposed on pharmaceutical companies in order to avoid these scenarios?

4. Should pharmaceutical companies advertise addictive opioids to physicians or offer non-research funding at all?

THE SANDUSKY ASSAULT

Alexander Hoffman

1. BACKGROUND

CONTROVERSY STRUCK PENNSYLVANIA STATE University in 2011 when Jerry Sandusky, the university's defensive coordinator for the football team, was charged with 40 counts of sex crimes against young boys.[1] Ten victims came forward, each claiming that Sandusky had approached them and either attempted to, or succeeded in, performing sexual acts upon them.[2] One victim claimed Sandusky had groomed him from the age of ten and continued to keep inappropriate contact over the course of four years.[3] Others claimed that Sandusky would take showers with them, coerce them into performing sexual acts, or outright rape them.[4]

Before the controversy, Jerry Sandusky was considered a legend at Penn State. Sandusky created a widely successful children's charity called "The Second Mile," which hosted summer camps for underprivileged kids. His likeness was portrayed on a mural across the street from Penn State campus, and he even had his own ice cream flavor created by Penn State Creamery.[5] Following Sandusky's official retirement in 1998, the result of similar complaints involving showers with a young boy, Penn State gave him a large compensation package and special designation as emeritus.[6]

During the official investigation of Sandusky in 2011, it became increasingly obvious that Sandusky's inappropriate conduct was known by several individuals working within the university.[7] Mike McQueary, a graduate student at the time, witnessed Sandusky raping a boy in the locker room showers in 2002. After telling the head coach, Joe Paterno, McQueary met with top university officials Tim Curley and Gary Schultz, the head of the athletics department and the overseer of campus police respectively, to explain what he had seen. After relating in detail what he had witnessed, Curley and Schultz responded by reportedly taking away Sandusky's keys to the locker room and reporting the incident to The Second Mile, the non-profit organization founded by Sandusky himself in 1977.[8] No report was filed with the police and Sandusky remained an active Penn State emeritus. Following the incident, Sandusky would continue to coach a summer camp at a satellite Penn State campus from 2002 to 2008 with almost daily contact with young boys throughout the entire period of time.[9]

After new reports of abuse came forward and an official investigation began, accusations were directed at Curley and Schultz for their negligence to address the 2002 controversy. In defense of the two university officials, Penn State President Graham Spanier expressed support for their testimony.[10] After insisting that they were never informed about a controversy in 2002, both Curley and Schultz were eventually charged with perjury and failure to report suspected child abuse.[11] Shortly afterwards Graham Spanier was also forced to resign from his position as president in response to accusations that Penn State administration failed to address several reports of Sandusky's abusive behavior.

In total, Jerry Sandusky was sentenced 30 to 60 years in prison and charged guilty on 45 counts of abuse.[12] The Sandusky scandal cost Pennsylvania State University roughly $237 million dollars in various legal fees, and the reputation of the university administration was tarnished.[13]

2. ANALYSIS

While there is no doubt that what occurred was wrong, the complexity in this case is exactly which things went wrong and what interests were at stake. Presented here is a partial list of one way the interests can be understood. I urge the reader to catalogue more nuanced or additional conflicts of interest in this case.

First, there is the interest of the children who had been abused, as well as those who were in danger of abuse by Sandusky in the future. The impetus of the outrage directed at this scandal mostly manifested in the way the university appeared to downplay the importance of the children. By continuing to employ Sandusky at a satellite campus after insufficiently dealing with early allegations of molestation, the faculty at Penn either weighed this interest too low or ignored it completely.

Second, there is the interest of the university's well-being, which the faculty members and students share. Of course, protecting the reputation of a university sports program is no excuse for covering up the crimes of a child molester. However, we can infer from the fame and prestige of Sandusky and his program (evidenced by his emeritus status and widely used name on campus) that the news of his transgressions would be a major blow to the university.

Finally, each individual who came across Sandusky's horrendous acts had their own personal interests in mind. Mike McQueary, the graduate student at Penn State, had interest staked both in his future success in the program and the continued support of Sandusky as his powerful superior. President of the university, Graham Spanier, supported the faculty members who covered up the Sandusky Assault because the reputation of his employees directly affected his own. The children's charity founded by Sandusky, The Second Mile, perhaps had an interest at stake if the information about Sandusky was made public due to their reputations being intertwined, and the abuses happening specifically to children in the program.

Obviously, no interest should weigh heavy enough to cover up the abuse of innocent children. Analyzing these interests is beneficial only for the purpose of understanding how the Sandusky Assault incident lasted for so long. The hope is to one day identify conflicts of interest before such serious damage can occur.

NOTES

1   Mark Viera, "Former Coach at Penn State Is Charged With Abuse," *The New York Times*, 5 November 2011, https://www.nytimes.com/2011/11/06/sports/ncaafootball/former-coach-at-penn-state-is-charged-with-abuse.html.

2   CNN Library, "Penn State Scandal Fast Facts," 28 October 2013, https://www.cnn.com/2013/10/28/us/penn-state-scandal-fast-facts/index.html.

3   Sarah Ganim, "Jerry Sandusky, Former Penn State Football Staffer, Subject of Grand Jury Investigation," *The Patriot News*, 31 March 2011, https://www.pennlive.com/midstate/index.ssf/2011/03/jerry_sandusky_former_penn_sta.html.

4   CNN Library 2013.

5   The Patriot News, "Penn State Creamery Pulls Jerry Sandusky Ice Cream Off Shelves, Menus," *The Patriot News*, 9 November 2011, https://www.pennlive.com/midstate/2011/11/penn_state_creamery_pulls_jerr.html.

6   Ken Belson, "Abuse Scandal Inquiry Damns Paterno and Penn State," *The New York Times*, 12 July 2012, https://www.nytimes.com/2012/07/13/sports/ncaafootball/13pennstate.html?_r=2&hp.

7   Jo Becker, "Inquiry Grew into Concerns of Cover-Up," *The New York Times*, 16 November 2011, https://www.nytimes.com/2011/11/17/sports/ncaafootball/internet-posting-helped-sandusky-investigators.html?pagewanted=all.

8   Becker, "Inquiry."

9   David Zucchino, "Penn State Sex Scandal: Jerry Sandusky Ran Boys Camp for Years," *Los Angeles Times*, 8 November 2011, https://latimesblogs.

latimes.com/nationnow/2011/11/sandusky-penn-state-.html.

10 Zucchino, "Penn State Sex Scandal."

11 John Taylor, "Penn State AD Charged With Perjury, Failure to Report in Sandusky Sex Case," *NBC Sports*, 5 November 2011, https://collegefootballtalk.nbcsports.com/2011/11/05/penn-state-ad-charged-with-perjury-failure-to-report-in-sandusky-sex-case/related/.

12 Tim Rohan, "Sandusky Gets 30 to 60 Years for Sexual Abuse," *The New York Times*, 9 October 2012, https://www.nytimes.com/2012/10/10/sports/ncaafootball/penn-state-sandusky-is-sentenced-in-sex-abuse-case.html?rref=collection%2Ftimestopic%2FSandusky%2C%20Jerry&action=click&contentCollection=timestopics&region=stream&module=stream_unit&version=latest&contentPlacement=63&pgtype=collection.

13 The Associated Press, "How Much Has the Sandusky Scandal Cost Penn State So Far?" *Pennsylvania Real-Time News*, 7 January 2017, https://www.pennlive.com/news/2017/01/how_much_has_the_sandusky_scan.html.

DISCUSSION QUESTIONS

1. What could the university have done to mitigate the damage caused by conflicts of interest in this case?

2. Are there any other conflicts of interest that have not been explicitly mentioned in the analysis of this case study?

3. Who are the bad actors in this case? Is everyone who knew about Sandusky's actions morally blameworthy?

4. How should the issue have been approached from the perspective of the individuals involved? What are some ways that they could have avoided being influenced by their various interests?

HONESTY, DECEPTION, AND TRUST

Fritz Allhoff and Jonathan Milgrim

1. INTRODUCTION

EVERYONE HAS, AT SOME TIME, EXPERIENCED the sting of being lied to or deceived. On an individual level this feeling of betrayal and injustice can lead to broken friendships, divorce, and an unwillingness to interact with the perceived violator. On a larger scale, honesty is seen as a necessary and needed trait for business and political leaders, and exemplary displays of honesty are likely to be rewarded with respect or even reverence. Stories of Abraham Lincoln's youth and pre-political life, which included instances of him walking miles to return a few pennies from accidental overpayment or working days to repay a neighbor for the accidental destruction of a loaned book, helped earn him the moniker Honest Abe.[1] This perception of honesty to a fault has helped him remain the most popular US president over 150 years after his death.[2] Likewise, we expect that our engineers, doctors, and even law enforcement professionals will be honest, oftentimes to a fault. The problem is that in the real world, the clarity of this desire for honesty falls apart.

With a little thought, there are some professional cases in which we are willing to acknowledge that honesty is not the best policy. For example, we allow police officers to use deception during their interrogation of suspects. Similarly, we oftentimes view (perhaps unfairly) lawyers as dishonest and we may even look down on them because of this. On the other hand, if we are trying to settle a legal dispute, as long as the lawyer is being honest *with us*, we are happy to have a lawyer skilled in deception. Even healthcare professionals are not immune from questions of when honesty is or is not the best policy. Should a doctor lie to a patient in order to ensure he chooses the correct treatment option? Should a nurse tell a patient mortally wounded in a car accident that their spouse or child was killed, ensuring the last moments of the patients' life are filled with grief? This brings into focus some issues with how we understand and treat honesty. It is not that we want our professionals to be honest to a fault. Instead, we want them to be honest unless they should not be. This unit explores the concept of honesty, as well as how and when we expect professionals to be deceptive or dishonest.

2. CONTENTS

The unit begins with the first three sections of Harry Frankfurt's work, "On Truth, Lies, and Bullshit." These sections explore what is meant by lying, and the harms that lying causes. These harms extend beyond simple betrayal and include harms to both the person being deceived and the deceiver as well. This is followed by Jonathan E. Adler's "Lying, Deceiving, or Falsely Implicating." In this work, Adler draws a distinction between simply lying, which is wrong in most cases, with deception or similar forms of untruthfulness that do not directly qualify as lies. This distinction is explored through various ethical theories to determine where the line might be drawn, if anywhere. The third article, "What Is Professional Integrity?" by Andreas Eriksen, explores the concept of integrity within the professional framework. It is difficult to discuss trust without evoking terms such as integrity. Eriksen explores what is meant by professional integrity as opposed to the more colloquial use of the term, arguing that it is a distinct virtue required of professionals.

Following these three articles related to honesty and lying in general, there are five articles that deal with honesty, deception, and trust in particular professions. The first, "The Ethics of Insider Trading" by Patricia H. Werhane, explores the breaches of trust present in insider trading, and counters arguments supporting the practice. The next article, "Ethically Challenged" by Lori Robertson, explores several cases of plagiarism in recent years, how those instances were handled, and why the cases might not be as straightforward as they first appear.

The final three articles of the unit involve instances that are less obvious than some of the previous cases, and they explore what the right course of action may be. The first, "Telling the Truth to Patients: A Clinical Ethics Exploration" by David C. Thomasma, explores kinds of truth, reasons for telling the truth, and then explores the various cases in the medical field in which telling the truth might be the most harmful and therefore wrong thing to do. The next, "Lies, Damn Lies and Unethical Lies: How to Negotiate Ethically and Effectively" by David Geronemus, examines how to conduct ethical, yet effective negotiations. The article is a series of short case-study questions, followed by discussion. While the article is written from the perspective of a business lawyer, the concerns and principles discussed apply to any profession involved in negotiation. The last article of the unit, "Liability to Deception and Manipulation: The Ethics of Undercover Policing" by Christopher Nathan, explores how the deception used by undercover police officers either does not infringe on the rights of potential crime suspects, or does so but is excused.

The first of the two case studies examines the Enron scandal and the related ethical concerns. This is followed by "The Ethics of Bluffing" which examines Oracle's takeover of PeopleSoft and the potential ethical issues related to Oracle's conduct during the takeover.

NOTES

1   William M. Thayer, *The Pioneer Boy and How He Became President* (Boston: Walker, Wise, and Company, 1864).

2   Brandon Rottinghaus and Justin Vaughn, "How Does Trump Stack Up Against the Best—and Worst—Presidents?" *The New York Times*, 19 February 2018, https://www.nytimes.com/interactive/2018/02/19/opinion/how-does-trump-stack-up-against-the-best-and-worst-presidents.html.

—31—

ON TRUTH, LIES, AND BULLSHIT

Harry Frankfurt

I

HOW *DO* LIES INJURE US? ACTUALLY, AS EVERYONE knows, there are many familiar circumstances in which lies are not truly injurious to us at all. They may sometimes be, on the whole, genuinely beneficial. For instance, a lie may protect us in one way or another from becoming aware of certain states of affairs, when no one (including ourselves) has anything in particular to gain from our being aware of them and when our awareness of them would cause us or others serious distress. Or a lie may divert us from embarking on a course of action that we find tempting but that would in fact lead to our doing ourselves more harm than good. Clearly, we must sometimes acknowledge that, all things considered, having been told a lie was actually helpful to us.

Even so, we often feel at such times that there was surely *something* bad about what the liar did. In the circumstances, it may be reasonable for us to be grateful for the lie. Whatever good the lie may turn out to have done, however, we believe at bottom that a better alternative would have been for the beneficial effects of the lie to have been achieved by sticking to the truth without any recourse to lying.

The most irreducibly bad thing about lies is that they contrive to interfere with, and to impair, our natural effort to apprehend the real state of affairs. They are designed to prevent us from being in touch with what is really going on. In telling his lie, the liar tries to mislead us into believing that the facts are other than they actually are. He tries to impose his will on us. He aims at inducing us to accept his fabrication as an accurate account of how the world truly is.

Insofar as he succeeds in this, we acquire a view of the world that has its source in his imagination rather than being directly and reliably grounded in the relevant facts. The world we live in, insofar as our understanding of it is fashioned by the lie, is an imaginary world. There may be worse places to live; but this imaginary world won't do for us, at all, as a permanent residence.

Lies are designed to damage our grasp of reality. So they are intended, in a very real way, to make us crazy. To the extent that we believe them our minds are occupied and governed by fictions, fantasies, and illusions that have been concocted for us by the liar. What we accept as real is a world that others cannot see, touch, or experience in any direct way. A person who believes a lie is constrained by it, accordingly, to life "in his own world"—a world that others cannot enter, and in which even the liar himself does not truly reside. Thus, the victim of the lie is, in the degree of his deprivation of truth, shut off from the world of common experience and isolated in an illusory realm to which there is no path that others might find or follow.

II

Some philosophers insist, with considerable vehemence, that lying decisively undermines

191

the cohesion of human society. Immanuel Kant, for example, declared that "without truth social intercourse and conversation became valueless" (*Lectures on Ethics*). And he argued that because lying threatens society in this way, "a lie always harms another; if not some particular man, still it harms mankind generally" ("On a Supposed Right to Lie from Altruistic Motives"). Michel Montaigne made a similar claim: "Our intercourse being carried on solely by means of the word, he who falsifies that is a traitor to society" ("Of Giving the Lie"). "Lying is an accursed vice," Montaigne declared. And then he added, warming to his subject with rather extraordinary intensity, "if we did but recognize the horror and gravity of … [lying], we should punish it with flames more justly than other crimes" ("Of Liars"). In other word, liars—more than criminals of any other sort—deserve to be burned at the stake.

Montaigne and Kant certainly had a point. But they exaggerated. Effective social intercourse does not strictly depend, as they maintained, on people telling one another the truth (not as, say, respiration *strictly depends* on oxygen, being *altogether impossible* without it); nor does conversation really lose *all* its value when people lie (some real information might come through, and the entertainment value of the conversation might even be increased). After all, the amount of lying and misrepresentation of all kinds that actually goes on in the world (of which the immeasurable flood of bullshit is itself no more than a fractional part) is enormous, and yet productive social life manages somehow to continue. The fact that people often engage in lies, and in other kinds of fraudulent behavior hardly renders it impossible to benefit either from living with them or from talking with them. It only means that we have to be careful.

We can quite successfully find our way through an environment of falsehood and fraud, as long as we can reasonably count on our own ability to discriminate reliably between instances in which people are misrepresenting things to us and instances in which they are dealing with us straight. General confidence in the truthfulness of others is not essential, then, as long as we are justified in having a certain sort of confidence in ourselves.

To be sure, we are rather easily fooled. Moreover, we know this to be the case. So it is not very easy for us to acquire and to sustain a secure and justifiable trust in our ability to spot attempts at deception. For this reason, social intercourse would indeed be severely burdened by a widespread and wanton disrespect for truth. However, our interest in shielding society from this burden is not what provides us with our most fundamental reason for caring about truth.

When we encounter people who lie to us, or who in some other way manifest a disregard for truth, it tends to anger and upset us. But it does not primarily do so, as Montaigne and Kant would presumably have had it, because we fear that the mendacity we have encountered threatens or encumbers the order of society. Our main concern is clearly not the concern of a citizen. What is most immediately aroused in our response to the liar is not public spirit. It's something more personal. As a rule, except perhaps when people misrepresent matters in which serious public interests are directly involved, we are dismayed far less by the harm liars may be doing to the general welfare than by their conduct toward ourselves. What stirs us against them, whether or not they have somehow managed to betray all of humankind, is that they have certainly injured us.

III

Truth and caring about truth concern us, then, in ways that do not bear simply on our quotidian practical interests. They have a deeper and more damaging significance as well. One of the most rewarding of contemporary poets, Adrienne Rich, offers an account of the malign effect that lying inevitably has—apart from its harmful effect on the person to whom the lie is told—on the liar herself. With poetic exactitude, she observes that "the liar leads an existence of unutterable loneliness,"[1] The loneliness is precisely *unutterable* because the liar cannot even reveal that she is lonely—that there is no one in her fabricated world—without disclosing, in doing so, that she has lied. She hides her own thoughts, pretending to believe what she does not believe, and thereby she makes it impossible for other people to be fully in touch with her. They cannot respond to her as she really is. They cannot even be aware that they are not doing so.

The liar refuses to permit himself to the extent that he lies, to be known. This is an insult to his victims. It naturally injures their pride. For it denies them access to an elementary mode of human intimacy that is normally taken more or less for granted: the intimacy that consists in knowing what is on, or what is in, another person's mind.

In certain cases, Rich notes, lies may cause an even more profound sort of damage. "To discover that one has been lied to in a personal relationship," she says, "leads one to feel a little crazy."[2] Here again, her observation is perspicuous. When we are dealing with someone whom we hardly know, we have to make a more or less deliberate assessment of her reliability in order to satisfy ourselves that what she tells us coincides with what she actually believes; and this assessment ordinarily pertains only to certain specific assertions that she has made. With our close friends, on the other hand, both of these conditions are usually relaxed. We suppose that our friends are generally honest with us, and we take this pretty much for granted. We tend to trust whatever they say, and we do so, mainly, not on the basis of a calculation establishing that they are currently telling us the truth, but because we feel comfortable and safe with them. As we familiarly put it, we "*just know* that they wouldn't lie to us."

With friends, the expectation of access and intimacy has become natural. It is grounded not in a calculated judgment but in our feelings—that is, in our subjective experience, rather than in any intellectual assessment based on pertinent objective data. It would be too much to say that our inclination to trust our friends belongs to our essential nature. But it could be properly enough said, as we sometimes do in fact say, that trusting them has come to be "second nature" to us.

That is why, as Rich observes, discovering that a friend has lied to us engenders in us a feeling of being a little crazy. The discovery exposes to us something about *ourselves*—something far more disturbing than merely that we have miscalculated, or that we have made an error of judgment. It reveals that *our own nature* (i.e., our *second* nature) is unreliable, having led us to count on someone we should not have trusted. It shows us that we cannot realistically be confident of our own ability to distinguish truth from falsity—our ability, in other words, to recognize the difference between what is real and what is not. Successfully deceiving a friend implies, needless to say, a fault in the one who tells the lie. However, it also shows that the victim of the deception is defective, too. The liar betrays him, but he is betrayed by his own feelings as well.

Self-betrayal pertains to craziness because it is a hallmark of the irrational. The heart of rationality is to be consistent; and being consistent, in action or in thought, entails at least proceeding so as not to defeat oneself. Aristotle suggested that an agent acts rational insofar as he conforms his actions to the "mean"—that is, to a point midway between excess and deficiency. Suppose that, for the sake of good health, someone follows a diet that is either so meager or so indulgent that it not only fails to improve her health but actually leads her to become *less healthy* than she was. Aristotle urges that it is in this defeat of her own purpose, in this self-betrayal, that the *practical irrationality* of the person's divergence from the mean consists.

Intellectual activity is undermined, similarly, by logical incoherence. When a line of thought generates a contradiction, its further progressive elaboration is blocked. In whatever direction the mind turns, it is driven back: it must affirm what it has already rejected or it must deny what it has already affirmed. Thus, like behavior that frustrates its own ambition, contradictory thinking is irrational because it defeats itself. When a person discovers that he has been told a lie by someone in whose reliability he had found it natural to have confidence, this shows him that he cannot rely on his own settled feelings of trust. He sees that he has been betrayed, in his effort to identify people in whom he can have confidence, by his own natural inclinations. These have led him to miss the truth rather than attain it. His assumption that he could guide himself in accordance with his own nature has turned out to be self-defeating, and hence irrational. Since he finds that he is by nature out of touch with reality, he may well feel that he is a little crazy.

NOTES

1. "Women and Honor: Some Notes on Lying," in Adrienne Rich, *Lies, Secrets and Silence* (New York: 1979), 191.
2. "Women and Honor: Some Notes on Lying," in Adrienne Rich, *Lies, Secrets and Silence* (New York: 1979), 186.

—32—

LYING, DECEIVING, OR FALSELY IMPLICATING[1]

Jonathan E. Adler

...

I

IN A WIDE RANGE OF CASES, PARTICULARLY those which pose tough problems for the view that lying is always or nearly always wrong, a (pragmatics) strategy is available to allow one to deceive rather than to lie.[2] If so, in those cases, you need not lie.

We concentrate on questions of the form 'Where is X?' as in the infamous case of the murderer at the door.[3] He wants to know where Joe is. You know that he intends to kill Joe, and that Joe is in the basement. You need an assertion that genuinely misleads as to Joe's whereabouts, which the murderer will accept. (Exploiting disjunctions or vague terms will generally fail on one of these criteria.)

Assume it is clearly after 11:00 a.m., though close to it. Imagine a plausible place to tell the murderer that Joe can be found, even though erroneous. If the murderer accepts it, he believes himself easily able to predict Joe's continued location, until he may intercept him—for example, being at the local bank. So you assert:

(1) If it is before 11:00 a.m. Joe is at the bank.

Since you believe the left-hand side to be false, and you accept the contentious, but credible, treatment of the truth conditions of indicative conditionals as that of the corresponding material conditional, you believe the statement to be true. So you have not lied. The murderer infers that though it is after 11:00 a.m., it is close enough so that Joe will still be there or in the vicinity, and so off he goes.

Arguably, however, in (1) ... speakers do not conversationally implicate the conclusion drawn by the hearer. Rather, the conclusion is closer to what is asserted (or said).[4]

Here is an alternative. Select any place, well away from the basement, but fairly nearby, where Joe spends a good deal of time—for example, the local diner, the Nevada—then assert:

(2) He's been hanging around the Nevada a lot.

The expectation is that since the murderer believes that you are being cooperative, your answer is meant to be relevant to his question. So he will take you as having conversationally implicated that Joe is at the Nevada now.

Case (2) differs from (1) in clearly implicating only what one believes false. The risk in this strategy, however, is less certainty that the murderer will be misled. (Even for (1), if the murderer becomes suspicious, he can foil you with the question, "What makes you think that, if it is before 11:00 a.m., Joe is at the bank?")

The responses (1) and (2) are independent. It is not as if one must learn complex rules of selection.

The factual information each requires is minimal and usually evident. Still, a little effort is needed to learn of these strategies. But were the alternative of lying as much worse as is alleged, we probably have an obligation to practice formulating such devious assertions.[5]

Other constructions designed to exploit what is implicated rather than stated or strictly entailed for similar ends are possible, and for other types of questions. But no claim is made that there are always feasible constructions. Also, this pragmatics strategy for deceiving cannot rival lying in ease and prospects for success. In fact, in section II, I take it as a telling difference between lying and deceiving that deceiving is more effortful. The claim is only that for answering a range of simple inquiries, this kind of linguistic deception is a workable alternative to lying.

But if these examples work in successfully misleading the murderer without lying, many will respond "So what?" At best, what I have offered is a gimmick of little, if any, ethical significance. Ordinarily understood, the intention is the same, and the means and consequences appear not terribly different.

In the passage from Immanuel Kant usually cited as capturing his view of lying within the framework of the *Grounding for the Metaphysics of Morals*,[6] he says of the false promise under the "rational beings as ends" formulation:

> For the man whom I want to use for my own purposes by such a promise cannot possibly concur with my way of acting toward him and hence cannot himself hold the end of his action (*ibid.*, Ak. 430).

The judgment applies to deception as well. Consent cannot be given, since the victim is deceived.

Still, the prohibition on asserting what one believes to be false is very strong, and on some views absolute. The prohibition on (even communicative) deception is much weaker. It is to be recommended as an admirable alternative to lying.[7]

The recommendation extends well beyond philosophers, as suggested by the opening example. Political discourse is rife with misleading implications and euphemism, as with such Orwellian examples as "pacification" for mass destruction.[8]

The desperate means to avoid lying, while going easy on deception is not accidental. For if it is never right to cooperate with evil and lying is a fundamental wrong, then only a strong distinction (where deception is not seriously bad at all) will help. The hardly liveable alternative is silence in a confrontation with evil or even lesser forms of ill intent.

II

If (or when) the above strategy works and the opening thesis is correct, why would anyone choose to lie rather than to deceive? One reason is the greater assurance of success with the lie;[9] another is belief that one's untruthfulness is justified.

Even if one does quickly come up with a misleading, but truthful, assertion, to take the first reason, we noted that there is greater uncertainty of correct inferences for implicatures than for lying. But there are other differences in assurance. It is a lot easier just to lie. Unless we renounce communication, there are few effective ways to immunize ourselves against the liar. The means to lie are readily at hand and the opportunities coeval with normal conversational assertion.

Consider why trickery (or fooling) is much more thorough deception than lying. In deceiving at all, there is a violation of a norm of truthfulness. So there has to be some excuse for it, such as a good, harmless joke. But in order for it to be a joke, there has to be some display of cleverness or ingenuity. Lying leaves little opportunity to display cleverness, except as a tease. It is a blunt instrument, easily found, promising an easy success. All it takes is a suitable (contextually believable) assertion incompatible with one's relevant belief.[10]

But the deceiver must keep his methods fresh. Consider the device proposed here (and illustrated by (1) and (2)). Once it becomes well known or it is even suspected, it will no longer be serviceable. In legal and quasilegal settings, the option of deception is virtually eliminated by the all purpose end question: To the best of your knowledge, are there any other relevant facts?

Choice of the lie, to move to the second advantage, can reflect the liar's belief that he is justified in his act.[11] He has no need to take a devious, more effortful route, beyond what is requisite for success. The belief that one's lying is justified allows the liar a kind of honesty about his lies that is barred from the deceiver (without renunciation).

The deceiver takes a more circuitous route to his success, where lying is an easier and more certain way to mislead. The deceiver's goal is to avoid blame; so he would not forthrightly want to defend his action publicly. He takes care lest he, and not just his deception be exposed.

The "honest" liar can be open toward others as to his act with the expectation of their endorsement.[12] But in her important article "The Right to Lie," Christine M. Korsgaard[13] effectively relegates the issue to a footnote, there to be dismissed:

> Sometimes it is objected that someone could assent to being lied to in advance of the actual occasion of the lie, and that in such a case the deception might still succeed. One can therefore agree to be deceived (*ibid.*, p. 333).

If we apply this claim to a doctor-patient relation, and if I do

> ... ask the doctor whether I am fatally ill, I cannot be certain whether she will answer me truthfully. Perhaps what's being envisioned is that I simply agree to be lied to, but not about anything in particular. Will I then trust the person with whom I have made this odd agreement (*ibid.*, p. 333)?

Contrary to Korsgaard, the answer to her rhetorically intended question, when applied realistically, is sometimes "yes." Even when the answer is "no," only full trust is eliminated. Sufficient trust may remain to sustain many social relations dependent upon it.

Social norms restrain criticism and favor complements; so we cannot be sure if a kind word is meant. But the trust is not absent, communication not dissolved. Deceptive social-science experiments proceed, even where experimenters have openly defended their studies.[14]

When practices are hardly avoidable, we accommodate. We draw rough distinctions among groups or reference classes as to whom to trust or how much, as well as when (for example, less so in matters of self-interest or privacy). Normal human psychology allows for selective attention and forgetting. We set our watches ahead, and ask others to mislead us as to the time. Certain accounts of character planning involve the unblinkered attempt to induce beliefs exploiting these shortcomings and abilities.[15]

Sometimes when one should not expect the truth, one does not know that one should not expect it. In these cases, the answer to Korsgaard's question is "yes."[16] Thus, a casual question to someone about how their family is faring can be intrusive when, unbeknownst to the questioner, there are serious marital difficulties. The trust and expectation of truthfulness are still present as the questioner does not believe that he is being intrusive, even when he endorses lies in such cases to protect privacy.[17]

But where the lie is not selected as an expression of one's belief that it is justified, lying reveals a more dangerous moral character—thus favoring the opening thesis. The deceiver, by his very effort to avoid the charge of lying, shows himself more respectful of morality, whether through honest respect or fear. The liar is more brazen. He too, of course, does not want to get caught. But what moves him is what will work best, not having the immorality attached to him after.

The deceiver can be made to feel shame or guilt but not, or much less so, the liar....

III

Even with this difference in character, however, the deceiver may be a greater social and moral threat than the liar. For the liar can be definitively exposed, and so, as with David Hume's[18] promise breaker, marked to the community. But thereby the deceiver is the more insidious threat (Iago being a paradigm). When exposed, he is not neatly categorized as a transgressor. After all, he never spoke falsely. He retains "plausible deniability" when he does not avoid blame altogether. Thus, "lying with statistics"[19] is attractive just because, aside from the persuasive force of precise, numerical values as the vehicle, the lying statistics are all true. That is, these are not (strictly!) lies, and that, of course, is their attraction as a way to circumvent blame.

These differences between the upfront path of the liar and the subterfuge of the deceiver are reflected in language. The liar lies. He is dishonest and not to be trusted. But the standard and slang terms for the deceiver and his means go well beyond these: sleazy, misleading, sneaky, underhanded, greasy, cunning, euphemistic, manipulative, sly, seductive, distorting, slanderous, evasive, deceitful.

Accordingly, victims do not experience lies and deception similarly. The victim of the liar, akin to the victim of coercion, has the anger and fear of one brutalized. But the brutality is clearly an external force imposed on him.

It is otherwise for the victim of the deceiver. Depending on the nature of the deception, the victim feels anything from foolish or tricked to corroded. Not only has he been misled, but the embarrassment or horror of it is that he has been duped into collaborating on his own harm. Afterward, he cannot secure the relief of wholly locating blame externally. (Consider Othello, at play's end.)

The hearer, in not demanding clarification can be held to accept the speaker's devious means, since communicational deception is overtly inference dependent. (The victim of a lie lacks even this minimal opportunity.) Of course, the deceiver is prudently betting that the hearer will not request clarification of the speaker's contribution. So, subsequently, should the hearer discover the deceit, he views himself as somewhat playing a role in it, even while his response to the assertion is natural.

To the victim, the deceiver's denial that he ever lied can have the familiarly hollow ring of "Well, I never promised" or "Okay, but I didn't give my word." These are excuses to mitigate blame by exploiting a lack of explicit agreement, even when there is a failure to live up to reasonable expectations.

Much of ethics depends upon commitments that are not explicit. We care very much about the spirit of our largely tacit moral code or norms.[20] You are new to the community, and we are going together to a social function, but I do not inform you that you are dressed too casually. What powerfully, though often imperceptibly, pulls me ethically to inform you is no promise or contract or giving of my word or right, but the vast range of "our ordinary, nonexplicit commitments."[21] ...

NOTES

1   Thanks to John Deigh, Georges Rey, Peter Unger, and especially Christopher Gowans for their comments, as well as to Jerrold Katz, Sidney Morgenbesser, and Frederic Schick for discussion on particular points. I am also grateful for comments by members of the audiences at the University of Miami and the Graduate Center/City University of New York.

2   Based on the work of H.P. Grice, *Studies in the Way of Words* (Cambridge: Harvard, 1989), essays 2–4.

3   See Kant, "On a Supposed Right to Lie from Altruistic Motives," in *Critique of Practical Reason and Other Writings in Moral Philosophy*, L.W. Beck, trans. and ed. (Chicago: University Press, 1949), pp. 346–50.

4   See Siegler, pp. 133–35; and the contrasting dissent from Grice's said/implicated distinction of

Francois Recanti, "The Pragmatics of What Is Said," in Steven Davis, ed., *Pragmatics: A Reader* (New York: Oxford, 1991), pp. 97–120; and Kent Bach, "Conversational Implicature," *Mind and Language*, IX (1994): 124–61.

5   Another construction akin to (1): when the basement where Joe is hiding is, say, ten miles east of the town, assert:

> Joe is two miles east of the town.

> Since being ten miles entails being two miles east, you have told the truth. But the murderer infers that Joe is exactly two miles east of the town.

6   J.W. Ellington, trans. (Indianapolis: Hackett, 1981).

7   See the second of Alasdair MacIntyre's lucid lectures, "Truthfulness, Lies, and Moral Philosophers," Grethe B. Peterson, ed., *The Tanner Lectures, Volume XVI* (Salt Lake City: Utah UP, 1995), pp. 309–61.

8   George Orwell, "Politics and the English Language," in his *A Collection of Essays* (New York: Doubleday, 1954), pp. 162–77, here p. 173. For many other (types of) examples, see John Wilson, *Politically Speaking* (Cambridge: Blackwell, 1990). See also *The New York Times* (September 27, 1995), B3.

9   As elsewhere, the claim assumes contexts in which no special beliefs hold as, for example, when a speaker believes that the audience does not think he will be truthful.

10   As Tyler Burge cryptically remarks: "lying for the fun of it is a form of craziness"—"Content Preservation," *Philosophical Review*, CII (1993): 457–88, here p. 474. So, too, though not as strongly, for linguistic deception. But Burge's insight overshoots if denying that sane persons can maliciously or, as a tease, lie for the fun of it.

11   On justifying lies, see Sissela Bok, *Lying* (New York: Vintage, 1979), chapter VII.

12   This possibility of a kind of openness about one's lying is helpful in Augustine's case of beneficent double-cross treated by Roderick M. Chisholm and Thomas D. Feehan—"The Intent to Deceive," [*The Journal of Philosophy*], LXXIV, 3 (March 1977): 143–59, here p. 154. Their answer will not do because it depends upon an unacceptable construal of assertion.

What separates this case from standard lies is that the speaker would be quite willing to allow the hearer to view openly his pertinent highest-order intention (the intention or purpose behind the intent to represent falsely what he believes); for his highest-order intention is for the hearer's belief to be correct.

13   "The Right to Lie: Kant on Dealing with Evil," *Philosophy and Public Affairs*, xv (1986): 325–49.

14   The case may be thought a counterexample to my contrasts between the liar and the deceiver. Many deceptive social-science experiments are lies, however. Additionally, the willingness to engage in public justification is partly a response to external pressures. On this topic, see Bok, chapter XIII.

15   See Jon Elster, *Sour Grapes* (New York: Cambridge, 1983), chapter IV.

16   Compare to Korsgaard's (*op. cit.*, pp. 328–34) own clever account of why lying to the murderer can circumvent violating the first formulation of the categorical imperative.

17   Similarly, placebos are still used in biomedical research, despite the requirement of prior consent.

18   *A Treatise of Human Nature*, L.A. Selby-Bigge, ed. (New York: Oxford, 1975), book III, part II, section v.

19   See Darrell Huff, *How to Lie with Statistics* (New York: Norton, 1954).

20   Thomas W. Pogge's argument—in "Loopholes in Moralities," [*The Journal of Philosophy*], LXXXIX, 2 (February 1992): 79–98—assumes a largely explicit moral code.

21   Stanley Cavell, *The Claim of Reason* (New York: Oxford, 1979), p. 298.

—33—

WHAT IS PROFESSIONAL INTEGRITY?

Andreas Eriksen

INTRODUCTION

INTEGRITY IS WIDELY REGARDED AS A KEY VIRTUE for professionals. Two main kinds of reasons are commonly offered to explain the value assigned to professional integrity. The first kind concerns *fidelity* to the fundamental goals of the role. For example, the appeal to professional integrity in cases of conscientious objection in the medical context is often described in terms of loyalty to profession-specific ends, such as life and health. The second kind of reason is *assurance*; when issues of corruption and conflict of interest are debated, professional integrity is often emphasized as the virtue that gives us reason to trust role holders to place professional standards above self-interest.

In this paper, I will develop an account of professional integrity as a distinct virtue (rather than just "ordinary" integrity in a special context), involving responsiveness to both fidelity and assurance. This view will be developed in a loosely Aristotelian way, as a response to two alternatives that turn out to be professional vices, which can be traced in the literature on professional integrity. One of these views emphasizes fidelity to the ends of a professional practice, as in health or education; this may be called the *teleological* view. The other alternative sees professional integrity as a matter of assurance and conceptually identical to

ordinary integrity; this may be called the *generic* view. As a third alternative, I develop the *interpretive* view. On this account, professional integrity is distinct from ordinary integrity but not because of a direct commitment to profession-specific ends. What makes professional integrity distinct is the way in which it calls for an interpretive judgment of what the role requires.

THE TELEOLOGICAL VIEW

The teleological view describes professional integrity as a commitment to key ends of professional practice, as in education or health. Dean Cocking and Justin Oakley (2001) provide a clear example of this approach: "For, characterising the goal of a profession in terms of the substantive good it undertakes to serve helps us better understand appeals to a notion of professional integrity as a reason for refusing to carry out certain requests for patients or clients" (Cocking & Oakley 2001: 83). Their main example is active voluntary euthanasia, which they claim "is to betray the goal of serving health which fundamentally defines their profession of medicine" (2001: 83). Even if it would be best for the patient to grant his or her autonomous request to be killed, doctors do not feel they act on this request in their capacity as doctors. In this way, the authors differentiate between personal and professional integrity. Active voluntary euthanasia may be compatible with personal integrity, but it must be performed with the "doctor's hat off" (Cocking & Oakley 2001: 83). Cocking and Oakley refer with approval to an article by Franklin G. Miller and Howard Brody (1995) that expresses similar ideas but with an even stronger emphasis on the conception of professional integrity as concerned with *profession-internal* values: "The acts of physicians of integrity must serve the proper ends or goals of medicine, and they must be ethically appropriate means to these ends in light of the values and norms internal to the practice of medicine" (Miller & Brody 1995: 11).

The insistence that professional integrity cannot be reduced to bureaucratic rule-following or mere responsiveness to client or patient requests is an attractive feature of this approach. The teleological view accepts rules and requests only insofar as they are sanctioned by a legitimating end. Oliver Wendell Holmes Sr., a physician renowned for his literary skills as well as for reforming medical practices of the day, elegantly elaborated on the importance of this point, expressing only disdain for "plain practical workmen" who "go about the work of the day before them, doing it according to the rules of their craft, and asking no questions of the past or of the future, or of the aim and end to which their special labor is contributing" (Holmes 1860: 8). Holmes drew a striking analogy to one of Sir William Edward Parry's Arctic expeditions. The expedition was supposed to be racing towards the North Pole, but the ice they travelled on was drifting towards the Equator, and this reverse travel would remain undiscovered if everyone kept their eyes strictly on the track they were plodding. Holmes used this story to illustrate the necessity of seeing practice in light of its larger purpose: "It is not only going backward that the plain practical workman is liable to, if he will not look up and look around; he may go forward to ends he little dreams of" (Holmes 1860: 8). Holmes's dreaded "plain practical workman" appears to be the opposite of an agent with professional integrity. The Arctic parable expresses the common understanding that professional integrity is a virtue

that demands that role holders lift their gaze and allow their judgments to be informed by a sense of purpose. The virtuous alternative to the plain practical workman is a role holder who makes responsible judgments with a reach that extends beyond the immediate task.

The teleological view would deny professional integrity to role holders who are unwilling to make evaluative judgments that reach beyond the immediate task. A doctor of integrity will see his actions in light of the overarching end of promoting health and not simply as performing assorted tasks without further connection. However, Holmes asked role holders to "look up and look around," and the teleological view fails on the "look around" part. The teleological view requires role holders to be faithful to profession-specific ends, but does not ask them to integrate these ends with the wider array of legitimate expectations.[1] Miller and Brody are very explicit about this: "Ethical considerations of respect for patient autonomy, social utility, and justice lie outside the domain of professional integrity, which constitutes the internal morality of medicine" (Miller & Brody 1995: 7; see also Lantos, Matlock, & Wendler 2011: 495).

A figure inspired by the main character of the TV show *House M.D.* serves to illustrate how this view is problematic. Let's call him Greg, and ignore the interpretive issues and various complexities in the series. Greg has exceptional diagnostic skills and a strong drive to solve medical puzzles. Understanding the nature of an illness is what matters to him, and he does not respect features of practice that constrain the pursuit of this end. According to Greg, procedural requirements, organizational hierarchy, collegial norms, and codes of ethics are more like annoying hurdles than genuine sources of reasons to moderate behavior.

Importantly, Greg's transgressions do not seem to be betrayals of a practice-internal good. That is, his failings as a professional are not due to a pursuit of goals foreign to the heart of medicine. Greg is not acting in the name of self-interest, nor is he pursuing money or fame. His disrespect for what he considers mere conventions of practice is a consequence of his sincere commitment to providing correct treatment according to his own judgment. Greg only violates norms regulating patient autonomy or confidentiality when he believes there is some medical gain.

Can defenders of the teleological view denounce Greg without altering their conception of professional integrity? That would seem to require a special claim about how the virtue can be possessed. Defenders of the teleological view could bite the bullet and grant Greg professional integrity despite his lack of other virtues. On this reading, Greg is a raw manifestation of professional integrity, purged of all kinds of external side-constraints and independent of other professional virtues. Certainly, this strategy identifies a distinct character trait, but it remains an open question as to whether this trait is a virtue. Do we value such behavior in the role holders we depend on? Advocates of this view might admit that we would not want professionals to be so anarchic and dismissive of shared norms but counter that integrity is only one of many virtues. At least Greg possesses this one virtue, although it would be preferable if he also had others, such as respectfulness and collegiality....

THE GENERIC VIEW

Let us now consider the opposite view—that professional integrity is not a special value commitment that transcends patient or client expectations but a virtue that gives us reason to trust professionals *in the same way* that ordinary integrity is a trait that gives us reason to rely on the words of friends and confidants. This view can be found in many accounts of professional integrity;[2] for present purposes, it will be useful to discuss a recent version of this view, developed by Greg Scherkoske in *Integrity and the Virtues of Reason* (2013). This account is especially rewarding because it emphasizes aspects of integrity that are of particular importance in the professional context.

Scherkoske argues that integrity belongs to the family of epistemic virtues, along with traits like intelligence, thoroughness, and open-mindedness. On his account, a commitment to the enterprise of excellent judging constitutes integrity (Scherkoske 2013: 88). Persons of integrity are willing and competent to hold and act upon their considered judgments. Unlike people who constantly question their own decisions or backslide in the face of social pressure, persons of integrity take their judgments seriously and are resolute in the face of temptation to waiver. They trust their own convictions when appropriate and suspend their decisions only in light of relevant reasons.

Central to this account is the idea of connecting integrity to responsibility in offering reasons to others. Agents of integrity have an adequate understanding of their epistemic position and of what kinds of judgment this position entitles them to. They use this understanding to constitute themselves as authors of dependable assurances: "People of integrity are constitutively *good on their word*: that is, they are good sources of competent and reliable reasons for action and belief" (Scherkoske 2013: 150, italics in original). In other words, persons of integrity are careful when they assert, promise, or use other performatives aimed at providing deliberative *assurance* to the receiver. They take the associated commitments seriously, taking care not to vouch for claims that they are not in a position to validate. In other words, they invite others to rely on their judgment only when it is responsible to do so.

Scherkoske's conception offers more than a phenomenological account of common perceptions of integrity; it also *vindicates* the idea that this is a genuine virtue—a character trait of value. His account builds on the plausible methodological assumption that both descriptive and normative adequacy are required in defending any conception of integrity (Scherkoske 2013: 16–20). According to Scherkoske, giving an account of integrity is not just about structuring common understandings; it is also about explaining why we are right to value integrity. What makes integrity a virtue in its own right is its importance in contexts where we depend on others: "Integrity is distinctive partly because of *why* we want it in the persons whom we surround ourselves with, specifically those mentors, friends and advisors upon whose judgment we rely" (Scherkoske 2013: 150, italics in original).

Professionals are perhaps the paradigm case of persons whose word is offered as trustworthy. It is constitutive of professional roles that they aim at being good sources of reasons for belief and action. As the sociologist Everett Hughes formulates the "essence of the professional idea," professionals "profess to know better" (Hughes 1984: 375). Physicians purport to know what is good for our health and offer their judgment as something to be relied upon. Teachers invite us to trust that they know how to educate our children. Lawyers take on our cases with the promise that their legal aid is dependable. In short, professions are institutions that present themselves as worthy of being entrusted with a key social responsibility.

In this vein, Andrew Abbott's influential sociological account describes professions as actively requesting the public to treat their word as singularly trustworthy: "In claiming jurisdiction, a profession asks society to recognize its cognitive structure through exclusive rights" (Abbott 1988: 59). The actual transactions may take many forms, of course. As Abbott explains, "In America it is ultimately through public opinion that professions establish the power that enables them to achieve legal protection. By contrast, on the Continent the state itself has traditionally been the professions' public" (Abbott 1988: 60). The relevant point here is that being good on one's word as a professional involves a responsiveness to public expectations engendered by the claim for a socially recognized jurisdiction.

On this reading, professional practice is constituted by its *assurance relation* to the public. This frames the virtue of professional integrity within a different conception of practice than that suggested by the teleological view. In particular, it is a deontic conception, emphasizing practice as a source of demands, as opposed to an axiological conception that focuses on the internal values of the profession. The general concept of professional practice seems to allow for both readings. Nevertheless, the deontic conception is more appropriate for understanding the value of professional integrity. Seeing professional practice as constituted by an assurance given to the public enables us to connect the virtue to our legitimate expectations. As Scherkoske argued, our reasons for seeking integrity in others is an important aspect of what makes it a distinct virtue. Given that the public entrusts professions with key social responsibilities, it is therefore reasonable to connect the virtue to the assurance relation that has been created.

So far, there has been little reason to doubt the generic view, to which Scherkoske's account is explicitly committed. He claims that distinctions commonly made between types of integrity serve only to "make clear the content of the relevant set of convictions, in the adherence to which a person expresses her integrity" (Scherkoske 2013: 101). That would imply that there are no interesting or substantive differences at the conceptual level, and this claim is not without plausibility, as Scherkoske has made a strong case that integrity is a matter of responsible assurance. Moreover, it has been argued that the notion of assurance is partly definitional of the professions. In other words, professionals are bound by the mechanisms of responsibility that Scherkoske has referred to in explaining integrity.

However, this view should also be considered in relation to Greg. Again, Greg only cares about getting the diagnosis right; routines, codes and norms are to be conformed to only insofar as they are instrumental in solving the case at hand. Although Greg fails to live up to the standard image of a doctor, he exhibits much of what we associate with ordinary integrity.[3] He sticks to his best judgment and ignores what he thinks are misguided conventions. He has the courage to put conviction over desire for approval, and he has the strength to hold and act upon his considered judgments. Certainly, he may deceive his patients and colleagues in order to find the key to a particular medical mystery. However, he is generally candid about his overall approach, and he is not afraid to state his actual reasons for action. He is an integrated agent in the sense that his mind is made up on matters of importance, and he speaks his mind when questioned. But is this sufficient to meet the standard of professional integrity?...

THE INTERPRETIVE VIEW

The central claim of the interpretive view is that for professional integrity to connect with assurance it must be an *interpretive* virtue. I develop this view by following the lead provided by Andrew Edgar and Stephen Pattison (2011). They characterize professional integrity as a mode of reasoning that calls for the role holder to engage critically and creatively with the varied and sometimes conflicting demands of practice. They describe the virtue as both an "interpretive stance" and a "deliberative capacity and competence which is deployed in the context of complex professional and organizational work to find appropriate answers and ways forward" (Edgar & Pattison 2011: 103). Daniel E. Wueste (2014) emphasizes something similar in his discussion of cheating and the duty to report it within academic institutions; integrity requires recognition that ethical decisions are "situated" in a "cluster of relationships that enriches but also, inevitably, makes things complicated rather than simple" (Wueste 2014: 20).

These approaches indicate a conception of professional integrity in which interpretive and evaluative engagement with practice is central. In developing the interpretive view, I will connect the notions of being "situated" and taking an "interpretive stance" more systematically to professional integrity. First, what is the fundamental normative relation that governs the situation? It is a promissory relation, where the profession has given its word to the public. Role holders are situated as promisors. What is the object of interpretation? It

is professional practice as a framework for decision-making. The main idea is that for professionals to be good on the word of their practice, they must act on a defensible interpretation of what their practice has promised.

The first step is to give Greg the proper moral diagnosis, and it has been argued here that the two preceding views could not do so. His main failure is not a betrayal of health, the key good of his practice. Nor is it a lack of willingness or competence to stand behind his considered judgments. Rather, he lacks professional integrity because he does not act in the name of his practice. Formal requirements, codes of ethics, institutional hierarchies, and collegial norms are among the features of professional practice that engender public expectations of professional role holders. For example, Greg's medical practice is subject to norms regarding respectful consultation and patient autonomy. Greg does not acknowledge the authority of these standards, which means that the word of the practice does not have the normative force to override his personal judgment.

Evidently, the alternative to Greg cannot simply be Holmes's dreaded "plain practical workman," who simply acts on the most straightforward and literal reading of role requirements. As already mentioned, professional integrity is often associated with a refusal to carry out certain role requirements (e.g. abortion and euthanasia). We do not wish to entrust key social goods such as health, education, and legal justice to role holders who surrender their ethical judgment in executing their role. In developing the interpretive view here, the goal is to provide an alternative to both Greg and the practical workman, both of whom fail to achieve an integrated understanding of the practice they represent. Greg does not integrate his sense of professional purpose with the existing features of practice. The practical workman, on the other hand, does not integrate his interpretation of practice with a sense of purpose. It is time to introduce a third character.

In articulating the interpretive view, it will be helpful to borrow the figure of a "chain novelist" from the theory of adjudication developed by Ronald Dworkin. He compares the task of judges to the task of authors engaged in a "chain novel" (Dworkin 1985: 158–162; 1986: 228–238). This comparison elicits a mode of reasoning that has general relevance in the professions. A chain novel is written one chapter at a time, and each finished chapter is passed along to a new author, who writes the next one. The task of each author is to make this the best novel it can be. It must unfold as a coherent story rather than as a mishmash of different visions. This calls for an integrated view of the story elements. The chain novelist "must take up some view about the novel in progress, some working theory about its characters, plot genre, theme, and point, in order to decide what counts as continuing and not as beginning anew" (Dworkin 1986: 230). According to Dworkin, this analogy is apt both to describe and to justify the actions of judges, who know that they are deciding disputes in the name of a practice that has given principled verdicts in similar cases. The good judge views earlier decisions "as part of a long story he must interpret and then continue, according to his own judgment of how to make the developing story as good as it can be" (Dworkin 1986: 239).

Why suppose that the figure of a chain novelist has relevance for professional integrity? Judges are continuing the "story" of law in a readily comprehensible sense, but their standard for decision-making is not obviously applicable to professional roles in general. In order to see the relevance of the chain novelist, we must consider why the analogy was introduced in the first place. The theory of legal adjudication is a response to the fact that judges have to decide "hard cases" that cannot be read straight off the books. How statutes should be applied or precedent invoked is usually open to argument when cases reach court. Judges must rule in favor of a particular reading of the law; the question is what makes one reading better than another. The key end of legal practice is justice, so one might suppose that decisions are better or worse according to the standard of justice. That is, good legal decisions aim for outcomes that conform to a vision of what is morally due to those involved. This sort of answer would suit Greg, if he were a judge. It fits his mode of operation, which is to focus directly on the key end of his profession. However, it would also reintroduce the problems we encountered above. What counts as a just outcome is open to considerable disagreement, and the direct application of justice therefore places too much responsibility on the role holder while failing to explain the authority of the decision.

Dworkin's standard for adjudication involves justice, but not as a direct measure of the quality of legal decisions. As he emphasizes, there is no "license for each judge to find in doctrinal history whatever he thinks should have been there" (Dworkin, 1985: 160). His figure of the chain novelist is opposed to the idea that judges should be guided directly by their perception of moral desert. Rather, their role is to reach an integrated view, where justice is draped "in workclothes," as one commentator has put it (Postema 1997). That is, judgments are informed by a conception of justice *contained within* the grounds of existing law. This conception is likely to be imperfect by the judge's own lights, just as a chain novelist will be disappointed with certain story developments. Nevertheless, neither role holder is entitled to start with a blank slate or make decisions untainted by compromise.

This barely scratches the surface of Dworkin's complex theory of legal adjudication, but it helps to show how the chain novelist represents a mode of reasoning that distinguishes professional integrity. Unlike being good on one's word as an ordinary agent, the professional agent represents a practice that has engendered a multifarious set of legitimate expectations. Professionals face the interpretive challenge of trying to understand how such provisions as codes, organizational procedures, and norms constitute the word of the profession. Like the chain novelist, they must make their decisions in light of an understanding of what others have done, why they have done it, and what this entitles the public to expect....

CONCLUSION

The interpretive view explains professional integrity as a virtue concerned with both fidelity to practice and assurance to the public, connecting these features by emphasizing the role of evaluative judgment. In being good on the word of their practice, professionals of integrity are responsive to the entrusted nature of their responsibility. From various sources of legitimate expectations, they extract the most compelling vision of how to realize the ends of their profession. Like chain novelists who must continue a partly written story, they recognize the normative force of even the flawed features of practice and integrate them into their conception of the role....

ACKNOWLEDGMENTS

The article has benefited from comments by Anders Molander, Edmund Henden, and members of the GPPS group at Centre for the Study of Professions. I am also grateful to Morten Magelssen for the opportunity to present an early version at the Centre for Medical Ethics.

NOTES

1   In this regard, we can distinguish between a *wide* and *narrow* reading of the teleological view. On the wide reading, the profession-specific good that professional integrity is concerned with includes considerations of justice, patient autonomy, etc. It is possible to argue that Cocking and Oakley belong in this wide category because of two features of their account: first, their inclusion of "side constraints" that regulate the means to pursue the internal goals of practice; second, their slightly paradoxically formulated idea that health as the proper goal of medicine is more than health (Cocking & Oakley 2001: 90–92). However, the wide reading leads to further questions concerning how integrity is conceived as a unified virtue when tied to a wider array of considerations. It is, at best, the beginnings of an account of professional integrity.

2   Cox, La Caze and Levine (2003: 103) attribute the generic view to Benjamin (1990, chs. 3 and 6), Calhoun (1995), Grant (1997), and Halfon (1989). To some extent, this attribution rests on implicit assumptions in the texts. Cox, La Caze and Levine provide a brief critical discussion of the view in general terms, but as Pritchard (2006: 67–68) has argued, their own alternative goes too far in the other direction, as they make professional integrity a distinct virtue for every individual profession.

3   Greg's disregard for general moral considerations does not disqualify him from being an agent of integrity on Scherkoske's account, in which the connection between integrity and moral conviction is allegedly "frequent but contingent" (Scherkoske 2013: 63). Scherkoske claims that standards of ordinary integrity can be understood in a non-moral sense. On his account, failure to be good on one's word is an "abuse of the illocutionary norms and commitments internal to assurance" (Scherkoske 2013: 179); so, lack of integrity amounts to abuse of perfomatives like promising or assertion, but supposedly, this does not necessarily involve moral standards.

REFERENCES

Abbott, A. (1988). *The system of professions: An essay on the division of expert labor.* Chicago, University of Chicago Press.

Benjamin, M. (1990). *Splitting the difference: Compromise and integrity in ethics and politics.* Lawrence, University Press of Kansas.

...

Cox D., La Caze M., Levine, M.P. (2003). *Integrity and the fragile self.* Aldershot, Ashgate.

Dare, T. (2009). *The counsel of rogues? A defence of the standard conception of the lawyer's role.* Burlington, Ashgate Publishing.

Dworkin, R. (1985). *A matter of principle.* Cambridge, Harvard University Press.

Dworkin, R. (1986). *Law's empire.* London, Fontana Paperbacks.

Edgar, A., Pattison, S. (2011). Integrity and the moral complexity of professional practice. *Nursing*

Philosophy 12(2): 94–106. http://dx.doi.org/10.1111/
j.1466-769X.2010.0048 1.x

Grant, R.W. (1997). *Hypocrisy and integrity: Machiavelli,
Rousseau, and the ethics of politics.* University
of Chicago Press. http://dx.doi.org/10.7208/
chicago/9780226305929.001.00 01

Halfon, M.S. (1989). *Integrity: A philosophical inquiry.*
Philadelphia, Temple University Press.

Holmes, O.W. (1860). *Currents and counter-currents
in medical science: An address delivered before
the Massachusetts Medical Society, at the Annual
Meeting,* May 30, 1860. Ticknor and Fields

Hughes, E.C. (1984). *The sociological eye: Selected papers.*
New Brunswick, Transaction Books.

...

Lantos, J., Matlock, A., Wendler, D. (2011). Clinician
integrity and limits to patient autonomy. *JAMA,*
305(5): 495–499. http://dx.doi.org/10.1001/
jama.2011.32

...

Miller, F.G., Brody, H. (1995). Professional integrity and
physician-assisted death. *Hastings Center Report*
25(3): 8–17. http://dx.doi.org/10.2307/3562107

Oakley, J., Cocking, D. (2001). *Virtue ethics and
professional roles.* Cambridge, Cambridge
University Press. http://dx.doi.org/10.1017/
CBO9780511487118.

Postema, G. (1997). Integrity: Justice in workclothes.
Iowa Law Review 82: 821–855

...

Scherkoske, G. (2013). *Integrity and the virtues of reason:
Leading a convincing life.* Cambridge, Cambridge
University Press. http://dx.doi.org/10.1017/
CBO9780511732270

...

Wueste, D.E. (2014). Promoting integrity integritively:
Avoiding the Scylla and Charybdis of
abdication and zealotry. Achieving ethical
excellence. *Research in Ethical Issues in
Organizations* 12: 5–27. http://dx.doi.org/10.1108/
S1529-209620140000012001

THE ETHICS OF INSIDER TRADING

Patricia H. Werhane

Insider trading is the reverse of speculation. It is reward without risk, wealth-generated—and injury done to others by an unfair advantage in information.... [T]he core principle is clear: no one should profit from exploitation of important information not available to the public.[1]

INSIDER TRADING IN THE STOCK MARKET IS characterized as the buying or selling of shares of stock on the basis of information known only to the trader or to a few persons. In discussions of insider trading it is commonly assumed that the privileged information, if known to others, would affect their actions in the market as well, although in theory this need not be the case. The present guidelines of the Securities and Exchange Commission prohibit most forms of insider trading. Yet a number of economists and philosophers of late defend this kind of activity both as a viable and useful practice in a free market and as a practice that is not immoral. In response to these defenses I want to question the value of insider trading both from a moral and an economic point of view. I shall argue that insider trading both in its present illegal form and as a legalized market mechanism violates the privacy of concerned parties, destroys competition, and undermines the efficient and proper functioning of a free market, thereby bringing into question its own raison d'être [i.e., reason for being]. It does so and therefore is economically inefficient for the very reason that it is immoral.

That insider trading as an illegal activity interferes with the free market is pretty obvious. It is like a game where there are a number of players each of whom represents a constituency. In this sort of game there are two sets of rules—one ostensive set and another, implicit set, functioning for some of the players. In this analogy some of the implicit rules are outlawed, yet the big players manage to keep them operative and actually often in control of the game. But not all the players know all the rules being played or at least they are ignorant of the most important ones, ones that determine the big wins and big losses. So not all the players realize what rules actually manipulate the outcome. Moreover, partly because some of the most important functioning rules are illegal, some players who do know the implicit rules and could participate do not. Thus not everyone in a position to do so plays the trading game the same way. The game, then, like the manipulated market that is the outcome, is unfair—unfair to some of the players and those they represent—unfair not only because some of the players are not privy to the most important rules, but also because these "special" rules are illegal so that they are adopted only by a few of even the privileged players.

But suppose that insider trading was decriminalized or not prohibited by SEC regulations. Then, one might argue, insider trading would not be unfair because anyone could engage in it with impunity. Although one would be trading on privileged knowledge, others, too, could trade on their privileged information. The market would function more efficiently since the best-informed and those most able to gain information would be allowed to exercise their fiscal capabilities. The market itself would regulate the alleged excesses of insider trading. I use the term "alleged" excesses because according to this line of reasoning, if the market is functioning properly, whatever gains or losses are created as a result of open competition are a natural outcome of that competition. They are not excesses at all, and eventually the market will adjust the so-called unfair gains of speculators.

There are several other defenses of insider trading. First, insider information, e.g., information about a merger, acquisition, new stock issue, layoffs, etc., information known only to a few, *should* be and remain private. That information is the property of those engaged in the activity in question, and they should have the right to regulate its dissemination. Second and conversely, even under ideal circumstances it is impossible either to disseminate information to all interested parties equally and fairly, or alternately, to preserve absolute secrecy. For example, in issuing a new stock or deciding on a stock split, a number of parties in the transaction from brokers to printers learn about that information in advance just because of their participation in making this activity a reality. And there are always shareholders and other interested parties who claim they did not receive information of such an activity or did not receive it at the same time as other shareholders even when the information was disseminated to everyone at the same time. Thus it is, at best, difficult to stop insider trading or to judge whether a certain kind of knowledge is "inside" or privileged. This is not a good reason to defend insider trading as economically or morally desirable, but it illustrates the difficulties of defining and controlling the phenomenon.

Third, those who become privy to inside information, even if they take advantage of that information before it becomes public, are trading on probabilities, not on certainties, since they are trading before the activity actually takes place. They are taking a gamble, and if they are wrong the

market itself will "punish" them. It is even argued that brokers who do not use inside information for their clients' advantage are cheating their clients.

Finally, and more importantly, economists like Henry Manne argue that insider trading is beneficial to outsiders. Whether it is more beneficial than its absence is a question Manne admits he cannot answer. But Manne defends insider trading because, he argues, it reduces the factor of chance in trading both for insiders and outsiders. When shares are traded on information probabilities rather than on rumor or whim, the market reflects more accurately the actual economic status of that company or set of companies. Because of insider trading, stock prices more closely represent the worth of their company than shares not affected by insider trading. Insider trading, then, actually improves the fairness of the market, according to this argument, by reflecting in stock prices the fiscal realities of affected corporations thereby benefitting all traders of the stocks.[2]

These arguments for insider trading are persuasive. Because outsiders are allegedly not harmed from privileged information not available to them and may indeed benefit from insider trading, and because the market punishes rash speculators, insider trading cannot be criticized as exploitation. In fact, it makes the market more efficient. Strong as these arguments are, however, there is something amiss with these claims. The error, I think, rests at least in part with the faulty view of how free markets work, a view which stems from a misinterpretation that derives from a misreading of Adam Smith and specifically a misreading of Smith's notions of self-interest and the Invisible Hand.

The misinterpretation is this. It is sometimes assumed that the unregulated free market, driven by competition and self-interest, will function autonomously. The idea is that the free market works something like the law of gravity—autonomously and anonymously in what I would call a no-blooded fashion. The interrelationships created by free market activities based on self-interested competition are similar to the gravitational relationships between the planets and the sun: impersonal, automatic interactions determined by a number of factors including the distance and competitive self-interest of each of the market components. The free market functions, then, despite the selfish peculiarities of the players just as the planets circle the sun despite their best intentions to do otherwise. Given that picture of the free market, so-called insider trading, driven by self-interest but restrained by competitive forces, that is, the Invisible Hand, is merely one gravitational mechanism—a complication but not an oddity or an aberration in the market.

This is a crude and exaggerated picture of the market, but I think it accounts for talk about the market *as if* it functioned in this independent yet forceful way, and it accounts for defenses of unrestrained self-interested actions in the market place. It allows one to defend insider trading because of the positive market fall-out from this activity, and because the market allegedly will control the excesses of self-interested economic activities.

The difficulty with this analysis is not so much with the view of insider trading as a legitimate activity but rather with the picture of economic actors in a free market. Adam Smith himself, despite his seventeenth-century Newtonian background, did not have such a mechanical view of a laissez-faire economy. Again and again in the *Wealth of Nations* Smith extols the virtues of unrestrained competition as being to the advantage of the producer and the consumer.[3] A system of perfect liberty he argues, creates a situation where "[t]he whole of the advantages and disadvantages of the different employments of labour and stock ... be either perfectly equal or continually tending to equality."[4] Yet for Smith the greatest cause of inequalities of advantage is any restrictive policy or activity that deliberately gives privileges to certain kinds of businesses, trades, or professions.[5] The point is that Smith sees perfect liberty as the necessary condition for competition, but perfect competition occurs only when both parties in the exchange are on more or less equal grounds, whether it be competition for labor, jobs,

consumers, or capital. This is not to imply that Smith favors equality of outcomes. Clearly he does not. But the market is most efficient and most fair when there is competition between equally matched parties.

Moreover, Smith's thesis was that the Invisible Hand works because, and only when, people operate with restrained self-interest, self-interest restrained by reason, moral sentiments, and sympathy, in Smith's case the reason, moral sentiments, and sympathies of British gentlemen. To operate otherwise, that is, with unrestrained self-interest, where that self-interest causes harm to others would "violate the laws of justice"[6] or be a "violation of fair play,"[7] according to Smith. This interferes with free competition just as government regulation would because the character of competition, and thus the direction of the Invisible Hand, depends on the manner in which actors exploit or control their own self-interests. The Invisible Hand, then, that "masterminds" the free market is not like an autonomous gravitational force. It depends on the good will, decency, self-restraint, and fair play of those parties engaging in market activities.[8] When self-interests get out of hand, Smith contends, they must be regulated by laws of justice.[9]

Similarly, the current market, albeit not Smith's ideal of laissez-faire, is affected by how people operate in the marketplace. It does not operate autonomously. Unrestrained activities of insider traders affect competition differently than Smithian exchanges which are more or less equal exchanges between self-interested but restrained parties. The term "insider trading" implies that some traders know more than others, that information affects their decision-making and would similarly affect the trading behavior of others should they become privy to that information. Because of this, the resulting market is different than one unaffected by insider trading. This, in itself, is not a good reason to question insider trading. Henry Manne, for example, recognizes the role of insider trading in influencing the market and finds that, on balance, this is beneficial.

Insider trading, however, is not merely a complication in the free market mechanism. Insider trading, whether it is legal or illegal, affects negatively the ideal of laissez-faire of *any* market, because it thwarts the very basis of the market: competition, just as "insider" rules affect the fairness of the trader even if that activity is not illegal and even if one could, in theory, obtain inside information oneself. This is because the same information, or equal information, is not available to everyone. So competition, which depends on the availability of equal advantage by all parties, is precluded. Insider trading allows the insider to indulge in greed (even though she may not) and that, by eschewing stock prices, works against the very kind of market in which insider trading might be allowed to function.

If it is true, as Manne argues, that insider trading produces a more efficient stock market because stock prices as a result of insider trading better reflect the underlying economic conditions of those companies involved in the trade, he would also have to argue that competition does not always produce the best results in the marketplace. Conversely, if competition creates the most efficient market, insider trading cannot, because competition is "regulated" by insiders. While it is not clear whether outsiders benefit more from insider trading than without that activity, equal access to information would allow (although not determine) every trader to compete from an equal advantage. Thus pure competition, a supposed goal of the free market and an aim of most persons who defend insider trading, is more nearly obtained without insider trading.

Insider trading has other ethical problems. Insider trading does not protect the privacy of information it is supposed to protect. To illustrate, let us consider a case of a friendly merger between Company *X* and Company *Y*. Suppose this merger is in the planning stages and is not to be made public even to the shareholders for a number of months. There may be good or bad reasons for this secrecy, e.g., labor problems, price of shares of acquired company, management changes, unfriendly raiders, competition in certain markets, etc. By law, management and others privy to knowledge about the possible merger cannot trade shares of either company during the negotiating period. On the other hand, if that information is "leaked" to a trader (or if she finds out by some other means), then information that might affect the merger is now in the hands of persons not part of the negotiation. The alleged privacy of information, privacy supposedly protected by insider traders, is now in the hands of not disinterested parties. While they may keep this information a secret, they had no right to it in the first place. Moreover, their possession of the information has three possible negative effects.

First, they or their clients in fact may be interested parties to the merger, e.g., labor union leaders, stockholders in competing companies, etc., the very persons for whom the information makes a difference and therefore are the objects of Company *X* and *Y*'s secrecy. Second, insider trading on privileged information gives unfair advantages to these traders. Even if outsiders benefit from insider trading, they are less likely to benefit as much nor as soon as insider traders for the very reason of their lack of proximity to the activity. Insider traders can use information to their advantage in the market, an advantage neither the management of *X* or *Y* nor other traders can enjoy. Even if the use of such information in the market makes the market more efficient, this is unfair competition since those without this information will not gain as much as those who have such knowledge. Even if insider trading does contribute to market stabilization based on information, nevertheless, one has also to justify the fact that insider traders profit more on their knowledge than outsiders, when their information becomes an actuality simply by being "first" in the trading of the stock. Do insider traders deserve this added profit because their trading creates a more propitious market share knowledge for outsiders? That is a difficult position to defend, because allowing insider trading also allows for the very Boeskyian greed that is damaging in any market.

Third, while trading X and Y on inside information may bring their share prices to the value most closely reflecting their real price-earnings ratio, this is not always the case. Such trading may reflect undue optimism or pessimism about the possible outcome of the merger, an event that has not yet occurred. So the prices of X and Y may be overvalued or undervalued on the basis of a probability, or, because insider traders seldom have all the facts, on guesswork. In these cases insider trading deliberately creates more risk in the market since the stock prices for X or Y are manipulated for not altogether solid reasons. So market efficiency, the end which allegedly justifies insider trading, is not guaranteed.

What Henry Manne's defenses of insider trading do show is what Adam Smith well knew, that the market is neither independent nor self-regulatory. What traders do in the market and how they behave affects the direction and kind of restraint the market will exert on other traders. The character of the market is a product of those who operate within it, as Manne has demonstrated in his defense of insider trading. Restrained self-interest creates an approximation of a self-regulatory market, because it is that that allows self-interested individuals and companies to function as competitively as possible. In the long run the market will operate more efficiently too, because it precludes aberrations such as those exhibited by Ivan Boesky's and David Levine's behavior, behavior that created market conditions favorable to no one except themselves and their clients.

NOTES

1   George Will, "Keep Your Eye on Guiliani," *Newsweek*, March 2, 1987, 84.

2   See Henry Manne, *Insider Trading and the Stock Market* (New York: The Free Press, 1966), especially Chapters X and XI.

3   Adam Smith, *The Wealth of Nations*, ed. R.A. Campbell and A.S. Skinner (Oxford: Oxford University Press, 1976), I.x.c, II.v.8–12.

4   *Wealth of Nations*, I.x.a.1.

5   *Wealth of Nations*, I.x.c.

6   *Wealth of Nations*, IV.ix.51.

7   Adam Smith, *The Theory of Moral Sentiments*, ed. D.D. Raphael and A.L. Macfie (Oxford: Oxford University Press, 1976), II.ii.2.1.

8   See Andrew Skinner, *A System of Social Science* (Oxford: Clarendon Press, 1979), especially 237ff.

9   See, for example, *The Wealth of Nations*, II.ii.94, IV, v.16.

-35-

ETHICALLY CHALLENGED

Lori Robertson

DENNIS LOVE DIDN'T NEED TO DO IT. HE WASN'T manufacturing unheard-of stories, amazing tales that astounded editors and readers alike. He was a good reporter.

His editor still says so. But, perhaps, Love wasn't satisfied with "good," and besides, with the wealth of information on the Internet, "it was very easy," he says. It was also easy to get caught. On November 21, the *Sacramento Bee* fired Love for plagiarizing and fabricating material in his stories on the presidential campaign.

At first, he told editors he didn't know why he did what he did. But he's had some time to think about it. "I think several things contributed to it in my situation," says Love, 47. "No. 1, it's just a simple human fallibility of taking a shortcut where one was available, concerning some stories that maybe I didn't care as much about as some other stories. I know that sounds maybe sort of cavalier. But I really do think that it was a character weakness." There's still an element of mystery, however. "This is not something that I have historically done."

Love had been a political writer with the *Bee* for 20 months. His previous employer, the *Orange County Register*, investigated his work there and found no signs of misappropriation. Love says this is the first time he's done such a thing, and the weird aspect is that some of the stuff he took—from *US News & World Report*, *USA Today*, the *Boston Globe* and the *Dallas Morning News*—didn't seem to be absolutely necessary for the story he already had—"filler quotes," he calls them. In at least one instance, he says, he had interviewed a

source but used somebody else's quotes from the same source anyway. Why would he do that?

Love's firing came at the outset of the most recent spate of plagiarism and fabrication episodes in the news industry. Northwestern University's Medill News Service said November 17 it could not verify information in two of its stories. (It did not name the author, Eric R. Drudis, a Northwestern journalism student.) Papers at which Drudis had previously interned—the *San Jose Mercury News*, the *Philadelphia Daily News* and the *San Francisco Examiner*—subsequently could not find proof that sources from 17 of Drudis' stories had existed. In late December, the *Detroit News* admitted to lifting a paragraph from a suburban weekly. Publisher and Editor Mark Silverman says a reporter and an editor were disciplined, though he would not provide details. About a week later, a *Mercury News* intern, David Cragin, was suspended—and shortly thereafter fired for plagiarizing material, including the words of the *Washington Post* and the *San Francisco Chronicle*. In its January 15 issue, *Business Week* apologized for using "information and wording without attribution" from the *Washington Post*. The column in question, by Marcia Stepanek, a journalist with about 20 years of experience, borrowed heavily from the *Post* article. After a two-month investigation, *Business Week* fired her. At Myrtle Beach, South Carolina's *Sun News*, Features Editor Mona Prufer stepped down January 15 after evidence of copying appeared in her weekly books column and a cooking column. And, on February 7, the

Bloomsburg, Pennsylvania, *Press Enterprise* fired reporter Steven Helmer after he admitted to fabricating at least one person in a story about a local shopping mall....

The understanding of what constitutes plagiarism is not universally held. When Dewitt taught a freshman journalism class at Kansas State University during the 1989–90 school year, one of her students lifted whole paragraphs from a *Newsweek* article. Dewitt told the student she would receive an automatic F; the student protested that she had mentioned the *Newsweek* article in her piece. The fact that she still couldn't swipe chunks of another person's story "seemed a very difficult concept for her to grasp," Dewitt says, adding that it's a problem she's heard of at other universities as well.

The *San Jose Mercury News'* David Cragin didn't get it either. When he admitted to using passages from a story by the *Post's* Ahrens, he told the *Merc*, "I know it's pretty similar obviously, but that's just a small piece of the story." He didn't think what he'd done was unethical, but said, "evidently, I guess I'm wrong." (*Mercury News* Executive Editor David Yarnold, however, disagrees with that statement. "My guess is he knew that it was wrong at the time," Yarnold says.)

In a December 26 story on San Francisco families living in hotels, Cragin wrote: "Most of these hotels in the city are more than half a century old; they were built for the solitary working men who streamed into the city to toil at the wharves and the railway lines. They were never meant for families." Ahrens had written November 27: "Most of these hotels are more than a half-century old; they were built as hives for the working men who streamed to this city to toil at the wharves and the railway lines. They were never meant for families."

Ahrens, who was out of town when the plagiarism news broke, received a hearty, "'Way to go, congratulations,'" from *Post* colleagues, he says. His own reaction was that "it was odd," to see his words under someone else's name. "Writers tend to remember what they wrote.... I remember where I was when I was writing things." He recalls sweating over a "short, powerful" line that would pull readers into a long story: "They were never meant for families."

"I could see," Ahrens says, "in his story, it was like boilerplate."

Writers do remember their turns of phrase, the right word that finally came to them in the shower, their rhythm, the decision to go back and put in periods to make short, choppy sentences.

All of which makes the "accidental" plagiarism, the "it got mixed up in my notes" excuse, a little harder to believe. Ahrens, for one, isn't buying it. "That's baloney," he says. "That's a big pile of sliced baloney.... If you're not a halfwit or a felon ... you know what's going on."

Meyer also brings up the carelessness excuse, but then adds, "it doesn't sound viable for me."

Others can see it happening, however, and news organizations have accepted that plea. Ruth Shalit, for one, admitted to being "a klutz" when charged with plagiarism in two stories in *The New Republic* in 1994 and 1995. She continued working at the magazine, faced another incident in 1996— after which she took a leave of absence—and eventually left in January 1999.

Whether the cut-and-paste ease and the mass of electronic information will lead to more cases of plagiarism—or more firings—is unclear. Some editors, such as Rosemary Armao, wouldn't accept the "mistaken ownership" excuse. "I just don't think we have any room for it," says the *Sarasota Herald-Tribune* managing editor. "There is something that has to be absolute, and that's that it's an original work product."

She continues, "The Internet has certainly increased the number of resources and sources you can use." That doesn't mean you can't name those sources.

Editors seem to be most forgiving when copying involves news briefs or items based on wire and other news accounts. That's when a bungled attribution becomes more understandable. In July, *San Antonio Express-News* Sports Editor Mitchell Krugel apologized to readers, as did Editor Robert Rivard, for not crediting four paragraphs in Krugel's piece on Tiger Woods to *Fort Worth Star-Telegram* columnist Gil LeBreton. The story carried Krugel's byline and the tag line: "Express-News wire services contributed to this report." The LeBreton piece ran on the Knight Ridder/Tribune News Service wire. Krugel wrote in his apology that he was not trying to use LeBreton's words as his own, but he should have better attributed his material.

As a result, an *Express-News* committee took a look at the paper's policy. "Given the landscape," one of information saturation, says Krugel, "we should examine and reexamine attribution consistently, and this is a situation that helped raise the consciousness on doing better journalism"....

Editors who have dealt with plagiarism or fabrication often try to institute a reform or ethical reinforcement in the aftermath....

After Julie Amparano was fired by the *Arizona Republic* for fabrication in August 1999, the paper reworked its corrections policy, says Reader Advocate Richard de Uriarte. Corrections are seen by the entire newsroom; the paper creates "an electronic paper trail of each call, each concern, its resolution ... by editor, by the section, that kind of thing," he says. The message behind these correction chronicles is, "Look what has gone wrong; look what can be done better."

The *Sacramento Bee* had halted its usual brown-bag ethics lunches for about a year while it altered its pagination process. In the wake of the Love incident, Editor Rodriguez says the paper reinstituted the sessions in January. The episode fostered many discussions at the paper on what constitutes plagiarism. A "high-profile, unfortunate incident reinforces to people that we take the issue very seriously, and we'll deal with it very seriously," Rodriguez says....

After Love was fired by the *Bee*, his former employer, the *Orange County Register*, held a series of internal training sessions in its bureaus. Ombudsman Dennis Foley and Training Editor Larry Welbom led discussions on plagiarism and ethics, aimed mostly at younger reporters. Foley saw it as a "good opportunity to remind everybody

that our craft and our ethics and our credibility ... is tied up in this," he says.

Other papers use high-profile cases to encourage discussion and awareness, as does Northwestern University. Ken Bode, the journalism school's dean, says the school would "stop the presses when anything like this happens in the real world of journalism," hosting ethics panels on the actual cases. "You hope that people don't have to learn the ethics and regulations of our profession on the run and on the road." (Bode was barred from talking about the Drudis case because of federal student privacy laws.)

But the idea that a news organization would implement plagiarism safeguards seems almost silly to some editors. "You're talking about one of the most basic sins in journalism, and we have a very detailed code of ethics," says *Business Week* Editor in Chief Stephen B. Shepard, "and it does not say, 'Do not steal,' on the assumption that anyone who works at *Business Week* bloody well knows that."

Some journalists may need a little reminding. "Maybe [news organizations] need to quit assuming that the basics are that well understood by people they hire," says SPJ's Fred Brown. "The other thing is to communicate with journalism schools to make sure they're teaching that lesson."

Business Week does fact-check stories, but only to verify the names of people, companies and institutions, says Shepard. The rest is the responsibility of the writer. Most newspapers, with daily deadlines, don't see fact-checking as a viable reform. And given Glass' ability to fool TNR's fact-checkers—he built a fake Web site, gave fake phone numbers—it's uncertain whether that would catch a determined fabricator or plagiarist before a story made it into print.

Since at least 1987, the *Orange County Register* has carried out accuracy checks. At first, the ombudsman would send out short surveys to news sources, asking how they had been treated by the paper, and then circulate the responses. Now, Foley sends letters inviting sources to call him or have him come talk to them. While it may help the paper's credibility and news practices, the policy is not designed to catch stolen words or made-up people. "It's not intended to be the internal affairs investigation accusing the reporters of doing wrong," Foley says....

But don't journalists corner the market on skepticism? Maybe not when it comes to one of their own. Geneva Overholser, a syndicated columnist with the Washington Post Writers Group and a journalism professor at the University of Missouri, says more skepticism may be what's needed. "At the very first suspicion you have to ask," she says, comparing editors to the spouses of alcoholics. They begin to suspect something. But they don't want to believe it.

When San Antonio's Krugel didn't give a columnist his proper credit, the paper gushed with apology to its readers. When the *Arizona Republic* fired Julie Amparano, it told readers on its front page and followed with a 2,800-word treatise on her ouster. When Rodriguez fired Love, he published a letter from the editor on the incident the next day. Most of the 30 to 40 calls and e-mails he then received from readers were supportive. "I think they were surprised that we dealt with it that directly and that publicly," he says. "Some of them thought we were being sanctimonious"....

Public embarrassment coupled with swift punishment may be the best deterrent to crimes of copying or out-and-out lying. It may also change the public's views: In an October 1998 survey by the Media Studies Center, 76 per cent of respondents believed that journalists often or sometimes plagiarize, and 66 per cent said they make stuff up.

To some observers, punishments dished out today tend to be more harsh than in the past. "I think there are more serious consequences than there used to be," says SPJ's Brown. He feels the Smith/Barnicle cases "raised the bar."

Meyer says some penalties in the last few years were "way too heavy." Many journalists thought *Globe* editorial page columnist Jeff Jacoby's four-month suspension in July wasn't warranted. Jacoby's July 3 column on the signers of the Declaration of Independence was hardly an original idea—the gist of it was zipping around the Internet. His version resembled several other accounts, including one in a 1975 book by Paul Harvey.

Imagine if today a writer included factual errors in a review of an Elton John concert, and it turned out that writer had never picked up her press ticket. When Patricia Smith did so in 1986 at the *Chicago Sun-Times*, she received a lecture— ironically from then *Sun-Times* Editor Storin— and wasn't allowed to write for several months. In 2001, most papers would launch a full-scale investigation into the matter as well as the writer's past works.

News organizations' commitment to deal with plagiarists and fabricators firmly and immediately and the subsequent revelations to the public can only raise credibility and instill a greater fear in would-be thieves. But—and this is a big but—the industry is more than willing to grant second chances. The list of past offenders who made a comeback is long: National Public Radio's Nina Totenberg; the *New York Times*' Fox Butterfield; Salon.com columnist Ruth Shalit; Mike Barnicle, who joined the *New York Daily News* in March 1999; and Patricia Smith, who was hired by *Ms. Magazine* to write a column in January 2000, among many others. Of course—as evidenced by this story—those charges will haunt those writers, quite possibly for the rest of their careers.

"It will probably never go away," says Barnicle, who adds that the *Globe* rescinded its accusation of plagiarism. (Storin says that's a fair statement. The columnist ultimately left amid fabrication charges.) "It's always out there lurking in some people's minds, not the readers', I don't think ... but in the business." It is a heavy scarlet letter to bear. It's indicative of not only the gravity of the offenses, but the very small percentage of journalists who commit them. The surprising thing is that only one person interviewed for this article said that under no circumstances would she offer a job to someone who had made up material or stolen words.

Says Rosemary Annao: "If I knew about it, I wouldn't hire them. There are so many good people in the market, why take somebody with that mark against them?" She says she can hardly even read *Ms.* since it hired Smith....

Dennis Love says he's "trying to just accept responsibility for what I did with as much dignity as I can and move on." He is freelancing for some trade magazines and working on a biography of Stevie Wonder. Asked if he will pursue a newspaper career again, he says he's not sure if it's up to him. "I don't know if somebody in my situation gets a second chance or not," Love says. "I could see it happening, I guess.... But I don't know the answer.... In the future, I think that I would like to."

His old boss, Rodriguez, says it would probably be difficult for Love to find a job in journalism in the near future. But he's a believer in second chances as well. "He's such a good writer that you would hope at some point he would use that craft again."

Judging from history, Love could find a second journalistic life. But, in five, maybe 10 years, when AJR inevitably does another piece on plagiarism, his name, along with many of the rest, doubtless will appear again.

—36—

TELLING THE TRUTH TO PATIENTS

A Clinical Ethics Exploration

David C. Thomasma

...

REASONS FOR TELLING THE TRUTH

IS THERE EVER A CIRCUMSTANCE IN HUMAN affairs when it might be better not to know the truth to protect our values? This question occurs now and then in our lives, and it is a traumatic one. For the most part, we assume that knowledge is power. It is important, we might reason, at all times to know the truth so that we can act on it by making informed choices. Perhaps the most significant form of this priority doctrine (the truth comes first) in healthcare is found in the principle of informed consent. Through it, all persons are guaranteed sufficient information to make intelligent decisions about their care based on their values. On the face of it, we would be hard pressed to consider any time or circumstance when the truth would not take precedence over other considerations. Not to receive the truth would be a form of unacceptable paternalism. Persons would be "protecting" us from harm by destroying our autonomy. This would hardly be a way of truly protecting us.[1]

The matter is more complex than that, however. In all human relationships, the truth is told for a myriad of reasons. A summary of the prominent reasons are that it is a right, a utility, and a kindness.

It is a right to be told the truth because respect for the person demands it. As Kant argued, human society would soon collapse without truth telling, because it is the basis of interpersonal trust, covenants, contracts, and promises.

The truth is a utility as well, because persons need to make informed judgments about their actions. It is a mark of maturity that individuals advance and grow morally by becoming more and more self-aware of their needs, their motives, and their limitations. All these steps toward maturity require honest and forthright communication, first from parents and later also from siblings, friends, lovers, spouses, children, colleagues, co-workers, and caregivers.[2]

Finally, it is a kindness to be told the truth, a kindness rooted in virtue precisely because persons to whom lies are told will of necessity withdraw from important, sometimes life-sustaining and life-saving relationships. Similarly, those who tell lies poison not only their relationships but themselves, rendering themselves incapable of virtue and moral growth[3]....

KINDS OF TRUTH

There are at least four broad categories of truth in human relationships. The first we might call direct truth. This is a response to an interrogatory question for which an answer is rather straightforward. A "yes" or "no" will suffice in most instances. "Are we going to the concert tonight?" might be a good example of such a question. A second, related type of truth might be called factual truth. This truth references objective reality. The fact that it is raining out is a truth to be told, should someone inquire. This would allow the inquirer to prepare to get an umbrella to go out to the car. Sometimes we might wish to withhold the truth or even lie about objective reality to tease a person. In any case, it is easily checked by the recipient of our joke, and little harm is done.

More important for our consideration are the next two types of truth, personal truth and interpretive truth.

Personal truth requires the speaker to inform the listener, and vice versa, about interior reality. It requires self-disclosure. Often self-disclosure is developmental; it is revealed over time as a relationship solidifies. Personal feelings are a good example of these truths. To tell another how one is truly feeling is important, so that lingering problems about feelings do not fester. If a husband says he does not mind if his beloved wants to dance with an old boyfriend but actually does mind a whole lot, that lack of truthfulness will spoil the evening for him and later, I am sure, for her, when his resentment comes out. If a patient does not truthfully reveal how she is feeling to her doctor, then the first step in diagnosis or therapy will be misled, to the detriment both of the patient and the relationship itself.

Interpretative or hermeneutical truth is the most complex of all truths, closely mirroring the complexity of human relationships and communication. In it, the responder tries to interpret the real reasons an individual makes an inquiry. This truth is important for how the other person, most often the caregiver in healthcare, thinks of us or how we respond to that other person. A good example might be those occasions during which values seem more important than the truth: a married couple might not be able sometimes to tell each other the truth about how they appear to one another for fear that that information needlessly might "crush" the other person. "Tell me how I look, honey" might become an open invitation to destroy the husband or wife who has gained 50 pounds over the years....

OVERRIDING THE TRUTH

When we stop and think of it, there are times when, at least for the moment, protecting us from the truth can save our egos, our self-respect, and even our most cherished values. Not all of us act rationally and autonomously at all times. Sometimes we are under sufficient stress that others must act to protect us from harm. This is called necessary paternalism. Should we become seriously ill, others must step in and rescue us if we are incapable of doing it ourselves. Consider how the comedian and actor John Belushi's family and friends watched him deteriorate on drugs but continued to say, "John's an adult; he can take care of himself."[4] But Belushi was not capable of making that move. He subsequently died without the intervention he needed....

In Healthcare Relationships

... Early in the 1960s, studies were done that revealed the majority of physicians would not disclose a diagnosis of cancer to a patient. Reasons cited were mostly those that derived from nonmaleficence. Physicians were concerned that such a diagnosis might disturb the equanimity of a patient and might lead to desperate acts. Primarily physicians did not want to destroy their patients' hope. By the middle 1970s, however, repeat studies brought to light a radical shift in physician attitudes. Unlike earlier views, physicians now emphasized patient autonomy and informed consent over paternalism. In the doctor-patient relation, this meant the majority of physicians stressed the patient's right to full disclosure of diagnosis and prognosis.

One might be tempted to ascribe this shift of attitudes to the growing patients' rights and autonomy movements in the philosophy of medicine and in public affairs. No doubt some of the change can be attributed to this movement. But also treatment interventions for cancer led to greater optimism about modalities that could offer some hope to patients. Thus, to offer them full disclosure of their diagnosis no longer was equivalent to a death sentence. Former powerlessness of the healer was supplanted with technological and pharmaceutical potentialities.

A more philosophical analysis of the reasons for a shift comes from a consideration of the goal of medicine. The goal of all healthcare relations is to receive/provide help for an illness such that no further harm is done to the patient, especially in that patient's vulnerable state.[5] The vulnerability arises because of increased dependency. Presumably, the doctor will not take advantage of this vulnerable condition by adding to it through inappropriate use of power or the lack of compassion. Instead, the vulnerable person should be assisted back to a state of human equality, if possible, free from the prior dependency.[6]

First, the goal of the healthcare giver-patient relation is essentially to restore the patient's autonomy. Thus, respect for the right of the patient to the truth is measured against the goal. If nothing toward that goal can be gained by telling the truth at a particular time, still it must be told for other reasons. Yet, if the truth would impair the restoration of autonomy, then it may be withheld on grounds of potential harm. Thus the goal of the healing relationship enters into the calculus of values that are to be protected.

Second, most healthcare relationships of an interventionist character are temporary, whereas relationships involving primary care, prevention, and chronic or dying care are more permanent. These differences also have a bearing on truth telling. During a short encounter with healthcare strangers, patients and healthcare providers will of necessity require the truth more readily than during a long-term relation among near friends. In the short term, decisions, often dramatically important ones, need to be made in a compressed period. There is less opportunity to maneuver or delay for other reasons, even if there are concerns about the truth's impact on the person.

Over a longer period, the truth may be withheld for compassionate reasons more readily.

Here, the patient and physician or nurse know one another. They are more likely to have shared some of their values. In this context, it is more justifiable to withhold the truth temporarily in favor of more important long-term values, which are known in the relationship....

CLINICAL CASE CATEGORIES

The general principles about truth telling have been reviewed, as well as possible modifications formed from the particularities of the healthcare professional-patient relationship. Now I turn to some contemporary examples of how clinical ethics might analyze the hierarchy of values surrounding truth telling.

There are at least five clinical case categories in which truth telling becomes problematic: intervention cases, long-term care cases, cases of dying patients, prevention cases, and nonintervention cases.

Intervention Cases

Of all clinically different times to tell the truth, two typical cases stand out. The first usually involves a mother of advanced age with cancer. The family might beg the surgeon not to tell her what has been discovered for fear that "Mom might just go off the deep end." The movie *Dad*, starring Jack Lemmon, had as its centerpiece the notion that Dad could not tolerate the idea of cancer. Once told, he went into a psychotic shock that ruptured standard relationships with the doctors, the hospital, and the family. However, because this diagnosis requires patient participation for chemotherapeutic interventions and the time is short, the truth must be faced directly. Only if there is not to be intervention might one withhold the truth from the patient for a while, at the family's request, until the patient is able to cope with the reality. A contract about the time allowed before telling the truth might be a good idea....

More complicated ... is a case of a young Hispanic woman, a trauma accident victim, who is gradually coming out of a coma. She responds only to commands such as "move your toes." Because she is now incompetent, her mother and father are making all care decisions in her case. Her boyfriend is a welcome addition to the large, extended family. However, the physicians discover that she is pregnant. The fetus is about 5 weeks old. Eventually, if she does not recover, her surrogate decision makers will have to be told about the pregnancy, because they will be involved in the terrible decisions about continuing the life of the fetus even if it is a risk to the mother's recovery from the coma. This revelation will almost certainly disrupt current family relationships and the role of the boyfriend. Further, if the mother is incompetent to decide, should not the boyfriend, as presumed father, have a say in the decision about his own child?

In this case, revelation of the truth must be carefully managed. The pregnancy should be revealed only on a "need to know" basis, that is, only when the survival of the young woman becomes critical. She is still progressing moderately towards a stable state.

Long-term Cases

Rehabilitation medicine provides one problem of truth telling in this category. If a young man has been paralyzed by a football accident, his recovery to some level of function will depend upon holding out hope. As he struggles to strengthen himself, the motivation might be a hope that caregivers know to be false, that he may someday be able to walk again. Yet, this falsehood is not corrected, lest he slip into despair. Hence, because this is a long-term relationship, the truth will be gradually discovered by the patient under the aegis of encouragement by his physical therapists, nurses, and physicians, who enter his life as near friends.

Cases of Dying Patients

Sometimes, during the dying process, the patient asks directly, "Doctor, am I dying?" Physicians are frequently reluctant to "play God" and tell the patient how many days or months or years they have left. This reluctance sometimes bleeds over into a less-than-forthright answer to the question just asked. A surgeon with whom I make rounds once answered this question posed by a terminally ill cancer patient by telling her that she did not have to worry about her insurance running out!...

Prevention Cases

A good example of problems associated with truth telling in preventive medicine might come from screening. The high prevalence of prostate cancer among men over 50 years old may suggest the utility of cancer screening. An annual checkup for men over 40 years old is recommended. Latent and asymptomatic prostate cancer is often clinically unsuspected and is present in approximately 30% of men over 50 years of age. If screening were to take place, about 16.5 million men in the United States alone would be diagnosed with prostate cancer, or about 2.4 million men each year. As of now, only 120,000 cases are newly diagnosed each year. Thus, as Timothy Moon noted in a recent sketch of the disease, "a majority of patients with prostate cancer that is not clinically diagnosed will experience a benign course throughout their lifetime."[7]

The high incidence of prostate cancer coupled with a very low malignant potential would entail a whole host of problems if subjected to screening. Detection would force patients and physicians to make very difficult and life-altering treatment decisions. Among them are removal of the gland (with impotence a possible outcome), radiation treatment, and most effective of all, surgical removal of the gonads (orchiectomy). But why consider these rather violent interventions if the probable outcome of neglect will overwhelmingly be benign? For this reason the US Preventive Services Task Force does not recommend either for or against screening for prostate cancer.[8] Quality-of-life issues would take precedence over the need to know.

Nonintervention Cases

This last example more closely approximates the kind of information one might receive as a result of genes mapping. This information could tell you of the likelihood or probability of encountering a number of diseases through genetic heritage, for example, adult onset or type II diabetes, but could not offer major interventions for most of them (unlike a probability for diabetes).

Some evidence exists from recent studies that the principle of truth telling now predominates in the doctor-patient relationship. Doctors were asked about revealing diagnosis for Huntington's disease and multiple sclerosis, neither of which is subject to a cure at present. An overwhelming majority would consider full disclosure. This means that, even in the face of diseases for which we have no cure, truth telling seems to take precedence over protecting the patient from imagined harms....

CONCLUSION

Truth in the clinical relationship is factored in with knowledge and values.

First, truth is contextual. Its revelation depends upon the nature of the relationship between the doctor and patient and the duration of that relationship.

Second, truth is a secondary good. Although important, other primary values take precedence over the truth. The most important of these values is survival of the individual and the community. A close second would be preservation of the relationship itself.

Third, truth is essential for healing an illness. It may not be as important for curing a disease.

That is why, for example, we might withhold the truth from the woman with ambiguous genitalia, curing her disease (having a gonad) in favor of maintaining her health (being a woman).

Fourth, withholding the truth is only a temporary measure. *In vino, veritas* it is said. The truth will eventually come out, even if in a slip of the tongue. Its revelation, if it is to be controlled, must always aim at the good of the patient for the moment.

At all times, the default mode should be that the truth is told. If, for some important reason, it is not to be immediately revealed in a particular case, a truth-management protocol should be instituted so that all caregivers on the team understand how the truth will eventually be revealed.

NOTES

1 Pellegrino, E.D., Thomasma, D.C., *For the Patient's Good: The Restoration of Beneficence in Health Care* (New York: Oxford University Press, 1988).

2 Bok, S., *Lying: Moral Choice in Public and Personal Life* (New York: Vintage Books, 1989).

3 Pellegrino, E.D., Thomasma, D.C., *The Virtues in Medical Practice* (New York: Oxford University Press, 1993).

4 Woodward, B., *Wired: The Short Life and Fast Times of John Belushi.* Book Club Ed (New York: Simon & Schuster, 1984).

5 See note 1, Pellegrino, Thomasma, 1988.

6 Cassell, E., "The Nature of Suffering and the Goals of Medicine," *New England Journal of Medicine* (1982) Vol. 306(11): 639–45.

7 Moon, T.D., "Prostate Cancer," *Journal of the American Geriatrics Society* (1992) Vol. 40: 622–27 (quote from 626).

8 Ibid.

—37—

LIES, DAMN LIES AND UNETHICAL LIES

How to Negotiate Ethically and Effectively

David Geronemus

WHAT ETHICS RULES APPLY WHEN LAWYERS ENTER the often sleight-of-hand world of negotiation? Ethical questions in negotiation present a unique problem. General notions of ethics encourage honesty. However, a rule of complete honesty in negotiation is plainly unworkable. Deception is at the core of many commonly accepted negotiating strategies. As Professor James White has observed, "Like the poker player, a negotiator hopes that his opponent will overestimate the value of his hand. Like the poker player, in a variety of ways he must facilitate his opponent's inaccurate assessment."

In addition, ethical dilemmas for business lawyers are complicated because they are negotiating on behalf of others. It is no doubt permissible for an individual negotiating on behalf of his or her own interest to eschew any tactic that he or she finds ethically distasteful. The situation is more difficult for lawyers who have a duty to seek the best results—within ethical limits—for their clients.

Not surprisingly, the limits of ethical behavior in negotiation are often murky. Surveys of lawyers, judges and academics about a variety of ethics issues in negotiation have shown that there is often little unanimity in views.

It is, however, not a sufficient answer for the lawyer to say that ethical lines are hard to draw. Negotiation is a pervasive activity for lawyers, and, as a result, understanding the relevant ethical precepts and making defensible ethical choices without unnecessarily sacrificing effectiveness is vital....

BOB'S LAWYER AND ETHICS: THE DISCUSSION

Question No. 1: Your Bottom Line

You are negotiating the sale of Bob's Books, to a major national chain, Kings and Boundaries. Your client, Bob, is shy and retiring (literally, as well as figuratively) and has asked you to conduct the negotiations. He has given you broad authority to sell the business as long as he gets at least $500,000 for it. After several hours of negotiation, counsel for the prospective buyer says, "Will your client accept $500,000?" You are certain that the buyer will pay more. Is it acceptable to say, "No, it will take at least $750,000"?

Discussion:

In my view, it is perfectly acceptable under the Model Rules of Professional Conduct and the Model Code of Professional Responsibility to tell the prospective buyer that your client's minimum price is greater than it really is.

Rule 4 .1 (a) of the Model Rules states that a lawyer shall not "knowingly ... make a false statement of material fact or law to a third person." DR7–102(A)(5) of the Model Code is similar. However, the comments to the Model Rules explain that the rules refer only to a statement of "fact," and that whether a statement is one of fact "can depend on the circumstances. Under generally accepted conventions in negotiation, certain types of statements are not taken as statements of material fact. Estimates of the price or value placed on the subject of a transaction and a party's intentions as to an acceptable settlement of a claim are in this category...."

There are justifications for this rule beyond negotiating conventions. One might argue that the statement that Bob will not take $500,000 is not misleading—that if Bob were sitting at the table and knew it was likely that the other side would pay more than $500,000, there is no way that he would accept $500,000. Or, one may contend that the law of fraud generally prohibits false statements of fact, and that you have been asked for your opinion about Bob's intention—not about any facts. (But see Shell, "When is it legal to lie in negotiations?" 32, *Sloan Management Rev.* 93 [1991] noting that courts have punished statements of intent or opinion as fraudulent in particularly egregious cases, but arguing that lies about reservation prices are not material.)

More important, misleading the other side about your reservation price is a key negotiating strategy. Unless a negotiator were to avoid the tactic of telling the other side that its bid was below his reservation price even when that were true, any evasion of the question whether $500,000 is acceptable might well be construed as an admission that it is acceptable.

Thus, if one could not misrepresent one's bottom line, negotiations between negotiators who follow the rule might well be negotiations in which both negotiators disclosed (at least implicitly by using evasive answers) their bottom lines and then proceeded to try to find a way to compromise on any overlap. While one may argue about

the relative merits and efficiency of such a system of negotiation, this is simply not how negotiations proceed.

Finally, it is probably rare that a party will discover whether the other party was telling the truth about its bottom line. Thus, a rule that did not permit misrepresentation of a bottom line would penalize honest, rule-following negotiators, and give advantage to the dishonest.

Question No. 2: *Your Authority*

Assume that the facts are the same as in question No. 1, except that the buyer's counsel asks you, "Are you authorized to accept $500,000?" Can you answer "No"?

Discussion:

This is a closer question than question No. 1. However, on balance, the better view is that you should be able misrepresent your authority consistent with the Model Rules and the Model Code.

The comments to the Model Rules do not directly address this question. Further, it is more difficult to argue that a negative response to this question is not a statement of fact, although one may at least construct an argument that a negative response is not misleading. Surely what Bob meant was that you have authority to accept $500,000 only if that is the most you can get. Thus, arguably, when you think that you can get more, you do not have the authority to take $500,000.

Some considerations are far more important than this argument, which is admittedly somewhat strained. Any distinction between the propriety of a false answer about your authority and your bottom line is both razor thin and hyper technical. The prospective buyer in both cases is seeking virtually the same information—can the sale be completed for $500,000? In my view, the two situations are so materially similar that it would be bad policy to treat them differently

Consider the effect of a rule that did not permit lies about authority. The question whether a lie about authority has been told is not more likely to be discovered than whether a lie about the bottom line has been told. Thus, a rule that required honesty in response to a question about one's authority might well aid the unscrupulous at the expense of those who follow the rules.

Alternatively, the honesty rule might simply be evaded by negotiators agreeing with their clients that they will not have final authority to make any deal. Efficiency considerations aside, I am not sure that any rule that requires such contortions on the part of negotiators is sensible.

There is nothing approaching consensus on this question. A 1988 survey (Lempert) asked nine law professors, five seasoned litigators, a federal judge and a federal magistrate about the propriety of misrepresenting authorized limits. "Of those willing to give a straight yes or no answer, six say no, you cannot say that. Seven say yes, you can—but all but one of these add that as a matter of personal ethics or strategy, they would not give such an answer."

In light of the Model Rules' rationale that lies about your bottom line are acceptable because "generally accepted conventions" of negotiating regard them as acceptable, this lack of unanimity cannot be wholly disregarded. However, I believe that the two inquiries—about bottom lines and about authority—are so similar that it does not make sense to develop different rules for them.

Question No. 3: The Other Offer

Let's change our hypothetical a bit. You are still trying to sell Bob's Books, with authority to accept $500,000. However, the lawyer for Kings and Boundaries is being far less forthcoming with money. To date, he has offered only $250,000. Bob has been attempting to sell the stores for some time and is getting very anxious to sell. He has, however, had no other offers. Since Bob also owns Bob's Boats (which you also represent) you are particularly anxious to keep Bob happy. Bob suggests a negotiating tactic—he asks you to tell the Kings and Boundaries' lawyer that he has another offer from
a competing national chain. Can you make Bob happy and convey this to Kings and Boundaries?

Discussion:

Although this is not an entirely uncommon practice, there is little doubt that it is unethical. Both the Model Rules and the Model Code prohibit knowing misstatements of fact (the Rules add a requirement of materiality). If Bob's lawyer conveys the fictional other offer, I believe he has made a knowing misstatement of material fact and violated his ethical obligations.

Indeed, there are cases that hold that such conduct amounts to fraud. For example, in *Kabatchnik v. Hanover Elm Building Corp.* (103 N.E.2d 692 (Mass. 1952)), a landlord used a false other tenant to induce a tenant to pay a higher rent. The tenant successfully sued for fraud. See generally Shell, "When is it legal to lie in negotiations," 32 *Sloan Management Rev.* 93 (1991).

Question No. 4: A Drafting Error

The negotiations for the sale of Bob's enter their final phase following an agreement on a sales price. Kings and Boundaries insists that Bob personally indemnify it for any breach of representations and warranties. After a lengthy discussion, Bob agrees. When you receive the final draft of the purchase and sale agreement from the buyer's lawyer (an old friend and former mentor), it omits the indemnity provision. Can you inform buyer's counsel of the mistake?

Discussion:

ABA Informal Opinion 86–1518 addresses the question of the inadvertent omission of a contractually agreed on provision and concludes, under the Model Rules, that "the error is appropriate for correction between the lawyers without client consultation." The Opinion notes that even if the information were considered "relating to the representation" and therefore presumptively confidential under Rule 1.6, disclosure would be permitted as one that is "impliedly authorized in order to carry out the representation." "The Comment to Rule 1.6 points out that a lawyer has implied authority to make 'a disclosure that facilitates a satisfactory conclusion'—in this case completing the commercial contract already agreed on and left to the lawyers to memorialize."

Although the Opinion does not clearly state that a lawyer must inform his or her adversary of the mistake, that is clearly the better practice. The Opinion cautions that the client does not have a right to try to capitalize on the error and that if the lawyer were to counsel the client to attempt to do so, he or she "might raise a serious question of the violation" of Rule 1.2(d)'s prohibition against counseling or assisting a client in fraudulent conduct. The Opinion concludes that the results would be the same under the Model Code....

JUST WHAT *ARE* THOSE RULES, ANYWAY?

Here are the texts of the Moral Rules and the Code of Professional Responsibility that are referred to in the accompanying article:

Model Rule 4.1: Truthfulness in statements to others

In the course of representing a client, a lawyer shall not knowingly:

1. make a false statement of material fact or law to a third person; or
2. fail to disclose a material fact to a third person when disclosure is necessary to avoid assisting a criminal or fraudulent act by a client, unless disclosure is prohibited by Rule 1.6

Code of Professional Responsibility, DR 7–102: Representing a client within the bounds of the law

3. In his representation of a client, a lawyer shall not: ...
4. (3) Conceal or knowingly fail to disclose that which he is required by law to reveal....
5. Knowingly make a false statement of law or fact....

BIBLIOGRAPHY OF LAW REVIEW ARTICLES

Dahl, "Ethics on the table: Stretching the truth in negotiations," 8 *Review of Litigation* 173 (1988)

Hazard, "The lawyer's obligation to be trustworthy when dealing with opposing parties," 33 *S.C.L. Rev.* 181 (1981)

Jarvis and Tellam, "A negotiation ethics primer for lawyers," 31 *Gonz. L. Rev.* 549 (1995)

Lempert, "In settlement talks, does telling the truth have its limits?," 2 *Inside Litigation* 1 (1988)

Lowenthal, "The bar's failure to require truthful bargaining by lawyers," 2 *Geo.J. Leg. Ethics* 411 (1988)

Perschbaker, "Regulating lawyers' negotiations," 27 *Ariz. L. Rev.* 75 (1985)

Rubin, "A causerie on lawyers' ethics in negotiations," 35 *La. L. Rev.* 577 (1975)

Rubin, "The ethics of negotiation: Are there any?" 56 *La. L Rev.* 447 (1995)

Shell, "When is it legal to lie in negotiations?" 32 *Sloan Management Rev.* 93 (1991)

Wetlaufer, "The ethics of lying in negotiations," 75 *Iowa L Rev.* 1219 (1980)

White, "Machiavelli and the bar: Ethical limitations on lying in negotiation," *Am. B. Found. Research J.* 926 (1980)

—38—

LIABILITY TO DECEPTION AND MANIPULATION

The Ethics of Undercover Policing

Christopher Nathan

INTRODUCTION

UNDERCOVER POLICE ACT IN WAYS THAT ARE, IN normal circumstances, ways of wronging people. Their actions cause several kinds of harms and setbacks to people's lives. Targets can be deceived, manipulated, have their privacy invaded, have their material interests set back, be encouraged to act in ways that are themselves wrong, and officers may omit to act in ways that would prevent harm. Being subject to acts of concerted deception and manipulation can lead to uncertainty about one's social sphere, and having the grounds for trust in this is constitutive of a general good, or is necessary for others. Consider the case of Mark Jenner, an undercover officer in the United Kingdom who gathered intelligence on the Colin Roach Centre, a group that had the goal of exposing police corruption and racism. He obtained information about the group by having a long-term relationship with one of its members. The victim of the deception now talks of her need for a 'grieving process', and of the way in which her relationship with him has coloured all of her subsequent relationships.[1] Even when people do not ever discover the fact of manipulation, it is arguable that a harm has occurred. If truth or success are elements of a good life, then deceptive police activity has the potential to set back people's interests by rendering their projects unfulfilled or corrupted.

What would an ideal structure of undercover policing activities look like? In this article I propose the notion of liability as a guiding ethical concept. According to this idea, those who engage in wrongdoing make themselves morally liable to preventive activities.[2] ...

THE LIABILITY MODEL AND SELF-DEFENCE

According to a natural viewpoint, we should have little sympathy for those whose interests are set back by covert policing, where those investigated are correctly suspected of involvement in crime. How can we account for this? It seems to be a case of a forfeiture of rights. The criminal's wrongful plans and behaviours cancel the moral complaint he would otherwise have. We can theorise this view by appeal to the principles that arise from considerations of personal self-defence. These cases provide a useful guide for our intuition, since they are structurally similar: they are also cases of rights-forfeiture.

Complaints

Distinguish first between an infringement and violation of a right. A 'rights violation' is a rights infringement that is not justified. A 'rights infringement' engages a right and gives rise to a complaint, but may on balance be justified.[3] In a paradigm case of self-defence, one is morally permitted to use force in order to overcome a culpable threat. In so doing, one does not infringe upon the rights of one's attacker. Rather, by culpably creating the threat, the attacker forgoes his right not to be harmed. In the case of an innocent threat, we respond differently. Suppose someone will harm you through no fault of her own—she is going to fall onto you—and you can divert her body away from you, thereby harming her and saving yourself. In that case, it seems that by defending yourself, you (arguably justifiably) infringe upon the rights of the innocent threat. The culpable attacker, on the other hand, by creating a threat, loses a right not to be harmed. This is not just because by harming one's attacker, one saves oneself, but because of the attacker's responsibility for creating the threat.

The intuition that guides these cases also appears to be at work in cases of manipulative or deceptive police investigation. The man who takes part in an online child pornography distribution ring makes himself liable to kinds of state action that set back his interests. These actions include his being systematically tricked, so that he reveals facts about himself and those using the ring. In taking part in the ring, he forgoes a number of rights, including his right against being deceived and manipulated. The harm that this person has unleashed is something that can be prevented or mitigated partly through means that impose direct costs upon him....

Compare that case to the known-innocent subject of useful deception. Sometimes it will be useful for covert police to deceive or manipulate those who are uninvolved in any criminal wrongdoing.[4] For example, police may spy on the family, sexual partners, or travel agent of their primary targets. Suppose that the intrusion is small and the security benefit is great. If such practices are ever on balance justified, many will still sense that those on the receiving end have their rights infringed. This contrasts with our sense that the culpable have no complaint at all.[5]

Proportionality

Proportionality constraints apply in self-defence cases. Suppose B threatens only a minor violation of A's personal space: B threatens to step on A's foot. In this case it is not permissible for A to shoot B dead as a preventive measure, even if this is the only way to avoid the threat. Similarly, ethical proportionality considerations apply in policing. The recent activities of police officers in infiltrating UK protest groups appears to the general public disproportionate—especially in going to the extreme depths of deception involved in having and raising children with their targets.[6] In these cases, the harm to be prevented was direct public protest action. Is this undercover action a proportionate measure against a group whose most clear plan is to close down a power station for a week, with the goal of seeking media attention on environmental issues? Many would think not.

Proportionality in self-defence involves comparing not only the harm threatened and the harm used to avert the threat, but also the attacker's culpability for the threat. One whose slight negligence gives rise to a threat of some small harm, H, makes himself liable to less defensive harm than one who maliciously aims at H. (I return to this in the following section.) On this view, then, just as a higher degree of culpability makes a threat liable to a greater self-defensive force, so also does a higher degree of culpability make a criminal liable to more intrusive or harmful investigative practices.

Innocent threats, of course, might warrant justified self-defensive force,[7] and so also in the case of policing does it seem that culpability for a possible harm is not a necessary condition for on-balance-justified manipulation or intrusion. Proportionality considerations apply. One does not forfeit all of one's rights against being harmed simply in virtue of being any threat at all; rather, one becomes more liable to intrusion and manipulation where, other things being equal, one is more responsible for the possible harm that is to be prevented.[8] The key point is that where the target of covert police work is culpable for a possible harm, intrusive and manipulative policing action can take place in a way that does not violate rights. In the governance of covert police work, this idea suggests that intrusion on the culpable ought to be less restricted than intrusion on the non-culpable.[9]

Imperfect Knowledge

Compare two cases. In the first, there are reasonable grounds to believe that person A is involved in serious criminal activity. The police infiltrate A's social grouping, and prevent A from acting in the way she intended. In the second, there are reasonable grounds to believe that person B is involved in serious criminal activity. The police infiltrate B's social grouping, and discover that B is not involved in serious criminal activity. Suppose that the infiltration creates setbacks for both A and B: they are manipulated, their privacy is intruded upon, their lives are affected in ways that they would not choose. What do we say about these cases? In the first case, we tend to feel that A has no ground for complaint regarding the setback she faces. She made herself liable to the harms of deception and manipulation. In relation to her planned acts, the harms she incurs in the course of the investigation do not just pale in comparison; a common intuition has no sympathy at all. It holds that A has not been wronged. On the other hand, in cases of the second sort, we tend to interrogate the facts of the case. Was there really reasonable suspicion? Was there an abuse of process? Did the police follow its own codes of best practice? Should these be altered? We are unlikely to hold that B has not been wronged at all. If the facts of the case are urged upon us—there were reasonable grounds for suspicion, these were faulty, and nobody acted, ex ante, in error—then we still feel sympathy for

B, and furthermore, sense that he has a legitimate complaint.

We can draw upon one prominent account of analogous intuitions in the context of self-defence in order to develop this thought.[10] Suppose X suspects that Y is culpable for some threat to X, and holds this belief with likelihood p. At some levels of p, it must be reasonable for X to engage in acts of self-defence. If X's beliefs turn out to be mistaken, and Y in fact posed no threat, then we want to say that X acted wrongly, at least in the sense that Y has been wronged. It also seems correct to say that X acted reasonably. Our norms cannot tell someone who reasonably but mistakenly believes he is under attack that he should not respond with force, and our norms also cannot say of someone who reasonably but mistakenly believed he was under attack that he acted rightly. If this is the correct view (bearing in mind that other positions on fact- and evidence-relative obligations are available),[11] then in our analogy to covert police work, the manipulation of an innocent infringes upon his rights, even if the fact of his innocence becomes accessible only after the manipulation. He has a complaint even where the manipulation is the result of reasonable but mistaken suspicion.

Apart from being culpable for a threat, one can also become liable to defensive force by being culpable for causing people to believe that one is a threat. Suppose that as part of a provocative conceptual art project someone dresses up as a bank robber, withdraws some of his own cash from the bank desk, and dashes out of the building with the money in a sack labelled 'swag.'[12] This may warrant some police attention. The analogy to self-defence is now helpful. This case is equivalent to one in which a person performs acts that create the impression of a threat, even when there is none. In both cases it will be a matter of degree and context how far we deem the act wrong in itself as a needless creation of fear and disruption, and how far we deem it a humorous poke at a culture of excessive security. In neither case is the person culpable for a threat. Now suppose police deploy intrusive methods upon the joke bank robber, on the grounds of the reasonable suspicion that he created. That is a case that we judge differently to one in which a target becomes subject to reasonable but mistaken suspicion through no fault of her own. And similarly, if we apply the reasoning of the previous paragraph, defensive harm to a person who one reasonably but falsely believes to be a threat does inflict a wrong, even if it was one that it was reasonable to inflict....

The liability model is attractive, and avoids the problems of the dirty hands and instrumentalist views. It allows us to say that at least some covert police work is not rights-infringing, and that other such work may be rights-infringing but justified on balance.[13] It makes a sharp distinction between police work that impacts harmfully on those who are culpable, and police work that impacts harmfully on the innocent. I suggest, further, that it provides a useful tool for thinking about policy. By abstracting away from the immediate politics of the question, it facilitates reflection on ideal practice. If we are to develop a plausible ethic of covert policing, this seems to be the correct path to follow....

CONCLUDING REMARK

In this article I have laid the groundwork for the liability view of undercover policing. It draws from our ideas about the ethics of personal self-defence. The view has the implication that police action in this area should be directly sensitive to the wrongs of its targets. Certain trends in policing, such as the shift towards intelligence models, and the lower cost of mounting online covert operations, imply that this implication will increasingly have practical manifestations....

NOTES

1   She states: 'Mark Cassidy, as [he] then was, joined the group in about 1994, and I started a relationship with him in about May 1995 ... I met him when I was 29, and he disappeared about three months before I was 35. It was the time when I wanted to have children, and for the last 18 months of our relationship he went to relationship counselling with me about the fact that I wanted children and he did not ... I have had recurring dreams ... I imagined being followed' Home Affairs Committee, 'Minutes of Evidence: HC 837', 2013 <http://www.publications.parliament.uk/pa/cm201213/cmselect/cmhaff/837/130205i.htm>.

2   I use 'liability' to refer to moral liability, not legal liability, throughout this article.

3   Judith Jarvis Thomson, 'Some ruminations on rights' in W. Parent (ed.) *Rights, Restitution, and Risk: Essays, in Moral Theory* (Cambridge, MA: Harvard University Press, 1986), p. 51.

4   The extent of 'wrongdoing' in which police can rightly get involved will depend upon the proper bounds of the criminal law: we do not tend to think that bad people are liable to more aggressive police intrusions, if their badness manifests itself only in non-criminalisable acts.

5   I do not commit to the claim that culpability is necessary for non-rights-infringing self-defensive harm; only, that our typical reactions to the kinds of case I describe involve a sense that a right has been infringed upon. Some argue that in personal self-defence cases, certain innocent threats and innocent attackers are liable to defensive force. That is, their rights are not infringed by self-defensive force. If this is the case, the analogy with policing will function differently. We should abandon our sense that the analogous innocent upon whom it is useful to spy is wronged. Nonetheless, as I propose below, proportionality permits greater intrusions upon and manipulations of those who are culpable.

6   Paul Lewis & Rob Evans, *Undercover: The True Story of Britain's Secret Police* (London: Guardian Faber Publishing, 2014).

7   Compare Jeff McMahan, 'Self-defense against morally innocent threats' in P.H. Robinson, S. Garvey & K.K. Ferzan (eds) *Criminal Law Conversations* (Oxford: Oxford University Press, 2011), pp. 384–406; and Judith Jarvis Thomson, 'Self-defense', *Philosophy & Public Affairs* 20,4 (1991): 283–310.

8   For an argument against this view, see Jonathan Quong, 'Proportionality, liability, and defensive harm,' *Philosophy & Public Affairs* 43,2 (2015): 144–73. On Quong's view, the mode of agency, and not responsibility, is a factor in determining a proportionate self-defensive response.

9   How much harm is it proportionate to use in fending off a threat? It is permissible to kill in self-defence against the person who threatens to severely harm but not kill you: see Suzanne Uniacke, 'Proportionality and self-defense,' *Law and Philosophy* 30,3 (2011): 253–72, at p. 261. If so, we can expect that police may similarly cause greater harm to those they pursue than the harm they are seeking to prevent.

10 Jeff McMahan, 'Self-defense and culpability,' *Law and Philosophy* 24,6 (2005): 751–74, at p. 771; see also Kimberly Kessler Ferzan, 'Justifying self-defense,' *Law and Philosophy* 24,6 (2005): 711–49, at p. 728.

11 For alternative views see Derek Parfit, *On What Matters* (Oxford: Oxford University Press, 2011), chapter 7; David McCarthy, 'Actions, beliefs, and consequences,' *Philosophical Studies* 90,1 (1998): 57–77.

12 Thanks to Victor Tadros for pointing me to this real life example.

13 One might also combine the metaethic of the dirty hands view with the liability view, and hold that it is more wrong to manipulate the innocent than the culpable, but that an ineliminable wrong remains where the culpable are manipulated. Analogously, one may believe that one wrongs a culpable aggressor even in harming him in proportionate self-defence.

EARNINGS AND ETHICS

Thinking about Enron

Daniel J. Wirth

1. BACKGROUND

IN 1985, KENNETH LAY FOUNDED ENRON Corporation in Omaha, Nebraska. At a later date, its corporate headquarters was relocated to Houston, Texas. As a public corporation in the energy industry, Enron employed approximately 21,000 workers by the end of 2001 and was the seventh largest company in the United States. It claimed to have earned $101 billion in profits in 2000 and enjoyed a reputation of stability and financial success in the business sector.

Such a reputation included earning the title of "America's Most Innovative Company" by *Fortune* magazine from 1996 to 2001 and a place on the magazine's list of "100 Best Companies to Work for in America" in 2000. Enron's profits in the stock market also enhanced this reputation. The corporation repeatedly garnered substantial financial earnings, and in 2000 its stock soared to a selling price of $85 per share. By all appearances Enron was a thriving business, and its future prospects looked promising in the eyes of its investors and employees.

Enron, however, stunned the global market by filing for bankruptcy at the end of 2001, amid controversy of its accounting practices. Investigations into the matter led to allegations of fraud, where Enron exaggerated its above earnings in reports, and simultaneously buried its debts and losses in an assortment of subsidiary partnerships known as the Raptors. Until this time the general public had little reason to doubt Enron's reported financial

transactions and success. Now, however, questions regarding the appropriateness of removing expenses from a parent company's ledgers to that of its subsidiaries to generate a more optimistic picture of the parent company's success are being asked. Enron's chief executive officers Kenneth Lay and Jeffrey Skilling went to trial in answer to the above charge in January 2006. [Both were convicted, though Lay died before his sentencing.]

Enron's actual financial performance in 2000 was poor, in contrast to what was reported. This was due, in part, to high-risk ventures that did not perform as well as expected. Such monetary losses amounted to millions of dollars in US currency, and affected investors and Enron employees alike. Company executives are paying back investors, but Enron's employees are not as fortunate. Since Enron stock was hit hard by the controversy, Enron employee benefits dependent on the company's stock were completely exhausted. Thus all employee retirement savings via the company's 401k program were lost, and apart from litigation such monies will not be restored.

Enron still manages some of its accounts until the company can be divided into smaller organizations in the industry. About 300 people are in its current employ.

2. ANALYSIS

One feature that is essential to understanding what is at stake in the Enron case is to recognize what a subsidiary partnership is and how these are typically used by corporations. Subsidiary partnerships, or Special Purpose Entities (SPEs), are a type of fund or trust that is created by a parent company with the aim of starting a new type of business venture. Such trusts allow the company to pursue these new business ventures with minimal risk attached. That is, if the new project does not work out financially, and the trust is drained, it would not jeopardize the parent company's financial status, because the very nature of SPEs prevent this. One advantage of such a financial entity, then, is to encourage a business's growth and development into new areas of industry.

Such financial ingenuity has other benefits as well. By creating an SPE, the parent company can gain a loan at a lower interest rate from a lender via an SPE than the parent company could ever have obtained through the lender otherwise. For the newly created SPE will have no debt from the parent company, enabling it to secure the loan. SPEs also afford a parent corporation the option of legitimately removing its debts and losses from its reports to its subsidiary accounts, and thus avoid reports that would show a decrease in earnings. Such moves appear to be in accordance with Generally Accepted Accounting Principles (GAAP), which are a standard set of reporting rules for companies to follow.[1]

Enron used SPEs to both boost earnings in reports and remove its debts and losses, making the crux of the issue whether or not ailing financial corporations should be able to use such accounting methods to make their numbers appear more attractive to investors than they might actually be. One element worth noting is that using SPEs in this manner might give a company like Enron an unfair market advantage over that of its competitors. By not reporting its earnings and losses in a more straight-forward fashion, a false impression of the company's performance is given, causing it to appear more successful than it actually is. Considering that investors are interested in thriving companies that generate profit, Enron would draw out more hopeful investors

with money to spend and gain more earnings than its competitors through this technique.

Also instructive is considering the other side of the issue. One of the commonly touted reasons for entering business is to make a profit. Surely there are times when a lack of candor is called for in such an industry. This is not uncommon. For example, one's resume often includes achievements and highlights one's skills. No one would seriously consider mentioning one's weaknesses or failures on such a document. The expectation is to advertise in a fashion that aids your objective: in this case getting the applied-for position. It may be that Enron's use of SPEs is not much different than another company's sale pitch.

NOTE

1   Mark P. Holtzman, Elizabeth Venuti, and Robert Fonfeder, "Enron and the Raptors," *CPA Journal*, (19 April 2006), http://www.nysscpa.org/cpajournal/2003/0403/features/f042403.htm. See also Tracy Byrnes, "Special-Purpose Entities Are Often a Clever Way to Raise Debt Levels," (21 February 2002), accessed 19 April 2006, http://pages.stern.nyu.edu/~adamodar/New_Home_Page/articles/specpurpentity.htm. Note also that these sources differ as to the appropriateness of Enron's actions in light of GAAP standards.

DISCUSSION QUESTIONS

1.   Imagine that the public never discovered Enron's reporting technique. Let's also say that Enron was able to pay off all its losses and debts through this strategy, and make a substantial profit. Would such a strategy be a moral course of action? Why or why not?

2.   When is candor expected in the business world, and when is it not? Are there other occasions outside of one's job when one would not want to be candid with others? When? How does this dynamic change in relation to those closest to you?

3. Would your opinion of Enron change if it retracted its earlier reports and fully disclosed its financial gains and losses while at the height of its popularity and purported earnings? Does changing the timing of this disclosure change the morality of the situation? If so, how?

4. In what ways is Enron's use of SPEs similar to other forms of advertising? In what ways is it not? Why or why not?

THE ETHICS OF BLUFFING

Oracle's Takeover of PeopleSoft

Patrick Lin

1. BACKGROUND

ON JUNE 6, 2003, ORACLE AMBUSHED PEOPLESOFT with an unsolicited $5.1 billion cash offer to buy the rival technology company. This set the stage for the two Silicon Valley giants—both operating under the leadership of giant-sized egos—to play out a tale about power, drama, and deceit.

First, to introduce the players: Larry Ellison is Oracle's chairman, a swash-buckling personality known for his extravagant financial gestures, such as his financing of the yacht-racing team that won the America's Cup in spring 2003. Equally aggressive is Craig Conway, PeopleSoft's CEO at the time of the takeover attempt, who had once described Oracle, his former employer, as a "sociopathic company."

Just days before Oracle's hostile takeover bid, PeopleSoft had announced its agreement to buy another rival, J.D. Edwards, for $1.7 billion in stock—a deal which would make it the world's second-largest business software company behind SAP. PeopleSoft rejected Oracle's $16-per-share offer as too low to be taken seriously and therefore simply a marketing ploy or distraction.

For more than a year, Oracle and PeopleSoft fought in the boardroom and the courtroom. Oracle successfully fended off an antitrust trial that examined whether the proposed takeover would be anti-competitive and harm the industry as well as customers. Shortly afterwards, PeopleSoft's board of directors announced a surprising vote of no-confidence in Conway, and he was fired in October 2004.

Over the course of that year, Oracle had changed its acquisition price several times, eventually tendering what the company called its "best and final" offer of $24 per share. PeopleSoft again rejected this offer, calling Oracle on its bluff. Finally, in December 2004, after more than twelve offers, PeopleSoft accepted Oracle's bid of $26.50 per share; the merger was completed in 2005.

It turned out that Oracle was not the only party that had bluffed in this bitter battle. Back in June 2003, PeopleSoft had implemented a "poison pill" plan stipulating that, should the company be taken over, its customers would be entitled to a refund of up to five times the licensing fees they had paid to the company. This tactic would commit the company to costly future obligations, and was intended to dissuade Oracle from its takeover ambitions. It took less than a year for PeopleSoft to let this policy expire.

A different kind of bluff had been played out in the AOL-Time Warner merger, another high-profile deal announced on January 10, 2000. The financial community was puzzled and shocked that a scrappy new economy start-up such as America Online was capable of making a bid for Time Warner, a decades-old media empire, in a deal originally worth $165 billion. Many considered AOL's stock to be severely overvalued, but AOL had convinced Time Warner otherwise.

The AOL-Time Warner merger was cleared by regulators in early 2001, but the impending stock market crash, led by overvalued dot-com and technology companies, forced AOL-Time Warner to write off $99 billion in losses in 2002—leading some to observe that AOL had successfully "bluffed" Time Warner into believing that AOL's 30 million dial-up Internet subscribers were worth more than Time Warner's much larger, better established, and more iconic global business.

2. ANALYSIS

In the Oracle-PeopleSoft case, the incentive to bluff is easy to understand. Not only were the two companies fierce adversaries, but there was also personal animosity between the two company chiefs. As a result, the usual niceties of negotiation—such as trust and honesty—were replaced by a no-holds-barred fight. If all is fair in love and war, and business is war (at least in this case), then bluffing seems a rather innocuous tactic compared to some other tactics that could have been employed.

Workforce negotiations also offer key opportunities for bluffing, since these relationships can be acrimonious. Some employee unions are quick to threaten a strike (or suggest that a strike is strongly possible) if their demands are not met. On the other side, a company may be bluffing when it refuses to negotiate further, insisting that its last offer was the best it could do or that it would be forced into bankruptcy or layoffs without more employee concessions. If one side has been bluffing, we would expect that a strike could be averted in last-minute negotiations—hiding the bluff by finding some token area of agreement or another face-saving reason.

But as the AOL-Time Warner deal shows, a negotiation need not involve adversaries. If "hype" or exaggeration counts as bluffing, then untold numbers of dot-com companies may have bluffed their way into key relationships and millions of dollars in private funding, ultimately unable to deliver on their sales and revenue forecasts. We might ask, however, whether a company that believes its own hype can be fairly accused of bluffing, as compared to a company that knowingly puts forward an exaggeration.

It is not just soulless corporations that bluff: ordinary individuals do it too. Any situation where one can claim "this is my final offer" or present a "do this, or else" threat provides an opportunity to bluff. From negotiating salaries to buying cars, many of us likely have experience bluffing our ways into better deals, such as by feigning an inability to accept a low offer, or afford a high price, when the given amount would in reality have been perfectly satisfactory.

It is important not to conflate bluffing with lying, since not all cases of bluffing involve the explicit making of false statements. Bluffing in poker, for example, does not; it simply involves misleading other players by taking an action that conceals the strength or weakness of one's cards—for instance, by betting a lot of money when one has a weak hand. Depending on how AOL made its case to Time Warner, they might not have made a false statement—perhaps they merely provided overly optimistic forecasts. PeopleSoft implemented a poison-pill policy that could be renewed after a given date, but it didn't seem to make any (false) warranty that it *would* renew it. On the other hand, when Oracle made what it called its "best and final" offer, the company appears to have been making a false statement, given that the offer was subsequently raised. But it is possible that company executives simple changed their minds.

These situations highlight how difficult it can be to identify even a failed bluff, let alone to discern whether a bluff is in progress.

DISCUSSION QUESTIONS

1. What exactly is bluffing—how should we define it? When it comes to bluffs that involve making false statements, where is the line between bluffing and lying, if one exists at all?
2. How else might one bluff in business without making an explicit claim or threat that one has no intention of carrying out? Does creating doubt in the other party's mind, when a decision has already been made in one's own mind, count as a bluff?

3. Since the two are often compared, what are some relevant similarities and differences between poker and business? If bluffing (and even lying) were allowed under the rules of a game, can we consider business to be a game in which bluffing is also allowed—or even necessary?

4. Does the creation of "hype" by making exaggerated claims count as bluffing? Why doesn't story-telling count as bluffing?

5. If bluffing is so pervasive and is often conducted by people we would consider to be otherwise ethical, does that suggest that it is morally permissible?

6. Could we argue that a bluff (at least in the form that involves making false statements) is simply a lie made under mitigating circumstances—such as when another party has bluffed first, or when one believes a car dealer to be earning an unfairly high profit? Or does this seem like an attempt to rationalize unethical behavior?

7. Can we distinguish between false-statement bluffs and outright lies by considering the intentions behind the statements made? If intentions are different, are they morally relevant?

PRIVACY AND CONFIDENTIALITY

Erika Versalovic and Anna Bates

1. INTRODUCTION

PRIVACY AND CONFIDENTIALITY ARE VALUES that play a critical role in both professional and personal ethics. However, the norms governing privacy and confidentiality in professional relationships often depart from the norms governing personal relationships. This unit challenges commonly held beliefs about privacy and confidentiality: When should professionals respect privacy? What are the limits of confidentiality? How should a professional weigh privacy and confidentiality against other values?

The professions considered in this unit all have a public role in society: journalism, law, medicine, and education. Individuals working in any of these professions have to consider the extent that privacy and confidentiality are or are not good for society at large, as well as whether privacy and confidentiality are good for themselves and their clients. The debates and decisions about confidentiality and privacy in these professions influence the value of privacy and confidentiality in society at large. For example, journalists face questions about whether private information should be published and have to weigh the privacy of individuals in the public eye against the needs of citizens in a democratic society.

This unit also questions the duty of professionals to ensure their clients or the public at large know the possible limits and threats to privacy and confidentiality. For example, lawyers must decide whether or not to inform clients about the exceptions to lawyer-client confidentiality. Disclosing limits to confidentiality may hamper the lawyer-client relationship, but this risk must be weighed against the importance of respecting a client's agency. Similarly, should tech companies, such as Google, disclose the possible threats to privacy to consumers?

2. CONTENTS

The first two readings in this unit provide a general introduction to the issues of privacy and confidentiality, explaining and examining the central concerns that underlie respect for these values. The first reading, "Privacy: Its Meaning and Value" by Adam D. Moore argues that privacy is physically, psychologically, and morally beneficial to humans and their societies. Looking towards the future, people and societies should be careful to maintain respect for privacy in an increasingly monitored world.

Next, "Confidentiality: A Comparison across the Professions of Medicine, Engineering, and Accounting" by Mary Beth Armstrong surveys the place of confidentiality in professional ethics. She describes a social contract between professions and society, in which professions are obligated to do what is in the interest of society. Traditionally, confidentiality has been considered good for society, but Armstrong exhorts all professionals to rethink the ethics of absolute confidentiality.

The following articles in this unit focus on privacy and confidentiality within the particular professions of journalism, law, medicine, and education. Dennis F. Thompson analyzes the degree to which the professional journalist ought to respect the privacy of elected officials in "Privacy, Politics, and the Press." He argues that journalists should disclose personal information about elected officials only if the information is relevant to their job performance.

Bruce M. Landesman and Lee A. Pizzimenti both discuss confidentiality between lawyers and clients. In "Confidentiality and the Lawyer-Client Relationship," Landesman argues that there must be limits to confidentiality and that absolute confidentiality is harmful to lawyers as moral agents. Next, in "Informing Clients about Limits to Confidentiality," Lee A. Pizzimenti focuses on whether lawyers ought to tell their clients about the limits to confidentiality and the potential consequences of providing that information.

Kenneth Kipnis discusses confidentiality in the medical profession in his article, "A Defense of Unqualified Medical Confidentiality," arguing that while confidentiality is necessary to encourage more patients to seek treatment, some doctors may fear that their personal ethics will conflict with their professional duty to confidentiality.

Bo Brinkman examines a privacy debate in professional education in his article, "An Analysis of Student Privacy Rights in the Use of Plagiarism Detection Systems." He insists professional educators must respect student privacy rights, when, for example, introducing new technology, such as plagiarism-detection systems.

Ira S. Rubinstein and Nathaniel Good's "Privacy by Design: A Counterfactual Analysis of Google and Facebook Privacy Incidents" explains the history of data protection and Internet-consumer privacy. They suggest that previous attempts to protect privacy were inadequate and suggest some improvements.

This unit closes with two case studies. Each begins by introducing a moral dilemma about privacy or confidentiality and ends with an ethical analysis. The first looks at a case from professional journalism: are journalists always obligated to keep their sources confidential? The second focuses on the potential conflict between a physician's duty to protect patients and the patient's rights to confidentiality.

—39—
PRIVACY
Its Meaning and Value

Adam D. Moore

INTRODUCTION

BODILY PRIVACY, UNDERSTOOD AS A RIGHT TO
control access to one's body, capacities, and powers, is one of our most cherished rights—a right
enshrined in law and notions of common morality.... Privacy, whether physical or informational, is
valuable for beings like us. Establishing the truth
of this claim will be the primary focus of this
article.... Before arguing for the claim that privacy
is a necessity for beings like us we must first clarify
the notion of privacy—alas there are numerous
competing conceptions of privacy.

DEFINING PRIVACY[1]

Privacy has been defined in many ways over
the last century. Warren and Brandeis called
it "the right to be let alone."[2] Pound and Freund
have defined privacy in terms of an extension of
personality or personhood.[3] Westin and others
including myself have cashed out privacy in terms
of information control.[4] Still others have insisted
that privacy consists of a form of autonomy over
personal matters.[5] Parent offers a purely descriptive account of privacy—"Privacy is the condition
of not having undocumented personal knowledge
about one possessed by others."[6] Finally, with all
of these competing conceptions of privacy some
have argued that there is no overarching concept

of privacy but rather several distinct core notions
that have been lumped together....

As noted in the opening paragraph, a "control"
based definition of privacy will be explicated and
defended—privacy has to do with control over
access to oneself and to information about oneself.[7]
Richard Parker writes:

> *privacy is control over when and by whom the
> various parts of us can be sensed by others.* By
> "sensed," is meant simply seen, heard, touched,
> smelled, or tasted. By "parts of us," is meant
> the part of our bodies, our voices, and the
> products of our bodies. "Parts of us" also
> includes objects very closely associated with
> us. By "closely associated" is meant primarily
> what is spatially associated. The objects which
> are "parts of us" are objects we usually keep
> with us or locked up in a place accessible only
> to us.[8]

One feature of such a conception is that it can
incorporate much of the aforementioned definitions. Controlling access to ourselves affords
individuals the space to develop themselves as they
see fit. Such control yields room to grow *personally*
while maintaining *autonomy* over the course and
direction of one's life....

This broad characterization holds of both
moral rights and legal rights. For example

property is a bundle of rights associated with an owner's relation to a thing where each right in the bundle is distinct.[9] Moreover rights are not free floating moral entities—rather, they are complex sets of claims, duties, obligations, powers, and immunities. Some have argued that if this is the case, then we should dispense with talk of rights and merely talk of duties, obligations, and claims. We could do this but then tedium also has costs and there is nothing wrong with talking in terms of rights so long as we do not lose sight of the fact that they are conceptually complex....

Moreover, if all rights are nothing more than sets of obligations, powers, duties, and immunities it would not automatically follow that we should dispense with talk of rights and frame our moral discourse in these more basic terms.[10] ...

A right to privacy can be understood as a right to maintain a certain level of control over the inner spheres of personal information and access to one's body, capacities, and powers. It is a right to limit public access to oneself and to information about oneself. For example, suppose that Ginger wears a glove because she is ashamed of a scar on her hand. If Fred were to snatch the glove away he would not only be violating her right to property— alas the glove is Ginger's to control—Fred would also violate her right to privacy; a right to restrict access to information about the scar on her hand....

PRIVACY RIGHTS AND PROPERTY RIGHTS

... In contrast to a *right* to privacy it may also be helpful to define what some have called a condition of privacy.[11] Here we are trying to be descriptive rather than normative. Weinstein provides a useful starting point. "If the condition is entered involuntarily, it is isolation when a matter of circumstance and ostracism when a result of the choice of others. Either isolation or ostracism may become loneliness when accompanied by a desire for communication."[12] Privacy, on the other hand, is a condition of voluntary seclusion or walling off. The condition obtains when an individual freely

separates herself from her peers and restricts access. For those entities that lack freewill we may talk of separation rather than privacy....

THE CULTURAL ROOTS OF PRIVACY

One could argue that privacy is a cultural phenomenon and its form or content depends on customs and social practices.[13] Independent of society—when we are by ourselves—there is no need for privacy. Thus there is nothing inherent in human nature that makes privacy valuable for all humans. This view is shown to be suspect as soon as it is admitted that we are, by nature, social animals. We need companionship and intellectual stimulation as much as food and shelter....

To continue, of the thousands of cultures studied there are a rare few that appear to contain no privacy. The Tikopia of Polynesia, Thlinget Indians of North America, Java of Indonesia, as well as a few others, have cultural systems that appear to leave everything open for public consumption. These are important cases because individuals in such societies may flourish in the absence of privacy—if true, we will have found a telling counterexample to the claim that privacy is necessary for human flourishing.

Before more closely examining these cases, it should be noted that one avenue of response would be to further relativize the central claim about privacy. Rather than maintaining that privacy is a necessary condition for human well-being full stop, the claim could be weakened to include only advanced cultures or societies that have moved beyond hunter gatherer or purely agricultural models. Such a restriction is not necessary, however, because while privacy may take many forms it appears everywhere. Consider the following cases.

Tikopia of Polynesia ... the Tikopia help the self to be continuous with its society.... They find it good to sleep side by side crowding each other, next to their children or their parents or their brothers and sisters, mixing sexes and generations; and if a widow finds herself alone in her one-room house she may adopt a child or a brother to allay her intolerable privacy....

Work among the Tikopia is also socially conceived and structured; and if a man has to work alone, he will probably try to take a little child along.[14]

Thlinget Indians of North America. There are no skeletons tucked away in native families, for the acts of one are familiar to all of the others. Privacy is hardly known among them. It cannot be maintained very well under their system of living, with families bunched together.... The Thlinget's bump of curiosity is well developed and anything out of the ordinary, as an accident, a birth, a death or a quarrel, never fails to draw a crowd.... They walk in and out of one another's homes without knocking on the door.[15]

Java of Indonesia. In Java people live in small, bamboo-walled houses.... [T]here are no fences around them ... and no doors. Within the house people wander freely just about any place any time, and even outsiders wander in fairly freely almost any time during the day and early evening.... Except for the bathing enclosure (where people change their clothes) no place is really private.[16]

Westin notes that these cases and others like them do not "prove that there are no universal needs for privacy and no universal processes for adjusting the values of privacy, disclosure, and surveillance within each society."[17] The Java still have bathing enclosures, while the Thlingets and Tikopia hide behind psychological walls to ensure private domains. Like viewing a stripper, we may see everything and nothing at all of the real person. Moreover, in each of these cultures there are time restrictions on access—for example, visiting someone in the middle of the night would be typically prohibited.

Cultural universals have been found in every society that has been systematically studied.[18]

Based on the Human Relations Area Files at Yale University, Westin argues that there are aspects of privacy found in every society—privacy is a cultural universal.[19]

Barry Schwartz, in an important article dealing with the social psychology of privacy, provides interesting clues as to why privacy is universal.[20] According to Schwartz, privacy is group-preserving, maintains status divisions, allows for deviation, and sustains social establishments. As such, privacy may be woven into the fabric of human evolution.

Privacy preserves groups by providing rules of engagement and disassociation. "If the distraction and relief of privacy were not available ... the relationship would have to be terminated...."[21] Without privacy or what may be called a dissociation ritual there could be no stable social relation. As social animals we seek the company of our fellows but at some point interaction becomes bothersome and there is a mutual agreement to separate. Thus having "good fences" would be necessary for having "good neighbors." James Rachels echoes this view:

We now have an explanation of the value of privacy in ordinary situations in which we have nothing to hide. The explanation is that, even in the most common and unremarkable circumstances, we regulate our behavior according to the kinds of relationships we have with the people around us. If we cannot control who has access to us, sometimes including and sometimes excluding various people, then we cannot control the patterns of behavior we need to adopt (this is one reason why privacy is an aspect of liberty) or the kinds of relations with other people that we will have.[22] ...

By protecting status divisions and determining association and disassociation rules privacy has a stabilizing effect on groups or social orders. Privacy also protects and leaves room for deviation within groups. Via deviation and experiments in living new ideas are introduced into groups and, if good, are adopted.[23] ...

Growing up can be understood as the building of a series of walls—the walls of privacy.[24] Infants are without privacy. As infants grow into toddlers and begin to communicate with language they express wishes for separation at times. This process continues as children grow into adults.[25] Toddlers and small children begin requesting privacy as they start the process of self-initiated development. More robust patterns of disassociation continue as children enter puberty. Finally as young adults emerge, the walls of privacy have hardened and access points are maintained vigorously.

Could we imagine, however, a culture that flourishes without individuals attaining any measure of accomplishment, autonomy, understanding, deep personal relationships, or privacy? Alexander Rosenberg writes,

> For all their desirability, could a just society get along without intimacy, friendship, and love? We can perfectly well imagine a desert island society and a scenario of impeccable justice and moral probity in which the inhabitants have no interest in the sort of social relations that moral social psychologists extol.... Alternatively, we can imagine a society replete with friendship, intimacy, and love, but without privacy.[26]

We can indeed imagine some of these things as we can imagine evolved humans who do not need protein or water to survive. Such entities would have different requirements for flourishing. It is arguably the case that we cannot imagine a society where friendship, intimacy, and love obtains but where privacy is non-existent. The very relation of association and disassociation that comprise friendship, intimacy, and love is central to the notion of privacy. It would seem impossible to have an "intimate" relationship where there was also no control over access.

CONCLUSION

While privacy may be a cultural universal necessary for the proper functioning of human beings, its form—the actual rules of association and disengagement—is culturally dependent.[27] The kinds of privacy rules found in different cultures will be dependent on a host of variables including climate, religion, technological advancement, and political arrangements. As with the necessities of food, shelter, and education we should not jump to the conclusion that because the forms of privacy are culturally dependent that privacy is subjective "all the way down." ...

Given all of this, one can, with great confidence claim that privacy is valuable for beings like us. The ability to regulate access to our bodies, capacities, and powers and to sensitive personal information is an essential part of human flourishing or well being. Modern surveillance techniques, data mining efforts, and media coverage are opening up private lives for public consumption. Technological advancements in monitoring and data acquisition are forcing us to rethink our views about the value of privacy. The unexamined life, as Socrates once said, is not worth living, but neither is the life examined by police or corporations, or the life open to inspection by anyone for any reason.[28]

NOTES

A draft of this article was completed during a summer fellowship (2002) at the Social Philosophy and Policy Center, Bowling Green State University. The author would like to thank Fred D. Miller Jr., Travis Cook, Edward Feser, Richard Timberlake, and George Selgin for their suggestions and comments.

1   Parts of this section draw from Adam D. Moore, "Intangible Property: Privacy, Power, and Information Control," *American Philosophical Quarterly*, vol. 35 (1998), pp. 365–378, esp. pp. 371–373; and Adam D. Moore, *Intellectual Property and*

Information Control (Piscataway, NJ: Transaction Pub., 2001), pp. 185–188.

2   S. Warren and L. Brandeis, "The Right to Privacy," *The Harvard Law Review*, vol. 4 (1890), pp. 193–220.

3   Roscoe Pound, "Interests in Personality," *Harvard Law Review*, vol. 28 (1915), pp. 343; Paul A. Freund, "Privacy: One Concept or Many?" *Privacy* (*Nomos*, vol. 13), ed. J. Roland Pennock and John W. Chapman (New York: Atherton Press, 1971), p. 182.

4   Alan Westin, *Privacy and Freedom* (New York: Atheneum, 1968); Moore, *Intellectual Property and Information Control*.

5   *Eisenstadt v. Baird*, 405 U.S. 438 (1972): 453. See also Louis Henkin, "Privacy and Autonomy," *Columbia Law Review*, vol. 14 (1974): 1410, 1425; Joel Feinberg, "Autonomy, Sovereignty, and Privacy: Moral Ideas in the Constitution?" *Notre Dame Law Review*, vol. 58 (1983), p. 445; Daniel R. Ortiz, "Privacy, Autonomy, and Consent," *Harvard Journal of Law and Public Policy*, vol. 12 (1989), p. 91; and H. Tristram Englehardt Jr., "Privacy and Limited Democracy," *Social Philosophy and Policy*, vol. 17 (Summer 2000), pp. 120–140. "Three different senses of privacy ... must be distinguished ... : (1) freedom from unwanted observation or collection of information, (2) freedom from the disclosure of personal information without one's consent, and (3) freedom from unwarranted government intrusion." Englehardt, "Privacy and Limited Democracy," p. 123.

6   W.A. Parent, "Privacy, Morality, and the Law," *Philosophy and Public Affairs*, vol. 12 (Autumn 1983), p. 269.

7   See also Charles Fried, *An Anatomy of Values* (Cambridge, Mass.: Harvard University Press, 1970), chap. 9; Richard Wasserstrom, "Privacy: Some Assumptions and Arguments," *Philosophical Law*, ed. R. Bronaugh (Westport, Conn.: Greenwood Press, 1979), p. 148; Hyman Gross, "Privacy and Autonomy," *Privacy* (*Nomos*, vol. 13), p. 170; Ernest Van Den Haag, "On Privacy," *Privacy* (*Nomos*, vol. 13), p. 147; and Richard Parker, "A Definition of Privacy," *Rutgers Law Review*, vol. 27 (1974), p. 280.

8   Richard Parker, "A Definition of Privacy," p. 281.

9   Honoré has provided a lucid account of full legal ownership. See A.M. Honoré, "Ownership," *Oxford Essays in Jurisprudence*, ed. A.G. Guest (London: Oxford University Press, 1961); and Becker, *Property Rights, Philosophic Foundations*, p. 19....

10 See also Jeffrey Reiman, "Privacy, Intimacy, and Personhood," Philosophy and Public Affairs, vol. 6 (Autumn 1976), pp. 26–44.

11 Parent's definition of privacy seems to be trying to capture this notion.

12 M. Weinstein, "The Uses of Privacy in the Good Life," *Privacy* (*Nomos*, vol. 13), p. 94.

13 See *A History of Private Life*, 5 volumes, eds. Philippe Aries and Georges Duby (Cambridge, Mass.: Belknap Press, 1987–91).

14 Dorothy Lee, *Freedom and Culture* (Englewood Cliffs, N.J.: Prentice Hall, 1959), p. 31.

15 Livingston Jones, *A Study of the Thlingets of Alaska* (New York, F.H. Revell, 1914), p. 58. Quoted in Westin, *Privacy and Freedom*, p. 12.

16 Clifford Geertz (unpublished paper), quoted in Westin, *Privacy and Freedom*, p. 16.

17 Westin, *Privacy and Freedom*, p. 12.

18 See George Murdock, "The Universals of Culture," in *Readings in World Anthropology*, eds. E.A. Hoebel, J.D. Jennings, and E.R. Smith (New York: McGraw-Hill, 1955).

19 This view is supported by John Roberts and Thomas Gregor, "privacy as a set of rules against intrusion and surveillance focused on the household occupied by a nuclear family is a conception which is not to be found universally in all societies. Societies stemming from quite different cultural traditions such as the Mehinacu and the Zuni do not lack rules and barriers restricting the flow of information within the community, but the management and the functions of privacy may be quite different." Roberts and Gregor, "Privacy: A Cultural View," *Privacy* (*Nomos*, vol. 13), p. 225 (italics mine).

20 Barry Schwartz, "The Social Psychology of Privacy," *American Journal of Sociology*, vol. 73 (May 1968), pp. 741–752.

21 Ibid., p. 741.

22 James Rachels, "Why Privacy is Important," p. 331. It would seem that Parent would agree: "if others manage to obtain sensitive personal knowledge about us they will by that very fact acquire power over us. . . . [A]s long as we live in a society where individuals are generally intolerant of life styles, habits, and ways of thinking that differ significantly from their own . . . our desire for privacy will continue unabated." Parent, "Privacy, Morality, and the Law," p. 276.

23 A classic treatment enumerating the benefits of free thought and experiments in living is John Stuart Mill's *On Liberty*.

24 "Both animals and humans require, at critical stages of life, specific amounts of space in order to act out the dialogues that lead to the consummation of most of the important acts of life." Rene Spitz, "The Derailment of Dialogue," *Journal of the American Psychoanalytic Association*, vol. 12 (1964), pp. 752–775.

25 "The door of openness closes perhaps halfway as a recognition of self development during childhood, it shuts but is left ajar at pre-puberty, and closes entirely—and perhaps even locks—at the pubertal and adolescent stages when meditation, grooming, and body examination become imperative." Schwartz, "The Social Psychology of Privacy," p. 749. See also Erik Erikson, *Childhood and Society* (New York: Norton, 1963), pp. 219–231; and Jane Kessler, *Psychopathology of Childhood* (Englewood Cliffs, N.J., Prentice-Hall, 1966).

26 Alexander Rosenberg, "Privacy as a Matter of Taste and Right," *Social Philosophy and Policy*, vol. 17 (Summer 2000), p. 71. Rosenberg also notes that "Anthropologists have even reported the existence of [such] societies" (p. 71). No citation is given for this claim and the work on cultural universals would point in the other direction. Moreover, later in the article, Rosenberg acknowledges the pervasiveness of privacy.

27 See Herbert Spiro, "Privacy in Comparative Perspective," *Privacy* (*Nomos*, vol. 13), pp. 121–148.

28 Paraphrasing John R. Silber in "Masks and Fig Leaves," *Privacy* (*Nomos*, vol. 13), p. 234.

—40—

CONFIDENTIALITY

A Comparison across the Professions of Medicine, Engineering, and Accounting

Mary Beth Armstrong

INTRODUCTION

PROFESSIONS ARE ORGANIZATIONS OF PEOPLE sharing a certain expertise (e.g., knowledge of medicine, law, accounting). The expertise is typically of a theoretical nature and requires extensive education and training. Thus, society restricts practice of the expertise to licensed individuals. But monopoly and special knowledge lead to power; and power in the hands of a few can result in harm to the many. Thus, at the heart of every profession is a service ideal, or promise to use the special knowledge and monopoly to benefit, not harm society. All professions, by their very nature, must be concerned with and must strive to advance the public interest.

Keeping professional secrets or confidences has long been considered to be in the public interest. Arguments defending professional confidentiality are both deontological and utilitarian. Deontological justifications for confidentiality are based on the notions of privacy, autonomy, promise keeping and loyalty, while utilitarian arguments stress the positive benefits to society when professionals can be trusted to keep confidences....

Deontological arguments are summarized well by Sissela Bok (1982). According to Bok (pp. 119–124), justification for confidentiality rests on four premises: individual autonomy over personal information, respect for relationships among human beings and for intimacy, the obligation created by a pledge of silence, and utility to persons and society. While these four premises are strong, creating the *prima facie* importance of the principle of confidentiality, they are not absolute, nor is the principle....

Since professional confidentiality is recognized as a *prima facie* duty, it therefore follows that it is morally binding on professionals unless it is in conflict with equal or stronger duties....

When individual decision makers or public policy formulators advocate the breaking of professional confidences, the principles most often evoked are those of "not causing harm" or "preventing harm." Thus, the interests of the client or patient, to whom the professional owes the *prima facie* duty of confidentiality, is pitted against the interests of others in society (or even society itself) who may be harmed if confidentiality is kept....

Beauchamp and Childress (1989, p. 337) ... [advocate] that "it is necessary to consider both the probability and the magnitude of harm and to balance both against the rule of confidentiality":

		Magnitude of Harm	
		Major	*Minor*
Probability of Harm	*High*	1	2
	Low	3	4

"As the health professionals' assessment of the situation approaches 1 in the above chart ... the weight of the obligation to breach confidentiality increases. As the situation approaches 4, the weight decreases." Cases 2 and 3 are more difficult to resolve. However, Beauchamp and Childress see no moral obligation to breach confidentiality in case 2 (high probability of a minor harm) and conclude that, in case 3, some form of risk/benefit analysis is called for, since judgement about probabilities and magnitudes are required. They also imply (p. 338) that reasonable doubts ought to be settled in favor of preserving confidentiality.

Unfortunately, Beauchamp and Childress do not give guidance to their readers to help them assess the probability of the risk of harm or its magnitude. Nor do they distinguish between types of harm (e.g., bodily harm, loss of wealth, damage to reputation). Ought all "harms" be treated equally? Presumably these distinctions and difficult assessments are to be made by individual professional practitioners in concrete situations, based upon guidelines by her/his professional organization....

One special form of confidence breaking, termed "whistleblowing," requires additional analysis. Whistleblowing can be internal, in the sense that one "goes over the head" of an immediate manager, perhaps even to the board of directors, or, as more commonly understood, one goes outside the organization in an act of external whistleblowing....

Bok, in describing the nature of whistleblowing, paints a ... dismal picture (1982, p. 213): "Three elements, each jarring, and triply jarring when conjoined, lend acts of whistleblowing special urgency and bitterness: dissent, breach of loyalty, and accusation...."

Thus Bok sees whistleblowing as a valid means of last resort to discharge a duty to protect the public from harm if 1) the threat is imminent and serious, 2) existing avenues for change within the organization have been exhausted, and 3) the whistleblower makes his/her accusations openly, so those criticized have the opportunity to defend themselves. This last requirement is particularly troublesome, since fairness to the accused may result in unfairness to the whistleblower. Some states and organizations, as well as the federal government, recognize this imbalance of power, and have enacted whistleblowers protection acts to safeguard the rights of whistleblowers....

In summary, confidentiality is a *prima facie* obligation, but not an absolute obligation. Ethicists may argue about when and under what circumstances confidentiality should yield to other duties, especially duties to protect the public from harm, but few ethicists, if any, would see professional confidentiality as an absolute duty. Whistleblowing, a special form of confidence breaking, is especially troublesome for professionals (as opposed to managers) in a corporate/employee relationship (as opposed to an external/consultant relationship). The remainder of this paper explores the extent to which three professions (medicine, engineering, and accounting) have attempted to give guidance to their members concerning when, and under what circumstances, to breach confidentiality.

THE MEDICAL PROFESSION

Confidentiality in the medical profession dates back to the fourth century B.C. and the Hippocratic Oath. "Whatsoever things I see or hear concerning the life of a man, in any attendance on the sick or even apart therefrom, which ought not to be noised about, I will keep silent thereon counting such things to be holy secrets."

In 1803, Thomas Percival published his Code of Medical Ethics which was the basis for the American Medical Association's (AMA) code, first promulgated in 1847. Over the next century several major revisions were made to the AMA code, the most dramatic coming in 1957. That year's Principles of Medical Ethics stated the following (section nine):

A physician may not reveal the confidence entrusted to him in the course of medical attendance ... unless he is required to do so by law or unless it becomes necessary in order to protect the welfare of the individual or the community.

The 1980 revision to the AMA's Principles of Medical Ethics ... ("5.05 Confidentiality") states:

> The obligation to safeguard patient confidences is subject to certain exceptions which are ethically and legally justified because of overriding social considerations. Where a patient threatens to inflict serious bodily harm to another person and there is reasonable probability that the patient may carry out the threat, the physician should take reasonable precautions for the protection of the intended victim, including notification of law enforcement authorities....

The change in language between the 1957 Code and the 1980 Code reflects a watershed event in the history of medical confidentiality; the *Tarasoff* case [*Tarasoff v. Regents of the University of California*]. This case involved one Prosenjit Poddar, a man obsessed with a student he met at a dance, Tatiana Tarasoff. Poddar revealed to Dr. Moore, the staff psychologist at the University of California, Berkeley student health services, that he thought of harming and maybe killing Tarasoff. When Poddar purchased a gun and discontinued therapy, Dr. Moore notified the campus police, who questioned and then released Poddar. Two months later Poddar killed Tarasoff.

In 1974 the California Supreme Court ruled that Dr. Moore had a duty to warn Tarasoff....

Shortly after [this] case, a series of cases followed both within and outside of California. For example, in 1980 in *Lipari v. Sears, Roebuck & Co.* the court extended the class of potential victims beyond those identifiable to the therapist to include the general public, since the harm was foreseeable.... State legislators have been busy redefining the law as it relates to medical confidentiality....

... The AIDS epidemic is [also] a particularly ripe arena for controversy regarding confidentiality. Some analysts may use a Tarasoff-type approach and argue that doctors have a duty to protect potential victims (including the general public) from the harm inflicted by this deadly disease. Others believe that, since the repercussions of disclosure of AIDS on the patient are so adverse, they outweigh even the potential contraction of the disease by a third party....

To date the AMA has, in effect, offered the following guidance to physicians relative to appropriate breaches of confidentiality: protect threatened victims and the general public, when required to do so by law.... Apparently, officials within the medical profession who are charged with the responsibility of making policy for its members have decided that courts and legislatures, rather than themselves, should grapple with issues such as resolving conflicts among *prima facie* duties, prioritizing duties (i.e., positive/negative), defining harm, assessing risks of harm, assessing strengths of loyalties, etc.... The medical profession is not unique in its struggle with confidentiality.

THE ENGINEERING PROFESSION

... One of the first sources of official ethical guidance for engineers was the 1912 Code of Ethics of American Institute of Electrical Engineers. In that code an engineer was told that he should consider "the protection of a client's or employer's interests his first professional obligation" (Peterson and Farrell, 1986, p. 8)....

The 1974 revision of the ECPD Canons of Ethics stated that "Engineers shall hold paramount the safety, health, and welfare of the public in the performance of their professional duties." (Peterson and Farrell, 1986, p. 8). Thus, in 62 years the engineers' thinking on the issues had evolved from a primary duty to clients and employers to simultaneous (and presumably equal, and sometimes conflicting) duties to clients, employers and public, to a primary duty to the general public.

Currently, the American Society of Civil Engineers, the American Society of Mechanical Engineers, the Institute of Industrial Engineers, and Tau Beta Phi have adopted language similar to the 1974 ECPD Canons. The American Association of Engineering Societies [AAES], an umbrella organization comprised of 22 engineering societies, uses even stronger language: "Engineers perceiving a consequence of their professional duties to adversely affect the present or future public health and safety shall formally advise their employers or clients and, if warranted, consider further disclosure" (Gorlin, 1990, p. 64)....

The BART case is a good example of engineering "society support of individuals who make disclosures" (Gorlin, 1990, p. 65). It involved the faulty design of the automatic train control system of the Bay Area Rapid Transit (BART) system that runs through three counties in northern California. Three engineers became concerned over a period of years with the way the system was being developed. All three expressed concerns to their respective managements, and all three received no significant response. Toward the end of 1971 the three engineers decided that the public safety could be in jeopardy if the system were implemented, so they decided to go over their managers' heads and take their concerns to the BART Board of Directors. The Board ruled in favor of management, who traced the complaints back to the three engineers and fired them.

One of the fired engineers enlisted the support of the California Society of Professional Engineers (CSPE), which began a study of the situation. The study brought to light many engineering and management problems which confirmed the claims of the three engineers....

A comparison of the AAES guidelines with those of the AMA reveals an interesting difference: the engineers appear more willing to break professional confidences in the absence of laws requiring them to do so.... This difference may, in part, be due to the catastrophic nature of engineering disasters, (magnitude of the harm) but medical epidemics can be equally devastating.

In grappling with the confidentiality problem, engineers have concluded that the duty to the public's safety, health and welfare is a higher duty than other, conflicting, *prima facie* duties. Although this conclusion does not satisfy the needed analysis nor does it give much guidance relative to risk assessment, definitions of harm, and the myriad other related questions, it is a foundation upon which to build.

THE ACCOUNTING PROFESSION

Accountants, like engineers, work for a variety of organizations and perform a variety of functions. This paper, however, will examine professional guidance from only two sources: the American Institute of Certified Public Accountants (AICPA), and the Institute of Management Accountants (IMA). AICPA members are licensed by the state (similar to physicians), while IMA members are not (similar to many engineers). The presence of a licensing requirement, or state certification, presumably gives stronger authority to confidentiality rules that are embedded in state business and professional codes than to similar rules promulgated by professional societies....

The AICPA membership is almost evenly divided between external, independent accountants who work for CPA firms, and internal accountants who work for large corporations or government as management (internal) accountants or internal auditors....

The AICPA Code of Professional Conduct is divided into two main sections, Principles and Rules. The former are aspirational in nature, while the latter are mandatory and violators are subject to disciplinary action....

The Principle entitled "The Public Interest" states: "In discharging their professional responsibilities, members may encounter conflicting pressures from among each of [several] groups [clients, credit grantors, governments, employers, investors, the business and financial community, and others]. In resolving those conflicts, members should act with integrity, guided by the precept that when members fulfill their responsibility to the public, clients' and employers' interests are best served...."

Rule 301 states "A member in public practice shall not disclose any confidential client information without the specific consent of the client...."

The negative duty to maintain client confidentiality does not allow for exceptions other than the following which are explicitly stated: Members have to disclose information if the promulgated accounting rules require it, if the information is subpoenaed, if it is part of a peer or quality review of the CPA firm, or is part of an AICPA or State investigation of the CPA's adherence to professional standards. Notably absent are exceptions for the public interest (e.g., the Savings and Loan crisis, where appropriate accounting rules may have been followed, but they did not tell an accurate story) and exceptions for compliance with the law (as the AMA code provides).

Case law relative to accounting confidentiality has been expanding rapidly, although not as rapidly as in the medical profession. In *Fund of Funds, Ltd. v. Arthur Andersen & Co.* (1982), the auditors were held liable when they did not reveal to one client that it was being defrauded by another client. Since the CPA firm audited both clients, it knew (or should have known) that one client was defrauding the other, and the courts held that it had a duty to warn the defrauded client. In a New York case, *White v. Guarente*, the auditor was held liable for not revealing to limited partners that they were being defrauded by a general partner (Causey, 1988, p. 30). Liability may even exist where newly discovered information reveals fraudulent client activity *after* financial statements are issued (for additional discussion of recent case law, see Causey, 1988). Thus the courts do not appear to be persuaded by the argument that CPAs (or medical doctors) who adhere to confidentiality rules promulgated by state business and professional codes are "obeying the law...."

The *Standards of Ethical Conduct for Management Accountants*, promulgated by the IMA, explicitly address the concerns of internal accountants. The IMA Standards state: "Management accountants have a responsibility to refrain from disclosing confidential information acquired in the course of their work except when authorized, unless legally obligated to do so...."

Thus, the official organization of management accountants, unlike organizations of engineers, do not allow for whistleblowing as an act of last recourse. Rather, management accountants are expected to resign and walk away. Some might argue that the threat to public safety exposed by an engineer is serious enough to warrant such drastic action as whistleblowing, while mere financial loss, the domain of the accountant, does not. In light of the dramatic losses incurred by the Savings and Loan industry, however, that distinction may no longer be appropriate.

CONCLUSION

The introduction to this paper described a social contract between professions and the larger society. At the heart of the contract is the profession's service ideal, or promise to act in the public's interest. Historically, professional confidentiality was deemed to be in the public interest and took on an almost sacred aura. In recent years, however, society, through its courts and legislators, has denied that confidentiality is *always* in the public interest. Professions, especially in the form of official guidance, have been slow to respond to society's new expectations relative to confidentiality, although some professions are moving faster than others.

The American Medical Association basically exhorts physicians to maintain confidentiality unless the law tells them to do otherwise. Medical ethicists, on the other hand, are calling for a complete reexamination of the confidentiality issue. Professional engineering societies, in their umbrella organization (AAES), have recently pledged to encourage disclosure necessary to protect public safety and to establish active society support of individuals who make disclosures. To date, however, their practical assistance to whistleblowers who have been blackballed is limited. The accounting profession, the author's own profession, is the slowest of the three professions examined to advocate change in its confidentiality rules. Accountants are traditionally conservative. But in their zeal to maintain client/employer confidences, accountants cannot lose sight of their pledge to fulfill their responsibilities to the public interest. The public no longer believes that *absolute* confidentiality is in their interest. It is time, therefore, for accountants, medical professionals, engineers, indeed all professionals, to work together and with ethical theorists to rethink and reformulate confidentiality guidance, from the ground floor up.

REFERENCES

Beauchamp, Tom L. and Childress, James F. (1989). *Principles of Biomedical Ethics*, 3rd Edition. Oxford: Oxford U.P.

Bok, Sissela. (1982). *Secrets: On the Ethics of Concealment and Revelation*. New York: Pantheon Books.

Causey, Denzil, Jr. (August, 1988). "The CPA's Guide to Whistleblowing." *The CPA Journal*, pp. 26–37.

De George, Richard. (Fall, 1981). "Ethical Responsibilities of Engineers in Large Organizations: The Pinto Case." *Business & Professional Ethics Journal*, 1(1): 1–14.

Fund of Funds, Ltd. v. Arthur Andersen & Co., 545 F. Supp. 1314 (SDNY 1982).

Gorlin, Rena, ed. (1990). *Codes of Professional Responsibility*. Washington, D.C.: Bureau of National Affairs.

—41—

PRIVACY, POLITICS, AND THE PRESS

Dennis F. Thompson

WHAT SHOULD THE PRESS REPORT ABOUT THE private lives of public officials? The most common answer is based on what may be called the relevance standard: Private conduct should be publicized only if it is relevant to the official's performance in public office. Although this standard is often invoked by journalists and politicians, its justification has often been misunderstood, and the interpretation of its scope has been incomplete and overly broad. If the standard were more firmly grounded in the requirements of the democratic process, it would better serve as a guide to making and criticizing decisions about what to publicize about the private lives of public officials.[1]

JUSTIFICATION: WHY SHOULD THE PRESS RESPECT THE PRIVACY OF PUBLIC OFFICIALS?

Any adequate justification for respecting the privacy of public officials must be based in part on what the democratic process requires. In virtually all conceptions of democracy, officials should be accountable to citizens. Citizens should be able to hold public officials accountable for their decisions and policies, and therefore citizens must have information that enables them to judge how well officials are doing, or are likely to do, their jobs.

This accountability requirement provides a reason to override or diminish the right of privacy that officials otherwise have. It is clear enough that the requirement justifies making some conduct public that is ordinarily private: the financial affairs of officials and their family members; health records; drug use; names of friends, relatives, and close associates; gifts received; outside employment; and sexual activity related to the job. Sexual harassment, as now defined in the law on the subject, is not a private matter.

The accountability requirement has another implication that is less noticed but no less important. The requirement provides a reason to *limit* publicity about private lives. When such publicity undermines the practice of accountability, the publicity should be limited. How can publicity undermine accountability? The most important way is through the operation of a political version of Gresham's law: Cheap talk drives out quality talk. This is not because people hoard the quality talk in the hope that they might be able to enjoy it later, as Gresham thought people would hoard higher-value currency, but because the cheap talk attracts readers and viewers, even those who, in their more reflective hours, would prefer quality talk....

SCOPE: WHAT PRIVACY OF PUBLIC OFFICIALS SHOULD THE PRESS RESPECT?

If the relevance standard is based on accountability, the scope of conduct that it would publicize is less than is often assumed. Two general features of the standard favor less publicity.

First, because the effects on accountability are a matter of degree, the standard focuses attention on questions of proportion. The issue should not be simply *whether*, but *to what extent*, private conduct should be publicized. The standard thus still has force in cases in which private conduct is relevant. Even when the standard does not prohibit coverage, it may require adjusting the amount of airtime or space devoted to private conduct compared to other issues.

A second consequence of basing the relevance standard on accountability is a shift in focus from conduct that affects job performance to conduct that citizens need to assess job performance. This shift builds into the standard some limits on intrusion. Citizens do not need to know, for example, about the drinking habits of an official because the alleged effects can be discovered by observing his actions on the job. More generally, in this interpretation of the standard, the press should concentrate more on the effects of private behavior and less on the behavior itself.

Four main types of conditions or considerations determine whether and to what extent private conduct is relevant.[2] The conditions refer to the publicness of the conduct, the character of the official in question, the reactions of the audience, and the effects on the political process. The significance of these conditions can be brought out by examining a case that has some parallels to recent events but is less cluttered with political contention. (The case also has the advantage of offering some insight into how editors think about this issue, because many spoke candidly about how they arrived at their decision to publish the story.)

In the mid-1980s, John Fedders, the chief of the enforcement division of the Securities and Exchange Commission (SEC), resigned shortly after the *Wall Street Journal* reported on its front page that he had repeatedly beaten his wife. Although his wife's charges had appeared in the public record at the start of the divorce proceedings nearly a year and a half earlier, virtually no one had taken notice until the *Journal*'s story appeared.[3] (The *Journal* had been told about the problem a year before but decided then against reporting it.) White House officials decided that once this information became so public, Fedders could not remain in office and asked for his resignation.

Can this disclosure be justified? The first refuge of a harried editor in face of such a story is to try to find some connection, however remote, between the private conduct and the job performance. The trouble was that Fedders's penchant for wife-beating had no noticeable effects on his job performance. By all accounts, Fedders's performance on the job had been exemplary.

Nevertheless, some editors, intent on publishing the story but not wanting to offend against the relevance standard, claimed that they *had* found an effect on performance. Demonstrating how far an editor is willing to stretch the relevance standard, Ben Bradlee of the *Washington Post* insisted that Fedders's private conduct "intrudes on his performance of his duties" because "the fact is that he's not at work, he's in court."[4] This argument is an abuse of the relevance standard because its claims can be shown to be false and can be shown to be so without publicizing anything about Fedders's private life. If the claim is that an official is distracted from his public duties, the press can simply report that he is not on the job. (They could give some general description of the reason, such as his appearance in court, if necessary to indicate how long the absence is likely to be and whether it is justifiable.)

The managing editor of the *Journal*, Norman Pearlstine, said the decision to run the story was "the toughest call I've had to make since I've been in the job."[5] He finally decided to override the paper's general rule respecting the privacy of public officials because of the whole set of facts surrounding the case:

[Fedders had] admitted in public the charges of wife-beating.... He is one of the important law enforcement officials in the country....

[There were] questions raised about his indebtedness.... The White House was aware of the issue of family violence and seemed to be concerned about it.[6]

Pearlstine's justification captures better than the claims of other editors the complexity of decisions of this kind and provides a useful start for analyzing the conditions that should be taken into account in applying the relevance standard.

PUBLICNESS OF THE CONDUCT

The first factor that almost all editors mentioned about this case is that the conduct was already on the public record. Abe Rosenthal, the executive editor of the *New York Times*, took this as a sufficient justification: "When stories of repeated wife-beating by a public official ... become part of the public record, they must be printed."[7]

Pearlstine was more careful. For him, Fedders's public admission of guilt, not just the publicness of the proceedings, was essential. This may be too strong a condition in some cases, as we may sometimes want an allegation of wrongdoing to be disclosed even if the accused denies it. But we ought to require some independent test of the plausibility of the charges beyond the fact that the charges are made in public....

UNITY OF CHARACTER

A second condition is that the private conduct must reveal important character flaws that are relevant to the official's job. That is presumably what Pearlstine had in mind when he connected Fedders's personal debts and spousal abuse with his role as a law enforcement official. Citizens may reasonably want to know about an official's tendency toward domestic violence and personal indebtedness when that person is responsible for enforcing the law and regulating the finances of others.

Pearlstine's claim here is more specific than the more common use of the character argument, which is undiscriminatingly general. The general claim that private conduct reveals character flaws that are bound eventually to show up on the job is a psychological version of the classical idea of the unity of the virtues: A person who mistreats his wife is likely to mistreat his colleagues; a person who does not control his violent temper is not likely to resist the temptation to lie.

We should be wary of this argument because many people, especially politicians, are quite capable of compartmentalizing their lives in a way that the idea of the unity of virtues denies. Indeed, for some people, the private misbehavior may be cathartic, enabling them to behave better in public. And private virtue is no sign of public virtue. We should remember that most of the leading conspirators in the Watergate scandal led impeccable private lives. So evidently did most of the nearly one hundred political appointees who were indicted or charged with ethics offenses during the early years of the Reagan administration.[8]

More generally, as far as character is concerned, we should be primarily interested in the political virtues—respect for the law and the Constitution, a sense of fairness, honesty in official dealings. These virtues may not be correlated at all with personal ones. And the vices that the press seems most interested in—the sins of sex—are those that are probably least closely connected with the political vices....

REACTIONS OF THE PUBLIC

Pearlstine's allusion to the Reagan administration's campaign against domestic violence introduces a third condition. It refers to reactive effects: The private conduct affects job performance not because of what the officials themselves do but because of the reaction of other people when they find out about the conduct. If the Reagan administration had allowed Fedders to stay on the job, his reputation might have made it more difficult to continue the campaign against domestic violence and, more generally, the effort to promote family values. Anticipating these effects, an editor might reasonably find the private conduct relevant.

But we should be careful about appealing to reactive effects. The anticipated reaction of other people should almost never count as a sufficient reason to publicize further what would otherwise be private. The missing step in the argument—the one factor that Pearlstine and none of the editors mention is the assumption that the private conduct itself is morally wrong and that the anticipated reactions of other people are therefore morally justified....

PRIORITY IN THE PROCESS

The fourth condition relates private conduct to other public issues: To what extent does knowing about this conduct help or hinder citizens' knowing about *other* matters they need to know to hold officials accountable?

In the Fedders case, it would be hard to argue that publicity about his private life distracted citizens from attending to more important traits or activities—whether his or those of the SEC or other officials and institutions. The publicity probably brought more attention to the SEC. (The number of people who learned for the first time that the SEC *had* an enforcement division must have increased substantially.) And the publicity indirectly gave a boost to the administration's campaigns against domestic abuse and for family values.

But in most cases—especially when they involve traditional personal vices such as drink, drugs, and sex—the Gresham effects are likely to be more salient. Even when this kind of private conduct has some clear relevance for judging the qualifications of a public official, it tends to assume more prominence than it deserves....

CONCLUSION

To return to Pearlstine's decision: Should he have run the story about Fedders? The decision was justified because Fedders's conduct satisfies the relevance standard: It is the kind of conduct about which citizens or their representatives need

to know to hold an official in Fedders's position accountable, and the extent of the publicity was proportionate to the relevance. More specifically, Fedders's conduct was already public, and legitimately so. The character flaws that the conduct revealed were closely and specifically connected to his job. There was reason to believe that the negative public reaction was morally justified because the conduct is a serious moral wrong. And most important, there were no significant Gresham effects.

Just as important as noting the factors that justify the story is recognizing the factors that should not count at all. Just because the conduct was already public does not justify publicizing it more widely. Just because the conduct reveals a character defect does not make it relevant to public office. And just because the public or some part of it is likely to react negatively does not license disclosing it.

Our interest is not in the conclusion about this particular case, but in the reasons for it. Those reasons can help identify some general principles that should guide journalists in making—and just as importantly, citizens in judging—decisions about reporting on the private lives of public officials. Those decisions affect not only what we read and watch, but also ultimately the quality of the discourse of the democratic politics we experience. That discourse is too important to be left to the vagaries of Gresham's law.

NOTES

1   For an earlier and more comprehensive discussion (written not only pre-Lewinsky, but even pre-Hart), see [Dennis F. Thompson. "The Private Lives of Public Officials," in *Public Duties: The Moral Obligations of Government Officials*, ed. Joel L. Fleishman, Lance Liebman, and Mark H. Moore. Cambridge, MA: Harvard University Press. 1981. Reprinted in *Essentials of Government Ethics*, ed. Peter Madsen and Jay Shafritz. New York: Penguin, 1992: 221–47]

2   For other institutional factors that should be considered, such as the level and type of office, see Thompson 1981: 129–32.

3   Brooks Jackson, "John Fedders of SEC Is Pummeled by Legal and Personal Problems," *Wall Street Journal*, Feb. 25, 1985.

4   Stuart Taylor, "Life in the Spotlight: Agony of Getting Burned," *New York Times*, Feb. 27, 1985.

5   Ibid.

6   Ibid. Pearlstine also mentioned two other factors: "that [Fedders] had indicated that he would resign his position at the S.E.C. if that would get his wife to take him back" and "the issues in the Southland case" (in which a former law client had been charged with a cover-up of a bribery scheme). Ibid.

7   Ibid.

8   George Lardner Jr., "Conduct Unbecoming an Administration," *Washington Post National Weekly Edition*, Jan. 3, 1988.

—42—

CONFIDENTIALITY AND THE LAWYER-CLIENT RELATIONSHIP

Bruce M. Landesman

I. INTRODUCTION

LAWYERS ARE EXPECTED TO KEEP INFORMATION learned from their clients confidential. This obligation has two parts: the narrower attorney-client privilege that bars lawyers from testifying in court, and a broader obligation not to reveal information in other contexts.[1] The grounds for this obligation are succinctly stated in *McCormick's Handbook on the Law of Evidence*:

> ... claims and disputes which may lead to litigation can most justly and expeditiously be handled by practised experts, namely lawyers, and ... such experts can act effectively only if they are fully advised of the facts by the parties whom they represent. Such full disclosure will be promoted only if the client knows that what he tells his lawyer cannot, over his objection, be extorted in court from the lawyer's lips.[2]

The same concern supports lawyer nondisclosure out of court as well. According to the American Bar Association's Code of Professional Responsibility, however, lawyers may sometimes reveal information learned in the course of the lawyer-client relationship. Thus lawyers may make known a client's intention to commit a crime and the information necessary to prevent the crime;[3] and lawyers may reveal information when necessary to collect their fee or to defend themselves against charges of wrongful conduct.[4] The code may also allow lawyers to reveal perjury, although this is a matter of dispute.[5] In any event, the obligation of confidentiality is not taken to be absolute. There is therefore a serious question about the *extent* and *limits* of the obligation. How much and what sorts of information should it cover? What sorts of information, if any, should be left unprotected? Where the confidentiality obligation exists, when, if ever, may it be overridden? I attempt to address these questions in this essay....

[W]hat is at issue is the lawyer's duty to his or her client as opposed to his or her duties to prevent harm or promote justice or as opposed to his or her right to protect his or her own interests. Thus an adequate view of the scope and limits of lawyer-client confidentiality requires an account that will enable us to weigh these competing values and interests. To make progress toward such an account, I think it best not to tackle the issues directly, but to look at confidentiality at a more fundamental level. Thus in Sections II and III, I make some suggestions about the moral basis, complexity, and limits of confidentiality. I focus in these sections on ordinary, nonprofessional contexts, leaving aside the attorney-client situation. I also consider the more general question of passing on information about other people, whether or not it has been given in confidence. In Section IV,

I return to the question of confidentiality in the legal context. I argue for the appropriateness of more liberalized disclosure provisions than are involved in the code or in current practice....

II. USE AND MISUSE OF PERSONAL INFORMATION

When one person conveys information about himself or herself to a second person, let's call the first person the *speaker*, the second person the *hearer*, and the sort of information conveyed *personal information*.[6] If the hearer discloses the information to a third person, let's call that person a *listener*. Such information might or might not be given with an understanding that it be kept confidential, and such an understanding might be explicit or implicit. It is explicit when the hearer has made a promise (in many but not all cases requested by the speaker) not to pass on the information, implicit when there is no expressed promise but, because of the relationship between the parties or the nature of the information, there is an unspoken understanding that the information is not to be transferred....

III. THE CASE FOR CONFIDENTIALITY

Confidentiality—the speaker's revelation of information with the explicit or implicit understanding that it will not be disclosed further—can be "attached" to many different sorts of information. I have restricted the discussion to personal information, that is, information about one's self. Other sorts of information might be kept confidential, but I am not dealing here with the questions these raise. I would now like to distinguish five different categories of confidential information and then turn to the basic reasons for confidentiality.

The first sort of information is *embarrassing* information, information that simply embarrasses or shames the speaker, but need not involve wrongful or illegal acts. From this, we can distinguish *guilty* information, information that the speaker has done something wrong that, if imparted to the appropriate listener, would cause the speaker to be sanctioned by formal punishment or by informal blame, disapproval, chastisement, etc. Information about a speaker's crime, a speaker's betrayal, or a child's mischievousness would all count as guilty information. Third, there is *dangerous* information, information that the speaker intends to commit some harm, injury, or other damage to the interests of a third party. A fourth category of information is *planning* information, information about a speaker's plans, intentions, projects, or purposes. The key reason for confidentiality here would be that revealing such information might cause the speaker's plans to be thwarted by others. The fifth and final category of information I call simply *positive* information, information involving good or indifferent facts about a person. Such information, though not intrinsically damaging, could be used by others to harm the speaker or his or her interests, as when the whereabouts of a diplomat are conveyed to an enemy terrorist.

These categories are not meant to be exhaustive or exclusive, but only a good rough classification for the purposes of understanding the limits of confidentiality. After making clear a conflict that I take to be inherent in confidentiality, I shall argue that the moral force of the obligation of confidentiality will differ with respect to these different types of information.

People may reveal embarrassing, guilty, or dangerous information for a number of reasons. They may wish advice, seek sympathy, desire the human response of another person, need to express what is on their mind, to confess or admit or just share their knowledge and feelings. Or they may want to boast or enlist hearers as confederates in some plan of action. The main point is that the speaker wishes both to retain the privacy of the information and at the same time to express it to someone else. Confidentiality is the device for doing this.

This dual nature of confidentiality can be understood in a somewhat metaphorical way: when a speaker delivers information in confidence, the speaker attempts to make the hearer a part of his or her own self, or "extended self," with respect to the information revealed. It is true that the speaker needs the hearer to be another person, another "ear" and mind who can register the information and respond to it; "revealing" a confidence to a wall or a dog is no substitute for telling a person. But at the same time, the speaker needs the hearer not to be another person, but to be a part of his or her own self so that the information will not be used except as he or she chooses. Dropping the metaphorical notion of an extended self, the idea is that the hearer is not an autonomous moral agent with regard to the piece of information revealed. This is not a merely arbitrary restriction on the hearer because the need to confide information in another person is a normal human need that the hearer may also be expected to experience on occasion. The information, in effect, still "belongs" to the speaker who would not have "lent" it without being sure of retaining control of it. I suggest that both the speaker and hearer in a situation in which information is imparted in confidence perceive the situation this way or at least realize that this is how it is supposed to be perceived.

The situation of the hearer just presented is characterized by inevitable moral conflict. On the one hand, the hearer has given up moral autonomy with respect to a certain piece of information. On the other hand, the hearer still remains an autonomous moral agent with the capacity for moral deliberation and choice. Morally speaking, his or her autonomy with respect to the information received cannot be given up. He or she remains a moral being and thus free to deliberate about what to do with the information once it has been received. That it has been revealed in confidence is a powerful reason for keeping it secret, but cannot settle the issue. The hearer cannot remain a moral agent without retaining the right to consider the information in light of other factors that may, all things considered, provide even stronger reasons for revealing it....

Just how strong are the reasons on both sides?... [T]wo of the reasons for an obligation of confidentiality are the needs that motivate the expression of information and the consequences, good and bad, of disclosure. I want to suggest that these also affect the strength of the obligation. To illustrate this, I want to compare some of the types of information mentioned above.

The speaker's need to reveal *guilty* information—information that the speaker has done some wrong for which he or she could be sanctioned—will often be deep and serious, deserving of respect. The speaker's need to reveal *dangerous* information—information that the speaker intends to harm another—will often be less compelling....

Furthermore, there is a difference with respect to consequences. Revealing dangerous information can often, with near certainty, have very good consequences: the prevention of injury and harm. The consequence of disclosing guilty information—usually the sanctioning of the offender—in many cases is less important to society than preventing impending harm....

The point ... is that it does matter what wants or needs give rise to expressing information and what consequences will follow disclosure. These features affect the strength of the obligation of confidentiality....

IV. CONFIDENTIALITY IN LEGAL CONTEXTS

To tackle the question of lawyer-client confidentiality, we need to note first that there are three possible categories of permissible disclosure of information...: (1) outside the domain of confidentiality, *totally unprotected*; (2) within the domain of confidentiality but permissible to reveal in certain circumstances, *prima facie protected*; and (3) within the domain of confidentiality and never to be revealed, *absolutely protected*. In elucidating a view on the scope of confidentiality, we need to be able to say into which of these categories various types of information should be put.

Let us distinguish three views concerning the scope of confidentiality, each of which has a strong and weak version. A very simple and natural view is that the information to be protected is *all* and *only* the information relevant to the particular case for which the client has sought the lawyer's aid. Let's call this the *particular case* theory. In a strong version, the information would be absolutely protected, under no conditions to be revealed. On a weaker version such information would be prima facie protected and might be revealed, for example, to prevent perjury. On either version many sorts of information would go unprotected, including information about past crimes, information about the intention to commit future crimes, and positive and negative information totally unrelated to the case. Examples of this might be the client's finances, occupational record, or prior mental or physical health history.

Because so much information is unprotected, many will find the particular case theory inadequate. A natural and opposed alternative is that *anything* the client tells the lawyer, whether or not it is relevant to the case, should be confidential. Let's call this the *holistic* theory. This, too, will have two versions: on the strong version the information will be absolutely protected, never to be revealed; on the weaker version it will be prima facie protected, with confidentiality overridden in certain instances. A third view, which falls between these two, brings all negative or detrimental information within the domain of confidentiality, whether or not it concerns the particular case, but leaves positive information unprotected. We can call this the *negative information* theory. And, in the obvious ways, it will also have strong and weak versions.

I am going to concentrate for now on the extent of the domain of confidentiality, with how much and what kinds of information should fall into it, and leave for later the question of whether information within the domain is absolutely or only prima facie protected.... [I]t is possible to give an argument that does invoke such demands and leads away from the particular case view to the holistic view. I will call the argument the "spread" argument because those who give it want to spread the veil of confidentiality from information about

the particular case to all information imparted to the lawyer.

The argument begins with the plausible assumption that for lawyers to present the best possible case for their client, they need to know everything of relevance to the case. From this premise it infers, also plausibly, that clients must be able to tell their lawyers, in confidence, anything they know that is relevant to the facts.... [Another] possibility is that the relevant information is often "intertwined" in the client's mind with other information that is not, logically, relevant to the case, and the client will be able to express the relevant information only if he or she also has the "space" to express a lot of nonrelevant information as well. The point is not that clients are not competent to assess relevance but that people need to express themselves in their own special ways and this requires freedom to go beyond the particular case. Whichever additional premise is used, it follows that clients must be free to say in confidence anything that is on their mind, leaving the assessment of relevance to the lawyer after all the facts have been brought out. If certain areas were exempted from the scope of confidentiality, clients would want to ensure that they did not reveal damaging information that falls into those areas. But since such information is, in one of the ways mentioned, connected with relevant information, clients are likely to omit relevant information as well. So any restrictions on the domain of confidentiality will make clients cautious and thus will have an unacceptable "chilling effect"; if lawyers are to represent clients effectively, confidentiality must therefore apply to all information.

... The first two versions of the crucial premise of the spread argument are implausible, as can be seen by rather obvious counterexamples. *A* is charged with robbing *B*. *A* can know with certainty that at least regarding this particular robbery his sister-in-law's maiden name or his favorite baseball team are irrelevant. *A* is not likely to be mistaken on this nor must he know everything in order to know this. On the other hand, whether *A* was or was not at the scene of the robbery when it occurred can be known with certainty by him to be relevant. So the claim that people cannot assess relevance at all or cannot assess it piecemeal is an implausible exaggeration.

The third version of the premise—the claim that relevant and irrelevant information is mentally "intertwined" for most people—is more satisfactory. It says, in effect, that people are not well-programmed computers who can communicate "the facts and nothing but the facts"; rather, in the course of giving out the facts, they need the freedom to express themselves in their own peculiar ways and this means bringing in more than the facts. Lawyers must therefore set up a situation in which clients feel free to talk about all sorts of things and the obvious condition of this freedom is that clients know they won't be betrayed. Thus it seems reasonable to think that, in the course of interviewing, lawyers are likely to learn not only the facts relevant to the case but other information that is embarrassing or otherwise detrimental or that is, though not negative, the sort of information that people usually keep private.

These psychological facts about the intertwining of information, if plausible, show that the particular case view is too restricted. Do they support the holistic theory? While people intertwine information and require freedom to talk about more than the particular case, they are not totally unable to discern differences, distinguish contexts, and categorize information. To say that they must be able to say *anything*, if they are to reveal relevant facts, is surely to overstate the case.[7] Most clients are unlikely to make fine distinctions among categories of information, however, and so may lose confidence in a lawyer who reveals information too freely, even information that has nothing to do with the present case. But likewise we are likely to lose confidence in friends who reveal even our trivial confidences too casually, though this certainly does not mean that a holistic duty of confidentiality holds among friends. Where information is clearly irrelevant to the case in hand and is in no way intertwined with information that is relevant to it, it would seem that the lawyer's duty of confidentiality to a client begins to approximate our ordinary assumptions discussed earlier regarding communications of personal information. What emerges from this, I think, is that the domain of confidentiality must be wider than the particular case theory allows, but its scope is not captured adequately by the holistic theory. Nor does the negative information theory do the job here. The trouble with the negative information view is that some nonnegative information should be included in the domain (the sort usually held private) and much negative information need not be included (the sort that is clearly not intertwined with the pertinent facts). So we have a vague domain of confidential information about the particular case plus other intertwined information "radiating out" from there. This additional information does not include everything known to the client, but it is difficult to give a precise demarcation of it that would fit every client's needs. This is probably why the extent of the domain of confidentiality is generally left quite vague in the various codes and systems of rules.

It might now be said that it is fine to speak of the domain of confidentiality as lacking clear boundaries, but this is not of much help to practitioners who need a rule to give them guidance. What then, for practical purposes, should the rule be? To answer this we need to stop talking about information in general and consider some of the controversial types of information mentioned in the introduction. I will focus, then, on the following two questions:

1. Should information about future crimes and/or acts that injure others fall within the domain of confidentiality?
2. Should the disclosure of information about the particular case be permitted or required in order to prevent or rectify perjury?

Discussing these issues will help us give a partial outline of the most plausible practical rule.

With respect to the client's intention to commit a crime, the major reason for disclosure is to prevent the harm and injury the crime involves. This is a compelling ground. Also relevant is a concern for the lawyer's own moral status: if such information may be disclosed the lawyer is not put in the morally difficult position of having to stand by while something dreadful happens....

In response, the case against revealing such information must, I think, appeal to three considerations. The first is the possibility that information about the intention to commit a crime may be intertwined with information directly relevant to the case. But while it is possible that some clients may be unable to discuss the particular case without revealing future criminal plans, I doubt this is very common. It is certainly not common enough to outweigh the considerations that favor disclosure.

Second, it may be held that the client's knowledge that the lawyer may report intentions to commit a crime will have a significant chilling effect, interfering with the confidence the client must have in the lawyer in order to reveal all pertinent information. I have already suggested that this sort of remark is an overstatement, most clients will not need this sort of immunity in order to have enough "space" to talk freely on the matter at issue. Nevertheless, this objection does suggest a general problem. It may be that allowing each one of a number of categories of information separately to be disclosed would have no significant chilling effect. But allowing all of them would have such an effect. So there may be a case for allowing disclosure of information of type A, of type B, of type C, etc., but not of A *and* B *and* C, etc. If all were disposable a threshold would be reached in which the client's "space" would be diminished enough so that confidence in the lawyer would disappear. This means we must take into account the combined results of various disclosure provisions, which may involve ranking the importance of various provisions and accepting only the most crucial. Since preventing imminent harm is a fundamental moral aim, this provision should survive this "combined effect" objection.

The third response to the argument is very interesting. If lawyers "blow the whistle" on clients' crimes, some harm will be prevented. But if clients come to know that lawyers will do this, most of them will cease informing lawyers of their criminal intentions. So the harm this disclosure is designed to prevent will not be prevented. Further, if disclosure is protected a lawyer will sometimes succeed in persuading a client not to follow through with criminal intentions. But if such disclosure is not protected, the information will not be revealed and the crime will be committed. So, it is argued, the long-term result of allowing disclosure of information about likely criminal acts, in terms of harm to others, is either no different or worse than the policy protecting such information.[8]

This is a powerful argument.... But something else is involved: the lawyer's own moral status and worth. If disclosure is not allowed, the lawyer will sometimes be forced to permit something quite evil to happen. The policy of disclosure avoids or minimizes this. I think that no one should be forced or required by social rules to stand by while genuine evil occurs; the damage to one's moral personality is unacceptable (and possibly habit-forming). I conclude that this weighty concern for the lawyer's own moral status tips the scales in favor of disclosure....

I now turn to the disclosure of perjury. Here we are concerned with information about the particular case that must be considered prima facie confidential. The question is whether confidentiality is overridden when the client commits perjury. The issue of perjury poses the question of what a lawyer may do for a client. Clearly, the lawyer may and should present the strongest and best case. But what is the strongest and best case? Although a case involving perjured testimony and manufactured evidence may be very strong, neither the client nor lawyer is entitled to present *this* case, despite its strength. On the other hand, they need not be confined to what they really believe, based on the evidence, is the strongest case. Uncounterfeit evidence may be treated with flexibility, welcome facts may be stressed, unwelcome facts played down, and the whole interpreted in the most favorable light.[9] The distinction between perjured or manufactured evidence and evidence that is given greater emphasis than the client or lawyer believes it deserves may or may not be arbitrary. Both cases involve a kind of deception. But perjury seems to be a reasonable place to draw the line, since permitting perjury may place impossible burdens on judges and juries, while forbidding any stretching of evidence would negate a person's day in court, also the adversary process arguably has the resources to correct such stretching. So the prohibition of perjury makes sense in terms of the nature of the adversary system and its aim of achieving justice while permitting people to present their case as they best see fit.

For these reasons there is a prima facie case for requiring lawyers not to allow perjury and for having a rule that requires them to attempt to dissuade clients from lying and to reveal the lie to the judge if a client goes through with it. What, then, are the arguments against this? The most typical is the familiar appeal to the "chilling effect": clients will not feel free to speak openly about the particular case if they know the lawyer can reveal perjury. To examine this, consider that we have two kinds of clients. The first have no intentions of committing perjury. These persons will not be chilled by the attorney's duty of disclosure. (And surely these clients are in the majority!) The second might want to commit perjury. They will be chilled. If they know in advance that they intend to lie, they will have to be very careful what they tell the lawyer and they may well omit relevant facts. And if they decide they want to commit perjury after they have revealed the damning facts, they won't be able to get away with it. So such people will suffer bad consequences if perjury may be disclosed. But why should this trouble any one else? They have, after all, no right to commit perjury, and if their attempt to do what

they have no right to do gets them into difficulties, the responsibility is theirs. They can simply avoid the difficulties by giving up the intention to lie.[10]

... I conclude then that there are good reasons for disclosing perjury to the court and the reasons that can be cited against this are unpersuasive.

V. CONCLUSION

I have argued that rules permitting or requiring the disclosure of information to prevent crimes and serious injuries and to reveal perjury are reasonable and will not damage the basic functions of confidentiality. Thus a social rule to guide practitioners should allow the disclosure of such information. Information about intended crimes should probably fall outside the domain of confidentiality, while information concerning perjury, being information about the particular case, will be prima facie confidential: it is in the domain, but it may be revealed when the client lies....

I said at the beginning that I would not present a complete and detailed argument for my conclusions and I have not. Much more needs to be said, but I believe progress has been made. Exclusive stress on confidentiality and on the obligation to the client leads to an unjustifiable surrender of moral autonomy and gives rise to the amorality and impersonality of the lawyer's role that has often been noticed.[11] By emphasizing moral autonomy and the moral status and worth of the lawyer, and by expressing some skepticism toward the systemic arguments for a wide and near-absolute domain of confidentiality (i.e., the "spread" argument, the chilling effect, etc.). I hope to have made plausible the idea that confidentiality must be restrained out of respect for autonomy and the lawyer's moral status, and that this can be done in a manner that achieves the important functions of confidentiality. In any case, I trust that enough has been said to show that "ideological" appeals either to zealous advocacy of the client's cause, on the one hand, or to the truth, on the other, are likely only to simplify the moral complexity of these issues.

NOTES

This paper is an extensively revised and expanded version of my "Confidentiality and the Lawyer-Client Relationship," *Utah Law Review* 1980 (1980): 765–86.

1   *ABA Code of Professional Responsibility* (1976 revision), DR 4-101.
2   Edward W. Cleary et al., *McCormick's Handbook on the Law of Evidence*, 2nd ed. (St. Paul, MN: West Publishing Co., 1972), 175.
3   *ABA Code*, DR 4-101 (C) (3).
4   Ibid., DR 4-101 (C) (4).
5   Ibid., DR 7-102 (A) (4), DR 7-102 (B) (1). An illuminating discussion of the ambiguities of the perjury rules can be found in "Note: Client Fraud and the Lawyer—An Ethical Analysis," *Minnesota Law Review* Vol. 62 (1977): 89–118.
6   There are of course other sorts of information that might be conveyed, e.g., about third parties, about the facts. I am simply not considering the disclosure of such information in this paper.
7   The claim that everything the client may feel inclined to say must be kept confidential has a great deal of cogency if applied to a psychotherapist; in such a context any information may have a symbolic meaning for the problem at hand. But the lawyer does not have the same job as a therapist. (In *Tarasoff v. Regents of University of California*, 551 P. 2d 334 [1976], however, it was ruled that psychotherapists are liable at tort if they don't reveal dangerous information that results in someone's death.)
8   An interesting version of this argument, applied to medical contexts, is given by Kenneth Kipnis, "Review Article: Alan Goldman's The Moral Foundations of Professional Ethics," *Westminster Institute Review* Vol. 1, No. 3 (October 1981): 8–10.
9   Criminal cases, civil cases, and negotiations will obviously need relatively different treatment in these respects.
10 [Monroe Freedman, *Lawyers' Ethics in an Adversary System* (Indianapolis: Bobbs-Merrill, 1975), 31.]
11 See [Richard Wasserstrom: "Lawyers as Professionals: Some Moral Issues," *Human Rights* Vol. 5 (1975): 1-24]. For another discussion that also emphasizes the lawyer's own autonomy, see John J. Flynn, "Professional Ethics and the Lawyer's Duty to Self," *Washington University Law Quarterly* 1976 (1976): 429–44.

—43—

INFORMING CLIENTS ABOUT LIMITS TO CONFIDENTIALITY

Lee A. Pizzimenti

THE LEGAL ETHICS RULES CONCERNING THE maintenance of client confidences are varied and confusing, and many exceptions exist allowing or mandating the lawyer to disclose confidences. For example, lawyers must disclose client perjury in many states, and they often have discretion to report future crimes, or to disclose information necessary to protect themselves or collect a fee.[1] Yet, clients expect lawyers to keep their secrets. Lawyers encourage that belief, either by misstating the scope of protections or by saying nothing to clients.[2] ... As a result, many clients believe that anything they tell their lawyers will never be disclosed to anyone.[3]

Suppose, then, that a lawyer discloses client information. The client may feel that the lawyer has misled him, or, at a minimum, has not provided him with an adequate opportunity to consider whether he should share information with the lawyer. That is, his decision to confide in the lawyer was not an informed one. The question then becomes whether the client should be the one to make that choice, and, if so, whether other considerations outweigh that right.

Rule 1.4 of the Model Rules of Professional Conduct recognizes that lawyers must provide information to the extent "reasonably necessary to permit the client to make informed decisions regarding the representation." However, not all decisions are to be made by the client. The

traditional approach is that "procedural," or tactical, decisions are to be made by the lawyer, while the client makes "substantive" decisions.[4] ...

While it may be concluded after consideration that lawyers should refrain from informing clients about confidentiality exceptions, it is improper to conflate the questions of making disclosures to third parties and giving clients information about that possibility. Just as a lawyer should not decide to disclose client information until after she undertakes a careful balancing of rights at stake, the lawyer should not withhold information from the client until she has made that analysis. I will undertake to consider that question now.

Using the substance/procedure analysis to determine what rights are at stake is not useful, because issues that are ostensibly procedural can have a profound impact upon clients. Professor David Luban provides the example of an innocent client being prosecuted for murder who forbade counsel from calling an alibi witness. While one might claim that choice of witnesses is a tactical matter, the client refused for what he viewed to be a "substantive" reason: the witness was his best friend's wife, who would testify that he had been with her during the time the crime had been committed.[5] A less provocative example might be that a client negotiating a long term contract would prefer that a lawyer be accommodating to the other party to assure a comfortable working

266

relationship with him, while the lawyer might wish to allow no compromise in order to effect the best possible agreement.

Recognizing the artificial distinction between substance and procedure, commentators agree that the appropriate focus should be on client expectations rather than upon whether the lawyer historically has made decisions of the type contemplated.[6] Instead, the lawyer should consider whether the client would view the information as material to his decisionmaking. Thus, to determine whether it is appropriate to withhold information, one must balance the rights implicated by the failure to allow informed consent against countervailing rights affected if clients are apprised of confidentiality's limits.[7]

A requirement of informed consent is necessary to protect the right of autonomy, which is derived from the Kantian notion of respect for persons as ends in themselves rather than as simply means to another goal.[8] ...

To assure that autonomy, lawyers must recognize their duty of veracity toward clients, which includes not only the duty to refrain from misstatements, but also the affirmative responsibility of candor.[9] Veracity is critical to the maintenance of autonomy, because a lack of it creates two obstacles to autonomous decisionmaking: limiting information limits choices, and, almost inevitably, the client may be manipulated if an attorney withholds or misstates information.[10] Thus, failure to share the material fact that secrets may be disclosed has an immediate and substantial impact on client autonomy.

In most cases, failure to disclose limits to confidentiality should be deemed an intentional act as a lawyer is bound to know the requirements of the code of ethics in her state.[11] Intentional deception creates additional strains upon the attorney-client relationship, even if the client is unaware of the deception. First, the lawyer may feel compelled to make additional false statements to avoid discovery of the original deception.[12] Moreover, the attorney may become less sensitive to the morality of her actions: "lies seem more necessary, less reprehensible; the ability to make moral distinctions can coarsen; the liar's perception of his chances of being caught may warp."[13] Finally, the lawyer who successfully deceives may view her client as being easily duped. Consequently, the attorney's respect for the client as an autonomous moral agent may be reduced.[14] Perhaps she may develop a general unwillingness to respect the client's rights, or those of other clients.[15] A lack of informed consent about limits on confidentiality also presents an interesting irony: the lawyer makes a misrepresentation regarding secrecy to clients to create an atmosphere encouraging candor. Such lawyers "would prefer, in other words, a 'free-rider' status, giving them the benefit of lying without the risks of being lied to."[16]

It is clear, then, that deception concerning confidentiality can immediately destroy the foundation of the attorney-client relationship and the client's right to autonomy. Of course, the right to autonomy is not absolute. Although increasing autonomy is good in the abstract, it may not be justified in cases where autonomous decisionmaking leads to immoral results.[17] Thus, one must also consider the rights of the lawyer or third parties at stake if the lawyer informs the client of exceptions to confidentiality and the client chooses to refrain from confiding in the lawyer.[18] However, autonomy is a "prima-facie" right entitled to great deference, and the lawyer attempting to justify deception must overcome a strong presumption that the client is entitled to information.

Deception is most justified when it prevents imminent bodily harm to a third party.[19] Such deception is justified for three reasons: there is a limited time available to evaluate alternatives; the right to bodily integrity is a strong countervailing one; and deception typically occurs in such isolated instances that it probably will not encourage others to lie.[20] Such a rationale might, for example, serve as a justification for failure to inform the parent of a child who is admitted to an emergency room with injuries clearly stemming from abuse that the incident must be reported. Otherwise, the parent may remove the child, who then would not receive care. In the attorney-client context, deception may be appropriate where the client has a history of violent behavior, making it more likely that third parties might be harmed.[21]

The difficulty with this analysis is that it assumes that clients will not inform of their intention to commit a harmful act absent a promise of confidentiality, and lawyers will therefore be unable to prevent harm. In fact, clients may tell lawyers anyway, either because they feel compelled to confess or because they recognize they will receive better representation if they talk to their lawyers.[22]

There is, in addition, an analytical problem with using the paradigm of avoidance of bodily harm as a blanket justification for deception. Deception about possible disclosure occurs from the commencement of the relationship, when it is unclear whether anyone's interests are implicated, let alone an innocent third party's interest in bodily integrity. Thus, the lawyer cannot evaluate the alternatives, nor can she determine the likelihood or severity of an infringement of a third party's rights at the time of the deception. Thus, the lawyer cannot evaluate the strength of the justification for the deception at the time it occurs. Moreover, a policy of not disclosing limits on confidences, if intentional, goes beyond the isolated incident that will not encourage others to lie. Rather, it reflects an ongoing practice of deception.

If the possibility of averting bodily injury does not serve to justify a policy of deception, it follows that deception is not justified by the possibility of perjury, or that a lawyer may avoid harm to herself if her competence is challenged or if she must collect a fee.[23] In fact, if situations invoking those exceptions arise more often than threats of bodily harm, the greater likelihood of occurrence makes the information more material to the client.

Lawyers may fear that informing clients of the limits to confidentiality will chill attorney-client communications. Other than the possibility of harm to the lawyer or third parties, which is too speculative to serve as support for deception, the only danger of a chilling effect is that the client may not confide information the attorney finds necessary for competent representation. One can analogize this argument to the discredited and paternalistic notion that patients should not be told of risks because they might not submit to procedures that are "good" for them.[24] So long as a client is made aware that the lawyer may be hampered in her representation if the client does not confide in her, the choice of whether to confide belongs to the client.

One exception to the notion that lawyers may not consider the chilling effect that informing the client might have is where the client appears extraordinarily nervous and mistrustful, and the lawyer feels immediate warnings will destroy the relationship before it is established. Commentators have recognized that short term paternalism may be necessary to enhance autonomy in the long run.[25] However, as David Luban indicates, there are strict limits to when deception is justified, even for a brief period: the decision-maker's capacity must be impaired; the constraint must be as limited and temporary as possible, and the threatened damage must be severe and irreversible.[26] I would add that if the attorney believes that confidences potentially damaging to the client are imminent, deception even in the short term is unjustified as the impact on autonomy would be irreversible. Absent these special circumstances, however, a presumption arises that informing clients about limits to confidentiality is necessary.

One obvious question that arises is how much information the lawyer should share. Providing the client with an equivalent of a law school education by explaining all of the nuances of confidentiality rules seems unnecessary and, in fact, would be counterproductive, as studies have shown that providing too much information reduces the recipient's ability to understand. However, the attorney should give a general explanation of the duty of confidentiality and its major exceptions. In that way, the client will have enough information to enable him to ask intelligent questions as specific confidentiality issues arise. If it becomes clear to the attorney as the representation progresses that the client needs more specific information because an exception may apply, she should raise the issue again.

Of course, not all information is material to every client. Three variables might be considered in determining when to inform the client. First, the lawyer might evaluate the relative sophistication of her client. A lawyer dealing with in-house corporate counsel may assume the client is aware of confidentiality sections. Although some cases have shown corporate officials are unaware of the nuances of legal representation,[27] one may assume they are generally more sophisticated than some other clients. Arguably, knowledgeable clients do not require warnings to make informed decisions.

Next, the lawyer could evaluate the likelihood that information might be confided.... For example, this factor would support a rule that lawyers should warn criminal clients about the potential for disclosure of future crimes or of fraud on a tribunal. If fee disputes are common, that exception should be disclosed.

Finally, the nature of the confidences to be shared is relevant. A client will be more concerned about disclosures involving highly private or harmful information than about more innocuous information. Perhaps, then, exceptions concerning crimes or frauds should be raised, but the fee exception need not be as only general information is disclosed. The client might also be interested in learning that a lawyer may exculpate herself by inculpating the client.

While use of these factors would be better than giving no consideration to client concerns, there are two grave problems with relying on them. First, selective information may be more misleading than no information at all. Recitation of some exceptions may lead the client to believe there are no others.

Second, use of the factors tends to treat clients as groups rather than as individuals, which is contrary to the central notion of the informed consent requirement. Rather than enhancing autonomy

of the individual client in an individual case, the lawyer relying on the factors above runs the risk of creating "a standardized person to whom he attributes standardized ends,"[28] and "acting for the hypothetical client rather than the one before him."[29] This approach depersonalizes the client and treats him as an object. To assure true autonomy, the lawyer must not decide what she thinks the client wants or needs, but must explore the client's actual goals with him.

As a result, while the above factors might be useful, they cannot be dispositive. The lawyer must engage the client in an ongoing, personal discussion to enable her to determine what matters to the client. Perhaps that discussion could begin with a statement such as the following one, which is drafted to apply to a criminal client:

> You should know that I work for you and that I consider it very important to keep your confidences. The attorney-client privilege essentially means that I cannot be forced to disclose information about discussions we have. For example, judges sometimes can order lawyers to disclose information, but they can't make me tell them about whether you committed the crime.[30] You should know about some limits to the privilege, however. I am an officer of the court, and I cannot help you commit any frauds upon the court. Therefore, if I learn that you will lie or have lied on the witness stand, I must report that.[31] I am also allowed to report if you tell me you are going to commit a crime. I may also report limited information to defend against claims made against me or to collect my fee, but I am allowed to report only that information necessary to meet those goals. For example, if we fight about my fee, I might be able to show my billing records, but I couldn't just reveal all the things I know about you. Although there are times I may feel it is necessary to report information, I want to remind you that I take the privilege very seriously and would never lightly decide to share information.

Those reading this suggested statement might believe all of this sounds terrible and the client would view the lawyer as greedy and self-protective.[32] This response is like shooting the messenger rather than wishing the message were different. The ethics rules provide for these exceptions, and if they sound as if ethical priorities are misplaced, the rules should be changed. So long as they exist, however, the client should be aware of them. Of course, absent modification of the rules, one alternative to revealing the more self-serving of those exceptions is that an individual attorney may decide as a matter of personal ethics not to warn regarding those exceptions, because she intends never to invoke them. In this way, no deception occurs.[33]

Assuming no explanation of exceptions occurs, and the client confides evidence he would not have absent a belief it would remain confidential, the client has lost the right to make autonomous decisions with adequate information. The lawyer should be held responsible for that loss. First, a lawyer may be disciplined for violation of Model Rule 1.4. Moreover, the client could bring an action for lack of informed consent. If there are no actual damages from the lack of informed consent, at least nominal damages and possibly attorney fees should be assessed.[34] Because an action for breach of the fiduciary duty of candor is a tort claim,[35] emotional distress damages, if proved, should be allowed. Punitive damages may be appropriate where reckless disregard is shown.[36]

Although informing clients of limitations on confidentiality might inhibit the rights of the lawyer or third parties, those rights are varied and speculative. Conversely, deception regarding limitations has an immediate impact of reducing autonomy and impairing the attorney-client relationship. Thus, an attorney is morally required, and should be legally required, to be forthright with a client and to allow the client to choose whether the risks of disclosure outweigh its benefits.

NOTES

1   See, e.g., *Model Code of Professional Responsibility* DR 4-101(c) (1980); *Model Rules of Professional Conduct* 1.6(b), 3.3 (1983) (hereinafter *Model Rules*). Confidentiality rules vary greatly among states. See Pizzimenti, "The Lawyer's Duty to Warn Clients About Limits on Confidentiality," *Cath. U.L. Rev.* Vol. 39: 801, 810 n.34; 829 n.126 (1990).

2   Zacharias, "Rethinking Confidentiality," *Iowa L. Rev.* Vol. 74: 351, 382–83 (1989).

3   Ibid. at 383. Of those clients surveyed regarding confidentiality, 42.4% believed that confidentiality requirements were absolute.

4   See *Model Rules*, *supra* note 1, at 1.2(a).

5   Luban, "Paternalism and the Legal Profession," *Wis. L. Rev.* 454, 456 (1981). For other examples of procedural issues with substantive impact, see Ibid. at 454–59.

6   See, e.g., Maute, "Allocation of Decision-making Authority Under the Model Rules of Professional Conduct," *U.C. Davis L. Rev.* Vol. 17: 1049, 1080–1105 (1984) (tactics/substance dichotomy not dispositive); Spiegel, "Lawyering and Client Decisionmaking: Informed Consent and the Legal Profession," *U. Pa. L. Rev.* Vol. 128: 41, 72–133 (1979) (same); Strauss, "Toward a Revised Model of Attorney-Client Relationship: The Argument for Autonomy," *N.C. L. Rev.* Vol. 65: 315, 336–49 (1987) (same).

7   I do not by suggesting the need for balancing rights implicated by an action mean to advocate adoption of a utilitarian standard....

8   Kant provided a deontological approach to determining morality. A deontological theory is one based on the notion that the "right, the obligatory and the morally good" are not determined by reviewing the consequences of an action, but by reviewing the intrinsic morality of the act itself. W. Frankena, *Ethics* 14 (1963)....

9   This right is drawn from the fiduciary nature of the attorney-client relationship. M. Bayles, *Professional Ethics* 72 (2nd ed. 1989).

10 [R. Wright, *Human Values in Health Care: The Practice of Ethics* 32 (1987)], at 94 (1987).

11 Nondisclosure may not be intentional, however, when an attorney mistakenly believes the information withheld is not relevant to a client. While such failure is not as morally culpable as deliberate nondisclosure, it still violates client autonomy, which is the value underlying an attorney's duty to inquire in order to determine what the client thinks is material. See [Martyn, "Informed Consent in the Practice of Law," *Geo. Wash. L. Rev.* Vol. 48 (1980)] at 323 (citing J. Story, *Commentaries on Equity Jurisprudence* § 208 [fiduciary has affirmative duty to disclose facts and circumstances principal would find important]).

12 S. Bok, *Lying: Moral Choice in Public and Private Life* 15 (1978).

13 Ibid.

14 The lawyer may reach this conclusion to reduce his or her own feelings of guilt. The attorney may conclude it is the client's "fault" that deception was necessary, or the client's "fault" that he is too dense to recognize the deception.

15 Disdain for the client's right or ability to make intelligent decisions may result even when the lawyer lies for the client's "own good." The lawyer may come to view the client as unable or unworthy to decide for himself. [S. Bok, *Lying: Moral Choice in Public and Private Life* 15 (1978)], at 76.

16 S. Bok, *supra* note [15] at 23. The fact that the client trusted the lawyer will exacerbate the inevitable feelings of betrayal that will result if the client learns the lawyer has disclosed private information, regardless of whether the lawyer intended to mislead.

17 See Luban, "The Lysistratian Prerogative: A Response to Stephen Pepper," *Am. B. Found. Res. J.* 637, 639 (1986).

18 Because apprising clients of confidentiality enhances the right of autonomy but may implicate other rights, one must determine which performance would result in the greatest balance of right over wrong. [W.D. Ross, *The Right and the Good* 21-23 (London: Oxford Press, 1930)], at 41. Recognizing that one should consider immoral results, as well as the intrinsic features of an act,

does not result in the adoption of a utilitarian theory....

19 S. Bok, *supra* note [15], at 105–09.

20 Ibid.

21 Although the rights of third parties are most clearly at issue in such a case, the information is also more material to the client, and of a more private nature than some confidences....

22 Subin, "The Lawyer as Superego: Disclosure of Client Confidences to Prevent Harm," *Iowa L. Rev.* Vol. 70: 1091, 1163–64 (1985); Zacharias, *supra* note 2, at 369.

23 For a discussion of the moral justifications for the various exceptions to confidentiality rules, see Pizzimenti, *supra* note 1, at 827–31, and sources cited therein.

24 The desire to do what is best for the client is a laudable one, based on the principle of beneficence, or providing benefits (which includes both prevention of harm and promotion of welfare). See [See T. Beauchamp and J. Childress, *Principles of Biomedical Ethics* (1979)], at 194–95. However, failure to provide informed consent for the client's "own good" creates a conflict between the principles of beneficence and autonomy. Ibid. at 210. In medical ethics, it is generally recognized that beneficence must give way to promotion of autonomy, at least where the patient is competent....

25 See T. Mappes and J. Zembaty, *Biomedical Ethics* 55 (2nd ed. 1986).

26 Luban, *supra* note [5], at 465.

27 See, e.g., *Brown v. E.F. Hutton*, 305 F. Supp. 371 (S.D. Tex. 1969) (corporate officer unaware attorney did not represent him as well as corporation).

28 Lehman, "The Pursuit of a Client's Interest," *Mich. L. Rev.* Vol. 77: 1078, 1087 (1977). See Anderson, "Informed Decisionmaking in an Office Practice," *B.C.L. Rev.* Vol. 28: 225, 233 (1987) (using the "reasonable client" approach to materiality assumes that clients fit into categories and that it is permissible to treat them alike).

29 Lehman, *supra* note [28], at 1087.

30 In another setting, the lawyer might say the court cannot force her to disclose her client's negligence,

breach of contract, or other past act which is the subject of the representation.

31 This statement assumes the lawyer lives in a jurisdiction where such disclosures are mandated....

32 It may also be argued that the client may be deterred from making disclosures....

33 An attorney may also decide as a matter of personal ethics to refrain from disclosing perjury, but she thereby runs the risk of violating an ethics rule and subjecting herself to discipline.

34 Anderson, *supra* note [28], at 250.

35 Cf. *Olfe v. Gordon* (breach of the fiduciary duty of following client instructions is malpractice).

36 Anderson, *supra* note [28], at 249–50.

—44—

A DEFENSE OF UNQUALIFIED MEDICAL CONFIDENTIALITY[1]

Kenneth Kipnis

THE INFECTED SPOUSE

THE FOLLOWING FICTIONALIZED CASE IS BASED ON an actual incident.

1982: After moving to Honolulu, Wilma and Andrew Long visit your office and ask you to be their family physician. They have been your patients ever since.

1988: Six years later the two decide to separate. Wilma leaves for the Mainland, occasionally sending you a postcard. Though you do not see her professionally, you still think of yourself as her doctor.

1990: Andrew comes in and says that he has embarked upon a more sophisticated social life. He has been hearing about some new sexually transmitted diseases and wants to be tested. He is positive for the AIDS virus and receives appropriate counseling.

1991: Visiting your office for a checkup, Andrew tells you Wilma is returning to Hawaii for reconciliation with him. She arrives this afternoon and will be staying at the Moana Hotel. Despite your best efforts to persuade him, he leaves without giving you assurance that he will tell Wilma about his infection or protect her against becoming infected.

Do you take steps to see that Wilma is warned? If you decide to warn Wilma, what do you say to Andrew when, two days later, he shows up at your office asking how you could reveal his confidential test results?

If you decide not to warn Wilma, what do you say to her when, two years later in 1993, she shows up at your office asking how you, her doctor, could possibly stand idly by as her husband infected her with a deadly virus. She now knows she is positive for the virus, that she was infected by her husband, and that you—her doctor—knew, before they reconciled, that her husband would probably infect her.

The ethical challenges here emerge from an apparent head-on collision between medical confidentiality and the duty to protect imperiled third parties. Notwithstanding Andrew's expectation of privacy and the professional duty to remain silent, it can seem unforgivable for anyone to withhold vital assistance in such a crisis, let alone a doctor....

... The conventional wisdom in medical ethics overwhelmingly supports either an ethical obligation to breach confidentiality in cases like this one or, occasionally and less stringently, the ethical permissibility of doing so (Lo 1995). Notwithstanding this consensus, it is my intention to challenge the received view. I will argue in what follows that confidentiality in clinical medicine is far closer to an absolute obligation than it has generally been taken to be; doctors should honor confidentiality even in cases like this one....

THE DUTY TO DIMINISH
RISKS TO THIRD PARTIES

There is an implication for the way in which we must now understand the problem in *The Infected Spouse*. The opening question "Do you take steps to warn Wilma?" has to be understood as a question about medical ethics and not about "you." We want to know what the "good doctor" should do under those circumstances. Each doctor is ethically required to do what a responsible doctor ought to do: in order to properly respect the core values of the profession. To become a doctor without a proper commitment to respect the profession's values is to be unfit for the practice of medicine. So how are trustworthiness and confidentiality to be understood in relationship to medicine's commitment to diminish risks to third parties?

The Infected Spouse poses its question in 1991, after the doctor-family relationship has been in place for a decade. The dilemma arises during and immediately after a single office visit, forcing a choice between calling Wilma or not, and having to explain to Andrew, in two days, why you disclosed his infection to his wife, or having to explain to Wilma, in two years, why you did not disclose his infection to her. Each option has a bad outcome: the betrayal of Andrew's trust or the fatal infection of Wilma. Either way, you will need to account for yourself.

Infection seems a far worse consequence for Wilma than betrayal is for Andrew. Much of the literature on confidentiality has been shaped by this fact, and perhaps the standard strategy for resolving the problem calls attention to the magnitude and probability of the bad outcomes associated with each option. While predictions of harm can sometimes be wrong, it can be evident that Tatiana Tarasoff and Wilma Long are at grave risk and, accordingly, it can seem honorable to diminish the danger to vulnerable parties like them. Justice Tobriner appeals to a version of this consequentialist argument in *Tarasoff*:

Weighing the uncertain and conjectural character of the alleged damage done the patient by such a warning against the peril to the victim's life, we conclude that professional inaccuracy in predicting violence [or deadly infection] cannot negate the therapist's duty to protect the threatened victim.

Beauchamp and Childress, in their widely read *Principles of Biomedical Ethics* (Beauchamp and Childress 2001), urge clinicians to take into account "the probability that a harm will materialize and the magnitude of that harm" in any decision to breach confidentiality. (While they also urge that clinicians take into account the potential impact of disclosure on policies and laws regarding confidentiality, they are not very clear about how this assessment is to be carried out.) In brief, the very bad consequences to Wilma—disease and death and the betrayal of her trust—outweigh the not-all-that-bad consequence to Andrew. Your explanation to Andrew could cover those points.

The preferred argument would go something like this: The state's interest in preventing harm is weighty. Medicine has an obligation to protect the well-being of the community. Because the seriousness of threatened grave injury to another outweighs the damage done to a patient by breaching confidentiality, the obligation of confidentiality must give way to a duty to prevent serious harm to others. Accordingly, despite confidentiality, warning or reporting is obligatory when it will likely avert very bad outcomes in this way. Of course clinicians should try to obtain waivers of confidentiality before disclosure, thereby avoiding the need to breach a duty. But the failure to obtain a waiver does not, on this argument, affect the overriding obligation to report.

A DEFENSE OF UNQUALIFIED
MEDICAL CONFIDENTIALITY

As powerful as this justification is, there are problems with it. Go back to 1990, when Andrew comes in to be tested for sexually transmitted diseases. Suppose he asks: "If I am infected, can I trust you not to disclose this to others?" If, following the arguments set out in the previous paragraphs, we are clear that confidentiality must be breached to protect third parties like Wilma, then the only truthful answer to Andrew's question is "No. You can't trust me." If the profession accepts that its broad promise of confidentiality must sometimes be broken, then any unqualified assurances are fraudulent and the profession should stop making them. If there are exceptions, clinicians have a duty to be forthcoming about what they are and how they work. Patients should know up front when they can trust doctors, and when they can't. To withhold this important information is to betray the value of trustworthiness.

Accordingly, the argument for breaching confidentiality has to be modified to support a qualified confidentiality rule, one that carves out an exception from the very beginning, acknowledging an overriding duty to report under defined circumstances. (In contrast, an unqualified confidentiality rule contemplates no exceptions.) Instead of undertaking duties of confidentiality and then violating them, doctors must qualify their expressed obligations so they will be able to honor them. Commentators who have walked through the issues surrounding confidentiality have long understood the ethical necessity of "Miranda warnings" (Bok 1983, Goldman 1980): A clinician would have to say early on: "Certain things that I learn from you may have to be disclosed to ... under the following circumstances: ..., and the following things might occur to you as a result of my disclosure...." If doctors are ethically obligated to report, they need to say in advance what will be passed along, when, to whom, and what could happen then. They should never encourage or accept trust only to betray their patients afterwards. To do so is to betray the value of trustworthiness.

But now a second problem emerges. If prospective patients must understand in advance that a doctor will report evidence of a threat to others, they will only be willing to disclose such evidence to the doctor if they are willing to accept that those others will come to know. If it is important to them that the evidence not be reported, they will have a weighty reason not to disclose it to those who are obligated to report it.

Some have questioned this proposition, arguing that there is no empirical evidence that prospective patients will avoid or delay seeking medical attention or conceal medically relevant information if confidentiality is qualified in this way. Despite widespread reporting practices, waiting rooms have not emptied and no one really knows if people stop talking openly to their doctors when confidentiality is breached....

Consider that Andrew belongs to one of two groups of prospective patients. Members of the first group are willing enough to have reports made to others. Members of the second are deterred from disclosure by the fear of a report. Of course we can't know in advance which type of patient Andrew is, but if both groups are treated alike, uncertainty will not be a problem. (While this division into two groups may be oversimplified, working through the qualifications would take us too far afield.)

Consider the first group: patients who would be willing to have a report made. Recall that the physician in *The Infected Spouse* tried to obtain assurance that Wilma would be protected. Under an unqualified confidentiality rule—no exceptions—if the patient were willing to have reports made to others, the doctor should be able to obtain a waiver of confidentiality and Wilma could then be informed. Once permission to report is given, the ethical dilemma disappears. Notice that for this group of patients an exceptionless confidentiality rule works just as well as a rule requiring doctors to override confidentiality when necessary to protect endangered third parties. At-risk parties will be warned just the same, but with appropriate permission from patients. In these cases there is no need to trim back the obligation of confidentiality since patients in this first group are, by definition, willing to have a report made.

Difficulties arise with the second type of patient: those who will not want credible threats reported. Notice that these prospective patients are in control of the evidence doctors need to secure protection for parties at risk. If a patient cannot be drawn into a therapeutic alliance—a relationship of trust and confidence—then doctors will not receive the information they need to protect imperiled third parties (at least so long as patients have options). As a result, doctors will not be able to mobilize protection. When one traces out the implications of a reporting rule on what needs to be said in 1990 (when Andrew asked to be tested and the doctor disclosed the limits to confidentiality), it becomes evident that Wilma will not be protected if Andrew (1) does not want her to know and (2) understands that disclosure to his doctor will result in her knowing. Depending on his options and the strength of his preferences, he will be careful about what he discloses to his doctor, or will go without medical advice and care, or will find another physician who can be kept in ignorance about his personal life.

We began by characterizing *The Infected Spouse* as an apparent head-on collision between the doctor's duty of confidentiality and the duty to protect imperiled third parties. But if the argument above is sound, there is no collision. The obligation to warn third parties does not provide added protection to those at-risk. In particular, a no-exceptions confidentiality rule has a better chance of getting the facts on the table, at least to the extent that honest promises of confidentiality can make it so. To be sure, clinicians would have to set aside the vexing "Should I report?" conundrum and search for creative solutions instead. These strategies will not always prevent harm, but they will sometimes. The nub of the matter is that these strategies can never work if they can't be implemented. And they can't be implemented if the fear of reporting deters patients from disclosure. Accordingly there is no justification for trimming back the obligation of confidentiality since doing so actually reduces protection to endangered third parties, increasing public peril.

The argument advanced here is that—paradoxically—ethical and legal duties to report make it less likely that endangered parties will be protected. Depending on the prospective patient, these duties are either unnecessary (when waivers can be obtained) or counterproductive (when disclosure to the doctor is deterred and interventions other than disclosure are prevented).

In part, the conventional wisdom on confidentiality errs in focusing on the decision of the individual clinician at the point when the choice has to be made to disclose or not. The decision to violate confidentiality reaches backwards to the HIV test administered years earlier and, as we shall see, even before. Perhaps little will be lost if one doctor betrays a single patient one time, or if betrayals are extremely rare. But medical ethics is not about a single decision by an individual clinician. The consequences and implications of a rule governing professional practice may be quite different from those of a single act. Better to ask, what if every doctor did that?

While it is accepted here that doctors have an overriding obligation to prevent public peril, it has been argued that they do not honor that obligation by breaching or chipping away at confidentiality. This is because the protective purpose to be furthered by reporting is defeated by the practice of reporting. The best public protection is achieved where doctors do their best work and, there, trustworthiness is probably the most important prerequisite. Physicians damage both their professional capabilities and their communities when they compromise their trustworthiness.

If, in choosing a governing ethical principle, the end-in-view is to protect vulnerable third parties; and if this can be done best, as I have tried to show, by honoring confidentiality and doing one's best to protect imperiled third parties within that framework; then what you must say to both Wilma and Andrew, when they enter your office in 1982, should be something like this:

There is an ethical problem physicians sometimes face in taking on a married couple as patients. It can happen that one partner becomes infected with a transmissible disease, potentially endangering the other. If the infected partner won't share information with me because he or she fears I will warn the other, there will be no protection at all for the partner at risk. There may, however, be things I can do if I can talk with the infected partner. What I promise both of you is, if that were to happen, I will do everything I possibly can to protect the endangered partner, except for violating confidentiality, which I will not do. You both need to remember that you should not count on me to guarantee the wholesomeness of your spouse, if doing this means betrayal.

It is in these words that the final explanation to Wilma can be found. If Wilma understands from the beginning that medical confidentiality will not be breached; if she (and the public generally) understand that the precariously placed are safer under unqualified confidentiality, she will understand she has final responsibility for her choices. If you are clear enough about it, she will grasp that she can't depend on you to protect her at the cost of betrayal, and that she is better off because of that. Both the doctor and the medical profession collectively need to work through these issues and fully disclose the favored standard to prospective patients before the occasion arises when a doctor must appeal to it. The view defended here is that the profession should continue to make an unqualified pledge of confidentiality, and mean it.

It is also appropriate to consider what should be said to Andrew as he is about to leave your office in 1991 to prepare for a romantic dinner with Wilma. I once spent part of an afternoon with a health care professional who had served in Vietnam. He had counseled married enlistees who had returned from visits with their wives and had been diagnosed with a venereal disease that was probably contracted before they left. These men may have infected their wives. This clinician had learned how to persuade these men to agree

to disclosure. He stressed that their wives would likely find out eventually and that the emotional and medical consequences would be far more severe because of the delay. More importantly—given the soldiers' tentative decisions not to let their at-risk spouses know—he would ask whether this was a marriage they really wanted to preserve? I recall that he claimed a near perfect record in obtaining permission to notify the at-risk spouses. It would be useful if there were skilled allied caregivers, bound by confidentiality, who could routinely conduct these specialized counseling sessions. While this is not the place to set out the full range of options for a profession reliably committed to trustworthiness, it will suffice to point out a direction for professional and institutional development.

CONCLUDING REMARKS

Even if the foregoing is accepted, what may trouble doctors still is a painful fear that they will learn about an endangered person and be barred by this no-exceptions confidentiality rule from doing anything. (Actually there is only one thing they cannot do: disclose. All other paths remain open.) Even if a reporting rule keeps many prospective patients out of the office, or silences them while they are there, the rule protects doctors from the moral risk of having to allow injury to third parties when a simple disclosure would prevent it. This distress is significant and has to be faced....

Many enter medicine believing that good citizens must prevent serious injury to others, even if that means violating other obligations. But the task of professional ethics in medicine is to set out principles that, if broadly followed, will allow the profession to discharge its collective responsibilities to patients and society. Confidentiality, I have argued, is effective at getting more patients into therapeutic alliances more quickly, it is more effective in bringing about better outcomes for more of them and—counter-intuitively—it is most likely to prevent serious harm to the largest number of at-risk third parties. Now it is ethically praiseworthy for honorable people to belong to a profession that, on balance, diminishes the amount of harm to others, even though these same professionals must sometimes knowingly allow (and sometimes even cause) harm to occur. Although doctors may feel guilty about these foreseeable consequences of their actions and inactions, they are not guilty of anything. They are acting exactly as it is reasonable to want doctors to act.

It is hard enough to create therapeutic alliances that meet patients' needs. But if doctors take on the added duty to mobilize protective responses without waivers of confidentiality, their work may become impossible in too many important cases. And all of us will be the worse for that. The thinking that places the moral comfort of clinicians above the well-being of patients and their victims is in conflict with the requirements of professional responsibility, properly understood. While it will be a challenge for many honorable physicians to measure up to this standard, no one ever said it was easy to be a good doctor.

NOTE

1   A longer version of this article will appear as "Medical Confidentiality" in *The Blackwell Guide to Bioethics*, edited by Rosamond Rhodes, Anita Silvers, and Leslie Francis (Oxford: Blackwell Publishers Ltd., 2006).

REFERENCES

Beauchamp, T.L., and J.F. Childress. 2001. *Principles of Biomedical Ethics* (New York: Oxford University Press).

Bok, S. 1983. *Secrets* (New York: Pantheon Books).

Goldman, A. 1980. *The Philosophical Foundations of Professional Ethics* (Totowa: Rowman & Littlefield).

Lo, B. 1995. *Resolving Ethical Dilemmas: A Guide for Clinicians* (Baltimore: Williams and Wilkins).

Tarasoff v. Regents of the University of California, Supreme Court of California: 529 P.2d 553 (Cal. 1974).

AN ANALYSIS OF STUDENT PRIVACY RIGHTS IN THE USE OF PLAGIARISM DETECTION SYSTEMS

Bo Brinkman

INTRODUCTION

THE PROBLEM OF PLAGIARISM IN STUDENT WORK has received a tremendous amount of attention. In recent years, services such as Google and TurnItIn.com have made it easier to find the sources of plagiarized material. At the same time, plagiarists have found a wealth of new material to plagiarize through the world-wide-web, including web-based "paper mills" that seemingly exist for no other purpose.

The adoption of plagiarism detection systems has been quite controversial. Many educators and authors worry about the legality and morality of forcing students to use them. In particular, TurnItIn.com has come under fire for the practice of archiving submitted student works for future use in plagiarism detection.

There is a growing (though still small) body of legal discourse that attempts to sort out whether or not this archiving of student work violates the student's copyrights. The United States District Court for the Eastern District of Virginia, for example, ruled that, at least when students submit their own work to the service, no copyright violation occurs (A.V. et al. v iParadigms LLC). In addition, the court found that students receive a direct benefit from submitting their work, and that being "forced" to submit work to TurnItIn.com was not illegal "duress" (A.V. et al. v iParadigms LLC, pp. 10–12).

Though many authors have also identified privacy rights as central to the debate over these services (Foster 2002; Townley and Parsell 2004),[1] privacy rights students have to their schoolwork have not been precisely defined. When plagiarism detection services archive[2] student work, as is currently practiced by the most popular such services, student privacy rights may be violated because the existence of these archives presents a risk of future harm to the students that cannot be overridden solely by the duty (of the professor) to fairly evaluate student work.

A DESCRIPTION OF THE TYPE OF PLAGIARISM DETECTION SERVICE ADDRESSED IN THIS PAPER

This paper focuses specifically on plagiarism detection services that make permanent archives of student work. Services of this type generally work as follows:

1. The student or professor uploads the student's work to the service.
2. The service automatically marks sections of the paper that are very similar to publicly available (on the Internet) web pages or papers.
3. The service automatically marks sections of the paper that are very similar to other student works that have been submitted in the past. Furthermore, the full text of the plagiarized work (which is often personally identifiable even if names are removed) may be provided to the professor.
4. The student's work is permanently archived for re-use in step 3 of this process (for future submissions).

Parts 3 and 4 of the process allow the plagiarism detection service to detect kinds of plagiarism that cannot be caught by step 2. For example, papers from paper mills are not usually posted on the "public" web. Though TurnItIn will not catch work from a paper mill the first time it is submitted, it will catch subsequent re-submissions of the same paper. This also allows the service to catch plagiarized sections from (non-digital) books, from papers kept by student organizations, and from similar sources of plagiarized material that are not openly posted on the Internet....

THE RIGHTS OF STUDENTS, AND DUTIES OF EDUCATORS, WITH RESPECT TO THE PRIVACY OF STUDENT WORK

Students have at least three distinct "privacy rights" related to their work:

1. Students have the right to expect that their submitted schoolwork will be treated as "personal" information. This means that the educational institution will take the same care in protecting it as it would in protecting the student's social security number or grades.
2. Educators have a duty to make sure students are fully informed about the potential privacy implications of using a plagiarism detection service. Note that, though phrased as a duty for the educator, this can be viewed as a claim right[3] for the students.
3. Students have the right to expect that work that is "risky" or "controversial" in nature will not be archived without some form of consent. Simply informing the student, as required in the previous rule, is not enough if the required work may expose the student to adverse effects.

In the following three sections I present my arguments for each of these. Each argument uses a different method. The first claim follows from a recent Supreme Court decision, the second from an analysis of the rights and duties of students, and the third from historical precedent and consequentialist arguments.

STUDENT WORK IS PERSONAL INFORMATION

It is clear, in US law, that a student's grades are personal and private (OWASSO ISD v. FALVO 2002). The decision of who can and cannot see their grades is left up to the student. But, what of the students' works, themselves? Is it just the grade that is private, or is student work also personal and private? TurnItIn.com (along with many educators) seems to believe that only the grades, not the works, are private (iParadigms LLC).[4,5] I argue that this belief is based on a misinterpretation of US privacy law. As I will show, the Supreme Court of the United States has stated that student work is indeed personal, and potentially shielded by privacy laws.

Under US law, a piece of information is usually only considered "private" if it is both specific to a particular person ("personal") and if it is unlikely to be publicly disclosed.[6] This understanding of privacy is at the core of TurnItIn's claims that their uses of student work do not infringe privacy rights. Their argument flows from an analysis of the Family Education Rights and Privacy Act (henceforth "FERPA," 20 U.S.C. § 1232 g), which is the US law that most directly addresses privacy issues for students. TurnItIn claims that "the work is not considered to be part of the student's education record because the work has not been graded. Thus, FERPA does not apply under the recent Supreme Court ruling Owasso Independent School District v. Falvo" (iParadigms LLC).

TurnItIn's claim is in error. The text of the SCOTUS (Supreme Court of the United States) ... decision they refer to also states:

> The parties disagree, however, whether peer-graded assignments constitute education records at all. The papers do contain information directly related to a student, but they are records under the Act only when and if they 'are maintained by an educational agency or institution or by a person acting for such agency or institution.' §1232 g(a)(4)(A) (OWASSO ISD v. FALVO 2002).

The "but" is very revealing. The court did not base its conclusion that the papers were not protected on the fact that the papers were not graded. Instead, the court asserts that, in Owasso, the papers themselves are not educational records because they are not permanently archived. The SCOTUS decision reports that "[the FERPA definition of personal records] covers ... those materials retained in a permanent file as a matter of course." TurnItIn's use of student work appears to meet this definition, while the Owasso Independent School District's use of student work did not. The archiving of student papers as a matter of course is a necessary part of the service that educational institutions are buying from TurnItIn.

It is not that TurnItIn violates FERPA, since it is quite legal to maintain such records, provided that the other provisions of FERPA are obeyed. Instead, this argument shows that SCOTUS considers submitted student work to be "personal data," contrary to TurnItIn.com's claims. One must conclude that, under US law, students have the right to expect that their submissions will be treated with the same respect as all other "personal" information....

THE DUTY TO FULLY INFORM THE STUDENT

An educator may feel that methods used in grading and detecting plagiarism should be kept secret. If students know that a particular plagiarism detection strategy is being used, they may find counter-measures to avoid detection. This leads to the second privacy problem. The use of automated plagiarism detection cannot be kept secret because educators have an especially strong duty to inform students about the privacy risks of plagiarism detection. Other authors have made similar claims.[7] The approach here differs in that fully informing students is in fact an unavoidable duty that is the natural "dual" (as defined below) of the student's duty not to plagiarize.

A definition of plagiarism is "copying that the copier claims (whether explicitly or implicitly, and deliberately or carelessly) is original with him and the claim causes the copier's audience to behave otherwise than it would if it knew the truth" (Posner 2007, pp. 106). Richard Posner's emphasis is that plagiarism revolves around the audience's (detrimental) reliance[8] on misinformation about the identity of the author....

Educators tend to feel that students have a duty and responsibility not to commit fraud of this type. Educators rely on students' claims of originality and authorship in order to fulfill the duty to fairly evaluate student work. What of the case when it is not the authorship that is uncertain, but the audience? In mathematics, "duality" between two statements exists when each statement can be transformed into the other simply by exchanging two words.[9] Swapping the roles of the audience and author, leads to the following claim:

> Dual Proposition: It is a fraud (of wrongful disclosure) to copy where the copier (whether intentionally or negligently) misrepresents himself/herself as the (sole) audience of a work, and this causes the author(s) to behave otherwise than they would if they knew the truth.

Here the "copier" is the educator, who is making copies of student work without informing the student. In the case of plagiarism, the copier is the student, who makes false claims regarding authorship, fooling the educator. In this new case, the educator makes false claims regarding the audience, fooling the student author. Educators should accept that they have a duty to fully inform students about the audience, and potential unintended audience, for their works....

PERMANENT ARCHIVES OF STUDENT WORK PLACE STUDENTS AT RISK OF HARM

Is there actually any harm if student work is archived permanently? The third privacy problem revolves around whether or not archives of student work, like TurnItIn.com, can ever negatively impact a student in later life. It might seem reasonable to think that student papers are trivial, and the student has no reason to worry about them being made public. However this is not true. In fact there is a documented case of a permanently archived student writing that came back to haunt its author.

The example is the role that Hillary Rodham-Clinton's undergraduate thesis played in her campaign for the presidential nomination in 2008. Secretary of State Clinton's thesis was archived, as a matter of course, in the archives of Wellesley College. Bill Dedman reports that former U.S. President William J. Clinton and his wife Hillary asked Wellesley to restrict access to the thesis (2007)....

When she wrote her thesis, Secretary Clinton was in her early 20s. By the time she ran for the Democratic presidential nomination 38 years had passed. Secretary Clinton likely regretted writing the paper, because it caused some members of the public to associate her with radical Marxism. Knowing what she knows now, she might have chosen a different topic for her thesis. It is also quite likely that her ideas, as expressed in the thesis, are no longer the ideas that she holds today. Permanent archives of student writing make it more difficult for individuals to grow and change, and to leave their young and immature selves in the past....

This example leads to the conclusion that there are times when a student may regret that her work has been permanently archived, as happens automatically and inescapably with plagiarism detection systems like TurnItIn.com. What must educators do to try to mitigate or prevent this from harming students? Should all use of plagiarism detection systems be prohibited due to this risk?...

If an educational institution uses TurnItIn.com for all student work, the case is very different. In such a situation, it is not just theses that are archived, but all student work. Furthermore, it is possible for students to be largely unaware of this process, leading them to choose risky or controversial topics that they would not have chosen if they knew TurnItIn.com was being used....

Students cannot honestly pursue challenging and significant questions if they are plagued by worries about the wide distribution of their work. As Townley and Parsell (2004) argue, students are only able to honestly engage when they are in a strong trust relationship with the audience, which is normally assumed to be (only) the instructor....

The result is a conflict between two goods. An effective deterrent against plagiarism would have a significantly positive impact on the goals of (liberal) education. At the same time, forcing students to write only for public consumption conflicts with those goals. The idea that students have a right to expect that work that is risky or controversial will not be submitted to plagiarism detection archives without (some form of) student consent strikes an acceptable balance between the good of deterring plagiarism and the good of encouraging intellectual risk-taking....

CONCLUSION

There are three specific privacy rights that students have in their submitted work. Under the law, student work is personal, and hence (all else being equal), private. Secondly, educators have a duty to fully inform students about the use of automated plagiarism detection, and this duty is the natural dual of the duty of the student not to plagiarize. Thirdly, concerns about archiving of student work are not purely speculative given the precedent of a student writing assignment that came back to haunt a prominent public figure. A problems-based approach to analyzing privacy issues is useful because it makes it possible to derive and justify rules that protect the privacy of students....

NOTES

1   Andrea Foster presents a broad overview of the controversies surrounding student rights. Cynthia Townley and Mitch Parsell comment on privacy only in passing, as one motivation for their proposed remedies for student plagiarism.

2   I use "archive" to mean a collection of documents that is systematic, centrally administered, and permanent. The copies of student work that might be inadvertently left behind on lab computers are not "archives," but the electronic submission features of courseware sites (like BlackBoard) are.

3   Claim rights are those rights that require someone else to act on our behalf. For example, one cannot exercise the right to a free primary education on one's own. Everyone else in society has to contribute some money in order for this to happen. This is contrasted with liberties, which are rights that one has as long as others do not interfere. Religious freedom is one example of a liberty.

4   Neither the authorship nor the date of this document are clear. Because it was posted on TurnItIn.com in 2008, authorship is attributed here to iParadigms LLC, the parent company of TurnItIn.com. The most likely date for the document is probably 2002 or 2003, since it talks about the Owasso decision as being "recent."

5   This document is no longer available from TurnItIn. com. Because the field of plagiarism deterrence is changing rapidly, many of the documents cited as evidence in this article have evolved over time. I use "as accessed on" in the bibliography entry to note the cases where I am referring to an older version of the document.

6   The reader should understand that the issue is intentionally simplified here. A detailed legal understanding of the principles involved is not necessary for this discussion, as long as the reader is aware that "personal" information receives special privacy protections under US law.

7   For example, Foster (2002) reports that UC San Diego required professors to inform students, though they did not have a uniform policy for what to do if students refused to comply. Townley and Parsell (2004) feel that it is not possible to get informed consent in this situation because of the unequal power structure in the student–teacher relationship. The Library at UMass Amherst recommends informing students through the syllabus, and provides standardized language for this purpose.

8   Readers familiar with US contract law may feel that "detrimental reliance" is out of place here. The term is adopted from Richard Posner's book (2007). I believe that he intentionally used this term to suggest that there is an implied contract between author and reader.

9   *Encyclopedia Britannica* (2012) defines "duality" as the "principle whereby one true statement can be obtained from another by merely interchanging two words." The definition has been reworded to emphasize the fact that the dual of a true statement might be false, and vice versa. Duality is most interesting, however, when both the statement and its dual are true.

REFERENCES

A.V. et al. v iParadigms LLC, US District Court for the Eastern District of Virginia, Civil Action No. 07-0293. Accessed 03 May 2012.

Dedman, B. (2007). Reading Hillary Rodham's hidden thesis. MSNBC.com. http://www.msnbc.msn.com/id/17388372/. Accessed 02 May 2012.

Foster, A. (2002). Plagiarism-detection tool creates legal quandary. *The chronicle of higher education.* 17 May 2002, pp A37. http://chronicle.com/free/v48/i36/36a03701.htm. Accessed 02 May 2012.

iParadigms LLC. (No date). TurnItin legal document. As Accessed 22 April 2008.

OWASSO INDEPENDENT SCHOOL DIST. NO. I—011 V. FALVO. (2002) 534 U.S. 426.

Posner, R.A. (2007). *The little book of plagiarism.* New York: Pantheon Books.

Townley, C., & Parsell, M. (2004). Technology and academic virtue: Student plagiarism through the looking glass. *Ethics and Information Technology,* 6(4), 271–277.

—46—

PRIVACY BY DESIGN

A Counterfactual Analysis of Google and Facebook Privacy Incidents

Ira S. Rubinstein and Nathaniel Good

... REGULATORS HAVE EMBRACED PRIVACY BY design.[1] Both the European Commission ("EC") and the Federal Trade Commission ("FTC") have recently called for a new approach to data protection and consumer privacy in which privacy by design plays a key role.[2] However, the details of what this means in practice will remain unclear until the EC completes its work on the delegated acts and technical standards anticipated by the proposed Regulation,[3] or until the FTC refines the meaning of "unfair design" through enforcement actions[4] and/or develops guidelines based on its ongoing dialogue with private firms.[5] Indeed, despite the strong expressions of support for privacy by design, its meaning remains elusive.

Presumably, the regulatory faith in privacy by design reflects a commonsense belief that privacy would improve if firms "designed in" privacy at the beginning of any development process rather than "tacking it on" at the end. And yet there is scant relevant data in support of this view. A few firms have adopted privacy guidelines for developing products and services;[6] however, a search of the literature reveals no before-and-after studies designed to determine if such firms have achieved better privacy results. We propose to examine this question in a different fashion—not by gathering empirical data but rather by conducting and reporting on case studies of ten major Google and Facebook privacy incidents.[7] We then consider whether the firms in question would have averted these incidents if they had implemented privacy by design.

This is a counterfactual analysis: we are asking a "what if?" question and will try to answer it by discussing what Google and Facebook might have done differently to better protect consumer privacy and thereby avoid these incidents. The proposed analysis has two prerequisites. First, we need ready access to a great deal of information about the selected incidents so that we have a reasonably clear idea of what happened as well as how and why the firms responded as they did (for example, by modifying certain features or even withdrawing a service entirely). Absent such information, it would be impossible to consider what the firm might have done differently if it had adopted privacy by design. Second, we need to identify a baseline set of *design* principles that will inform our discussion of alternative outcomes.

The first task is easy because there are so many well-documented major Internet privacy incidents. A non-exhaustive list would include privacy gaffes by AOL, Apple, DoubleClick, Facebook, General Motors, Google, Intel, Microsoft, MySpace, Real Networks, Sony, and Twitter.[8] This Article focuses on a series of related incidents—five each from Google and from Facebook—for several reasons. To begin with, both firms have experienced serious privacy incidents and suffered major setbacks ranging from negative publicity and customer indignation to government scrutiny, regulatory actions, and law suits. Second, their travails have been well documented by investigative journalists, privacy advocates, and various regulators. And, third, both firms have all of the necessary resources—engineering talent, financial wherewithal, and business incentives—to prevent future incidents by implementing a leading-edge program of privacy by design. Moreover, studying a range of incidents at each company—Gmail, Search, Street View, Buzz (and Google+), and changes in privacy policies for Google; and News Feed, Beacon, Facebook Apps, Photo Sharing, and changes in privacy policies and settings for Facebook—makes it possible to observe patterns and compare how the two companies think about privacy, especially in similar services such as social networking.

The second task—identifying design principles to rely on for purposes of a counterfactual analysis—is far more difficult. An obvious starting point for understanding what it means to design products and services with privacy in mind is the set of internationally recognized values and standards about personal information known as the Fair Information Practices ("FIPs").[9] The FIPs define the rights of data subjects and the obligations of data controllers; most privacy laws throughout the world rely on FIPs.[10] This Article argues that although the FIPs allocate rights and responsibilities under applicable legal standards, the present task requires something different, namely, *design* principles and related practices.

Another possible source of guidance is the work of Ann Cavoukian, the Information and Privacy Commissioner ("IPC") of Ontario, Canada. Cavoukian is a tireless champion of privacy by design (or "PbD" to use her preferred acronym) and has authored or coauthored dozens of papers describing both its origins and its business and technology aspects.[11] In 2009, Cavoukian advanced the view that firms may accomplish privacy by design by practicing seven "foundational" principles:

1. Proactive not Reactive; Preventative not Remedial;
2. Privacy as the Default Setting;
3. Privacy Embedded into Design;
4. Full Functionality—Positive-Sum, not Zero-Sum;
5. End-to-End Security—Full Lifecycle Protection;
6. Visibility and Transparency—Keep It Open; and
7. Respect for User Privacy—Keep It User-Centric.[12]

Although Cavoukian's many publications offer valuable lessons in how the public and private sector might apply the "PbD approach" to new information systems and technologies, it is not at all clear for present purposes that her seven principles are of any greater assistance than the FIPs.

To begin with, Cavoukian's seven principles are more aspirational than practical or operational. Principles 1–3 provide useful, if somewhat repetitive, guidance about the importance of considering privacy issues early in the design process and setting defaults accordingly, but they stop far short of offering any design guidance. Granted, Cavoukian offers more practical advice in several of her technology-specific papers,[13] but she makes little effort to systematize or even summarize the design principles found therein.[14] Principle 4 seems unrealistic in an era when some view personal data as the "new oil" of the Internet and privacy controls only tend to limit the exploitation of this valuable commodity.[15] Principle 5 emphasizes lifecycle management, which is a key aspect of privacy engineering. Principle 6 resembles the familiar transparency principle found in all versions of FIPs, while Principle 7 functions primarily as a summing up of the earlier principles. Moreover, Cavoukian associates PbD with many other concepts, including accountability,[16] risk management,[17] FIPs,[18] and privacy impact assessments ("PIAs").[19] This breadth tends to dilute, rather than clarify, Cavoukian's definition of PbD. As several

European computer scientists recently concluded, the principles as written do not make it clear "what 'privacy by design' actually is and how it should be translated into the engineering practice."[20]

Of course, various commentators have taken different approaches to privacy by design. Some see PbD as an offshoot of privacy-enhancing technologies ("PETs");[21] others in terms of a life cycle approach to software development and/or data management (i.e., one that considers privacy at all stages of product design and development);[22] and still others in terms of implementing "accountability based mechanisms" such as risk-based privacy impact assessments.[23] Some regulators combine all of these ideas under the umbrella of privacy management programs that include policies, procedures, and systems architecture; several recent FTC consent decrees have required companies like Google, Facebook, Twitter, and MySpace to adopt identical five-part programs combining accountability, risk assessment, design processes, due diligence in selecting vendors, and ongoing program adjustments.[24] But the FTC offers firms no guidance about how to implement such programs.

Fortunately, a few private sector firms have developed more detailed privacy guidelines, explaining how to integrate privacy into the several stages of the software development process (requirements, design, implementation, verification, and release).[25] For example, in 2006 Microsoft published a comprehensive set of guidelines that explores nine specific development scenarios and identifies over 120 required and recommended practices for "creating notice and consent experiences, providing sufficient data security, maintaining data integrity, offering customers access [to their data], and supplying [other privacy] controls."[26] Although the guidelines are full of sound advice and would benefit both established and start-up firms, they also have several shortcomings. First—and this is not a problem limited to Microsoft—the tools and techniques concerning "privacy by design" are quite immature, especially as compared with those relied upon for "security by design."[27] Second, the guidelines have not kept up with the transition from client-server products to social media and Web 2.0 services and largely omit this topic, which makes them badly outdated. Finally, the guidelines allow business units within Microsoft to balance privacy requirements against business purposes but offer limited guidance on this delicate task.[28] For example, while "essential" actions such as processing of real-time location data, waiver of certain notice requirements, and transfer of sensitive personal information require "Company Approval,"[29] there is little discussion of the relevant factors for granting or withholding such approval. Similarly, the guidelines state that when data transfers or updates are "essential" to the functioning of a product (as defined by Microsoft), this justifies a weaker "all-or-nothing" form of user controls.[30] More generally, Microsoft's internal decision-making process under the guidelines remains opaque to customers and policy makers, which has led to accusations that business or competitive considerations sometimes overwhelm privacy requirements.[31]

All of these varied attempts at fleshing out the meaning of privacy by design are valuable and we have no wish to disparage them.... We contend that although FIPs underlie privacy by design, they are not self-executing. Rather, privacy by design requires the translation of FIPs into engineering and design principles and practices. An example helps illustrate what we have in mind. One of the FIPs, the purpose specification principle, is the basis for limits on how long a company may retain personal data. But there is a vast difference between a company promising to observe reasonable limitations on data retention and designing a database that automatically tags personal and/or sensitive information, keeps track of how long the information has been stored, and deletes it when a fixed period of time has expired. To adapt a familiar distinction, one is just words, while the other is action realized through code.

We argue that FIPs must be translated into principles of privacy engineering and usability and that the best way to accomplish this task is to review the relevant technical literature and distill the findings of computer scientists and usability experts. This is a departure from most discussions of privacy by design, which tend to slight the small but significant design literature in favor of advocating broad discourse on policy principles and business practices. We seek to remedy this omission and put the design back into privacy by design....

NOTES

1   See Ira S. Rubinstein, *Regulating Privacy by Design*, 26 BERKELEY TECH. L.J. 1409, 1410–11 (2012) (describing statements by regulators in Canada, Europe, and the United States).

2   See *Proposal for a Regulation of the European Parliament and of the Council on the Protection of Individuals with Regard to the Processing of Personal Data and on the Free Movement of Such Data (General Data Protection Regulation)*, Recital 61, art. 23, COM (2012) 11 final (Jan. 25, 2012), available at http://ec.europa.eu/ justice/data-protection/document/review2012/ com_2012_11_en.pdf [hereinafter *Proposed E.U. Regulation*] (requiring data controllers to implement mechanisms ensuring "data protection by design and by default"); FED. TRADE COMM'N, PROTECTING CONSUMER PRIVACY IN AN ERA OF RAPID CHANGE: RECOMMENDATIONS FOR BUSINESSES AND POLICYMAKERS (2012), http://www.ftc.gov/ os/2012/03/120326privacyreport.pdf (hereinafter FTC FINAL REPORT) (urging companies to "build in privacy at every stage of product development").

3   *Proposed E.U. Regulation, supra* note 2, art. 23(3)–(4).

4   See, *e.g.*, Complaint for Permanent Injunction and Other Equitable Relief at 13, 19, F.T.C. v. Frostwire LLC, No. 1:11-CV-23643, 2011 WL 9282853 (S.D. Fla. 2011) (describing default setting of Android application that allowed sharing of all existing files on the device in terms of "unfair design").

5   See Kenneth A. Bamberger & Deirdre K. Mulligan, *Privacy on the Books and on the Ground*, 63 STAN. L. REV. 247, 287–89 (2011) (describing various

"deliberative and participatory processes promoting dialogue with advocates and industry").

6   See *The Role of Privacy by Design in Protecting Consumer Privacy*, CTR. FOR DEMOCRACY & TECH. (Jan. 28, 2010), https://www.cdt.org/ policy/role-privacy-design-protecting-consumer-privacy [hereinafter *Role of Privacy by Design*] (explaining that IBM, Sun Microsystems, Hewlett-Packard, and Microsoft have adopted privacy by design into their business models and product development procedures).

7   As used here, the term "incident" is descriptive rather than normative. Thus, a "privacy incident" is no more than an episode or event that raises privacy concerns. Not every privacy incident results from a design failure or causes harm. However, because privacy is highly cherished and causes anxiety if violated, many privacy incidents are associated with negative press coverage, reputational harm, regulatory investigations, and/ or enforcement actions.

8   We identified these incidents based on general knowledge and by reviewing the websites of leading privacy organizations for discussion of privacy issues; we also conducted a LexisNexis® search.

9   The FIPs are a set of internationally recognized privacy principles that date back to the 1970s. They have helped shape not only the main U.S. privacy statutes but also European data protection law...; see *generally Fair Information Practice Principles*, FED. TRADE COMM'N, http://www.ftc.gov/ reports/privacy3/fairinfo.shtm (last visited Mar. 15, 2013).

10   See, *e.g.*, Marc Rotenberg, *Fair Information Practices and the Architecture of Privacy (What Larry Doesn't Get)*, 2001 STAN. TECH. L. REV. 1, ¶ 44 (2001).

11   These publications are available on the IPC website. *Discussion Papers*, IPC, http://www.ipc.on.ca/ english/Resources/Discussion-Papers (last visited Mar. 6, 2013).

12   ANN CAVOUKIAN, PRIVACY BY DESIGN: THE 7 FOUNDATIONAL PRINCIPLES (2011), www. privacybydesign.ca/content/uploads/2009/08/7 foundationalprinciples.pdf.

13 Among the topics covered are smart grids, Radio Frequency Identification ("RFID"), biometric systems, mobile communications, Wi-Fi positioning systems, and mobile near field communications ("NFC"). See *Publications: Papers*, PBD, http://www. privacybydesign.ca/index.php/publications/papers (last visited Mar. 15, 2013).

14 Instead, many of the papers merely restate or elaborate the seven foundational principles. See, *e.g.*, ANN CAVOUKIAN, OPERATIONALIZING *PRIVACY BY DESIGN*: A GUIDE TO IMPLEMENTING STRONG PRIVACY PRACTICES (Dec. 4, 2012), http://www.ipc.on.ca/images/Resources/operationalizing-pbd-guide.pdf; ANN CAVOUKIAN, ACCESS BY DESIGN: THE 7 FUNDAMENTAL PRINCIPLES (May 10, 2010), http://www.ipc.on.ca/images/Resources/accessbydesign_7fundamentalprinciples.pdf; ANN CAVOUKIAN & MARILYN PROSCH, PRIVACY BY REDESIGN: BUILDING A BETTER LEGACY (May 20, 2011), http://www.ipc.on.ca/images/Resources/PbRD-legacy.pdf.

15 See Meglena Kuneva, European Consumer Commissioner, Keynote Speech, Roundtable on Online Data Collection, Targeting and Profiling 2 (Mar. 31, 2009), http://europa.eu/rapid/press-release_SPEECH-09-156_en.htm; see also Julia Angwin & Jeremy Singer-Vine, *Selling You on Facebook*, WALL ST. J. ONLINE (Apr. 7, 2012), http://online.wsj.com/article/SB10001424052702303302504577327744009046230.html.

Angwin and Singer-Vine wrote:

This appetite for personal data reflects a fundamental truth about Facebook and, by extension, the Internet economy as a whole: Facebook provides a free service that users pay for, in effect, by providing details about their lives, friendships, interests and activities. Facebook, in turn, uses that trove of information to attract advertisers, app makers and other business opportunities.

Id.

16 See ANN CAVOUKIAN, SCOTT TAYLOR & MARTIN ABRAMS, PRIVACY BY DESIGN: ESSENTIAL FOR ORGANIZATIONAL ACCOUNTABILITY AND STRONG BUSINESS PRACTICES 3 (Nov. 2009), http://www.privacybydesign.ca/content/uploads/2009/11/2009-11-02-pbd-accountability_HP_CIPL.pdf (describing accountability as a business model wherein "organizations tak[e] responsibility for protecting privacy and information security appropriately and protecting individuals from the negative outcomes associated with privacy-protection failures").

17 See ANN CAVOUKIAN, INFO. & PRIVACY COMM'N, PRIVACY RISK MANAGEMENT: BUILDING PRIVACY PROTECTION INTO A RISK MANAGEMENT FRAMEWORK TO ENSURE THAT PRIVACY RISKS ARE MANAGED, BY DEFAULT 17 (Apr. 2010), http://www.ipc.on.ca/images/Resources/pbd-priv-risk-mgmt.pdf (asserting that privacy risks may be "[m]anaged in a fashion similar to conventional risks... by employing the principles of privacy by design").

18 See ANN CAVOUKIAN, THE 7 FOUNDATIONAL PRINCIPLES: IMPLEMENTATION AND MAPPING OF FAIR INFORMATION PRACTICES (2011), http://www.ipc.on.ca/images/Resources/pbd-implement-7found-principles.pdf (comparing FIP principles with privacy by design principles).

19 See PAT JESELON & ANITA FINEBERG, A FOUNDATIONAL FRAMEWORK FOR A PBD-PIA (Nov. 2011), http://privacybydesign.ca/content/uploads/2011/11/PbD-PIA-Foundational-Framework.pdf (offering a framework for a privacy by design privacy impact assessment).

20 Seda Gürses et al., *Engineering Privacy by Design*, International Conference on Privacy and Data Protection ("CPDP") (2011), http://www.dagstuhl.de/mat/Files/11/11061/11061.DiazClaudia.Paper.pdf (arguing that many of the seven principles include the term "privacy by design" in the explanation of the principle itself resulting in recursive definitions).

21 See generally Rubinstein, *supra* note 1, at 1414–26.

22 See FTC FINAL REPORT, *supra* note 2, at 46–47.

23 See E.U. ARTICLE 29 DATA PROTECTION WORKING PARTY, OPINION 3/2010 ON THE PRINCIPLE OF ACCOUNTABILITY (WP 173) 3 (July 2010) [hereinafter WP 173], http://ec.europa.eu/justice/policies/privacy/docs/wpdocs/2010/wp173_en.pdf; see also Paula J. Bruening, *Accountability: Part of the International Public Dialogue About Privacy Governance*, BNA INT'L WORLD DATA PROTECTION REP. 2 (October 2010) (describing the work of an expert group convened by the Irish Data Protection Commissioner for the purpose of defining the essential elements of accountability).

24 See, *e.g.*, Agreement Containing Consent Order, Google, Inc., F.T.C. No. 102–3136, 4–5 (Mar. 30, 2011) [hereinafter Google Settlement], http://www.ftc.gov/os/caselist/1023136/110330googlebuzz agreeorder.pdf; Agreement Containing Consent Order, Facebook, Inc., F.T.C. No. 092–3184, 5–6 (Nov. 29, 2011) [hereinafter Facebook Settlement], http://www.ftc.gov/os/caselist/0923184/111129fa cebookagree.pdf. The third element specifically requires firms to engage in "the design and implementation of reasonable controls and procedures to address the risks identified through the privacy risk assessment." *Id.*

25 See *Role of Privacy by Design*, *supra* note 6.

26 *Privacy Guidelines for Developing Software Products and Services, v. 3.1*, MICROSOFT, 5 (Sept. 2008), http://www.microsoft.com/en-us/download/details.aspx?id = 16048 [hereinafter *Microsoft Privacy Guidelines*]. Ira Rubinstein was an Associate General Counsel at Microsoft when these guidelines were first developed but did not contribute to them.

27 In security engineering, there is consensus on the meaning of key concepts and there are tried-and-true design principles and canonical texts, international standards, and a large cadre of certified security experts. Additionally, security professionals may draw upon a variety of technical resources including sophisticated threat-modeling processes, secure coding practices, and automated development and testing tools. Privacy professionals enjoy few of these advantages or resources.

28 *Microsoft Privacy Guidelines, supra* note 27, at § 1.2; see also *infra* notes 456, 461–63 and accompanying text (discussing balancing)....

29 The Microsoft Privacy Guidelines define "Company Approval" as "[t]he consent of the authorized privacy council or privacy decision makers within the Company, which may include legal counsel." *Microsoft Privacy Guidelines, supra* note 27, at 26.

30 *Id.* at 30, 33, 36.

31 See Nick Wingfield, *Microsoft Quashed Efforts to Boost Online Privacy*, WALL ST. J. ONLINE (Aug. 1, 2010), http://online.wsj.com/article/SB 10001424052 748703467304575383530439838568.html (describing an internal debate in 2008 over privacy features in Microsoft's Internet Explorer ("IE") 8 browser that the advertising division feared would undermine both Microsoft's and its business partners' targeted advertising abilities). Microsoft later reversed this decision and added a very similar feature to IE 9. See Nick Wingfield & Jennifer Valentino-DeVries, *Microsoft To Add 'Tracking Protection' to Web Browser*, WALL ST. J. ONLINE (Dec. 7, 2010), http://online.wsj.com/article/SB10001424052 748703296604576005542201534546.html.

BREAKING A PROMISE TO PREVENT A LIE

Aaron Quinn

1. BACKGROUND

JOURNALISM IS REPLETE WITH ETHICAL CONTRO-versy and no time more than in the recent past. Special federal prosecutor Patrick J. Fitzgerald was assigned to investigate the senior George W. Bush Administration source(s) who had apparently leaked confidential information that potentially threatened national security and the safety of an undercover CIA agent to journalists. Subsequently, at least two journalists were ordered by a federal grand jury to reveal the confidential source (or sources) who had leaked the identity of CIA agent Valerie Plame. Matthew Cooper of *Time Magazine* and Judith Miller of *The New York Times* were ordered to reveal the identity of a source or sources who, apparently out of political revenge, had leaked Plame's name to reporters because of her husband's role in publicly criticizing the Bush Administration's rationale for going to war in Iraq.

Plame's husband, Joseph C. Wilson, had been commissioned to investigate whether it was likely the pre-invasion Iraqi government had either attempted to acquire or succeeded in acquiring uranium for the purpose of making weapons of mass destruction. Wilson concluded that there was no evidence that uranium had been acquired or even sought by the Iraqi government or military officials. In an op-ed column he authored for *The New York Times*, Wilson criticized the Bush Administration for attempting to justify the invasion of Iraq on the grounds that it had, or was developing, weapons of mass destruction.

The ethical controversy first gained prominence after Plame's name was published in an article written by conservative columnist Robert Novak, because it sparked worry in the intelligence community of further dangerous intelligence leaks. When contacted by the special federal prosecutor Fitzgerald, Novak agreed to give testimony about his source(s), but both Cooper and Miller initially refused, citing their interest in maintaining their confidentiality agreements. Though *Time Magazine* and its reporter Matthew Cooper relented to the judicial pressure and threat of imprisonment, Miller was eventually jailed for 85 days for her refusal to comply with the grand jury's order, despite having never published a story mentioning Plame.

Fitzgerald, meanwhile, continued to seek information about what role Vice President Dick Cheney's chief of staff, I. Lewis Libby, and senior Bush advisor Karl Rove, might have played in the leak. Though Libby claimed he had not participated in leaking information, he was indicted on charges of obstruction of justice, perjury, and making false statements. [In 2006, prosecutors decided that there were no grounds to charge Rove; however, he remained involved in subsequent investigations.] Several reporters, including *Time Magazine*'s Viveca Novak (no relation to Robert Novak), told Fitzgerald that Rove was Cooper's source for information about Plame.

2. ANALYSIS

There are a number of moral matters at issue in this case, and we will focus on those most crucial to journalists. First and foremost is the matter of whether journalists are always bound to confidentiality agreements with their sources. Legally, it has become increasingly common for journalists to make written agreements with sources regarding the conditions of their confidentiality. Miller claims to have been legally bound to maintain her confidentiality agreement based on one such contract, but later agreed to offer limited testimony once her source(s) relieved her of her contractual obligation. It is less clear with Cooper or either of the Novaks whether their agreements were written contracts or more traditional oral agreements.

Nevertheless, there is the additional matter of what a journalist's moral obligation ought to be when confidentiality agreements bring about conflicting duties. On the one hand, journalists are morally obligated to keep their promises, which include maintaining confidentiality agreements. On the other hand, there may be legitimate duties that conflict with those agreements, such as aiding law enforcement when there are few or no alternative sources of information for authorities. In the Plame affair, many journalists and media critics alike have suggested that Miller's stronger duty might have been to reveal her confidential source(s) because maintaining the confidence would make her complicit in a moral and legal wrong—leaking intelligence information that might threaten both national security and the safety of an innocent, Valerie Plame.

Journalists, as many of their ethics codes and traditions reveal, rarely if ever are comfortable in breaking confidentiality agreements. Most journalists think breaking confidences undermines the very trust on which journalism's social value rests. Conversely, many in the judiciary believe journalists have the same legal and moral obligation as all citizens, which is to comply with grand jury and judicial subpoenas that aim to bring justice. Ultimately, this impasse boils down to a disagreement about what costs journalists ought to incur in such moral conflicts— does one risk losing public trust by breaking confidentiality agreements, or does one instead weaken the justice system by failing to contribute crucial information to it?

Journalists have long argued that complying with subpoenas in instances in which they are not protected by "shield laws"—state statutes that sometimes allow journalists to refuse testimony without legal penalty—makes them an unofficial branch of law enforcement to be used (or abused) at will. Moreover, journalists have never had an official professional status—other than scattered shield laws—that recognizes them as anything other than ordinary citizens who have a legal and moral obligation as citizens to promote justice. Conversely, medical doctors and lawyers have a legal obligation to maintain confidential information about their patients and clients.

Journalists' confusion about moral conflicts in confidential sourcing represents part of an interesting debate in professional ethics between what is commonly labeled role morality—following the moral mandates and guidelines specific to the goals and purposes of an occupation—and universalizable ethics—mandates and guidelines to be followed in any circumstance, occupational or otherwise. As mentioned above, journalists are typically inclined to follow a journalistic role morality that emphasizes maintaining confidentiality agreements and by extension their public trust. Nevertheless, critics decry this steadfast adherence to journalistic convention because of its occasional incompatibility with the more universal pursuit of justice.

DISCUSSION QUESTIONS

1. Should journalists maintain confidential sources under all conditions, or are there circumstances that mitigate their promise-keeping obligations?

2. Are the contractual obligations of journalists (legal or moral) nullified when their sources lie to or mislead them?

3. What is a more important goal for journalists when their journalistic duties conflict with their duties as ordinary citizens: to achieve ends that best advance the profession or to achieve ends that a good citizen would promote?

4. Should journalists be afforded special legal and social privileges like absolute shield laws because of their special duties related to informing the public?

TO SHARE OR NOT TO SHARE

When Patient Confidentiality and Physicians' Duties to Protect Conflict

Erika M. Versalovic

1. BACKGROUND

AFTER MONTHS OF TESTING AND THE ACCOMPA-nying uncertainty, Mrs. Jefferson sat down with Dr. Nichols to receive her official diagnosis: invasive epithelial ovarian cancer.[1] While Dr. Nichols made clear there was no clear cause, the genetic testing that had accompanied her other tests revealed her to be a carrier for the BRCA1 mutation—a genetic variant that significantly increases a person's risk for both breast and ovarian cancers. After allowing Mrs. Jefferson time to ask questions about treatment options and begin processing the new reality of the diagnosis, Dr. Nichols moved to another important consideration: the strong possibility that others in her family were carriers of this gene as well. Because this variant increases women's risk of developing breast cancers from 12 to 72 per cent,[2] some women who discover they are carriers choose to get mastectomies, or have their breasts removed, to lower their chances of developing breast cancer. Seeing the overwhelmed look in Mrs. Jefferson's eyes, Dr. Nichols left the topic at that and turned his attention towards sharing comforting words.

Later, when Mrs. Jefferson met with her primary care physician, Dr. Garcia, he asked her if she'd had the opportunity to speak with her family, not only about the diagnosis, but about the genetic component as well. Mrs. Jefferson said that, while she had spoken extensively to her husband and children about it, there was one person who held a significant risk of being a carrier who she had not shared the news with—her sister. She explained they had had a bad falling out years previously and had not spoken since. While she recognized the importance of having the discussion with her sister, she said that she did not want the reason for their reconciliation to be rooted in pity for the diagnosis she'd received and the treatment she was undergoing. If her sister chose to reach out, she might consider it. But, she explained that it was taking all the energy she had just to care for herself, let alone attempt to work through an old conflict she had no intention of resolving.

Dr. Garcia said he respected her wishes, but also pushed her to consider whether or not she would attempt to contact a stranger who she knew might be able to take preventative action if they knew their genetic carrier status. Even if she did not feel a strong familial tie to her sister, perhaps she should consider the obligation she might feel to someone with whom there was no connection whatsoever. Mrs. Jefferson proceeded to shake her head: "I hear what you're saying, but it does not make me any more comfortable with the idea of reaching out to her. I have chosen to continue through my life without a connection to her and, especially with everything I am trying to handle right now, I just don't feel comfortable with either me or you having that conversation with her."

The Hippocratic Oath he had taken those years ago when he first donned his white coat echoed back into his mind: "I will prevent disease whenever I can, for prevention is preferable to cure." But, other words of that same oath closely followed: "I will respect the privacy of my patients."[3] Mrs. Jefferson was his patient, but Dr. Garcia considered the fact that these responsibilities seemed to extend beyond his currently enrolled patients. Invasive breast cancers like Mrs. Jefferson's could kill someone in cases of late-stage diagnoses. "Surely the potential of saving or lessening the potential suffering of her sister outweighs respecting a request for confidentiality?" he thought to himself. His eyebrows furrowed and he felt himself tense as he deliberated on how to act amid these conflicting duties.

2. ANALYSIS

In thinking through this case, both consequentialist and deontological, or value-driven, frameworks can illuminate important considerations for Dr. Garcia. In the former, an act utilitarian approach asks him to compare the outcomes of each of his potential actions and determine which outcome works towards the highest overall level of well-being. In the latter, actions are evaluated according to the ways they align with particular ethical principles.

First, taking a more utilitarian, consequence-driven approach, one could consider the outcomes of each of Dr. Garcia's potential choices. If he chooses to respect her confidentiality and not make contact with her sister, Mrs. Jefferson's desires will be respected, but, there is an increased chance that the sister could develop a life-threatening form of breast cancer that could have been prevented through taking preventative actions like a mastectomy. This decision will, however, bode the better for his physician-patient relationship with Mrs. Jefferson as he continues to walk her through her care. If he makes contact with the sister, he will have broken the trust of his patient. Even if he does reach out to her sister, there is a chance that she will not choose to act on the suggestion to get genetic testing or, even if she does, that she chooses not to take preventative action. Depending on how one chooses to weigh the resulting well-being of

the parties involved, act utilitarianism could lead one to rule in either direction.

If one takes a more deontological approach, it is helpful to turn towards Beauchamp and Childress' four principles that are widely cited in Western bioethics.[4] They propose thinking through cases in terms of four principles: autonomy, justice, beneficence, and non-maleficence. Respect for autonomy pushes the healthcare team to maximally empower the patient's decision-making capacities and respect their involvement in directing the course of care. Justice calls for providers to consider the equitable distribution of treatments across societal demographic groups. Beneficence requires that there be intent for doing good for the patient involved. Finally, non-maleficence requires physicians to do no harm, or minimize harm, for the patient involved.

Considerations of beneficence and non-maleficence apply in considering the complexities of this case. Concerning beneficence, it seems that preserving the confidentiality of Mrs. Jefferson's diagnosis and obeying her wishes to not contact her sister fall in line with attempting to do good to the patient. However, while Mrs. Jefferson is the main patient, it seems that considerations of beneficence could extend to her sister and that her sister could be viewed as a potential patient. Weighing the considerations of non-maleficence leads to similar uncertainty. Breaching the confidentiality of Mrs. Jefferson is a harm to her that could be prevented. However, giving her sister the opportunity to get the same genetic testing could lead to her taking preventative steps, such as the mastectomy Dr. Nichols had mentioned, and thus finding a way to alert her could be seen as a significant step towards preventing harm for her. While far from providing a formula for determining the course of action Dr. Garcia should take, the principles provide a way of breaking down and examining the most relevant aspects of the case. Ethical dilemmas like this one make decision-making difficult, but also make deliberation all the more important in order to sufficiently respect the complexities involved.

NOTES

1   This case study was inspired by Clint Parker's piece, "Disclosing Information about the Risk of Inherited Disease," in the *AMA Journal of Ethics* 17, no. 9 (September 2015): 819–825.

2   "BRCA Mutations: Cancer Risk and Genetic Testing," National Cancer Institute, last modified 30 January 2018, https://www.cancer.gov/about-cancer/causes-prevention/genetics/brca-fact-sheet.

3   "The Hippocratic Oath and Others," McMaster University Health Sciences Library, last modified 17 May 2018, https://hslmcmaster.libguides.com/c.php?g=306726&p=2044095.

4   Tom L. Beauchamp and James F. Childress, *Principles of Biomedical Ethics* (New York: Oxford University Press, 2008).

DISCUSSION QUESTIONS

1. What are the most pertinent ethical considerations in this case?

2. In what ways does Dr. Garcia being a physician affect his responsibilities to the parties involved?

3. Does Dr. Garcia have a responsibility to Mrs. Jefferson's sister? If so, in what ways may it differ (or not) to Mrs. Jefferson?

4. What kinds of considerations and obligations outweigh the duty to respect physician-patient confidentiality?

PROFESSIONALISM, DIVERSITY, AND PLURALISM

Jill Gatfield

1. INTRODUCTION

NOW MORE THAN EVER, WE LIVE WITH AN AWARE-ness of diversity—globally, and within our own countries, cities, and neighborhoods. "Diversity" refers to the fact that people are different from one another but, more to the point, different from one another in ways that are socially significant. Recognizing diversity is a matter of recognizing the ways that groups of people are, actually or allegedly, different from other groups of people in their beliefs and values. "Pluralism," in our current context, refers to these differences in beliefs and values.

Professionals of every kind will encounter situations where diversity and pluralism generate ethical concerns and challenges, whether within professionals' own practices and workplaces or, on yet larger scales, in relation to professional associations, organizational policies, or laws that affect professional domains. Challenges may arise at the level of an individual professional serving a client. Consider, for example, a doctor, devotedly Christian, who works in a remote community and is the only available professional to perform a patient's abortion. Also, challenges pertaining to diversity may need to be addressed on institutional levels. Consider the question of whether affirmative action programs supporting racial diversity in public universities should be legally permitted or, to the contrary, judged as unconstitutional. This last question is taken up by two of our readings in this unit.

Many of us, as members of the public, adopt a general view that diversity and pluralism are good things, but some of us do not share this view. An attitude of being either "for" or "against" diversity, however, is too simplistic. We need to command robust understandings of the particular challenges that arise. The articles presented in this unit help us to do this. Their analyses of pertinent concepts and issues facilitate our being able to reach defensible judgments about whether and when, within professional contexts, it is morally right to support actions and policies that promote pluralism and whether and when diverse ways of living and being should not be endorsed or accommodated.

2. CONTENTS

Our first two articles address general concepts and lay groundwork for deliberations about professionalism and the challenges posed by diversity. Subsequent articles focus on particular ethical issues encountered by professionals, beginning with a general critique of Human Resources across both professional and business fields, followed by discussion of particular issues in medicine, education, public service, and pharmacy.

First, Carina Fourie, Fabian Schuppert, and Ivo Wallimann-Helmer analyze the concept of social equality in the article "The Nature and Distinctiveness of Social Equality." Given the basic egalitarian belief that all people deserve equal rights and opportunities, how should equality be understood and promoted? Is it enough to equally distribute important social goods and services, such as political rights, opportunities for education, and access to basic resources? The authors discuss why social egalitarians believe there is more to equality than just equal distributions of goods and services, and examine whether social egalitarianism is a distinct and viable perspective.

Next, Anita Superson, in "A Feminist Definition of Sexual Harassment," offers an objective definition of sexual harassment based on the idea that sexual harassment harms all women and not only the particular women who are harassed. She rejects subjective definitions that are currently used in court deliberations and judgments, and claims that her definition both more accurately captures the nature of sexual harassment and avoids significant ethical problems that standard subjective definitions invite.

Caitlin Flanagan's "The Problem with HR," then offers a general critique of Human Resource departments. This article explores how HR offices tasked with solving sexual harassment issues often have goals other than what we might expect. While we might expect HR departments to advocate for employees, they are really a tool used by organizations to protect their own interests. Using the backdrop of the #MeToo movement, Flanagan's ultimate critique is that HR departments have failed magnificently at protecting employees but have been wildly successful at protecting the interests of companies themselves.

Our next two readings address the question of whether affirmative action relating to race and admissions policies in post-secondary education is unconstitutional or otherwise unethical. First, Ronald Dworkin, in "Why Bakke Has No Case," discusses the precedent-setting case of *Allan Bakke v. the University of California at Davis*. This is followed by an examination of the US Supreme Court justices' opinions in the case of *Fisher v. The University of Texas at Austin*. In both cases, a Caucasian university applicant who was not accepted subsequently claimed that their constitutional right, under the Fourth Amendment, had

been violated. These readings detail arguments about the permissibility of universities using "race conscious" admissions policies as opposed to policies that may be considered "race neutral."

Should people be granted special accommodations in their professions and workplaces for their religious commitments and, if so, why? John Corvino, in "'Under God's Authority': Professional Responsibility, Religious Accommodation, and the Culture Wars," addresses this question, discussing whether there are justifiable reasons to accommodate religious beliefs as compared with providing the same sorts of accommodations for people's arguably just-as-important secular beliefs.

In "Should Educators Accommodate Intolerance: Mark Halstead, Homosexuality and the Islamic Case," Michael S. Merry argues that educators, specifically in the area of sex education, should aim to provide genuinely empathetic and respectful encounters among students with diverse values. He focuses on the work of Mark Halstead who supports accommodating "the Islamic view" against teaching homosexuality as an "acceptable alternative lifestyle." Merry rejects Halstead's view, noting, for example, that value pluralism not only exists within our larger society, but also within groups. He argues that Halstead is wrong to think that Islam is monolithic, and also wrong to think that educators should accept mere tolerance as an educational goal for their students who are challenged with understanding others' cultures and values, when they could promote genuine understandings and empathetic relations.

Thomas A. Hemphill and Waheeda Lillevik, lastly, examine ethical issues relating to emergency contraceptives in cases where pharmacists or businesses that employ pharmacists object to dispensing such drugs, in "U.S. Pharmacists, Pharmacies, and Emergency Contraception." Patients/consumers have a right to access emergency contraceptives, yet pharmacists may invoke "conscience clauses" to avoid being required to provide them. The authors discuss how the diverse needs and interests of various stakeholders may best be served.

The unit concludes with two case studies. The first explores the moral and legal complexities of the case involving Terri Schiavo and the fight to remove her feeding tubes after years in a vegetative state. The second case explores the case of a Colorado baker refusing to bake a cake for a gay couple and the ensuing legal battles.

THE NATURE AND DISTINCTIVENESS OF SOCIAL EQUALITY

Carina Fourie, Fabian Schuppert, and Ivo Wallimann-Helmer

EQUALITY IS NOT ONE IDEA, AND ONE CAN ADVO-cate or criticize a number of forms of egalitarianism. Many egalitarians advocate the equal distribution of one of a range of *equalisanda*—in other words, what it is that should be equalized, such as political power, human rights, primary goods, opportunities for welfare, or capabilities. This notion that equality is best described according to some "thing" that should be distributed equally has been subject to criticism by a range of schools of thought. Of these critics, a number of prominent contemporary philosophers insist that, while the ideal of equality clearly has distributive implications and may well match certain distributive notions of equality, equality is foremost about relationships between people. The structure of relationships can be more or less egalitarian, more or less hierarchical. When we appeal to the value of equality, we mean the value primarily of egalitarian and nonhierarchical relationships, and not of distributions, which may only be instrumentally valuable in terms of how well they reflect or help to achieve egalitarian relationships. This form of egalitarianism is known as social or relational egalitarianism.[1] ...

SOCIALLY EGALITARIAN RELATIONSHIPS

What ... is social equality? We can answer the question by elucidating which kinds of relationships, or structures of relationships, are compatible with or exemplify equality and by determining which kinds of asymmetrical relationships, which kinds of social hierarchies, egalitarians should oppose. Examples of social egalitarian interactions and relationships might be the use of "Mr." and "Ms." to address everyone, rather than distinguishing according to rank, education, or marital status, for example....

Claims are made that social equality is violated by, for example, slavery, class systems, hierarchies of social status based on race or gender, orders of nobility, behavior that is "either, on the one hand, noticeably flattering or deferential or approbatory or obsequious or, on the other hand, noticeably disparaging or deprecatory or insulting or humiliating,"[2] and any kinds of relationships between superiors and inferiors.

What is it about these interactions and relationships that make them socially egalitarian or inegalitarian? A popular response is to associate social equality with relationships that express respect (usually respect for persons) or recognition.[3] In this case, an important part of determining what social equality is would be to identify the relevant notions of respect and to unpack how egalitarian relationships constitute or reflect this form of respect. Whether respect exhausts social equality is a question that social egalitarians need to answer and that they are likely to answer in various manners. The asymmetrical relationships that social egalitarians oppose also include (certain kinds of) hierarchies of prestige, honor, and esteem, as well as those of power, command and domination—why and under what circumstances these should be opposed, and whether these hierarchies can all be categorized as constituting violations of respect, requires further analysis.

The high emphasis social egalitarians place on *relationships* raises a number of questions about the subject and scope of social equality. The subject of justice is often confined to major social institutions such as the constitution and the form of the economy—personal choice, social norms, and civil society are often seen to be excluded from the regulation of principles of justice.[4] If social equality is about social relationships, surely even private, interpersonal relationships should be subject to norms of equality?...

Many discussions of social equality are particularly concerned with the implications of equality on a political and an institutional level. The claim is that as citizens or, even merely as human beings, we should be treated as social equals, and the state and its institutions should not express, establish, or reinforce (certain kinds of) inegalitarian and hierarchical relationships between individuals or groups of individuals. However, even the fact that social equality could be seen as a significant moral value at the level of individual behavior and informal social structure ..., and as a significant political value, raises a number of significant questions. Is social equality one value that can be reflected on both a personal and an informal level, as well as on a formal and political level? What can we learn from social equality on an informal level that could apply formally, or vice versa?

These questions about the subject of social equality also raise challenges about whether we may be justified to intervene in personal relationships—if we aim to achieve social equality, and if this form of social equality is reflected in or determined by personal relationships, then do we not have reason to try to establish equality in personal relationships? Of course, this may not mean that social egalitarians, even if they agree that many personal relationships should be egalitarian, will necessarily promote intervention all things considered, but it does raise the question of whether the subject of social equality should indeed include informal relations, or whether it need be limited in range in the same way that justice often is.

This can be seen to be a case of asking *which* relationships should be socially equal.... If social equality is what is owed fellow citizens, or if social equality is constitutive of or necessary for civic friendship,[5] then what does this imply in terms of our relationships with noncitizens and residents of other nation-states?[6] Can social equality be said to be what we owe all other human beings, or need it be confined to residence or citizenship? Could we justify cosmopolitanism on the basis of social equality?

THE DISTINCTIVENESS OF SOCIAL EQUALITY

... While social egalitarians often relate social equality to equal moral worth or to what it means to treat people with respect and concern, they do not *equate* social equality with these other forms of equality. Many distributive egalitarians (or prioritarians) follow on from what they see as a foundational claim (or basic intuition) that people are equals and should be treated as such, to providing distributive principles that they claim are an expression of this fundamental notion of equality.[7] Social egalitarians could claim that while social equality may well be an expression of equal moral worth or treating people with respect and concern, it is a substantive ideal in itself that needs to be fleshed out, and this fleshing out will help to determine which distributive principles are compatible with equality.[8] ...

Two of the most significant questions in terms of the distinctiveness of social equality are whether and how this form of equality can be distinguished from justice, or, relatedly, from questions associated with distribution.[9] ...

David Miller has argued particularly influentially for drawing a distinction between equality and justice, claiming that there are two valuable forms of equality, the first, and which is indeed directly related to justice, is distributive equality at times, justice may require equality in distribution. Social equality, however, is not directly related to justice but rather "identifies a social ideal, the ideal of a society in which people regard and treat one another as equals, in other words a society that is not marked by status divisions such that one can place different people in hierarchically ranked categories, in different classes for instance."[10] Such a distinction indicates that justice and equality are two separate values implying, for example, that social equality could make moral claims besides, and even in conflict with, the claims made by a theory of justice.[11]

While one might disagree with Miller about whether equality and justice should be seen as separate, one might still accept that Miller has identified an important distinction between concerns of social equality and concerns of distribution. Social egalitarians often distance themselves from an emphasis on distribution as being the primary concern of egalitarianism. While social equality is likely to have significant implications for distribution, many egalitarians insist that social equality cannot be captured foremost according to a description of the distribution of goods or some other relevant currency.[12] ...

First, for example, the moral concern of social equality often presupposes the existence of a relationship; in contrast, distributions can exist even if there are no relationships, but these are irrelevant from the perspective of social equality. Second, social equality or inequality is conveyed through, among other things, attitudes, and evaluations, and their expressions via behavior and institutions, which seem difficult to subsume under a wholly distributive paradigm at the least, such a paradigm would need to try to make room explicitly for these kinds of phenomena, if indeed it is able to do so. Last, it seems doubtful that what social equality will require can be captured by singular descriptions of distributive patterns as it is likely to make nuanced demands in terms of esteem,

power, or social cooperation, which will not be properly characterized by claims that these should (simply) be equalized....

A further significant aspect of the potential distinction between questions of distribution and social egalitarianism is the relationship between distributive *patterns* and social equality. A primary debate within social justice is whether we really require equality, at least as an ideal that is valuable in itself, or whether some other distributive pattern might not be our ultimate aim, such as, for example, providing the worst off with the best possible position, or providing individuals with "enough," with a sufficient amount. This debate has led many to question whether equality is valuable at all.[13] Social egalitarians could respond by emphasizing that this debate is too focused on only certain forms of (distributive) equality, in isolation from the social egalitarian commitments that could underlie them. Indeed, we could distinguish at least two ways in which social egalitarians could make claims to establishing the value of equality.

First, ... it seems, at least at first glance, to make more sense to claim that we value equal social relations per se, in contrast to making similar claims about equal distributions. Second, however, social equality could provide *egalitarian* grounds for equal distributions.[14] While [distributive egalitarians] could indeed promote equality in the distribution of certain social goods, they would argue that the reasons why we should prefer these distributions are actually ultimately *inegalitarian*. For example, we may still prefer an equal distribution of goods if our ultimate aim is to achieve the best possible opportunities for welfare for the worst off, and not equality per se.

However, a number of egalitarians have pointed out that there seem to be a range of reasons why we might prefer equal distributions of at least certain kinds of goods, and although some of these, such as a concern for the absolute position of the worst off, are not egalitarian, a number of them, including reasons that correspond to social equality, are indeed egalitarian. So, for example, when we are concerned that inequalities in social goods lead to "stigmatizing differences in status, whereby the badly off feel like, and are treated as, inferiors ... [or they create] objectionable relations of power and domination" we have egalitarian reasons, specifically, *socially egalitarian reasons*, to value distributive equality.[15] ...

While there is no singular account of social or relational egalitarianism, certain overlapping concerns stand out, such as an emphasis on determining the structure of egalitarian relationships.... [We have] aimed to highlight some of the significant questions that can be asked of this form of egalitarianism and indicated some of the potential ways in which they can be answered....

Two primary kinds of questions can be distinguished based on the discussion [above]: First, what is the nature social equality? Second, what is its relationship with theories of justice and with politics?...

[Theorists concerned with articulating the nature of social equality] investigate the relevance of respect, esteem, love, deliberative practices, power, and domination for conceptions of social equality. In so doing, the contributions aim to flesh out which kind of relationships, which social hierarchies, and which social practices are compatible with social equality and which are not....

What is the relationship between the concept of social equality and justice? What is the subject and range of social equality? What is the scope of social equality? What is the politics of social equality?...

[Studying these questions generates] two broad camps: justice-based relational egalitarianism and pluralist social egalitarians. Defenders of justice-based relational egalitarianism have a somewhat narrower conception of social equality than pluralist social egalitarians, who hold that the idea of social equality is of independent value above and beyond justice.

If social egalitarians are right in claiming that many hierarchies of esteem and inegalitarian personal relationships are morally objectionable, we should also consider the question of what we can do about it and whose responsibility it is (if anybody's) to regulate such relationships....

NOTES

1   For the purposes of this introduction, we take social and relational equality to be equivalent and use mainly "social equality" as the umbrella term to refer to both social and relational equality. There are a number of different understandings of social and relational equality, and some theorists may be tempted to describe these different understandings according to a distinction drawn between social equality, on the one hand, and relational equality, on the other. We believe, however, that there are enough similarities between what some theorists call relational equality and some call social equality to merit referring to them as equivalent. It is an open question, and one that social egalitarians may answer variously, as to whether there is a need to distinguish between social and relational equality.

2   W.G. Runciman, "'Social' Equality," *The Philosophical Quarterly* 17, no. 68 (1967): 223.

3   Runciman, "'Social' Equality"; [David] Miller, "Equality and Justice" [Ratio 10, no. 3 (1997)]; Jonathan Wolff, "Fairness, Respect, and the Egalitarian Ethos," *Philosophy & Public Affairs* 27, no. 2 (1998): 97–122; Elizabeth Anderson, "What Is the Point of Equality?" *Ethics* 109, no. 2 (1999): 287–337; Christian Schemmel, "Why Relational Egalitarians Should Care about Distributions," *Social Theory and Practice* 37, no. 3 (2011): 365–390.

4   John Rawls, *A Theory of Justice* (Oxford: Oxford University Press, 1999), Part 2, 6–10, & Part 14, 73–78; John Rawls, *Justice as Fairness: A Restatement* (Cambridge, MA: Belknap Press of Harvard Univ. Press, 2001), 10–12. Confining justice in this way is not without its critics: see, for example, G.A. Cohen, *If You're an Egalitarian, How Come You're So Rich?* (Cambridge, MA: Harvard University Press, 2001), 117–147.

5   Anderson, "What Is the Point of Equality?"; Elizabeth Anderson, "Justifying the Capabilities Approach to Justice," in *Measuring Justice Primary*

Goods and Capabilities, ed. Harry Brighouse and Ingrid Robeyns (Cambridge and New York: Cambridge University Press, 2010), 81–100; Andrew Mason, *Living Together as Equals: The Demands of Citizenship* (Oxford: Oxford University Press, 2012).

6   Richard Norman, "The Social Basis of Equality," *Ratio* 10, no. 3 (1997): 238–252; Rekha Nath, "Equal Standing in the Global Community," *Monist* 94, no. 4 (2011): 593–614.

7   See, for example, Scheffler's discussion of this tendency. Samuel Scheffler, "Choice, Circumstance, and the Value of Equality," *Politics, Philosophy & Economics* 4, no. 1 (2005): 5–28.

8   Anderson, "What Is the Point of Equality?"; Samuel Scheffler, "What Is Egalitarianism?" *Philosophy and Public Affairs* 31, no. 1 (2003): 5–39; Scheffler, "Choice, Circumstance, and the Value of Equality."

9   While theories of social justice are often concerned with distribution (of resources or opportunities for welfare, for example), we cannot necessarily equate concerns of justice with concerns about distribution.

10 Miller, "Equality and Justice," 224.

11 Not all social egalitarians agree. Christian Schemmel, for example, insists that relational egalitarianism should be seen as an ideal of social justice—the problem with inegalitarian relationships is precisely that "they constitute unjust treatment" (Schemmel, "Why Relational Egalitarians Should Care About Distributions," 366).

12 Here, Young and Fraser's criticisms of distributive models of justice can be understood to back up the social egalitarian concern with reducing social equality to distribution: [Iris Marion] Young, *Justice and the Politics of Difference* [(Princeton University Press, 1990)]; [Nancy] Fraser, *Justice Interruptus*[: *Critical Reflections on the Postsocialist Condition* (Routledge, 1996)].

13 Even an only partially comprehensive set of references here would be too numerous. For early contemporary statements of the sufficientarian, egalitarian, and prioritarian positions see, respectively, Harry Frankfurt, "Equality as a Moral Ideal," *Ethics* 98, no. 1 (1987): 21–43; Larry S. Temkin, *Inequality* (Oxford University Press, USA, 1993); [Derek] Parfit, "Equality and Priority[," *Ratio* 10, no. 3 (1997)].

14 For example, [T.M.] Scanlon, "The Diversity of Objections to Inequality," [in *The Ideal of Equality*, ed. Matthew Clayton and Andrew Williams (Basingstoke: Palgrave Macmillan, 2002)]; Martin O'Neill, "What Should Egalitarians Believe?" *Philosophy & Public Affairs* 36, no. 2 (2008): 119–156; Daniel M. Hausman and Matt Sensat Waldren, "Egalitarianism Reconsidered," *Journal of Moral Philosophy* 8, no. 4 (2011): 567–586; Jonathan Wolff, "Scanlon on Social and Material Inequality," *Journal of Moral Philosophy*, 2012.

15 O'Neill, "What Should Egalitarians Believe?" 126.

—48—

A FEMINIST DEFINITION OF SEXUAL HARASSMENT

Anita M. Superson

INTRODUCTION

... MY PRIMARY AIM IN THIS PAPER IS TO OFFER an objective definition of [sexual harassment (SH)] that accounts for the group harm all forms of SH have in common. Though my aim is to offer a moral definition of SH, I offer it in hopes that it will effect changes in the law....

My goal in this paper is merely to defend my definition against the definitions currently appealed to by the courts in order to show how it is more promising for victims of SH. I define SH in the following way:

> Any behavior (verbal or physical) caused by a person, A, in the dominant class directed at another, B, in the subjugated class, that expresses and perpetuates the attitude that B or members of B's sex is/are inferior because of their sex, thereby causing harm to either B and/or members of B's sex....

THE SOCIAL NATURE OF SEXUAL HARASSMENT

Sexual harassment, a form of sexism, is about domination, in particular, the domination of the group of men over the group of women.[1] Domination involves control or power which can be seen in the economic, political, and social spheres of society. Sexual harassment is not simply an assertion of power, for power can be used in beneficial ways. The power men have over women has been wielded in ways that oppress women. The power expressed in SH is oppression, power used wrongly.

Sexual harassment is integrally related to sex roles. It reveals the belief that a person is to be relegated to certain roles on the basis of her sex including not only women's being sex objects, but also their being caretakers, motherers, nurturers, sympathizers, etc. In general, the sex roles women are relegated to are associated with the body (v. mind) and emotions (v. reason).

When A sexually harasses B, the comment or behavior is really directed at the group of all women, not just a particular woman, a point often missed by the courts. After all, many derogatory behaviors are issued at women the harasser does not even know (e.g., scanning a stranger's body). Even when the harasser knows his victim, the behavior is directed at the particular woman because she happens to be "available" at the time, though its message is for all women....

Hughes and May claim that women are a disadvantaged group because

1. they are a social group having a distinct identity and existence apart from their individual identities,

2. they occupy a subordinate position in American society, and

3. their political power is severely circumscribed.

They continue:

> Once it is established that women qualify for special disadvantaged group status, all practices tending to stigmatize women as a group, or which contribute to the maintenance of their subordinate social status, would become legally suspect.[2]

This last point, I believe, should be central to the definition of SH....

Because SH has as its target the group of all women, this group suffers harm as a result of the behavior. Indeed, when any one woman is in any way sexually harassed, all women are harmed.... The group harm has to do primarily with the fact that the behavior reflects and reinforces sexist attitudes that women are inferior to men....

The harm women suffer as a group from any single instance of SH is significant.... Though there is nothing wrong with being a caretaker or nurturer, etc., *per se*, it is sexist—and so wrong— to assign such roles to women. The group harm SH causes is different from the harm suffered by particular women as individuals: it is often more vague in nature as it is not easily causally tied to any particular incident of harassment. The belief that women must occupy certain sex roles is both a cause and an effect of their oppression. It is a cause because women are believed to be more suited for certain roles given their association with body and emotions. It is an effect because once they occupy these roles and are victims of oppression, the belief that they must occupy these sex roles is reinforced....

Women are harmed by SH in yet another way. The belief that they are sex objects, caretakers, etc., gets reflected in social and political practices in ways that are unfair to women. It has undoubtedly meant many lost opportunities that are readily available to men. Women are not likely to be hired for jobs that require them to act in ways other than the ways the sex roles dictate, and if they are, what is expected of them is different from what is expected of men. Mothers are not paid for their work, and caretakers are not paid well in comparison to jobs traditionally held by men. Lack of economic reward is paralleled by lack of respect and appreciation for those occupying such roles. Certain rights granted men are likely not to be granted women (e.g., the right to bodily self-determination, and marriage rights).

Another harm SH causes all women is that the particular form sex stereotyping takes promotes two myths: (1) that male behavior is normally and naturally predatory, and (2) that females naturally (because they are taken to be primarily bodily and emotional) and even willingly acquiesce despite the appearance of protest.[3] Because the behavior perpetuated by these myths is taken to be normal, it is not seen as sexist, and in turn is not counted as SH.

The first myth is that men have stronger sexual desires than women, and harassment is just a natural venting of these desires which men are unable to control. The truth is, first, that women are socialized *not* to vent their sexual desires in the way men do, but this does not mean these desires are weaker or less prevalent.... But second, SH has nothing to do with men's sexual desires, nor is it about seduction; instead, it is about oppression of women. Indeed, harassment generally does not lead to sexual satisfaction, but it often gives the harasser a sense of power.

The second myth is that women either welcome, ask for, or deserve the harassing treatment. Case law reveals this mistaken belief. In *Lipsett v. Rive-Mora*[4] (1987), the plaintiff was discharged from a medical residency program because she "did not react favorably to her professor's requests to go out for drinks, his compliments about her hair and legs, or to questions about her personal and romantic life."[5] The court exonerated the defendant because the plaintiff initially reacted favorably by smiling when shown lewd drawings of herself and when called sexual nicknames as she thought she had to appease the physician. The court said that "given the plaintiff's admittedly favorable responses to these flattering comments, there was no way anyone could consider them as 'unwelcome.'"[6] ...

The idea that women welcome "advances" from men is seen in men's view of the way women dress. If a woman dresses "provocatively" by men's standards, she is said to welcome or even deserve the treatment she gets.... The myth that women welcome or encourage harassment is designed "to keep women in their place" as men see it. The truth of the matter is that the perpetrator alone is at fault.

Both myths harm all women as they sanction SH by shifting the burden on the victim and all members of her sex: women must either go out of their way to avoid "natural" male behavior, or establish conclusively that they did not in any way want the behavior.... Instead of the behavior being seen as sexist, it is seen as women's problem to rectify.

I have spoken so far as if it is only men who can sexually harass women, and I am now in a position to defend this controversial view. When a woman engages in the very same behavior harassing men engage in, the underlying message implicit in male-to-female harassment is missing. For example, when a woman scans a man's body, she might be considering him to be a sex object, but all the views about domination and being relegated to certain sex roles are absent. She cannot remind the man that he is inferior because of his sex, since given the way things are in society, he is not. In general, women cannot harm or degrade or dominate men as group, for it is impossible to send the message that one dominates (and so cause group harm) if one does not dominate. Of course, if the sexist roles predominant in our society were reversed, women could sexually harass men. The way things are, any bothersome behavior a woman engages in, even though it may be of a sexual nature, does not constitute SH because it lacks the social impact present in male-to-female harassment. Tort law would be sufficient to protect

against this behavior, since it is unproblematic in these cases that tort law fails to recognize group harm.

SUBJECTIVE V. OBJECTIVE DEFINITIONS OF SEXUAL HARASSMENT

Most definitions of "sexual harassment" make reference to the behavior's being "unwelcome" or "annoying" to the victim.... The EEOC [Equal Employment Opportunity Commission] *Guidelines* state that behavior constituting SH is identified as "unwelcome sexual advances, requests for sexual favors, and other verbal or physical conduct of a sexual nature."[7] In their philosophical account of SH, Hughes and May define "harassment" as "a class of annoying or unwelcome acts undertaken by one person (or group of persons) against another person (or group of persons)."[8] ...

The criterion of unwelcomeness or annoyance present in these subjective accounts of harassment puts the burden on the victim to establish that she was sexually harassed. There is no doubt that many women are bothered by this behavior, often with serious side-effects including anything from anger, fear, and guilt, to lowered self-esteem and decreased feelings of competence and confidence, to anxiety disorders, alcohol and drug abuse, coronary disturbances, and gastro-intestinal disorders.

Though it is true that many women are bothered by the behavior at issue, I think it is seriously mistaken to say that whether the victim is bothered determines whether the behavior constitutes SH. This is so for several reasons.

First, we would have to establish that the victim was bothered by it, either by the victim's complaints, or by examining the victim's response to the behaviour. The fact of the matter is that many women are quite hesitant to report being harassed for a number of reasons. Primary among them is that they fear negative consequences from reporting the conduct. As is often the case, harassment comes from a person in a position of institutional power, whether he be a supervisor, a company-president, a member of a dissertation committee, the chair of the department, and so on. Unfortunately for many women, as a review of the case law reveals, their fears are warranted. Women have been fired, their jobs have been made miserable forcing them to quit, professors have handed out unfair low grades, and so on. Worries about such consequences means that complaints are not filed, or are filed years after the incident.... But this should not be taken to imply that the victim was not harassed.

Moreover, women are hesitant to report harassment because they do not want anything to happen to the perpetrator, but just want the behavior to stop. Women do not complain because they do not want to deal with the perpetrator's reaction when faced with the charge. He might claim that he was "only trying to be friendly." Women are fully aware that perpetrators can often clear themselves quite easily, especially in tort law cases where the perpetrator's intentions are directly relevant to whether he is guilty. And most incidents of SH occur without any witnesses—many perpetrators plan it this way. It then becomes the harasser's word against the victim's. To complicate matters, many women are insecure and doubt themselves. Women's insecurity is capitalized upon by harassers whose behavior is in the least bit ambiguous. Clever harassers who fear they might get caught or be reported often attempt to get on the good side of their victim in order to confuse her about the behavior, as well as to have a defense ready in case a charge is made. Harassers might offer special teaching assignments to their graduate students, special help with exams and publications, promotions, generous raises, and the like. Of course, this is all irrelevant to whether he harasses, but the point is that it makes the victim less likely to complain. On top of all this, women's credibility is very often questioned (unfairly) when they bring forth a charge. They are taken to be "hypersensitive." There is an attitude among judges and others

that women must "develop a thick skin."[9] Thus, the blame is shifted off the perpetrator and onto the victim. Given this, if a woman thinks she will get no positive response—or, indeed, will get a negative one—from complaining, she is unlikely to do so.

Further, some women do not recognize harassment for what it is, and so will not complain.... Given that women are socialized into believing their bodies are the most important feature of themselves, it is no surprise that a fair number of them are complacent about harassing behavior directed at them.... It would be incorrect to conclude that the behavior is not harassment on the grounds that such victims are not bothered....

An *objective* view of SH avoids the problems inherent in a subjective view. According to the objective view defended here, what is decisive in determining whether behavior constitutes SH is not whether the victim is bothered, but whether the behavior is an instance of a practice that expresses and perpetuates the attitude that the victim and members of her sex are inferior because of their sex....

In various cases the courts have invoked a reasonable man (or person) standard, [which is meant to be an objective standard,] but not to show that women who are not bothered still suffer harassment. Instead, they used the standard to show that even though a particular woman was bothered, she would have to tolerate such behavior because it was behavior a reasonable person would not have been affected by. In *Rabidue v. Osceola Refining Co.*[10] (1986), a woman complained that a coworker made obscene comments about women in general and her in particular. The court ruled that "a reasonable person would not have been significantly affected by the same or similar circumstances,"[11] and that "women must expect a certain amount of demeaning conduct in certain work environments."[12] ...

[U]nlike women, men can take sexual overtures directed at them to be complimentary because the overtures do not signify the stereotyping that underlies SH of women. A reasonable man standard would not succeed as a basis upon which to determine SH, as its objectivity is outweighed by the disparity found in the way the sexes assess what is "reasonable."

Related to this last topic is the issue of the harasser's intentions. In subjective definitions this is the counterpart to the victim's being bothered. Tort law makes reference to the injurer's intentions: in battery tort, the harasser's intent to contact, in assault tort, the harasser's intent to arouse psychic apprehension in the victim, and in the tort of intentional emotional distress, the harasser's intent or recklessness, must be established in order for the victim to win her case.

But like the victim's feelings, the harasser's intentions are irrelevant to whether his behavior is harassment. As I just pointed out, many men do not take their behavior to be bothersome, and sometimes even mistakenly believe that women enjoy crude compliments about their bodies, ogling, pinching, etc.... Also, as I have said, many men believe women encourage SH either by their dress or language, or simply by the fact that they tolerate the abuse without protest (usually out of fear of repercussion). In light of these facts, it would be wrongheaded to allow the harasser's intentions to count in assessing harassment, though they might become relevant in determining punishment.... [I]t is the attitudes embedded and reflected *in the practice* the behavior is an instance of, not the attitudes or intentions of *the perpetrator*, that makes the behavior SH....

IMPLICATIONS OF THE OBJECTIVE DEFINITION

[An] implication of my definition is that it gives the courts a way of distinguishing SH from sexual attraction. It can be difficult to make this distinction, since "traditional courtship activities" are often quite sexist and frequently involve behavior that is harassment. The key is to examine the practice the behavior is an instance of. If the behavior reflects the attitude that the victim is inferior because of her sex, then it is SH. Sexual harassment is not about a man's attempting to date a woman who is not interested, as the courts have tended to believe; it is about domination, which might be reflected, of course, in the way a man goes about trying to get a date. My definition allows us to separate cases of SH from genuine sexual attraction by forcing the courts to focus on the social nature of SH.

Moreover, defining SH in the objective way I do shifts the burden and the blame off the victim. On the subjective view, the burden is on the victim to prove that she is bothered significantly enough to win a tort case, or under Title VII, to show that the behavior unreasonably interfered with her work. In tort law, where the perpetrator's intentions are allowed to figure in, the blame could easily shift to the victim by showing that she in some way welcomed or even encouraged the behavior thereby relinquishing the perpetrator from responsibility. By focusing on the practice the behavior is an instance of, my definition has nothing to do with proving that the victim responds a certain way to the behavior, nor does it in any way blame the victim for the behavior.

Finally, defining SH in a subjective way means that the victim herself must come forward and complain, as it is her response that must be assessed. But given that most judges, law enforcement officers, and even superiors are men, it is difficult for women to do so. They are embarrassed, afraid to confront someone of the same sex as the harasser who is likely not to see the problem. They do not feel their voices will be heard. Working with my definition will I hope assuage this. Recognizing SH as a group harm will allow women to come to each other's aid as co-complainers, thereby alleviating the problem of reticence. Even if the person the behavior is directed at does not feel bothered, other women can complain, as they suffer the group harm associated with SH.

NOTES

1   This suggests that only men can sexually harass women. I will defend this view later in the paper.

2   [John C. Hughes and Larry May, "Sexual Harassment," *Social Theory and Practice*, Vol. 6, No. 3 (Fall, 1980),] 265.

3   These same myths surround the issue of rape. This is discussed fruitfully by Lois Pineau in "Date Rape: A Feminist Analysis," *Law and Philosophy*, Vol. 8 (1989), 217–43.

4   *Lipsett v. Rive-Mora*, 669 F.Supp. 1188 (D. Puerto Rico 1987).

5   Dawn D. Bennett-Alexander, "Hostile Environment Sexual Harassment: A Clearer View," *Labor Law Journal*, Vol. 42, No. 3 (March, 1991), 135.

6   *Lipsett*, op. cit., Sec. 15.

7   EEOC Guidelines [on Discrimination Because of Sex, 29 C.F.R] Sec. 1604.11(a) (1980).

8   Hughes and May, op. cit., 250.

9   See [Ellen] Frankel Paul, ["Sexual Harassment as Sex Discrimination: A Defective Paradigm," *Yale Law & Policy Review*, Vol. 8, No. 2 (1990)], 333–65. Frankel Paul wants to get away from the "helpless victim syndrome," making women responsible for reporting harassment, and placing the burden on them to develop a tough skin so as to avoid being seen as helpless victims (362–63). On the contrary, what Frankel Paul fails to understand is that placing these additional burdens on women detracts from the truth that they are victims, and implies that they deserve the treatment if they do not develop a "tough attitude."

10 *Rabidue v. Osceola Refining Co.*, 805 F2d (1986), Sixth Circuit Court.

11 Ibid., at 622.

12 Ibid., at 620–22.

—49—

THE PROBLEM WITH HR

Caitlin Flanagan

IN APRIL 2018, I SPENT THREE DAYS IN AUSTIN, Texas, in the company of more than 2,500 people, most of them women, who are deeply concerned about the problem of workplace sexual harassment. The venue was the city's convention center, and when a man named Derek Irvine took the vast stage and said that there had been "an uprising in the world of those who refuse to be silent," the crowd roared its support. He introduced a panel of speakers[1] who have been intimately involved with the #MeToo movement: Tarana Burke, the creator of the original campaign and hashtag; Ronan Farrow, who broke the Harvey Weinstein story in *The New Yorker*; and Ashley Judd, one of the actors who says she was harassed by Weinstein. Adam Grant, the author of many highly regarded books on management theory and a professor at the Wharton School, interviewed them, and their remarks were often interrupted by loud, admiring applause.

The session ended to a standing ovation, which was not surprising, given the moral authority of the speakers. What *was* surprising, however, was the makeup of the audience: This was a gathering not of activists, but of professionals who work in human resources. The event was a convention called Workhuman, put on by a software company.

For 30 years, ever since Anita Hill testified at Clarence Thomas's Supreme Court confirmation hearings, HR has been almost universally accepted as the mechanism by which employers attempt to prevent, police, and investigate sexual harassment. Even the Equal Employment Opportunity Commission directs Americans to their HR offices if they experience harassment. That the #MeToo movement kept turning up so many shocking stories at so many respected places of employment seemed to me to reflect a massive failure of human resources to do the job we have expected it to perform. Even Harvey Weinstein's company, after all, had an HR department.

I went to Texas to get a sense of how the people who work in the field were feeling about this exposure of their profession's shortcomings. Each morning at the convention, I fished around in my suitcase for something that looked businessy and then clip-clopped across the street to the convention center, joining a stream of similarly attired women. (HR is a profession of women; 75 percent of the field's workers are female—as, of course, are the overwhelming majority of employees who experience sexual harassment.) Our numbers grew in strength until we became a river of Banana Republic blazers and Ann Taylor wrap dresses and J.Crew slingbacks, a crowd of professional women, ages 25 to 60, all in an aggressively upbeat mood, many in chunky jewelry.

As I got to know them, I found the Workhuman attendees to be extremely personable and helpful, eager to wave me over to lunch tables and coffee groups. But they evinced an oddly disinterested attitude toward #MeToo. On the one hand, they were inspired by the movement. On the other hand, they did not exhibit any particular sense of responsibility for the kinds of failures that have allowed harassment to flourish. When Farrow said that #MeToo was about the "elaborate systems in place that could be utilized by the most powerful, the wealthiest, men" and Grant replied that the "reporting systems in companies tend not to work very well," I thought the crowd might take offense, but no one seemed insulted.

The problem of sexual harassment wasn't merely one of "bad apples," Grant continued, but also of "bad barrels." I looked around the hall, thinking that in this analogy the harassing men were the apples, and the systems that protect them—such as HR—were the bad barrels. But no one else appeared to take his remark that way. The audience members applauded graciously when Farrow paid them a high compliment: He was "so happy to be speaking to this room," to people who took preventing sexual harassment as their "sacred charge."

No one called for reforming or replacing HR. Just the opposite: The answer to the failures of HR, it seemed, was more HR.

The experience left me with a question: If HR is such a vital component of American business, its tentacles reaching deeply into many spheres of employees' work lives, how did it miss the kind of sexual harassment at the center of the #MeToo movement? And given that it did, why are companies still putting so much faith in HR? I returned to these questions many times over the course of the following year, interviewing workplace experts, lawyers, management consultants, and workers in the field.

Finally, I realized I had it all wrong. The simple and unpalatable truth is that HR isn't bad at dealing with sexual harassment. HR is actually very good at it.

In the old days, there was personnel: payroll, hiring, and—should things go terribly awry—pink slips. It was an office where the clatter of a typewriter signaled that volumes of paperwork were being shifted from inbox to outbox, and where employees could be just as bloodlessly reshuffled from "in" to "out." It was women's work, and in the popular imagination it was the terrain of the spinster: humorless, a stickler.

Human resources performs all of these old functions, along with a host of new ones.

Employees often imagine that the "resources" on offer are the benefits that flow to them from that department, but in the term's 19th-century origins, it is the workers themselves who are the resources, one more asset—along with equipment, factories, and capital—at the company's disposal. Most HR reps today would never dream of speaking about employees as a type of commodity (at least not to their face), although it can be hard to understand what, exactly, these reps are talking about, because the field is rich with jargon: *onboarding, balanced scorecards, cultural integration, the 80/20 rule.*

In a strong job market, HR is the soul of generosity, making employees feel valued and significant. But should the economy change, HR can just as quickly become assassin as friend.

On *The Office*, Michael Scott once said of Toby, the Dunder Mifflin HR rep: "If I had a gun with two bullets, and I was in a room with Hitler, bin Laden, and Toby, I would shoot Toby twice."[2] Over the past year, every time a friend asked what I was working on and I mentioned the letters *HR*, there was a remarkably consistent response: a quiet groan and a brief, skyward look—not a two-bullet look, but not a one-bullet look, either.

Fairly or not, HR is seen as the division of the company that slows things down, generates endless memos, meddles in employees' personal business, holds compulsory "trainings," and ruins any fun and spirit-lifting thing employees come up with. A notorious *Fast Company* cover story, published in 2005, is called "Why We Hate HR."[3] Its author, Keith H. Hammonds, laid out a string of damning questions that have resonated with businesspeople ever since:

Why are annual performance appraisals so time-consuming—and so routinely useless? Why is HR so often a henchman for the chief financial officer, finding ever-more ingenious ways to cut benefits and hack at payroll? Why do its communications—when we can understand them at all—so often flout reality? Why are so many people processes duplicative and wasteful, creating a forest of paperwork for every minor transaction? And why does HR insist on sameness as a proxy for equity?

But the real reason many workers don't love human resources is that while the department often presents itself as functioning like a union—the open door for worker complaints, the updates on valuable new benefits—it is not a union. In a strong job market, HR is the soul of generosity, making employees feel valued and significant. But should the economy change, or should management decide to go in another direction, HR can just as quickly become assassin as friend. The last face you'll see is Jane's—your pal from HR, who hands out the discounted tickets to Knott's Berry Farm and sends the blast emails about Chipotle Friday—and she'll be dry-eyed while collecting your employee badge and invoking the executioner's code: COBRA.

Jane's not a bad person—she's just carrying out orders from far up the ladder. And when it comes to sexual harassment, women understand that Jane reports to upper management, not some neutral body that stands in allegiance with right moral action. If employers judged HR departments by their ability to prevent sexual harassment, most would have gotten a failing grade long ago. What HR is actually responsible for—one of the central ways the department "adds value" to a company—is serving as the first line of defense against a sexual-harassment lawsuit. These two goals are clearly aligned, but if the past year has taught us anything, it's that you can achieve the latter without doing much of anything at all about the former.

In October 2014, Ellen DeGeneres did something on her talk show that we can hardly imagine in today's environment: She made an extended joke about sexual harassment. "Last week we had our mandatory sexual-harassment training seminar," she told the audience. "We have it every year for all of the employees, and it combines frank discussions about the workplace behavior and ... mind-numbing boredom." The people in the audience laughed appreciatively—they knew exactly what she meant. Then she introduced a game: "Sexual-Harassment Training or Late-Night Movie?"[4] And, with the eager participation of the audience, she read lines of dialogue and asked the crowd to guess their source.

Ellen's joke depended on our common understanding that in the decades since Anita Hill's testimony, HR has created a huge body of instructional films, computer training modules, seminar scripts, and written policies on sexual harassment. That a subject as urgent and—in its own, lurid way—bound with eros, fear, and guilt created an oeuvre known primarily for its stupefying dullness should have been a clue that the serious issue of harassment was being funneled through a bureaucracy whose aim was not (at least not purely) protecting women workers.

At solving the problem, HR is not great. At creating protocols of "compliance" to defend a company against lawsuits? By that criterion, it has been a smashing success.

Hill's testimony riveted the nation. It occurred years before the forensically prurient Starr Report became part of breakfast-table discourse; before hard-core pornography became a subject of open conversation; before sex workers were interviewed, respectfully, on staid national news programs. It was unprecedented: a dignified and extremely well-educated woman testifying before a group of male senators about pubic hair on a Coke can, all while the camera whirred before her and the entire country looked on. It was, in other words, exactly the kind of sui generis event that should not have resonated on a deeply personal level with any woman, save perhaps some of Clarence Thomas's law clerks. Yet it did resonate with women—millions of them. Their response was nonpartisan, unifying, nationwide, and—for many men—eye-opening. The concept, if not the linguistic formation, of "Me too" was born almost overnight. Hill's composure in the face of withering and often humiliating male commentary (including, let us not forget, that of Joe Biden) was stirring. "I am not given to fantasy," she said simply. "This is not something I would have come forward with if I were not absolutely sure."

Hill's testimony gave American women a way of understanding something that the Supreme Court had decided four and a half years earlier, in the famous *Meritor Savings Bank v. Vinson* case, which established that sexual harassment is a form of discrimination as defined by Title VII of the Civil Rights Act.[5] A potent combination of factors was born: Women could sue for sexual harassment, and their employer could be on the line for big damages. That last fact caught the attention of American employers and is the true father of the system that Ellen and so many other Americans have mocked.

At solving the problem, HR is not great. At creating protocols of "compliance" to defend a company against lawsuits? By that criterion, it has been a smashing success. How do we know? Partly because employers are so devoted to it; the first thing many an executive will do when a company is under scrutiny for sexual harassment is heap praise on its crackerjack HR team, and describe the accused men as outliers.

Pam Teren, an employment lawyer in Los Angeles, graduated from law school and began working at a firm in 1990. "I thought I'd probably never have a sexual-harassment case," she told me. The next year, Anita Hill testified, and these cases poured in. She told herself, "This is a five-year window. Because how simple is this? *Don't grab women. Don't stare at their chests.*" We both laughed—it really was pretty obvious. She figured that men would catch on quickly and the window would close. But she was wrong. Like thousands of lawyers across the country, she has been taking sexual-harassment cases ever since. Her entire career has been devoted to this work.

One aspect of the #MeToo movement that has puzzled observers is the nature of its inciting incident: the reports of Harvey Weinstein's alleged sexual harassment.[6] Why is it that such a singular bit of horror—with its luxury hotels, its glamorous locales, its involvement of famous actors, and its promises of Hollywood stardom—launched a movement that united women from all walks of life and all types of jobs?

The reality is that #MeToo was waiting to happen. Women's anger and frustration had been a simmering pot, its lid jittering. Something was going to cause it to boil over soon enough. The anger was about harassment; the frustration was about the system that had been created to address it.

In the months before Weinstein's crimes were revealed, in October 2017, three prominent American women spoke out against human-resources departments. In February, an Uber engineer named Susan Fowler wrote a 3,000-word blog post alleging sexual harassment at the company.[7] She described her experiences with a male manager who propositioned her and wrote that she "expected that I would report him to HR, they would handle the situation appropriately, and then life would go on." It didn't. On April 6, Nancy Erika Smith, who represented Gretchen Carlson in her harassment suit against Fox News chief Roger Ailes, spoke at the annual Women in the World conference and told the audience a stark truth: "HR is not your friend. HR will not help you."[8] That same day, Anita Hill wrote in *The Washington Post*, "There are still companies that pay lip service to human-resources departments while quietly allowing women to be vilified when they come forward."[9] All of this set the table for what has happened in the wake of Weinstein.

In fact, the movement could have begun a full year earlier, in 2016, when a special task force from the EEOC released its findings on sexual harassment.[10] The occasion was the anniversary of the *Meritor* case. The task force had been charged with determining how much progress the country had made since that historic decision. Its finding: very little. "Much of the training done over the last 30 years has not worked as a prevention tool," the task force found. That's an incredible statement—three decades of failure.

Making a show out of tossing harassers to the curb proved good for business during the early and middle phases of #MeToo. But social change that is dependent on a popular movement is destined to fade.

The EEOC report is a government white paper for the ages: sprawling, maddeningly unfocused, almost willfully opaque. But wade through it with pen in hand, and you realize it is also a startling document. It reveals that sexual harassment is "widespread" and "persistent," and that 85 percent of workers who are harassed never report it. It found that employees are much more likely to come up with their own solution—such as avoiding the harasser, downplaying the harassment, or simply enduring it—than to seek help from HR. They are far more likely to ask a family member or co-worker for advice than to file a complaint, because they fear that they will face repercussions if they do.

Anti-harassment training, and the centrality of HR in resolving women's problems, has been an ever-growing part of employees' lives since 1998, when a pair of Supreme Court decisions, *Faragher v. City of Boca Raton* and *Burlington Industries, Inc. v. Ellerth*, changed the way courts look at harassment claims. If a company uses a Faragher-Ellerth defense, it is asserting that despite clear policy and regular training, the employee who was harassed failed to make a report to HR and so the employer was unable to resolve the problem. This is why all of that training—the videos and online courses and worksheets—seems so useless: because it's designed to serve as a defense against an employment lawsuit.[11] The task force cited a study that found "no evidence that the training affected the frequency of sexual harassment experienced by the women in the workplace." The task force also said that HR trainings and procedures are "too focused on protecting the employer from liability," and not focused enough on ending the problem. The findings are depressing. Yet in a PowerPoint presentation accompanying the report, the task force maintains a hopeful, at times even chipper, tone. "The good news," it pronounces after delivering the dire facts, is that "we have some creative ideas."

One of these ideas comes in a bold assertion: "An 'It's On Us' campaign in the workplace could be a game changer." Here the EEOC is referring to a campaign that was introduced during President Barack Obama's administration to reduce sexual assault on college campuses. There's no indication that the campaign did anything at all to reduce sexual assault, and after an exciting and widely publicized launch it has been largely forgotten. Other suggestions include bystander-intervention training and civility training—the latter of which even the EEOC admits hasn't been "rigorously evaluated" as a tool for preventing harassment.

"Creative ideas"? A year before Weinstein, the agency ultimately responsible for fighting sexual harassment in America was grasping at straws.

When I was in Austin, I asked conference attendees why HR has accomplished so little. Over and over, they gave me a version of the same answer: They don't have power. They can deliver the trainings and write the policies, they can take reports and conduct investigations, but unless the harasser is of relatively low status within the organization, they have little say in the outcome. Most of the time, if the man is truly important to the company, the case is quickly whisked out of HR's hands, the investigation delivered to lawyers and the final decision rendered by executives. These executives are under no legal imperative to terminate an alleged offender or even to enforce a particular sanction, only to ensure that the woman who made the report is safe in the future.

Making a show out of tossing highly placed harassers to the curb proved good for business during the early and middle phases of #MeToo. But social change that is built on a popular movement is destined to fade when that movement becomes less fashionable. Already the country has begun to move on. The steady drumbeat of famous men being fired has slowed, and a backlash against what are perceived as unfair punishments has gathered strength. In April, Taffy Brodesser-Akner wrote a *New York Times Magazine* cover story about allegations of an extensive pattern of sexual harassment and discrimination at Sterling Jewelers, a chain of retailers that includes Kay, Jared, and Zales.[12] Here was a major writer reporting on an important subject—it was the kind of piece that a year earlier would have gotten the attention of the country. But as the #MeToo movement wanes, outrage has turned to resigned acceptance.

Like everyone else who understands the problem, including the EEOC, the HR workers I met at the conference reported that there is only one way to eradicate harassment from a workplace: by creating a climate and culture that starts at the very top of the company and establishes that harassment is not tolerated and will be punished severely. Middle managers can't change the culture of a company; only the most senior people can do that. And expecting an HR worker—with a car loan, a mortgage, college tuition around the corner—to risk her job in a fight against management on behalf of an employee she barely knows is unrealistic.

Throughout the course of writing this article, I encountered many alternatives to the traditional system of dealing with sexual harassment. I talked with one hugely successful high-stakes litigator in Los Angeles named Mark Baute. "I'm brutal in a courtroom," he told me cheerfully, "and I've got the goods." Baute has sometimes been asked to speak to executives at big companies. When he is introduced, none of the men in the audience takes much notice of him, because the subject is HR. But then, in his booming courtroom voice, he says, "I'm here so that this company doesn't hire someone like me to come in and destroy your career." The men put down their phones. He hammers them with every possible outcome of harassing a co-worker, and then he shames them: "Tell me something. If you're such a stud, why do you only date women who depend on you for employment? Why can't you walk outside of this building and find someone else to date?"

Baute's approach is aggressive, unconventional, and apparently very effective. It struck me as exactly the kind of "creative idea" that the EEOC might have been looking for. But no one is talking about taking it mainstream. Instead, we can expect to see HR deploy new techniques aimed more at protecting companies than at protecting employees.

So-called love contracts are becoming popular, requiring employees who are dating to report to HR to sign paperwork affirming that they are willingly taking part in a consensual relationship.

It is like a posting of the banns: a semipublic profession of intention, HR squirreling away one more signed document to indemnify the company from the human impulses of its workers. This could be understood as HR mission creep. Or it could be understood as another mile marker of the journey we are all on, as religion falls away and customs erode, and new norms of behavior are reverse-engineered from employment law. Title VII is the Bible, compliance training is the sermon, and the HR office is the confessional.

HR is no match for sexual harassment. It pits male sexual aggression against a system of paperwork and broken promises, and women don't trust it. For 30 years, we've invested responsibility in HR, and it hasn't worked out. We have to find a better way.

NOTES

1   Globoforce Press Release. "Globoforce Announces Historic #MeToo Panel at WorkHuman 2018 on Sexual Harassment in the Workplace." Feb. 18, 2018.

2   "The Chump." *The Office*. Dir. Randall Einhorn. Perf. Steve Carell. NBC, 13 May 2010.

3   "Why We Hate HR." *Fast Company* Aug. 1, 2005.

4   *The Ellen DeGeneres Show*. Perf. Ellen DeGeneres. Telepictures, 6 Oct 2014.

5   Brown, DeNeen L. "She said her boss raped her in a bank vault. Her sexual harassment case would make legal history." *The Washington Post* 13 Oct. 2017.

6   Farrow, Ronan. "From Aggressive Overtures to Sexual Assault: Harvey Weinstein's Accusers Tell Their Stories." *The New Yorker* 23 Oct. 2017.

7   Fowler, Susan. "Reflecting on one very, very strange year at Uber." susanjfowler.com, 19 Feb. 2017.

8   Symons, Emma-Kate. "Gretchen Carlson: 'In 2017, every damn woman still has a story.'" *Women in the World* 6 Apr. 2017.

9   Hill, Anita. "Fox News, Bill O'Reilly and how to stop companies that tolerate harassment." *The Washington Post* 6 Apr. 2017.

10 U.S. Equal Employment Opportunity Commission. *Select Task Force on the Study of Harassment in the*

Workplace: Report of Co-Chairs Chai R. Feldblum & Victoria A. Lipnic. Jun. 2016.

11   Lauren B. Edelman. "How HR and Judges Made It Almost Impossible for Victims of Sexual Harassment to Win in Court." *Harvard Business Review* 22 Aug. 2018.

12   Brodesser-Akner, Taffy. "The Company That Sells Love to America Had a Dark Secret." *The New York Times Magazine* 23 Apr. 2019.

—50—

WHY BAKKE HAS NO CASE

Ronald Dworkin

ON OCTOBER 12 THE SUPREME COURT HEARD oral argument in the case of *The Regents of the University of California v. Allan Bakke.* No lawsuit has ever been more widely watched or more thoroughly debated in the national and international press before the Court's decision. Still, some of the most pertinent facts set before the Court have not been clearly summarized.

The medical school of the University of California at Davis has an affirmative action program (called the "task force program") designed to admit more black and other minority students. It sets sixteen places aside for which only members of "educationally and economically disadvantaged minorities" compete. Allan Bakke, white, applied for one of the remaining eighty-four places; he was rejected but, since his test scores were relatively high, the medical school has conceded that it could not prove that he would have been rejected if the sixteen places reserved had been open to him. Bakke sued, arguing that the task force program deprived him of his constitutional rights. The California Supreme Court agreed, and ordered the medical school to admit him. The university appealed to the Supreme Court.

The Davis program for minorities is in certain respects more forthright (some would say cruder) than similar plans now in force in many other American universities and professional schools. Such programs aim to increase the enrollment of black and other minority students by allowing the fact of their race to count affirmatively as part of the case for admitting them. Some schools set a "target" of a particular number of minority places instead of setting aside a flat number of places. But Davis would not fill the number of places set aside unless there were sixteen minority candidates it considered clearly qualified for medical education. The difference is therefore one of administrative strategy and not of principle.

So the constitutional question raised by *Bakke* is of capital importance for higher education in America, and a large number of universities and schools have entered briefs *amicus curiae* urging the Court to reverse the California decision. They believe that if the decision is affirmed then they will no longer be free to use explicit racial criteria in any part of their admissions programs, and that they will therefore be unable to fulfill what they take to be their responsibilities to the nation.

It is often said that affirmative action programs aim to achieve a racially conscious society divided into racial and ethnic groups, each entitled, as a group, to some proportionable share of resources, careers, or opportunities. That is a perverse description. American society is currently a racially conscious society; this is the inevitable and evident consequence of a history of slavery, repression, and prejudice. Black men and women, boys and girls, are not free to choose for themselves in what roles—or as members of which social groups—others will characterize them. They are black, and no other feature of personality or allegiance or ambition will so thoroughly influence how they will be perceived and treated by others, and the range and character of the lives that will be open to them.

The tiny number of black doctors and professionals is both a consequence and a continuing cause of American racial consciousness, one link in a long and self-fueling chain reaction. Affirmative action programs use racially explicit criteria because their immediate goal is to increase the number of members of certain races in these professions. But their longterm goal is to *reduce* the degree to which American society is over-all a racially conscious society.

The programs rest on two judgments. The first is a judgment of social theory: that America will continue to be pervaded by racial divisions as long as the most lucrative, satisfying, and important careers remain mainly the prerogative of members of the white race, while others feel themselves systematically excluded from a professional and social elite. The second is a calculation of strategy: that increasing the number of blacks who are at work in the professions will, in the long run, reduce the sense of frustration and injustice and racial self-consciousness in the black community to the point at which blacks may begin to think of themselves as individuals who can succeed like others through talent and initiative. At that future point the consequences of nonracial admissions programs, whatever these consequences might be, could be accepted with no sense of racial barriers or injustice.

It is therefore the worst possible misunderstanding to suppose that affirmative action programs are designed to produce a balkanized America, divided into racial and ethnic subnations. They use strong measures because weaker ones will fail; but their ultimate goal is to lessen not to increase the importance of race in American social and professional life.

According to the 1970 census, only 2.1 percent of US doctors were black. Affirmative action programs aim to provide more black doctors to serve black patients. This is not because it is desirable that blacks treat blacks and whites treat whites, but because blacks, for no fault of their own, are now unlikely to be well served by whites, and because a failure to provide the doctors they trust will exacerbate rather than reduce the resentment that now leads them to trust only their own. Affirmative action tries to provide more blacks as classmates for white doctors, not because it is desirable that a medical school class reflect the racial makeup of the community as a whole, but because professional association between blacks and whites will decrease the degree to which whites think of blacks as a race rather than as people, and thus the degree to which blacks think of themselves that way. It tries to provide "role models" for future black doctors, not because it is desirable for a black boy or girl to find adult models only among blacks, but because our history has made them so conscious of their race that the success of whites, for now, is likely to mean little or nothing for them....

Professor Archibald Cox of Harvard Law School, speaking for the University of California in oral argument, told the Supreme Court that this is the choice the United States must make. As things stand, he said, affirmative action programs are the only effective means of increasing the absurdly small number of black doctors. The California Supreme Court, in approving Bakke's claim, had urged the university to pursue that goal by methods that do not explicitly take race into account. But that is unrealistic. We must distinguish, as Cox said, between two interpretations of what the California court's recommendation means. It might mean that the university should aim at the same immediate goal, of increasing the proportion of black and other minority students in the medical school, by an admissions procedure that on the surface is not racially conscious.

That is a recommendation of hypocrisy. If those who administer the admissions standards, however these are phrased, understand that their immediate goal is to increase the number of blacks in the school, then they will use race as a criterion in making the various subjective judgments the explicit criteria will require, because that will be, given the goal, the only right way to make those judgments. The recommendation might mean, on the other hand, that the school should adopt some non-racially conscious goal, like increasing the number of disadvantaged students of all races, and then hope that that goal will produce an increase in the number of blacks as a by-product. But even if that strategy is less hypocritical (which is far from plain), it will almost certainly fail because no different goal, scrupulously administered in a non-racially conscious way, will in fact significantly increase the number of black medical students....

A racially conscious test for admission, even one that sets aside certain places for qualified minority applicants exclusively, serves goals that are in themselves unobjectionable and even urgent. Such programs are, moreover, the only means that offer any significant promise of achieving these goals. If these programs are halted, then no more than a trickle of black students will enter medical or other professional schools for another generation at least.

If these propositions are sound, then on what ground can it be thought that such programs are either wrong or unconstitutional? We must notice an important distinction between two different sorts of objections that might be made. These programs are intended, as I said, to decrease the importance of race in the United States in the long run. It may be objected, first, that the programs will in fact harm that goal more than they will advance it. There is no way now to prove that that is not so....

Affirmative action programs seem to encourage, for example, a popular misunderstanding, which is that they assume that racial or ethnic groups are entitled to proportionate shares of opportunities, so that Italian or Polish ethnic minorities are, in theory, as entitled to their proportionate shares as blacks or Chicanos or American Indians are entitled to the shares the present programs give them. That is a plain mistake: the programs are not based on the idea that those who are aided are entitled to aid, but only on the strategic hypothesis that helping them is now

an effective way of attacking a national problem. Some medical schools may well make that judgment, under certain circumstances, about a white ethnic minority. Indeed it seems likely that some medical schools are even now attempting to help white Appalachian applicants, for example, under programs of regional distribution....

In the view of the many important universities who have such programs, however, the gains will very probably exceed the losses in reducing racial consciousness over-all. This view is hardly so implausible that it is wrong for these universities to seek to acquire the experience that will allow us to judge whether they are right. It would be particularly silly to forbid these experiments if we know that the failure to try will mean, as the evidence shows, that the status quo will almost certainly continue. In any case, this first objection could provide no argument that would justify a decision by the Supreme Court holding the programs unconstitutional. The Court has no business substituting its speculative judgment about the probable consequences of educational policies for the judgment of professional educators.

So the acknowledged uncertainties about the long-term results of such programs could not justify a Supreme Court decision making them illegal. But there is a second and very different form of objection. It may be argued that even if the programs *are* effective in making our society less a society dominated by race, they are nevertheless unconstitutional because they violate the individual constitutional rights of those, like Allan Bakke, who lose places in consequence. In the oral argument Reynold H. Colvin of San Francisco, who is Bakke's lawyer, made plain that his objection takes this second form....

But can he be right? If Allan Bakke has a constitutional right so important that the urgent goals of affirmative action must yield, then this must be because affirmative action violates some fundamental principle of political morality. This is not a case in which what might be called formal or technical law requires a decision one way or the other.

There is no language in the Constitution whose plain meaning forbids affirmative action. Only the most naïve theories of statutory construction could argue that such a result is required by the language of any earlier Supreme Court decision or of the Civil Rights Act of 1964 or of any other congressional enactment. If Mr. Colvin is right it must be because Allan Bakke has not simply some technical legal right but an important moral right as well.

What could that right be? The popular argument frequently made on editorial pages is that Bakke has a right to be judged on his merit. Or that he has a right to be judged as an individual rather than as a member of a social group. Or that he has a right, as much as any black man, not to be sacrificed or excluded from any opportunity because of his race alone. But these catch phrases are deceptive here, because, as reflection demonstrates, the only genuine principle they describe is the principle that no one should suffer from the prejudice or contempt of others. And that principle is not at stake in this case at all. In spite of popular opinion, the idea that the *Bakke* case presents a conflict between a desirable social goal and important individual rights is a piece of intellectual confusion.

Consider, for example, the claim that individuals applying for places in medical school should be judged on merit, and merit alone. If that slogan means that admissions committees should take nothing into account but scores on some particular intelligence test, then it is arbitrary and, in any case, contradicted by the long-standing practice of every medical school. If it means, on the other hand, that a medical school should choose candidates that it supposes will make the most useful doctors, then everything turns on the judgment of what factors make different doctors useful. The Davis medical school assigned to each regular applicant, as well as to each minority applicant, what it called a "benchmark score." This reflected not only the results of aptitude tests and college grade averages, but a subjective evaluation of the applicant's chances of functioning as an effective doctor, in view of society's present needs for medical service. Presumably the qualities deemed important were different from the qualities that a law school or engineering school or business school would seek, just as the intelligence tests a medical school might use would be different from the tests these other schools would find appropriate.

There is no combination of abilities and skills and traits that constitutes "merit" in the abstract; if quick hands count as "merit" in the case of a prospective surgeon, this is because quick hands will enable him to serve the public better and for no other reason. If a black skin will, as a matter of regrettable fact, enable another doctor to do a different medical job better, then that black skin is by the same token "merit" as well. That argument may strike some as dangerous; but only because they confuse its conclusion—that black skin may be a socially useful trait in particular circumstances—with the very different and despicable idea that one race may be inherently more worthy than another.

Consider the second of the catch phrases I have mentioned. It is said that Bakke has a right to be judged as an "individual," in deciding whether he is to be admitted to medical school and thus to the medical profession, and not as a member of some group that is being judged as a whole. What can that mean? Any admissions procedure must rely on generalizations about groups that are justified only statistically. The regular admissions process at Davis, for example, set a cutoff figure for college grade-point averages. Applicants whose averages fell below that figure were not invited to any interview, and therefore rejected out of hand.

An applicant whose average fell one point below the cutoff might well have had personal qualities of dedication or sympathy that would have been revealed at an interview, and that would have made him or her a better doctor than some applicant whose average rose one point above the line. But the former is excluded from the process on the basis of a decision taken for administrative convenience and grounded in the generalization, unlikely to hold true for every individual, that those with grade averages below the cutoff will not have other qualities sufficiently persuasive.... Mr. Colvin, in oral argument, argued the third of the catch phrases I mentioned. He said that his client had a right not to be excluded from medical school because of his race alone, and this as a statement of constitutional right sounds more plausible than claims about the right to be judged on merit or as an individual. It sounds plausible, however, because it suggests the following more complex principle. Every citizen has a constitutional right that he not suffer disadvantage, at least in the competition for any public benefit, because the race or religion or sect or region or other natural or artificial group to which he belongs is the object of prejudice or contempt.

That is a fundamentally important constitutional right, and it is that right that was systematically violated for many years by racist exclusions and anti-Semitic quotas. Color bars and Jewish quotas were not unfair just because they made race or religion relevant or because they fixed on qualities beyond individual control. It is true that blacks or Jews do not choose to be blacks or Jews. But it is also true that those who score low in aptitude or admissions tests do not choose their levels of intelligence. Nor do those denied admission because they are too old, or because they do not come from a part of the country underrepresented in the school, or because they cannot play basketball well, choose not to have the qualities that made the difference.

Race seems different because exclusions based on race have historically been motivated not by some instrumental calculation, as in the case of intelligence or age or regional distribution or athletic ability, but because of contempt for the excluded race or religion as such. Exclusion by race was in itself an insult, because it was generated by and signaled contempt.

Bakke's claim, therefore, must be made more specific than it is. He says he was kept out of medical school because of his race. Does he mean that he was kept out because his race is the object of prejudice or contempt? That suggestion is absurd. A very high proportion of those who were accepted (and, presumably, of those who run the admissions program) were members of the same race. He therefore means simply that if he had been black he would have been accepted, with no suggestion that this would have been so because blacks are thought more worthy or honorable than whites.

That is true: no doubt he would have been accepted if he were black. But it is also true, and in exactly the same sense, that he would have been accepted if he had been more intelligent, or made a better impression in his interview, or, in the case of other schools, if he had been younger when he decided to become a doctor. Race is not, in *his* case, a different matter from these other factors equally beyond his control. It is not a different matter because in his case race is not distinguished by the special character of public insult. On the contrary the program presupposes that his race is still widely if wrongly thought to be superior to others....

We have now considered three familiar slogans, each widely thought to name a constitutional right that enables Allan Bakke to stop programs of affirmative action no matter how effective or necessary these might be. When we inspect these slogans, we find that they can stand for no genuine principle except one. This is the important principle that no one in our society should suffer because he is a member of a group thought less worthy of respect, as a group, than other groups. We have different aspects of that principle in mind when we say that individuals should be judged on merit, that they should be judged as individuals, and that they should not suffer disadvantages because of their race. The spirit of that fundamental principle is the spirit of the goal that affirmative action is intended to serve. The principle furnishes no support for those who find, as Bakke does, that their own interests conflict with that goal....

-51-

FISHER V. UNIVERSITY OF TEXAS AT AUSTIN

Concurrence

Clarence Thomas[*]

Cite as: 570 U.S. _____ (2013)

THOMAS, J., concurring

SUPREME COURT OF THE UNITED STATES

No. 11–345

ABIGAIL NOEL FISHER, PETITIONER v. UNIVERSITY OF TEXAS AT AUSTIN ET AL.

ON WRIT OF CERTIORARI TO THE UNITED STATES COURT OF APPEALS FOR THE FIFTH CIRCUIT

[June 24, 2013]

JUSTICE THOMAS, concurring.

I join the Court's opinion because I agree that the Court of Appeals did not apply strict scrutiny to the University of Texas at Austin's (University) use of racial discrimination in admissions decisions. *Ante*, at 1. I write separately to explain that I would overrule *Grutter v. Bollinger*, 539 U.S. 306 (2003), and hold that a State's use of race in higher education admissions decisions is categorically prohibited by the Equal Protection Clause.

I

A

The Fourteenth Amendment provides that no State shall "deny to any person... the equal protection of the laws." The Equal Protection Clause guarantees every person the right to be treated equally by the State, without regard to race. "At the heart of this [guarantee] lies the principle that the government must treat citizens as individuals, and not as members of racial, ethnic, or religious groups." *Missouri v. Jenkins*, 515 U.S. 70, 120–121 (1995) (THOMAS, J., concurring). "It is for this reason that we must subject all racial classifications to the strictest of scrutiny." *Id.*, at 121.

Under strict scrutiny, all racial classifications are categorically prohibited unless they are "'necessary to further a compelling governmental interest'" and "narrowly tailored to that end." *Johnson v. California*, 543 U.S. 499, 514 (2005) (quoting *Grutter, supra*, at 327). This most exacting standard "has proven automatically fatal" in almost every case. *Jenkins, supra*, at

---

[*]   Editor's note: Thomas was confirmed as Supreme Court justice despite allegations from a former co-worker, Anita Hill, that he had sexually harassed her over a period of years. It may strike some readers as ironic or inappropriate for material drafted by someone whose own professional ethics have been called into question to be included in an anthology on the subject of professional ethics. The editors and the publisher have in this case carefully weighed the issues involved, and have concluded that, on balance, the material merits inclusion in this volume, given that Thomas's arguments here concern only the issue of affirmative action and that they express the reasoning underlying his Supreme Court vote in this historic case.

121 (THOMAS, J., concurring). And rightly so. "Purchased at the price of immeasurable human suffering, the equal protection principle reflects our Nation's understanding that [racial] classifications ultimately have a destructive impact on the individual and our society." *Adarand Constructors, Inc. v. Peña*, 515 U.S. 200, 240 (1995) (THOMAS, J., concurring in part and concurring in judgment). "The Constitution abhors classifications based on race" because "every time the government places citizens on racial registers and makes race relevant to the provision of burdens or benefits, it demeans us all." *Grutter, supra*, at 353 (THOMAS, J., concurring in part and dissenting in part).

B

1

The Court first articulated the strict-scrutiny standard in *Korematsu v. United States*, 323 U.S. 214 (1944). There, we held that "[p]ressing public necessity may sometimes justify the existence of [racial discrimination]; racial antagonism never can." *Id.*, at 216.[1] Aside from *Grutter*, the Court has recognized only two instances in which a "[p]ressing public necessity" may justify racial discrimination by the government. First, in *Korematsu*, the Court recognized that protecting national security may satisfy this exacting standard. In that case, the Court upheld an evacuation order directed at "all persons of Japanese ancestry" on the grounds that the Nation was at war with Japan and that the order had "a definite and close relationship to the prevention of espionage and sabotage." 323 U.S., at 217–218. Second, the Court has recognized that the government has a compelling interest in remedying past discrimination for which it is responsible, but we have stressed that a government wishing to use race must provide "a 'strong basis in evidence for its conclusion that remedial action [is] necessary.'" *Richmond v. J.A. Croson Co.*, 488 U.S. 469, 500, 504 (1989) (quoting *Wygant v. Jackson Bd. of Ed.*, 476 U.S. 267, 277 (1986) (plurality opinion)).

In contrast to these compelling interests that may, in a narrow set of circumstances, justify racial discrimination, the Court has frequently found other asserted interests insufficient. For example, in *Palmore v. Sidoti*, 466 U.S. 429 (1984), the Court flatly rejected a claim that the best interests of a child justified the government's racial discrimination. In that case, a state court awarded custody to a child's father because the mother was in a mixed-race marriage. The state court believed the child might be stigmatized by living in a mixed-race household and sought to avoid this perceived problem in its custody determination. We acknowledged the possibility of stigma but nevertheless concluded that "the reality of private biases and the possible injury they might inflict" do not justify racial discrimination. *Id.*, at 433. As we explained, "The Constitution cannot control such prejudices but neither can it tolerate them. Private biases may be outside the reach of the law, but the law cannot, directly or indirectly, give them effect." *Ibid.*

Two years later, in *Wygant, supra*, the Court held that even asserted interests in remedying societal discrimination and in providing role models for minority students could not justify governmentally imposed racial discrimination. In that case, a collective-bargaining agreement between a school board and a teacher's union favored teachers who were "'Black, American Indian, Oriental, or of Spanish descendancy.'" *Id.*, at 270–271, and n. 2 (plurality opinion). We rejected the interest in remedying societal discrimination because it had no logical stopping point. *Id.*, at 276. We similarly rebuffed as inadequate the interest in providing role models to minority students and added that the notion that "black students are better off with black teachers could lead to the very system the Court rejected in *Brown v. Board of Education*, 347 U.S. 483 (1954)." *Ibid.*

2

Grutter was a radical departure from our strict-scrutiny precedents. In *Grutter*, the University of Michigan Law School (Law School) claimed that it had a compelling reason to discriminate based on race. The reason it advanced did not concern protecting national security or remedying its own past discrimination. Instead, the Law School argued that it needed to discriminate in admissions decisions in order to obtain the "educational benefits that flow from a diverse student body." 539 U.S., at 317. Contrary to the very meaning of strict scrutiny, the Court *deferred* to the Law School's determination that this interest was sufficiently compelling to justify racial discrimination. *Id.*, at 325.

I dissented from that part of the Court's decision. I explained that "only those measures the State must take to provide a bulwark against anarchy, or to prevent violence, will constitute a 'pressing public necessity'" sufficient to satisfy strict scrutiny. *Id.*, at 353. Cf. *Lee v. Washington*, 390 U.S. 333, 334 (1968) (Black, J., concurring) (protecting prisoners from violence might justify narrowly tailored discrimination); *J.A. Croson, supra*, at 521 (SCALIA, J., concurring in judgment) ("At least where state or local action is at issue, only a social emergency rising to the level of imminent danger to life and limb ... can justify [racial discrimination]"). I adhere to that view today. As should be obvious, there is nothing "pressing" or "necessary" about obtaining whatever educational benefits may flow from racial diversity.

II
A

The University claims that the District Court found that it has a compelling interest in attaining "a diverse student body and the educational benefits flowing from such diversity." Brief for Respondents 18. The use of the conjunction, "and," implies that the University believes its discrimination furthers two distinct interests. The first is an interest in attaining diversity for its own sake. The second is an interest in attaining educational benefits that allegedly flow from diversity.

Attaining diversity for its own sake is a non-starter. As even *Grutter* recognized, the pursuit of diversity as an end is nothing more than impermissible "racial balancing." 539 U.S., at 329–330 ("The Law School's interest is not simply 'to assure within its student body some specified percentage

of a particular group merely because of its race or ethnic origin.' That would amount to outright racial balancing, which is patently unconstitutional" (quoting *Regents of Univ. of Cal. v. Bakke*, 438 U.S. 265, 307 (1978); citation omitted)); see also *id.*, at 307 ("Preferring members of any one group for no reason other than race or ethnic origin is discrimination for its own sake. This the Constitution forbids"). Rather, diversity can only be the *means* by which the University obtains educational benefits; it cannot be an end pursued for its own sake. Therefore, the *educational benefits* allegedly produced by diversity must rise to the level of a compelling state interest in order for the program to survive strict scrutiny.

Unfortunately for the University, the educational benefits flowing from student body diversity—assuming they exist—hardly qualify as a compelling state interest. Indeed, the argument that educational benefits justify racial discrimination was advanced in support of racial segregation in the 1950's, but emphatically rejected by this Court. And just as the alleged educational benefits of segregation were insufficient to justify racial discrimination then, see *Brown v. Board of Education*, 347 U.S. 483 (1954), the alleged educational benefits of diversity cannot justify racial discrimination today.

1

Our desegregation cases establish that the Constitution prohibits public schools from discriminating based on race, even if discrimination is necessary to the schools' survival. In *Davis v. School Bd. of Prince Edward Cty.*, decided with *Brown, supra*, the school board argued that if the Court found segregation unconstitutional, white students would migrate to private schools, funding for public schools would decrease, and public schools would either decline in quality or cease to exist altogether. Brief for Appellees in *Davis v. School Bd. of Prince Edward Cty.*, O.T. 1952, No. 191, p. 30 (hereinafter Brief for Appellees in *Davis*) ("Virginians ... would no longer permit sizeable appropriations for schools on either the State or local level; private segregated schools would be greatly increased in number and the masses of our people, both white and Negro, would suffer terribly ... [M]any white parents would withdraw their children from the public schools and, as a result, the program of providing better schools would be abandoned" (internal quotation marks omitted)). The true victims of desegregation, the school board asserted, would be black students, who would be unable to afford private school. See *id.*, at 31 ("[W]ith the demise of segregation, education in Virginia would receive a serious setback. Those who would suffer most would be the Negroes who, by and large, would be economically less able to afford the private school"); Tr. of Oral Arg. in *Davis v. School Bd. of Prince Edward Cty.*, O.T. 1954, No. 3, p. 208 ("What is worst of all, in our opinion, you impair the public school system of Virginia and the victims will be the children of both races, we think the Negro race worse than the white race, because the Negro race needs it more by virtue of these disadvantages under which they have labored. We are up against the proposition: What does the Negro profit if he procures an immediate detailed decree from this Court now and then impairs or mars or destroys the public school system in Prince Edward County").[2]

Unmoved by this sky-is-falling argument, we held that segregation violates the principle of equality enshrined in the Fourteenth Amendment. See *Brown, supra,* at 495 ("[I]n the field of public education the doctrine of 'separate but equal' has no place. Separate educational facilities are inherently unequal"); see also *Allen v. School Bd. of Prince Edward Cty.*, 249 F. 2d 462, 465 (CA4 1957) (*per curiam*) ("The fact that the schools might be closed if the order were enforced is no reason for not enforcing it. A person may not be denied enforcement of rights to which he is entitled under the Constitution of the United States because of action taken or threatened in defiance of such rights"). Within a matter of years, the warning became reality: After being ordered to desegregate, Prince Edward County closed its public schools from the summer of 1959 until the fall of 1964. See

R. Sarratt, The Ordeal of Desegregation 237 (1966). Despite this fact, the Court never backed down from its rigid enforcement of the Equal Protection Clause's antidiscrimination principle.

In this case, of course, Texas has not alleged that the University will close if it is prohibited from discriminating based on race. But even if it had, the foregoing cases make clear that even that consequence would not justify its use of racial discrimination. It follows, *a fortiori*, that the putative educational benefits of student body diversity cannot justify racial discrimination: If a State does not have a compelling interest in the *existence* of a university, it certainly cannot have a compelling interest in the supposed benefits that might accrue to that university from racial discrimination. See *Grutter*, 539 U.S., at 361 (opinion of THOMAS, J.) ("[A] marginal improvement in legal education cannot justify racial discrimination where the Law School has no compelling interest either in its existence or in its current educational and admissions policies"). If the Court were actually applying strict scrutiny, it would require Texas either to close the University or to stop discriminating against applicants based on their race. The Court has put other schools to that choice, and there is no reason to treat the University differently....

NOTES

1 The standard of "pressing public necessity" is more frequently called a "compelling governmental interest." I use the terms interchangeably.

2 Similar arguments were advanced unsuccessfully in other cases as well. See, *e.g.*, Brief for Respondents in *Sweatt v. Painter*, O.T. 1949, No. 44, pp. 94–95 (hereinafter Brief for Respondents in *Sweatt*) ("[I]f the power to separate the students were terminated, ... it would be as a bonanza to the private white schools of the State, and it would mean the migration out of the schools and the turning away from the public schools of the influence and support of a large number of children and of the parents of those children ... who are the largest contributors to the cause of

public education, and whose financial support is necessary for the continued progress of public education.... Should the State be required to mix the public schools, there is no question but that a very large group of students would transfer, or be moved by their parents, to private schools with a resultant deterioration of the public schools" (internal quotation marks omitted)); Brief for Appellees in *Briggs v. Elliott*, O.T. 1952, No. 101, p. 27 (hereinafter Brief for Appellees in *Briggs*) ("[I]t would be impossible to have sufficient acceptance of the idea of mixed groups attending the same schools to have public education on that basis at all.... [I]t would eliminate the public schools in most, if not all, of the communities in the State").

—52—

"UNDER GOD'S AUTHORITY"

Professional Responsibility, Religious Accommodations, and the Culture Wars

*John Corvino**

CONSIDER THE FOLLOWING CASE: AFTER CONverting to Islam, a flight attendant on a mid-sized airline concludes that serving alcohol is immoral. Citing her religious beliefs, she requests exemption from that particular job duty. Her airline offers an accommodation, allowing her to signal other flight attendants when alcohol service is needed. Eventually, however, a coworker complains to management; the coworker also mentions the flight attendant's "headdress" and her book with "foreign writings." The airline terminates the flight attendant's employment.

This is the real-life case of Charee Stanley, an ExpressJet employee.[1] Stanley has filed a complaint with the Equal Employment Opportunity Commission (EEOC) under Title VII of the 1964 Civil Rights Act, which requires employers to accommodate religious practices unless doing so would impose an "undue hardship" on the employer.

Now consider ... [an] additional case:

... After years of witnessing drunken passengers behave badly—not to mention drunken fellow employees, at hotel bars during overnight layovers between assignments—a flight attendant develops serious moral qualms about alcohol. This flight attendant, whom we'll call Ms. Temperance, starts reading books about alcohol abuse and the history of the temperance movement. It's worth noting, however, that Ms. Temperance rejects that movement's religious underpinnings: She identifies as agnostic. Ms. Temperance eventually concludes that it is morally wrong not only to drink alcohol but also to serve it. Citing her (non-religious) conscience, she requests an accommodation from her employer....

We may posit that Ms. Stanley [and] Ms. Temperance are ... sincere in their objections to serving alcohol: They are not slackers who refuse this job duty out of laziness. Serving alcohol would be personally difficult for each employee, although for slightly different reasons: religious conscience for Ms. Stanley, non-religious conscience for Ms. Temperance.... Furthermore, the burden imposed on their employers appears similar in each case: in order to satisfy customers' requests while accommodating the objecting employee, the airline must require other employees to do a bit of extra work. The amount of extra work, and thus the difficulty of the accommodation, will depend on a variety of contextual factors: How large are the aircraft on which these employees work—how many flight attendants per flight, and per beverage cart? How many other employees seek similar accommodations? How long are the flights? How impatient are the customers? And so on.

---

* Reprinted with permission by the author.

There are also differences between the cases, some of which have to do with the messiness inherent in real-life situations like Ms. Stanley's as compared to hypotheticals. The wording of Ms. Stanley's coworker's complaint, which mentioned her "headdress" and book of "foreign writings," suggests anti-Islamic sentiment: After all, virtually no one in the U.S. would refer to the Judeo-Christian Bible, which was originally written in ancient Hebrew, Aramaic, and Greek, as a book of "foreign writings."

The bigger difference, however, is in the likelihood of accommodation. Ms. Stanley is expected to win her EEOC complaint, given Title VII's explicit guidelines on religious accommodations. Ms. Temperance does not have similar recourse: There is no law mandating accommodation in cases like hers, where the objection is based on non-religious conscience....

In this essay I have two, relatively modest aims. First, I want to explore the question of whether employers ought to give special treatment to specifically *religious* requests for accommodations.... Second, I want to compare cases like Ms. Stanley's to a more controversial case: that of Kim Davis, the Kentucky clerk who cited religious objections in refusing to grant marriage licenses to same-sex couples. In the process, I want to tease out some general principles for addressing such cases, navigating between an inflexible "Just do your job!" on the one side, and treating religion as a "Get out of your job free" card on the other.

PART I. WHY RELIGIOUS ACCOMMODATIONS?

Why single out religious commitment for special protection in the workplace? Let us consider four possible answers to this question:

(1) *Religion as a proxy for deep and important moral commitments.* One reason we might single out religion is that it provides evidence for deep and important commitments. Consider employment accommodations for Saturday Sabbath-observers. Most people would prefer not to work on Saturdays—weekends are fun!—but some people have better reasons than others. Because it would be difficult for the state to weigh each reason individually, it must instead use rough categories. "Religious reasons" are such a category, allowing people to point to their membership in a larger community which shares the commitment.

A major problem with this answer is that not all deep and important commitments are shared by a larger religious community, and not all commitments shared by a larger religious community are deep and important; thus, religion is both over- and under-inclusive as a proxy. Of course, virtually all proxies are imperfect: We use them because the targeted category—in this case, "deep and important commitments"—is hard to measure directly. But there are better proxies than religion in capturing this target, especially given that neither courts nor regulatory agencies require believers to point to a shared communal tradition in order to establish a religious claim. As the EEOC guidelines now put it, "[a]n employee's belief or practice can be 'religious' under Title VII even if the employee is affiliated with a religious group that does not espouse or recognize that individual's belief or practice, or if few—or no—other people adhere to it."[2]

Of course, the ability to point to a larger tradition may be useful in establishing a religious claim's *sincerity*, which is indeed a relevant requirement. Suppose a professor at Midwestern university tells his dean that during the holy month he is religiously bound to make a pilgrimage to the Holy Land, and thus must receive an accommodation—he must teach his classes remotely, via Skype, during that time. Oh, and by the way: The holy month is February and the Holy Land is Puerto Vallarta. Most deans would balk at such a request (as did mine, sadly) because they would rightly suspect that it had nothing to do with religion at all: The combination of self-interested motive and the lack of any recognizable religious tradition makes the insincerity apparent. But other cases are more difficult. Keep in mind that every religion was new at some point. Mormonism is only 200 years old. Scientology is less than 75 years old. The founders of both were regarded as charlatans by many of their contemporaries, not to mention ours. Yet no one doubts that both religions have many sincere adherents. How long a tradition is necessary, and how many followers, to provide the requisite evidence of sincerity?

(2) *Religious believers experience religious objections as particularly binding.* Another possible reason for privileging religion is the fact that religious believers may experience their dictates of conscience as especially binding. The general idea is that religious conscience is derived from an external authority, God, who holds people accountable. The believer thus experiences such dictates as "non-optional." ...

The problem with this rationale, as with the previous one, is that it is both over- and under-inclusive. Not all claims that people experience as morally binding are religious, and not all religious claims are experienced as morally binding. Not all faiths subscribe to belief in a personal God, much less one who metes out eternal reward and punishment in an afterlife. Even religions that do posit such a God contain various "optional" practices, such as whether to wear certain religious garb. Because courts rightly wish to avoid adjudicating "the place of a particular belief in a religion or the plausibility of a religious claim,"[3] they typically defer to believers' self-reporting on this matter. But there is no reason to think that believers are more candid or sincere than non-believers in reporting whether they experience a claim as morally mandatory....

(3) *Religion is a fundamental good.* Maybe the reason for privileging religion when granting accommodations is that religion—like health, education, family, and so on—is a fundamental good worth promoting. It engages the distinctively human capacity for grappling with basic questions about meaning and existence. It binds people together, often for charitable purposes which promote the general welfare. It provides a way to mark major life events ... and offers solace in times of grief and despair. Just as employers sometimes provide gym memberships to promote employees' physical health, maybe they should provide religious accommodations to promote employees' "spiritual health."

There is no doubt that religion promotes the goods just mentioned, and does so well. One could scarcely explain its pervasiveness and endurance otherwise. There is also no doubt that it promotes great evil. The same fervor that makes some willing to die for their faith makes others willing to kill for it—witness, for example, the 9–11 attacks, or the Salem Witch Trials, or the Crusades. Regarding religion, the Nobel-winning physicist Steven Weinberg has said: "With or without it, you would have good people doing good things and evil people doing evil things. But for good people to do evil things, that takes religion." The reason is that it leads people to think that they have infallible backing for their all-too-fallible judgments.

Some will object that religion that does evil is not true religion. This objection just ignores the problem by defining it away: It's like arguing that there's no such thing as spousal abuse because anyone who abuses is not a true spouse. Okay, but what about the "spouses" who do? And what about the "religion" that has been, and continues to be, the cause of so much sectarian strife? In any case, secular employers cannot be in the business of distinguishing between "true" and "false" religion, and so this rationale is a non-starter....

(4) *Religious minorities have been historically burdened.* A fourth possible reason for providing special treatment to religious claims is that people have historically suffered discrimination on account of religion; thus, exemptions or accommodations function as a kind of corrective measure. This discrimination is not necessarily intentional. As Martha Nussbaum notes, "Majority thinking is usually not malevolent, but is often obtuse, oblivious to the burden [its] rules impose on religious minorities."[4] Such burdens tend to sharpen divisions between in-groups and out-groups, divisions that are bad for the workplace and for society at large.

I'm reminded here of how my university requires that professors make reasonable accommodations for students who miss exams for religious reasons. Initially I feared that this policy would pose an administrative nightmare: I work at a large, diverse public institution, and I often teach large classes; my students observe a plethora of holidays. But then the following thought occurred: Christian students never have to take an exam on Christmas day. Why is that? After all, we're a state school, not a sectarian one. The answer is that official holidays are chosen by the majority, and the majority observes Christmas: a Christian holy day that has, due to Christianity's prevalence in the U.S., also become a secular holiday. Our university schedule thus places a burden on minority faiths that it does not place on Christians. Realizing that, I came to see the accommodations policy as a reasonable way to correct such imbalances. Perhaps religious accommodations should be entertained because they restore fairness in this way.

There is much to be said for this argument, with some important caveats.

The first caveat is that while religion is *special* in this regard, it is not *unique*. It is, rather, one among several axes according to which majorities have historically disadvantaged minorities.

Again, such discrimination is frequently unintentional. Guidelines regarding appropriate workplace hairstyles often disadvantage racial and ethnic minorities whose hair textures and cultural traditions make "appropriate" hairstyles difficult. The design of public facilities often disadvantages people with disabilities, not to mention those at height and weight extremes. Blue laws, which prohibit various kinds of commerce on Sundays, disadvantage not only Saturday Sabbath observers but also the poor: A coordinated, forced day of rest may sound wonderful, unless you're truly desperate for income. When laws and policies implicate such characteristics, they deserve heightened scrutiny.

A second caveat is that heightened scrutiny need not result in an accommodation. Whether it does will depend not only whether the policy disproportionately affects minorities, but also, on what other values are at stake—including, of course, the value of consistent treatment. While policies

should not arbitrarily disadvantage the religious, nor should they arbitrarily favor them.

Consider again Ms. Stanley's case. It is true that anti-Islamic sentiment—and even simply ignorance of Islamic practices—sometimes disproportionately burdens Muslim employees in Western nations. Ms. Stanley's case may thus deserve somewhat more scrutiny than Ms. Temperance's.... On the other hand, alcohol service is a standard job requirement for flight attendants, and accommodations given to Ms. Stanley will likely result in extra work for her coworkers—including people like Ms. Temperance..., whose burdens are similar, and who may thus have a similar argument for accommodation.... So while the religious nature of Ms. Stanley's claim provides some reason for giving it extra attention, it does not entail that her claim should prevail, let alone that it is substantially stronger than that of [Ms. Temperance].

A third caveat is that accommodations should not remove burdens from some disadvantaged minorities only to place burdens on other, possibly even more disadvantaged, minorities. Otherwise, we undermine the very reason for considering such accommodations in the first place—at least, the reason we've identified as strongest. Which brings us to the case of Kim Davis.

PART II. KIM DAVIS AND THE CULTURE WARS

Kim Davis is a Rowan County, Kentucky, Clerk who was jailed for five days in September 2015 after refusing to obey a Federal District Court order to issue marriage licenses to same-sex couples or to allow her deputy clerks to do so, claiming she was acting "under God's authority." After she was jailed, deputy clerks began issuing the licenses; two months later, Kentucky Governor Matt Bevin issued an executive order eliminating the requirement that clerks' names appear on them.

Ms. Davis's case sparked considerable controversy. At the time, many (including me) argued that she ought to do her job or resign. As I put it then, her stance made little more sense "than that of an Amish person who expects to retain a job as a bus driver," or a Christian Scientist who wanted to retain a job as a surgeon.[5] To be fair, the cases are not precisely analogous: Issuing marriage licenses is but one of several functions that county clerks perform; by contrast, an Amish bus driver couldn't do their job *at all*. Still, the centrality of the job function is relevant, as is the fact that Ms. Davis refused to let her deputy clerks issue licenses in her place. So too is the fact that Ms. Davis is an elected official, who is supposed to act on behalf of all citizens. By refusing to issue the licenses or allow others to do so, Davis didn't merely inconvenience coworkers or customers, as Charee Stanley may have: She denied citizens a fundamental right.

Some have argued that Ms. Davis's case is actually more sympathetic than Ms. Stanley's, for the following reason: Ms. Stanley's job requirements did not change, whereas Ms. Davis's did. The conflict for Ms. Stanley arose when she voluntarily converted to Islam, a year after taking the job, whereas the conflict for Ms. Davis arose when the U.S. Supreme Court ruled in *Obergefell v. Hodges* that same-sex couples have the right to marry in every state. In other words, unlike Ms. Stanley, Ms. Davis didn't change: the law did.

I answer that the change in the law is not tantamount to a change in Davis's job requirements, much less an unjustified one. Laws change all the time: Legislatures enact, repeal, and modify them, and sometimes (as in this case) courts overrule them. Ms. Davis surely knew all of this when she ran for office and accepted her position....

In substituting her own religious understanding of marriage for state law, Ms. Davis also imposed a burden on gay and lesbian Kentuckians, a historically marginalized group. (She initially recommended that they drive to another county in order to receive a license.) Kim Davis is not a religious minority member who wished to be left alone to practice her faith: She is a member of a powerful religious majority who tried to impose her views on others. That, too, is an important difference from Ms. Stanley's case.

Before concluding, I want to address one final objection. Some have argued that there are ways to accommodate people like Davis without generating burdens for same-sex couples or anyone else: Simply eliminate the legal requirement that the clerk's name appears on marriage licenses, and the conflict disappears.[6] As already noted, that solution has since been provided by Kentucky Governor Matt Bevin. Thus same-sex couples get their licenses, Davis keeps her job, and no one's conscience is burdened: an apparent "win-win." ...

Yet I worry about the message sent by changing Kentucky law in order to accommodate Davis. To see why, imagine a slightly different case. Suppose Mr. Burqa is a religious fundamentalist who believes that women ought never to show their faces in public; furthermore, he insists that they ought never to go out unless accompanied by their husbands, fathers, or other male "authority figures." As County Clerk, he objects to granting licenses to women who enter his office unveiled or unaccompanied. Moreover, he refuses to let his deputy clerks do so as long as his name appears on the licenses, as current law requires.

Should we change our licensing procedures to accommodate Mr. Burqa? I'm inclined to say no. The reason is that Mr. Burqa's belief that women may not enter the public on their own authority is sexist; it contributes to the subjugation of women. The state should show it no deference. In a similar way, Kim Davis's beliefs about marriage reflect heterosexist views that have long harmed gays and lesbians, views that the U.S. Supreme Court rejected in *Obergefell* when ruling in favor of legal marriage equality.

Or consider another, real-world case: In 2009, Keith Bardwell, a Louisiana justice of the peace, refused to officiate at an interracial wedding. Bardwell claimed, and no doubt sincerely believed, that he was not a racist: "I have piles and piles of black friends," he told reporters. "They come to my home, I marry them, they use my bathroom. I treat them just like everyone else."[7] But Bardwell personally objected to interracial marriages, and he refused to sign licenses or perform weddings for them.[8]

When word got out about Bardwell's position, he was pressured to resign—and rightly so. Notwithstanding his protestations, Bardwell's moral qualms both reflected and reinforced the racist subjugation of blacks in this country. That he even saw it as a live question whether his "piles and piles of black friends" should be permitted to use his bathroom is evidence of just how deep that racism runs.... We expect better of our public officials.

Whether you see Kim Davis as analogous to Bardwell and Mr. Burqa will depend on how bad you think anti-gay discrimination is. Here, I simply point out that just because people's religious beliefs *can* be easily accommodated, it does not follow that they *should* be. Some accommodations reinforce sentiments that deserve repudiation.

CONCLUSION

The United States has a long (if not always consistent) tradition of striving for religious liberty, tolerance, and fairness, and workplace accommodations are a key element of that tradition. It is important, however, that religious liberty does not morph into religious favoritism, and that religious accommodations do not remove burdens from some individuals only to impose them, sometimes even more harshly, on others. Kim Davis's demands crossed that line; the judge in her case was right to deny them. The case of Charee Stanley is more difficult. In my view, the argument for accommodating her is strong but not decisive, and in any case, it is not substantially stronger than that for accommodating Ms. Temperance.... Whether the accommodation should be granted hinges less on her claim's religious character than on various contextual factors related to others' burdens.

NOTES

1   "Muslim flight attendant suspended for refusing to serve alcohol files federal complaint," *The Washington Post*, https://www.washingtonpost.com/news/morning-mix/wp/2015/09/08/muslim-flight-attendant-suspended-for-refusing-to-serve-alcohol-files-federal-complaint/; accessed March 10, 2016.

2   EEOC, "Questions and Answers about Religious Discrimination in the Workplace," http://eeoc.gov/policy/docs/qanda religion.html; accessed March 7, 2016.

3   *Employment Div., Dept. of Human Resources of Ore. v. Smith*, 494 US 872, 887 (1990)....

4   Martha Nussbaum, *Liberty of Conscience: In Defense of America's Tradition of Religious Equality* (Basic Books, 2010), p. 116.

5   John Corvino, "It's Time to Remove Kentucky Clerk Kim Davis," *Detroit Free Press*, http://www.freep.com/story/opinion/contributors/2015/09/01/s-time-remove-kentucky-clerk-kim-davis/71505026/; accessed March 9, 2016.

6   See for example Ryan T. Anderson, "We Don't Need Kim Davis to Be in Jail," *The New York Times*, http://www.nytimes.com/2015/09/07/opinion/we-dont-need-kim-davis-to-be-in-jail.html?_r = 0.

7   "Interracial couple denied marriage license in Tangipahoa Parish," http://www.nola.com/crime/index.ssf/2009/10/interracial_couple_denied_marr.html; accessed March 9, 2016.

8   Bardwell's reason was not overtly religious; he claimed, rather, that such unions were bad for the resulting children, who might be rejected by both black and white society. But one need not look far to find religious objections to interracial relationships.

—53—

SHOULD EDUCATORS ACCOMMODATE INTOLERANCE?

Mark Halstead,[1] Homosexuality, and the Islamic Case

Michael S. Merry

... THOUGH NOT A MUSLIM HIMSELF, MARK Halstead has eloquently articulated the moral views of Muslims for a quarter of a century. In general, Halstead has attempted to elaborate the Muslim concern for nurturing commitment to a shared way of life; more particularly, he has endeavoured to demonstrate various ways in which the democratic aims of liberals—especially as they pertain to education—must take account of the moral claims of Muslims living in Western societies. The ideological interface between Muslims and liberal educators undoubtedly is strained in the realm of sex education, and perhaps on no topic more so than homosexuality. Halstead argues that schools should not try to undermine the faith of Muslims, who object to teaching homosexuality as an 'acceptable alternative lifestyle'. Rather, insofar as schools concern themselves with private values, they should adopt a neutral stance, purveying information *about* different values but not condoning one to the exclusion of the other (1999b, p. 276).

Halstead begins by positing two basic claims. First, the increasing acceptance of homosexuality in Western culture, he tells us, is due to certain philosophical assumptions. These assumptions buttress the values of liberal education and they include the unflinching support of individual freedom, equality of respect, tolerance, and a celebration of diversity. Second, Halstead insists that not all people who reject homosexuality are 'homophobic'; they simply may disagree in principle with a) an acknowledgement of a homosexual orientation, or b) 'acts' that one might associate with homosexuality. While there are several groups one might use to represent these principled objections, Halstead chooses Muslims to stand opposite the 'gay agenda', i.e., the view that sex educators ought to present homosexuality as an acceptable lifestyle. Halstead briefly acknowledges a diversity of opinion within the homosexual community, but proceeds with a portrayal of a 'gay agenda' based on what he believes are 'the beliefs and values which unite at least the majority of western homosexuals' (Halstead & Lewicka, 1998, p. 51)....

[Halstead] follows the logic of the cultural coherence model. The basic concern behind cultural coherence is the emotional and social stability of the child whose parents may adhere to a set of cultural and religious values lacking endorsement by the society in which they live. While cultural coherence may apply to *all* families, including those whose values receive widespread approval, it is especially relevant to minority communities, whose specific values and beliefs are more likely to be ignored or even forbidden in certain cultural contexts. Where education is concerned, cultural coherence theory assumes that a learning environment culturally (and/or religiously) consonant with the parents is more likely to produce healthy learning outcomes for young children and is more likely to foster a firmer sense of self. Implicitly assumed in cultural coherence theory is that parents have the fundamental right to raise their children according to their customs, beliefs and values.

The second stage to Halstead's pedagogy involves the aim of enabling 'different communities with different values and ways of understanding the world to live together in harmony and to enable each in their different ways to contribute to the well-being of the broader society' (Halstead & Lewicka, 1998, p. 62). Halstead recognizes that it is in Muslim children's best interest to be knowledgeable about certain Western attitudes toward homosexuality if they are to cultivate appropriate responses to it....

... In Halstead's own words,

> [E]ven if certain beliefs do not make sense from one's own cultural perspective, one should try to see them through the eyes of others, and this involves learning about the underlying values of others so that one can understand how certain beliefs fit into their world view. (1999a, pp. 135–136)

Halstead recognizes that his proposals are a tall order. He knows, for instance, that there is likely to be tension if a 'gay agenda' can seek to promote homosexuality as an alternative expression of one's sexual identity when conservative Muslims do not espouse beliefs capable of accommodating such views.... [He] genuinely hopes that sensitive teaching about homosexuality will lead Muslim students to be 'better informed and more sympathetic to other people's positions and may help them to clarify their own values and attitudes'. Nevertheless, throughout Halstead's argument there is the implicit assumption that Muslims *cannot* and perhaps even *should not* be encouraged to think about homosexuality empathically. This

is because he does not question the widely held view that homosexuality is morally wrong from an 'Islamic point of view'.

Halstead unequivocally asserts that Muslims 'think in terms of acts, not inclinations' (Halstead & Lewicka, 1998, p.58), thereby premising his claim that Muslims cannot *conceive* of a homosexual 'orientation' owing to its fundamental 'incoherence' within an Islamic frame of reference. Not only is a sexual orientation inconceivable, we are told that Islam also cannot abide homosexual deeds.... [T]he upshot of Halstead's constructed antagonism suggests that a) Muslims share a 'coherent and unified worldview', including a unanimous set of beliefs about homosexuality; and b) if Muslims are to receive sensitive education concerning homosexuality it ought to be presented as controversial, as something that 'some people believe'. However, before this education takes place, Muslim children must 'have been adequately initiated into the beliefs and values of their own community during primary socialisation' (Halstead & Lewicka, 1998, p. 62). Finally, c) Halstead's stark opposition presumes there to be some concerted and unified homosexual front attempting to squeeze out the hegemonic heterosexual norm. In what follows, I will argue against Halstead's odd defence[2] of an Islamic understanding of homosexuality and I will show three things:

1. Halstead endorses a questionable understanding of Islam that considers homosexuality to be forbidden;
2. He neglects gay and lesbian Muslims who are particularly vulnerable to the unrepentant hostilities of their own communities;
3. He delimits the range of options available to sex educators in such a way as to discourage genuine encounters between homosexuals and Muslims.

DISCUSSION

... [Halstead] ignores the unwarrantable conclusion that sexual orientation is supposed to follow from one's being born a man or a woman. Halstead claims that in Islam sexual identity is ultimately not a matter of being either heterosexual or homosexual. The key distinction, he tells us, is between what is permitted (*halal*) and forbidden (*haram*). Halstead expands on this:

> Islam teaches that if people have sinful desires they should keep them to themselves and control them in order to avoid doing what God has forbidden. It may, for example, be quite natural for anyone to find handsome boys attractive (and indeed the Qur'an promises that in paradise the faithful will be attended by young men like pearls: Sura 56:37 and Sura 76:19), but if this attraction becomes sexual desire it must be resisted. (Halstead & Lewicka, 1998, p. 59)

Because Halstead limits his discussion to a (particular) religious framework, he does not flesh out the cultural underpinnings of homophobia, nor does he acknowledge the relatively recent beginnings of widespread anti-homosexual attitudes within Islam. Rather he chooses to focus on what he calls 'the religious perspective', setting in terminal opposition Islam, *as a religion*, against homosexuality. In concluding that the Islamic 'worldview' cannot admit of any notion of 'orientation' but can only conceive of 'acts', Halstead permits conservative Muslim scholars to remain stubbornly indolent where there is room for Islam to expand its conception with ever-increasing knowledge and experience....

When it comes to the germane religious sources, Judaism, Christianity and Islam share many of the same narratives. Still, it is discomfiting that Halstead covers the obligatory exegesis of the Sodom and Gomorrah story without referencing alternate interpretations,[3] welcomed by many Muslims, Jews, and Christians, which suggest that the 'sin' of Sodom is not homosexuality but *inhospitality* (see Boswell, 1980, pp. 91–99), a grave offence in Near Eastern cultures....

Islam has come to inhabit many cultural spaces wherein homosexuality is commonly practised. Halstead admits to the fact (Halstead & Reiss, 2003, p. 101), though he unfailingly assumes the most orthodox Islamic view when he refers to these occurrences as 'lapses' and 'deviations'.[4] One anticipates, then, Halstead's sympathy with parents who wish to withdraw their children from sex education classes whose content may conflict with the values of the home, but he wisely acknowledges the tremendous burden such a choice invites for parents who must take up this daunting responsibility. Halstead also knows that no matter how strictly Muslim parents attempt to regulate their children's knowledge of sexuality, the formidable influences of popular culture, purveyed through various media and the hidden curriculum[5] (not excluding children taken out of the state school system and placed in comprehensive religious schools) will exert considerable influence on a child's thinking. He also knows that simplistic moralizing and Islamic prohibitions, to which many immigrant Muslim children are exposed in after-school and weekend Qur'ānic classes, will not suffice to counter these influences, nor will they be likely to appeal to the Muslim child without more culturally-sensitive lessons that take account of non-Muslim societies. Nevertheless, concerning homosexuality as a 'morally acceptable way of life', Halstead defends the right of conservative religious groups, in particular Muslims, to object to 'the gay and lesbian perspective'....

Because of the austere prohibitions against homosexuality in Islamic *teaching*, gay and lesbian Muslims must choose to live an irreconcilable double identity, repress or deny their homosexual feelings, or turn their back on Islam in order to be true to themselves....

Halstead's insistence that Muslims learn about homosexuality as a controversial subject is problematic for three reasons: first, by merely learning 'about' different opinions and experiences with no effort to foster empathy (i.e., the ability to 'take on' or profoundly relate to another's situation) and mutual respect, one can do little more than provide exposure to another point of view without cultivating respect for persons *qua* persons. Second, this approach does little to alleviate the stigmatization and fear that attend Muslim youth who identify as gay or lesbian but are unable to be public about it because that view is presented only as an option *for others*.... Muslim children might learn to show *sympathy* toward homosexuals, but Halstead does not address the needs of gay and lesbian Muslim youth who may find themselves 'trapped' by highly intolerant attitudes towards homosexuality within their own communities.

Third, Halstead's characterization of homosexuality as an 'abomination' and deserving of condemnation according to the 'Muslim worldview' not only foists a monolithic reading of homosexuality onto Islam, but it also delimits the range of topics morally acceptable to Muslims.... [What is] essential is that we consider the experiences of gay and lesbian people and consider why it is that his or her religion would appear to condemn a sexual identity so many people possess, including many within the Muslim world.[6] ...

... [C]onsidering that Halstead does recognize that Muslim children are raised according to views uncompromisingly intolerant toward homosexuality, one would hope to find him a little more sceptical of the traditions that maintain and justify anti-homosexual attitudes.... Ataullah Siddiqui asserts that many Muslim scholars trained in *madrassahs* and seminaries are 'out of touch with developments in the field of science, technology and even other areas of thought and society' (Siddiqui, 1997, p. 426). This seems a more plausible explanation for 'incoherence' from an Islamic view than any argument suggesting there not to be an implicit understanding of what is *meant* by a particular sexual orientation....

[Halstead] unequivocally states:

[A] pluralist democratic society has a duty to respect and take account of the beliefs and values of minority groups within it except where, as in the case of racist beliefs, for example, those beliefs are in conflict with the fundamental principles on which the democratic society itself is based. (1997, p. 327)

... Halstead is correct to cast aside racist beliefs as unworthy of respect, but why does he stop there? The fact that racist beliefs are abhorrent and unworthy of respect while homophobic attitudes ascribed to a religion *deserve* our respect seems astonishingly incongruent. [Also,] Halstead's attempts to 'preserve Muslim values intact within the Muslim community' unwittingly sanction *internal* intolerance as well, because some of these 'values'[7] often include militant bigotry toward homosexuals, and this will inevitably include many Muslims.

Finally, tensions persist between liberalism and illiberal communities. 'Clearly', Halstead comments, 'the state cannot both claim to welcome diversity and at the same time try to ensure that its non-liberal citizens adopt liberal values' (1999a, p. 133). Halstead assumes here that diversity and the adoption of liberal values are somehow incompatible. Yet this would only be true if the state welcomed *all* kinds of diversity, including those that systematically interfere with the freedom of others to pursue life and liberty. We know this *not* to be the case; the state does not sanction *unfettered* diversity. Still, there is another way in which Halstead, mistakenly, understands liberal values to be neutral. Halstead claims that a liberal education stresses equality of respect and refuses 'to side with any contestable conception of the good' (1999a, p. 132). I concur with Halstead that in one sense a neutral stance is necessary in order to teach controversial subject matter. Therefore, one ought to encourage students to think from multiple perspectives about stem cell research, gun control, and euthanasia but not condone or promote any particular take on this subject matter. Similarly, one ought to be just as objective concerning religious belief as one would be about homosexuality. Not only is there widespread ignorance about religions among non-religious people, but also it is unsurprising that gay and lesbian groups can be equally intolerant of conservative religious groups. As John Beck says, 'moral offence is experienced on *both* sides' (1999, p. 125).[8]

Even so, in another sense one cannot be neutral when entertaining *all* points of view. A liberal education worthy of its name simply cannot give equal time to views that tout superiority or monopolies on truth when they pertain to the basic virtues of tolerance and respect. Most liberals are also famously interested in pursuing justice and fairness, hardly a neutral position. Halstead is correct, therefore, to stress that an education for democratic citizenship necessarily entails 'the rejection of racism, prejudice, and discrimination as an affront to individual dignity' (Halstead, 2003, p. 289; cf. Halstead & Reiss, 2003, p. 160). Where Halstead's view becomes problematic is in his insistence that persons' primary identities, i.e., their religious and cultural 'commitments', are more constitutive of who they are than any identity derived from citizenship (2003, p. 280) *if* and *when* these primary identities become the bane of all that stands in the way of a liberal education....

[Stephen Macedo believes that] neutrality is a clever ruse to which no one, including liberals, can afford to acquiesce. He adds:

> Liberal education should not stand for a neutral educational environment, one that is 'nonjudgmental' with respect to the choices people make or to the forms of good and valuable lives: to the contrary, we want children to learn that there are better and worse ways to using their freedom. What is crucial from a liberal standpoint is that no one educational authority should totally dominate; that children acquire a measure of distance on all claims to truth in order to be able to think critically about our inclusive political ideals and detect conflicts between those inclusive ideals and their more particular moral and religious convictions. (Macedo, 2000, p. 238)

Macedo's point is important and Halstead would doubtless agree. Yet Halstead never actually says that Muslims ought to attain a critical distance from their beliefs or repudiate the (cultural)

prejudice of homophobia.[9] ... Halstead does not work out the tension wrought by an equality of respect for *cultures* with a concern for the equality of respect for persons. He seems to favour the former when he says, for instance, that the failure to pass on the 'beliefs and customs' of the community to the next generation has 'every appearance of the wilful self-destruction of the community' (1995a, p. 39). Though I recognize the cultural embeddedness of all persons, I am frankly more concerned with the latter and see no need to be uncritical about one's inherited culture....

EDUCATIONAL CHALLENGES

I concur with Halstead that in a pluralist society there will be many issues on which reasonable persons can and will respectfully disagree. I would also endorse Halstead's view that it is the responsibility of the common school to avoid what he calls a 'potentially oppressive situation where children are expected to accept values in school [that] are directly in conflict with their own values or those of their family' (Halstead, 1999a, p. 132). Yet to claim, as Halstead does, that the most we can hope for is 'an enlightened live-and-let-live' is to despair of fostering more than mere tolerance. It also avoids any responsibility to confront crass prejudices and hatred. Beck writes,

> Irrational prejudice against [homosexuals] should be shown to be irrational; intimidation of such minorities should be met with firm but rational sanctions and the reasons why their rights to self-expression and self-actualization ought to be upheld should be explained. (Beck, 1999, p. 127)

Furthermore, 'an enlightened live-and-let-live' falls far short of the encounter I am suggesting will be conducive to reciprocity and mutual respect. This would be an encounter where persons espousing different points of view and having different experiences can learn from one another in an atmosphere of trust and respect. Religious persons opposed to homosexuality need to encounter gay and lesbian students in an atmosphere of mutual trust and respect, just as gay and lesbian students need to encounter devout religious persons who do not approve of their sexual identification.[10] ...

... Hearing from informed Muslim students who believe[11] that heterosexual relations are only permissible within marriage will do at least three things: a) it will force children with different opinions to reflect upon the reasons why they disagree; b) it will oblige Muslim (and other religious) children to provide reasons for holding the views on sexuality that they do; and c) finally, taking this approach will engender an atmosphere of inclusion, tolerance, and mutual respect by taking account of different perspectives.[12] ...

CONCLUSION

In this article, I have challenged three aspects of Halstead's opposition of homosexuality to Islam. First, I have shown that he has not properly taken into consideration the problems associated with homophobic prejudice by leaving unchallenged the fundamentalist views of some Muslims. Many Muslims are seeking for new ways, as have Jews and Christians with their own scriptures, for understanding passages in the *hadīth* and the Qur'ān that seem to reject homosexuality. Halstead ignores the problems associated with narrow, decontextualized interpretations. Secondly Halstead does not address the problem of gay and lesbian Muslims who suffer shame and rejection from within their own communities because of these interpretations. In some cases, there is even fear of death. Halstead does not successfully reconcile his interests in children's autonomy and his defence of Islam's proscriptive disposition toward homosexuality. Finally, I have shown that Halstead's approach to teaching *about* homosexuality is too limiting and permits groups to exercise a tremendous power over Muslim young people by uncritically initiating children into a highly intolerant religious value system (Halstead & Lewicka, 1998, p. 61)....

NOTES

1. In the principal article this paper will reference, Halstead co-authors with Katarzyna Lewicka, but I shall speak only to Halstead in this paper, as his work spans more than twenty years, and he alone responds to one of the critics of the article he co-authored with Lewicka.

2. By 'defence', I do not mean that he agrees with it personally, but that he does very little if anything to challenge the view.

3. Halstead considers several interpretations in *Values in sex education* (Halstead & Reiss, 2003), but only in reference to Christianity.

4. Halstead explains that the executions of Iranian homosexuals during the Islamic Revolution between 1979–1984 probably had more to do with 'an attack on western decadence and the public transgression of morality than with homosexuality per se' (Halstead & Lewicka, 1998, p. 59).

5. The hidden curriculum, for my purposes here, will refer to the *implicit* messages conveyed to schoolchildren through the attitudes and actions of school staff, peers, and materials used in classrooms.

6. Halstead correctly notes that the number of homosexuals in Britain is roughly equivalent to the number of Roman Catholics, i.e., about 6% of the population, though this figure only reflects those who *exclusively* identify as homosexuals. See Halstead & Reiss (2003, p.160).

7. In many places Halstead refers to 'core Islamic values', 'fundamental beliefs and values' and 'distinctive beliefs and values'. See, for example, Halstead (1995a, p. 27; 2003, pp. 283, 292).

8. The reasons for this usually have to do with the malicious attitudes towards homosexuality among many conservative religious groups. One could surmise gays and lesbians to be rather indifferent to these religious groups if these groups were not so wont to cast scorn on homosexuals.

9. He does say that education for democratic citizenship would require that children be taught that 'homophobic *bullying* is always wrong, an affront to individual dignity, and a failure

to respect fundamental rights and freedoms'
(Halstead, 2003, p.292; emphasis mine).

10 I choose 'identification' over 'lifestyle' or
'preference' because the latter imply far more
choice in the matter than most people attest to *vis-
à-vis* their sexuality.

11 Of course, not *all* Muslim children believe this.

12 I am aware that this last point is controversial. It
is very possible that such encounters will have the
opposite effect.

REFERENCES

Beck, J. (1999) Should homosexuality be taught as
an acceptable alternative lifestyle? A Muslim
perspective: a response to Halstead and Lewicka,
Cambridge Journal of Education, 29(1), 121–130.

Halstead, J.M. (1995a) Towards a unified view of Islamic
education, *Islam and Christian–Muslim Relations*,
6(1), 25–43.

Halstead, J.M. (1997) Muslims and sex education,
Journal of Moral Education, 26(3), 317–329.

Halstead, J.M. (1999a) Teaching about homosexuality:
a response to John Beck, *Cambridge Journal of
Education*, 29(1), 131–136.

Halstead, J.M. (1999b) Moral education in family life:
the effects of diversity, *Journal of Moral Education*,
28(3), 265–281.

Halstead, J.M. (2003) Schooling and cultural
maintenance for religious minorities in the
liberal state, in: K. McDonough & W. Feinberg
(Eds) *Citizenship and education in liberal-
democratic societies* (Oxford, Oxford University
Press), 273–295.

Halstead, J.M. & Lewicka, K. (1998) Should
homosexuality be taught as an acceptable
alternative lifestyle? A Muslim perspective,
Cambridge Journal of Education, 28(1), 49–63.

Halstead, J.M. & Reiss, M.J. (2003) *Values in
sex education: from principles to practice*
(London, Routledge).

Macedo, S. (2000) *Diversity and distrust* (Cambridge,
Cambridge University Press).

Siddiqui, A. (1997) Ethics in Islam: key concepts and
contemporary challenges, *Journal of Moral
Education*, 26(4), 423–431.

—54—

U.S. PHARMACISTS, PHARMACIES, AND EMERGENCY CONTRACEPTION

Thomas A. Hemphill and Waheeda Lillevik

IN THE UNITED STATES (U.S.), THE DEVELOPMENT of health provider "conscience clauses" first appeared as a response to the United States Supreme Court's decision in the *Roe v. Wade* case, 410 U.S. 113 (1973), the landmark legal decision establishing that most state laws forbidding an abortion violate a constitutional right to privacy—thus voiding all state laws outlawing or restricting abortion (Flynn, 2008).[1] A "conscience" or "refusal-to-provide health care" clause is a legal or ethical codicil which allows a health care provider the right to not participate in certain professional health care activities based on personally held moral, ethical or religious beliefs. Since the *Roe v. Wade* decision, 46 of 50 state governments have subsequently passed legislation designed to allow physicians, nurses and other health care providers to refuse to perform or assist in an abortion; and 43 states allow health care institutions (including 15 states private only and one religious only) to refuse to allow abortions to take place on their premises (Guttmacher Institute, 2006a). Furthermore, professional associations, such as the American Medical Association (AMA) (2001) and the American Nurse Association (ANA) (2001), have established "conscience clauses" in their respective codes of ethics which allow for physicians and nurses not to participate in abortions on "freedom to choose" or moral grounds.[2]

In recent years, the use of "conscience clauses" has expanded beyond physicians and nurses to pharmacists, many of whom are now refusing to fill routine contraceptive prescriptions (so called "Plan A") and emergency contraceptive prescriptions (so called "Plan B") authorized by a licensed physician for his/her patients. The present policy debate, however, has centered on the issue of emergency contraception used to prevent a pregnancy, and describes several different types of birth control pills used in increased doses within seventy-two hours of unprotected intercourse.[3] While physicians and nurses are primarily employed in hospitals and private practices, pharmacists are generally employed in the for-profit sector—with the majority of pharmacies (58 percent) operated by major discount retailers, and the remainder (42 percent) independently owned drug stores (Dallard, 2005).[4] ...

The ethical (or "managerial") questions confronting the American business community regarding emergency contraceptive prescriptions are complex and contentious. Does a pharmacist have the legal and ethical right to refuse to dispense a legal drug ("emergency contraceptive") based on moral reasons ("prevents conception" or "aborts a living human being")? Are retailers ("pharmacies") required (by law or due to activist political advocacy pressure) to carry a product ("pharmaceutical") contrary to the policy established by firm management? Should a pharmacist's decision override those of the patient or the doctor who provided the prescription, i.e., should the pharmacist intervene in what may be considered the "best interests" of the patient, a decision that has already been made by both the patient and doctor? What corporate responsibility does firm management have to the pharmaceutical needs of the consumer; to meet the legal requirements of state public policy; and accommodate the ethical/moral beliefs held by the pharmacist? Pharmacists are often employees of a company or small business owners, and are state-licensed health care providers who abide by a professional code of ethics. Consequently, where does the pharmacist's allegiance to the employer end and the personal right to refuse begin? Where does the professional code of ethics pertaining to responsibility to the patient end and the individual morality of the pharmacist begin? What is the pharmacist's social responsibility as a business owner to the consumer?...

THE PROFESSIONAL ROLES OF THE PHARMACIST

Pharmacist as Professional

The primary professional association which represents state-licensed pharmacists in the U.S. is the American Pharmacists Association ("APhA")....
In 1998, APhA developed a Pharmaceutical Conscience Clause, which states:

> 1. APhA recognizes the individual pharmacist's right to exercise conscientious refusal and supports the establishment of systems to ensure patient's access to legally prescribed therapy without compromising the pharmacist's right of conscientious refusal.[5]

> 2. APhA shall appoint a council to serve as a resource for the profession in addressing and understanding ethical issues. [American Pharmacists Association, 2006]

While this "right-of-refusal" for a pharmacist is clearly stated, there is also a clear limit to this right-of-refusal, i.e., involving responsibility to the patient, as explained in the following quote from an APhA policy report:

> [P]harmacists [should] be allowed to excuse themselves from dispensing situations which they find morally objectionable, but that removal from participation must be accompanied by responsibility to the patient and performance of certain professional duties which accompany the refusal ... ensuring that the patient will be referred to another pharmacist or be channeled into another available health system.... Pharmacists and their employers will need to develop processes that support the decision of the individual pharmacists while still providing the appropriate service the patient seeks. (American Pharmacists Association, 1998; Sonfield, 2005)

Thus, the professional ethics code of the pharmacist allows for the individual exercise of conscience (to refuse to fill an emergency contraceptive prescription), but this refusal must be matched with the assurance that the patient has relatively seamless access to the emergency contraceptive prescription in a timely fashion.[6,7] ...

Pharmacist as Employee

The overwhelming majority of pharmacists in the U.S. are employees of major retailers, hospital pharmacies, or independently owned pharmacies. Unless the pharmacist is a small business owner, the pharmacist will be operating under the employment rules established by his/her employer.... One important [legal] development at the Federal level was the passage of the 1964

Civil Rights Act, especially Title VII of this Act which prevents wrongful discharge based on race, religion, sex, age, and national origin (Muhl, 2001). The aspect of "religion" in Title VII of the 1964 Civil Rights Act, as pertains to dispensing emergency contraceptives, could be relevant to employee (pharmacist) behavior and how it tracks management policy.... (Baldas, 2005).

Notwithstanding state law, which supersedes management policy, managerial guidelines concerning a pharmacist's dispensing of ethical drugs—in this case emergency contraceptives—can take three generic forms:

- An employer (pharmacy owner) can require that all pharmaceuticals kept in store stock be made available to customers by employees (pharmacists)—without exception.
- An employer can recognize that a pharmacist has a professional right not to dispense emergency contraceptives to customers (based on moral, ethical or religious convictions), but require that the pharmacist refer the prescription to another pharmacist (co worker) or manager (for referral to another pharmacist or pharmacy) so customers' needs are accommodated.
- As business policy, management can decide not to stock emergency contraceptives, thus alleviating the potential for an employee-employer confrontation over refusal-to-dispense the emergency contraceptive.

Examples of the above generic forms of management policy are extant in today's retail pharmacy environment. In 1996, Karen L. Brauer was fired from a Kmart pharmacy in Delphi, Ohio, for refusing to fill birth control prescriptions, contrary to Kmart's policy that pharmacists employed by the company must dispense all drugs stocked (Brauer, 1996; Stein, 2005). However, Rite Aid Corporation, Target Corporation, Walgreen Corporation and Winn-Dixie Stores, Inc., allow pharmacists to refuse to dispense emergency contraceptives, except where state law requires

that such pills be dispensed to a customer (Zimmerman, 2006). Walgreen's policy requires the pharmacist who refuses to dispense emergency contraceptives to notify the manager that he/she has decided not to fill the prescription, and the manager is responsible for the customer to have access to the emergency contraceptive through other means (Stein, 2005). Until March 2006, Wal-Mart, as a matter of management policy, had refused to stock contraceptive pills, although management's present policy allows a pharmacist to refuse to dispense birth control or emergency contraceptive pills (with the managerial caveat that if another Wal-Mart pharmacist is not available to dispense the prescription, another pharmacy willing to dispense the prescription will be recommended to the customer) (Zimmerman, 2006).[8]

Pharmacist as Business Owner

As stated in the introduction of this article, 42 percent of U.S. pharmacies are independently owned and operated. Many, if not most of these independently owned and licensed pharmacies are the businesses of statelicensed pharmacists.[9] The management policy of these pharmacists may be to refuse to stock and dispense emergency contraceptive pills (even if they stock other birth control pills). [Here,] the potential exists for women who rely on those independently owned-andoperated pharmacies that do not carry emergency contraceptives, specifically those who reside in rural and geographically isolated areas who may not have easy access to alternative sources, to be placed in a situation where their health can be adversely affected by not getting the prescription in a timely fashion (Dallard, 2005).

As a small business owner, what social responsibility does the pharmacist have to its customers? While there are numerous definitions of social responsibility (or corporate social responsibility (CSR)),[10] one popular definition developed by Archie B. Carroll, the Robert W. Seherer Chair of Management and Corporate Public Affairs, Terry College of Business, University of Georgia and seminal thinker in the field of business and society, is as follows:

> CSR involves the conduct of a business so that it is economically profitable, law abiding, ethical, and socially supportive. To be socially responsible ... then means that profitability and obedience to the law are foremost conditions to discussing the firm's ethics and the extent to which it supports the society in which it exists with contributions of money, time and talent. Thus CSR is composed of four parts: *economic, legal, ethical* and *voluntary* or *philanthropic*. (Carroll, 1983)

... The ethical responsibility part of the social responsibility of business, says Carroll (1998b), includes the dictum that management should "do no harm" through its business operations. Such an underlying premise of business to "do no harm" to its stakeholders relates directly to the key issue of whether a customer can have reasonable access to her (emergency contraceptive) prescription. How such a social responsibility is properly managed, i.e., whereby a customer's health is not adversely affected, will define whether this ethical responsibility has been met by the pharmacist/business owner.

Identity and Belief System

... The choice that pharmacists have in involving their personal beliefs in their daily work may be seen in whether they see themselves merely as instrumental means to execute doctors' prescriptive orders (i.e., as 'amoral technicians' (Vischer, 2006)) or whether they choose to use a reflective moral perspective, where pharmacists make decisions based on what they perceive to be their patients' true moral perspective (Vischer, 2006). Should they choose the latter, they will likely inject their own values and beliefs and exercise power and discretion into the decision already made between the doctor and patient, depending on what they feel are appropriate and inappropriate

mitigating circumstances. At the organizational level, organizational context may also contribute to resolving moral dilemmas (Moberg, 2006), as pharmacists may or may not suppress personal identity depending on their sense of identification with their employer and possible constraints such as distance of a nearby pharmacy or reason for the contraception request.... [T]hose who choose to become pharmacists are and should be aware of the possible moral and religious dilemmas that could arise within the course of their employment, and as such may be required to act within the larger constraints of the organization, profession and legislation. However ... when a pharmacist finds him/herself in a position where he/she is morally at odds with a professional decision, he/she may choose not to dispense these contraceptives by pushing the personal identity to the forefront of the decision.

Another issue with which pharmacists may have to contend regarding identity is the possible moral conflict between their personal identity and the 'common good' intent of the current legislation (Elsbernd, 2005). Common morality theory would purport that there are norms shared by all who are dedicated to the objectives of morality, or the minimizing of conditions that would diminish one's quality of life (Beauchamp, 2003).... Overall then pharmacists are governed by rules and regulations that support common morality theory. Those pharmacists who feel morally obligated to withhold emergency contraceptive prescriptions may however feel that they are contributing to the development of a more 'just and humane' community through 'correcting' what they see as an injustice (Elsbernd, 2005; Hinga, 2002) within this common morality....

The proposed legislation runs the gamut: in some states, such as Maryland, New York, Kentucky and Illinois, state-licensed pharmacists would have the right to dispense emergency contraception without a physician-issued prescription: some states would require that pharmacies stock and pharmacists dispense emergency contraceptives; and more than 20 states are considering bills that give pharmacy management the right not to stock emergency contraceptives and pharmacists the right not to dispense it....

On August 24, 2006, the FDA announced approval of Plan B emergency contraceptives as an over-the-counter option for women aged 18 and older (FDA News, 2006). Plan B will, however, remain available as a prescription-only drug for women age 17 or younger.[11] Packaging designed to hold both OTC and prescription Plan B will be stocked by pharmacies behind the counter—because it cannot be dispensed without a prescription or proof of age....

CONCLUSIONS AND RECOMMENDATION

... As Dallard (2005) notes, there are two related, yet distinct, problem areas to be addressed in this controversy; the first, whether pharmacists should be allowed to refuse to fill valid prescriptions on moral, ethical or religious grounds, and the second, what social obligation the pharmacy has to the patient/customer when its employee (pharmacist) refuses to dispense emergency contraceptives. A sub-set of this second problem area, while receiving less media attention, concerns the important management prerogative to not stock emergency contraceptives—ostensibly, in the case of Wal-Mart, for "business reasons" (Zimmerman, 2006). This latter problem area, if such a management policy is instituted by a corporation or business owner, effectively negates the former two problem areas of concern for pharmacy managers/owners.

From the vantage point of the pharmacists, the professional code of ethics developed by APhA recognized his/her right of refusal to dispense emergency contraceptives—but only if there is assurance that the patient's prescription needs are met by referral.[12] Similarly, the pharmacy manager/owner is socially responsible for "doing no harm" to a customer in the operation of the pharmacy/business, thus, the customer's timely medical needs should also be met—either by an employee/pharmacist of the pharmacy or by

referral to another pharmacy where the prescription can be filled. Public policy, whether by statute, executive order, or administrative ruling, has generally indicated that "conscience clauses" for health care personnel (including pharmacists) to refuse-to-participate should be respected. However, in no instances are such personal or managerial decisions (by, respectively, a pharmacist or pharmacy manager/business owner) intended to restrict patients from getting access to ethically prescribed drugs in a timely fashion. Where state law or regulation has established clear guidelines for access or referral for emergency contraceptives, management/pharmacy owners must comply. Yet even in states where there are such laws and regulations in place, there exist managerial interpretations (that fall under management prerogatives) which must be codified in company policy.

With the overwhelming majority of pharmacists employed by major retailers (either in discount retail store chains, e.g., Wal-Mart or Target, or pharmacy store chains, e.g., CVS or Rite-Aid) or independently owned pharmacies (by a licensed pharmacist), managing the issue of emergency contraceptives is a significant challenge for strategic/human resource management policy. To assist business owners/managers in developing a workable strategic/human resource management policy, the following set of business policy recommendations (framed within an ethical, legal and human resource management framework) is presented for managerial consideration:

- *The Business Prerogative of Not Stocking a Pharmaceutical: Design a Management System Which Refers Customers in a Timely Fashion.* The management prerogative of not stocking emergency contraceptives largely remains a business policy decision in the U.S. In 49 of 50 states there is no legal, regulatory or administrative requirement that a pharmacy stock any contraceptives (the exception being Massachusetts). Nevertheless, with the recent pronouncement by

Wal-Mart that it would now stock emergency contraceptives nationwide in its pharmacies (after an intense activist campaign that labeled the retail giant as "anti-woman"), all major retail discounters and pharmacy chains in the U.S. have made the business decision to stock emergency contraceptives (Zimmerman, 2006). This, of course, does not preclude independently owned-and-operated pharmacies in rural areas (where there may be few options to have prescriptions filled) from not stocking emergency contraceptives, creating a potential hardship for women needing such a prescription filled in a timely fashion. The ethical aspect of corporate social responsibility includes "doing no harm" to the customer; in the case of a business decision (which certainly can be based on ethical, moral or religious foundations, as well as traditional market-based considerations) not to stock emergency contraceptives, a responsible business should be able to refer a customer to another pharmacy which does stock and will dispense emergency contraceptives, or where this is not practicable, a hospital, clinic or physician where the valid prescription can be readily filled. This aligns with the notion that the best interest of the patient lies in having the necessary resources readily available irrespective of the decision made by the pharmacist in charge (Sandman & Nordmark, 2006).

- *Recognize "Conscience Clauses," But "Do No Harm" to the Consumer....* While recognizing the legal and/or professional right to not dispense emergency contraceptives to customers, management/business owners simultaneously have the responsibility to meet their customers' needs. Thus, management/business owners should require that their employees (either pharmacist or store manager) refer a customer to another pharmacy or facility (retail pharmacy, or if not easily available, health care facility or physician) which dispenses emergency

contraceptives if the pharmacy cannot fill the prescription in a timely fashion.... The professional responsibility to refer is also codified in the APhA *Pharmaceutical Conscience Clause* and is recognized as a business responsibility in the ethical component of corporate citizenship ("to do no harm" to customers).

- *Disseminate Management "Best Practices" on "Conscience Clauses" Through Joint Professional/Industry Sponsorship....* Is it a reasonable expectation for management/ business owners to ask a pharmacist who is seeking employment with a company or business what drugs they will refuse to dispense? Is it legal? In the recent case of pharmacist Neil T. Noesen, who was brought up on state administrative charges for rejecting a woman's request for a refill of a prescription for oral contraceptives (because of his moral opposition as a Roman Catholic to the use of birth control), the Wisconsin Pharmacy Examining Board found him in violation of professional statutory requirements, and, as part of his penalty, required him to provide advance written notification to employers about what pharmacy practices he will decline to perform. It may be a managerial "stretch" to move from state penalties for violations of professional practice standards to a standard practice of employers requiring information on what prescription drugs a potential new hire will not dispense. This could result in an employer violating Title VII of the Civil Rights Act of 1964, the federal statute prohibiting religious discrimination by private employers (in this case, in the process of hiring). But how far must an employer neutralize the effect of the ethical, moral or religious beliefs of an employee—in this case, a pharmacist—before it affects the performance of the business and/or the needs of the customers? This question has yet to be answered, although management/business owners have apparently been able to generally establish workable referral systems to accommodate pharmacists who refuse to dispense particular drugs. By having co-workers fill these prescription drugs (which involves managerial employee work scheduling decisions), or in certain circumstances, referring a customer to another pharmacy where access to emergency contraceptives is assured, this issue has not caused any widespread problems for customers (although there have been some scattered instances of problems) in isolated geographic areas. This issue, regarding patient/customer access to emergency contraceptives, should be handled through retail industry dissemination of business "best practices" (with joint sponsorship of "best practices" symposia by the American Pharmacists Association, National Association of Retail Druggists, National Association of Boards of Pharmacy and the National Association of Chain Drug Stores). Furthermore, discount retail chains and independently owned pharmacies should work with appropriate agencies of state government to ensure reasonable access by patients/customers to emergency contraceptives, especially in geographic locations where there are a limited number of providers of these prescriptions.

With a national shortage of professionally trained and licensed pharmacists, the retail pharmacy industry has strong market-based incentives (to complement ethical and legal incentives) to recognize the claims of conscience that will affect the work performance of their highly skilled employees.[13] Yet this issue may resonate beyond the highly contentious realm of birth control and reproductive rights that presently exists in the U.S. For example, Karen Pearl, President of the Planned Parenthood Association of America, argues:

This [conscience clauses] is a very, very slippery slope. When pharmacists become an intermediary between the patient and the doctors to impose their ideology and their position on the relationship that the doctor and the patient have very, very carefully thought about—where does that stop? (CBS News, 2005)[14]

Essentially, pharmacists are now given some latitude in intervening in other care professionals' decisions and potentially the best interests of the patient, in the name of protecting (and asserting) their personal identities and belief systems (Sandman and Nordmark, 2006).

The broader issues of conscience clauses and the lack of boundaries on to what extent such clauses should be respected by retail pharmacy management/business owners may be the next level for management to strategically address, although this will more likely than not need to be resolved through the legal and political institutions of American society. On a conceptual level, this discussion falls under the wider debate of whether common morality will be sufficient enough to allow businesses, government agencies and professional organizations to adopt and adhere to blanket policies on the availability and dispensing obligations of pharmacists.

NOTES

1   The Church Amendment, passed in 1973, prevents the U.S. government (as a condition of a federal grant) from requiring health care providers or institutions to perform or assist in abortion or sterilization procedures against their moral or religious beliefs (Sonfield, 2005).

2   According to the AMA's Principles of Medical Ethics:
VI. A physician shall, in the provision of appropriate patient care, except in emergencies, be free to choose whom to serve, with whom to associate, and the environment in which to provide medical care.
According to the ANA's *Code of Ethics for Nurses with Interpretive Statement*:
5.4 Preservation of integrity—

Where a particular treatment, intervention, activity, or practice is morally objectionable to the nurse, whether intrinsically so or because it is inappropriate for the specific patient, or where it may jeopardize both patients and nursing practice, the nurse is justified in refusing to participate on moral grounds.

3   According to the American College of Obstetricians and Gynecologists, "the primary contraceptive effect of all the non-barrier methods, including emergency use of contraceptive pills, is to prevent ovulation and/or fertilization. Additional contraceptive actions for all of these also may affect the process beyond fertilization but prior to pregnancy" (Dallard, 2005). Both these definitions view implantation in the uterine wall as the point at which a viable life begins; others believe that life begins at conception. Emergency contraception is not the same as Mifeprex, the brand name of mifepristone in the U.S. and is sometimes referred to as non-surgical abortion, or RU-486. Pharmacists do not play a role in administering these medications (National Conference of State Legislatures, 2007a).

4   There are 57,000 drug stores in the U.S. (Dallard, 2005). On average, says Dallard (2005), the independently owned pharmacies employ 2.5 pharmacists, including the small business owner....

5   In a November 18–21, 2004 *CBS News/New York Times* poll, only 16 percent of 885 adults interviewed by telephone told surveyors that they think pharmacists should be able to refuse to dispense birth control pills on religious grounds (statistical error is +/- 3 percentage points) (CBS News, 2004).

6   According to Susan C. Winkler, Vice-President, Policy and Communications and Staff Counsel, APhA, "[T]his policy works. It is only if the policy is not implemented properly that the patient or the right of conscience of the pharmacist would not both be properly acknowledged (Winkler, 2004)."

7   In June of 2005, the AMA passed a resolution at its Annual Meeting to
Support legislation that requires referral to other pharmacies if a pharmacist objects to filling a legal prescription, work with state medical societies to support legislation that would protect a patient's ability to fill a legal and valid prescription, and work with other associations to guarantee individual pharmacists' right to conscientious objection while ensuring referral to another pharmacy (Champlin, 2005a).
In October of 2006, the American Association of Family Physicians passed a resolution stating "that a pharmacist's right of conscientious objection should be reasonably accommodated" but that governmental policies must be in place to protect patients' right to obtain legally prescribed and medically indicated treatment (Champlin, 2005b)....

8   Previous to its recent change in management policy, Wal-Mart's was "to refer customers to another specific source for this prescription, just as we would for any other requested medication that we do not have available," according to the company's policy statement (Dallard, 2005: 11).

9   In the U.S., the standard practice is for state governments to license both individuals ("pharmacists") who dispense ethical drugs, as well as license and regulate sites ("pharmacies") that distribute, manufacture and sell ethical drugs (National Association of Boards of Pharmacy, 2006).

10   The issue of defining "corporate social responsibility" has been a long-standing topic of debate. For a history of this term's definitional evolution, see Carroll (1999)....

11   Proponents of those pharmacy access programs believe that minors will not see any change in those states already allowing women of any age to buy Plan B without a physicians' prescription because the pharmacist already technically writes the prescription (National Conference of State Legislatures, 2007b)....

12   In April 2005, the Wisconsin Pharmacy Examining Board, acting on a recommendation made in February 2005 by a state administrative law judge, reprimanded and limited the license of pharmacist Neil T. Noesen, for rejecting a woman's request for a refill of a prescription for oral contraceptives (Forster, 2005). The board required Noesen to

provide advance written notification to employers about what pharmacy practices he will decline to perform, and the steps he will take to be sure the patient/customer's access to necessary medications isn't impeded. Noesen was also required to pay $20,000 for the costs of the proceedings and undergo six hours of continuing education in pharmacy practice....

13   According to the National Association of Chain Drug Store Foundation (2006), there are 4,925 pharmacy and pharmaceutical industry jobs available in the U.S. as of June 3, 2006. To place this jobs figure in perspective, the Pharmacy Manpower Project (2006), located at Western University of Health Sciences, Pomona, CA, has constructed an "Aggregate Demand Index" which measures national pharmacists labor demand in the U.S. (High Surplus: 1 and High Demand: 5). According to the February 1, 2006 Aggregate Demand Index, national pharmacist demand registered 4.21 (out of 5.0).

14   According to a report from Planned Parenthood of America, a Dallas pharmacist refused to fill a mother's prescription for her son's Ritalin; a pharmacist in Denton, Texas, was fired after refusing to fill a rape victim's prescription for emergency contraceptives; and a pharmacist in North Richland Hills, Texas, refused to fill a prescription for birth control (Baldas, 2005).

REFERENCES

American Medical Association. 2001. *Principles of Medical Ethics*, adopted by the AMA's House of Delegates, June 17.

American Pharmacists Association. 1998. *1997–1998 Policy Committee Report: Pharmacists Conscience Clause*, Washington, DC.

——. 2006. *Code of Ethics for Pharmacists*. www.aphanet. org/AM/Template.cfm?Section=Pharmacy_ Pharmacy_Practice_Resources&Template ... on July 21, 2008.

Baldas, T. 2005. "The Push to Protect Pro-Life Medical Providers." *National Law Journal*, February 7.

www.aclj.org/News/Read.aspx?ID=ll 85 ... on May 14, 2006.

...

Beauchamp, T.L. 2003. "A Defense of the Common Morality." *Kennedy Institute of Ethics Journal*, 13(3), pp. 259–274.

Brauer, K.L. 1996. "K-Mart Pharmacist Fired for Refusing to Dispense Abortifacient." *Repression of Conscience*, www.consciencelaws.org/Repression-Conscience/Conscience-Repression-08.html ... on May 15, 2006.

——. 1983. "Corporate Social Responsibility: Will Industry Respond to Cutbacks in Social Program Funding?" *Vital Speeches of the Day*, 49, July 15, pp. 604–608.

——. 1998b. "Social Responsibility." In *Blackwell Encyclopedic Dictionary of Business Ethics*, ed. P.H. Werhane and R.E. Freeman. Malden, MA: Blackwell Publishers, Inc., pp. 593–595.

——. 1999. "Corporate Social Responsibility: Evolution of a Definitional Construct." *Business and Society*, (38)3, pp. 268–295.

CBS News. 2004. "Religion at the Drugstore." November 3. www.cbsnews.com/stories/2004/11/23/opinion/ polls/printables657413.shtml ... on May 15, 2006.

——. 2005. "Are Pharmacists Right to Choose." March 29. www.cbsnews.com/stories/2005/03/29/early show/ health/printable683753.shtml ... on May 14, 2006.

Champlin, L. 2005a. "AMA Acts to Protect Access to Prescriptions." *AAFP News Now*, July 22. www. aafp.org/x35982.xml?printxml ... accessed April 24, 2006.

——. 2005b. "Delegates Confirm Policy on Pharmacists Conscientious Objection." *AAFP News Now*, October 6. www.aafp.org/x38744.xml?printxml ... accessed March 30, 2006.

Dallard, C. 2005. "Beyond the Issue of Pharmacist Refusals: Pharmacies that Won't Sell Emergency Contraceptives." *The Guttmacher Report on Public Policy*, 8(3), pp. 10–12.

...

Elsbernd, M. 2005. "Social Ethics." *Theological Studies*, 66, pp. 137–158.

FDA News. 2006. "FDA Approves Over-the-Counter Access for Plan B for Women 18 and Older;

Prescription Remains Required for Those 17 and Under," August 24, U.S. Food and Drug Administration, U.S. Department of Health and Human Services, Washington, DC.

Flynn, D.P. 2008. "Pharmaceutical Conscience Clauses and Access to Oral Contraceptives." *Journal of Medical Ethics*, 34, pp. 514–520.

Forster, S. 2005. "Pharmacist Rebuked: He Refused to Refill Birth Control Prescription." *Milwaukee Journal Sentinel*, April 14. www.jsonline.com/story/index.aspx?id=318188 ... on May 15, 2005.

Giddens, A. 1991. *Modernity and Self-Identity: Self and Society in the Late Modern Age*. Cambridge: Polity Press.

Graafland, J., M. Kapstein, and C.M. v. Schouten. 2006. "Business Dilemmas and Religious Belief: An Explorative Study among Dutch Executives." *Journal of Business Ethics*, 66, pp. 53–70.

Hinga, T.M. 2002. "African Feminist Theologies, the Global Village, and the Imperative of Solidarity across Borders: The Case of the Circle of Concerned African Women Theologians." *Journal of Feminist Studies in Religion*, 18, pp. 79–86.

...

National Association of Boards of Pharmacy. 2006. *Model State Pharmacy Act and Model Rules of the National Association of Boards of Pharmacy*, January. Mount Prospect, Illinois.

National Conference of State Legislatures. 2007a. *Pharmacist Conscience Clauses: Laws and Legislation*, March. www.ncsl.org/programs/health/conscienceclauses.htm ... on November 22, 2007.

——. 2007b. *50 State Summary of Emergency Contraception Laws*, September. www.ncsl.org/programs/health/ecleg.htm on November 22, 2007.

Pharmacy Manpower Project. 2006. "Aggregate Demand Index-National Pharmacist Demand" February 2006. www.pharmacymanpower.com ... on June 3, 2006.

Sandman, L., and A. Nordmark. 2006. "Ethical Conflicts in Prehospital Emergency Care." *Nursing Ethics*, 13(6), pp. 592–607.

Sonfield, A. 2005. "Rights vs. Responsibilities: Professional Standards and Provider Refusals." *The Guttmacher Report on Public Policy*, 8(3), pp. 7–9.

Stein, R. 2005. "Pharmacists' Rights at Front of New Debate." *The Washington Post*, March 28, p. A01.

Vischer, R.K. 2006. "Legal Advice as Moral Perspective," *The Georgetown Journal of Legal Ethics*, 19 (1), pp. 225–273.

...

Winkler, S. 2004. "APhA Responds to Media Coverage: Letters to the Editor: Letter to the Editor Submitted to *Prevention* Magazine," July 1. www.aphanet.org/AM/Template.cfm?Section= Resources_ For_Reporter&Template ... on March, 22, 2006.

Zimmerman, A. 2006. "Morning After Pill Comes to Wal-Mart." *The Wall Street Journal*, March 18–19, p. A2.

THE SCHIAVO CASE AND END-OF-LIFE DECISIONS

Wally Siewert

1. BACKGROUND

ON FEBRUARY 25, 1990 FLORIDA RESIDENT Theresa (Terri) Schiavo, daughter of Robert and Mary Schindler, and wife of Michael Schiavo, suffered a cardiac arrest leading to brain damage from a lack of oxygen. During the course of the following hospitalization and attempts at rehabilitation Michael Schiavo was appointed as Ms. Schiavo's guardian and the Schindlers did not object. Over the next few years Ms. Schiavo received intensive therapy at various institutions, including experimental brain and thalamic stimulator treatments. In November of 1992 Ms. Schiavo was awarded over a million dollars in two malpractice suits against doctors involved in her treatment. Of which $300,000 went to Michael Schiavo, and another $750,000 was placed in a trust fund for Ms. Schiavo's medical care.

In 1993 Ms. Schiavo's parents and Michael Schiavo had a disagreement over the course of Ms. Schiavo's therapy. As a result, on July 29, the Schindlers petitioned the courts to have Mr. Schiavo removed as guardian for the first time. A guardian ad litem, who had no decision-making power, but who was to represent Terri's best interests before the court, was appointed. The guardian's report stated that Michael Schiavo acted appropriately and attentively towards Terri and the petition to remove Michael as guardian was later dismissed.

In May of 1998 Michael Schiavo petitioned the court for the first time to authorize the removal of Terri's feeding tube (known as a PEG tube). His petition was opposed by the Schindlers, who maintain that Terri would have wanted to stay alive. A second guardian ad litem was appointed. He agreed that Ms. Schiavo was in a persistent vegetative state without possibility of improvement, but stated that Michael Schiavo's decision making may be influenced by his prospective inheritance of her estate.

On February 11, 2000 Pinellas-Pasco County Circuit Court Judge George Greer ruled that Ms. Schiavo would have chosen not to live in such a condition and ordered the PEG tube removed. On April 24, 2001, upon the denial of several appeals, the PEG tube was removed for the first time. Two days later the Schindlers filed a new civil suit against Michael Schiavo, and the tube was re-inserted.

During the ensuing court battle the Schindlers alleged that Ms. Schiavo was abused by her husband, leading to her condition, an attempt at mediation between the Schindlers and Michael Schiavo failed, and Governor Jeb Bush filed a federal court brief in support of the Schindler's efforts. On October 15, 2003 the PEG tube was removed once again on the court's orders. On October 20 and 21 respectively, the Florida House of Representatives and Senate passed "Terri's Law," allowing the governor to issue a "one time stay in certain cases." As a result, Governor Bush issued an executive order and the PEG tube was reinserted for the second time. By this time, in addition to a maze of court proceedings, the case had become a national media event. President Bush publically praised his brother Jeb Bush's handling of the case. Pope John Paul II spoke out on "Life Sustaining Treatments and Vegetative state," defending the obligation to keep Ms. Schiavo alive. And Randall Terry, the founder of the nationally recognized pro-life group Operation Rescue, made media appearances with the Schindlers. In both the Florida and the US congresses bills were introduced which would, to varying degrees, limit the right of legal guardians in such cases to remove sustenance without the express written consent of the patient themselves.

On September 23, 2004 the Florida Supreme Court declared Terri's Law unconstitutional, and on March 18 of the following year Ms. Schiavo's PEG tube was removed for the third and final time. In the resulting scramble to have the tube re-inserted Governor Jeb Bush reported that a neurologist, Dr. William Cheshire, claimed that Ms. Schiavo was not, after all, in a persistent vegetative state. Despite this, several federal and state appeals failed and on March 31 at 9:05 a.m. Terri Schiavo died. A post-mortem revealed that she was indeed in an irreversible vegetative state.

2. ANALYSIS

There are three primary areas of ethical concern involved in the Terri Schiavo case. First is the question of decision-making procedures at the end of life. The initial consideration in such cases is always the autonomous will of the patient herself. The right of Ms. Schiavo to request the removal of her PEG tube had been established by the Nancy Cruzan case. Ms. Cruzan's feeding tube was removed and she died in December 1990, after her family presented what was considered clear and convincing evidence that this would have accorded with her wishes. Since Ms. Schiavo left no written evidence of her preferences

regarding continued treatment, or the abrogation thereof, the decision was left entirely up to her legal guardian. Michael Schiavo was Terri's legal guardian during the entire period from her cardiac arrest to her death. He maintained consistently that the removal of the PEG tube was what Terri herself would have wanted. The court's acceptance of his decisions regarding Ms. Schiavo's treatment were blocked, however, by the legal actions of her parents. Robert and Mary Schindler repeatedly claimed themselves as the rightful legal guardians, and the courts were obligated to hear their case before acceding to Mr. Schiavo's requests for euthanasia. The Schindlers also claimed that, contrary to Mr. Schiavo's testimony, their daughter would have preferred to stay alive. The court's discretion in deciding whose legal guardianship is in the best interests of an incapacitated patient placed it in a very difficult position.

The second area of ethical concern involved in the Terri Schiavo case is the question of the scope of the right to privacy. The courts were petitioned by the litigants in the case, Robert and Mary Schindler and Michael Schiavo. They were therefore rightful participants in the dispute. Governor Jeb Bush, the Florida Congress, and the US Congress were not petitioned as such and had, by some accounts, no business inserting themselves into what should have been a private decision. Others claim that the removal of the PEG tube and Terri Schiavo's subsequent death was an act against moral law, and therefore the activities of said politicians, as well as other public personalities such as Pope John Paul II and Randall Terry, were justified.

Finally we must consider the status of Terri's "right to die." While precedent has established such a right under certain circumstances, its implementation is still limited to the removal or withholding of treatment. The removal of a PEG tube commences the slow and painful process of starvation. While it is unclear if Terri could do so, it is clear that some patients who ask to die in this manner can feel this pain. Terri began this process and was abruptly re-nourished twice. If what patients in these situations seek is a "good death" (the very definition of euthanasia) would a less painful and quicker injection be preferable?

DISCUSSION QUESTIONS

1. Given clear testimonial evidence that the removal of the PEG tube is what the patient would have wanted, but lacking a written statement by the patient to that effect, should the courts and/or medical establishment allow the removal of PEG tubes, or euthanasia of any kind? What guidelines could you recommend to make such decisions easier in the future?

2. Regardless of the outcome, should end-of-life decisions be private? Does the fact that the decision involves the intentional, though presumably voluntary, ending of a life justify the involvement of politicians? Why or why not?

3. How should religious considerations factor into decisions such as the right to die? In the absence of a written order, should a patient's religious preference (provided it is known) play a role in medical decisions?

4. If you were in a persistent vegetative state, would you want be unplugged? Would you perhaps prefer an injection? Why or why not? Since we are afforded a right to die, should this right be extended to the right to die in the most humane way possible?

RELIGIOUS COMMITMENTS IN THE WORKPLACE

T.J. Broy

1. BACKGROUND

IN 2012 DAVID MULLINS AND CHARLIE CRAIG vis-ited Masterpiece Cakeshop in Lakewood, Colorado to order a wedding cake for their wed-ding reception.[1] Because same-sex marriage was not yet legal in Colorado, the couple planned to marry in Massachusetts and then celebrate their wedding with family and friends in Colorado. Expert baker and owner of Masterpiece Cakeshop, Jack Phillips, refused to sell the couple a wedding cake due to his religious commitments. Phillips is a conservative Christian and believes marriage is intended by God to be between a man and a woman. For Phillips, baking a cake for a same-sex marriage would amount to an endorsement of a celebration that runs counter to his deeply held religious beliefs.

The Colorado Anti-Discrimination Act (CADA) makes it illegal for anyone to refuse access to goods and services in a place of public accommodation due to disability, race, creed, color, national origin, ancestry, religion, sex, marital sta-tus, or sexual orientation. When violations of the CADA are alleged to have occurred, the Colorado Civil Rights Commission investigates to determine whether or not a violation has in fact taken place. If the commission determines a violation has taken place, then remedial measures (excluding fines or monetary damages) can be ordered. Mullins and Craig filed a complaint with the commission, which found Phillips had violated the CADA

when he refused to provide a cake for Mullins and Craig's wedding reception and ordered Phillips to cease and desist discriminating against same-sex couples, as well as remedial measures including staff training on the CADA and the preparation of quarterly compliance reports detailing the number of customers denied service and the reasons for such denial.

Phillips appealed all the way to the Supreme Court, which decided in his favor. The Court determined the Colorado Civil Rights Commission violated Phillips's rights under the First Amendment by displaying "clear and imper-missible hostility toward the sincere religious beliefs that motivated [Phillips's] objection [to same-sex marriage]."[2] When considering other cases where bakers had refused to decorate cakes with messages critical of same-sex marriage or containing Bible passages used to support criti-cism of same-sex marriage, the commission ruled in those bakers' favor noting that because the nature of the message was offensive, those bakers had no obligation to provide the service. When dealing with Phillips's case, one commissioner called the invocation of religious belief to justify exemption to anti-discrimination law "one of the most despicable pieces of rhetoric that people can use."[3] The Supreme Court saw this language as evidence the commission was neither fair nor impartial toward Phillips.

According to Phillips, his baking amounts to a form of artistic expression. Where in the other cases of bakers refusing to write messages on cakes, the objection was to the content of the message; in Phillips's case the objection was to the exercise of Phillips's artistic abilities in baking and decorating the cake. Whether or not the cakes were decorated with text Phillips found objectionable, Phillips sees his baking of cakes as a form of expression. To force Phillips to provide cakes would then be a case of forced expression and so a violation of Phillips's free-speech rights.

The Court did not rule that the only way to respect Phillips's First Amendment rights was to allow him to refuse service to same-sex couples. Rather, the Court ruled that the Colorado Civil Rights Commission violated Phillips's First Amendment rights in the way they treated him during the proceedings. This leaves open the possibility that a suitably neutral treatment of Phillips's case might reach the same conclusion, that he must serve same-sex and opposite-sex couples alike, and not in so doing violate his First Amendment rights.

There is little doubt that Phillips's religious beliefs are sincere. Phillips told Mullins and Craig that he would provide any other service (cookies, brownies, birthday cakes, etc.), his only objection was to a wedding cake for a same-sex wedding. Phillips also closes his bakery on Sundays, refuses to bake cakes containing alcohol, and refuses to make cupcakes for Halloween, all as a result of his religious beliefs.[4]

2. ANALYSIS

This case brings two values into tension. First, professionals should have the right to adhere to their sincere religious beliefs. Second, clients should not be discriminated against on the basis of their sexual orientation. When these two values collide, how should we decide what to do?

One might think that sincere religious beliefs amount to a reason for granting exemptions to the law so long as no one is harmed by the exemption. For example, you might think the state has good reasons for restricting alcohol use by minors. It seems likely that a child taking a sip of wine as part of a religious ceremony will not undermine those reasons. So, it seems plausible that an exemption can be made to the law banning alcohol consumption by minors so that minors can participate in certain religious ceremonies. Is this what the Masterpiece Cakeshop case is like?

Whether or not the *Masterpiece Cakeshop* case is sufficiently similar to the communion wine case will likely depend on how one understands what it is to harm someone. One might think the only way to harm someone is by depriving them of some good. Should the only baker available refuse to bake cakes for a same-sex marriage, then it is plausible to say the same-sex couple was harmed. So long as there is another baker available, however, one might think no one is harmed by the baker refusing to bake the wedding cake. On the other hand, one might think there is another type of harm besides being deprived of some good. Someone might suffer dignitary harm if they are treated unequally relative to their fellow citizens. The disrespect inherent in not treating someone like they deserve as a result of their sexual orientation might constitute a kind of harm. If there is such a category of harm, there is good reason to consider the *Masterpiece Cakeshop* case as distinct from the communion wine case. In the *Masterpiece Cakeshop* case, someone suffers dignitary harm. In the communion wine case, no one suffers dignitary harm. So, in the one case an exemption to the law is not permissible and in the other case an exemption to the law is permissible.

There are ways one might approve of some cases of a baker refusing services to a same-sex couple and yet disapprove of others. Take Phillips's argument that his baking a cake amounts to a case of expression. It seems reasonable to suppose that it would be permissible for a gay baker to refuse to print Leviticus 20:13 on a cake.[5] If this is right, then there is reason to think it would be permissible for a baker like Jack Phillips to refuse to print "Congratulations David and Charlie" on a cake for Mullins and Craig's wedding celebration. So, it might be that it is permissible for Phillips to refuse to print congratulatory messages on a wedding cake for a same-sex marriage and yet be impermissible for Phillips to refuse to sell a blank sheet cake to a same-sex couple. Plausibly, Phillips is expressing something by printing on a cake and not expressing something by ringing a transaction through a cash register.

If this analysis is correct, then it is plausible there would be some cases where a baker's right to free expression would outweigh the dignitary harm done to a same-sex couple and some cases in which the dignitary harm done to a same-sex couple would outweigh the curtailing of a baker's right to free expression. It might be that forcing a baker like Phillips to bake a custom cake is asking too much, that it amounts to a violation of the baker's First Amendment right to free expression. It might still be reasonable, however, to demand the baker sell a cake out of a catalog of standard cakes rather than create a custom cake for a same-sex wedding. The larger the gap between the baker's serving a same-sex couple and his act being an act of expression, the less harm is done to the baker. In this sort of case, the dignitary harm done to the same-sex couple might be greater than the harm done to the baker and so the baker ought to sell the standard, catalog cake.

NOTES

1 *Masterpiece Cakeshop v. Colorado Civil Rights Commission* U.S. 548 ___ (2018).

2 *Masterpiece Cakeshop v. Colorado*, p. 12.

3 *Masterpiece Cakeshop v. Colorado*, p. 13.

4 *Masterpiece Cakeshop v. Colorado*, (Thomas, J., concurring), p. 10.

5 "If a man lies with a male as with a woman, both of them have committed an abomination; they shall surely be put to death; their blood is upon them."

DISCUSSION QUESTIONS

1. How would you balance religious freedom and freedom of expression with the demands of anti-discrimination in this case?

2. Is baking a cake a form of expression? How does that affect the analysis of this case?

3. Is dignitary harm a sort of harm? How does that affect the analysis of this case?

4. Does it matter for the analysis of the case whether or not bakers are professionals? Why or why not?

PROFESSIONALISM IN A GLOBAL CONTEXT

Kyle J. Yrigoyen and Anand J. Vaidya

1. INTRODUCTION

ONE OF THE CENTRAL QUESTIONS THAT PROFESsional ethics tries to answer is: What is it to be a professional? There are two ways in which this question can be approached. On the one hand, one can take a domestic approach, where one looks at professionalism from within the purview of a given nation, such as the United States. On the other hand, one can take an international or global approach by either comparing professional standards across nations or by compiling information about professions across nations. Although the domestic approach to thinking about professions has its strengths, it is increasingly becoming the exception rather than the rule. Vast numbers of people travel and trade across international boundaries, many of whom are professionals of one kind or another. And many professions that once only existed in several countries, are now present in almost all countries: take bankers, for example. The global approach, then, appears to be better equipped at addressing the challenges that professionals face in our contemporary setting.

In the following unit of study, we look at the prospects of professional ethics in a global context. We believe that as professionals are increasingly faced with the demands of navigating a literal international landscape, the concerns and challenges associated with performing in accordance with codes of ethics is perhaps becoming more important than ever before. Faced with these challenges, we might then ask: What would professional codes in a global context look like? Will each and every profession face the same sort of challenges, or might it be that the challenges are context-dependent to each profession? After all, whatever criteria we may use to identify a profession in general, the troubles and their respective solutions may still be unique to each profession in particular.

2. CONTENTS

In the readings that follow, we look to the professions of accounting, journalism, law, engineering, social work, and medicine to examine how each deals with issues relating to an increasingly global context. Some professions already possess a rich tradition of ethical deliberation among their members, and these dispositions easily align with universally shared values at the international level. Some professions, however, may also find it challenging to adapt to the norms and demands required by differing cultural values. Such differences, it should be noted, are not always matters of mere disagreement, but rather of prioritization: for example, cultural norms of individualism and communitarianism may cause problems within professions not due to any explicit disagreement about what is considered valuable or worth doing, but rather because some groups rank the priority of norms differently than others. But this fact should not discourage us; rather, it should invite a more careful examination of the concerns and commitments that professionals face in a global context.

Vivian Weil illustrates this point well in examining a historical case in early twentieth-century Russia. By telling the story of Russian engineer Pavel Palchinsky, she portrays moral exemplars as trailblazers in the development of professional codes of ethics, noting that individuals play a role in global contexts.

In the next reading, Thomas Donaldson considers one approach to grounding the possibility of global professional codes. He does so by appealing to a minimum of universally held values; values which he thinks are shared across all cultures, in order to secure a moral foundation for a globalized professional ethics.

Once we've examined arguments for the possibility of doing professional ethics in a global context, we turn to specific professions to explore the challenges and concerns faced by professionals in their respective fields.

Curtis E. Clements et al. offer an empirical analysis of how ethical standards within the accounting profession are taking on a more nuanced international character. They cite, for example, recent trends showing successful convergence of ethical standards in the revised International Federation of Accountant's "Code of Ethics for Professional Accountants."

Michael Perkins grounds the need for international standards of journalism in both international law and the United Nation's 1948 Universal Declaration of Human Rights.

Andrew Boon and John Flood consider the normative grounding of an international code of ethics for lawyers, and the subsequent challenges that the legal profession may face due to cultural differences and globalization. Different forms of legal engagement, such as "zealous advocacy" vs. "inquisitorial" approaches, for example, find their origin in cultural norms, thus generating the difficulty of creating an international code of ethics.

Hengli Zhang and Michael Davis offer a narrative for the development of a robust code of ethics among Chinese engineers dating back to the early twentieth century and its influence leading up to the present.

Ndungi wa Mungai et al. explore the possibility, and challenges, of doing social work in Kenya within the framework of Afrocentricity. In the Kenyan context, the Afrocentric approach grounds the moral basis for doing social work in the local philosophical traditions of Africa.

Lastly, Nurbay Irmak details the moral obligations medical workers have to patients undergoing a hunger-strike, appealing to international guidelines for medical professionals. This has become a pressing issue for medical professionals that transcends merely domestic approaches to moral codes, especially since hunger-strikes are fast becoming a popular form of protest across the globe.

The unit closes with two cases studies. The first details the case of tech-company workers who refuse to work on military projects, or projects that may in the future be militarized. The second case explores the issues surrounding the arrests of journalists who are working in foreign countries in apparent efforts to prevent reporting on sensitive topics.

—55—

PROFESSIONAL STANDARDS

Can They Shape Practice in an International Context?

Vivian M. Weil

AS THE PACE OF GLOBALIZATION INCREASES—IN business, academia, communications, and professions—the question persists whether internationally accepted standards can govern activity. From one point of view, it seems easy to answer affirmatively. After all, there is enough common ground to support the rapid pace of internationalization. Why should not international standards follow? However, as new connections between countries are formed, encounters between different practices and styles, not to mention misunderstandings and conflicts, keep the question alive. Given that observers ponder whether governments can devise regulations for international business, the question of whether international professional standards can shape the practice of engineers has force.

The question has two parts: 1) can professional ethical standards that cross national borders be formulated and 2) if they can be, how can they shape practice? This response will divide into two parts. In answer to the first part, I offer an exemplar, a model of responsible engineering practice in an international context. The career of a Russian engineer who began practicing engineering just about a hundred years ago provides the model. Considering his career and what it shows about the possibility of international standards for professional engineers will lay the groundwork for answering the second part, for explaining how professional standards can shape practice in an international context.

PAVEL PALCHINSKY: AN EXEMPLAR

The story of the career of the engineer, Pavel Palchinsky, comes from a recently published volume titled, *The Ghost of the Executed Engineer*, by historian Loren Graham, based on his archival research.[1] This engineer's practice reflected a concept of engineering that has direct application to the concern with international ethical standards for engineering in business and industry. Palchinsky was born in 1875 and grew up in Kazan, a city on the Volga River. In 1893, he began his engineering studies at the Mining Institute in St. Petersburg.[2] To put himself through school, he worked as a laborer on railroads, in coal mines, and in factories; he graduated in 1900 with honors. After his graduation, his first assignment was to study the decline of coal production in Ukraine's Don Basin; 70% of Russia's coal came from the Don Basin. At a time of intense economic competition among the European powers, coal was critical for Russia's industrial expansion.

Palchinsky proceeded by collecting information on workers and mines. He discovered that the mine operators did not know the number of workers, the number of work days, or the living conditions of the workers. He had formed the principle: good industrial policy requires full and reliable statistics. Working for two years, Palchinsky put together a great wealth of information on workers' housing, population density, transportation networks, and so on. The information revealing the shameful living conditions of workers proved to be politically inflammatory and resulted in Palchinsky's transfer to Siberia. To escape the political turmoil in Russia, he eventually fled to Western Europe in 1908.

For five years, Palchinsky had a successful career as a consultant to industry in Germany, France, England, the Netherlands, and Italy. During this period, he articulated a second principle: view engineering plans in their political, social, and economic context. He became a respected specialist on world seaports, including London, Amsterdam, and Hamburg. To improve productivity and efficiency of seaport operations, he insisted, there is a need not only for cranes, rail spurs, deep sea channels, wharves, and warehouses, but also for workers' housing, schools, public transportation, medical care, recreational facilities, adequate wages, and social insurance. Palchinsky viewed each seaport as a vast system of services interlocking in such a way as to make it possible for workers to get maximum results with the least effort.

During his stay in the west, Palchinsky learned European languages and wrote articles, including pieces advising Russia how to improve as an industrial power. He recommended that Russia attend to political, social, legal, and educational contexts of industrial development. For example, he pointed to the need to straighten out legal land titles in order to build railroads and mines—a recommendation strikingly applicable in Russia today. Palchinsky offered a critique of engineering education in Russia and elsewhere, observing that as a result of the heavy emphasis on natural science, mathematics, and "descriptive technology", students emerge thinking every problem is merely technical.[3]

In 1913, Palchinsky received a pardon from the Tsar and returned to Russia. He quickly resumed his engineering career, founding two institutions, the Institute of Surface and Depths of the Earth and a journal, *Surface and Depths of the Earth*. Again Palchinsky could not avoid becoming embroiled in the turmoil of politics. He was saved from execution in 1918 as a result of a letter written to Lenin by a socialist colleague in Switzerland who knew Palchinsky's engineering work.

Released from prison in 1919, he became a valued specialist eager to help the new government, but he was also suspect for being a capable organizer and an independent expert. Palchinsky became very prominent in the All Russian Association of Engineers, and he became a professor in the Mining institute from which he had graduated. He assisted government agencies, and he wrote reports. When the Association of Engineers was forced to accept communist party control in the early 20's, he resigned. He would belong only to an independent organization.

Palchinsky criticized communist party policies related to engineering. He was critical of: 1) policies that promoted projects valuable for image rather than substance, e.g. gushing oil extraction as against coal and gas that were more economical; 2) policies that blindly endorsed centralized command and ignored local conditions; 3) blind commitment to mammoth projects; and 4) inadequate safety restrictions for the protection of workers and others, objecting that emphasis on theft, which was, in any case, illegal, took precedence over rules for safety. He was also critical of trends in the U.S., Taylorism and Fordism,[4] practices that produced mind-numbed workers as cogs in factories. He argued that an uneducated, unhappy worker would not be productive.

As Stalin became more powerful, 'gigantism'[5] carried the day and governed engineering projects, and there came a crackdown on independent engineers. Stalin reportedly said to H.G. Wells, "The engineer does not work as he would like to but as he is ordered." In 1921, Palchinsky had written that coercion of engineers would produce flawed, even "monstrous", results. For the mammoth White Sea Canal project, which was part of the first five-year plan of 1927, almost all the workers, including supervising engineers, were prisoners. Analysis for that project did not include the point that the canal would be frozen half the year and that modernizing the existing railroad would make it usable the year round. To notice that point would mean to recognize the error of building the canal. The canal was constructed with coerced labor, a "monstrous" enterprise, and the results were "monstrous".

In 1928 Palchinsky was arrested, and in 1929, having refused to confess to crimes he had not committed, he was executed in secrecy, without even a show trial. From the career of this engineer trained in the time of the Tsar, Russia today has much to learn. There are a number of lessons for us as well.

LESSONS FROM PALCHINSKY'S HISTORY

The first point is that in spite of the differences in history, government, ways of life and business between western European countries and Russia, there was nonetheless legal common ground that Palchinsky found. Legal constraints of ordinary life were intelligible across national borders; Palchinsky did not land in jail in western Europe.

The second point is that his skills and standards, technical and ethical, were transferable. He was hired as an engineer; his competence made him valuable. The specific principles of responsibility that he stressed were understood by his clients. These principles are comprehensible everywhere and serve engineers and industries well, wherever they are situated. Recall that the first principle was: gather full and reliable information about the specific situation. The second was: view engineering plans and projects in context, taking into account impacts on workers, the needs of workers, systems of transportation and communication, resources needed, resource accessibility, economic feasibility, impacts on users and on other affected parties, such as people who live downwind.

The third lesson concerns a third principle which Palchinsky evidently accepted though I do not know whether he wrote about it: engineers and their organizations must be left free enough to exercise their judgment. He understood the importance to society and to engineering of protecting the engineer's independent judgment. In the communist party's assumption of control over the engineering society, Palchinsky's story offers an example of gross interference with the ability of engineers to organize. His history also furnishes an example of the bravest, most persistent resistance to such control and of insistence on independent judgment. The history of the White Sea Canal and other mammoth Soviet projects makes very vivid the disastrous outcomes for business and government enterprises when they make it impossible for engineers to exercise independent judgment.

A fourth lesson relates to our common morality. The policy under Stalin of using coercion, even employing prisoners at every level of engineering projects, and showing no respect for the well being or lives of workers, indeed, sacrificing millions, was a violation of basic respect for human beings. We can call these violations of human rights, rights that we have by virtue of our humanity, regardless of differences in societies, when or where we live. Because of the kind of beings we are, that is, because of features that humans have in all societies, humans are entitled to be treated in certain ways and not treated in certain ways. The right not to be tortured is such a right....

Palchinsky is an exemplar of the technological talent and of the expertise (comprising technical and ethical standards, as well as knowledge) that engineers can bring to internationally-based, as well as nationally-based technological organizations. He made plain, in recommendations he set forth, what measures were required to respect the rights of workers.

ENGINEERING STANDARDS AND CODES OF ETHICS

Turning now to the question of formulating engineering professional standards for international practice, it will help to look first at the development of standards—technical, and then ethical—at the national level. A key feature of the evolution of the engineering profession in the U.S. since before the middle of the 19th century is the articulation of technical standards for practice, in continuation of patterns established earlier in France and England. Among the factors driving the formulation of such standards in the United States was the need to assure safety and reliability in the new technologies of the industrial revolution.

For instance, injuries, loss of life and property in steam boat boiler explosions eventually led to systematic research and the articulation of standards for the materials, designs, and construction of steamboat boilers. From 1831 to 1836, under the auspices of the Franklin Institute in Philadelphia, a committee of volunteers carried out a program of experiments, employing a small experimental boiler for most of the work.[6] They determined, for example, that the gauge cocks commonly used to ascertain the water levels inside boilers were not reliable indicators. Rather, a glass tube gauge was much more reliable, if kept free from sediment. Another committee, using a sophisticated tensile testing machine, investigated the strength of boiler materials. One finding was that with increase in temperature, there was a swift decrease in the ultimate strength of both copper and wrought iron, the two materials that were in use. The committee made quantitative determinations, demonstrating, for example, that the strength of iron parallel to the direction of rolling was six percent greater than in the direction at right angles to it.

The Franklin Institute issued reports on the committees' methods and findings in which it "laid down sound guidelines on the choice of materials, on the design and construction of boilers, and on the design and arrangement of appurtenances added for their operation and safety."[7] The report also made recommendations regarding provisions that any regulatory legislation should incorporate. After additional research by others that led to recommendations substantially the same as those issued in 1836 by the Franklin Institute, the United States Congress responded in 1852 with appropriate legislation to regulate steamboat boilers. Rules such as the one setting the maximum allowable working pressure for any boiler at 110 p.s.i. and the one requiring every boiler to be tested yearly at one and one-half times its working pressure became law.

In subsequent decades, engineering societies became active in formulating technical standards. They have seen their codified technical knowledge influence customer specifications and acquire legal force in government regulations. Other technical standards for engineers have been issued by such bodies as the American Concrete Institute and the American Institute of Steel Construction. It should be noted that technical standards, whether in manuals, technical codes, standards of practice, or legal rules, are both descriptive and prescriptive, and oriented toward ethical concerns—safety and reliability.

In 1912, engineering societies in the United States began to formulate codes of ethics (in precisely the period during which Palchinsky worked in western Europe), several decades after the first efforts in Britain. Those societies of 1912 are the ancestors of contemporary engineering professional societies, such as the American Society of Civil Engineers (ASCE) and the American Society of Mechanical Engineers (ASME). The evolution of engineering codes of ethics in the United States, ongoing throughout this century, has been punctuated by periods of heightened activity, as in the aftermath of World War I and World War II, and in the ferment of the 1970's. One important revision of the mid 70's was the change from enjoining engineers to have "due regard" for the public welfare to stating as Canon One in most codes that "Engineers shall hold paramount the safety, health and welfare of the public in the performance of their professional duties." Currently under discussion in some societies is the question of adding a provision addressing protection of the environment.

Ethical codes, like technical codes, respond to circumstances of practice and to problems engineers commonly encounter. At each stage in their development, ethical codes represent the judgements of a collectivity of engineering practitioners, and they in turn, help define a community of engineering professionals. A distinguishing feature of professions generally is that they are occupational groups which have organized with a commitment to serve society and have adopted ethical standards to support that commitment. In recognizing their special ethical standards, engineers identify themselves with their profession. One engineering professional society, the Institute of Electrical and Electronics Engineers, has been successful in acquiring membership and disseminating its publications internationally.

Both ethical and technical standards are part of and expressions of the expertise of engineers. The Wright brothers, working just before the promulgation of the first ethical codes, did not begin the experiments that led to their success with aircraft before they studied the codified knowledge of European predecessors and tried to obtain similar resources from the Smithsonian. They understood that such information was crucial to their safety and the safety of others. Safety is a leading ethical concern in engineering, a concern that underlies technical standards and is made explicit in codes of ethics. Hence, tables, codes, standards, and rules can be arrayed on a continuum from the technical to the ethical. All this guidance is translated into routines of practice that shape practitioners' discretionary space, while leaving room for individual judgement....

SOME OBSTACLES

Yet it might seem that differences in local conditions bar the way to developing general standards on a broad international scale. Structural engineers in earthquake prone regions have to meet standards not required elsewhere. Technical standards for certain technologies may differ across national boundaries. For example, the Chernobyl disaster revealed that standards covering containment structures for nuclear reactors in the U.S.S.R. did not match those that were in place in the United States. There appear to be differences around the world in levels of safety that are accepted in transportation, construction, pollution from chemicals in air and water, and so on. In some places, the resources to make standards affordable are available, and in other places they are not.

Confronting these differences, it is useful to notice some features of standards. First, they should not be thought of as categorical statements of the form "Do 'X'." Rather, standards should be understood as incorporating relevant local conditions in a *conditional* statement of the form, "If you want 'X', under conditions 'Y', then do 'Z'."[8] Thus, if you are an engineer designing a building for a locale that is not earthquake-prone, you can ignore certain conditions that an engineer in such a locale must take into account. There are differences in the level of risk that people in different places will live with at specific times. Those differences too can be taken account of under "conditions 'Y'." In this way, we can make sense of general standards while acknowledging differences in local conditions. At the same time, the conditional statement allows agreement on means and ends to be represented.

Second, in the clarification it provides, the conditional statement helps to deal with other quandaries. It may make it easier to see that general standards are not rigid rules making engineers into machines. And the conditional also helps to show that in leaving room for interpretation and judgment, standards are not empty and meaningless. Yet, the claims made for what standards can accomplish should be realistically modest. Standards provide rough boundaries for practice and a vocabulary for carrying on discussion. They contribute to predictability and a degree of uniformity and thereby make it possible for certain efficiencies and other benefits to be realized. The debates considered earlier offer a window on a part of the process. Given the messiness of most human undertakings, modest claims for uniformity achieved by standards should not cause surprise. The complexities of formulating and using standards are what we should expect.

CONCLUSION

For direction about what to include in engineering codes of ethics covering international practice, the principles enunciated and exemplified by Palchinsky make a good starting point. The imperative to gather full and reliable information about the specific situation is fundamental. Back in 1972, in ignorance of conditions in Japan, the Lockheed Company blundered into a bribery scheme that eventually brought down high officials of the Japanese government. For practice in countries other than one's own, this principle often requires information gathering with added dimensions, such as learning about certain business practices.

The imperative to view engineering plans and projects in context—taking into account impacts on workers, consumers, and third parties, as well as economic feasibility, resource and transportation requirements and the like—is at last gaining recognition in engineering education. It is critical to articulate this imperative for engineering practice as globalization advances and impacts are increasingly recognized to be global. It will be useful to develop routines for incorporating aspects of context.

The weight Palchinsky gave to independent judgment should be emphasized; it should not be obscured in the complexities of practice in an international context. The institutions important to the profession—engineering education, professional societies, journals and other periodicals, codes of all kinds, boards of ethical review—have an important role to play in preparing engineers to exercise judgment as professionals in global enterprises. International standards should give support to this element of professionalism, for it is ultimately critical.

In the international context, the imperative to respect human rights has special salience because of the very poor living and working conditions in countries to which global operations are spreading. Palchinsky's maxim to make it possible for workers to get maximum results with the least

effort should govern. His argument that uneducated workers living in misery are unproductive is sound. But the imperative to respect human rights cuts more deeply. Even if workers living and working in miserable circumstances could do their jobs, respect for human beings should not allow it.

Finally, Palchinsky's activities during his sojourn in western Europe provide an example of how to approach international practice. He learned European languages and published his recommendations in sources in Western Europe, as well as in sources for Russia. Palchinsky reflected on engineering education and advocated broadening it so that students learn not to see every problem as merely technical. Perhaps his experience on railroads, in coal mines, and factories, while still a student, helped him acquire the breadth of understanding he displayed as an engineer and should be considered part of his education.

There are no good reasons to think that there is a fundamental divide to prevent international standards of ethics from being formulated and shaping practice in an international context. Some transnational agreements on ethical standards have already been fashioned or are in process. Incorporating Palchinsky's insights in the education of engineering students should help to bring recruits to engineering who will appreciate the importance of international standards of professional ethics and will help formulate them.

NOTES

1   Graham, L. (1993) *The Ghost of the Executed Engineer*, Harvard University Press, Cambridge, MA, USA.

2   From recent research by a Russian historian of science and engineering, we learn that in Russia in the 19th century, there were some excellent engineering schools, among them, the Mining Institute in St. Petersburg. Tarasova, Y. (1998) "Engineering Education in Russia," English translation from an unpublished paper.

3 Graham, *The Ghost of the Engineer*, p. 14.

4 'Taylorism' is a term for a scheme that introduced time-and-motion studies as a basis for revolutionizing machine-shop practice in the U.S. in the early decades of this century. The originator of this scheme, Frederick Winslow Taylor, also "rationalized" workers' use of machinery and tools, in a system that treated workers themselves like machines. In 1913, Henry Ford introduced the assembly line, putting into practice his principle of production flow. The tasks to be performed in automobile production were divided into a series of small pieces, arranged in order. Requiring workers with minimum skills, the pieces consisted of repetitive tasks and made workers interchangeable. Soviet industrializers were attracted to "Fordism" and "Taylorism."

5 Gigantism refers to the policy of promoting and carrying out large-scale, costly projects with high visibility.

6 John G. Burke provided this history in 1966 "Bursting Boilers and the Federal Power," *Technology and Culture* 7/1: 1–23. The article won the Payson Usher prize of the Society for the History of Technology.

7 Ibid.

8 I owe this analysis to a suggestion made by my colleague Warren Schmaus.

—56—

VALUES IN TENSION

Ethics Away from Home

Thomas Donaldson

WHEN WE LEAVE HOME AND CROSS OUR NATION'S boundaries, moral clarity often blurs. Without a backdrop of shared attitudes, and without familiar laws and judicial procedures that define standards of ethical conduct, certainty is elusive. Should a company invest in a foreign country where civil and political rights are violated? Should a company go along with a host country's discriminatory employment practices? If companies in developed countries shift facilities to developing nations that lack strict environmental and health regulations, or if those companies choose to fill management and other top-level positions in a host nation with people from the home country, whose standards should prevail?

Even the best-informed, best-intentioned executives must rethink their assumptions about business practice in foreign settings. What works in a company's home country can fail in a country with different standards of ethical conduct. Such difficulties are unavoidable for businesspeople who live and work abroad.

But how can managers resolve the problems? What are the principles that can help them work through the maze of cultural differences and establish codes of conduct for globally ethical business practice? How can companies answer the toughest question in global business ethics: What happens when a host country's ethical standards seem lower than the home country's?...

BALANCING THE EXTREMES: THREE GUIDING PRINCIPLES

Companies must help managers distinguish between practices that are merely different and those that are wrong. For relativists, nothing is sacred and nothing is wrong. For absolutists, many things that are different are wrong. Neither extreme illuminates the real world of business decision making. The answer lies somewhere in between.

When it comes to shaping ethical behavior, companies must be guided by three principles.

1. Respect for core human values, which determine the absolute moral threshold for all business activities.
2. Respect for local traditions.
3. The belief that context matters when deciding what is right and what is wrong.

Consider those principles in action. In Japan, people doing business together often exchange gifts—sometimes expensive ones—in keeping with long-standing Japanese tradition. When US and European companies started doing a lot of business in Japan, many Western businesspeople thought that the practice of gift giving might be wrong rather than simply different. To them, accepting a gift felt like accepting a bribe. As Western companies have become more familiar with Japanese traditions, however, most have come to tolerate the practice and to set different limits on gift giving in Japan than they do elsewhere.

Respecting differences is a crucial ethical practice. Research shows that management ethics differ among cultures; respecting those differences means recognizing that some cultures have obvious weaknesses—as well as hidden strengths. Managers in Hong Kong, for example, have a higher tolerance for some forms of bribery than their Western counterparts, but they have a much lower tolerance for the failure to acknowledge a subordinate's work. In some parts of the Far East, stealing credit from a subordinate is nearly an unpardonable sin.

People often equate respect for local traditions with cultural relativism. That is incorrect. Some practices are clearly wrong. Union Carbide's tragic experience in Bhopal, India, provides one example. The company's executives seriously underestimated how much on-site management involvement was needed at the Bhopal plant to compensate for the country's poor infrastructure and regulatory capabilities. In the aftermath of the disastrous gas leak, the lesson is clear: companies using sophisticated technology in a developing country must evaluate that country's ability to oversee its safe use. Since the incident at Bhopal, Union Carbide has become a leader in advising companies on using hazardous technologies safely in developing countries.

Some activities are wrong no matter where they take place. But some practices that are unethical in one setting may be acceptable in another. For instance, the chemical EDB, a soil fungicide, is banned for use in the United States. In hot climates, however, it quickly becomes harmless through exposure to intense solar radiation and high soil temperatures. As long as the chemical is monitored, companies may be able to use EDB ethically in certain parts of the world.

DEFINING THE ETHICAL THRESHOLD: CORE VALUES

Few ethical questions are easy for managers to answer. But there are some hard truths that must guide managers' actions, a set of what I call *core human values*, which define minimum ethical standards for all companies. The right to good health and the right to economic advancement and an improved standard of living are two core human values. Another is what Westerners call the Golden Rule, which is recognizable in every major religious and ethical tradition around the world. In Book 15 of his *Analects*, for instance, Confucius counsels people to maintain reciprocity, or not to do to others what they do not want done to themselves.

Although no single list would satisfy every scholar, I believe it is possible to articulate three core values that incorporate the work of scores of theologians and philosophers around the world. To be broadly relevant, these values must include elements found in both Western and non-Western cultural and religious traditions....

WHAT DO THESE VALUES HAVE IN COMMON?

... Despite important differences between Western and non-Western cultural and religious traditions, both express shared attitudes about what it means to be human. First, individuals must not treat others simply as tools; in other words, they must recognize a person's value as a human being. Next, individuals and communities must treat people in ways that respect people's basic rights. Finally, members of a community must work together to support and improve the institutions on which the community depends. I call those three values *respect for human dignity*, *respect for basic rights*, and *good citizenship*.

Those values must be the starting point for all companies as they formulate and evaluate standards of ethical conduct at home and abroad. But they are only a starting point. Companies need much more specific guidelines, and the first step to developing those is to translate the core human values into core values for business. What does it mean, for example, for a company to respect human dignity? How can a company be a good citizen?

I believe that companies can respect human dignity by creating and sustaining a corporate culture in which employees, customers, and suppliers are treated not as means to an end but as people whose intrinsic value must be acknowledged, and by producing safe products and services in a safe workplace. Companies can respect basic rights by acting in ways that support and protect the individual rights of employees, customers, and surrounding communities, and by avoiding relationships that violate human beings' rights to health, education, safety, and an adequate standard of living. And companies can be good citizens by supporting essential social institutions, such as the economic system and the education system, and by working with host governments and other organizations to protect the environment.

The core values establish a moral compass for business practice. They can help companies identify practices that are acceptable and those that are intolerable—even if the practices are compatible with a host country's norms and laws. Dumping pollutants near people's homes and accepting inadequate standards for handling hazardous materials are two examples of actions that violate core values....

CONFLICTS OF DEVELOPMENT AND CONFLICTS OF TRADITION

Managers living and working abroad who are not prepared to grapple with moral ambiguity and tension should pack their bags and come home. The view that all business practices can be categorized as either ethical or unethical is too simple. As Einstein is reported to have said, "Things should be as simple as possible—but no simpler." Many business practices that are considered unethical in one setting may be ethical in another. Such activities are neither black nor white but exist in what Thomas Dunfee and I have called *moral free space*.[1] In this gray zone, there are no tight prescriptions for a company's behavior. Managers must chart their own courses—as long as they do not violate core human values....

How can managers discover the limits of moral free space? That is, how can they learn to distinguish a value in tension with their own from one that is intolerable? Helping managers develop good ethical judgment requires companies to be clear about their core values and codes of conduct. But even the most explicit set of guidelines cannot always provide answers. That is especially true in the thorniest ethical dilemmas in which the host country's ethical standards not only are different but also seem lower than the home country's. Managers must recognize that when countries have different ethical standards, there are two types of conflict that commonly arise. Each type requires its own line of reasoning.

In the first type of conflict, which I call a *conflict of relative development*, ethical standards conflict because of the countries' different levels of economic development.... The second type of conflict is a *conflict of cultural tradition*....

To resolve a conflict of relative development, a manager must ask the following question: Would the practice be acceptable at home if my country were in a similar stage of economic development? Consider the difference between wage and safety standards in the United States and in Angola, where citizens accept lower standards on both counts. If a US oil company is hiring Angolans to work on an offshore Angolan oil rig, can the company pay them lower wages than it pays US workers in the Gulf of Mexico? Reasonable people have to answer yes if the alternative for Angola is the loss of both the foreign investment and the jobs....

But there are many instances when the answer to similar questions is no. Sometimes a host country's standards are inadequate at any level of economic development. If a country's pollution standards are so low that working on an oil rig would considerably increase a person's risk of developing cancer, foreign oil companies must refuse to do business there. Likewise, if the dangerous side effects of a drug treatment outweigh its benefits, managers should not accept health standards that ignore the risks.

When relative economic conditions do not drive tensions, there is a more objective test for resolving ethical problems. Managers should deem a practice permissible only if they can answer no to both of the following questions: Is it possible to conduct business successfully in the host country without undertaking the practice? and Is the practice a violation of a core human value? Japanese gift giving is a perfect example of a conflict of cultural tradition. Most experienced businesspeople, Japanese and non-Japanese alike, would agree that doing business in Japan would be virtually impossible without adopting the practice. Does gift giving violate a core human value? I cannot identify one that it violates. As a result, gift giving may be permissible for foreign companies in Japan even if it conflicts with ethical attitudes at home. In fact, that conclusion is widely accepted, even by companies such as Texas Instruments and IBM, which are outspoken against bribery.

Does it follow that all nonmonetary gifts are acceptable or that bribes are generally acceptable in countries where they are common? Not at all. What makes the routine practice of gift giving acceptable in Japan are the limits in its scope and intention. When gift giving moves outside those limits, it soon collides with core human values. For example, when Carl Kotchian, president of Lockheed in the 1970s, carried suitcases full of cash to Japanese politicians, he went beyond the norms established by Japanese tradition. That incident galvanized opinion in the United States Congress and helped lead to passage of the Foreign Corrupt Practices Act. Likewise, Roh Tae Woo went beyond the norms established by Korean cultural tradition when he accepted $635.4 million in bribes as president of the Republic of Korea between 1988 and 1993.

GUIDELINES FOR ETHICAL LEADERSHIP

Learning to spot intolerable practices and to exercise good judgment when ethical conflicts arise requires practice. Creating a company culture that rewards ethical behavior is essential. The following guidelines for developing a global ethical perspective among managers can help.

Treat corporate values and formal standards of conduct as absolutes. Whatever ethical standards a company chooses, it cannot waver on its principles either at home or abroad. Consider what has become part of company lore at Motorola. Around 1950, a senior executive was negotiating with officials of a South American government on a $10 million sale that would have increased the company's annual net profits by nearly 25 per cent. As the negotiations neared completion, however, the executive walked away from the deal because the officials were asking for $1 million for "fees." CEO Robert Galvin not only supported the executive's decision but also made it clear that Motorola would neither accept the sale on any terms nor do business with those government officials again. Retold over the decades, this story demonstrating Galvin's resolve has helped cement a culture of ethics for thousands of employees at Motorola.

Design and implement conditions of engagement for suppliers and customers. Will your company do business with any customer or supplier? What if a customer or supplier uses child labor? What if it has strong links with organized crime? What if it pressures your company to break a host country's laws? Such issues are best not left for spur-of-the-moment decisions. Some companies have realized that. Sears, for instance, has developed a policy of not contracting production to companies that use prison labor or infringe on workers' rights to health and safety. And BankAmerica has specified as a condition for many of its loans to developing countries that environmental standards and human rights must be observed.

Allow foreign business units to help formulate ethical standards and interpret ethical issues. The French pharmaceutical company Rhône-Poulenc Rorer has allowed foreign subsidiaries to augment lists of corporate ethical principles with their own suggestions. Texas Instruments has paid special attention to issues of international business ethics by creating the Global Business Practices Council, which is made up of managers from countries in which the company operates. With the over-arching intent to create a "global ethics strategy, locally deployed," the council's mandate is to provide ethics education and create local processes that will help managers in the company's foreign business units resolve ethical conflicts.

In host countries, support efforts to decrease institutional corruption. Individual managers will not be able to wipe out corruption in a host country, no matter how many bribes they turn down. When a host country's tax system, import and export procedures, and procurement practices favor unethical players, companies must take action....

Exercise moral imagination. Using moral imagination means resolving tensions responsibly and creatively. Coca-Cola, for instance, has consistently turned down requests for bribes from Egyptian officials but has managed to gain political support and public trust by sponsoring a project to plant fruit trees. And take the example of Levi Strauss, which discovered in the early 1990s that two of its suppliers in Bangladesh were employing children under the age of 14—a practice that violated the company's principles but was tolerated in Bangladesh. Forcing the suppliers to fire the children would not have ensured that the children received an education, and it would have caused serious hardship for the families depending on the children's wages. In a creative arrangement, the suppliers agreed to pay the children's regular wages while they attended school and to offer each child a job at age 14. Levi Strauss, in turn, agreed to pay the children's tuition and provide books and uniforms. That arrangement allowed Levi Strauss to uphold its principles and provide long-term benefits to its host country.

Many people think of values as soft; to some they are usually unspoken. A South Seas island society uses the word *mokita*, which means, "the truth that everybody knows but nobody speaks." However difficult they are to articulate, values affect how we all behave. In a global business environment, values in tension are the rule rather than the exception. Without a company's commitment, statements of values and codes of ethics end up as empty platitudes that provide managers with no foundation for behaving ethically. Employees need and deserve more, and responsible members of the global business community can set examples for others to follow. The dark consequences of incidents such as Union Carbide's disaster in Bhopal remind us how high the stakes can be.

NOTE

1   Thomas Donaldson and Thomas W. Dunfee, "Toward a Unified Conception of Business Ethics: Integrative Social Contracts Theory," *Academy of Management Review*, April 1994; and "Integrative Social Contracts Theory: A Communitarian Conception of Economic Ethics," *Economics and Philosophy*, Spring 1995.

THE IMPACT OF CULTURAL DIFFERENCES ON THE CONVERGENCE OF INTERNATIONAL ACCOUNTING CODES OF ETHICS

Curtis E. Clements, John D. Neill, and O. Scott Stovall

INTRODUCTION

THE FINANCIAL ACCOUNTING STANDARDS BOARD has an expressed goal of converging U.S. Generally Accepted Accounting Principles (U.S. GAAP) with International Financial Reporting Standards (IFRS) promulgated by the International Accounting Standards Board. In recent years, we have seen numerous examples in which previous differences between U.S. GAAP and IFRS have disappeared. While we are currently nowhere near total convergence, much progress has been made in the past few years. As an example of a recent move toward harmonization of international accounting standards, in 2007 the U.S. Securities and Exchange Commission (SEC) changed a longstanding requirement by allowing foreign registrants to submit financial statements based on IFRS without the need to reconcile those statements to U.S. GAAP. There has even been recent discussion by the SEC of the possibility of allowing U.S. domestic corporations to use IFRS in annual filings with the SEC.

In a similar vein, international convergence is also occurring for *ethical* standards for professional accountants. The International Federation of Accountants (IFAC) has recently issued a revised "Code of Ethics for Professional Accountants" (IFAC Code). According to Farrell and Cobbin (2000, p. 182), the IFAC Code is "intended as a model code directed at national associations of accountants." In other words, the model IFAC Code can potentially serve as a universal code of conduct for professional accountants throughout the world and prior research suggests that the IFAC's harmonization efforts have indeed been successful.

Recent empirical evidence demonstrates that the IFAC Code has currently been adopted by slightly over 50% of IFAC member organizations (Clements et al., 2009). Clements et al.'s (2009, p. 182) analysis also indicates that "numerous non-adopting accounting organizations are striving to minimize the differences between their code of ethics and the IFAC Code and still others are planning on adopting the IFAC Code at some later date." They therefore conclude that international convergence of accounting ethical standards is currently a reality and will only increase in future years.

Even so, given that almost 50% of member organizations have not yet adopted the IFAC Code, it seems relevant to study possible explanations for such lack of participation to date. For example, thus far, the United States' American Institute of Certified Public Accountants has not adopted the IFAC Code. Why is this so? Are there differences in the environments in which adopter and non-adopter member organizations operate (e.g., cultural and socio-economic differences), that are associated with their present IFAC Code adoption decision? If one wishes to explore the efficacy of the IFAC's efforts to converge ethical standards internationally, it seems appropriate to explore possible explanations as to why member organizations have chosen to adopt or not adopt the IFAC Code.

We contend that culture is likely to play an important role in explaining why a particular IFAC member organization may or may not have adopted the IFAC Code. There is a great deal of theory in the social sciences that predicts that culture may influence choices such as the one we explore in this article. For example, institutional economics suggests that various institutions, including national culture, help establish the customs and norms that economic actors use to make choices. In sociology, culture plays a role in forming and modifying both individual and collective social interaction. We use Hofstede's (Hofstede, 1980, 2008; Hofstede and Hofstede, 2005) work that bridges organizational management literature and social anthropology to formulate measurable variable constructs that represent national cultural dimensions. Specifically, we investigate whether Hofstede's (2008) cultural dimensions are correlated with adopter/non-adopter positions with respect to the IFAC Code.

In this article, we empirically examine the influence that cultural differences may play in a national accounting organization's decision as to whether to adopt the model IFAC Code as their own. Cohen et al. (1992, p. 687) provide "a framework for the examination of cultural and socioeconomic factors that could impede the acceptance and implementation of a profession's international code of conduct." They specifically apply their analysis to the decision about whether to adopt the IFAC Code version that was current at the time of their analysis. It is important to note that Cohen et al. (1992) do not empirically test for relationships between cultural and socioeconomic factors and the IFAC Code adoption decision. Previously, Clements et al. (2008) examined socioeconomic influences on the IFAC Code of Ethics decision. However, they were unable to empirically demonstrate a significant relationship between the socioeconomic status of a national accounting organization's home country and its IFAC Code adoption decision.

In this article, we extend prior research by empirically examining how cultural factors influence the convergence of international accounting ethical standards. Our results reveal that the IFAC Code adoption decision is significantly correlated with two of the four cultural dimensions described by Hofstede (1980). Specifically, our results indicate that the IFAC Code adoption decision is significantly negatively associated with the cultural dimensions labeled Individualism and Uncertainty Avoidance by Hofstede (1980). Our results are thus consistent with the notion that a national accounting organization's IFAC Code adoption decision is influenced by various aspects of the nation's culture. Since cultural factors differ across countries, an implication of our results is that cultural differences may serve as a hindrance to the total convergence of accounting ethical standards across the world.

MOTIVATION AND EXPECTED CONTRIBUTIONS

This appears to be a virtually unexamined area of business ethics research. To the best of our knowledge, there has never been an empirical analysis of the relationship between cultural factors and national accounting organizations' decisions on whether to adopt the model IFAC Code or not. We find this surprising since Cohen et al.'s analysis, which was published in 1992, suggests the importance of such an empirical examination. With the growth of the global economy and international financial markets, we believe that examinations of cultural differences across the world are needed inputs in discussions on topics such as international harmonization of accounting standards, as well as harmonization of ethical standards.

We also believe that it is vitally important that accounting firms and practitioners (particularly those with international practices and/or multinational clients) understand the divergent ethical climates and ethical expectations of the countries in which they practice. Specifically, one might reasonably expect that the ethical obligations present in accounting practice would vary across national borders due to varying nationalistic, socioeconomic, cultural, and political concerns. For example, while it is generally accepted that the shareholder is the dominant stakeholder group for firms operating in the United States (Stovall et al., 2006), other cultures may perceive other constituents to be just as legitimate (e.g., employees and/or the environment may be viewed as a primary stakeholder in Europe). Multinational accounting firms must be able to meet the culturally dependent ethical obligations of their international practices to function effectively. Our study is a first step in the necessary process of understanding some of the cultural differences in countries across the world and the impact of those cultural differences on accounting ethical codes worldwide. This in turn will aid international accounting firms in understanding differing ethical cultures and expectations in various countries in which they practice.

THE IFAC CODE OF ETHICS

The International Federation of Accountants currently has 134 members and 24 associate member organizations. IFAC members are national accounting organizations rather than accounting firms or individual professional accountants. For example, the three IFAC member organizations in the United States are the American Institute of Certified Public Accountants, the Institute of Management Accountants, and the National Association of State Boards of Accountancy.

According to the IFAC Code, the mission of the International Federation of Accountants is "the worldwide development and enhancement of an accountancy profession with harmonized standards, able to provide services of consistently high quality in the public interest" (IFAC, 2005, p. 2). International harmonization of accounting standards, including ethical standards for professional accountants, is therefore a major objective of the IFAC. Pursuant to that aim, the IFAC issued a revised "Code of Ethics for Professional Accountants" in June 2005. As previously mentioned, Farrell and Cobbin (2000) describe the IFAC Code as a model code of ethics directed at national accounting associations. It is important to note that adoption of the IFAC Code is not necessary for membership in the IFAC. However, the IFAC Code states that "A member body of IFAC or firm may not apply less stringent standards than those stated in this Code" (IFAC, 2005, p. 2). Therefore, IFAC member organizations may adopt an organization-specific code of conduct for their members, provided that the adopted code is not "less stringent" than the IFAC Code.

HOFSTEDE'S CULTURAL DIMENSIONS AND HYPOTHESIS DEVELOPMENT

Hofstede (2008) has conducted a multi-year "comprehensive study of how values in the workplace are influenced by culture." Specifically,

> From 1967 to 1973, while working at IBM as a psychologist, he collected and analyzed data from over 100,000 individuals from 50 countries and 3 regions. Subsequent studies validating the earlier results have included

commercial airline pilots and students in 23 countries, civil service managers in 14 counties, 'up-market' consumers in 15 countries and 'elites' in 19 countries. From the initial results, and later additions, Hofstede developed a model that identifies four primary Dimensions to assist in differentiating cultures: Power Distance—PDI, Individualism—IDV, Masculinity—MAS, and Uncertainty Avoidance—UAI (Hofstede, 2008).

These four cultural dimensions have been utilized extensively in prior research efforts, both empirical and theoretical. For example, Rallapalli (1999) employs Hofstede's cultural variables in the context of the development of a global marketing ethics code, while Williams and Zinkin (2008) use these cultural dimensions in a corporate social responsibility context. Other examples include the works of Arnold et al. (2006) and Vitell et al. (1993), who each employ Hofstede's cultural framework in an ethical decision making environment.

We will next describe each of the four cultural dimensions. Included in this discussion will be the development of a research hypothesis about how each cultural dimension should impact a national accounting organization's decision about whether to adopt the model international accounting code of ethics or to retain their present organization-specific code of conduct.

Power distance (PDI)

According to Hofstede and Hofstede (2005, p. 46), power distance is defined "as the extent to which the less powerful members of institutions and organizations within a country expect and accept that power is distributed unequally." In high power distance countries, there is a clear delineation between the roles of "superiors" and "subordinates." According to Williams and Zinkin (2008, p. 213), "Societies with high power distance expect to receive and take orders from authorities."

In the context of the IFAC Code adoption decision, the International Federation of Accountants would likely be seen as an authoritative body in regards to international accounting standards, including ethical standards for professional accountants. Thus, our first hypothesis is that national accounting organizations in high power distance countries will be more likely to yield control of ethical standard setting to an authoritative international body. Hypothesis 1 may therefore be stated as:

> H_1: The greater power distance present in the culture, the more likely it is for a national accounting organization in that country to adopt the model IFAC Code of Ethics.

Individualism (IDV)

Hofstede's second cultural dimension is labeled Individualism, while the opposite of Individualism is referred to as Collectivism. Hofstede and Hofstede (2005, p. 76) define these concepts as follows:

> Individualism pertains to societies in which the ties between individuals are loose: everyone is expected to look after himself or herself and his or her immediate family. Collectivism as its opposite pertains to societies in which people from birth onward are integrated into strong, cohesive in-groups, which throughout people's lifetimes continue to protect them in exchange for unquestioning loyalty.

Typically, individuals in collectivist societies such as Japan are concerned with the impact of an action or decision on society at large or on an organization. Conversely, individuals in more individualist societies such as the United States or Canada tend to concentrate on the impact of decisions or actions on themselves or their immediate family.

In terms of the IFAC Code adoption decision, we propose that national accounting organizations in societies with a high degree of Individualism will not turn over control of the ethical standard setting process to an outside international organization, while Collectivist cultures would more readily yield to an international standard setting body. Our second hypothesis is therefore:

> H2: The greater individualism present in the culture, the less likely it is for a national accounting organization in that country to adopt the model IFAC Code of Ethics.

Masculinity (MAS)

Masculinity and its opposite Femininity comprise Hofstede's third cultural dimension. These constructs are defined as follows:

> A society is called masculine when emotional gender roles are clearly distinct: men are supposed to be assertive, tough, and focused on material success, whereas women are supposed to be more modest, tender, and concerned with the quality of life.

> A society is called feminine when emotional gender roles overlap: both men and women are supposed to be modest, tender, and concerned with the quality of life (Hofstede and Hofstede, 2005, p. 120).

In a high masculinity society, individuals would likely prefer autonomy to dependence on others. In addition, there would most likely be an aversion to following rules in high masculinity societies, especially rules mandated by an outside international organization such as the IFAC. Therefore, our third hypothesis is:

> H3: The more masculinity is present is a society, the less likely it is for a national accounting organization in that country to adopt the model IFAC Code of Ethics.

Uncertainty Avoidance (UAI)

The final cultural dimension that we will examine is labeled Uncertainty Avoidance. Hofstede and Hofstede (2005, p. 167) define uncertainty avoidance as "the extent to which the members of a culture feel threatened by ambiguous or unknown situations." Members of a high uncertainty avoidance culture would therefore prefer stable, familiar situations to new and possibly unknown situations. In other words, if one seeks to avoid uncertainty and ambiguity, then one would prefer the status quo to change. Therefore, we hypothesize that national accounting organizations in high uncertainty avoidance cultures would be reluctant to change from their current organization-specific code of ethics by adopting the IFAC Code. Hypothesis 4 can be stated as:

> H4: The more uncertainty avoidance present in the culture, the less likely it is for a national accounting organization in that country to adopt the model IFAC Code of Ethics....

CONCLUSIONS AND IMPLICATIONS

Harmonization of international accounting ethical standards is occurring and increased convergence will likely occur in future years.... In this article, our goal was to explain the IFAC Code adoption decision by employing four different dimensions of a society's culture. Our results indicate that national accounting organizations in high Individualism and Uncertainty Avoidance cultures are less likely to adopt the IFAC Code. In other words, national accounting organizations in both high Individualism and Uncertainty Avoidance societies are less likely to surrender the setting of ethical standards to an outside, worldwide organization.

An implication of our findings is that due to cultural differences throughout the world that it will be difficult, if not virtually impossible, for the IFAC to expect to gain universal acceptance of its model code of ethics. A "one size fits all" international code of conduct appears unlikely to be appropriate for all national accounting organizations since cultures vary considerably throughout the world.

Why are IFAC member organizations in cultures with high Individualism and Uncertainty Avoidance less likely to have adopted the IFAC Code? One potential answer to this question may involve the fact that the IFAC has adopted a "principles-based" approach to ethical issues in their model code of ethics. By definition, principles-based approaches to financial reporting standards or codes of ethics allow considerable latitude and the exercise of judgment among professional accountants. Such an approach is in direct contrast to a more "rules-based" approach in which standard setters provide a list of detailed rules that should be followed in particular situations. Accounting professionals in cultures with lower Uncertainty Avoidance may tolerate and even welcome the flexibility afforded by the IFAC's principles-based approach, while individuals in cultures with higher Uncertainty Avoidance scores might favor codified, standardized ethics rules which discourage or even prohibit such flexibility. For example, in addressing the issue of auditor independence, accounting professionals in cultures with lower Uncertainty Avoidance might prefer a broad, interpretable definition of independence. Conversely, professional accountants in cultures with high Uncertainty Avoidance might favor specific rules dictating when an auditor is or is not independent. These individuals might go so far as to reject the more uncertain, subjective principles-based approach outright.

The IFAC's principles-based approach to ethics may help explain why IFAC member organizations in countries with higher Individualism scores are also less likely to adopt the IFAC Code. It seems plausible to assume that a principles-based approach to setting ethics standards would require a more compromising, community-oriented approach than a more standardized, rules-based system that focuses on individual compliance.

The results of this article, which help to provide a basic understanding of cultural differences between countries and their effect on various codes of ethics that accounting firms may be subject to in their international practices, have several potential uses. First, firms performing work with multinational exposure may require practitioners to comply with several different national codes of ethics in one client engagement. Due to cultural differences, some national codes of conduct may be similar in nature, while others will likely differ, and still others may even conflict. Accounting practitioners thus need to be aware that they may face different codes of ethics across national boundaries. Second, multinational accounting firm cultures may necessitate the need for accounting firms to adapt their own internal codes of ethics to conform to the codes of the professional bodies within the countries that they operate. A firm with a decentralized, locally governed structure may find it easier to adapt to various codes of ethics across practices in several countries than a firm that has adopted a more centralized "one-firm" approach.

In response to this initial investigation into the effects of culture on the IFAC Code adoption decision, we would encourage additional research on the role that culture may play in decision making in the accounting profession. Specifically, we suggest that in addition to more investigation into decisions regarding the adoption and compliance with ethics codes, more research investigating the potential effects of national culture on accounting policy decisions is warranted. As discussed at the outset of this article, international convergence in financial accounting and reporting standards is occurring rapidly. The decision of accounting governing bodies and standard setters about whether to adopt/not adopt IFRS is currently a relevant topic worldwide. It would be interesting indeed to see whether one could generalize the effects of culture on the IFAC Code adoption choice demonstrated in this study to the IFRS adoption process as well.

REFERENCES

Arnold, D., R. Bernardi, P. Neidermeyer and J. Schmee: 2006, 'The Effect of Country and Culture on Perceptions of Appropriate Ethical Actions Prescribed by Codes of Conduct: A Western European Perspective among Accountants', *Journal of Business Ethics* 70(4), 327–340.

Clements, C., J. Neill and O. Stovall: 2009, 'An Analysis of International Accounting Codes of Conduct', *Journal of Business Ethics* 87(Suppl. 1), 173–183.

Cohen, J., L. Pant and D. Sharp: 1992, 'Cultural and Socioeconomic Constraints on International Codes of Ethics: Lessons from Accounting', *Journal of Business Ethics* 11(9), 687–700.

Farrell, B. and D. Cobbin: 2000, 'A Content Analysis of Codes of Ethics from Fifty-Seven National Accounting Organizations', *Business Ethics: A European Review* 9(3), 180–190.

Hofstede, G.: 1980, *Culture's Consequences* (Sage Publications, Beverly Hills, CA).

Hofstede, G.: 2008, 'Geert Hofstede Cultural Dimensions', http://www.geert-hofstede.com/hofstede_dimensions.php.

Hofstede, G. and G.J. Hofstede: 2005, *Cultures and Organizations* (McGraw-Hill, New York).

IFAC: 2005, 'Code of Ethics for Professional Accountants', http://www.ifac.org/Members/Downloads/2005_ Code_of_Ethics.pdf.

IFAC: 2008, 'Responses to the Member Body Compliance Program', http://www.ifac.org/Compliance Assessment/published_surveys.php.

Rallapalli, K.: 1999, 'A Paradigm for Development and Promulgation of a Global Code of Marketing Ethics', *Journal of Business Ethics* 18(1), 125–137.

Stovall, O., J. Neill and B. Reid: 2006, 'Institutional Impediments to Voluntary Ethics Measurement Systems', *Journal of Business Ethics* 66(2/3), 169–175.

Vitell, S., S. Nwachukwu and J. Barnes: 1993, 'The Effects of Culture on Ethical Decision-Making: An Application of Hofstede's Typology', *Journal of Business Ethics* 12(10), 753–760.

Williams, G. and J. Zinkin: 2008, 'The Effect of Culture on Consumers' Willingness to Punish Irresponsible Corporate Behaviour: Applying Hofstede's Typology to the Punishment Aspect of Corporate Social Responsibility', *Business Ethics: A European Review* 17(2), 210–226.

–58–

INTERNATIONAL LAW AND THE SEARCH FOR UNIVERSAL PRINCIPLES IN JOURNALISM ETHICS

Michael Perkins

[I]N THIS ARTICLE I EXAMINE THE PROFESSIONAL ethical assumptions and issues presented in the free-press guarantees of international human rights law. Human rights treaties deserve examination in this line of inquiry because they are excellent means of identifying universally recognized and accepted moral standards across cultures. As Hamelink (1999) noted,

> Despite the temptations of normative relativism and the justified suspicion about unitary value judgments, it is possible to infer people's interests from universally accepted standards. These are the standards of international human rights. Human rights provide currently the only available set of standards for the dignity and integrity of all people. (p. 264)

[I]n this article I evaluate the protection for free expression and freedom of the press in international human rights treaties. I then argue that the international legal norms for free expression make certain assumptions about the role of journalism in society and the ethical principles that will guide that journalism. Finally, I propose that local cultural conditions can frustrate even basic international and cross-cultural agreement about free expression....

INTERNATIONAL LAW AND INTERNATIONAL ETHICS

Law and ethics are both normative lenses through which the role of journalism and the news media in a society can be analyzed. Each offers a distinct focus, but they are complementary, because both law and ethics can advance the interests of societal and individual flourishing and can contribute to the resolution of conflicts. Of course, important differences also exist between law and ethics: Some valid laws might still be immoral, and law can impose sanctions against violators while ethics generally cannot. But the most significant difference for purposes of this study is that law cannot address some dimensions of human action that morality can regulate (Pojman, 2002). The old saw is largely accurate in saying that law tells us what we can and can't do, whereas ethics tells us what we ought and ought not to do; law sets a minimum standard below which our actions must not fall if we fear the opprobrium that accompanies such a violation, whereas ethics sets a higher standard to which we ought to aspire.

International law can be created a number of different ways, but the one of interest for this study is bilateral or multilateral treaties. International law arising from a signed and ratified treaty between two or more nations—whether on trade, arms control, human rights or any other subject—binds each nation just as that nation's domestic law binds it. International human rights treaties, then, are not a violation of the sovereignty of the nations that have signed and ratified the treaties, despite the rhetoric sometimes heard in international diplomatic debates. A nation is expected to respect and carry out the commitments it makes regarding human rights when it signs a treaty. This principle is captured in the Vienna Convention on the Law of Treaties (1969): "Every treaty in force is binding upon the parties to it and must be performed by them in good faith" (Article 26). In the sphere of free expression, that principle means that a nation signing a human rights treaty that protects free expression and freedom of the press in certain ways spelled out in the treaty cannot legally refuse to protect free expression and freedom of the press within its borders. Of course, free expression does not have a single, universally accepted definition, but human rights treaties worldwide that protect free expression and freedom of the press operate on the assumption that local traditions and domestic law cannot be invoked as an excuse for failing to protect free expression according to the terms of the treaty (Gross, 1978).

PRESS FREEDOM IN INTERNATIONAL LAW

The granddaddy of modern free-expression norms in international law is Article 19 of the United Nations' 1948 Universal Declaration on Human Rights, which expresses its protections in absolute terms:

> Everyone has the right to freedom of opinion and expression; this right includes freedom to hold opinions without interference and to seek, receive and impart information and ideas through any media and regardless of frontiers. (Brownlie, 1992, p. 25)

The free-press and free-expression provisions in international treaties more typically protect a broad range of news media communications while at the same time including specific exemptions to those liberties as regional circumstances or history might dictate. Article 19 of the United Nations' International Covenant on Civil and Political Rights (1966) is an excellent example of pairing broad guarantees for free expression with explicit limitations on that freedom—limitations born of the duties and responsibilities that accompany the right of free expression:

> Everyone shall have the right to freedom of expression; this right shall include freedom to seek, receive and impart information and ideas of all kinds, regardless of frontiers, either orally, in writing or in print, in the form of art, or through any other media of his choice.
>
> The exercise of the rights provided for in … this article carries with it special duties and responsibilities. It may therefore be subject to certain restrictions, but these shall only be such as are provided by law and are necessary:
>
> • For respect of the rights or reputations of others.
> • For the protection of national security or of public order or of public health and morals. (Brownlie, 1992, p. 132)

Significantly, also, Article 20 of the International Covenant on Civil and Political Rights (1966) includes two kinds of expression explicitly prohibited: "Any propaganda for war shall be prohibited by law. Any advocacy of national, racial or religious hatred that constitutes incitement to discrimination, hostility or violence shall be prohibited by law" (Brownlie, 1992, p. 132).

The two United Nations' documents share common elements—even wording—with regional human rights treaties in Europe, Latin America, and Africa. There is no regional human rights treaty in effect in Asia. The European Convention on Human Rights (1953) guarantees in Article 10:

> Everyone has the right to freedom of expression. This right shall include freedom to hold opinions and to receive and impart information and ideas without interference by public authority and regardless of frontiers. This article shall not prevent States from requiring the licensing of broadcasting, television or cinema enterprises....

FOUNDATIONAL ASSUMPTIONS

In articulating the international legal protection for free expression, these treaties make certain assumptions about human nature and the social structure in which humans flourish. First regarding the human: Human rights treaties generally, and these provisions about press freedom in particular, assume that all individuals are fundamentally equal and that individuals belonging to any minority group are not less human or deserving of less respect than anyone else (Donnelly, 1999, p. 96). All the international and the regional treaties emphasize that the right of free expression is held individually, which includes the right to receive and to circulate matters of fact and personal opinion. This emphasis on the individual as the entity vested with rights arises from the "recognition [that] the inherent dignity and ... the equal and inalienable rights of all members of the human family is the foundation of freedom, justice and peace in the world" and "that these rights derive from the inherent dignity of the human person" (International Covenant, 1966, Preamble)....

Furthermore, as regards human nature, the human rights treaties assume that humans are rational beings capable of reasoned discourse and understanding regarding their own self-interest. In other words, individuals are capable of—indeed, responsible for—choosing the conditions they want for their own well-being and flourishing....

Such a view of the individual leads logically to a second assumption inherent in human rights treaties, which is that human rights will be respected best within a democratic social order....

The democratic implication here is not necessarily of a system with multiparty parliamentary-style elections; nothing so specific is required. But generally speaking, the kind of social system required to respect individuals will also offer individuals sufficient choice in pursuing their economic, political, and social well-being. Donnelly (1998) identified the liberal state—in contrast to authoritarian regimes or communally-oriented societies—as the essential political structure for respecting human rights because such a democratic social structure is most consistent with both the respect for the individual as rights-holder and the "international normative universality of human rights" (p. 88), that is the sense of international standards and enforceability of human rights....

JOURNALISM AND HUMAN RIGHTS

Based on these assumptions about human nature and democracy, certain characteristics of the journalism envisioned by the human rights apparatus can be identified.

First, the free-expression guarantees in the treaty language cited above provide for a journalism free of censorship and other forms of governmental intervention. First and foremost, the journalism of the human rights treaties enjoys a negative liberty that acknowledges the threat to the spread of information and ideas that accompanies the accumulation of political power....

Second, the kind of journalism to be inferred from the treaties' language can be—though it is not required to be—adversarial to government in the sense that it fills the role as the Fourth Estate or a counterpoint to government. In particular, the treaties imply that sufficient "breathing space" must be granted to journalists to do their job, and as a result the reporting and writing might be aggressive, caustic, or critical—even to the point of offending those in positions of power. In short, the protection of free expression intends to create a vibrant journalism that equips citizens to make informed decisions as part of their democratic stewardship and self-determination....

The final characteristic of the journalism implied by international human rights treaties is that the news media play a systemic role within democracy that justifies the broad grant of freedom of media expression. The news media deserve the protection that the treaties provide because media inform the public of essential democratic information. Under all the international human rights treaties, freedom of the press has a dual nature: The press is protected so it can report news, information, and opinion, and the public is co-equally protected—that is, freedom of the press inheres in the public as much as in the press—because the public has a need to receive the news, information, and opinion that the press publishes (Nordenstreng, 1998; Perkins, 2002)....

In sum, the journalism that can be envisioned within the interstices of international human rights norms is a journalism largely free from government intrusion and censorship, it is a vibrant and vigorous—perhaps even aggressive—journalism, and it is a journalism that is expected to play a public-service role in a democracy to justify the broad protection it has been granted. A fairly clear principle exists then in characterizing this kind of journalism, namely, that there is a difference between the legally defined and legally accountable free press and the journalistic practices and standards not covered legally but left in the realm of professional ethics.

UNIVERSAL PRINCIPLES IN JOURNALISM ETHICS

The contours of freedom of the press canonized in the international human rights treaties and the implications it holds for the practice of journalism offer up several principles for journalism ethics than can be reliably said to transcend national or cultural boundaries.

Truthtelling. The first of these is truthtelling, the origin of which in moral philosophy is also the

origin of one foundational assumption of the human rights movement: that each individual intrinsically deserves respect. Truthtelling, in this discussion of journalism ethics under international human rights treaties, certainly includes factual accuracy, but it must include more. Because this imperative of truthtelling arises from the news media's responsibility to give readers democratically necessary information, it also must include the need to provide context for the news so as to give readers and viewers fuller meaning or understanding about particular events or information.

Included also in truthtelling, and related to context, would be the need for news media to present the news in a balanced or fair way. Intentionally one-sided, slanted, or partisan news accounts would seem to fall short of the requirement that news serve readers' and viewers' need for information they require to help structure their democratic society. Could the argument be made that this ethical requirement would be satisfied if within a city or nation newspaper readers had access to both the daily organ of the socialist workers party and the daily voice of the bankers and financial markets? Probably not under the journalism ethics inferred from the international human rights order. The freedom of expression affixes to individual journalists and publishers under the treaties (as well as individual readers and viewers, as noted previously), and it is through those individual rights that a system of free expression is created. And if legal rights attach individually under the treaties, so it would seem must the duties—moral duties—that justify the rights in the international law. So the ethics of the news media in stressing truthtelling must emphasize that all journalists and publishers must tell the truth as completely and broadly as journalistically possible in order to fulfill partially their public-service role....

Independence. The second universal ethical principle to be inferred from the human rights treaties is independence. The independence principle grows out of the treaties' legal imperative that journalism is to be free from government interference or censorship. Similarly, the ethical principle of independence addresses the clear inference that journalism operates only in the public interest: As with partisan political interests, commercial, ethnic, linguistic, religious, or other interests ought not be allowed to predominate in the practice of journalism. On a personal level, the principle of independence also addresses questions of personal integrity, such as not accepting bribes, gifts, or favors. Such compromising conflicts cloud the public service mission of journalism as envisioned by the international law. In all these ways, independence is also similar to truthtelling in at least one regard, that the presentation of news ought not to be slanted to promote or ought not to be written in service to partisan viewpoints.

Responsible freedom. The final cross-cultural ethical principle inferable under the human rights treaties is freedom with responsibility. The essential acknowledgment in this regard is the recognition by journalists that they as individuals are guaranteed legal protections on the assumption that they will use those liberties in a moral way, primarily in the broad public interest. The obverse is also a part of this principle: Individual journalists and media organizations ought not to use this freedom in a solely self-interested way. Restricting self-interest and promoting the public interest, according to the system of journalism implied by the treaties, is to be achieved through the news media's providing the public with news and information essential for self-governance and self-determination in a democratic society. The international law implies nothing about the specific stories that news outlets should provide for the public day in and day out; this principle is not a matter of daily news judgment, reporters' beats, or front-page meetings. Rather, the essential factor in freedom with responsibility is just this acknowledgment on the part of journalists that they are part of a system of journalism essential to the promotion, advancement, and perpetuation of democracy.

This is the common theme running through all these values discussed here. Truthtelling and

independence no less than responsible freedom are part of this system of democratic journalism envisioned by—or at least inferable from—the international law. The three values become a seamless web sustaining the conclusion that journalism is a kind of public calling within the system of democracy and respect for the individual that the international human rights order creates.

CULTURAL PLURALISM

This analysis of international human rights norms has inherent limitations that deserve further study. Not the least among these is the fact that the cross-culturally endorsed principles for journalism ethics discussed here are inferred from international treaties agreed to by national governments, but these principles do not necessarily arise— indeed, may never be found to exist—organically within the cultures that reside within the signatory nations. For this reason, the Western orientation of human rights treaties and the concept of free expression they contain can become problematic. The treaties logically anticipate that these principles will hold sway, but cultural traditions and practices in the many nations signing the treaties may be violated by the kind of journalism that follows these principles....

[A] nation's ratification of a human rights treaty will not necessarily change these kinds of social and cultural barriers that might be offended by the journalistic values and practices implied by the treaties. A full anthropological exploration of these cultural differences would be a diversion from the thesis of this article, but the issue of cultural pluralism is essential to mention in an effort to identify an important area for future research.

CONCLUSION

In this article I proposed that the international law protecting freedom of expression and freedom of the press provides a cross-culturally reliable foundation from which to launch a consideration of universal principles in journalism ethics. The treaties that canonize protection for human rights internationally offer the advantage of being humanistically based, regionally and globally accepted statements of moral principles.

These universal principles for journalism ethics inferable from the international human rights accords—truthtelling, independence, and freedom with responsibility—are consistent with the findings of other scholars who have pursued other methods to identify universal values in communications ethics generally. The identification of such universal principles, of course, does not mean that journalism ethics will be identical in Brazil and Belgium, or in Swaziland and Switzerland. But it is not unreasonable to consider that the culturally specific ways that journalists in different countries recognize, analyze, and address ethical dilemmas can arise from a common concern for the three principles here proposed.

REFERENCES

American Convention on Human Rights (1969). Adopted November 22, 1969, by the Organization of American States. Entered into force July 18, 1978.

Brownlie, I. (1992). *Basic documents on human rights* (3rd ed.). Oxford, England: Clarendon.

Christians, C. (1989). Ethical theory in a global setting. In T.W. Cooper, C.G. Christians, F.F. Plude, & R.A. White (Eds.), *Communication ethics and global change* (pp. 3–19). White Plains, NY: Longman.

Donnelly, J. (1998). *International human rights* (2nd ed.). Boulder, CO: Westview.

Donnelly, J. (1999). Social construction of international human rights. In T. Dunne & N. Wheeler (Eds.), *Human rights in global politics* (pp. 71–102). Cambridge, England: Cambridge University Press.

European Convention on Human Rights (1953). Adopted November 4, 1950, by the Council of Europe. Entered into force September 3, 1953.

Gross, L. (1978). International law aspects of the freedom of information and the right to communicate. In P.C. Horton (Ed.), *The third world and press freedom* (pp. 55–73). New York: Praeger.

Hamelink, C.J. (1999). Media monitoring and individual duties under international law. In K. Nordenstreng & M. Griffin (Eds.), *International media monitoring* (263–274). Cresskill, NJ: Hampton.

International Covenant on Civil and Political Rights (1966). Adopted December 16, 1966. Entered into force March 23, 1976.

Nordenstreng, K. (1998). Hutchins goes global. *Communication Law and Policy, 3,* 419–438.

Perkins, M. (2002). Freedom(s) of the press in Latin America: Reconciling societal and individual rights in international law. *Gazette: The International Journal of Communications Studies, 64*(1), 5–19.

Pojman, L. (2002). *Ethics: Discovering right and wrong* (4th ed.). Belmont, CA: Wadsworth.

Vienna Convention on the Law of Treaties (1969). Adopted May 22, 1969. Entered into force January 27, 1980.

—59—

GLOBALIZATION OF PROFESSIONAL ETHICS?

The Significance of Lawyers' International Codes of Conduct

Andrew Boon and John Flood

1. INTRODUCTION

IS A TRANSCENDENT ETHICS FOR A GLOBAL LEGAL profession feasible? Increasing activity in two areas has given credence to the idea. The first is the participation by lawyers in international deal-making and international commercial dispute resolution. In turn, this may be seen to provide the momentum for the growth of multi-national law firms and multi-disciplinary practices. The second area of activity concerns attempts to establish international codes of ethics by international bodies such as the International Bar Association (IBA) and the Council of the Bars and Law Societies of the European Union (CCBE)....

Our path through the issues is as follows. First, we examine the activity of the CCBE and IBA, the contexts in which they function, and the codes that they have produced, as case studies of the production of international codes of ethics. These two codes are among the more mature attempts in the production of international ethical codes and therefore provide sufficient material for analysis and comparison. Secondly, we ... examine the three functions of the promulgation of ethical codes that constitute their sociological comprehensiveness: the deontological function, the legitimation function and the political function, and the extent to which these provide the momentum for globalisation of lawyers' ethics.[1] We conclude with a discussion of the wider issues raised by exploring the interplay of ethics and globalisation.

2. THE COUNCIL OF THE BARS AND LAW SOCIETIES OF THE EUROPEAN UNION (CCBE)

The CCBE is the liaison body for the legal professions of the countries comprising the European Community (EC).[2] The CCBE studies questions affecting the legal profession of the Member States and formulates "solutions designed to coordinate and harmonize professional practice". It maintains contacts with other international organisations of lawyers, including the IBA, submits comments prepared by specialist committees to European institutions,[3] and maintains permanent delegations to the European Court of Justice, the Court of First Instance of the European Communities and the "European Jurisdictions of Human Rights".[4] The adoption of the "common code of conduct" in 1988 followed the promulgation of the fundamental principles of professional conduct applicable to EC lawyers in the Declaration of Perugia in 1977 and, following the decision to create a code, six years of discussion between representatives of the different legal traditions of the EC.[5] The result, the "Code of Conduct for Lawyers in the European Community", applies to the cross-border activities of lawyers within the EC and has been accepted by most of the EU professional bodies.[6] As discussed below, however, it is intended to have a wider impact than this.

The creation of the CCBE code followed the policy of the European Community towards eliminating internal restrictions on the free movement of goods and services.[7] Part of the CCBE's early agenda was the application of the directive on lawyers' services and the preparation of a directive on the exercise by lawyers of rights of establishment.[8] It necessarily brought to the fore issues of conduct, and led directly to the consideration of inconsistencies in etiquette between the European bars. These were most clearly identified, *inter alia*, as problems relating to professional privilege, specialisation and advertising, information relating to fees, the protection of the consumer of legal services and the education of young lawyers.[9] The aim of harmonisation was to be pursued by each local bar or law society in relation to the cross-border activities of EC lawyers. No date was set for the adoption of a common code by all the member associations, and the extent to which it is a realistic goal is debatable. The CCBE code is, for example, less comprehensive than the rules of conduct promulgated by the Law Society of England and Wales. In most instances, the Law Society would argue, its own rules are more extensive and detailed than the CCBE code can aspire to be. This is itself anomalous, in that the Law Society conspicuously refuses to call its own provisions "a code".[10] Were the CCBE Code to stand alone as a code for European lawyers it would reflect considerable confidence in the ability of lawyers to interpret and observe broad ethical principles, as opposed to detailed rules of conduct.[11] Conversely, a European code more detailed than the national codes would be more effective in stimulating debate in national professional associations. It would also force the pace of harmonisation, if, indeed, that is regarded by the European legal professions as a desirable end.

3. THE INTERNATIONAL BAR ASSOCIATION'S INTERNATIONAL CODE OF ETHICS AND GENERAL PRINCIPLES

The International Bar Association was founded in 1947 in New York.[12] Notionally, it brings together lawyers and bar associations from around the world but, in reality, it primarily represents elite lawyers. Its strength lies in its section and committee structure; each section reflects a broad area of work and contains a raft of committees devoted to substantive and procedural issues.[13] Despite its lack of representative status it has influence. For example, it played a signal role in promoting the establishment of a permanent international criminal court. Similarly, although the IBA has no official status in the regulation of lawyers, its effort to create an international code of ethics for lawyers reflects a strong aspiration to represent the global legal profession. There are two main components in the IBA's initiative; the Code of Ethics and the General Principles of Ethics. The IBA International Code of Ethics, which has been adopted by the Law Society (of England and Wales),[14] "applies to any lawyer of one jurisdiction in relation to his contacts with a lawyer of another jurisdiction or to his activities in another jurisdiction".[15] The General Principles of Ethics do not presume directly to affect practitioners (see Appendix). Rather, they serve as a yardstick against which members can judge the rules of their own national associations "without prejudice to the direct application of any such Code of Ethics which Member Organizations may currently have in house".[16]

Both the code and the general principles tread familiar ethical ground covering obligations of loyalty to clients, candour in general and, particularly, as part of a duty to the court. The IBA Code is an even shorter document than the CCBE Code, comprising 21 brief paragraphs, and, like the CCBE Code, it contains nothing remarkable in terms of the ethical principles espoused. Its prohibitions are often subject to national codes, for example, in relation to advertising and soliciting and the delegation of work to non-qualified personnel.[17] ...

5. THE FUNCTIONS OF INTERNATIONAL CODES

Here we identify three functions, deontology, legitimacy and politics, which capture the potential motivational forces in the production of ethical codes. We also try to excavate deeper into the problematics of ethical codes before we move onto the theorising involved.

5.1 *The Deontological Function*

The IBA's *General Principles of Ethics* is most clearly directed to ensuring that, world-wide, the codes of lawyers, and particularly the professions of Europe and North America, are brought into line. Its International Code of Ethics moves only slightly beyond the expression of broad principles, to specific instances, for example, the setting of fees, the seeking of deposits and the terms on which retainers are terminated.[18] This is not only ambitious, because the IBA has little or no regulatory muscle, it also runs counter to the attempt of the CCBE code to harmonise the ethics of European lawyers. Were lawyers working in Europe to take the IBA code seriously there would, in some small but significant areas, be a risk of "triple deontology": the home code, the CCBE code and the IBA code could all claim jurisdiction.[19] Nevertheless, the similarity between these documents is so great, and their contents so general, that this risk is negligible. To assess their validity as a framework for a universal code of ethics for lawyers, it is necessary to explore the scale of the problem of "double deontology", that is, multiple allegiances to national codes....

5.2 *The Legitimation Function*

Analysts hold very different views on the role of ethics in the evolution of legal professions. Early sociological analysis regarded the development of rules of conduct and disciplinary procedures as a prerequisite for the end state of professionalism and a necessary response to the increasing heterogeneity of the professional group. Professionalism, the control of producers of professional services by their peers, was a benign force operating in the public interest. Recent emphasis in the sociology of the legal profession is on the manipulation of markets in the self-interest of professionals.[20] Within this tradition, professional claims to ethical practice, including codes of conduct and the other paraphernalia of self-regulation, are conceived of as means to securing and retaining legal jurisdiction over preferred areas of work.[21] Their principal mode of operation is through claims of legitimacy articulated by means of a professional ideology that emphasises the responsibility for defending the rule of law and individual rights against the intrusions of the State....

The development of international codes of ethics by international lawyers may therefore be seen as an ideological claim reflecting the strategies of dominance used by the commercial clients that they serve. This reflects the increasing dominance of an internationalist ruling class whose ideology is founded on corporate liberalism and Atlantic unity, characterised by the international replication of institutions and corporate forms.[22] So powerful is this economic elite that anti-trust and competition law is inadequate at the national level, let alone in the international sphere. One of the recent strategies of the elite for addressing the perception that regulatory mechanisms are inadequate is its promotion of "international economic soft law", such as codes of conduct for international business. In general these codes can be seen as largely symbolic, "a reaction to and an attempt to contain the growing criticisms of and actions against transnational corporations from the 1960s onwards".[23]

The development of lawyers' international codes of ethics can be seen as part of a similar process of emulation. Like international businesses, international lawyers are suspicious of, even fearful of, an effective system of regulation of their activities. They produce codes to create the impression that professionalism is an adequate mechanism of control. Yet, the justification of double deontology is dubious. The confidentiality of correspondence between lawyers apart, problems do not arise in the spheres of activity, or in relation to the client groups, that are used as means of legitimating the codes. They react to the perceived absence of regulation of international lawyers but they articulate an ideology that furthers the political objectives of legal professions.

5.3 *The Political Function*

The legitimation of professional structures and professional action is not an end in itself. It is deployed in pursuit of political goals. In broader terms, the agenda of the legal profession could be seen as the furtherance of the goal of professional autonomy, and the restriction of the role of the State.[24] At a micro-political level legitimacy protects professions from incursions into their work and autonomy. The relationship between legal professions and the state can be seen as one in a condition of permanent tension. Historically, strong legal professions were influential in the broader political sphere and achieved privileges such as self-regulation because of the relative weakness of the state bureaucracy.[25] ...

What are the connections between professional aspirations and state activity? Professions such as the French and English bars, which were both well organised and founded on a prestigious medieval past had played a significant role in the evolution of the democratic liberal State.[26] Professional activities mirrored state aspirations. Thus, under imperial rule, professions co-opted local elites to the goals, standards and interests of the metropolitan centres, laying potential foundations for a global legal culture. In the new global market, governments and lawyers again share the aspiration of and opportunity for global domination. Liberal States may have eschewed overt imperial domination but, with the agglomeration of corporate power in business, and its virtual eclipse by supra-national companies, corporate imperialism now rides on the back of liberal democracy. World political movements towards democracy, in Latin America and Eastern Europe, provide ample opportunities for liberal democracy, corporatism and lawyers. Market theories of professions have moved from the national to the international sphere.[27] While in domestic markets the relationship between the State and publicly funded private lawyers is under considerable strain, in the international sphere lawyers and their national governments march in step....

Images of the beneficence of law are part of a myth of globalisation that Silbey calls the story of the enlightenment. Science and technology facilitate increasingly rational forms of social organisation, "in the end overcoming ignorance, superstition, myth, religion, and scarcity to create relative abundance, human freedom and worldwide mobility".[28] But one of the narratives of globalisation is the spectre of the increasing domination of the social and the political by economics.[29] The State itself is forced to shrink as private property is recognised as paramount: "[b]y subordinating reason and law to desire, the market narrative is a parable about lowering expectations about what collectives can or should do".[30] Governments are increasingly impatient of the attempts of law to mediate the operation of markets.

But the need for some form of political mediation becomes increasingly necessary as globalising forces produce casualties among those who cannot adapt to the demands of globalisation. The legal profession could be one such casualty and is therefore, perhaps, in a weak position to play a mediating role. There are, however, opportunities for the professions to fill a niche in the neo-liberal State and the new supra-national state systems. As in the nineteenth century, the bureaucratic machinery of the nation state, and the supra-national state system, is relatively weak in relation to the massive tasks of integration it assumes. This provides scope for professional influence, both national and transnational, particularly for the normative professions, like law, whose authority transcends its disciplinary boundaries.[31] This creates the conditions in which Johnson's view, that world-wide alliances of professional associations could provide important checks on the accumulation of state power in the interests of trade and the service of corporations, could be realised. Professions could "provide an important channel of communications with the intellectual leaders of other countries, thereby helping to maintain world order."[32] ...

6. TOWARDS A THEORY OF THE GLOBALISATION OF ETHICS

It is, of course, possible that codes of conduct exist to serve all of these purposes we have identified and more. But, motive aside, is the idea of a global ethic for legal professions realistic? Supporters of the idea acknowledge differences in the ethical codes of legal professions in the United States and Western Europe, but, as in the case of Toulmin, feel that "they are like two trains on the same track with the US train in the lead".[33] Incompatibility in key areas, including secrecy and confidentiality, advertising, conflicts of interest and contingency fees, are, he suggests, "greater in theory than they are in practice".[34] Expressed at the level of the international codes this may be so. For example, the traditional Anglo-American values of loyalty to clients, confidentiality and candour to the court, harmonising the legal profession's affiliations to clients and the judiciary, are similar elsewhere.[35] But stating these duties is one thing; their manifestation in practice differs significantly, even in relation to the most fundamental obligations....

The USA has a strong tradition of "zealous advocacy" on behalf of clients. Over a period of years it has been argued that this creates for lawyers a partisan role, and a distinctive role morality, that, in certain operations, negotiation for example, justifies the pursuit of client desires irrespective of their validity or conduct implications.[36] Similarly, there have been debates about the role of lawyers in the empowerment of clients through collaborative decision making. In the UK, in contrast, these debates are more muted, if they exist at all.[37] Practice Rule 1, the cornerstone of the solicitors' code, talks of a duty to act in the client's best interests, there are specific provisions in the code against pursuing certain client goals[38] and, recently, a clear indication that the public interest is the key to interpreting conflicting principles of conduct.[39] The fact that the American Bar Association has softened the obligation of "zeal", and that streams of academics have opposed the more extreme claims made for role-morality,[40] cannot disguise the deep roots of partisanship in the United States. We must confront a number of possibilities here. Do lawyers in the United Kingdom have a more paternalistic attitude towards clients? Is the identity of European lawyers less likely to be collapsed into that of their clients than in the USA? Or are the processes of lawyer/client interaction in the USA and Europe substantially different even though the results for clients are the same? Each possibility suggests significant differences in the ethical stance of lawyers in Europe and the United States. It is likely however, that these and other differences are found amongst the European countries.

It is not credible to imagine that the practice cultures that underlie the codes of lawyers can be changed by diktat. The ethics of the legal professions of different countries are deeply rooted, reflecting different conceptions of the judicial process and its purpose, different theories and ideologies about procedure and substantive justice and different ideologies relating to the role of judges and legal professionals. The ethics of any particular legal profession will be pitched at a point along a continuum marked by obligations to protect client interests to the exclusion of other interests,[41] and wider obligations to administer and to facilitate the operation of law.[42]

In the western democracies, we surmise, the ethical orientation of different legal professions varies greatly, producing different responses to standard hypotheticals applying the same rules. If this is not sufficiently problematic for the prospect of a "universal ethic", the fact that the three main legal cultures of the world, Common Law, Civil Law and Islamic Law, produce legal professions

with profoundly different traditions surely is....
The interjection of culture represents a significant
constraint on the evolution of a universal ethic for
legal professions.[43] ...

8. CONCLUSION

... In this article, we have attempted to broaden the
notion of globalisation typically articulated in legal
professional discourse. In terms of the international codes, we identify the relative absence of
discourse as the barrier to the opportunity for the
globalisation of professional ethics presented by
the growing practice of international law. This is
reflected in the absence of mechanisms to legitimate ethical norms through consulting groups
marginal to their formation, and the absence of
any attempt to universalise such norms through
educational activity. We speculate that, at present,
the international codes operate at a symbolic and
ideological level. If they are to become more, legal
professions must seek new ways to articulate, legitimate and transmit their ethical vision.

APPENDIX: THE INTERNATIONAL BAR ASSOCIATION GENERAL PRINCIPLES

These General Principles were drafted by the
Professional Ethics Standing Committee of the IBA
and were endorsed by a number of IBA member
organizations. The principles state that:

1. Lawyers shall at all times maintain the highest
   standards of honesty and integrity towards all
   those with whom they come into contact.
2. Lawyers shall treat the interests of their
   clients as paramount, subject always to
   their duties to the Court and the interests of
   justice, to observe the law and to maintain
   ethical standards.
3. Lawyers shall honour any undertaking given
   in the course of their practice, until the
   undertaking is performed, released or excused.
4. Lawyers shall not place themselves in a
   position in which their clients' interests

conflict with those of themselves, their
partners or another client.
5. Lawyers shall at all times maintain
   confidentiality regarding the affairs of their
   present or former clients, unless otherwise
   required by law.
6. Lawyers shall respect the freedom of clients to
   be represented by the lawyer of their choice.
7. Lawyers shall account faithfully for any of
   their clients' money which comes into their
   possession, and shall keep it separate from
   their own money.
8. Lawyers shall maintain sufficient
   independence to allow them to give their
   clients unbiased advice.
9. Lawyers shall give their clients unbiased
   opinion as to the likelihood of success of their
   case and shall not generate unnecessary work.
10. Lawyers shall use their best efforts to carry
    out work in a competent and timely manner,
    and shall not take on work which they do not
    reasonably believe they will be able to carry
    out in that manner.
11. Lawyers are entitled to a reasonable fee for
    their work. A demand for fees should not be
    a condition of the lawyer carrying out the
    necessary work if made at an unreasonable
    time or in an unreasonable manner.
12. Lawyers shall always behave towards their
    colleagues with integrity, fairness and respect.

NOTES

1   There has been a recent increase in attention to
    the issue of how codes of ethics might best be
    analysed and compared (see D. Nicolson, "Mapping
    Professional Legal Ethics: The Form and Focus
    of the Codes" [1998] *Legal Ethics* 51 and L.E. De
    Groot-Van Leeuwen & W.T. De Groot, "Studying
    Codes of Conduct: A Descriptive Framework for
    Comparative Research" [1998] *Legal Ethics* 155). We
    have not adopted the structures outlined by these
    authors but agree broadly that production, audience,
    focus, communication and function are central.

It will be seen that this article deals with these issues pervasively.

2. The professions originally represented were *Avocat/Advocaat/Rechtsanwald* (Belgium), *Advokat* (Denmark), *Avocat* (France), *Rechtsanwalt* (Germany), *Dikigoros* (Greece), Barrister or Solicitor (Ireland), *Avvocato* or *Procuratore* (Italy), *Avocat-Avoué/Rechtsanwalt* (Luxembourg), *Advocaat* (Netherlands), *Advogado* (Portugal), *Abogado* (Spain), Advocate, Barrister or Solicitor (United Kingdom). The Bars of Austria, Cyprus, Finland, Norway, Sweden, Switzerland and Czechoslovakia had observer status (CCBE pamphlet, 1992).

3. "... on such subjects as competition and intellectual property, company law and lawyers' pensions" (*id.*).

4. *Id.*

5. See L.S. Terry, "An Introduction to the European Community's Legal Ethics Code Part 1: An Analysis of the CCBE's Code of Conduct" (1993) 7 *Georgetown Journal of Legal Ethics* 1 for a detailed account of the process of drafting the code, starting with a draft prepared by a Scottish solicitor in 1983, and J. Toulmin, "Ethical Rules and Professional Ideologies", Paper for the Cornell Law School seminar in Paris, 4–5 July 1997 at p.13.

6. "CCBE Code of Conduct for Lawyers in the European Community" in N. Taylor (ed), *The Guide to the Professional Conduct of Solicitors* (7th edn., London, Law Society, 1996), p.172 and para. 1.5.

7. The CCBE Code refers to the "... continued integration of the European Community and the increasing frequency of the cross-border activities of lawyers within the community ..." (Preamble, para. 1.3). The Services Directive (EC Directive of 1977 on Lawyers' Services) permits the rendering of occasional legal services in the host State rather than establishment. The Diplomas Directive (EC Directive of 1989 on Mutual Recognition of Diplomas) provides for the recognition of legal qualifications gained in one EU State in another EU State subject to either an aptitude test or adaptation period (most States have opted for the latter).

8. *Supra* n. [2].

9. *Id.*

10. Hence the *"Guide", supra* n. [6].

11. Terry, *supra* n. [5], and "An Introduction to the European Community's Legal Ethics Code Part II" (1993) 7 *Georgetown Journal of Legal Ethics* 348.

12. See the IBA Website at http://www.ibanet.org.

13. For example, Committee J of the Section on Business Law has been central to the adoption of international practices relating to cross-border insolvency.

14. "International Code of Ethics of the International Bar Association" (see *The Guide, supra* n.6, p.159).

15. *Id.*, "Preamble".

16. International Bar News, Summer 1995, p.47.

17. *Supra* n. [14], paras. 8 and 20 (hereafter "IBA Code").

18. IBA Code, Rules 17–18, 16 and 10.

19. A mischievous suggestion, but one with some substance in that the drive towards convergence/harmonisation is in fact driving lawyers to divergence in following codes (see Terry, *supra* n. [11]).

20. M.S. Larson, *The Rise of Professionalism: A Sociological Analysis* (Berkeley, Los Angeles, Cal., University of California Press, 1977), R. Abel, *The Legal Profession in England and Wales* (Oxford, Blackwell, 1988).

21. In Abbot's analysis ([A. Abbott, *The Systems of Professions: An Essay on the Expert Division of Labor* (Chicago, Ill., University of Chicago Press, 1988)]) professions are territorial: they protect their sphere of work against rival occupations using specialist knowledge. Their objectives are both economic and social; power, material and social capital. See also T.C. Halliday & L. Karpik (eds), *Lawyers and the Rise of Western Political Liberalism* (Oxford, Clarendon Press, 1997).

22. S. Picciotto, "The Control of Transnational Capital and the Democratisation of the International State" (1998) 15 *Journal of Law and Society* 58 at p.64.

23. *Id.*, at pp.70–1.

24. In most jurisdictions, professional ethics reflect the desire of professionals to be independent, particularly from state control, and the demand for

autonomy in the way work is conducted. This trend is probably less pronounced in civil law countries and reversed in the communist countries during the cold war. In Eastern Europe the lawyer was not bound solely by client loyalty but by loyalty to the State. Lawyers were formerly under a duty to persuade clients to avoid proceedings which conflicted with the interests of the community or society, an orientation which will change as lawyers in the former Soviet bloc now redefine their basic affiliations (M. Bohlander, M. Blacksell & K.M. Born "The Legal Profession In East Germany—Past, Present and Future" (1996) 3:3 *International Journal of the Legal Profession* 255), hence the interest of lawyers from these States in issues of professionalism.

25 D. Sugarman, "Bourgeois Collectivism, Professional Power and the Boundaries of the State: The Private and Public Life of the Law Society, 1825–1914" (1996) 3 *International Journal of the Legal Profession* 81.

26 Abel, *supra* n. [20] at p.353.

27 *Id.*, p.349.

28 [S.S. Silbey, "'Let Them Eat Cake': Globalization, Postmodern Colonialism, and the Possibilities of Justice" (1997) *Law & Society Review* 207] at p.212.

29 *Id.*

30 *Id.*, at p.217.

31 See T.C. Halliday, *Beyond Monopoly: Lawyers, State Crises and Professional Empowerment* (Chicago, Ill., University of Chicago Press, 1987), Halliday and Karpik, *supra* n. [21], and [T.J.] Johnson[, *Professions and Power* (London, Macmillan, 1972)].

32 *Ibid.*, at p.14 quoting K. Lynn, "The Professions" [1963] *Daedalus* 653.

33 [Toulmin, *supra* n. 5]

34 *Id.* at p.16.

35 [G.C.] Hazard, ["The Future of Legal Ethics" (1991) 100 *Yale Law Journal*] at p.1246.

36 G. Condlin, "Bargaining in the Dark: The Normative Incoherence of the Lawyer Dispute bargaining Role" 51 *Maryland Law Review* 1 at pp.68–78.

37 A. Boon, "Client Decision Making in Personal Injury Schemes" (1995) 23 *International Journal of the Sociology of Law* 253.

38 The *Guide* obliges a solicitor to "refuse to take action which he or she believes is solely intended to gratify a client's malice or vindictiveness" (para.12.01 note 6).

39 The latest edition of the *Guide* explicitly states that "where two or more of the principles in practice rule 1 come into conflict, the determining factor in deciding which principle should take precedence must be the public interest and especially the public interest in the administration of justice" (para. 1.02, note 6, "Basic principles—additional guidance" p.2: note the examples given in the *Guide* under para. 7 of situations where a solicitor may find a conflict between rule 1(c) (client's best interests) and 1(b) choice of solicitor where "the public interest demands that the latter takes precedence ...").

40 Hazard, *supra* n. [35], and see J. Noonan, "The Purposes of Advocacy and the Limits of Confidentiality" (1966) 64 *Michigan Law Review* 1485.

41 J. Weinstein, "On the Teaching of Legal Ethics" (1972) 72 *Columbia Law Review* 452, and J.F. Sutton & J.S. Dzienkowski, *Cases and Materials on the Professional Responsibility of Lawyers* (St. Paul, Minn, West Publishing Co, 1989) at p.3.

42 T.W. Giegerich, "The Lawyer's Moral Paradox" (1979) 6 *Duke Law Journal* 1335.

43 [J.] Flood, ["Megalawering in the Global Legal Order: The Cultural, Social, and Economic Transformation of Global Legal Practice" (1996) 3 *International Journal of the Legal Profession* 169].

—60—

ENGINEERING ETHICS IN CHINA

Hengli Zhang and Michael Davis

THE COMMON VIEW TODAY SEEMS TO BE THAT codes of professional ethics in general, and codes of engineering ethics in particular, were until recently, say, the last three decades, a phenomenon largely confined to English-speaking countries. The very idea of professionalism is thought to be a recent export of the English-speaking countries.[1]

This article should raise doubts about that view. It sketches China's century-long concern with the professional ethics of engineers, especially a succession of codes of engineering ethics going back at least to 1933. For convenience of exposition, we divide that century-long story into three periods: 1912 to 1933 (modernization), 1934 to 1948 (war), and 1949 to today (after the communist revolution). What makes this division convenient should become evident as we proceed....

THE FIRST PERIOD: MODERNIZATION, 1912–1933

... For engineers in this early period, the leader was Zhan Tianyou, known as "the Father of China's Railroads."[2] In 1912, he founded the Institute of Zhong Hua Engineers in Guangzhou. This seems to have been the first engineering society in China. Elected its president in 1913, Zhan soon united the Institute of Zhong Hua Engineers with two other engineering societies (the Gongji Society of Railroad Engineers and the Zhong Hua Engineering Institute) to form the Zhong Hua Engineers Society, moving the Society's office to Hankou city in Hubei province.[3] ("Zhong Hua"

means China in a cultural or literary sense, as opposed to a geographical or political sense, much as "America" means the United States.)

The constitution of the Zhong Hua Engineer Society prescribed three missions for the Society:

1. Standardize project construction, draw up rules and regulations, and leave no margin for differences in engineering products.
2. Fully develop the engineering industry and use it to promote social well-being.
3. Update technology in the field of engineering, innovate new approaches, and don't be confined to conventions.[4]

The Society's three missions together underlined the importance to engineering of technical standards, public welfare ("social well-being"), and technological innovation.

This mission statement may be considered, if not the first code of engineering ethics in China, at least a proto-code, that is, a formal statement of ethical standards. Of course, "ethics" has at least three senses. It can refer, first, to ordinary morality (those standards of conduct that apply to all moral agents) or, second, to a field of philosophy (the attempt to understand morality as a reasonable undertaking). But, most relevant here, "ethics" can also refer to those morally binding standards of conduct that apply to members of a group simply because they are members of that group (for example, engineers or members of the Zhong Hua Engineer Society). It is in this third sense that the mission statement of the Zhong

Hua Engineer Society may best be considered a code of ethics (or, given its brevity, a proto-code).[5] The statement sought to guide individual engineers, the members of the Society, as well as the Society itself, but not every moral agent—or even every Chinese moral agent. Engineers (non-Chinese as well as Chinese) might well consider it a statement of morally binding standards without being members of the Society.

About the same time that Zhan was founding the Zhong Hua Engineer Society, he was thinking more broadly about how engineers should act. For example, in a 1918 lecture, he called on engineers to develop in four areas: business, morality, rules, and relationships. He urged engineers "to promote invention on the basis of accurate scientific research," "to heighten morality by respecting morally upright persons and acts," "to proceed in an orderly way and step by step, and not beyond what conditions allow," and "to plan in accurate detail and be more careful in their work."[6] In this way, Zhan sought to improve the moral sense, abilities, and conduct of the engineers of that time. As more engineers understood engineering ethics better, Zhan became a model for other engineers.[7]

Zhan died in 1919. After his death, the Zhong Hua Engineer Society grew slowly. But another engineering society, the Engineering Institution of China—founded in New York City in 1918—soon replaced it as the most important engineering society in China.[8] With more engineering students returning to China, the Institution also returned in 1920. Its journal, *Engineering*, was founded in 1923, eventually becoming a forum for discussion of ethical as well as technical matters. For example, one 1928 article argued that engineers should always study hard, be diligent, care about technology, and seek to improve the welfare of human beings.[9] Another, published the same year, claimed that "the missions of engineers" were two: first, to promote the happiness of life; second, to develop production, improve the daily life of people, and make them more comfortable. Engineers should be responsible for leading workers, should constantly exchange experience and knowledge with colleagues, and

should honestly pursue common interests of engineers, even if that means sacrificing personal interests. Engineers should be loyal, honest in their work, and have "exalted minds."[10]

In 1931, the Institution joined with the Zhong Hua Engineer Society and other engineering societies to form the Chinese Institution of Engineers (CIE).[11] The CIE initially included fifteen engineering societies, the most prominent of which were the Chinese Engineering Society, the Chinese Institution of Civil Engineers, the Chinese Mechanical Engineering Society, and the Chinese Electrical Engineers Society. These fifteen societies became subdivisions of the CIE, but had their own rights. The CIE did its best to promote engineering. It connected engineers across China, sponsored speeches to tell the public about the significant roles of engineers, called for public emphasis on engineers, and set some industry standards. Chinese engineers thus achieved a unified professional society in 1931, something that American engineers have yet to achieve, though they have envied the unity of lawyers in the American Bar Association and of physicians in the American Medical Association for more than a century.

In 1932, the CIE held one of its annual meetings in Tianjin city. There Li Shutian, Wang Huatang, and others proposed establishing "the Engineering Code of Ethics Committee" to draft "an engineering code of ethics."[12] The motion passed and Li Shutian, Hua Nangui, and Qiu Lingyun were appointed to the new committee. The committee soon proposed a code consisting of seven rules:

1. Be as loyal to the duty as a soldier to military service.[13]
2. Do not accept improper pay.
3. Do no harm, directly or indirectly, to the reputation or business of counterparts.
4. Internal strife with other engineers is absolutely prohibited.
5. Do not get business or position by dirty methods.
6. Do not arbitrarily comment on the work of colleagues in front of their employer.

7. Do not publicize in self-laudatory language or do anything to damage the dignity of the profession.[14]

This first proposal resembles the Code of Ethics of the American Society of Civil Engineers (ASCE) insofar as it is short, gives priority to "loyalty," and is most concerned with assuring good relations among engineers.[15] It is, however, not necessarily a good indication of what Chinese engineers at the time thought their ethics should be. CIE member Yun Zhen soon responded to this proposal with a shorter alternative having a somewhat different emphasis:

1. Be loyal to the profession.
2. Seek truth from facts.
3. Work hard and be able to endure hardship.
4. Neither accept nor give in an unfair way.
5. Collaborate with others, not jostle against one another or push somebody out.
6. Do not criticize others recklessly and exaggerate your own merits.[16]

The CIE discussed the two proposal, published them in *Engineering Weekly*, and mailed letters to members asking for comments.[17] After a year of discussion, the CIE (meeting in Wuhan city) let Hu Shuhua, Ling Hongxun, and Shao Yizhou modify their original proposal and adopted the resulting "Ethics Code of CIE."[18]

While apparently written after studying codes of engineering ethics from Western countries, especially the ASCE code, this early Chinese code was not a mere translation of any Western document. It was, in part at least, based on a local understanding of what a code should be and what engineers should do. It consisted of six rules:

1. Don't abandon one's commitment or loyalty to duties.
2. Don't grant or accept rewards overstepping one's bounds.
3. Don't engage in internal strife or jostling against counterparts.

4. Don't harm, directly or indirectly, the reputation or business of counterparts.
5. Don't resort to despicable means to compete for business or position.
6. Don't engage in false speech or conduct that may damage one's professional reputation.[19] ...

THE SECOND PERIOD: WAR, 1934–1948

... As part of promoting industrial development, military technology, and efficient standards of engineering, the CIE rewrote its ethics code to encourage engineers to work appropriately in this new context. In 1940 in Chengdu city, at its ninth annual meeting, the CIE discussed the idea that the chief responsibility of engineers should be to the nation. In 1941, the CIE formally adopted a new code of ethics consisting of eight rules, all stated positively.[20] This may well be the only (formally adopted) code of engineering ethics ever to be stated entirely in positive form:

1. Comply with the policies of national defense and economic development to carry out the industrial plan of our Founding Father.
2. Be aware of the priority of the national interests and willing to sacrifice one's freedom for them.
3. Promote the national industrialization for self-sufficiency in main goods.
4. Develop industrial standardization to meet the needs of national defense and people's livelihood.
5. Resist the temptation of fame and fortune, safeguard the professional dignity, and abide by professional ethics.
6. Seek truth from the facts, and pursue perfection, independent innovation and collaborative achievements.
7. Undertake challenges, adhere to professional obligations and, most of all, value cooperation.
8. Be disciplined with oneself and lenient towards others, and develop such living habits as being neat, thrifty, responsive, and honest.[21]

Plainly, the 1941 code, or rather the first half, was designed for wartime and related political needs. Hence, the use of "national" in Rules 1–4 and the reference to "our Founding Father" in Rule 1. The remaining Rules (5–8) could have appeared in the 1933 code—or, indeed, in a Japanese or American code of engineering ethics. Of course, the last Rule (8) is unusual insofar as it specifies virtues not generally mentioned in codes of engineering ethics ("such living habits as being neat, thrifty, responsive, and honest"). Here perhaps is a Confucian influence....

THIRD PERIOD: TAIWAN AFTER THE REVOLUTION, 1949–TODAY

The third period of the history of engineering ethics in China (1949 to today) has two main branches: the Mainland branch and the Taiwanese branch. On the Mainland, there were many engineering societies but no formal code of engineering ethics for almost half a century. On Taiwan, the CIE rebuilt after its flight from the Mainland in 1949, becoming an important means for Taiwanese engineers "to strengthen close ties and interactions between members and professional institutes worldwide" and "to advance technology, expertise, and professionalism in engineering."[22]

The CIE maintained its 1941 code unchanged until 1976 (perhaps because Taiwan considered itself still to be at war, though with Mainland China rather than Japan). Then, in 1976, it made only one small change (apparently, a clarification), replacing "one's freedom" in Rule 2 with "oneself" so that the amended rule read "Be aware of the priority of the national interest; be willing to sacrifice oneself for it."[23]

Then, on November 10, 1994, at its 59th annual meeting, the CIE set up a committee both to formulate a new ethics code and to do research on engineering ethics in Taiwan—to clear up misunderstandings of engineers, improve the reputation of engineers, and maintain the dignity of engineering. After much work, including the study of codes of ethics of many foreign countries, the CIE

adopted a new code of ethics in 1996.[24] The 1996 code seems to owe little to either CIE's 1933 or 1941 code. The 1996 code distinguished four kinds of responsibility: to society, to the profession, to employers, and to colleagues:

Engineer's Social Responsibility

Lawfulness and dedication: follow laws and regulations, protect public safety, and improve all citizens' well-being.

Respect nature: maintain the ecological balance, cherish natural resources, and preserve cultural heritage.

Engineer's Professional Responsibility

Professional Dedication: apply professional knowledge and skills, maintain professional discipline, and enforce engineering practices.

Innovation and perfection: absorb advanced technology knowledge, commit to perfection, and improve product quality.

Engineer's Employer Responsibility

Sincere services: contribute all your talents and wisdom to provide the best service, and achieve job objectives.

Mutual trust and benefit: establish mutual trust, foster win-win consensus, and accomplish engineering goals.

Engineer's Colleague Responsibility

Cooperation and collaboration: collaborate professionally, emphasize cooperation, and coordination and improve operational efficiency.

Heritage continuation and future inspiration: engage in self and mutual encouragement, inherit technological know-how and experience from predecessors, and develop new talents....

THIRD PERIOD: REVOLUTION ON THE MAINLAND, 1949–TODAY

On the Mainland, the period between 1949 and today can be divided into three sub-periods. During the first, the People's Republic came into being and began building a socialist economy. This sub-period lasted about thirty years, ending with the collapse of the Cultural Revolution in 1978. During those thirty years, there was no formal code of ethics for engineers. All occupations, including engineering, were to do their best for the nation under the direction of the new government. Central administration left no room for voluntary associations like professions—or for their special standards. Indeed, during much of this period, especially, during the Great Leap Forward and the Cultural Revolution, even technical expertise was suspect. In the second sub-period, starting with the policy of Reform and Opening-up (1978), China began to develop a market economy, reducing considerably the control that government exercised over society. Technical organizations slowly changed their role, coming increasingly to resemble their counterparts in the West. Engineering education improved. In the third sub-period, beginning near the end of the twentieth century, professional organizations again began adopting codes of ethics. There was also considerable effort put into accrediting engineering programs using international standards. Among these international standards were requirements for teaching engineering ethics.[25] ...

CONCLUSION

Codes of engineering ethics are not a recent import to China. Their roots go back more than a century, that is, at least to the founding of Zhong Hua Engineer Society in 1912. The first formal code of engineering ethics was adopted in 1933, radically revised in 1941, and again radically revised in

Taiwan in 1996. There was also a slow and independent development of codes of engineering ethics on the Chinese Mainland after the reforms of 1978. While code writers in China plainly learned from Western codes, the Chinese codes were not mere copies of their Western counterparts. Indeed, the Chinese codes sometimes differed inventively from Western codes in form (for example, being wholly positive) or content (for example, protecting "cultural heritage")....

NOTES

1   See, for example, the Wikipedia entry for "Engineering Ethics" (https://en.wikipedia.org/wiki/Engineering_ethics), which mentions only one non-English code of engineering ethics (a German document dating from 1950), though a document in French (from Quebec) does appear in the list of codes at the entry's end. Whatever its failures as a scholarly source, Wikipedia is pretty reliably a place to find "the common view." Compare the discussion of "profession" in Harris et al. 2014: 189–190.

2   Zhan (b. 1861) began his modern education in America in 1872. He graduated from the Sheffield Engineering School of Yale University in 1881, majoring in civil engineering. From 1905 to 1909, Zhan designed and built the Jing-Zhang railway, the first railway designed and constructed in China without foreign assistance. Zheng Fang, "'Civic Leaders' of Modern Engineer Groups—The Study of Chinese Institute of Engineers (1912–1950)" (近代工程师群体的 "民间领袖"—中国工程师学会研究 (1912–1950)) (Beijing: China Economy Daily Press, 2014).

3   Zhan Tongji, Huang Zhiyang, and Deng Haicheng, eds., "A Biographical Note on Tianyou Zhan" (詹天佑生平) (Guangzhou: Guangdong People's Press, 1995), 235–252; Chinese Civil Engineering Society (CCES), ed., *The History of Chinese Civil Engineering Society* (中国土木工程学会史) (Shanghai: Shanghai Jiaotong University Press, 2008), 15–16.

4   *The Report of Zhong Hua Engineers Society* (中华工程师会报告), November 11, 1913. The original Chinese reads:

1. 统一工程营造, 规定正则制度, 使无参差杆格之患;
2. 发达工程事业, 俾得利用厚生, 增进社会之幸福;
3. 日新工程学术, 力求自阐新途, 不至囿于成法.

5 Michael Davis, "Codes of Ethics," in *Encyclopedia of Science, Technology, and Ethics*, ed. Carl Mitcham (New York: Macmillan Reference, 2005), 350–353.

6 Zhan Tianyou, "Announcements of the Younger Engineers in the Transportation Engineering" (敬告交通界青年工学家), *Transportation Newspaper* (August 1918): 19–22; Zhan Tongji, ed., *The Business Writings and Business Philosophy Research of Tianyou Zhan* (詹天佑创业著述精选和创业思想研究) (Guangzhou: Guangdong Map Press, 1999), 23–25.

7 Zhan Tianyou Development Foundation for Science and Technology, ed., *The Corpus of Commemorating the 150th Birthday Anniversary of Zhan Tianyou* (纪念詹天佑先生诞辰 150 周年纪念文集) (Beijing: China Railway Press, 2011); Zhan Tongji, *Critical Biography of Zhan Tianyou* (詹天佑评传) (Zhuhai: Zhuhai Press, 2008).

8 CCES 2008: 16.

9 Huang Yan, "Review of the Last Hundred Years of Engineering Enterprises" (工程事业最近一百年来之回顾), *Engineering* 4 (1928): 3–5.

10 Cheng Wendong, "The Mission of Chinese Engineers" (中国工程师之使命), *Engineering* 5 (1930): 463–465.

11 Liu Hua, *The Research of Establishment, Development and History Position of Chinese Institute of Engineering* (中国工程学会的创建、发展及其历史地位的研究) (Beijing: Tinghua University, 2002).

12 "Summary of Yearly Meeting of Chinese Institute of Engineer (2)" (中国 工程学会年会之纪要 (二)), *Shen Newspaper*, August 28, 1932.

13 The reference to "military service" disappeared from later drafts. We do not know why. But one obvious answer is that later drafts seem to avoid analogies and similes altogether.

14 "21st Meeting General Report of Chinese Institute of Engineer" (中国工程 师学会二十一年度会务总报告), *Engineering Weekly* 12(2) (September 1933).

15 American Society of Civil Engineers, "ASCE Code of Ethics, 1914," http://ethics.iit.edu/ecodes/node/4093 (accessed September 10, 2016).

16 "21st Meeting."

17 Ibid.

18 Ibid.

19 This is our translation. The original Chinese reads:
1. 不得放弃责任或不忠于职务;
2. 不得授受非分之报酬;
3. 不得有倾轧排挤同行之行为;
4. 不得直接或间接损害同行之名誉及其业务;
5. 不得以卑劣之手段，竞争业务或位置;
6. 不得作虚伪宣传或其他有损职业尊严之举动.
(Chinese Institute of Engineers (CIE), "Code of Ethics" [中国工程师信守规 条], Wuhan Annual Meeting Record of CIE, *Engineering Weekly* 12 [September 1933]: 178)

20 Mao Yisheng, "A Brief History of Chinese Institute of Engineers" (中国工 程师学会简史), in *Selected Writings of Cultural and Historical Material*, No. 34, Vol. 99–100, Chinese Cultural and Historical Press, 2011.

21 Chinese Institute of Engineers (CIE), "The Norms of CIE (中国工程师信 条)," *Shen Newspaper*, October 28, 1941.

22 CIE 2012: 11. Why did the CIE "flee" to Taiwan? Why did it not stay on the mainland? The answer seems simple. While most engineers may have remained on the mainland, most important Chinese institutions retreated to Taiwan with the Nationalist government. The CIE was just one of these.

23 "Summary of the 30th Anniversary Meeting of the Reestablished CIE" (中 国工程师学会在台湾重建 30 周年纪念会务纪要), CIE Library (1984), 3.

24 CIE 1996a.

25 Qin 2010: 86–87, 97–99.

REFERENCES

American Society of Civil Engineers (ASCE). 1914. "Engineering Ethics." http://ethics.iit.edu/ecodes/node/4093 (accessed September 10, 2016).

Cheng Wendong. 1930. "The Mission of Chinese Engineers" (中国工程师之使命). *Engineering* 5: 463–465

Chinese Civil Engineering Society (CCES), ed. 2008. *The History of Chinese Civil Engineering Society* (中国土木工程学会史). Shanghai: Shanghai Jiaotong University Press.

Chinese Institute of Engineers (CIE). 1933. "Code of Ethics" (中国工程师信守规 条), Wuhan annual meeting record of CIE. *Engineering Weekly* 12(2) (September): 178.

Chinese Institute of Engineers (CIE). 1941. "The Norms of CIE" (中国工程师信 条). *Shen Newspaper*, October 28.

Chinese Institute of Engineers (CIE). 2012. "The 2021 Development Strategic of the Chinese Institute of Engineers" (中工会 110 年发展策略白皮书), April 27. http://www.cie.org.tw/cms/upload/files/2012%20 Development%20Strategy%20of%20CIE(2).pdf (accessed September 22, 2016).

Chinese Institute of Engineers (CIE). 1996a. "Code of Ethics." http://www.cie.org.tw/Important?cicc_id=3 (accessed May 25, 2016).

Chinese Institute of Engineers (CIE). 1996b. "Operating Procedures" (中国工程 师信条实行细则). http://www.cie.org.tw/Important/ImportantDetail?cic_id=15&cic_cicc_id=4 (accessed May 25, 2016).

Davis, Michael. 2005. "Codes of Ethics." In *Encyclopedia of Science, Technology, and Ethics*, ed. Carl Mitcham, 350–353. New York: Macmillan Reference.

Fang Zheng. 2011. "A Study of Chinese Institute of Engineers (1912–1950)" (中国 工程师学会研究). Doctoral thesis, Fu Dan University.

Huang Yan. 1928. "Review of the Last Hundred Years of Engineering Enterprises" (工程事业最近一百年来之回顾). *Engineering* 4: 3–5.

Liu Hua. 2002. *The Research of Establishment, Development and History Position of Chinese Institute of Engineering* (中国工程学会的创建、发展及其历史 地位的研究). Beijing: Tinghua University.

Mao Yisheng. 2011. "A Brief History of Chinese Institute of Engineers" (中国工程 师学会简史). In *Selected Writings of Cultural and Historical Material*, No. 34, Vol. 99–100. Chinese Cultural and Historical Press.

Qin Zhu. 2010. "Engineering Ethics Studies in China: Dialogue between Traditionalism and Modernism." *Engineering Studies* 2(2) (August): 85–107. https://doi.org/10.1080/19378629.2010.490271

Wikipedia. "Engineering Ethics." https://en.wikipedia.org/wiki/Engineering_ethics (accessed May 25, 2016).

Zhan Tianyou. 1918. "Announcements of the Younger Engineers in the Transportation Engineering" (敬告交通界青年工学家). *Transportation Newspaper* (August): 19–22.

Zhan Tianyou Development Foundation for Science and Technology, ed. 2011. *The Corpus of Commemorating the 150th Birthday Anniversary of Zhan Tianyou* (纪念詹天佑先生诞辰 150 周年纪念文集). Beijing: China Railway Press.

Zhan Tongji, ed. 1999. *The Business Writings and Business Philosophy Research of Tianyou Zhan* (詹天佑创业著述精选和创业思想研究), 23–25. Guangzhou: Guangdong Map Press.

Zhan Tongji. 2008. *Critical Biography of Zhan Tianyou* (詹天佑评传). Zhuhai: Zhuhai Press.

Zhan Tongji, Huang Zhiyang, and Deng Haicheng, eds. 1995. "A Biographical Note on Tianyou Zhan" (詹天佑生平), 235–252. Guangzhou: Guangdong People's Press.

Zhang Fuliang. 1928. "The Speech Records of the 10th Annual Conference of CIE" (中国工程学会第 10 届年会演讲记录). *Engineering* 3: 168–174.

REPORTS

Report of Zhong Hua Engineers Society, The (中华工程师会报告), November 11, 1913.

"Summary of the 30th Anniversary Meeting of the Reestablished CIE." 1984. (中 国工程师学会在台湾重建 30 周年会务纪要). (CIE Library). "Summary of Yearly Meeting of Chinese Institute of Engineer (2)." 1932. (中国工程学会年 会之纪要 (二)). Shen Newspaper, August 28.

"21st Meeting General Report of Chinese Institute of Engineer." 1933. (中国工程师 学会二十一年度会务总报告), Engineering Weekly 12(2) (September).

-61-

THE CHALLENGES OF MAINTAINING SOCIAL WORK ETHICS IN KENYA

Ndungi wa Mungai, Gidraph G. Wairire, and Emma Rush

INTRODUCTION

THE CHALLENGES OF MAINTAINING PROFES-sional social work ethics derived from a Western base of knowledge and practice in the Kenyan African context have not been fully explored, yet they are key to social work identity and standing in the country. Banks (2008) acknowledges that while social work values may have a Western base and even bias, they also have potential for international application. Banks' (2008) argument is that social work is an international social movement committed to promoting social justice, but it is also a situated practice that takes place within a context of national laws, policies and culture. Social workers have always emphasised the importance of location and context (Parton and Kirk 2010). This outlook is shared by other social scientists. For example, Nyambedha (2008) stresses the importance of using and adding to local knowledge through research with vulnerable groups (including for instance, communities affected by HIV/AIDS in Kenya) and using the knowledge gained to guide and inform their advocacy work. Recognising the way socio-cultural issues affect, for example, public health, and the importance of creating positive relationships with individuals and communities in social research, are important ethical aspects in engaging vulnerable communities in Africa (Molyneux *et al.* 2009). In other words, working with respect with people includes respecting their history and culture.

Recognising African histories and cultures is important given the continent's colonial legacy of neglecting the needs of the indigenous peoples and disrespecting their cultures. African social workers are faced with the challenge of rebuilding from this difficult past, and welcome support and collaboration with other social workers to find solutions to the problems they face as they adapt social work to African conditions (Asamoah and Beverly 1988). The profession's core value of mutual respect is the basis of such collaboration (Asquith, Clark, and Waterhouse 2005). As an example of what such mutual respect and collaboration might look like, and the promise this might hold for the intended beneficiaries of social work intervention, this article explores the challenges of working ethically within the Kenyan situation. It considers the reality of the challenges within the Kenyan laws, policies and cultural context. It argues that while the interventions have to be considered in context, social workers in Kenya and Africa can also learn from ethical approaches by social workers in other countries. This learning needs to occur on the basis of mutual exchange as partners in pursuit of social justice....

THE KENYAN CONTEXT

[T]he challenge for Kenyan social workers is how to maintain the ethics of their predominantly Western-based profession while working in African cultural contexts. There is currently a gap in the academic literature regarding social work ethics in Kenya (during 2012, our searches of 15 relevant international journal databases produced no results at all). Therefore, a brief review of the international development of social work ethics as well as the general challenges for social workers in Africa opens this section. This is followed by a longer discussion of specific issues for social work training and practice in the Kenyan context, drawn from one of the authors' 21 years of experience 'on the ground'. The contextual issues discussed here contribute significantly to the challenges social workers in Kenya face in maintaining professional social work ethics, highlighting the importance of an Afrocentric perspective in responding productively to such challenges.

Social Work Values, Ethics and Morality

From its beginnings, social work has been a value-based profession (Dubois and Miley 2011). While the definition and expression of these values has evolved over time, the core value of concern for humanity remains the defining feature of social work. Values are important as they shape our beliefs, emotions and attitudes; in turn, our beliefs, emotions and attitudes shape our values (Dubois and Miley 2011). In other words, values are implicit or explicit beliefs concerning what is 'good' and 'right', guiding our understanding of what actions may be considered ethical. Our behaviour or conduct, thus influenced by our values, can be regarded as a reflection of our individual sense of morality. Morality is hard to define but one attempt at a definition suggests that the moral system is 'the system people use, often unconsciously, when they are trying to make a morally acceptable choice among several alternative actions or when they make moral judgements about their own actions or those of others' (Gert 2005, 3). Morality in many Western conceptualisations appears therefore to be demonstrated through action, or inaction, and the judgements we make of ourselves or others. This approach is increasingly challenged as alternative concepts, such as communitarian ethics (with emphasis on community, responsibility and cooperation), critique this dominance (Banks 2008). Social workers in Africa are confronted by similar ethical issues, and have to decide whether or not to take action as individual social workers, as employees of an organisation, or as members of a community.

In the course of social work's development as a profession, there has been a shift from focusing on the morality of the poor as the source of problems to a concern with the morality or ethics of the social workers and the constraints imposed by social systems (Reamer 1993; DuBois and Miley 2011). Professional codes of ethics have now been developed in a wide range of developing and developed countries in which social work is practiced (Banks 2008). The International Federation of Social Workers (IFSW) and International Association of Schools of Social work (IASSW) note that ethical awareness is a fundamental part of social work practice (IFSW 2012). Their definition of social work states that:

> The social work profession promotes social change, problem solving in human relationships and the empowerment and liberation of people to enhance well-being. Utilising theories of human behaviour and social systems, social work intervenes at the points where people interact with their environments. Principles of human rights and social justice are fundamental to social work. (IFSW 2012)

By adopting principles of human rights and social justice, social work emphasises the right of people to be treated with dignity when using social work services. Abbot (1999), in a study conducted in four parts of the world (USA, Asia, Europe and Australasia) has grouped social work values into four categories: respect for human rights, social responsibility, commitment to individual freedom (social justice), and self-determination. The research identifies that social workers throughout the world share the values of respect for basic rights and support for self-determination, but there is no such unanimity around social responsibility and commitment to individual freedom (Abbot 1999). This confirms that social work is both 'an international social movement concerned to promote social justice across the world, and a situated practice that takes place in a context of national laws, policies and cultures' (Banks 2008, 243). In other words, context makes a significant difference in how social workers in different places will address the issues facing them in the process of helping their clients.

Social Work in Africa

In Africa, general challenges for social workers arise from the legacy of colonisation that disrupted, undermined, and sometimes destroyed the cultural fabrics of its people; weak public sectors unable to meet the needs of the people; underdeveloped institutions including legal institutions unable to guarantee the rule of law; widespread and absolute poverty; and violent conflicts causing mass displacements (Maathai 2009). These are broad generalisations and different populations in Africa are affected differently, so while some people live comfortable lifestyles, others find themselves in desperation. Nonetheless, these broad generalisations speak to the lived experiences of many Africans. Such vast problems cannot be solved by social workers alone, but social workers must play their role. As MacCormack (1996) notes, the suffering caused by psychological wounds sustained from structural and interpersonal

violence—including poverty, deprivation and war—affect not only the well-being of individuals but also that of communities and societies. It is important therefore that social workers base their interventions on a deep-enough understanding of the cultures, histories, traditions and politics of the affected people.

Traditional Support Networks in Kenya

Traditional social support networks in Kenya were embedded within the social cultural practices of each community. Social responsibilities were clearly defined for different community members, and the necessary knowledge and understanding thereof were passed on through socialisation. Individual needs were largely addressed at the extended family and community levels. The family unit had clear structures for assisting someone in need and whenever necessary, other community members would intervene. Household heads and village elders assumed many of the roles now occupied by modern social workers, particularly with regard to enhancing the social functioning of individuals. Heads of age sets and group mentors equally played significant roles in helping particular individuals or groups to manage problems of living. The kind of individualism prevalent in Kenya today did not exist in traditional societies, and individuals readily accepted counsel, advice or direction from their seniors whenever a problem of living was experienced.... [E]veryone was linked in some specific way to the society.

Social Work Training in Kenya: Issues and Challenges

The establishment of the first training institution for social work education in Kenya (Kenya-Israel School of Social Work) in 1962 introduced professional social work where only traditional networks had existed. The school was later integrated with the Kenya Institute of Administration where social work training continued at the Diploma level. The training offered then was limited, but it equipped aspiring social workers with skills relevant for interventions in predominantly rural communities still recovering from colonialism (Wairire, personal communication). Social work education at Bachelor degree level was started in 1976 at the University of Nairobi in the then Department of Sociology. The focus was to equip social work personnel with skills that training at the diploma level could not provide, particularly interventions requiring research, policy formulations, project planning and management. There were a combination of factors—including the impact of globalisation, a weakening of traditional family structures and traditions, and population increase—that contributed to the further weakening of the pre-colonial support networks, and created more space and need for professional social work practice in Kenya (Wairire, personal communication).

There are currently six universities and eight colleges offering Bachelor of Arts (Social Work) degrees in the country (KenyaPlex.com 2012). At the time of writing this paper, no university in Kenya, either public or private, offered higher degrees in social work. And yet, social workers with postgraduate social work qualifications could play a significant role in research, teaching and provision of specialised social work services. Without the research training provided at postgraduate level, very little Kenyan research is directly related to social work, yet ideally, classroom content should be informed by social work research. Social work curricula that are therefore heavily based on subject matter derived from the West, but intended for social workers who will work in Africa may raise both relevance and ethical concerns (Mwansa 2011). Moreover, the lack of opportunities at the postgraduate level means that frequently, academics teaching social work do not have social work training beyond a Bachelor of Social Work degree. There have been instances where people with no basic qualification in social work end up teaching social work units simply because people with relevant qualifications are not available. The problem is more acute in institutions that are located in remote areas and

hence cannot compete for the limited number of lecturers with relevant social work backgrounds, leaving teaching positions to non social work graduates. Finally, as noted below, there is demand for specialised social work services in Kenya, but in most cases only generic services can be provided, due to lack of social work practitioners who have completed specialised postgraduate training. These concerns at the training level raise more ethical issues at the practice level.

Social Work Practice in Kenya: Issues and Challenges

The scope for professional social work practice in Kenya has changed as the country has undergone different phases of development and reels under the impact of globalisation (Wairire 2008). Professional social workers now practice in a variety of sectors in Kenya, including child welfare services, probation services, hospital settings, school social work, industrial social work, community development and micro finance institutions (Wairire 2008). However, this practice is largely generic. Specialised social work has not fully taken shape as specialist postgraduate training is unavailable, and the profession is still developing at the same time as needs for intervention are overwhelming. Social work services cover both urban and rural areas, and the mode of service delivery may vary depending on the agency, its focus, mandate and the responsiveness of intended beneficiaries, among other factors (Wairire 2008).

Social work has not yet gained due recognition as a fully fledged profession. To date, Kenya has no social work professional association enjoying universal allegiance among social workers and social work academics. Social workers in Kenya have no mutually agreed formal code of ethics to guide them. For teaching purposes, social work training institutions rely on codes of ethics from other associations, particularly the National Association of Social Workers in the United States of America. Nonetheless, some training institutions have made efforts to fill this gap. A good example is the

Kenya Institute of Social Work and Community Development (KISWCD) which has developed what is called 'Code of Ethics and Professional Conduct for KISW' to guide social workers and community development workers in the face of ethical dilemmas (KISWCD n.d.).

Besides this, the relatively low numbers of qualified social work personnel, practitioners and academics, may explain the near invisible nature of professional social work in some sectors in Kenya, leading to a situation where many social work jobs and roles are allocated to people with non-social work qualifications. A case in point is Kenya's Vision 2030 that serves as Kenya's blueprint for national development by 2030 (Government of the Republic of Kenya 2007) in which only a few social workers are fully involved even though the blue-print is largely interdisciplinary. Social work voices and aspirations may therefore not be fully heard, rendering social workers practically powerless to make any significant contribution to the national social development agenda (Lombard and Wairire 2010).

Finally, in Kenya as elsewhere, the influence of neo-liberalism is felt in both research and education through the pressure to meet market needs. The risk is of an erosion of the basic values of social justice, empowerment, emancipation and community engagement (Wehbi and Turcotte 2007). South Africa's experience shows that the social work profession is forced to operate within an interaction of the three discourses of professionalism, managerialism and the market, while the forces of globalisation increasingly challenge post-apartheid development ideals (Sewpaul and Hölscher 2004). Similar pressures are felt around the world with the most vulnerable—including the indigenous people who have historically been marginalised as a result of colonialism—being the most affected....

CONCLUSION

This paper has provided some insights into the challenges of maintaining professional social work ethics that are Western-based in an African context, with a specific focus on the Kenyan experience. There is also an argument that supports the view that common themes exist in traditional African societies which would allow for the generalisation of this discussion beyond the Kenyan situation (Schiele 2000; Agulanna 2007). This view has informed the discussion in this paper. The term Afrocentricity represents a standpoint in which the actor consciously chooses to regard the world within an African frame of reference (Schiele 2000). This worldview, while emphasising African particularities, is also universal as it emphasises the spiritual, collective nature of African people and humanity in general (Swignoski 1996). Schiele (2000) suggests that Afrocentricity supports a move from knowledge to knowledge-informed action as part of ethics for social workers. From this perspective, social workers in Africa should not stop at identifying problems but should act to address those problems.

There is a need to increase the amount and scope of social work-led research in African contexts, but the knowledge accumulated by social workers elsewhere is also relevant to Africa as long as it is translated to render it relevant to, and compatible with, the needs and cultures of African people. The danger here is that African cultures were suppressed, demonised or banned outright under colonialism. That meant that even people's names, their languages, their environment, their heritage, their belief in themselves and their capacities were derogated (Wa Thiong'o 1986). It is therefore critically important that social work is not seen as a continuation of this colonial endeavour but as a tool to improve people's lives....

REFERENCES

Abbot, A.A. 1999. "Measuring Social Work Values: A Cross-cultural Challenge for Global Practice." *International Social Work* 42 (4): 455–470. doi:10.1177/002087289904200407.

Agulanna, C. 2007. "Moral Thinking in Traditional African Society: A Reconstructive Interpretation."

Prajna Vihara: Journal of Philosophy and Religion 8 (1). Accessed March 12, 2013 http://agulanna. blogspot.com.au/2008/06/hh.html

Asamoah, Y.W., and C.C. Beverly. 1988. "Collaboration Between African Schools of Social Work: Problems and Possibilities." *International Social Work* 31 (3): 177–193. doi:10.1177/002087288803100304.

Asquith, S., C. Clark, and L. Waterhouse. 2005. "The Role of Social Worker in the 21st Century—a Literature Review." Accessed October 25, 2012 http://www.scotland.gov.uk/Publications/ 2005/12/1994633/46334

Banks, S. 2008. "Critical Commentary: Social Work Ethics." *British Journal of Social Work* 38 (6): 1238–1249. doi:10.1093/bjsw/bcn099.

Dubois, B., and K.K. Miley. 2011. *Social Work: An Empowering Profession*. Boston: Allyn & Bacon.

Gert, B. 2005. *Morality: Its Nature and Justification*. Cary: Oxford University Press.

Government of the Republic of Kenya. 2007. *Kenya Vision 2030, A Globally Competitive and Prosperous Kenya*. Nairobi: Ministry of State for Planning, National Development and Vision 2030.

International Federation of Social Work. 2012. "Code of Ethics." Accessed May 25, 2012 http://ifsw.org/ policies/code-of-ethics/

Kenya Institute of Social Work and Community Development (KISWCD). (n.d.) Membership Code of Ethics and Professional Conduct. Accessed March 5, 2014 http://www.kiswcd. co.ke/code_of_ ethics.html

KenyaPlex.com. 2012. Colleges and Universities Offering Bachelor of Arts (Social Work). Accessed October 25, 2012 http://www.kenyaplex.com/ courses/4-bachelor-of-arts-social-work.aspx

Lombard, A., and G. Wairire. 2010. "Developmental Social Work in South Africa and Kenya: Some Lessons for Africa." *Social Work Practitioner-Researcher, Special Issue* April: 98–111.

Maathai, W. 2009. *The Challenge for Africa: A New Vision*. London: William Heinemann.

MacCormack, C. 1996. "Promoting Psychosocial Well-Being among Children Affected by Armed Conflict and Displacement: Principles and Approaches."

Working Group on Children Affected by Armed Conflict and Displacement, ISCA Working Paper No. 1. Accessed May 24, 2012 http://www.unicef. org/wcaro/SCF_psychsocwellbeing2.pdf

Molyneux, C., J. Goudge, S. Russell, J. Chuma, T. Gumede, and L. Gilson. 2009. "Conducting Health-Related Social Sciences Research in Low Income Settings: Ethical Dilemmas Faced in Kenya and South Africa." *Journal of International Development* 21 (2): 309–326. doi:10.1002/jid.1548.

Nyambedha, E.O. 2008. "Ethical Dilemmas of Social Sciences Research on AIDS and Orphanhood in Western Kenya." *Social Sciences & Medicine* 67 (5): 771–779. doi:10.1016/j.socscimed.2008.02.024.

Parton, N., and S. Kirk. 2010. "The Nature and Purpose of Social Work." In *The Sage Handbook of Social Resarch*, edited by I. Shwa, K. Briar-Lawson, J. Orme, and R. Ruckdeschel, 23–36. Los Angeles: Sage.

Reamer, F.G. 1993. *Ethical Dilemmas in Social Service: A Guide for Social Workers*. New York: Columbia University Press.

Schiele, J.H. 2000. *Human Services and the Afrocentric Paradigm*. New York: Haworth Press.

Sewpaul, V., and D. Hölscher. 2004. *Social Work in Times of Neoliberalism: A Postmodern Discourse*. Hatfield: Van Schaik.

Swignoski, M.E. 1996. "Challenging Privilege through Africentric Social Work Practice." *Social Work* 41 (2): 153–161.

Wa Thiong'o, N. 1986. *Decolonising the Mind: The Politics of Language in African Literature*. London: James Currey.

Wairire, G.G. 2008. "The Challenge for Social Work in the Kenyan Context of Political Conflict." In *Social Work facing Political Conflict*, edited by S. Ramon, 101–122. London: Venture Press.

Wehbi, S., and P. Turcotte. 2007. "Social Work Education: Neoliberalism's Willing Victim?" *Critical Social Work* 8 (1). Accessed May 28, 2008 http://www.uwindsor.ca/criticalsocialwork/ social-work-education-neoliberalism%E2%80%99s-willing-victim

—62—

PROFESSIONAL ETHICS IN EXTREME CIRCUMSTANCES

Responsibilities of Attending Physicians and Healthcare Providers in Hunger Strikes

Nurbay Irmak

HUNGER STRIKE OR FOOD REFUSAL AS A FORM OF protest has never been as prevalent as it is today. A quick search reveals that an increasing number of people from all over the world, in various settings, for various reasons, are going on hunger strikes or refusing food to protest or react against the circumstances in which they find themselves [1–4]. Just within the last two years [2012–2013], there have been several massive collective hunger strikes that have attracted a lot of attention, such as the strikes in California prisons [5] and Guantanamo Bay [6] and a strike by Kurdish prisoners in Turkey [7]. Although hunger strikes in absolute terms are rare, their increasing frequency suggests that there will be more cases in which the risks of significant harm for participants are serious.[1] Hunger strikes potentially present a serious ethical challenge for physicians as obligations of beneficence and autonomy seem to conflict in caring for hunger strikers, especially in custodial settings. On the one hand, physicians have a duty to preserve life, which, in this context, might entail intervening before the hunger striker loses his or her life. On the other hand, physicians have a duty to respect the autonomy of their patients who refuse medical interventions, which, in this case, might imply that attending physicians have to respect hunger

strikers' decision to refuse food and artificial feeding. There are several international guidelines to assist physicians who attend hunger strikes and a number of proposals to solve this dilemma offered by physicians, philosophers, and international organizations [8–12]. In this article, among other things, I address a situation, though rare, in which current guidelines are too vague to provide sufficient guidance to the attending physician when confronted with a hunger striker who is unconscious or otherwise no longer competent. In the absence of clear, informed, and unpressured advance directives, said guidelines leave the final decision to the physician to judge what is in the striker's best interest [8, 9]. I argue that the moral principles that ground said guidelines can be supplemented so that physicians have clearer guidance.

DEFINING A HUNGER STRIKE

Not all food refusals are hunger strikes. A hunger strike is a refusal of nutrition for a significant amount of time to establish certain goals.[2] It is essentially a form of protest or of expressing demands, which is appealed to by detainees as a last resort to raise public awareness and put pressure on the authorities. Hunger strikers must be competent, having full understanding of the nature of their decision and its reversible and irreversible consequences. Fasting, when it is a manifestation of mental illness, such as clinical depression or anorexia nervosa, is not a hunger strike. It is rather a medical condition that should be treated accordingly. Hunger strikes are not always voluntary. Especially in collective hunger strikes, individuals might be coerced to participate in (by their peers) or to end (by the authorities) the strike. Hunger strikes do not have to be total fasting. In most cases, hunger strikers accept fluids, but there are cases in which the striker refuses both food and water. Dry hunger strikes (refusal of food and water) are very rare, yet there have been a few recently reported cases without any fatal consequences [16]. The main reason why dry hunger strikes are not common is that it does not leave enough time (since a human body cannot survive more than a few days without fluid intake) to make demands known to the public and to continue negotiations. Sometimes, food refusal is not total; protestors can take some form of nutrition usually to gain more time for negotiations [12]. However, as the second major collective hunger strike in Turkey in 2000 has shown, hunger strikes do not have to take the form of total fasting in order to lead to fatal consequences [10]. For these reasons, I follow the World Medical Association's (WMA's) broader definition in this article; I do not limit hunger strike to mean only voluntary total fasting. Defined in this way, it is clear that hunger strikes do not always pose moral dilemmas for attending physicians and healthcare providers. The fact that the cases of hunger strikes that pose a serious potential threat are rare does not, of course, mean that the moral and the medical responsibilities of attending physicians need not be thought about. The international guidelines and the debates surrounding them clearly illustrate that the issue has been rightly taken very seriously, and comprehensive moral and medical guidance has been provided by national and international organizations. The main purpose of this article is to suggest

a further clarification of or a supplementation to those guidelines with respect to certain perhaps rare or exceptional situations....

RESPONSIBILITIES OF PHYSICIANS

There are certain duties of physicians who attend in caring for hunger strikes that are quite uncontroversial. I will begin with those and continue with the issues that are more complicated and controversial, such as what a physician should do when the patient loses consciousness. I will follow the WMA's Declaration of Malta on Hunger Strikes as it provides the most current international ethical guideline for physicians. The following is an outline of the responsibilities of physicians attending hunger strikes.

- Physicians must assess the decision-making capacity of individuals and acquire a detailed medical history of them as early as possible. If a prisoner is not competent, that is, if his ability to make an informed decision is impaired, he cannot be considered a hunger striker.
- Physicians should interview the prisoner in a private and an unmonitored setting before and during the strike in order to establish that their decision to fast is voluntary and not made under coercion. Physicians should conduct these interviews on a regular basis (daily if the conditions permit) to establish whether or not the striker wishes to continue fasting.
- Physicians should inform the strikers about the possible, reversible, and irreversible physical and psychological consequences of fasting.
- Physicians should provide counseling.
- Physicians have a duty to establish and preserve confidentiality.
- Physicians should remain objective and independent.
- Physicians should ask the striker what he wants to be done as he loses his

consciousness or is no longer able to communicate meaningfully.

- Artificial feeding can be ethically appropriate if competent hunger strikers give consent to it.
- Force-feeding is never ethically acceptable.

Good communication and establishing a relationship based on trust and confidentiality are essential for physicians if they are to assess whether the patient is competent and his hunger strike is voluntary. This is especially difficult in collective political hunger strikes in prisons, as the protestors tend to perceive prison doctors as part of the detaining authority. If it is impossible for prison doctors to build a reliable dialogue with the strikers, it might be helpful to bring in external physicians for assistance who have no connection with the detaining system. Local medical associations and/or international organizations, such as the ICRC and the WMA, can be consulted about the possibility of providing such assistance.[3] Patients who suffer from a psychiatric or mental disorder, such as anorexia or clinical depression, should not be allowed to fast in a way that might endanger their health. Fasting, in those cases, is a consequence of a medical condition and should be treated accordingly. However, psychological changes in hunger strikers induced by starvation, such as increased levels of aggression, anger, and impulsivity should not be taken to undermine their competence [17, 18]. It is important to notice that the assessment of competence is not necessarily all or none. As the fasting progresses, especially after the first four weeks of a total hunger strike, the degree of competence will vary depending on the previous physical and psychological state of the striker. Therefore, a formal and continuing psychological assessment in different stages of fasting is crucial to determine competency.

It is especially difficult for physicians to establish whether a hunger strike in prison is voluntary, as there are various ways in which and degrees to which one might be coerced into participating in the strike. As most of the political hunger strikes are collective, there is a question of peer pressure,

and coercion by the group or its leader. Families or relatives could inadvertently play a coercive role in political strikes, as they try to publicize the strike through the media and raise support for the strikers' demands, which could in turn make it very difficult for some of the strikers to opt out without losing face. In addition to the discussion of the previous section about difficulties of establishing voluntariness in the context of force-feeding, I would like to reflect a bit more on what physicians could do in cases where there is a significant worry that individual prisoners might be coerced to participate in political collective hunger strikes. The importance of gaining trust cannot be overemphasized. Physicians should do their best to have a frank and private discussion about the striker's goals and his or her reasons for going on a strike. In custodial settings, this is not an easy task, as privacy is under constant threat by other members of the group, fellow prisoners, or prison authorities and staff. One solution might be to separate those individuals whom physicians suspect could be under duress from the group under a medical pretext and to have a confidential discussion about an individual's intention to continue fasting [12]. If there are serious obstacles for attending physicians to gain the strikers' trust to determine if they are fasting voluntarily, physicians could bring in independent doctors, or ask the patient to nominate physicians who are in a better condition to assess whether the strikers' decision to fast is indeed autonomous. Even though physicians try their best to assess voluntariness in collective hunger strikes, it is unfortunately possible that some cases of coercion will escape notice. If there is not enough evidence to conclude that the patient is under significant duress, physicians should follow the patient's explicit instructions [12].

It is not uncommon in some countries for hunger strikers to be transferred to a hospital only after they lapse into a critical condition, but while still conscious. In most cases, the prison authorities do not inform physicians about the advance directives of the patient. Even if they are presented with written directives, for the reasons discussed above, the attending physicians should talk to the patients about their intentions. If the patient is unable to communicate (due to his medical condition), the physician has a duty to intervene so that it becomes possible to have a meaningful conversation with the patient about what should be done in case they are incapacitated. The physician should make sure that the conversation between them is confidential and unmonitored. It is considerably easier for the physician to establish confidentiality in a hospital compared to a prison. Before asking the patient about his decision, the physician should inform him about the possible reversible and irreversible consequences of continuing fasting. It is reasonable to assume that given the critical medical condition that the patient is in, which, in a way, helps him to realize the significance of his condition, his decision to continue or stop fasting reflects his autonomous will. The physician ought to respect the wishes of her patient....

The controversy I would like to focus on in the rest of this article is over what physicians should do as the striker loses his or her consciousness or ability to communicate meaningfully. The discussion of this question has also significant consequences for the kind of worries about coercion raised above. I would like to separate two issues here: (a) what should be done when the striker has clear and unpressured advance directives not to be fed artificially as he lapses into unconsciousness, and (b) what should be done when the striker has already lost his decision-making capacity, before the physician takes over the case, and there is no known advance directives or there is a reasonable doubt that the striker was coerced to take part in the hunger strike.

It is very important to notice that these are rare cases. Most hunger strikes end before posing serious health risks for the protestors. The current moral and medical guidelines are sufficient to resolve most of the questions physicians might have. However, albeit rare, cases of (a) and (b) have occurred before, and they, unfortunately, are likely to occur in the future. Therefore, it is important to have, if possible, clear and comprehensive

guidelines for attending physicians and health-care providers....

... According to the WMA's Malta Declaration, "when the hunger striker has become confused and is therefore unable to make an unimpaired decision or has lapsed into a coma, the doctor shall be free to make the decision for his patient as to further treatment which he considers to be in the best interest of that patient." The most straightforward interpretation of "the best interest of the patient" in the case of an unconscious hunger striker who will soon die due to extreme starvation is to feed him artificially and preserve his life. However, the WMA also emphasizes that the physician should honor the decision freely made by the competent striker.... The second international statement, the latest version of the Malta Declaration (October 2006), attempts to clarify what should be done in such circumstances:

> When a physician takes over the case, the hunger striker may have already lost mental capacity so that there is no opportunity to discuss the individual's wishes regarding medical intervention to preserve life. Consideration needs to be given to any advance instructions made by the hunger striker. Advance refusals of treatment demand respect if they reflect the voluntary wish of the individual when competent. In custodial settings, the possibility of advance instructions having been made under pressure needs to be considered. Where physicians have serious doubts about the individual's intention, any instructions must be treated with great caution. If well informed and voluntarily made, however, advance instructions can only generally be overridden if they become invalid because the situation in which the decision was made has changed radically since the individual lost competence. [8] ...

One might argue that even without a formal advance directive, the hunger strikers' previously expressed wishes, and their personal and cultural values, indicate the strikers' preferences.

This may well be true, but the physician obviously cannot act on them, partly because they do not constitute enough evidence for the striker's decision as he might have changed his mind or revised his decision, etc. More importantly, it is very difficult, if not impossible, for physicians to acquire such information about their patients' previously expressed wishes in the kind of setting and urgency under consideration. Therefore, I argue that if there is a reasonable doubt that the advance directives were given under duress, or if such advance directives are absent, unconscious strikers should be resuscitated and artificially fed if necessary. It is important to note that the primary purpose of resuscitation at this stage is not a full recovery, but to take a temporary measure to establish voluntariness.[4] Once the striker regains consciousness, the physician has a responsibility to explain to him why he was resuscitated, and to ask if he wishes to continue the strike or the treatment. If the striker wishes to continue fasting, and gives the advance directive so as not to be resuscitated again, the physician should honor the striker's decision to refuse treatment and feeding, and should not medically intervene if the striker loses his competence again. The physician has a further responsibility to make the required arrangements that are in his power in order to ensure that a new physician of the patient is not confronted with the same question.

CONCLUSION

I have argued that the international guidelines and, more specifically, the Malta Declaration of the WMA give us a good understanding of the responsibilities of physicians attending hunger strikes. The Malta Declaration deems force-feeding to be ethically unacceptable and emphasizes the need to respect the autonomy and dignity of hunger strikers. In the absence of unpressured advance directives, the Malta Declaration leaves room for physicians facing an unconscious striker to decide between the values and previously expressed wishes of the striker and the striker's best interests.

I have argued that given the Declaration's reasons for rejecting force-feeding, there is no need to be vague about the cases in question. When facing a striker who has already lost his competence, and there are no advance directives, or there is a reasonable doubt that the striker was under coercion or had changed his mind during the strike, the physician has the responsibility to resuscitate the striker. Once the striker regains consciousness, he should be asked about his decision, and if he wants to continue the strike and refuses treatment, the physician should respect this decision and follow the patient's directives.

NOTES

1   Even though there are no available data to support this claim; thousands of detainees have gone on a hunger strike in the last few years in countries like the US, the UK, Turkey, Israel, and Iran, but only a very limited number of hunger strikes were reported to have reached a life threatening level for the participants, and even fewer cases were reported to have had fatal consequences.

2   See Brockman [13] for a discussion of various motivations behind food refusals in prisons based on actual case examples.

3   There are a few examples that illustrate how the involvement of outside doctors might be beneficial [12, 15, 16].

4   I would like to thank an anonymous referee for bringing this up.

REFERENCES

1.   Laxmidas, Shrikesh. 2013. Angola teenager held for insulting president starts hunger strike. *Reuters*, November 6. http://www.reuters.com/article/2013/11/06/us-angola-youth-idUSBRE9A50PP20131106. Accessed Nov. 2014.

2.   Iranian prisoners launch hunger strike. 2013. *Al Jazeera*, November 5. http://www.aljazeera.com/news/middleeast/2013/11/iranian-prisoners-launch-hunger-strike-2013115143246356619.html. Accessed Nov. 2014.

3. Bigg, Claire, and Natalya Dzhanpoladova. 2013. Defendant in Russia's "Bolotnaya" case on hunger strike for 50 days. *Radio Free Europe*, November 6. http://www.rferl.org/content/bolotnaya-krivov-feature/25160206.html. Accessed Nov. 2014.

4. Kurdish mayor on hunger strike against "wall of shame." 2013. *Al Jazeera*, November 5. http://stream.aljazeera.com/story/201311052100-0023166. Accessed Nov. 2014.

5. California prison hunger strike: 30,000 inmates refuse meals. 2013. *Huffington Post*, July 9. http://www.huffingtonpost.com/2013/07/09/california-prison-hunger-strike-30000_n_3567639.html. Accessed Nov. 2014.

6. Reilly, Ryan J. 2013. Guantanamo Bay hunger strike numbers grow. *Huffington Post*, April 15. http://www.huffingtonpost.com/2013/04/15/guantanamo-bay-hunger-strike_n_3087299.html. Accessed Nov. 2014.

7. Jones, Sophia. 2012. More than 700 Kurdish prisoners now on hunger strike in Turkey. *NPR*, October 24. http://www.npr.org/blogs/thetwo-way/2012/10/24/163569699/more-than-700-kurdish-prisoners-now-on-hunger-strike-in-turkey. Accessed Nov. 2014.

8. World Medical Association. 2006. *WMA declaration of Malta on hunger strikers*. http://www.wma.net/en/30publications/10policies/h31/. Accessed Nov. 2014.

9. Johannes Wier Foundation for Health and Human Rights. 1995. *Assistance in hunger strikes: A manual for physicians and other health personnel in dealing with hunger strikers*. Amersfoort: JWFHHR.

10. Reyes, Hernan. 2007. Force-feeding and coercion: No physician complicity. *Virtual Mentor* 9(10): 703–708.

11. Annas, George J. 2006. Hunger strikes at Guantanamo: Medical ethics and human rights in a 'legal black hole'. *New England Journal of Medicine* 355: 1377–1382.

12. WMA declaration of Malta—a background paper on the ethical management of hunger strikes. 2006. *World Medical Journal* 52(2): 36–43.

13. Brockman, Bea. 1999. Food refusal in prisoners: A communication or a method of self-killing? The role of the psychiatrist and resulting ethical challenges. *Journal of Medical Ethics* 25: 451–456.

14. Woman jailed in Iran for attending volleyball match on 'dry' hunger strike. 2014. *The Guardian*, November 4. http://www.theguardian.com/world/2014/nov/04/ghoncheh-ghavami-jailed-iran-volleyball-match-hunger-strike. Accessed Nov. 2014.

15. Reyes, Hernan. 1998. Medical and ethical aspects of hunger strikes in custody and the issue of torture. In *Maltreatment and torture*, ed. M. Oehmichen. Lubeck: Verlag Schidt-Romhild. https://www.icrc.org/eng/resources/documents/article/other/health-article-010198.htm. Accessed June 15, 2015.

16. Soyer, Ata. 2000. Açlık grevleri/ölüm oruçları, TTB ve son tartışmalar [Hunger strikes/death fasts, TMA and the recent discussions]. *Toplum ve Hekim* 15(6): 1–15.

17. Fessler, D.M.T. 2003. The implications of starvation induced psychological changes for the ethical treatment of hunger strikers. *Journal of Medical Ethics* 29: 243–247.

18. Kalk, W.J., M. Felix, E.R. Snoey, and Y. Veriawa. 1993. Voluntary total fasting in political prisoners: Clinical and biochemical observations. *South African Medical Journal* 83(6): 391–394.

STANDING ON PRINCIPLE

Tech Workers Refusing Projects with Military Applications

Jonathan Milgrim

1. BACKGROUND

EACH YEAR THE US MILITARY SPENDS BILLIONS OF dollars on research and development.[1] These contracts, for obvious financial reasons, are in high demand by companies, many of whom rely heavily on military contracts for business. Tech giants such as Amazon, Google, and Microsoft also compete for these contracts, but recently there has been pushback—from their own employees. In 2018 Google chose not to renew a contract with the Pentagon that involved development of artificial intelligence for use in interpreting video images.[2] The technology has potential uses in drone guidance and target acquisition. The decision not to renew the contract was due to pressure from Google's own employees, many of whom worried the "do-no-evil" policy of the company was being put at risk. This change in policy is in stark contrast to Amazon and Microsoft, who routinely work with the Pentagon without objection. However, that also appears to be changing.

In February of 2019, Microsoft employees published an open letter objecting to the development of the Integrated Visual Augmentation System (IVAS). The Pentagon hopes to expand on the Microsoft HoloLens technology to provide night vision, thermal sensing, and vital sign monitoring in both training and battlefield situations. In their objection, the employees worried that, "the application of HoloLens within the IVAS system is designed to kill people. It will be deployed on the battlefield, and works by turning warfare into a simulated 'video game,' further distancing soldiers from the grim stakes of war and the reality of bloodshed."[3] Additionally, military technology is often passed down to other government agencies such as Immigration and Customs Enforcement (ICE) and civilian agencies such as local law enforcement departments. This creates an additional worry for those who work in the technology sector: that they will see their technology being used to enforce domestic policies they consider misguided or even immoral.

A final worry for the companies pursuing these contracts is the potential for widespread public backlash in the event their technology becomes famous, or infamous, due to military use. This was the case of Dow Chemical, the maker of Saran Wrap, when it developed napalm for the US military during the Vietnam War.[4] They soon found themselves associated with the nightly news images of civilians with terrible burns, fleeing in terror. In the age of Internet and instant news coverage, such worries are only exacerbated.

2. ANALYSIS

For those that see the professions as requiring obligations above those of non-professionals, these cases serve as ready examples of professionals attempting to fulfill those obligations. Professionals, such as those who subscribe to Google's do-no-evil policy, may see technology developments that aid in war as an evil that should be avoided. The Microsoft employees expressed a specific worry, that the development of this specific technology might dehumanize the targets in war, taking away from the horror that should be present when we take a life, whether that taking be justified or not. As societies become more global in nature, these concerns become even more pressing. In short order, similar technology may show up on the other side of the battlefield, leaving tech professionals feeling responsible for the death of American soldiers. Many professionals may feel obligated to object and perhaps even leave their company.

At the same time, there is an understanding that military technology is necessary. Though there are certainly some passivist technology professionals, most people agree that some level of military capability is necessary, and in an increasingly technological world, the major advancements will require the specific sort of expertise that technology professionals possess. This creates a potential no-win situation. On one hand the tech workers can, to some extent, influence how their individual companies act and what contracts are pursued. However, once technology leaves the parent company, they have no control over how the technology will be used. It is one thing to demand that Google not accept a contract, but if Amazon then develops the technology and passes it on to the military, nothing has been gained.

NOTES

1   Jeff Stein, "U.S. military budget inches closer to $1 trillion mark, as concerns over federal deficit grow," *The Washington Post*, 19 June 2018, https://www.washingtonpost.com/news/wonk/wp/2018/06/19/u-s-military-budget-inches-closer-to-1-trillion-mark-as-concerns-over-federal-deficit-grow/?noredirect=on&utm_term=.92d9dbc404bf.

2   Daisuke Wakabayashi and Scott Shane, "Google Will Not Renew Pentagon Contract That Upset Employees," *The New York Times*, 1 June 2018, https://www.nytimes.com/2018/06/01/technology/google-pentagon-project-maven.html.

3   Jason Evangelho, "Microsoft Employees Upset about HoloLens as U.S. Military Weapon," *Forbes*, 23 February 2019, https://www.forbes.com/sites/jasonevangelho/2019/02/23/ microsoft-employees-upset-about-hololens-as-u-s-military-weapon/#3a3b36464822.

4   Kevin Roose, "Why Napalm Is a Cautionary Tale for Tech Giants Pursuing Military Contracts," *The New York Times*, 4 March 2019, https://www.nytimes.com/2019/03/04/technology/technology-military-contracts.html.

DISCUSSION QUESTIONS

1.   Do you agree or disagree with the Google and Microsoft workers who objected to working on the military projects? Why?

2.   Do technology professionals have an obligation to avoid developing technology that will be used for harm (by the military or otherwise)? If so, does that also apply to all other companies (such as Boeing or Lockheed Martin that develop military aircraft that may be used in combat)? What about other professions, such as those in the medical field?

3.   Operating under the assumption that military technology is a necessity, should technology professionals who refuse to work on such projects be punished (through termination or reassignment to lesser projects)?

4.   Do you find the specific worry regarding the development of the HoloLens compelling?

RIGHTS AND RESPONSIBILITY

Arrests of International Journalists

Chad Watson

1. BACKGROUND

IN MAY 2017 TURKISH POLICE ARRESTED REPORTER Meşale Tolu Çorlu at her residence in Istanbul. The Turkish government charged Tolu Çorlu with involvement in a terrorist organization and spreading terrorist propaganda. Tolu Çorlu was detained in prison by officials for fear of her fleeing the country before her trial. In December 2017 Tolu Çorlu was released from prison but ordered to remain in Turkey. Her travel ban was subsequently lifted in August 2018 and she returned to Germany.

Meşale Tolu Çorlu was born in Germany to second-generation-emigrated Turkish parents. She received German citizenship in 2007 and renounced her Turkish citizenship. In 2014 Tolu Çorlu moved to Istanbul, Turkey to work as a reporter and translator. Tolu Çorlu worked for the radio station Özgür Radyo until its 2016 government-decreed shutdown, as well as the left-leaning news agency Etkin Haber Ajansı.

Tolu Çorlu's arrest came as part of a spate of arrests stemming from Turkish government crackdown following a 2016 coup d'état attempt to depose Turkish president Tayyip Erdoğan. Citing displeasure with government policy and actions, a faction of the Turkish Armed Forces attempted to wrest control of key locations in Ankara, Istanbul, and other areas of Turkey in July 2016. Forces loyal to the ruling party were able to break the coup attempt. In the months-long aftermath of the coup attempt, thousands of military personnel, civil servants, educational staff, and journalists were jailed under the power of sweeping new anti-terror policies and charged with aiding or otherwise being tied to a terrorist organization. These regulations also resulted in the shuttering of many news outlets and television and radio stations critical of the Turkish government, including Tolu Çorlu's former employer, Özgür Radyo.

Tolu Çorlu was officially charged with being a member of a terrorist organization and distributing terrorist propaganda. The group Tolu Çorlu was charged with associating with is the Marxist-Leninist Communist Party, a political party described as a terrorist organization by the Turkish government and outlawed in 2007. The Marxist-Leninist Communist Party is one of eleven outlawed political parties in Turkey. Tolu Çorlu denies the allegations of the Turkish government.

Özgür Radyo was one of dozens of media outlets shutdown due to alleged ties to Fethullah Gülen, a Turkish cleric self-exiled to the United States. Gülen is the founder of the Gülen Movement, a transnational Islamic social movement blamed by the Turkish government for the 2016 coup attempt. Among the journalists and reporters arrested for alleged involvement with the Gülen movement, outlawed political parties, or other organizations considered terrorist groups by the Turkish government, were several German citizens, in addition to Meşale Tolu Çorlu, and several United States citizens. At the time of Tolu Çorlu's release, many of these other foreign journalists were still being held in Turkey.

Meşale Tolu Çorlu returned to Turkey for her trial in October 2018. Tolu Çorlu was facing a prison sentence up to fifteen years. At the time of writing, no verdict had been reached in the trial.

2. ANALYSIS

Meşale Tolu Çorlu's arrest in Turkey is one case out of many where foreign journalists have been arrested in the country they are working in. While these cases have clear political and legal elements, navigating the moral features of these cases requires appreciating the broad scope of concerns involved. The press is an important institution globally. We rely on journalists, reporters, and news outlets to deliver important information about global and domestic affairs and expect that information to be presented truthfully and without unjust interference. To successfully analyze cases like Tolu Çorlu's arrest, we should identify those who have a stake in the situation and what their roles are. Primarily, the relevant parties in these cases are consumers of news media, the reporters themselves, and national governments.

Consumers of news media, the citizens of the relevant country, and the wider global community, have an interest in having access to truthful reporting from a variety of sources. Turning to the press to gain information about current events, citizens deserve factual reporting about these events and goings-on. Distortions of the facts are disrespectful to those looking to the press for information. For domestic citizens, they have an interest not only in being informed themselves, but in having the affairs of their country accurately portrayed to the global community. Similarly, those outside the country have an interest in the honest representation of events taking place in foreign countries. In cases like that of Turkey, where high acuity events have taken place, this interest is especially important; these events have significant effects globally and domestically and relevant reporting must be done carefully.

Gathering and presenting this information is the role of foreign reporters. In their important role, international journalists have a responsibility to maintain the integrity of their reporting while exercising their granted independence. Though we may value free press, this freedom should be used in service of the public interest in honest reporting and not merely to the individual ends of the journalists or news agencies. Regardless of these role-specific concerns, the fact remains that journalists are people and deserve *their* fundamental rights respected as well. While attitudes toward and regulations of the press may vary internationally, these differences should not constrain the fundamental rights of the foreign journalists in those countries.

This matter, then, falls primarily to the government. As the public has an interest in open access to information, governments have an obligation to protect and promote this interest. Part of this entails allowing citizens to access a variety of information from different sources and standpoints. However, there may be some reasonable limitations regarding foreign journalists. Dissemination of war propaganda or libelous publications may be limited out of concern for public interest; publication of such pieces shirks the responsibility held by international journalists and media outlets. In cases like that of the Turkish government, determining whether the limitations imposed are reasonable and in the public interest will require sensitive examination of current affairs and the reasoning behind the regulations. As noted above, however, journalists as persons maintain a certain degree of fundamental rights that ought not be violated. Whatever punishment is imposed, then, on international journalists violating legal press regulations should not severely infringe on these rights.

Cases like that of Meşale Tolu Çorlu's arrest in Turkey under charges of being part of and distributing propaganda for a terrorist organization involve many competing moral concerns. Navigating these problems to come up with a satisfying answer for the moral standing of these events requires not only a firm grasp of the facts of the scenario but also careful attention to these varied moral interests.

DISCUSSION QUESTIONS

1. Journalism does not always involve purely factual articles, but opinion pieces and analyses as well. What extra considerations, if any, are relevant to these pieces in the realm of international journalism?

2. If a foreign journalist has good reason to think the country he or she is working in has overly strict press regulations, is it acceptable to publish pieces in conflict with these regulations?

3. Domestic and international citizens have similar interests in the reporting of foreign journalists. Where do these interests overlap and where do they differ? For international reporting, do either set of interests take precedence over the other? Why or why not?

4. On global ethical standards, as opposed to the standards of the country in question, what kinds of reporting should we disallow or be suspicious of from international journalists?

CLIENT-BASED PROFESSIONS

Luke Golemon and T.J. Broy

1. INTRODUCTION

THE PREVIOUS UNITS FOCUSED ON SUBJECTS THAT cut across professions as a whole. No matter which profession one finds oneself in, one will have to deal with issues of privacy and confidentiality. Units 9 and 10, however, split professions into two categories: client-based professions and institution-based professions. This division is meant to allow a deeper delve into some of the specifics of certain professions without having an entire unit on, for example, lawyers.

This division is imperfect, however. There are professions that do not appear to fit into either category, such as engineering,[1] as well as professions that appear to fit in both categories, such as nurses or other medical professionals. Though the distinction between client-based and institution-based professions is sometimes blurry, there are still relevant differences and important insights to be had in exploring the space within each.

Client-based professions differ from other professions in that the relationship between the professional and their client involves a certain kind of knowledge that grants unique power to the professional. The lawyer knows much more about the law than their client, and the client relies on the lawyer to provide the information needed for the client to make decisions in their interest. The lawyer could, for example, withhold information in order to get the client to make one decision over another. This sort of abuse and others like it is what distinguishes client-based professions from categories like institution-based professions, in which the moral locus is the tension between doing what is good for an individual over doing what is good for the institution, which itself is good for the public at large.

The readings follow this taxonomy. After exploring the theory of client-based professions in more depth, the ethical framework and exploration find their focus in the relationship between the professional and their client. Finally, two case studies consider other aspects of the client-based professional, like loyalty to client as a value or being beholden to an institution as well as one's client.

2. CONTENTS

The readings begin with Michael Bayles's analysis of a client-based profession. He first considers paternalism, in which the professional does what is best for the client due to superior knowledge. He points out this is fair to the client's autonomy only when the client does not have any autonomy, and so settles on the fiduciary model of trust and information access as the analysis of choice.

In the second reading, Edmund Pellegrino argues that history alone could tell us there is more to being an ethical physician than duties or rules, but he goes on to give further reasons why we should expect physicians to be virtuous people over and above their duties.

Next, Pamela Grace explains three interrelated parts of nursing: what nursing is (e.g., how it differs from being a physician), what this means for professional responsibility, and finally the implications of the previous two parts for nursing ethics. This sheds light on how a parallel process might go in other client-based professions as well.

In the reading after, Michael Davis defends engineering as a profession. He first takes on critiques of engineering as a profession before building a positive case for why it should be considered so.

The fifth reading by Yotam Lurie and Shlomo Mark gives an interesting account of how to build an ethical framework for software engineers. Along the way, they emphasize the unique aspects of software engineering as a profession and how the correct framework plays into the kind of practice common in software engineering.

Following this, Domènec Melé shows how to integrate the interrelated values, rules, and virtues in accounting. The insights and implications drawn from accounting's example are then easily generalizable to other professions.

Frederic Reamer takes on the ethics and values of social work in the next reading. He shows how rules in social work that prevent abuse can sometimes interfere with what might seem like the right thing to do. This sort of tension is not limited to social work and can present itself in places like the medical field.

In the first case study, Hans Allhoff considers the complex issue of loyalty in a professional framework. Because the relationship between client and professional is so unique in these cases, loyalty can be an important part of the relationship. One question Allhoff explores is where the line should be drawn such that unethical conduct is not unwittingly performed.

In the second case study, Luke Golemon presents the case of a nurse who criticizes an institution for the elderly in which her grandfather was not properly cared for. Although she did not work at the institution, the nurse was reprimanded for her actions, citing violations of professional conduct.

NOTE

1   Although engineering is included in this unit, the discussion leading up to whether it is a profession at all also indicates how it is similar to a client-based profession (expertise and knowledge unavailable to the client) and how it differs (the relationship is not the primary locus of moral problems) in an enlightening fashion.

—63—

THE PROFESSIONAL-CLIENT RELATIONSHIP

Michael Bayles

... MANY ANALYSES HAVE BEEN OFFERED OF THE professional-client relationship. Some analyses are empirical; they describe the relationship as it normally exists. That is not the purpose of this section. Rather, the purpose here is to develop an ethical model that should govern the professional-client relationship. However, ethical models and norms often assume certain facts. For example, an ethical model of the appropriate relationship between parent and child makes certain assumptions about a child's abilities. A model of full equality would not work for very young children simply because they lack the physical and mental abilities to engage in such a relationship. Thus, although an ethical model of the professional-client relationship is not simply to describe it, a model can be inappropriate because it makes false empirical assumptions about one or the other parties.

The impulse of philosophy is to generalize. The present aim is to develop general statements of obligation that can require different conduct depending on the situation. The obligations to keep promises and make reparations for past injustice remain constant although the required conduct varies with the situation. There is no a priori reason why general obligations of professionals to clients cannot be established even though their application to particular cases requires different conduct in different situations. This does not imply ethical relativism.

To develop an ethical model that has the broadest scope, the model should not be based on unusual situations, such as a defendant charged with a capital crime or an unconscious patient. Unusual situations are so simply because they lack features of the usual or have additional features. An analysis based on unusual situations is therefore likely to distort normal situations. Professional ethics should be based on the usual sort of contact average clients have with professionals. Individual citizens are most likely to see lawyers in connection with real estate transactions, divorces, making wills, and personal injury negligence cases. Lawyers also spend much time drafting commercial contracts and advising about business matters. The average client will probably have a physician's attendance during a fatal illness or injury, but most physician-patient contacts are for more mundane matters such as a bacterial infection or a broken bone. Only gross neglect by the patient or physician—for example, the failure of a patient to take any medicine at all or of a physician to ask whether the patient is allergic to penicillin before prescribing it—is apt to turn these matters into seriously life-threatening illnesses or injuries. Engineers are apt to be consulted by companies or governments that want a project designed. Similarly, certified public accountants are most often hired to audit the books of a corporation. Both accountants and architects also deal with individuals for such purposes as income tax preparation and designing houses.

The central issue in the professional-client relationship is the allocation of responsibility and authority in decision making—who makes what decisions. The ethical models are in effect models of different distributions of authority and responsibility in decision making. One may view the professional-client relationship as one in which the client has most authority and responsibility in decision making, the professional being his employee; one in which the professional and client are equals, either dealing at arm's length or at a more personal level; or as one in which the professional, in different degrees, has the primary role. Each of these conceptions has been suggested by some authors as the appropriate ethical model of the relationship. Each has some commonsense support.

AGENCY

According to this view, the client has most of the authority and responsibility for decisions; the professional is an expert acting at the direction of the client.[1] The client hires a professional to protect or act for some interest; the professional provides services to achieve the client's goal—purchase of a house, removal of a gallbladder, design of a building. According to this conception, not only does the professional act for or in behalf of the client, but also acts under the direction of the client as in bureaucratic employer-employee relationships. This conception is especially plausible for lawyers. In filing a complaint or arguing for a client, a lawyer acts for and in behalf of the client. According to some people, a lawyer is merely a "mouthpiece" or "hired gun." It is not a plausible view of accountants performing public audits, for they are supposed to provide an independent review and statement of the clients' financial conditions.

In some contexts, professionals are prone to adopt the agency view of the professional-client relationship. Professionals are sometimes "identified" with their clients and charged with the client's alleged moral failings. Lawyers offer the defense that in representing clients, they do not thereby ascribe to or support clients' goals or aims.[2] They are merely employees hired to perform a specific task. If the projects are bad or immoral, the fault lies with the clients, or perhaps with the legal system for permitting them.

The agency model most clearly exemplifies what has been called the "ideology of advocacy." This ideology has two principles of conduct: (1) that the lawyer is neutral or detached from the client's purposes, and (2) that the lawyer is an aggressive partisan of the client working to advance the client's ends.[3] This ideology is readily applicable to physicians, architects, and engineers. A physician, for example, should not evaluate the moral worth of patients but only work to advance their health. The second element of the ideology does not apply to accountants performing audits, for they are to present independent statements of clients' financial conditions. It applies in other accounting activities though. For example, an accountant preparing a client's income tax statement should try to take every plausible deduction on behalf of the client.

Some aspects of this ideology appear inescapable in professional ethics. If professionals accepted only clients whose purposes they approved of and did not consider clients' interests any more than those of others, many persons with unusual purposes (such as wanting an architectural style of a building that is completely inconsistent with those nearby) might be unable to obtain professional services. And even if they did, the services might not be worth much, as no special consideration would be paid to their interests.[4] The chief problem with the ideology of advocacy, where it does become an ideology, is that sometimes devotion to a client's interests is thought to justify any lawful action advancing the client's ends, no matter how detrimental the effect on others.

The agency view of the professional-client relationship is unduly narrow. A number of considerations indicate limits to a professional's proper devotion to a client's interests, and consequently to a client's authority in decision making.

1. *... Professionals have obligations to third persons that limit the extent to which they may act in behalf of client interests.*
2. *The agency view arises most often in the context of defending professionals, especially lawyers, from attribution of client sins. This focus is too narrow to sustain a general account of the professional-client relationship. It best pertains to an adversarial context in which two opposing parties confront one another. In counseling, a lawyer's advice "need not be confined to purely legal considerations.... It is often desirable for a lawyer to point out those factors which may lead to a decision that is morally just as well as legally permissible."[5]*
3. *Professionals emphasize their independence of judgment. Unlike a soldier who is not expected to think for himself but to do things the army's way, professionals should exercise their training and skills to make objective judgments. The agency view ignores this feature.*
4. *Except in cases of dire need—medical emergencies, persons charged with crimes— professionals may accept or reject specific clients. With a few restrictions, they may also stop the relationship. Consequently, the agency view is too strong. Professionals must also be ethically free and responsible persons. For their own freedom and the protection of others, they should not abdicate authority and responsibility in decision making.*

The strongest possible claim of supremacy has been suggested, namely, that, like the common law doctrine of the merging of the identity of the husband and wife, the attorney and client are similarly merged in the identity of the client.[6] The proposal was made in the context of attempts by the Internal Revenue Service to obtain possibly incriminating documents from a client's attorney. By the Fifth Amendment to the U.S. Constitution, clients need not surrender possibly incriminating documents in their own possession. The IRS contends this Fifth Amendment privilege does not extend to lawyers,

just as it does not extend to tax accountants. If the identities of client and attorney are merged, then the rights and privileges of a client would apply to the attorney.

Although this "legal fiction" could be useful in this narrow context, strong reasons are against adopting it. Fictions should be avoided in law and ethics if straightforward arguments lead to similar results. Once admitted, fictions can bewitch the understanding and lead to unjustifiable results in other areas. The analogy with the common law doctrine of the identity of husband and wife is quite weak. Except for dowry and a few other matters, the identities of husband and wife were completely merged for legal purposes. In contrast, the merger of attorney and client identities would be very limited. As the considerations against the agency view indicate, good grounds exist for separating the attorney and client in many contexts. Even with respect to incriminating materials, professionals should be permitted or even required to reveal confidences indicating a client's intention to commit a crime.[7]

CONTRACT

If a client ought not to be viewed as having most authority and responsibility, then perhaps the authority and responsibility should be shared equally. In law, a professional-client relationship is based on a contract, and the ethical concept of a just contract is of an agreement freely arrived at by bargaining between equals. If the relationship is a contractual one, then there are mutual obligations and rights, "a true sharing of ethical authority and responsibility."[8] As it recognizes the freedom of two equals to determine the conditions of their relationship, the contract model accords well with the liberal values of freedom and equality of opportunity.

However, no gain results from treating as equals people who are not relevantly equal in fact or from assuming a nonexistent freedom. The history of contract of adhesion (the standard forms offered by monopolies or near monopolies such as airlines) indicates the injustice that can result from falsely assuming contracting parties have equal bargaining power. Many commentators have noted relevant inequalities between professionals and clients, especially in the medical context.[9] First, a professional's knowledge far exceeds that of a client. A professional has the special knowledge produced by long training, knowledge a client could not have without comparable training. Second, a client is concerned about some basic value—personal health, legal status, or financial status—whereas a professional is not as concerned about the subject matter of their relationship. The client usually has more at stake. Third, a professional often has a freedom to enter the relationship that a client lacks. A professional is often able to obtain other clients more easily than a client can obtain another professional. Especially if a potential client has an acute illness or has just been charged with a crime, he or she is not free to shop around for another professional. From this point of view, the bargaining situation is more like that between an individual and a public utility.

These considerations are not as important for the usual situation in architecture, accounting, and engineering. The clients of these professionals are often better informed about the subject matter of the transaction than are clients of lawyers and physicians. For example, businesses and corporations have accountants working for them who can give advice about auditors. Often firms hiring consulting engineers have had previous experience working with engineers in that field. Governments, even local ones, frequently have one or two engineers working for them who can advise and help. Moreover, they are freer than the professional to conclude an arrangement with another firm. Thus, in these situations the factual basis for the contract model is most nearly present. However, the consulting engineer or architect has some special knowledge and ability the client lacks, or else a professional would probably not be hired, so the contract model's empirical assumptions do not quite hold even in these cases.

FRIENDSHIP

Instead of viewing the relationship as one between two free and equal persons dealing at arm's length, some authors suggest that the relationship is more personal. One does not relate to a professional as one does to a grocer or public utility. The personal element is most closely captured by viewing the relationship as one of pals or friends. According to this view, professional and client have a close relationship of mutual trust and cooperation; they are involved in a mutual venture, a partnership.

Perhaps the most sophisticated version of this conception is that proposed by Charles Fried.[10] He is primarily concerned with the legal and medical professions. Fried seeks to justify professionals devoting special attention and care to clients and sometimes seeking ends and using means that they would not seek or use for themselves. Friends are permitted, even expected, to take each others' interests seriously and to give them more weight than they do those of other persons. Fried suggests that the attorney-client relationship is analogous to a one-way limited friendship in which the lawyer helps the client secure legal rights. The lawyer helps the client assert his autonomy or freedom within the bounds society permits. Others have suggested that the physician-patient relationship should similarly be viewed as a cooperative effort of friends or pals to deal with the patient's illness or injury.

The many dissimilarities between friendship and the professional-client relationship, however, destroy the analogy. First, as Fried recognizes, the professional-client relationship is chiefly in one direction; the professional has a concern for the client's interests but not vice versa. Second, friendship is usually between equals. Even in friendships between employer and employee, the employer's superiority in the office is changed to a position of equality in the bar for a drink. As the above discussion of the contract model indicates, professionals and clients are not equals. Third, the affective commitment of friendship is usually lacking.[11] Professionals accept clients for a fee, not out of concern for individuals. Thus, one commentator concludes that "Fried has described the classical notion, not of friendship, but of prostitution."[12] As the factual assumptions of this model are incorrect and the analogy supporting it is weak, its ethical implications are unfounded.

The friendship analogy is not needed to justify a professional paying special attention to a client's interests. The role of a professional is to provide services to clients, and the acceptance of a client is sufficient to justify the special attention. A barber who accepts a customer pays special attention to a customer's hair over that of others who need a haircut more. One need not postulate the barber as friend to justify this attention. It is presupposed by any system of services for a fee.

PATERNALISM

Once one abandons models that assume the professional and client are equal and accepts that the professional is to some extent in a superior position to the client, one faces the problem of the proper extent of professional authority and responsibility in decision making. Parents have knowledge and experience that children lack, and it is often ethically appropriate for them to exercise their judgment on behalf of their children. Similarly, as a professional has knowledge and experience a client lacks and is hired to further the client's interests, perhaps the relationship should be viewed as one of paternalism.

Paternalism is a difficult concept to analyze. A person's conduct is paternalistic to the extent his or her reasons are to do something to or in behalf of another person for that person's well-being. What is done can be any of a number of things, from removing an appendix to preventing the person from taking drugs. One can also have a paternalistic reason for acting in behalf of a person—for example, filing a counterclaim or asserting a legal defense. The key element of paternalism derives from the agent, X, acting regardless of the person's, Y's, completely voluntary and informed consent. X's reason is that he or she judges the action to be for Y's well-being regardless of Y's consent to it. Y may be incapable of consent, as when a physician treats an unconscious patient in an emergency, or Y may never have been asked, or may have refused to consent to the act.

Conduct can be paternalistic even when Y in fact consents.[13] For example, if X is prepared to do something to Y regardless of Y's consent, then X's reason is paternalistic even if Y does consent. Parents frequently manipulate a child into assenting to actions, although they were prepared to do them without the child's assent. The key element is that X would have done the action, if he could, even if Y had not consented. Such claims are difficult to establish, but this difficulty is a practical problem and does not affect the conceptual matter. In manufacturing consent, information can be withheld, false information provided, or more emphasis placed on some facts than others. Professionals sometimes manufacture consent when action cannot legally be taken without client consent, such as accepting a settlement or performing an operation. The concept of doing something to or in behalf of someone includes failure to do something. Suppose Y requests X to do something for him, but X refuses because she thinks it would be detrimental to Y's well-being; for example, a physician refuses to prescribe a tranquilizer for a patient. This also counts as doing something to or in behalf of a person without his consent; Y does not consent to the tranquilizers being withheld.

A voluminous literature exists concerning the justification of paternalism. The brief discussion here will outline only the major arguments. Paternalism requires justification because it involves doing something to or in behalf of another person regardless of that person's consent. It thus denies people the freedom to make choices affecting their lives. They lack the freedom of self-determination.... The loss of control over their own lives, especially to professionals, is one reason for people's concern about professional ethics. Thus, paternalism is of central importance in professional ethics.

Three arguments are often offered to justify paternalism.

1. *The agent has superior knowledge as to what is in a person's best interest. Because the agent knows better than the person what is best, the agent is justified in acting to avoid significant harm to, or to procure a significant benefit for, the person. This argument is perhaps the central one in favor of paternalism by professionals. As noted before, a professional possesses a relevant knowledge the client lacks, so he or she is better able to perceive the advantages and disadvantages of alternative actions. Consequently, the professional rather than the client should have primary authority and responsibility for decisions.*

2. *The client is incapable of giving a fully free and informed consent. By "fully free" is meant without duress, psychological compulsion, or other emotional or psychological disturbance. By "informed" is meant with appreciation of the consequences of a course of conduct and its alternatives. If people cannot give such consent, then their decisions will not adequately reflect their reasonable desires and will not be expressions of their "true selves." This argument, which in some respects is a subcase of the previous one, is also popular in the professions, especially medicine. It is often claimed that people who are ill have a strong feeling of dependency, are worried by their illness, and are in a weakened state, and so lack their usual mental command. A somewhat similar argument can be made about lawyers' clients. If charged with a criminal offense, a person is fearful and disturbed. Even in civil suits, a client's emotions might be aroused, preventing an objective view of the situation.*

3. *A person will later come to agree that the decision was correct. Although the person does not now consent, he will later. For example, an unconscious accident victim with a broken limb will agree that a physician was correct to set the bone. Parents often require their children to do things, such as take music lessons, on the ground that later the children will be glad they did—"You'll thank me later!" An engineer might see a way to improve an agreed-upon rough design to better serve a client's needs, although it involves a significant alteration from the rough design. She might make the change in the belief that the client will agree when he sees the completed design.*

To decide whether these justifications support viewing the professional-client relationship as paternalistic, it is useful to consider when reasonable people would allow others to make decisions for them. First, a person might not wish to bother making decisions because the differences involved are trivial. For example, an executive authorizes a secretary to order any needed office supplies, because the differences between brands of paper clips and so forth are not important. Second, the decisions might require knowledge or expertise a person does not possess. For example, an automobile mechanic knows whether a car's oil filter needs changing. One goes to a mechanic for knowledge and service. Third, a person might allow others to make judgments if he or she is or will be mentally incompetent. Some people voluntarily enter mental hospitals. The first of these reasons does not directly relate to the arguments for paternalism, but the second and third do relate to the first two arguments for paternalism. Reasonable persons would allow others to make decisions for them when they lack the capacity to make reasonable judgments. However, most clients do not have sufficiently impaired judgment to reasonably allow others to make important decisions for them. This incapacity argument has little or no plausibility for the common clients of architects, engineers, and accountants. Business and corporate clients of lawyers are unlikely to have significantly impaired judgment, even if they are biased. Moreover, even with individuals, the view is not plausible for the common legal and medical cases. A person who wants to purchase a house or make a will, or who has the flu or an infection, is rarely so distraught as to be unable to make reasonable decisions. Consequently, the argument from incapacity does not support adopting a paternalistic conception of the professional-client relationship for most cases, although it supports using that conception in special cases. The first argument for paternalism, that from superior knowledge, fits with reasonable persons allowing others to make decisions when they lack knowledge. Moreover, clients go to professionals for their superior knowledge and skills; such knowledge and skill is a defining feature of a profession. However, many decisions require balancing legal or health concerns against other client interests. As many authors have noted, crucial professional decisions involve value choices.[14] They are not simple choices of technical means to ends, and even choices of means have a value component. Professionals have not had training in value choices. Even if they had, they might not know a client's value scheme sufficiently to determine what is best for him when everything is considered. An attorney might advise a client that he or she need not agree to such large alimony or child support payments, but the client might decide that for personal relations with the former spouse or the welfare of the children, the larger payments are best. Similarly, a physician can advise bed rest, but because of business interests a client can decide her overall interests are best promoted by continuing to work on certain matters. The client might especially need the income or be on the verge of completing a business deal that will earn a promotion. Physicians sometimes fail to realize that a patient's other concerns, even a vacation trip with the family, can precede health. They write and speak of the problem of patient noncompliance just as parents speak of noncompliance by children. Yet, one does not have everything when one has health. Similarly, a client might want an engineering or architectural design to use one type of construction rather than another because its subsidiary supplies such materials. Although a professional and client are not equals, sufficient client competence exists to undermine the paternalistic model as appropriate for their usual relationship. Clients can exercise judgment over many aspects of professional services. If they lack information to make decisions, professionals can provide it. Sometimes professionals argue that clients can never have the information they have. This is true, but not directly to the point.

Much of the information professionals have is irrelevant to decisions that significantly affect client values. The precise name of a disease and its manner of action are not relevant to deciding between two alternative drug therapies, but the fact that one drug reduces alertness is. Similarly, clients of engineers do not need to know the full weight a structure will bear, only that it is more than sufficient for all anticipated stress. To deny clients authority and responsibility by adopting the paternalistic model is to deny them the freedom to direct their own lives. Clients are not capable of determining the precise nature of their problem, or of knowing the alternative courses of action and predicting their consequences or carrying them out on their own. They need and want the technical expertise of a professional to do so. However, they are capable of making reasonable choices among options on the basis of their total values. They need professionals' information in order to make wise choices to accomplish their purposes. Finally, when the professional-client relationship is conducted on the paternalistic model, client outcomes are not as good as when the client has a more active role. Douglas E. Rosenthal studied settlement awards in personal injury cases.[15] The actual awards received were compared to an expert panel's judgments of the worth of the claims. The less the client participated in the case by not expressing wants or seeking information from the lawyers, and so on, the more the awards fell short of the panel's estimates of the worth of claims. Not only does the paternalistic model sacrifice client freedom and autonomy, but as a result client values and interests are also often sacrificed.

FIDUCIARY

As a general characterization of what the professional-client relationship should be, one needs a concept in which the professional's superior knowledge is recognized, but the client retains a significant authority and responsibility in decision making. The law uses such a conception to characterize most professional-client relationships, namely, that of a fiduciary. In a fiduciary relationship, both parties are responsible and their judgments given consideration. Because one party is in a more advantageous position, he or she has special obligations to the other. The weaker party depends upon the stronger in ways in which the other does not and so must *trust* the stronger party.

In the fiduciary model, a client has more authority and responsibility in decision making than in the paternalistic model. A client's consent and judgment are required and he participates in the decision-making process, but the client depends on the professional for much of the information upon which he gives or withholds his consent. The term *consents* (the client consents) rather than *decides* (the client decides) indicates that it is the professional's role to propose courses of action. It is not the conception of two people contributing equally to the formulation of plans, whether or not dealing at arm's length. Rather, the professional supplies the ideas and information and the client agrees or not. For the process to work, the client must trust the professional to accurately analyze the problem, canvass the feasible alternatives, know as well as one can their likely consequences, fully convey this information to the client, perhaps make a recommendation, and work honestly and loyally for the client to effectuate the chosen alternatives. In short, the client must rely on the professional to use his or her knowledge and ability in the client's interests. Because the client cannot check most of the work of the professional or the information supplied, the professional has special obligations to the client to ensure that the trust and reliance are justified.

This is not to suggest that the professional simply presents an overall recommendation for a client's acceptance or rejection. Rather, a client's interests can be affected by various aspects of a professional's work, so the client should be consulted at various times. The extent of appropriate client participation and decision making can be determined by advertence to the reasons for allowing others to make decisions for one. Professionals do not have expertise in a client's values or in making value choices. Their superior knowledge

and expertise do not qualify them to make value choices significantly affecting a client's life plans or style. However, they do have knowledge of technical matters. A patient will certainly let a physician determine the dosage of medicines. A client can reasonably allow an engineer to determine the general specifications of materials for a job. A lawyer may decide whether to stipulate facts, object to testimony, or agree to a postponement.[16] Clients allow professionals to make these judgments, because the effects on their values are small and they do not wish to be bothered. In short, client consent and involvement are not necessary when (1) the matter is chiefly a technical one or (2) the value effect is not significant.

The appropriate ethical conception of the professional-client relationship is one that allows clients as much freedom to determine how their life is affected as is reasonably warranted on the basis of their ability to make decisions. In most dealings of business and corporate clients with accountants, architects, engineers, and lawyers, the relationship is close to a contract between equals. As clients have less knowledge about the subject matter for which the professional is engaged, the special obligations of the professional in the fiduciary model become more significant. The professional must assume more responsibility for formulating plans, presenting their advantages and disadvantages, and making recommendations. Because of the increased reliance on the professional, he or she must take special care to be worthy of client trust. Thus, although the fiduciary model is appropriate throughout the range of competent clients and services, the less a client's knowledge and capacity to understand, the greater the professional's responsibilities to the client.

Finally, some clients are not competent to make decisions. In this case, the paternalistic model becomes appropriate. These cases of an incompetent client will almost always be restricted to members of the legal and health professions. Even then it does not follow that the professional should make the decisions. If a client is incompetent, a legal guardian should be appointed to make decisions. When this is done, the professional has a fiduciary relationship to the guardian. Consequently, the appropriate occasions for professionals to adopt a paternalistic role are restricted to those in which a client is incompetent and a guardian has not yet been appointed....

NOTES

1 See [Robert M. Veatch, "Models for Ethical Medicine in a Revolutionary Age," *Hastings Center Report* 2 (June 1972)], p. 5. Veatch calls this the engineering model of the physician, but this assumes it is appropriate for engineers.

2 See [American Bar Association. *Model Rules of Professional Conduct*. Chicago: American Bar Association, 1983], 1.2(b).

3 [William H. Simon, "The Ideology of Advocacy: Procedural Justice and Professional Ethics," *Wisconsin Law Review* (1978)], p. 36.

4 Simon's proposed alternative to the ideology of advocacy suffers these defects to some extent. He does not allow for professional roles. Thus, all professional obligations are at best specifications of ordinary norms. "The foundation principle of non-professional advocacy is that problems of advocacy be treated as a matter of *personal* ethics....Personal ethics apply to people merely by virtue of the fact that they are human individuals. The obligations involved may depend on particular circumstances or personalities, but they do not follow from social role or station." Ibid., p. 131.

5 [American Bar Association, ABA, *Code of Professional Responsibility and Code of Judicial Conduct*, Chicago: American Bar Association, 1983], EC 7–8; see also ABA, Commission, *Model Rules*, 2.1 and comment.

6 [Roger M. Grace, "Invading the Privacy of the Attorney-Client Relationship," *Case and Comment* 81 (July–August 1976)], p. 47.

7 ABA, *Code of Professional Responsibility*, DR 4–101(C) (3): ABA, Commission, *Model Rules*, 1.6(b).

8 Veatch, "Models for Ethical Medicine," p. 7.

9 See, for example, [Roger D. Masters, "Is Contract an Adequate Basis for Medical Ethics?," *Hastings Center Report* (December 1975)], p. 25; [William F. May, "Code, Covenant, Contract, or Philanthropy?," *Hastings Center Report* 5 (December 1975)], p. 35; [H. Tristram Englehardt Jr., "Rights and Responsibilities of Patients and Physicians," in *Medical Treatment of the Dying: Moral Issues*, edited by Michael D. Bayles and Dallas M. High, Cambridge, Mass.: G.K. Hall and Schenkman, 1978], pp. 16–17; Richard Wasserstrom, "Lawyers as Professionals: Some Moral Issues," in *1977 National Conference on Teaching Professional Responsibility*, ed. Goldberg, pp. 120–122.

10 Charles Fried, "The Lawyer as Friend: The Moral Foundations of the Lawyer-Client Relationship," in *1977 National Conference on Teaching Professional Responsibility*, ed. Goldberg, pp. 129–158; and [Charles Fried, *Right and Wrong*, Cambridge, Mass.: Harvard University Press, 1978], chap. 7; see also Veatch, "Models for Ethical Medicine," p. 7.

11 Edward A. Dauer and Arthur Allen Leff, "The Lawyer as Friend," in *1977 National Conference on Teaching Professional Responsibility*, ed. Goldberg, p. 164.

12 Simon, "The Ideology of Advocacy," p. 108.

13 Cf. Joseph Ellin, "Comments on 'Paternalism and Health Care,'" in *Contemporary Issues in Biomedical Ethics*, ed. Davis, Hoffmaster, and Shorten, pp. 245–246.

14 See, for example, Glenn C. Graber, "On Paternalism and Health Care," in *Contemporary Issues in Biomedical Ethics*, ed. Davis, Hoffmaster, and Shorten, p. 239; [Allen Buchanan, "Medical Paternalism," *Philosophy & Public Affairs* 7 (1978)], p. 381; and [Alan H. Goldman, *The Moral Foundations of Professional Ethics*, Totowa, N.J.: Rowman and Littlefield, 1980], pp. 179–186.

15 [Douglas E. Rosenthal, *Lawyer and Client: Who's in Charge?* New York: Russell Sage Foundation, 1974], chap. 2.

16 See ABA, *Code of Professional Responsibility*, EC 7–7; but see ABA, Commission, *Model Rules*, 1.2(a), 1.4.

—64—

THE VIRTUOUS PHYSICIAN AND THE ETHICS OF MEDICINE

Edmund D. Pellegrino

... IN MOST PROFESSIONAL ETHICAL CODES, VIRTUE and duty-based ethics are intermingled. The Hippocratic Oath, for example, imposes certain duties like protection of confidentiality, avoiding abortion, not harming the patient. But the Hippocratic physician also pledges: "... in purity and holiness I will guard my life and my art." This is an exhortation to be a good person and a virtuous physician, in order to serve patients in an ethically responsible way.

Likewise, in one of the most humanistic statements in medical literature, the first century AD writer, Scribonius Largus, made *humanitas* (compassion) an essential virtue. It is thus really a role-specific duty. In doing so he was applying the Stoic doctrine of virtue to medicine [Cicero, Pellegrino].

The latest version (1980) of the AMA "Principles of Medical Ethics" similarly intermingles duties, rights, and exhortations to virtue. It speaks of "standards of behaviour," "essentials of honorable behavior," dealing "honestly" with patients and colleagues and exposing colleagues "deficient in character." The *Declaration of Geneva*, which must meet the challenge of the widest array of value systems, nonetheless calls for practice "with conscience and dignity" in keeping with "the honor and noble traditions of the profession." Though their first allegiance must be to the Communist ethos, even the Soviet physician is urged to preserve "the high title of physician,"

"to keep and develop the beneficial traditions of medicine" and to "dedicate" all his "knowledge and strength to the care of the sick."

Those who are cynical of any protestation of virtue on the part of physicians will interpret these excerpts as the last remnants of a dying tradition of altruistic benevolence. But at the very least, they attest to the recognition that the good of the patient cannot be fully protected by rights and duties alone. Some degree of supererogation is built into the nature of the relationship of those who are ill and those who profess to help them.

This too may be why many graduating classes, still idealistic about their calling, choose the Prayer of Maimonides (not by Maimonides at all) over the more deontological Oath of Hippocrates. In that "prayer" the physician asks: "... may neither avarice nor miserliness, nor thirst for glory or for a great reputation engage my mind; for the enemies of truth and philanthropy may easily deceive me and make me forgetful of my lofty aim of doing good to thy children." This is an unequivocal call to virtue and it is hard to imagine even the most cynical graduate failing to comprehend its message.

All professional medical codes, then, are built of a three-tiered system of obligations related to the special roles of physicians in society. In the ascending order of ethical sensitivity they are: observance of the laws of the land, then observance of rights and fulfillment of duties, and finally the practice of virtue.

A legally based ethic concentrates on the minimum requirements—the duties imposed by human laws which protect against the grosser aberrations of personal rights. Licensure, the laws of torts and contracts, prohibitions against discrimination, good Samaritan laws, definitions of death, and the protection of human subjects of experimentation are elements of a legalistic ethic.

At the next level is the ethics of rights and duties which spells out obligations beyond what law defines. Here, benevolence and beneficence take on more than their legal meaning. The ideal of service, of responsiveness to the special needs of those who are ill, some degree of compassion, kindliness, promise-keeping, truth-telling, and non-maleficence and specific obligations like confidentiality and autonomy, are included. How these principles are applied, and conflicts among them resolved in the patient's best interests, are subjects of widely varying interpretation. How sensitively these issues are confronted depends more on the physician's character than his capability at ethical discourse or moral casuistry.

Virtue-based ethics goes beyond these first two levels. We expect the virtuous person to do the right and the good even at the expense of personal sacrifice and legitimate self-interest. Virtue ethics expands the notions of benevolence, beneficence, conscientiousness, compassion, and fidelity well beyond what strict duty might require. It makes some degree of supererogation mandatory because it calls for standards of ethical performance that exceed those prevalent in the rest of society [Reader].

At each of these three levels there are certain dangers from over-zealous or misguided observance. Legalistic ethical systems tend toward a justification for minimalistic ethics, a narrow definition of benevolence or beneficence, and a contract-minded physician-patient relationship. Duty- and rights-based ethics may be distorted by too strict adherence to the letter of ethical principles without the modulations and nuances the spirit of those principles implies. Virtue-based ethics, being the least specific, can more easily lapse into self-righteous paternalism or an unwelcome over-involvement in the personal life of the patient. Misapplication of any moral system even with good intent converts benevolence into maleficence. The virtuous person might be expected to be more sensitive to these aberrations than someone whose ethics is more deontologically or legally flavored.

The more we yearn for ethical sensitivity the less we lean on rights, duties, rules, and principles and the more we lean on the character traits of the moral agent. Paradoxically, without rules, rights, and duties specifically spelled out, we cannot predict what form a particular person's expression of virtue will take. In a pluralistic society, we need laws, rules and principles to assure a dependable minimum level of moral conduct. But that minimal level is insufficient in the complex and often unpredictable circumstances of decision-making, where technical and value desiderata intersect so inextricably.

The virtuous physician does not act from unreasoned, uncritical intuitions about what feels good. His dispositions are ordered in accord with that "right reason" which both Aristotle and Aquinas considered essential to virtue. Medicine is itself ultimately an exercise of practical wisdom—a right way of acting in difficult and uncertain circumstances for a specific end, i.e., the good of a particular person who is ill. It is when the choice of a right and good action becomes more difficult, when the temptations to self-interest are most insistent, when unexpected nuances of good and evil arise and no one is looking, that the differences between an ethics based in virtue and an ethics based in law and/or duty can most clearly be distinguished.

Virtue-based professional ethics distinguishes itself, therefore, less in the avoidance of overtly immoral practices than in avoidance of those at the margin of moral responsibility. Physicians are confronted, in today's morally relaxed climate, with an increasing number of new practices that pit altruism against self-interest. Most are not illegal, or, strictly speaking, immoral in a rights- or duty-based ethic. But they are not consistent with the higher levels of moral sensitivity that a virtue-ethics demands. These practices usually involve opportunities for profit from the illness of others, narrowing the concept of service for personal convenience, taking a proprietary attitude with respect to medical knowledge, and placing loyalty to the profession above loyalty to patients.

Under the first heading, we might include such things as investment in and ownership of for-profit hospitals, hospital chains, nursing homes, dialysis units, tie-in arrangements with radiological or laboratory services, escalation of fees for repetitive, high-volume procedures, and lax indications for their use, especially when third party payers "allow" such charges.

The second heading might include the ever decreasing availability and accessibility of physicians, the diffusion of individual patient responsibility in group practice so that the patient never knows whom he will see or who is on call, the itinerant emergency room physician who works two days and skips three with little commitment to hospital or community, and the growing over-indulgence of physicians in vacations, recreation, and "self-development."

The third category might include such things as "selling one's services" for whatever the market will bear, providing what the market demands and not necessarily what the community needs, patenting new procedures or keeping them secret from potential competitor-colleagues, looking at the investment of time, effort, and capital in a medical education as justification of "making it back," or forgetting that medical knowledge is drawn from the cumulative experience of a multitude of patients, clinicians, and investigators.

Under the last category might be included referrals on the basis of friendship and reciprocity rather than skill, resisting consultations and second opinions as affronts to one's competence, placing the interest of the referring physician above those of the patients, looking the other way in the face of incompetence or even dishonesty in one's professional colleagues.

These and many other practices are defended today by sincere physicians and even encouraged in this era of competition, legalism, and self-indulgence. Some can be rationalized even in a deontological ethic. But it would be impossible to envision the physician committed to the virtues assenting to these practices. A virtue-based ethics simply does not fluctuate with what the dominant social mores will tolerate. It must interpret benevolence, beneficence, and responsibility in a way that reduces self-interest and enhances altruism. It is the only convincing answer the profession can give to the growing perception clearly manifest in the legal commentaries in the FTC ruling that medicine is nothing more than business and should be regulated as such.

A virtue-based ethic is inherently elitist, in the best sense, because its adherents demand more of themselves than the prevailing morality. It calls forth that extra measure of dedication that has made the best physicians in every era exemplars of what the human spirit can achieve. No matter to what depths a society may fall, virtuous persons will always be the beacons that light the way back to moral sensitivity; virtuous physicians are the beacons that show the way back to moral credibility for the whole profession.

Albert Jonsen, rightly I believe, diagnoses the central paradox in medicine as the tension between self-interest and altruism [Jonsen]. No amount of deft juggling of rights, duties, or principles will suffice to resolve that tension. We are all too good at rationalizing what we want to do so that personal gain can be converted from vice to virtue. Only a character formed by the virtues can feel the nausea of such intellectual hypocrisy.

To be sure, the twin themes of self-interest and altruism have been inextricably joined in the history of medicine. There have always been physicians who reject the virtues or, more often, claim them falsely. But, in addition, there have been physicians, more often than the critics of medicine would allow, who have been truly virtuous both in intent and act. They have been, and remain, the leaven of the profession and the hope of all who are ill. They form the seawall that will not be eroded even by the powerful forces of commercialization, bureaucratization, and mechanization inevitable in modern medicine.

We cannot, need not, and indeed must not, wait for a medical analogue of MacIntyre's "new St. Benedict" to show us the way. There is no new concept of virtue waiting to be discovered that is peculiarly suited to the dilemmas of our own dark age. We must recapture the courage to speak of character, virtue, and perfection in living a good life. We must encourage those who are willing to dedicate themselves to a "higher standard of self effacement" [Cushing]. We need the courage, too, to accept the obvious split in the profession between those who see and feel the altruistic imperatives in medicine, and those who do not. Those who at heart believe that the pursuit of private self-interest serves the public good are very different from those who believe in the restraint of self-interest. We forget that physicians since the beginnings of the profession have subscribed to different values and virtues. We need only recall that the Hippocratic Oath was the Oath of physicians of the Pythagorean school at a time when most Greek physicians followed essentially a craft ethic [Edelstein]. A perusal of the Hippocratic Corpus itself, which intersperses ethics and etiquette, will show how differently its treatises deal with fees, the care of incurable patients, and the business aspects of the craft.

The illusion that all physicians share a common devotion to a high-flown set of ethical principles has done damage to medicine by raising expectations some members of the profession could not, or will not, fulfill. Today, we must be more forthright about the differences in value commitment among physicians. Professional codes must be more explicit about the relationships between duties, rights, and virtues. Such explicitness encourages a more honest relationship between physicians and patients and removes the hypocrisy of verbal assent to a general code, to which an individual physician may not really subscribe. Explicitness enables patients to choose among physicians on the basis of their ethical

commitments as well as their reputations for technical expertise.

Conceptual clarity will not assure virtuous behavior. Indeed, virtues are usually distorted if they are the subject of too conscious a design. But conceptual clarity will distinguish between motives and provide criteria for judging the moral commitment one can expect from the profession and from its individual members. It can also inspire those whose virtuous inclinations need reinforcement in the current climate of commercialization of the healing relationship.

To this end the current resurgence of interest in virtue-based ethics is altogether salubrious. Linked to a theory of patient good and a theory of rights and duties, it could provide the needed groundwork for a reconstruction of professional medical ethics as that work matures. Perhaps even more progress can be made if we take Shakespeare's advice in *Hamlet*: "Assume the virtue if you have it not.... For use almost can change the stamp of nature."

BIBLIOGRAPHY

1   Cicero: 1967, *Moral Obligations*, J. Higginbotham (trans.), University of California Press, Berkeley and Los Angeles.

2   Cushing, H.: 1929, *Consecratio Medici and Other Papers*, Little, Brown and Co., Boston.

3   Edelstein, L.: 1967, "The Professional Ethics of the Greek Physician," in O. Temkin (ed.), *Ancient Medicine: Selected Papers of Ludwig Edelstein*, Johns Hopkins University Press, Baltimore.

4   Jonsen, A.: 1983, "Watching the Doctor," *New England Journal of Medicine* Vol. 308: 25, 1531–35.

5   Pellegrino, E.: 1983, "*Scribonius Largus* and the Origins of Medical Humanism," address to the American Osler Society.

6   Reader, J.: 1982, "Beneficence, Supererogation, and Role Duty," in E. Shelp (ed.), *Beneficence and Health Care*, D. Reidel, Dordrecht, Holland, 83–108.

—65—

NURSING ETHICS AND PROFESSIONAL RESPONSIBILITY

Pamela J. Grace

The professional must respond ... if practices in his field are inadequate at any stage of the rendering of the service: if the client the ultimate consumer is unhappy; if he is happy, but unknowing, badly served by shabby products or service; or if he is happy and well served by the best available product but the state of the art is not adequate to his real needs.

—L.H. NEWTON, "Lawgiving for Professional Life: Reflections on the Place of the Professional Code," 1988

Let whoever is in charge keep this simple question in her head (not, how can I always do this right thing myself, but) how can I provide for this right thing to be always done?

—FLORENCE NIGHTINGALE, *Notes on Nursing: What It Is and What It Is Not,* 1946

NURSING AS A PROFESSION

The Status of Nursing as a Profession

CONCERNS

WHY SHOULD NURSES BE CONCERNED WITH THE quality and intent of all clinical judgments and the actions that follow from them? Is it not true that some actions are purely routine? Why should everything about nursing practice be subject to ethical appraisal (nursing ethics)? The answer lies partly in the idea that nursing is one of those professions that caters to the sores of human needs that left unmet make subjects more than ordinarily vulnerable to their environments and partly in the idea that all actions are in some way directed toward the care of a human individual with unique needs. Thus, even tasks that at first glance seem simple, such as giving an intravenous (IV) medicine or taking a blood pressure, will have a different meaning for that patient than for any other. APNs are responsible for responding to patients as unique individuals with unique needs. And when circumstances do not allow for this, for whatever reason, nurses are responsible for recognizing the ethical nature of the obstruction to what they know to be good care. In addition, problems that have often been assumed to be out of the purview of nurses, such as institutional obstructions to patient care, inadequate staffing, poor inter- and/or intradisciplinary communication about a patient, all have ethical aspects for the same reason: they obstruct efforts to provide good care.

Therefore, in addition to responsibilities related to direct care, there is logical support for the idea that nurses have broader societal responsibilities as outlined in the ICN's (2012) and ANA's

(2001) codes of ethics and in the ANA's (2010) *Social Policy Statement*. Furthermore, individuals on entering a profession and achieving professional status are implicitly promising to fulfill the goals of the profession. The profession's code of ethics applies to the practice of each professional. It supersedes all other institutional policies and cannot be negated by other professions, by administrators, or by the demands of the workplace (ANA, 1994). In advanced practice settings, where APNs so often find themselves working side by side and on a par with colleagues from other disciplines, they may find it hard to resist the "pull" of the other profession's particular aims, or of economic interests, and lose sight of the importance to individual and societal health of prioritizing nursing goals (Bryant-Lukosius, DiCensio, Browne, & Pinelli, 2004; Hagedorn & Quinn, 2004). Additionally, nurses working in research and correctional facilities may experience pressures to prioritize the goals of research or of the prison system over nursing goals.

Therefore, it is critically important that APNs understand that advanced practice, although it may bring with it augmented responsibilities, is nevertheless specific to nursing practice, and they must be able to articulate what this means. One way to think about this is that further education enables nurses to meet professional goals of good patient care more comprehensively because they are then able to provide for a wider array of patient needs. This lessens the fragmentation that can occur with multiple providers attending to different problems or systems and makes it easier to elicit the real needs of patients both for care and information.

Finally, some have noted the problem of dual loyalties arising for professionals working in certain circumstances such as military service (Gross, 2010; Williams, 2009). The question revolves around primary duties. Is the military nurse a nurse first—subject to the nursing code of ethics—or a member of the armed forces first and subject to military rules as a priority? The practical answer is probably that military service (unlike correctional service) provides an exception to the rules of professional (medical, nursing, or allied healthcare) conduct. A military nurse is bound first by military ethics rules and nursing ethics rules second. Moreover, the military nurse is not free to change her job and is subject to different legal sanctions than civilian nurses. The problem of military nursing and divided loyalties has not been sufficiently explored in the philosophical or ethics literature. Nevertheless, the ethical decision-making tools provided throughout this text provide strategies for military nurses to practice well in spite of their sometimes conflicting loyalties.

Changes in Contemporary Healthcare Settings

Changes in contemporary healthcare settings both in the United States and elsewhere, resulting from a shift of emphasis to the economic bottom line and expediency and away from the patient and/or societal good, lend urgency to the need for all professional nurses to understand that the basis for their work is firmly attached to the goals of their profession. Unless this is taken seriously, the goals of other professions or institutions will dominate nursing work at all levels—this is a problem for the reasons given in more detail shortly but mostly because nursing serves a distinct purpose and has a distinct perspective that is crucial to the well-being of individuals and for societal health. Should nursing merge with another healthcare profession or its goals become subsumed under the goals of another profession, the gains that have been made over the last century in professional autonomy, and thus the ability to directly influence nursing care, will be lost.

Not only do contemporary healthcare delivery systems both in the United States and elsewhere present a danger that nursing will lose its hard-won autonomy, but the autonomy of other professions is also at risk. Thus it is more vital than ever that the healthcare professions in general, including nursing, retain their societal status as professions—they are, arguably, the last line of defense against the political and/or business interests of contemporary health care and other major shifts that have been projected in healthcare delivery internationally (Anscombe, 2008; Bruhn, 2001; Dougherty, 1992; Mechanic, 1998).

Interdisciplinary work and action are becoming more common because collaboration is often needed to address or research complex health issues. The danger is that a blurring of professional boundaries will occur. Nursing is perhaps more vulnerable to this than other professions, yet nursing's perspective is important because of its unique emphasis on the person as contextual and continuously evolving.

Ambiguity about Nursing as a Profession

The question of whether nursing is a full-fledged or mature profession is still somewhat open for debate. Achieving generally accepted professional status within a society is important because it is accompanied by a certain amount of control or autonomy of practice. In some countries nursing is accorded professional status and with that status the ability to regulate itself. In some countries other more established professions have ignored or are unaware of nursing's particular knowledge about, and contributions to, the health of persons and the larger society. The troubled history of nursing as a female profession, the progress of which "has echoed the status of women in society" (Grace, 2004b, p. 285) as an oppressed group, is well documented (Andrist, Nicholas, & Wolf, 2006; Group & Roberts, 2001). Nursing as a predominantly female discipline has been subject to "gender discrimination" (Andrist et al., 2006, p. 1), lessening its ability either to realize its political potential or be taken seriously by others as a political force. Wuest (2006) highlights the paradox that a key factor of professions historically is that they excluded women. When women did enter professions such as nursing, their motivations did not tend to include the acquisition of power. This has

led to relatively easy domination by other groups working within the same environments, such as physicians and administrators. This statement is not intended to denigrate the significant contributions of some eminent members of the profession who managed Herculean tasks of nursing and healthcare reform, but rather to highlight the idea that nurses as the largest workforce within most healthcare systems could have significant power to improve the lot of individuals and society related to health....

NURSING POSSESSES THE ESSENTIAL CHARACTERISTICS OF A PROFESSION

Although no agreement has been reached about the precise nature of professions, there is nevertheless a general consensus that professions serve an important purpose in democratic societies and that they have certain characteristics in common. The discipline of nursing possesses these characteristics and thus fits the description of a profession. Professions have responsibilities to society that should not be circumvented by economic or business interests. Professions direct and monitor their own activities independent of those who might wish to subvert professional goals. The loss of professional status would not bode well for the population nursing serves, for reasons highlighted later. And yet there is great concern among nursing scholars that nursing, instead of realizing its potential for societal good, is in danger of becoming weakened by lack of attention to, or concern for, the philosophical and theoretical work that draws upon and contributes to nursing practice (Fawcett, Newman, & McAllister, 2004).

The Relationship of Nursing's Goals and Nursing Ethics

In the preceding discussion, not much distinction was made between medicine and nursing in regard to goals because the greater point of focus was the importance of certain professions to individuals and society. This section concentrates more on laying out the distinct nature of nursing goals and nursing perspectives as they have developed over the last century or so.

There is an inevitable relationship between nursing's goals and nursing ethics that has not always been as well recognized as it is currently. Nursing's philosophers and scholars over the past 150 years or so have been diligently involved in trying to determine and describe what the purpose of nursing is, who is served, what knowledge is needed for addressing these goals, and the responsibilities of nursing's membership in keeping these goals as the focus of their endeavors. This quest to define nursing and its unifying purpose is well documented in nursing literature (Donaldson & Crowley, 1978; Milton, 2005; Newman, Sime, & Corcoran-Perry, 1991; Packard & Polifroni, 1992, Willis et al., 2008) and represents the self-reflective nature of the discipline. Interestingly, medicine as a discipline has not been so self-reflective—much of what has been written about the nature and goals of medicine has come from philosophers and historians who for the most part are not physicians....

Evolution of Nursing and Consolidation of Nursing Goals

NURSING THEORY AND DISCIPLINARY KNOWLEDGE DEVELOPMENT

... "The (foundational) goal of the nursing profession is generally agreed to be that of promoting a 'good' which is health. Health may be variously defined depending on philosophical and theoretical perspectives guiding practice" (Grace, 2001, p. 155) and on the particular contexts of practice. Nevertheless, nursing has espoused a perspective of human beings that grounds the discipline's activity in the assumption that humans are contextual beings whose needs cannot be conceptualized in isolation from the larger contexts of their lives, histories, relationships, projects, and values. Additionally, many of nursing's philosophers have noted the importance of the nurse-patient

relationship and engagement with patients to facilitate meaning-making in difficult and fluid circumstances. The relationship and engagement are important even in cases of those who have profound cognitive challenges that prevent the individual's direct input.

Some have criticized nursing's perspective, noting that certain allied professions could also lay claim to this perspective. Indeed, in the past 20 years or so, some physicians have moved to adopt what they call the "new medicine" or an "integrative medicine" approach to patient care (Blumer & Meyer, 2006). This is good for patients. Even so, the new medicine fails to draw on the copious previous work done in nursing, and "new medicine" practitioners cannot necessarily be found in all the disparate settings where nurses practice in advanced roles, and they do not stand in the same relationships to patients. Additionally, it is doubtful that many physicians see integrative medicine as a realistic approach, given the limits of current healthcare environments and their emphasis on cure, along with a narrow view of what constitutes a good outcome. Still, it is an encouraging movement and one where nurses are well equipped to provide leadership.

REVISITING NURSING ETHICS AS PROFESSIONAL RESPONSIBILITY

In light of the preceding discussion, it is clear that an examination of nursing ethics is appropriately addressed "via the explications of nursing's theorists and scholars" (Grace, 2006, p. 68). In turn, nursing's theorists and scholars can realistically be called nursing philosophers because their theories or thoughts emerge from their philosophical attempts (informed by practice experiences) to find reasonable answers to the following questions: What is nursing? Why is nursing necessary? How can it best be done? What is needed to do it (including knowledge, characteristics, and skills required of practitioners as well as the environments in which it can be done)? Hence the two main goals of theorizing in nursing are

(1) "To describe and explain (all levels of) nursing" (Grace, 2006, p. 68), and (2) to provide a structure or framework that facilitates practice, guides research endeavors aimed at expanding nursing's knowledge base, and underpins practitioner development and education.

The use of philosophies, models, and theories as guides for nursing practice and the reverse influence of practice experiences on theory development are factors critical to the development of nursing's knowledge base and thus to the maturation and evolution of the discipline. However, it is the discipline's explicit aim of contributing both to the health of individuals and the overall health of society that makes nursing itself a moral endeavor. Flaming (2004) has argued that because theories of nursing say what nursing is (ontology), they represent ethical imperatives. Take, for example, the goal of nursing to promote an individual's health. Because nursing views of health all include the understanding that human beings are complex entities, inseparable from the environment in which they live and connected to countless important others in their lives, promoting health means taking into account the person in context. Failure to do so represents a failure of nursing ethics or, alternatively stated, a failure of professional responsibility. Willis and colleagues (2008) synthesized a central unifying focus of the discipline that is implicit in almost all theoretical and philosophical nursing works and that gives nurses a way to articulate their work. This focus, as noted earlier, is facilitating humanization, meaning, choice, quality of life, and healing in living and dying. The central theme evident in the historical nursing literature is that nurses facilitate humanization for patients and patient groups. "Nursing facilitates humanization by engaging experiential human beings [persons who experience life and its events] in practice and modeling humane relating for other human beings. Humanization ... is manifested when the nurse works with [any] human being [and views them as] relational, experiential, valuable, respect-worthy, meaning-oriented, flawed, imperfect, vulnerable,

fragile, complex, and capable of health and healing even if not capable of being cured" (p. E34)....

REFERENCES

American Nurses Association. (1994). *Ethics and human rights position statements: The nonnegotiable nature of the ANA Code for Nurses with interpretive statements.* Washington, DC: Author. Retrieved from http://www.nursingworld.org/positionstatements

American Nurses Association. (2001). *Code of ethics for nurses with interpretive statements.* Washington, DC: Author.

American Nurses Association. (2010). *Social policy statement.* Washington, DC: Author.

Andrist, L.C., Nicholas, P.K., & Wolf, K.A. (2006). *A history of nursing ideas.* Sudbury, MA: Jones and Bartlett.

Anscombe, J. (2008). Healthcare out of balance: How global forces will reshape the health of nations. Report of A.T. Kearney Inc. Retrieved from http://www.atkearney.com/documents/10192/dced09b1745b-4934-be20-3dec90d8195e

...

Blumer, R.H., & Meyer, M. (2006). *The new medicine.* Ashland, OH: Atlas Books.

...

Bruhn, J.G. (2001). Being good and doing good: The culture of professionalism in the health professions. *Health Care Manager*, 19(4), 47–58.

Bryant-Lukosius, D., DiCensio, A., Browne, G., & Pinelli, J. (2004). Advanced practice nursing roles: Development, implementation and evaluation. *Nursing and Healthcare Management and Policy*, 48(5), 519–529.

...

Donaldson, S.K., & Crowley, D.M. (1978). The discipline of nursing. *Nursing Outlook*, 26(2), 113–120.

...

Dougherty, C.J. (1992). The excesses of individualism. For meaningful healthcare reform, the United States needs a renewed sense of community. *Health Progress Journal*, 73(1), 22–28.

...

Fawcett, J., Newman, D.M.L., & McAllister, M. (2004). Advanced practice nursing and conceptual models of nursing. *Nursing Science Quarterly*, 17(2), 135–138.

...

Flaming, D. (2004). Nursing theories as nursing ontologies. *Nursing Philosophy*, 5(3), 224–229.

Grace, P.J. (2001). Professional advocacy: Widening the scope of accountability. *Nursing Philosophy*, 2(2), 151–162.

...

Grace, P.J. (2004b). Philosophical considerations in nurse practitioner practice. In S.K. Chase (Ed.), *Clinical judgment and communication in nurse practitioner practice* (pp. 279–294). Philadelphia, PA: F.A. Davis.

Grace, P.J. (2006). Philosophies, models, and theories: Moral obligations. In M.R. Alligood & A. Marriner-Tomey (Eds.), *Nursing theory: Utilization and application* (3rd ed., pp. 67–85). St. Louis, MO: Elsevier/Mosby.

Gross, M.L. (2010). Teaching military medical ethics: Another look at dual loyalty and triage. *Cambridge Quarterly of Healthcare Ethics*, 19, 458–464.

Group, T.M., & Roberts, J.I. (2001). *Nursing, physician control and the medical monopoly*. Bloomington, IN: Indiana University Press.

Hagedorn, S., & Quinn, A.A. (2004). Theory-based nurse practitioner practice: Caring in action. *Topics in Advanced Practice Nursing*, 4(4).

...

International Council of Nurses. (2012). *Code of ethics for nurses*. Geneva, Switzerland: Author. Retrieved from http://www.icn.ch/icncode.pdf

...

Mechanic, D. (1998). The functions and limitations of trust in the provision of medical care. *Journal of Health Politics, Policy and Law*, 23, 661–686.

Milton, C. (2005). Scholarship in nursing: Ethics of a practice doctorate. *Nursing Science Quarterly*, 18(2), 113–116.

...

Newman, M.A., Sime, A.M., & Corcoran-Perry, S.A. (1991). The focus of the discipline of nursing. *Advances in Nursing Science*, 14(1), 1–6.

Newton, L.H. (1988). Lawgiving for professional life: Reflections on the place of the professional code. In A. Flores (Ed.), *Professional ideals* (pp. 47–56). Belmont, CA: Wadsworth.

Nightingale, F. (1946). *Notes on nursing: What it is and what it is not*. Philadelphia, PA: Lippincott. (Original work published in 1859.)

Packard, S.A., & Polifroni, E.C. (1992). The nature of scientific truth. *Nursing Science Quarterly*, 5(4), 158–163.

...

Williams, J.R. (2009). Dual loyalties: How to resolve ethical conflict. *South African Journal of Bioethics and Law*, 2(1), 8–11.

Willis, D.B., Grace, P.J., & Roy, C. (2008). A central unifying focus for the discipline: Facilitating humanization, meaning, choice, quality of life and healing in living and dying. *Advances in Nursing Science*, 31(1), E28–E40.

...

Wuest, J. (2006). Professionalism and the evolution of nursing as a discipline: A feminist perspective. In W.K. Cody (Ed.), *Philosophical and theoretical perspectives for advanced nursing practice* (4th ed., pp. 85–98). Sudbury, MA: Jones and Bartlett.

—66—

IS THERE A PROFESSION OF ENGINEERING?

Michael Davis

I DO NOT TAKE UP THE QUESTION OF ENGINEER-ing's status as a profession because I doubt there is a profession of engineering. Instead, I take up the question because those who have maintained that engineering is not a profession seem to rely on one of two methods of defining "profession"—"conceptualism" and "sociology"—causing unnecessary confusion among those who do practical ethics. Doubt about the professional status of engineering has more to do with these methods than with any important difference between engineering and the "traditional," "classic," or "true" professions (law, medicine, and so on). The way to dispose of doubts about engineering's status as a profession is to describe, defend, and apply a better method of defining profession. I shall do that here—after explaining what is wrong with the other two methods....

I. ENGINEERING AS A "PSEUDO-PROFESSION"

Timo Airaksinen, a Finnish philosopher, offers a good example of the first argument I want to consider: Medicine, which everyone agrees is a profession, clearly has a distinctive aim, health. This aim is, he claims, distinctive not because other occupations (such as politics or engineering) are not also concerned with it, but for two other reasons. First, medicine *defines* health: "without medicine, we are not ill. We just suffer and die."[1]

Second, medicine itself is inconceivable without health as its object. So, for example, "if a doctor works to undermine health, she does not work as a doctor but as an impostor and charlatan."[2] In these two respects, medicine's aim, the ideal it serves, is internal to its practice. The connection between health and doctoring is not a mere consequence of social decision or historical accident but of relations among concepts.

Engineering's ideal of service, Airaksinen continues, lacks this conceptual relation to engineering. Suppose, for example, that the engineers' ideal of service is "using their knowledge and skill for the enhancement of human welfare," a description of their work common to many codes of engineering ethics. Such an ideal fails to be internal to engineering in either way in which health, according to Airaksinen, is internal to medicine. First, engineering does not define human welfare in the way medicine defines health. To some degree, each of us defines human welfare for himself; to a large degree, we do it together through public debate, legislation, judicial decision, and administrative ruling, processes in which engineers have only a small part. Second, even if engineering did define human welfare for its own practice in the way medicine defines health, we could point to engineers who ignore human welfare in their work, for example, the engineers who designed the Nazis' gas chambers.[3] Unlike the doctor who pays no attention to health, such an engineer, however reprehensible, is not obviously an impostor or charlatan. To any charge that he is an impostor or charlatan, he could answer that his work embodies the knowledge and skill characteristic of engineering. He has served his client well—and that is enough to be a good engineer, if not a good person. So, Airaksinen concludes:

> any attempt to introduce internal values and ideals into engineering is bound to fail. Engineering and similar pseudo-professions are technical by nature. They deal with methods by means of which the client/employer can realize his own values [rather than with methods designed to achieve values—like health—internal to the profession itself].[4]

What is wrong with this argument? Every discussion of what constitutes a profession begins—at least implicitly but often explicitly—with a list of clear cases, the "traditional," "classic," or "true" professions.... Airaksinen's list differs from [others]: along with the perennials, law and medicine, his includes two rather controversial items, teaching and social work.[5] ... [W]hat is important is that Airaksinen's list includes "law"—by which, I assume, he means lawyering.

The reason Airaksinen's inclusion of law among the traditional professions is important is that lawyers do not, as far as I can see, stand in the same relation to justice, even to legal justice, as (according to Airaksinen) doctors stand to health. First, in no country does the legal profession as such define legal justice, much less justice as such. Legislatures, courts, and administrative bodies have a large part. Most of what lawyers do is present evidence and arguments to such bodies, prepare documents for use in such bodies, advise clients what to expect of such bodies, and so on. Second, a lawyer who, without breaking the law herself, gets her clients what they want, ignoring considerations of (legal) justice, seems no more an impostor or charlatan than do the engineers who designed the Nazis' gas chambers. Generally, we reserve the terms "impostor" and "charlatan"

for those whose practice routinely falls well short of what they promise, whether through incompetence or malice. That is not our objection to either the Nazi engineer or the lawyer indifferent to justice.

To admit that law is only a pseudo-profession would reduce Airaksinen's list of traditional professions to medicine, teaching, and social work, a sufficiently eccentric ensemble to put in doubt any analysis relying on it.

To save the status of law as a profession, Airaksinen would, it seems, have to revise the profession of law to include judges, administrators, and others who help to define legal justice. Such a revision seems hard to justify. Even in the United States, not all judges or administrators are lawyers. In some countries, such as Switzerland, most are not. To combine into one legal profession those learned in the law and those who are not, simply because all have a part in defining legal justice, would be to give theoretical passion precedence over common sense. It would certainly ignore the almost universal view that part of what distinguishes lawyers from non-lawyers is being learned in the law....

V. PROFESSIONS WITHOUT AN ARCHIMEDEAN POINT

Archimedes is supposed to have said that, with a bar long enough and strong enough and a place to stand, he could move the earth. He understood that finding "the Archimedean point," the appropriate place to stand, is not all there is to making practical the theoretician's dream of moving the earth. One must also have a bar long enough and strong enough (and a suitable fulcrum on which to set it).

In practice, we could not move the earth even if we could find a place to stand. We would still need a bar many times longer than the earth's diameter—and, given the strength of materials, many times the earth's mass. In practice, we must restrict our leveraging to relatively small objects with relatively short bars.... The approach I shall now sketch and sketchily defend avoids this problem of conceptualism by working much closer to practice. The concept of profession it develops is, like sociology's, historically conditioned, but not, as sociology's is supposed to be, historically given....

Here is the definition of profession that [my] approach has so far yielded:

> A profession is a number of individuals in the same occupation voluntarily organized to earn a living by openly serving a certain moral ideal in a morally-permissible way beyond what law, market, and morality would otherwise require.

This definition has, I believe, at least five advantages over definitions that sociology or conceptualism have so far produced. First, it seems to fit what most professionals (or, at least, my sample of them) now think about their own profession. Second, this definition helps us to understand the relatively high opinion we have of professions as such, as the sociological definition does not. Third, it can help us understand the criticism we make of actual professions, and of particular members of a profession as members of that profession. Fourth, it provides a plausible framework for explaining the empirical relationship between profession and professional monopoly—without making monopoly a criterion of profession. And last, and most important here, the definition will allow us to explain why engineering is plainly a profession in just the sense law and medicine are. I shall now show that the definition does all that, taking up its interrelated elements more or less in order....

Professions are voluntary in two respects. First, there is no requirement that any occupation be a profession. Becoming a profession is one morally permissible option; doing no more than what law, market, and morality demand is another. Second, individual members of a profession both join and remain in the profession voluntarily. Indeed, one must claim membership—whether by seeking a license to practice the profession, by applying for a job calling for a member of that profession (for example, "engineer"), or just by declaring oneself a member of that profession (for example, "I am an engineer"). One can also leave a profession simply by giving up the license if there is one, withdrawing from practice, and ceasing to claim membership. (The voluntariness of professions is, as we shall see, crucial for explaining the special moral obligations—the ethics—of professionals)....

What is a *moral ideal*? A moral ideal may be simple (health) or complex (cure the sick, comfort the dying, and preserve the health of those who are well). The "moral" in "moral ideal" is meant to exclude both such immoral ideals as the perfect crime and such non-moral ideals as art for art's sake. A moral ideal is moral both in the minimal sense of being morally permissible to pursue—as, for example, the perfect crime is not—and in the stronger sense of being morally good to pursue, that is, its pursuit tends to support morally right conduct—as art for art's sake does not. But a moral ideal is also moral in a stronger sense. A moral ideal is a state of affairs which, though not morally required, is one that everyone (that is, every rational person at his rational best) wants pursued, wanting that so much as to be willing to reward, assist, or at least praise its pursuit if that were the price for others to do the same. If we think of morality as consisting of those standards of conduct everyone wants everyone else to follow even if that means having to do the same, then morality gives us a reason to support by reward, assistance, or at least praise anyone pursuing a moral ideal.

Because moral ideals have this moral claim on us and each profession, by definition, serves a moral ideal, professions are, by definition, morally praiseworthy, that is, activities we always have good moral reason to praise. The relationship between moral ideals and (what we have called) rational ideals is therefore tricky. On the one hand, a moral ideal is necessarily a rational ideal, whether intrinsic or technical. We always have good reason to pursue a moral ideal because achieving it would be morally good. That cannot be said of all rational ideals. Prudence is an example of a rational ideal of which this cannot be said. Prudence certainly is a rational ideal. That an act is prudent is, all else equal, reason enough to do it. But a prudent act does not deserve the reward, assistance, or even praise an act in pursuit of a moral ideal does. It does not, in part, because we do not have the same pressing reasons to encourage prudence in our enemies that we have to encourage morality in them. Because rational ideals are not necessarily moral ideals, there can be no profession serving a mere rational ideal.

How Airaksinen formulates a rational ideal is therefore quite important to whether what he calls a profession can be one in the sense I have given "profession." For example, health understood merely as one's own health is a rational ideal but not a moral one. To be a moral ideal, health must be understood as a state of affairs we all share in, "public health." So, if there is to be a profession serving health, it will have to aim at everyone's health, not just at the health of some individuals, its patients. Insofar as it in fact focuses its efforts on individual patients, as medicine does, a profession of health will have to do that as part of a strategy for serving everyone's health, that is, as a "public service." Only seeking to serve everyone's health will deserve the moral praise, assistance, and rewards appropriate to a profession. For this reason. I think, the Preamble to the AMA's Principles of Medical Ethics explicitly recognizes a "responsibility not only to patients, but also to society," a recognition that led the AMA to call for legislation restricting handguns, to condemn smoking, and to take other stands for public health.[6] ...

To be a member of a profession is to be subject to a set of special, morally binding standards beyond what law, market, and morality (otherwise) demand. To act as a member of a profession is openly to carry on one's occupation according to those higher standards—for example, to declare by word and deed, "I work as an engineer [that is, as engineers are supposed to work]." There is no "profession" without such professing.

To declare that one will carry on one's occupation by a higher standard than law, market, and morality otherwise demand is, of course, morally praiseworthy, in the way any morally good resolution is. Actually to carry on one's occupation in accordance with one's declaration is morally praiseworthy too, in the way doing one's duty is. But such potential praise has its price. The professional whose deeds fall short of her profession's standards is open to moral criticism she would not be open to had she not declared her commitment to those standards. To be a professional is to be open to a range of moral criticism to which a non-professional doing identical work is not. A member of a profession must satisfy a higher standard than a mere practitioner of the underlying occupation just to do what she is supposed to do.

Having compared members of a profession and mere practitioners of the underlying occupation, a society may conclude that it will be better off if practice of that occupation is restricted to members of the profession. Members of a profession may also properly urge that practice of their occupation be so restricted if they believe that the public will be better off if practice is so restricted. Whether the public will be better off depends on a number of considerations, not least of which is the sophistication and bargaining power of those who must hire or otherwise choose practitioners of that sort. So, for example, the large companies that employ most engineers seem in a much better position to protect themselves from the incompetent, the indifferent, and the dishonest than the lawyer's client or doctor's patient typically is. Because licensing as such is a social expense—that is, an administrative burden and a restriction of liberty—there is always a presumption against it. Licensing is justified, when it is, because the society benefits overall from imposing its own controls on practice. Such benefits have little bearing on what is or is not a profession.

If we re-examine what Airaksinen and Zussman said, we shall find nothing suggesting that engineering fails to satisfy the definition of profession offered here. Engineers constitute a number of individuals in a single occupation (engineering) voluntarily organized to earn their living by openly serving a certain moral ideal—in Airaksinen's formulation, "good control of the artificial environment"—in a morally-permissible way beyond what law, market, and morality would otherwise demand, that is, according to engineering's special standards, including its code of ethics....

VII. PROFESSIONAL ETHICS AND MORAL THEORY

... My approach to professional ethics thus resembles Airaksinen's conceptualism in being relatively independent of "moral foundations." It nonetheless differs from Airaksinen's in two respects, both of which I consider to be advantages.

First, my approach is not as independent of moral theory as Airaksinen's. I have explicitly understood professions in a way recognizing moral constraints on the pursuit of a professional ideal. I have also understood professional standards in a way making them morally binding (in the sense that promises bind). I have therefore left room for moral theory insofar as moral theory can enlighten us concerning how morality makes professional ethics binding and what professional ethics can bind us to.

Second, my approach is not as independent of the social sciences as Airaksinen's. As I understand professions, the social sciences may help us to distinguish "true professions" from "pseudo-professions." True professions are those organized occupations that largely live up to the special standards they profess; pseudo-professions, those organized occupations that, though having professional standards, fall too far short of them, whether by incompetence, indifference, or venality, to count as professions. I have, however, not understood professions in a way making the social sciences the arbiter of what is a profession. My approach allows us to conclude, for example, that engineering is a profession even if social scientists say it is not. Indeed, I have provided a definition that might help the social sciences to understand the professions better and so help the rest of us to do the same....

NOTES AND REFERENCES

1   Airaksinen, Timo (1994) "Service and Science in Professional Life," in Chadwick, Ruth F. (ed) *Ethics and the Professions* (Aldershot, England: Avebury), 9.
2   Airaksinen (1994) 9.
3   Harris, Nigel G.E. (1994) "Professional Codes and Kantian Duties," in Chadwick, 107.
4   Airaksinen (1994) 10.
5   Airaksinen (1994) 1.
6   Gorlin, Rena A. (ed) (1986). *Codes of Professional Responsibility* (Washington, DC: Bureau of National Affairs), 101....

—67—

PROFESSIONAL ETHICS OF SOFTWARE ENGINEERS

An Ethical Framework

Yotam Lurie and Shlomo Mark

INTRODUCTION

FAMILIAR CASES OF FAULTY ENGINEERING, LIKE the Ford Pinto gasoline tank (De George 1981), the Space Shuttle Challenger disaster caused by an O-ring seal that failed at liftoff (Boisjoly et al. 1989), or the 1997 collapse of the pedestrian bridge erected especially for the Israeli Maccabiah games (Schmemann 1997), have given rise to numerous discussions about engineering ethics (Dodig-Crnkovic and Feldt 2009). These cases pertain to the classical engineering branches of electrical, mechanical and civil engineering. However, as technology shapes and drives the world in which we live, software has become an integral element in many of our day to day activities. Indeed, the ubiquity of software is such that it can be found in almost every aspect of our lives, including, but not limited to our children's electronic toys, our smartphones, our HD plasma or LED televisions, and our cars' onboard computer systems, to name but a few examples. Software also plays an essential role in providing business information (BI) solutions for enterprise resource planning (ERP), enabling, organizing, and protecting the activities of large, medium and small organizations alike, including, among others, department stores, banks, government agencies and the military.

As a result, the impact of software errors and software bugs can be dramatic and can often have catastrophic consequences. In fact, it is increasingly being recognized that the source of many technological failures originates from software issues. Software plays an essential role in both our private and professional lives. Basically, people have become increasingly dependent in their daily lives (indeed, for their very survival) on computers and software, which together provide a service we cannot do without—for example, it is quite simply impossible to manually gather data and perform the calculations needed to process all the data we have without the proper software. In fact, as the foundation of any computer-based system or product, the software package is practically the "mind" of the product, without which computer systems would be rendered useless heaps of metal and plastic. Moreover, what this means is that the quality and dependability of the software package determines, in turn, the quality, usability, reliability, accuracy, serviceability, and safety of the product in which it is installed.

At the 1968 NATO convention the notion of *Software Crisis* was coined to express the gap between the ability to systematically (i.e., from an engineering perspective) develop a "quality software" product—correct, understandable, reliable, stable and verifiable—and the rapid expansion in computing power. The *software crisis* is reflected in irregular schedules, budget overruns, software that is inefficient or of low quality, non-compliance, and programs that are not delivered. It was found that 75% of large software products sent to customers are considered failures in the sense that they are either not used or they do not meet customer requirements (Mullet 1999). The cost of repairing software bugs in the U.S. each year is estimated at $59.5 billion (NIST 2002). Published findings of the consulting firm "The Standish Group", which systematically and continuously surveys the field of software engineering and IT, show that over time, only one-third of software development projects end successfully and on time. About 15% of projects fail almost immediately with the start of development, and almost half of the projects run into problems and end with significant deviations from both forecasted budgets and schedules. In addition, more than half of the projects that end successfully and are delivered to customers require significant post-delivery changes, since typically only about half of the required features purported to be supported by the software were actually functioning. The 2009 Standish report on the success of IT projects shows an increase over previous years in the incidence of IT project failure:

> This year's results show a marked decrease in project success rates, with 32% of all projects succeeding which are delivered on time, on budget, with required features and functions" says Jim Johnson, chairman of The Standish Group, 44% were challenged which are late, over budget, and/or with less than the required features and functions and 24% failed which are cancelled prior to completion or delivered and never used. (StandishGroup n.d.)

Analyses of the software crisis have led researchers to associate it with a wide variety of causes ultimately rooted in the software company's abilities and organization. Among the typical drivers are the complexity of the software package, exaggerated expectations, poor planning, a lack of clear goals and objectives or objectives that are suddenly changed mid-project, changing requirements, unrealistic time and cost estimates, lack of cooperation, impaired communication and faulty teamwork, and lack of skill (Tilmann and Weinberger 2004). Over time, the software crisis has been dealt with, to varying degrees of success, using a range of approaches—the development of dedicated software tools, computer aided software engineering (CASE), frameworks, tools, programming paradigms, and programming languages; the implementation of improved modeling and design; changes to process and project management and software architecture; augmented software development and testing methodologies, principles and maintenance—but the inevitable conclusion is that there is no "silver bullet" solution (Brooks 1986) to the software crisis, and software development continues and grows, while facing future challenges, including various failures. Meanwhile, software engineers and producers must internalize the lessons learned from past failures and recognize where and how to implement the myriad of minor changes and improvements required to bridge the gap between increasing computation power and lagging software development.

This paper suggests the notion of an *ethical framework*, adopted from the concept of a framework in software engineering, to deal with challenges, non-successes and failures in software development processes. Although it is a professional challenge, it is related to the engineer's interconnectedness with clients and other stakeholders. A viable approach to combatting the effects of the crisis entails increasing the ethical professionalism of software engineers through the use of a software development approach termed Ethical-Driven Software Development (EDSD). This approach constitutes an alternative to the classical model expressed by the traditional stand-alone engineering codes of ethics....

THE SYNERGY BETWEEN ETHICAL AND PROFESSIONAL SKILLS IN SOFTWARE ENGINEERING

A software package is in many respects like a "black box" to most of its end users, who have no idea how it works or how to interact with it. Often the software package includes infrastructure, features and functions that are far beyond what the end user needs or comprehends. However, its black-box status notwithstanding, in practical terms the fundamental quality of the software product and of its design will determine whether it will fulfill the needs of the consumer. Our increasing **dependence** on computers and software packages in essential infrastructures, on the one hand, together with the profound **lack of understanding** (i.e., a knowledge gap) among most end users regarding the operation of the software package, on the other hand, entails a critical dependence of the end-user/consumer on the professionalism of the software experts. Due to this dependence, it makes sense to instill in, and promote among, software professionals a professional code of ethics. Because software engineers provide an essential service to end-users, their work resembles that of the other service professions in the sense that the service they provide is more important than the tangible good delivered, and consequently, there should be no separation between the software professional's practical and ethical skills. In other words, the ethical and professional skills associated with software engineering should [synergize] (Figure 1).

Figure 1 Synergistic Relationship between Ethical and Professional Skills

Approaching the issue from a slightly different angle, the relationship between the software developer and the consumer can be characterized as asymmetrical in the sense that the end-user/consumer is dependent and relies on a software product s/he cannot understand. The software developer, who holds the keys to this black box, i.e., software package, must have sufficient knowledge, expertise and skills to control the product upon which the consumer is so dependent. Such a relationship, commonly termed a relationship of power, which in this case is between the software developer (the professional) and the end-user (the customer), necessarily requires ethical checks and balances to regulate it and assure that it is not abused....

[T]his paper adopts a somewhat different direction. The idea is to sketch out an ethical framework within which software engineers make use of EDSD: Ethical-Driven Software Development. The concept of a framework has been defined as following: "a framework generally provides a skeletal abstraction of a solution to a number of problems that have similarities.... A framework generally outlines the steps or phases that must be followed in the implementation of a solution without getting into the details of what activities are done in each phase" (Mnkandla 2009). In other words, the framework has to be a reusable, extendable and abstract set of basic components (objects) that characterizes the area of the problem. The user can adopt the object as-is, can change it, ignore it or add new objects to it.

By proposing an *ethical framework*, which is inherently connected to the life cycle of a software product, rather than suggesting another "stand alone ethics code" for software engineers, the paper breaks down the dichotomy between the technical and ethical aspects of the profession, thereby explicitly linking the technical and ethical aspects of software engineering. Through the development of an *ethical framework for software engineers*, the occupation moves one step closer to becoming a professional occupation. The goal of this paper, therefore, is to articulate the details of an *ethical framework* that will be woven into the life cycle of the software development process and become an integral part of the professional life of software engineers. This approach is unique in that the proposed *ethical framework* is inherently connected to the day-to-day professional activity of software engineers and the software development process, regardless of the development life cycle, e.g., Agile (scrum, XP, RUP etc.) iterative waterfall and others, which is adopted. Indeed, the efficacy of this framework depends on it being incorporated as part of the daily work routine of the software engineer. By adopting the concept "ethical framework" as a skeleton abstraction of a solution to integrate ethical concepts in the software development process we enable the user to tailor ethical objects for his/her project, as well as for her/his development process and team....

ETHICAL-DRIVEN SOFTWARE DEVELOPMENT (EDSD): AN ETHICAL FRAMEWORK

Engineers and ethicists are "programmed" to think in vastly different ways. Whereas ethicists strive for meaningful "codes of ethics" that are often inspirational but that lack standardized procedures, engineers approach the world via protocols and checklists (Farrell 2002; Gaumnitz 2004). As a result, the engineering codes of ethics, which are not ingrained into the day-to-day practice of the profession, have only random and contingent effects on the day-to-day practice of engineering. All too often the professional code of ethics is conceived merely as an inspirational-normative ideal without practical bearings.

This matter bears upon a deeper philosophical point which should not be overlooked. David Hume (1711–1776) and much of modern moral philosophy contrast between factual judgments and value judgments in what has come to be known as the fact-value distinction, maintaining that these are two separate realms of judgment and that one cannot infer value judgments based on fact judgments and vice versa. The fact-value distinction is closely related to the naturalistic fallacy, according to which it is a fallacy to make claims about what ought to be on the basis of statements about what is. Insofar as this relates to the ways codes of ethics supposedly function, the profession has rules (protocols and standard procedures) of rational judgment regarding factual matters, but these are distinct from the value judgments expected of professional software engineers.

Contemporary moral philosophers (Foot 1978; MacIntyre 1981; Putnam 2002) have challenged these distinctions, arguing that facts and values are deeply entangled and that the dichotomy is based on a misunderstanding of the nature of fact. As an alternative to this typical separation between the ethical values of the profession and the practical protocols and checklists according to which the engineering profession operates, it is possible to connect the professional ethics of software engineers as a *practical tool* inherently linked to their day to day work. The EDSD approach allows for this by introducing an ethical framework into the development process. The notion of an *ethical framework* is a rich metaphor. Within the world of software development, a framework is a "sub-system design made up of a collection of abstract and concrete classes and the interfaces between them ... frameworks are generic and extended to create a more specific application or subsystem" (Sommerville 2004). In other words, a framework can be presented as an engineering-aided tool to support or guide the developer under the rules of the development approach. On the other hand, within the world of applied ethics, an *ethical framework* denotes both the ethical limits/boundaries of a normative system as well as its situational constraints and directives.

By way of analogy, similar to how the World Medical Association has developed the *Declaration of Helsinki* that is the cornerstone for ethics in medical research involving human subjects, the *ethical framework* for software engineers should provide an ethical checklist that will be integral to the software's life cycle. The *Declaration of Helsinki* is an ethical guideline that requires the physician to follow a certain protocol in the research design. Similarly, the use of a practical tool, such as cue cards specifically designed for each stage of the development life cycle, can augment the awareness and commitment of the software engineer to think ethically about the stakeholders and risks involved. And when the client understands that the developer uses such tests, the tension that can potentially develop between client and developer is defused. In so doing, software engineers can provide the assurance needed that the development process abides by certain ethical standards.

More particularly, software life cycle models describe phases in the development of software and the order in which these phases are executed. There are many models, processes and methodologies for the software life cycle (waterfall, iterative, Agile etc.), and although each company (or project) adopts its own model and methodology, all are characterized by similar elements (artifacts). At each phase there are fundamental ethical requirements that must be met, which are derived from the specifics of the relevant stage. In all software development life cycles there are five major phases or, their incidence and terminology obviously depends on the specific rules of the life cycle methodology adopted: e.g., in waterfall methodology the phases appear one after the other as a sequence, while in Agile processes all five phases are concentrated to shorter time boxes depending on the methodology....

1. Initiation stage—in the **initiation phase**, the client articulates what s/he wants.
2. Setting requirements—in the **requirement phase**, the software engineer defines the client's needs. Much more than mere communication is at stake, the requirement phase entails a complex, interpretive process in which software engineers attempt to understand and match the needs of the client with the best technical response. One must be aware that there are a variety of methods, depending on the lifecycle methodology, to achieve the goals of this phase.

3. Design stage—in the **design phase**, the client's "wants" that have been defined as "needs" receive a technical solution based on the technical abilities of the software engineer. Diagrams can be used to illustrate the functional operation of the system for the client. However, when obtaining the client's consent for a particular design, it is important to bear in mind that this is not *informed consent*, which requires that the software engineer confirm the client indeed understands what is at stake, including matters pertaining to information security, information back up, etc.
4. Development stage—in the **Development phase**, the software engineer puts the technical solution into practice, after which the product enters the testing phase to be validated and verified, to determine where it succeeded and whether there were any failures in its operation.
5. **Testing and maintenance phase**—there are three types of maintenance: corrective, perfective and adaptive. At each phase, there are fundamental ethical considerations that must be taken into account, the resulting products, and deliverables that are required in the next phase in the life cycle. Requirements are translated into design. Code produced during Development is driven by the design. Testing verifies the deliverable of the Development phase in terms of whether it fulfills the requirements of that stage.

One must understand that the engineering of the development process is first and foremost connected to quality. Developing "quality software" is much more difficult than simple code development, especially when the definition of the term "software quality" is vague, equivocal and subject to different translations. In his book, Pressman (2010) preferred to define software quality by defining certain measures. Accordingly, software quality is measured by the software's degree of compliance with functional and performance requirements, development standards, and with all prerequisites required in professional software development. In other words, "how is the development process engineered?"

EDSD is a software engineering framework that is independent of the lifecycle development methodology, the specific project and the development team. Its goal is to obtain a quality engineering perspective by adopting ethical objects for all software development cycles, irrespective of specific development methodology and project. The *ethical framework* is a supportive software engineering tool that supports the EDSD approach and serves as a guide in the entire development process. There are several studies in order to determinate ethics interventions and rules for software developments (Braude 2011; Miller 2011; Friedman 2012; Basart 2013), but in a study conducted in parallel to this work and continued and expanded these days (the results will be compiled and published shortly) in order to seek and explore the necessity of ethical interventions in a software development life cycle it was found (Amity 2014) that more than 77.86% of the respondents (sample size over 200 people) agrees with (33.59% strongly agree and 44.27% agree) the statement that in a software development project, working in accordance to a defined set of rules and procedures is not enough to guarantee the success of the project; furthermore 76.17% of the respondents agree with (32.31% strongly agree and 43.86% agree) the statement that familiarity with the ramifications of every action taken within the development process is a necessary precondition for the process' success. And lack of awareness is one of the factors that hinder and harm the development process. Arguments that led us to the main idea beyond the EDSD approach ... emerged out of the claim that ethical processes are no different from any other development process and therefore adding ethical rules and procedures is not enough and in most cases software development decisions are made without considering the ethical effects and implications of the decision as part of the quality process. In other words, the status quo

reflects a lack of awareness, which when present, will inevitably lead to proactive approaches that will ensure "quality software" and improve the quality of the final product. Therefore, all it takes is to raise the awareness and understanding of ethical interventions as a necessary component of the development process. Therefore, the ethical framework is a set of YES/NO ethical awareness questions that accompany each of the five phases in the development process, and of which every major stakeholder, including customer, administrator, team leader, designer, developer and quality member must be aware, before beginning any phase of software development. As such, the EDSD framework will not only increase the commitment of developers to produce high quality and dependable software, it may also substantially reduce the potential for tension developing between the stakeholders.

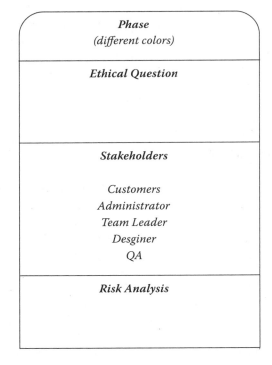

Figure 2 Ethically-Driven Software Development Ethically—(EDSD) Index Card

Practically speaking, the ethical framework suggests using EDSD index cards as a tool to aid and facilitate the development process, each phase of which has a specific set of such cards that could be color coded to distinguish between the phases. Each card contains only one yes/no ethical question, specific and focused, relevant to the specific development phase at hand that all relevant stakeholders are asked to answer. In general, the questions raise stakeholder awareness about the ethical considerations and implications relevant to each development phase....

CONCLUSION

From the perspective of professional software engineering, EDSD is a novel and practical approach to software development that bridges the gap and creates a link between ethical and professional skills, thus proposing a process of software development that is more transparent and brings better awareness of the risks and limitations in the process of software development. Taking ethical questions into consideration thus becomes part of the process required for the development of "quality software" products. The ethical framework sketched out is very rudimentary and can be further adapted and expanded within the context of different software development protocols.

Philosophically, through the specific case of professional ethics in software engineering, a broader and more significant argument has been made regarding ethics in the professions. This approach is a *process* centered approach to ethics in the professions, which we demonstrated has advantages over principle and rule based approaches to ethics, as manifest in formal codes of ethics. Moreover, by integrating the ethical considerations with the professional considerations a more robust conception and manifestation of professionalization emerges.

REFERENCES

Amity, E. (2014). *Agile and professional ethics*. M.Sc. Thesis in software engineering. SCE–Shamoon College of engineering, Israel.

Basart, J.M. (2013). Engineering ethics beyond engineers' ethics. *Science and Engineering Ethics*, 19(1), 179–187.

...

Boisjoly, R.P., Curtis, F.E., & Mellican, E. (1989). Roger Boisjoly and the Challenger disaster: The ethical dimensions. *Journal of Business Ethics*, 8(4), 217–230.

Braude, E.J. (2011). *Software engineering: Modern approaches*. New York: Wiley.

Brooks, F.P. (1986). No silver bullet—Essence and accident in software engineering. In *Proceedings of the IFIP Tenth world computing conference* pp. 1069–1076.

...

De George, R.T. (1981). Ethical responsibilities of engineers in large organizations: The Pinto case. *Business and Professional Ethics Journal*, 1(1), 1–14.

Dodig-Crnkovic, G., & Feldt, R. (2009). Professional and ethical issues of software engineering curriculum applied in Swedish academic context. In *HAoSE 2009 first workshop on human aspects of software engineering*. Orlando, Florida.

Farrell, B.C. (2002). Codes of ethics: Their evolution, development and other controversies. *Journal of Management Development*, 21(2), 152–163.

Foot, P. (1978). *Virtues and vices and other essays in moral philosophy*. Berkeley and Oxford: University of California Press and Blackwell.

...

Friedman, B. (2012). The envisioning cards: A toolkit for catalyzing humanistic and technical imaginations. In *Proceedings of the SIGCHI conference on human factors in computing systems*. ACM.

Gaumnitz, B.R. (2004). A classification scheme for codes of business ethics. *Journal of Business Ethics*, 49(4), 329–335.

...

MacIntyre, A. (1981). *After virtue: A study in moral theory.* Notre Dame, IN: University of Notre Dame Press.

Miller, K.W. (2011). Moral responsibility for computing artifacts: The rules. *IT Professional*, 13(3), 57–59.

Mnkandla, E. (2009). About software engineering frameworks and methodologies. In *AFRICON, 2009.* AFRICON'09. IEEE.

Mullet, D. (1999). The software crisis. *Benchmarks Online—A monthly publication of Academic Computing Services of the University of North Texas Computing Center,* 2(7). https://www.unt.edu/ benchmarks/archives/1999/july99/crisis.htm.

...

NIST. (2002). *New Release of June 28, 2002.* The National Institute of Standards and Technology.

...

Pressman, R. (2010). *Software engineering: A practitioner's approach* (7th ed.). New York: McGraw Hill.

Putnam, H. (2002). *The collapse of the fact/value dichotomy and other essays.* Cambridge: Harvard University Press.

Schmemann, S. (1997). *2 die at games in Israel as bridge collapses.* Retrieved from http://www.nytimes.com/ 1997/07/15/world/2-die-at-games-in-israel-as-bridge-collapses.html

Sommerville, I. (2004). *Software engineering, international computer science series* (7th ed.). Boston: Addison Wesley, Pearson Education.

...

Tilmann, G., & Weinberger, J. (2004). Technology never fails, but project can. *Baseline*, 1(26), 28.

—68—

ETHICAL EDUCATION IN ACCOUNTING

Integrating Rules, Values, and Virtues

Domènec Melé

INTRODUCTION

ETHICS IN ACCOUNTING HAS SEEN AN INCREASED interest in the last decade, although it is not by any means a new subject. In the USA, public accounting has had some form of ethical standards since at least the beginning of the twentieth century (Casler, 1964, mentioned by Loeb, 1988). Issues regarding ethics in accounting are briefly touched on in some early European textbooks on business ethics (e.g., Azpiazu, 1964; Baudhuin, 1954). However, specific training on accounting ethics for accounting students or a systematic presentation of this matter had rarely been undertaken until the 1970s (Loeb and Bedingfield, 1972). In 1978, Loeb edited *Ethics in the Accounting Profession*, a pioneering monograph on this topic....

[C]onsiderable steps have been made in ethical accounting education, but, after the well-known recent accounting scandals, it seems absolutely essential to pay increasing attention to ethics in accounting and to improve ethical education for accountants. In line with this, this paper aims to contribute to a better understanding of accounting ethics and to provide some insights on ethical education in accounting.

First, this article examines some relevant current approaches in accounting ethics and ethical education in accounting and the corresponding role given to rules and principles, ethical theories, values, and virtues. Second, it presents an approach in which rules, values and virtues are presented in an interrelated consistent manner. Finally, some implications of this approach for ethical education in accounting are discussed....

VALUES AND VIRTUES

... Pioneers in ethical education in accounting, in spite of their praiseworthy task, focused on dilemmas and ethical theories rather than on the role of virtues.... Although Loeb (1988, 322) included "setting the stage for" a change in ethical behavior, "he does not go so far as to imply accounting educators have the power to bring about good or bad behavior on the part of students" (Armstrong et al., 2003, 10)....

Several scholars have strongly criticized those approaches which reduce ethical education to presenting ethical theories to solve ethical dilemmas without considering personal virtues and behavior. Pincoffs (1986, 4–6) pointed out the problems with theories used to solve ethical dilemmas. He stated deontological or utilitarian ethical theories are reductive, since they eliminate what is morally relevant (character) and they legislate the form of moral reflection (duties and consequences)....

As an alternative to teaching ethical theories, Pincoffs (1986, 150) presented the primary objective of moral education as encouraging the development of the person. This means encouraging the development of virtues, that is to say, permanent dispositions that favor ethical behavior.

Subsequently, other scholars have presented significant insights into the role of virtue in accounting, both in practice and education. Francis (1990) emphasized the role of the agent beyond rules and the capacity of accounting to be a virtuous practice. Mintz (1995, 1996), following Pincoffs (1986) and MacIntyre (1984), presented significant pedagogical insights in the teaching of virtue to accounting students and mentioned several virtues which enable accountants to withstand environment pressures and to act in accordance with the moral point of view: (1) benevolence and altruism; (2) honesty and integrity; (3) impartiality and open-mindedness; (4) reliability and dependability; (5) faithfulness and trustworthiness.

THE CRUCIAL IMPORTANCE OF THE AGENT'S CHARACTER

Regarding practical judgments, Armstrong (2002, 145) affirms that "accounting is an art, not a science. It requires significant judgments and assumptions and 10 accountants, given complex circumstances, will probably arrive at several different net income or taxable income figures." Accountants must determine the significance of each situation while acting with objectivity, independence, professional competence, due care, professional behavior, confidentiality, integrity, and so on. Rules cannot determine what to do in every situation. Universal principles can give guidelines, but each situation is unique. Accountants have to judge each situation and judge what objectivity,

integrity, etc. mean in a given situation; and then act according to this judgment.

It has been rightly said that a "practical judgment is, at the very least, crucially dependent upon perception" (Koehn, 2000, 4). The ethical perception depends on certain human capacities, related with character, which is different from others, such as logic or aesthetics. This capacity to perceive the ethical dimension of the reality is no more than practical wisdom or prudence (in the moral sense), an intellectual virtue, called "phronesis" by Aristotle (*Nichomachean Ethics*, bk 5, chap. 7). Practical wisdom may be expressed, for instance, in being sincerely objective, truly unbiased and independent, and in following the "spirit of the law" rather than the letter of the law.

Character of a person, in which practical wisdom forms an important part, is made up of habits (good habits, or virtues, or bad habits, or vices). Habits shape personal character, which combines with personality (understanding by personality mainly the innate features and non-moral qualities)....

The virtue of man is "the state of character which makes a man good and which makes him do his own work well" (*Nichomachean Ethics*, bk 2, chap. 6; 1106a22). In other words, virtuous individuals habitually perform moral actions. Thus, courage drives us to do what is good and justice to give to each what is his or hers by right.

To sum up, virtues should be introduced in ethical education as a crucial element to overcome the limitations previously discussed. However, a new problem arises: how to harmonize virtues with rules and values. Some versions of "virtues" only judge as virtues those which foster outcomes: industriousness for a productive life: justice for achieving good relations: loyalty to maintain a sound adhesion: truthfulness to garner more the reputation of being a reliable person....

Another problem is found in certain approaches in which virtues are proposed without any reference to norms or principles, which according to some authors is a failure to supply the means to resolve moral dilemmas (Messerly, 1994, 109; among others).

Both problems arise from considering virtues apart from rules and values or principles instead of simultaneously considering rules, values and virtues. But, are rules, values and virtues really interrelated?

UNDERSTANDING THE INTERRELATION BETWEEN RULES, VALUES AND VIRTUES

Rules, values and virtues are indeed interrelated if one accepts the basic anthropological and ethical concepts presented by Aristotle and his main commentator, Thomas Aquinas (MacIntyre, 1993). A crucial point in this approach is that values have to be considered as "intrinsic moral values," or "moral goods" rooted in human nature.

This makes sense, since values, although frequently considered either as subjective or as social agreements, can also be understood objectively. Some scholars have even distinguished values, in general, from "moral or ethical values." The latter are defined as those which, when one lives in accordance with them, contribute to "the good of the person," that is to say, to the perfection or flourishing of individuals as human beings. In this sense, Guardini (1999, 30–31) wrote that the good (of the person) "is different from any other values." These other values "drive our behavior here and now, depending on the situation, while the good compels us always.... In other words, the requirements of values are always specific; the requirements of good are universal. The former is presented to men and women in certain circumstances ..., while the requirement of good drives men and women for the simple fact of being human." If moral values, relate to "the good of the person," they can be distinguished from other values (technical, economics, aesthetics, etc.)....

Humans are responsible for their own acts and, therefore, for their human development, which at the same time produces a good society. It requires the following of rules associated with

moral goods. Some rules need extensive study due to complicated issues in each profession or environment. But there are some elemental moral rules relatively easy to learn. Thus, practically everyone can discover the "golden rule" (treat others in the same way you would like to be treated), the rule of respecting human dignity, "giving people their rights," honoring promises and fulfilling contracts, and some others. Likewise, abusing power by exploiting human need, manipulating people and considering persons as mere instruments for the sake of one's own interests, are ethical rules regarding what must be avoided.

By acting in accordance with these rules and consequently in accordance with moral goods, the individual acquires virtues. These virtues acquired by acting according to moral goods and the corresponding rules can be called "human virtues." Understanding rules, goods (values), and virtues in this way is, by definition, interrelated.

Because human virtues are habits, they provide promptness or readiness to do good, ease or facility in performing a good action and joy or satisfaction while doing it. Human virtues, or virtues proper to human beings as such, are traditionally grouped in four major categories called "cardinal virtues": practical wisdom (or prudence); justice, which includes all "transitive virtues" or virtues related with dealing with others; and two self-master virtues: fortitude (sometimes known as courage) and temperance (or moderation) (Houser, 2004; Pieper, 1965), which many consider genuine human virtues (Geach, 1977).

Moral values (goods) entail rules and acting in accordance with these rules develops human virtues, and these virtues make it easier to grasp moral values (see Figure 1). In grasping moral values, practical wisdom has a crucial role, since this virtue provides the capacity for perceiving human good in every action and to determine what is the content of each virtue (e.g., pointing out what does it mean to be courageous in a particular situation). Other human virtues are united among them, and practical wisdom requires the existence

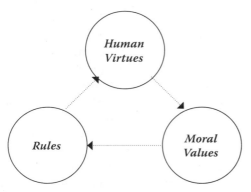

Figure 1 Interdependence of Moral Values, Rules, and Human Virtues

of the other virtues. For Aristotle, "it is not possible to be good in the strict sense without practical wisdom, or practically wise without moral virtues" (*Nichomachean Ethics*, bk 6, chap. 13; 1144b31).

In other words (see Figure 2), practical wisdom points out what is the right means in each situation regarding transitive and self-mastering virtues. Practicing these latter virtues develops practical wisdom as a necessary condition. Finally, transitive and self-mastering virtues have reciprocal influences (e.g., fairness requires courage, and being fair is fostered by the development of courage needed to act fairly). Rules, goods and virtues, understood in

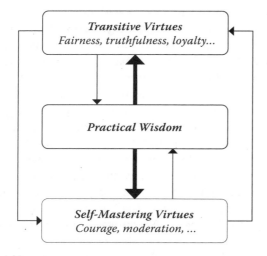

Figure 2 Practical Wisdom as a Driver of Moral Virtues

this way, are indeed interconnected. Furthermore, "virtues, rules and goods … have to be understood in their relationship or not at all"; and "rules, conceived apart from virtues and goods, are not the same as rules conceived in dependence upon virtues and goods; and so it is also with virtues apart from rules and good and good apart from rules and virtues" (MacIntyre, 1993, 144).

ETHICAL EDUCATION FOR GOOD BEHAVIOR

In line with the Aristotelian tradition, I suggest ethical behavior of a person in accounting, as in any other human activity, depends on (see Figure 3)

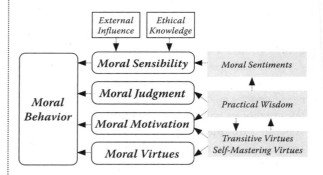

Figure 3 Constituent Factors and Virtues for a Moral Behavior

- *Moral [sensibility]*, which could be described as how the subject comprehends the ethical dimension of a situation. Human beings have a certain capacity to feel other people's needs. In the face of certain situations we experience feelings of compassion, solidarity, sympathy for a noble cause, and other moral sentiments. In accounting, one can feel that a practice can adversely or favorably affect some people. But there are also sentiments of greed, self-sufficiency or even fear which can be stronger than those related to good behavior. Sentiments can also lead to attitudes of sentimentalism, the morality of which could be questioned. Therefore, moral sentiments seem not sufficient for an authentic moral sensibility; they need practical wisdom to bring about moral sensibility. Practical wisdom helps one to grasp the moral good in each particular action. External influences, including the perceptions of peers, education, and ethical knowledge can cultivate (or discourage) moral sentiments.

- *Moral judgment*, or capacity to judge which alternatives are ethically acceptable and which are not and to determine the uprightness of the intention. Good behavior requires deliberation and deciding to carry out an action. Making sound moral judgments is previous to making a good decision. In this deliberation, practical wisdom plays a crucial role. It fosters upright moral reasoning by taking into account universal principles and the pertinent circumstances of each situation. Furthermore, some other relevant virtues in accounting, such as objectivity, open-mindedness, insight and perspicacity can be considered as integrated within practical wisdom.

    Ethical knowledge, including a right understanding of rules, principles and values, which could be seen as accumulation of wisdom throughout time, can also help one to make sound ethical judgments. This latter is especially valuable for those without experience and with low practical wisdom. However, rules, principles and values have to be considered only as an aid and not as a substitute for practical wisdom.

- *Moral motivation*, understood as willingness to take the moral course of action, placing moral values (human goods) above other values, and taking personal responsibility for moral outcomes. Frequently, moral motivation is the driving force for making good moral judgments but it plays a crucial role in selecting the right action and in executing it. Practical wisdom and transitive moral virtues (indirectly also self-mastering virtues) foster moral motivation, since they give a permanent motivation for acting well. External motivation, such as moral role modeling, ethical leadership, culture, education, etc., can also play a significant role in motivating people towards moral behavior.

- *Moral virtues* or permanent attitudes and interior strength for moral behavior. Among these virtues, those which have special relevance to accounting are fairness, integrity, truthfulness, honesty, loyalty, faithfulness, trustworthiness, service to the common good, gratitude and benevolence ("transitive virtues" or justice in a broad sense). Courage, perseverance, competence, diligence, professional will, humility, and other self-mastering virtues help to defeat inner resistance to act as one should. Practical wisdom, as has been said, provides capacity to perceive the right means for each virtue.

If this sketch is correct, character, shaped by the virtues of the subject, is crucial for moral behavior....

CONCLUSION

... This paper ... holds that the main goal for ethical education in accounting—and of course, in any other professional field—should be to impact on the ethical behavior of those receiving this education and not only to provide a set of theories tools to solve ethical dilemmas. Ethical behavior primarily has to do with character, although ethical knowledge and external motivation must also be an influence. Consequently, ethical education has to be oriented toward motivating moral behavior and acquiring virtues, as some scholars have pointed out in recent years. However, virtues are not a matter of knowledge but personal moral development. What ethical education can do is to show virtues, exhort and motivate the student to acquire them and explain how to do so. This includes the presentation and discussion of rules, generally from codes, principles and values which are necessary for acquiring virtues.

From a practical perspective, this proposal requires, first of all, changing the status quo of teaching which exclusively presents rules and enlightened ethical theories. Teaching material should also seek a different focus than what is common in many places, which is presenting dilemmas based on cases and providing little or no information about the people involved. What I have proposed is a comprehensive ethical approach interrelating rules, values and virtues. Case studies should include not only dilemmas but also descriptions of specific people involved in a particular situation, significant facts of their life, traits of their character, as well as other relevant information about factors with an influence on moral behavior, such as how people are motivated by their organization (incentives, moral role modeling, leadership, organizational culture and so on) and by the socio-cultural environment....

REFERENCES

Aristotle, *Nichomachean Ethics* in R. McKeon (ed.), 1941, *The Basic Works of Aristotle* (New York: Random House).

Armstrong, M.B.: 2002, "Ethics Issues in Accounting," in N.E. Bowie (ed.), *The Blackwell Guide to Business Ethics* (Oxford: Blackwell).

Armstrong, M.B., J.E. Ketz and D. Owsen: 2003, "Ethics Education in Accounting: Moving Toward Ethical Motivation and Ethical Behavior," *Journal of Accounting Education* 21(1), 1–16.

Azpiazu, J.: 1964, *La moral del hombre de negocios* (Zaragoza: Fax).

Baudhuin, F.: 1954, *D'ontologie des affaires*, 4th edition (Bruxelles: Universelle).

Francis, J.R.: 1990, "After Virtue? Accounting as a Moral and Discursive Practice," *Accounting, Auditing and Accountability Journal* 3(3), 5–17.

Geach, P.T.: 1977, *The Virtues* (Cambridge: Cambridge University Press).

Guardini, R.: 1999, *Ética. Lecciones en la Universidad de Munich* (BAC, Madrid). Original: 1993, *Ethik. Vorlesungen an der Universitat München* (Mainz: Matthias-Grünerwald-Verlag).

Houser, R.E. (ed.): 2004, *The Cardinal Virtues. Aquinas, Albert and Philip the Chancelor* (Toronto: Pontifical Institute of Mediaeval Studies).

Koehn, D.: 2000, "What is Practical Judgment?" *Professional Ethics Journal* 8(3/4), 3–18.

Loeb, S.E. and J.P. Bedingfield: 1972, "Teaching Accounting Ethics," *The Accounting Review*, October, 811–13.

Loeb, S.E. (ed.): 1978, *Ethics in the Accounting Profession* (New York: Wiley).

Loeb, S.E.: 1988, "Teaching Students Accounting Ethics: Some Crucial Issues," *Issues in Accounting Education* 3(2), 316–29.

MacIntyre, A.: 1984, *After Virtue. A Study in Moral Theory*, 2nd edition (Notre Dame, IN: Notre Dame University Press).

MacIntyre, A.: 1993, "Plain Persons and Moral Philosophy: Rules, Virtues and Goods," *Convivium* (2nd series) 5, 63–80.

Messerly, J.G.: 1994, *An Introduction to Ethical Theories* (Lanham, New York, London: University Press of America).

Mintz, S.M.: 1995, "Virtue Ethics and Accounting Education," *Issues in Accounting Education* 10(2), 247–67.

Mintz, S.M.: 1996, "The Role of Virtue in Accounting Education," *Accounting Education: A Journal of Theory, Practice and Research* 1, 67–91.

Pieper, J.: 1965, *Four Cardinal Virtues* (Notre Dame, IN: Notre Dame University Press).

Pincoffs, E.L.: 1986, *Quandries and Virtues* (Lawrence: University Press of Kansas).

—69—

SOCIAL WORK VALUES AND ETHICS

An Overview

Frederic Reamer

... [S]ITUATIONS SOMETIMES ARISE IN SOCIAL work in which core values in the profession conflict, and this leads to ethical dilemmas. An ethical dilemma is a situation in which professional duties and obligations, rooted in core values, clash. This is when social workers must decide which values—as expressed in various duties and obligations—take precedence.

To make these difficult choices social workers need to be familiar with contemporary thinking about ethical decision making....

As I shall explore shortly, the phenomenon of ethical decision making in the professions has matured considerably in recent years. Professionals trained today have far more access to helpful literature and concepts related to ethical decision making than did their predecessors. This is particularly true in social work, which has experienced a noticeable burgeoning of interest in ethical decision making.

Finally, social workers must be concerned about the risk-management ramifications of their ethical decisions and actions, particularly the possibility of professional malpractice and misconduct. Is it acceptable for a social worker to knowingly and willingly violate a law, even if she has only noble motives involving service to clients? What consequences should there be for a social worker who does not act in a client's best interests?

What legal risks—in the form of criminal penalties, ethics complaints, formal adjudication by ethics disciplinary committees or state licensing boards, and lawsuits—do social workers face as a result of their actions?...

THE ETHICAL THEORY AND DECISION-MAKING PERIOD

Until the late 1970s the profession focused primarily on social work's core values and value base. Then the profession underwent another significant transition in its concern about values and ethical issues. The 1970s saw a dramatic surge of interest in the broad subject of applied and professional ethics (also known as practical ethics). Professions as diverse as medicine, law, business, journalism, engineering, nursing, social work, psychology, and criminal justice began to devote sustained attention to the subject. Large numbers of undergraduate and graduate training programs added courses on applied and professional ethics to their curricula, professional conferences witnessed a substantial increase in presentations on the subject, and the number of publications on professional ethics increased dramatically (Callahan and Bok 1980; Reamer and Abramson 1982).

The growth of interest in professional ethics during this period was the result of a variety of factors. Controversial technological developments in health care and other fields certainly helped to spark ethical debate involving such issues as termination of life support, organ transplantation, genetic engineering, psychopharmacological intervention, and test-tube babies. What criteria should be used to determine which medically needy patients should receive scarce organs, such as hearts and kidneys? When is it acceptable to terminate the life support that is keeping a comatose family member alive? To what extent is it appropriate to influence the sex of a fetus through laboratory intervention? Is it ethically justifiable to implant an animal's heart into the body of an infant born with an impaired heart?

Widespread publicity about scandals in government also triggered considerable interest in professional ethics. Beginning especially with Watergate in the early 1970s, the public has become painfully aware of various professionals who have abused their clients and patients, emotionally, physically, or financially. The media have been filled with disturbing reports of physicians, psychologists, lawyers, clergy, social workers, nurses, teachers, pharmacists, and other professionals who have taken advantage of the people they are supposed to serve. Consequently, most professions take more seriously their responsibility to educate practitioners about potential abuse and ways to prevent it.

In addition, the introduction, beginning especially in the 1960s, of such terminology as patients' rights, welfare rights, women's rights, and prisoners' rights helped shape professionals' thinking about the need to attend to ethical concepts. Since the 1960s members of many professions have been much more cognizant of the concept of rights, and this has led many training programs to broach questions about the nature of professionals' ethical duties to their clients and patients.

Contemporary professionals also have a much better appreciation of the limits of science and its ability to respond to the many complex questions professionals face. Although U.S. society has placed science on a pedestal since the 1930s and widely regards it as the key to many of life's mysteries, modern-day professionals acknowledge that science cannot answer questions that are fundamentally ethical in nature (Sloan 1980).

Finally, the well-documented increase in litigation and malpractice, along with publicity about unethical professionals, has forced the professions to take a closer look at their ethics traditions and training. All professions have experienced an increase in claims and lawsuits against practitioners, and a substantial portion of these complaints alleges some form of unethical conduct....

THE ETHICAL STANDARDS AND RISK-MANAGEMENT PERIOD

The most recent stage in the development of social work ethics, especially in the United States, reflects the dramatic maturation of social workers' understanding of ethical issues. This stage is characterized mainly by the significant expansion of ethical standards to guide practitioners' conduct and by increased knowledge concerning professional negligence and liability....

Compared to most other nations, the United States has a relatively high incidence of lawsuits filed against professionals in general (doctors, dentists, psychologists, etc.). As a result of increased litigation against social workers—a significant portion of which alleges some kind of ethics violation—many social work education programs, social service agencies, licensing boards, and professional associations are sponsoring special training and education on ethics-related risk management, especially as it relates to such issues as confidential and privileged information, informed consent, conflicts of interest, dual relationships and boundary issues, use of non-traditional and unorthodox interventions, termination of services, and documentation. This training and education typically focuses on common ethical mistakes, procedures for handling complex ethical issues and dilemmas, forms of ethical misconduct, and prevailing ethical standards.

Social workers in the United States are particularly concerned about ethical issues and related liability risks that result from managed care (Reamer 2001a; Strom-Gottfried 1998). Managed care, which began in earnest in the United States in the 1980s, includes large-scale efforts by the insurance industry and service providers to deliver mental health and social services in the most cost-effective and efficient way possible. One major feature of managed care is that social workers must obtain approval from managed care organizations and insurance companies before commencing services. This process typically requires social workers to disclose confidential clinical and personal information about clients. Social workers must be familiar with potential confidentiality risks associated with the disclosure of information to managed care organizations.

Managed care has created other ethical issues as well. Social workers sometimes are unable to obtain authorization for services that they think are essential for vulnerable or troubled clients. In some instances social workers may be tempted to exaggerate clients' clinical symptoms, a form of fraud and deception, in an effort to obtain approval for services from managed care organizations (Kirk and Kutchins 1988). Social workers also sometimes find themselves caught between their obligation to serve clients and their right to be paid for their professional services. The possibility of premature termination of services (known in legal circles as abandonment) is a serious ethical and liability risk. And social workers are sometimes required to refer clients to treatment programs that seem inadequate in light of clients'

clinical needs. This may occur when a managed care organization has entered into an agreement with the treatment program to provide services at an attractive cost, as opposed to allowing clients and their social workers to locate the most appropriate, and perhaps more expensive, program based solely on clinical criteria.

The burgeoning interest in professional values and ethics is the product of a variety of circumstances. These factors have combined to produce a remarkable and sustained growth of interest in the subject across professions, one that has fundamentally changed the way professionals are educated and trained....

WORKS CITED

Callahan, Daniel and Sissela Bok, eds. 1980. *Ethics Teaching in Higher Education*. New York: Plenum.

Kirk, Stuart A. and Herb Kutchins. 1988. "Deliberate Misdiagnosis in Mental Health Practice." *Social Service Review* 62 (2): 225–37.

Reamer, F.G. "Ethics and Managed Care Policy." In N.W. Veeder and W. Peebles-Wilkins, eds., *Managed Care Services: Policy, Programs, and Research*, pp. 74–96. New York: Oxford University Press.

Reamer, F.G. and M. Abramson. 1982. *The Teaching of Social Work Ethics*. Hastings-on-Hudson, N.Y.: Hastings Center.

Sloan, Douglas. 1980. "The Teaching of Ethics in the American Undergraduate Curriculum, 1876–1976." In D. Callahan and S. Bok, eds., *Ethics Teaching in Higher Education*, pp. 1–57. New York: Plenum.

Stom-Gottfried, K.J. 1998. "Is 'Ethical Managed Care' an Oxymoron?" *Families in Society* 79(3): 297–307.

WILLFUL IGNORANCE AND THE LIMITS OF ADVOCACY

Hans Allhoff

1. BACKGROUND

DANIEL KELLINGTON WAS A LAWYER IN PRIVATE practice in Medford, Oregon, specializing in personal injury law and trusts and estates.

One Saturday afternoon, a United States Marshal phoned Kellington to tell him a former client of his, "Richard Parker," was really Peter MacFarlane, a fugitive wanted in Vermont on drug trafficking charges. MacFarlane had been arrested in Appelgate, Oregon, was in jail, and wished to speak with Kellington. Kellington took his call. He had represented MacFarlane about a year previous in a few matters connected with MacFarlane's business, Metalhead Boat Works.

Kellington told MacFarlane he was not a criminal lawyer, but agreed to visit MacFarlane anyway regarding, in MacFarlane's words, "some matters related to a boat business." Their meeting lasted for about ten minutes. MacFarlane admitted to Kellington he was in fact Peter MacFarlane and not Richard Parker. He also told him he owed time for a prior drug conviction and intended to serve it. MacFarlane then asked Kellington to contact an employee named Norm Young, and to have Young remove some things from MacFarlane's home. Those things included: stereo equipment, files, a black attaché case, money stuffed underneath a mattress, a laptop computer, electronic organizers, and a boat. In addition, MacFarlane wrote out some instructions for Young, which read, "Chair in bedroom,

right side of arm, envelope. Please destroy as soon as possible."

Kellington returned to his office, immediately called Young, and began to pass on instructions from his conversation with MacFarlane. Young asked him how he should destroy the envelope; Kellington said he could burn it. Young also asked Kellington why he was calling him and not Mr. "Parker"; Kellington told him Mr. "Parker" was in jail, but said nothing more. When Young asked Kellington if he could get into any kind of trouble for doing what MacFarlane was asking of him, Kellington told him he could not—but also to stop if he ran into police or "somebody bigger than you."

Young, more or less, did as he was instructed. But, after discovering a driver's license with MacFarlane's picture and another name (not Parker or MacFarlane) in the envelope he was told to burn, as well as $20,000 in cash in a bag he removed, Young panicked and drove home. When he later drove back to MacFarlane's house to put things back in their place, he was confronted by federal officials who were there to execute a search warrant. Young told them what, through Kellington, MacFarlane had instructed him to do.

The federal officials then arranged for Young to initiate a tape-recorded phone call to Kellington. During this call, Young told Kellington about the fake I.D. and the large amount of money. When Kellington asked Young if he had "heard from anybody," Young said he had not. Kellington then suggested they take an inventory of everything, and he would then take possession. When Young asked Kellington whether they should report this to authorities, Kellington said, "Well, I don't think you have to do that." Kellington said, "I have a duty to my client to protect his assets that, that they can't get and when they … If they, if somebody uh, come and, comes and says hey we're attaching that money because it's ill-gotten gains or something … Well then I have to turn it over to them, but in the meantime it's his money, and it's his money and he may need to defend uh, you know pay a lawyer." When Kellington left Young's house with MacFarlane's belongings, federal agents detained him.

2. ANALYSIS

These facts, names included, are taken almost verbatim from a real case, *United States v. Kellington*, in which Kellington was arrested and, along with MacFarlane, charged with obstructing justice by "knowingly … engaging in misleading conduct toward another person, with intent to alter, destroy, mutilate, or conceal an object with intent to impair the object's integrity or availability for use in an official proceeding."

At trial, Kellington played dumb. For all he knew, the envelope he was directing Young to destroy contained a love letter. In hindsight, he admitted, he should have been more inquisitive of MacFarlane's demands, but when he and MacFarlane met he assumed MacFarlane merely wanted to make sure his things were in good hands. Why did he tell Young so little? Because, Kellington maintained, it is his policy not to disclose to third parties information he learns in confidence from clients.

The real issue at trial, and on appeal, was whether Kellington, unlike MacFarlane, could avail himself of a defense grounded in legal ethics norms. Specifically, the trial judge, in his instruction to the jury, said, "[T]his is not a case on legal lawyer ethics. A crime has been charged and I'm not going to permit ethics type of arguments

here." On appeal, the Ninth Circuit Court of Appeals rejected this framing. An expert on legal ethics had testified on Kellington's behalf, and the Ninth Circuit thought his testimony was quite relevant: "When you have a lawyer who has been in private practice on the civil side—and Mr. Kellington has been for the better part of 30 years—it does not come as a surprise to me that in this context he did not immediately flash upon what I think would be known to you or to maybe others, that, by God, this is a—you know, I'm being asked to destroy evidence here." On this analysis, Kellington's ignorance, naïveté—call it what you will—coupled with his sense of client loyalty, would seem to rebut an obstruction of justice charge.

DISCUSSION QUESTIONS

1. During his taped phone conversation with Kellington, Young asked Kellington whether they should alert authorities, against what MacFarlane's wishes obviously would have been. Kellington replied, "I have a duty to my client to protect his assets that, that they can't get and when they … If they, if somebody uh, come and, comes and says hey we're attaching that money because it's ill-gotten gains or something … Well then I have to turn it over to them, but in the meantime it's his money, and it's his money and he may need to defend uh, you know pay a lawyer." What do you make of Kellington's response? Can Kellington's claim of naïveté be accepted?

2. It certainly would not have been a crime for Kellington to have gone straight to the police after his initial phone conversation with MacFarlane. Should he have? Or are you satisfied with a rule saying, "If you're a lawyer and you don't know that what your client is asking you to do is illegal, you can go ahead and do it"?

3. Kellington said MacFarlane was a client of his. But was he? Once a lawyer for MacFarlane, always a lawyer for MacFarlane? Doesn't this

amount to conscripting Kellington into an ethical dilemma?

4. In connection with this case and the readings in this section, ask yourself whether lawyering requires an ethics of its own. Is common-sense moral philosophy just not enough? Do we want lawyers to have certain moral duties and exemptions beyond those we have as ordinary people?

PROFESSIONAL MISCONDUCT WHILE OFF-DUTY

Luke Golemon

1. BACKGROUND

CAROLYN STROM'S GRANDFATHER DIED IN January of 2015 after receiving palliative care from St. Joseph's Health Facility in Macklin, Saskatchewan. Strom, a registered nurse, took to Facebook and Twitter to decry what she took to be inadequate care at the facility in February of 2015:

> My grandfather spent a week in palliative care before he died and after hearing about his and my family's experience there, it is evident that not everyone is "up to speed" on how to approach end of life care or how to help maintain an ageing senior's dignity. I challenge the people involved in decision making with that facility to please get all your staff a refresher on this topic and more. Don't get me wrong, "some" people have provided excellent care so I thank you so very much for your efforts, but to those who made Grandpa's last years less than desirable, please do better next time ... As an RN [registered nurse] and avid health care advocate myself, I just have to speak up. Whatever reasons/excuses people give for not giving quality of life care, I do not care. It just needs to be fixed.[1]

Although Strom did not work at the facility herself, members of the St. Joseph's Health Facility staff saw the post and felt shamed and attacked. Strom's status as an RN came up later during discussion of the post, and the Saskatchewan Registered Nurses Association (SRNA) was notified of the social media comments via a formal complaint, alleging professional misconduct.

After investigation, the SRNA concluded Strom was guilty of professional misconduct. They note the lack of outreach to the staff at the facility prior to the social media post as a key part of their decision: "Ms. Strom engaged in a generalized public venting about the facility and its staff and went straight to social media to do that."[2] Even though Strom stated she was venting from the perspective of an aggrieved granddaughter, the SRNA maintained she had overstepped the boundaries of what is acceptable for a registered nurse to say regarding her fellow nurses. The SRNA also concluded that while Strom was guilty of professional misconduct, her misconduct was not in any way malicious; she really was being sincere in attempting to improve the state of medical care at St. Joseph's Health Facility and healthcare for elderly persons more broadly. This appeared to factor into the severity of the penalty the SRNA decided to levy on Strom.

Strom appealed her verdict, but the judge dismissed the case. The costs of the case, including the appeal proceedings, were enormous: over $150,000. Strom's penalty was a $1000 fine and one-sixth of the cost of the court proceedings—which added up to $26,000. A GoFundMe campaign set up by sympathizers raised $27,000 to cover her fine.[3]

2. ANALYSIS

Strom's guilty verdict caused significant outcry. Many objected the punishment was excessive; $26,000 was an exorbitant fine for such a small infraction. Others did not see it as an infraction at all. Still others thought the first instance of holding someone accountable for activities ruled unethical after the fact can be controversial, but needs to be done. Broadly, there appear to be two issues at stake here. First, should the SRNA have sanctioned Strom? Second, were Strom's actions unethical in any way?

Many have defended Strom from the SRNA's sanction on freedom-of-expression grounds, but freedom of expression usually concerns itself with interactions between the government and its citizens, not private entities and their interactions in the private sphere. Still, the moral principles undergirding freedom of expression carry some weight here. Worse cases have received leniency regarding freedom of expression in the past. To give one example, Bill Whatcott, a practical nurse, picketed Planned Parenthood clinics in Regina in 2002 and 2003. Although he was found guilty of professional misconduct, he won his appeal on the grounds of freedom of expression.[4] Because he situated his protest as a dutiful citizen rather than as a nurse, his appeal succeeded. It is unclear if this should hold for Strom. She did mention her credentials as a registered nurse, but did not try to situate herself as a nurse at St. Joseph's nor to tag the post as from the perspective of a nurse rather than a granddaughter.

The SRNA assumed Strom's duties as a nurse in this case did extend to her comments on Facebook. Even if we agree with the SRNA on this point, it does not resolve the ethical issues. One serious concern is the inconsistency of the decision with two of the Canadian Nursing Association's provisions in their code of ethics.

Listed under ethical responsibilities in the Canadian Nursing Association's Code of Ethics is that a nurse shall "advocate for persons receiving care if they believe the health of those persons is being compromised by factors beyond their control, including the decision-making of others."[5] A nurse owes her clients—patients—a certain protection and advocacy. When on duty, for example, nurses *must* speak up on the behalf of their patients if the system, visitors, circumstances, or even other medical professionals are endangering or are not properly caring for the patient in some way. Even when a medical professional is not working as such, their increased medical knowledge comes with an increase in obligations. For example, when a medical emergency occurs near an off-duty medical professional, she is often the best qualified among the bystanders to provide medical care; therefore, she ought to provide the emergency medical care over the other bystanders.[6] This is listed in the Canadian Nursing Association Code of Ethics and carried over into the SRNA's own list of standards.

By the SRNA's own principles, they appear to be committed to the permissibility of Strom's post if she was striving to improve the conditions of St. Joseph's workplace and attempting to protect and promote the rights and health of patients there. If anyone has the expertise to criticize these institutions, surely it is medical professionals. If this is right, then stifling Strom's speech by finding her guilty of professional misconduct violates ethical principles that all nurses should accept. Medical institutions certainly should not stand in the way of nurses fulfilling their ethical duty. Therefore, if Strom's post was within the realm of appropriately improving the quality of care for her clients (broadly construed), then she should not be found guilty of professional misconduct.

In response to the two concerns above, the SRNA can point out Strom was not employed at St. Joseph's and therefore is unlikely to know details integral to improving the environment for patients. Considering she did not give specific recommendations for St. Joseph or its staff to improve, it is difficult to see how she is concretely improving the patients' environment there. Additionally, Strom may have hurt the environment of St. Joseph's by airing her grievances publicly first, rather than working with the staff at the facility.[7] Prospective patients might feel uncomfortable about going to St. Joseph's or might stop going to St. Joseph's altogether. Especially considering the gravitas Strom lent her post by mentioning her medical credentials, those who read the post might seriously consider getting their healthcare elsewhere. Although these concerns appear to be strong enough to show Strom should have thought more about what she was going to do and perhaps pursue other alternatives, it is less clear Strom should be found guilty of professional misconduct.

The above issues assume Strom was acting in the role of a registered nurse, but this too is contentious. Although she mentioned her role as a nurse, she neither worked at the facility nor did she engage in the sort of feedback a nurse would give if she had worked at the facility. The post itself was inspired by grief at the death of her grandfather, and many have complaints about how their elders' healthcare has been managed. Airing these sorts of complaints publicly may be neither nice nor fair, but it does not seem like professional misconduct. If Strom was playing *that* role, then accusations of professional misconduct miss completely. Nevertheless, concerns about how easily a professional can don and doff the role of their profession muddy the waters. Just because I do not intend for others to see me as a professional does not guarantee others will in fact see me as renouncing my role.

However, as noted before, medical professionals (and other professionals as well) receive additional duties in the course of receiving their training and knowledge, duties that extend beyond when and where one is employed or on duty. If a certain sort of respect for fellow medical professionals is one of these duties, then Strom does seem to have done something wrong. It is possible, however, that the SRNA should not have sanctioned her and yet Strom is still blameworthy; the two issues appear somewhat independent.

NOTES

1   Victoria Dinh, "Facebook Post Leaves Prince Albert, Sask., Nurse Charged with Professional Misconduct," *CBC*, 12 January 2016, https://www.cbc.ca/news/canada/saskatoon/facebook-post-prince-albert-nurse-charged-professional-misconduct-1.3400676.

2   CBC News, "Nurse Who 'Vented' Online Found Guilty of Professional Misconduct," 3 December 2016, https://www.cbc.ca/news/canada/saskatchewan/srna-discipline-social-media-nurse-saskatchewan-1.3880351.

3   Ashley Martin, "Prosecution Draws Parallel Between Registered Nurse Carolyn Strom's Case and Bill Whatcott's in Disciplinary Hearing," *Regina Leader-Post*, 4 March 2016, https://leaderpost.com/news/local-news/prosecution-draws-parallel-between-registered-nurse-carolyn-stroms-case-and-bill-whatcotts-in-disciplinary-hearing.

4   Martin, "Prosecution Draws Parallel."

5   Canadian Nurses Association, "Code of Ethics," (2017), https://cna-aiic.ca/en/nursing-practice/nursing-ethics .

6   Canadian Nurses Association, "Code of Ethics." One can also see this in the SRNA "Standards and Foundations" statement, under "Standard IV: Service to the Public" in Saskatchewan Registered Nurses Association, *Standards and Foundations Competencies for the Practice of Registered Nurses* (Regina, 2013).

7   While the SRNA now has guidelines developed from this case, at the time of the incident the guidelines only referred to one's own workplace.

DISCUSSION QUESTIONS

1.   Professionals certainly have obligations toward their clients, but do they also owe potential or ostensive clients (such as the patients of a medical facility where one does not work) anything beyond the norm?

2. Should client-based professions require a certain code of conduct even when their members are not "on-duty"? Should it preclude them from conduct that would otherwise be appropriate?

3. Do client-based professionals have a "whistle-blower" obligation?

4. Medical professionals are not legally required to give aid while off duty, ostensibly because they are not in the role of a medical professional at that time. What might we say about such roles on social media, where one's credentials are almost always visible on one's profile?

UNIT 10

INSTITUTION-BASED PROFESSIONS

T.J. Broy and Luke Golemon

1. INTRODUCTION

INSTITUTION-BASED PROFESSIONS ARE DISTIN-
guished from client-based professions by the
moral questions that are typically involved in each.
Thinking about client-based professions involves
a special focus on the relationship between a
professional and his or her client. Thinking
about institution-based professions, on the other
hand, involves a special focus on the relationship
between individuals, institutions, and society.

The institutions that will be considered in this
unit all have a social function to serve. That is to
say, the good of society is served by these institutions functioning well. Examples include the military, the Church, universities, police, and media
organizations. The existence of these institutions
puts professionals working within them in unique
moral situations. Where conflicts of interest in
business might be easy to adjudicate morally,
conflicts of interest within institution-based
professions are often far from easy to judge. What
is good for the institution is good for society, but
it might not be good for the individuals involved.
For example, army officers know they put their
soldiers at risk by ordering them into combat. It is
in the soldier's best interest that they not fight. It
is in the army's best interest that they accomplish
their mission. A balance has to be struck between
what is good for individuals and what is good for
the institutions with which they interact.

Institutions also raise questions regarding
blame and harm. Some harms seem particular to
institutions. Without the reputability of a news
station, a journalist might not cause much harm
by lying. When those lies are broadcast to trusting
viewers during prime time, however, the harm can
be tremendous. Without the authority of a police
force, the individual officer would not be able to
abuse his power. Abuses of power by police only
exist because the institution grants officers the
power they have. Institutions can also perpetuate
harms by seeking their own interests. If Catholic
priests abuse children, it is in the Church's best
interest that this not become public knowledge. By
seeking to promote its own interests, the Church
might put abusive priests in situations where they
can inflict even greater harm. Is the institution
responsible for these harms? If so, how should the
institution be held accountable? There are no easy
answers to these questions.

2. CONTENTS

The readings in this unit will explore several
institution-based professions, the moral challenges particular to each, and the roles of these
professionals both within their institutions and
within society.

In the first reading, Chelsey and Anderson
examine the role of university professors in
teaching ethics. Should business professors teach

business ethics? Chelsey and Anderson consider several ethical challenges unique to university professors and argue that university professors must understand the ethical challenges of their own profession in order to effectively teach ethics.

The second reading examines research ethics for academic researchers. In this reading Resnik explores some of the common ethical concerns regarding scientific research and the way different ethical principles and values shape how research ought to be done.

In the third reading, Detmer considers the role of journalists in society and their effect on political life. Detmer explores ways in which journalists can be complicit in the actions of their governments rather than objective purveyors of fact and how these failures might be remedied.

The fourth reading examines the professional nature of the military. Cook argues that the unique characteristics of the military profession make for unique moral challenges. In addition to the moral concerns common to all professions, the nature of the military gives it further moral challenges to deal with.

In the fifth reading, Ciulla explores leadership ethics and makes clear the relationship between society and institution-based professions. Ciulla considers various definitions of leadership as well as how normative theories of good leadership might impact the relationships between leaders and the groups they lead.

The Miller reading is a survey of some of the moral challenges facing police. Because police occupy a unique place in society, they must be aware of the effect their actions will have on society—from the use of force to building trust in communities.

In the seventh reading, Kipnis examines the ethical challenges of having professional ethics consultants working in hospitals. There are few agreed-upon standards for clinical ethics consultants, which makes it unclear how well patients are being served. Kipnis suggests some core features of ethics consulting and considers how those features might inform the accreditation of ethics consultants.

The final reading by Camenisch examines whether or not members of the clergy are professionals and how our answer to that question might impact the ethics of vocational ministry. Camenisch considers historical and analytical models for defining the profession of religious ministry and how an application of the professional ethics framework might function for members of the clergy.

The case studies invite exploration of the ways in which institutions interact with society and the professionals who serve in them. The first case study is of the My Lai massacre in which American soldiers killed hundreds of Vietnamese civilians during the Vietnam War. The second case study is of the sexual abuse perpetrated by Catholic priests and the Church's role in covering up the abuse. Both these cases ask the reader to reflect on how features of institutions interact with the actions of individuals to result in moral credit and blame.

—70—

ARE UNIVERSITY PROFESSORS QUALIFIED TO TEACH ETHICS?

G.R. (Dick) Chesley and Bruce Anderson

IN RECENT YEARS THE FIELD OF ETHICS HAS grown rapidly in Canadian universities. New positions have been created and research centres devoted to studying ethics have been established. Philosophers and theologians have led the way in medical ethics, environmental ethics, legal ethics, and business ethics. At our own university—Saint Mary's [Halifax, Canada]—the study of ethics takes various forms. The philosophy department offers a course in business ethics and members of the accounting department address ethical issues in their courses when they teach topics such as fraud, negligence, the GAAP, and tax.

With this growing concern with ethics in Canadian universities, professors in our business schools can be heard talking about the importance of teaching business ethics and calling for ethics courses relevant to today's business world. In fact, many business professors now believe that business ethics should be taught by people who know business and not left to philosophers and theologians. In their opinion, the general discussions and abstract pronouncements of philosophers and theologians on business do not meet the needs of business students. Rather, they argue that the ethical dilemmas found in actual business situations are complex and require a comprehensive knowledge of business in order to understand and to resolve them. Their position can be summed up as: how can you teach business ethics if you don't know anything about business.

But do our business professors have the qualifications required to teach business ethics? To address this question, begin by considering how formal professional groups—lawyers, doctors, accountants, engineers—deal with ethics in their profession. Formal codes of ethics are a key part of the structure of their self-regulated associations. Their codes serve them as a guide and justification for both official and unofficial regulation of members. Such shared codes of ethics, whether formal or not, represent a guide to the extra-legal behaviour of persons operating in complex social and institutional arrangements. Not only do they spell out behaviour that is unacceptable, but they also demand that members of these professions perform to the very best of their technical abilities with the highest degree of honesty and integrity. Evidently, explicitly addressing behaviour in a formal code of conduct and demanding that members operate in accord with it is a crucial part of the ethics of these professional groups.

By contrast, the behaviour of university professors who are not members of a formal professional association is not guided by a formal code of conduct. In fact, we do not even share an informal code of ethics. Given the complex nature of the interactions and relationships among university professors, and the growing concern with ethics in Canadian universities, this state of affairs is surprising.

What do university professors use to guide their behaviour? A vague notion of what is legal and what is illegal may be part of a decision whether or not to use stationery supplies for personal use, to make personal long distance phone calls at work, or to use work time for paid consulting. On the other hand, the criteria for a decision may be whether or not one believes there is a reasonable risk of being caught. However, these types of ethical questions don't seem very difficult because criminal law offers some guidance.

Other questions for a professor may be far harder to answer. For example, what should a professor consider before telling a student about the approach used by a colleague, especially when the comment could be perceived by the student as pejorative? Other examples occur when administrators use student responses as a basis for renewing, promoting or tenuring faculty, when many people believe that such data are unreliable measures of teaching abilities. Also, professors may be tempted to influence the results of student evaluations of their teaching.

The collegial environment of a university requires professional assessments of colleagues. Such actions pose ethical conflicts involving many elements. Issues related to competence, confidentiality, integrity, and objectivity may be entwined. While universities make efforts to protect the records of students from inappropriate disclosure by faculty, what about administrator or colleague confidentiality? For example, can or should a professor comment about the character of a colleague if the statement is conjecture or hearsay? What if a decision about tenure is required and the decision maker was previously voted against by the colleague under review? What if the decision maker needs the support of the colleague under review in a future decision? What about letters of reference for colleagues or informal telephone responses? Must the activities of faculty be assessed solely by using objective evidence? How confidential should discussions of colleagues be? Should comments by a professor about the character of another student,

professor, or administrator be made in meetings with colleagues?

The point is not simply that such ethical issues will go away if university professors adopt a set of rules to govern our behaviour. In fact, we may not even be ready for a formal code of ethics. The point here is that ethical dilemmas exist in the interpersonal environment of a collegial milieu. To ignore ethical questions in this environment means that the experiences to be learned from ethical experiences will be lost and thus the benefits of these experiences cannot be conveyed to students. The guidance of a code of ethics in a university setting may avoid the need for external regulation while providing the experiential practice needed to teach students about the importance of ethics.

Adequately dealing with such situations does not necessarily call for a code, but rather for the cultivation of intelligence and the invention and implementation of strategies to effectively deal with the bias of self-interested individuals and groups that arise in particular situations in the university. The highest possible degree of intellectual competence and integrity are demanded of us. It does not mean that we follow a set of rules or procedures in a simple-minded fashion yet a set of rules may help to provide the stimulation academics may need.

Academics operating in a self-regulated environment where they are concerned with conveying ethics to students need to understand ethics themselves. To do this they must act ethically in their own day to day activities. The minimum, then, for those professors who want to teach business ethics is that they must notice, and effectively deal with, the complex ethical situations at the university in which they find themselves. Part of that challenge involves coming to grips with the factors that influence and shape their own judgments and decisions. Otherwise, academics become like company executives who preach ethics to employees while abusing perquisites associated with their positions. If ethics are to become a meaningful part of the educational process they must be lived by professors who convey them.

—71—

WHAT IS ETHICS IN RESEARCH AND WHY IS IT IMPORTANT?

David B. Resnik

WHEN MOST PEOPLE THINK OF ETHICS (OR MORals), they think of rules for distinguishing between right and wrong, such as the Golden Rule ("Do unto others as you would have them do unto you"), a code of professional conduct like the Hippocratic Oath ("First of all, do no harm"), a religious creed like the Ten Commandments ("Thou Shalt not kill ..."), or ... wise aphorisms like the sayings of Confucius. This is the most common way of defining "ethics": **norms for conduct** that distinguish between acceptable and unacceptable behavior.

Most people learn ethical norms at home, at school, in church, or in other social settings. Although most people acquire their sense of right and wrong during childhood, moral development occurs throughout life and human beings pass through different stages of growth as they mature. Ethical norms are so ubiquitous that one might be tempted to regard them as simple commonsense. On the other hand, if morality were nothing more than commonsense, then why are there so many ethical disputes and issues in our society?

One plausible explanation of these disagreements is that all people recognize some common ethical norms but interpret, apply, and balance them in different ways in light of their own values and life experiences. For example, two people could agree that murder is wrong but disagree about the morality of abortion because they have different understandings of what it means to be a human being.

Most societies also have legal rules that govern behavior, but ethical norms tend to be broader and more informal than laws. Although most societies use laws to enforce widely accepted moral standards and ethical and legal rules use similar concepts, ethics and law are not the same. An action may be legal but unethical or illegal but ethical. We can also use ethical concepts and principles to criticize, evaluate, propose, or interpret laws. Indeed, in the last century, many social reformers have urged citizens to disobey laws they regarded as immoral or unjust laws. Peaceful civil disobedience is an ethical way of protesting laws or expressing political viewpoints.

Another way of defining 'ethics' focuses on the **disciplines that study** standards of conduct, such as philosophy, theology, law, psychology, or sociology. For example, a "medical ethicist" is someone who studies ethical standards in medicine. One may also define ethics as a **method, procedure, or perspective** for deciding how to act and for analyzing complex problems and issues. For instance, in considering a complex issue like global warming, one may take an economic, ecological, political, or ethical perspective on the problem. While an economist might examine the cost and benefits of various policies related to global warming, an environmental ethicist could examine the ethical values and principles at stake.

Many different disciplines, institutions, and professions have standards for behavior that suit their particular aims and goals. These standards also help members of the discipline to coordinate their actions or activities and to establish the public's trust of the discipline. For instance, ethical standards govern conduct in medicine, law, engineering, and business. Ethical norms also serve the aims or goals of research and apply to people who conduct scientific research or other scholarly or creative activities. There is even a specialized discipline, research ethics, which studies these norms.

There are several reasons why it is important to adhere to ethical norms in research. First, norms **promote the aims of research**, such as knowledge, truth, and avoidance of error. For example, prohibitions against fabricating, falsifying, or misrepresenting research data to promote the truth and minimize error.

Second, since research often involves a great deal of cooperation and coordination among many different people in different disciplines and institutions, ethical standards promote the **values that are essential to collaborative work**, such as trust, accountability, mutual respect, and fairness. For example, many ethical norms in research, such as guidelines for authorship, copyright and patenting policies, data sharing policies, and confidentiality rules in peer review, are designed to protect intellectual property interests while encouraging collaboration. Most researchers want to receive credit for their contributions and do not want to have their ideas stolen or disclosed prematurely.

Third, many of the ethical norms help to ensure that researchers can be held **accountable to the public**. For instance, federal policies on research misconduct, conflicts of interest, the human subjects protections, and animal care and use are necessary in order to make sure that researchers who are funded by public money can be held accountable to the public.

Fourth, ethical norms in research also help to build **public support** for research. People are more likely to fund a research project if they can trust the quality and integrity of research.

Finally, many of the norms of research promote a variety of other important **moral and social values**, such as social responsibility, human rights, animal welfare, compliance with the law, and public health and safety. Ethical lapses in research can significantly harm human and animal subjects, students, and the public. For example, a researcher who fabricates data in a clinical trial may harm or even kill patients, and a researcher who fails to abide by regulations and guidelines relating to radiation or biological safety may jeopardize his health and safety or the health and safety of staff and students.

CODES AND POLICIES FOR RESEARCH ETHICS

Given the importance of ethics for the conduct of research, it should come as no surprise that many different professional associations, government agencies, and universities have adopted specific codes, rules, and policies relating to research ethics. Many government agencies, such as the National Institutes of Health (NIH), the National Science Foundation (NSF), the Food and Drug Administration (FDA), the Environmental Protection Agency (EPA), and the US Department of Agriculture (USDA) have ethics rules for funded researchers. Other influential research ethics policies include Singapore Statement on Research Integrity, the American Chemical Society, The Chemist Professional's Code of Conduct, Code of Ethics (American Society for Clinical Laboratory Science), American Psychological Association, Ethical Principles of Psychologists and Code of Conduct, Statements on Ethics and Professional Responsibility (American Anthropological Association), Statement on Professional Ethics (American Association of University Professors), the Nuremberg Code, and the World Medical Association's Declaration of Helsinki. The following is a rough and general summary of some ethical principals that various codes address:

Honesty

Strive for honesty in all scientific communications. Honestly report data, results, methods and procedures, and publication status. Do not fabricate, falsify, or misrepresent data. Do not deceive colleagues, research sponsors, or the public.

Objectivity

Strive to avoid bias in experimental design, data analysis, data interpretation, peer review, personnel decisions, grant writing, expert testimony, and other aspects of research where objectivity is expected or required. Avoid or minimize bias or self-deception. Disclose personal or financial interests that may affect research.

Integrity

Keep your promises and agreements; act with sincerity; strive for consistency of thought and action.

Carefulness

Avoid careless errors and negligence; carefully and critically examine your own work and the work of your peers. Keep good records of research activities, such as data collection, research design, and correspondence with agencies or journals.

Openness

Share data, results, ideas, tools, resources. Be open to criticism and new ideas.

Respect for Intellectual Property

Honor patents, copyrights, and other forms of intellectual property. Do not use unpublished data, methods, or results without permission. Give proper acknowledgement or credit for all contributions to research. Never plagiarize.

Confidentiality

Protect confidential communications, such as papers or grants submitted for publication, personnel records, trade or military secrets, and patient records.

Responsible Publication

Publish in order to advance research and scholarship, not to advance just your own career. Avoid wasteful and duplicative publication.

Responsible Mentoring

Help to educate, mentor, and advise students. Promote their welfare and allow them to make their own decisions.

Respect for Colleagues

Respect your colleagues and treat them fairly.

Social Responsibility

Strive to promote social good and prevent or mitigate social harms through research, public education, and advocacy.

Non-Discrimination

Avoid discrimination against colleagues or students on the basis of sex, race, ethnicity, or other factors not related to scientific competence and integrity.

Competence

Maintain and improve your own professional competence and expertise through lifelong education and learning; take steps to promote competence in science as a whole.

Legality

Know and obey relevant laws and institutional and governmental policies.

Animal Care

Show proper respect and care for animals when using them in research. Do not conduct unnecessary or poorly designed animal experiments.

Human Subjects Protection

When conducting research on human subjects, minimize harms and risks and maximize benefits; respect human dignity, privacy, and autonomy; take special precautions with vulnerable populations; and strive to distribute the benefits and burdens of research fairly.*

*[This list of ethical principals is] adapted from Shamoo A. and Resnik D. 2015. *Responsible Conduct of Research*, 3rd ed. (New York: Oxford University Press).

...

PROMOTING ETHICAL CONDUCT IN SCIENCE

Most academic institutions in the US require undergraduate, graduate, or postgraduate students to have some education in the responsible conduct of research (RCR). The NIH and NSF have both mandated training in research ethics for students and trainees. Many academic institutions outside of the US have also developed educational curricula in research ethics.

Those of you who are taking or have taken courses in research ethics may be wondering why you are required to have education in research ethics. You may believe that you are highly ethical and know the difference between right and wrong. You would never fabricate or falsify data or plagiarize.

Indeed, you also may believe that most of your colleagues are highly ethical and that there is no ethics problem in research.

If you feel this way, relax. No one is accusing you of acting unethically. Indeed, the evidence produced so far shows that misconduct is a very rare occurrence in research, although there is considerable variation among various estimates. The rate of misconduct has been estimated to be as low as 0.01% of researchers per year (based on confirmed cases of misconduct in federally funded research) to as high as 1% of researchers per year (based on self-reports of misconduct on anonymous surveys). See Shamoo and Resnik (2015), cited above.

Clearly, it would be useful to have more data on this topic, but so far there is no evidence that science has become ethically corrupt, despite some highly publicized scandals. Even if misconduct is only a rare occurrence, it can still have a tremendous impact on science and society because it can compromise the integrity of research, erode the public's trust in science, and waste time and resources. Will education in research ethics help reduce the rate of misconduct in science? It is too early to tell. The answer to this question depends, in part, on how one understands the causes of misconduct. There are two main theories about why researchers commit misconduct. According to the "bad apple" theory, most scientists are highly ethical. Only researchers who are morally corrupt, economically desperate, or psychologically disturbed commit misconduct.

Moreover, only a fool would commit misconduct because science's peer review system and self-correcting mechanisms will eventually catch those who try to cheat the system. In any case, a course in research ethics will have little impact on "bad apples," one might argue.

According to the "stressful" or "imperfect" environment theory, misconduct occurs because various institutional pressures, incentives, and constraints encourage people to commit misconduct, such as pressures to publish or obtain grants or contracts, career ambitions, the pursuit of profit or fame, poor supervision of students and trainees, and poor oversight of researchers (see Shamoo and Resnik 2015). Moreover, defenders of the stressful environment theory point out that science's peer review system is far from perfect and that it is relatively easy to cheat the system. Erroneous or fraudulent research often enters the public record without being detected for years. Misconduct probably results from environmental and individual causes, i.e. when people who are morally weak, ignorant, or insensitive are placed in stressful or imperfect environments. In any case, a course in research ethics can be useful in helping to prevent deviations from norms even if it does not prevent misconduct. Education in research ethics can help people get a better understanding of ethical standards, policies, and issues and improve ethical judgment and decision making. Many of the deviations that occur in research may occur because researchers simply do not know or have never thought seriously about some of the ethical norms of research. For example, some unethical authorship practices probably reflect traditions and practices that have not been questioned seriously until recently. If the director of a lab is named as an author on every paper that comes from his lab, even if he does not make a significant contribution, what could be wrong with that? That's just the way it's done, one might argue. Another example where there may be some ignorance or mistaken traditions is conflicts of interest in research. A researcher may think that a "normal" or "traditional" financial relationship, such as accepting stock or a consulting fee from a drug company that sponsors her research, raises no serious ethical issues. Or perhaps a university administrator sees no ethical problem in taking a large gift with strings attached from a pharmaceutical company. Maybe a physician thinks that it is perfectly appropriate to receive a $300 finder's fee for referring patients into a clinical trial.

If "deviations" from ethical conduct occur in research as a result of ignorance or a failure to reflect critically on problematic traditions, then a course in research ethics may help reduce the rate of serious deviations by improving the researcher's understanding of ethics and by sensitizing him or her to the issues.

Finally, education in research ethics should be able to help researchers grapple with the ethical dilemmas they are likely to encounter by introducing them to important concepts, tools, principles, and methods that can be useful in resolving these dilemmas. Scientists must deal with a number of different controversial topics, such as human embryonic stem cell research, cloning, genetic engineering, and research involving animal or human subjects, which require ethical reflection and deliberation.

—72—

THE ETHICAL RESPONSIBILITIES OF JOURNALISTS

David Detmer

INTRODUCTION

DEMOCRACIES CANNOT FUNCTION WITHOUT AN effective system of political communication. For if citizens are not aware of the policies that are carried out in their name, they are powerless to oppose them. Consequently, one of the chief responsibilities of journalists in a democracy is to provide their readers (or viewers or listeners) with news accounts that are accurate, reasonably comprehensive, and free from subordination to governmental or corporate power (or to that of other "special interests").

Certainly, most mass media journalists in the United States accept such a characterization of their responsibility, which they interpret as entailing an obligation on their part to present news in an "objective," "nonpartisan," "unbiased," "balanced," "nonideological," and "neutral" manner. Other journalists, however, interpret this same responsibility as justifying their adoption of a highly specific bias—that of acting as a "counter-weight" to, or "watchdog" of, governmental power.[1] Despite this disagreement, there is a consensus among journalists holding it to be a serious breach of their professional ethics to tilt their news coverage heavily in *favor* of official US government perspectives, thus depriving their audience of the information needed to evaluate governmental poli-cies critically. And yet these earnest professionals

often do, though usually unwittingly, end up behaving in precisely this unethical fashion, and do so virtually without exception in the sphere of coverage of international affairs. In this essay I wish to (a) document that this is indeed the case, (b) offer an explanation as to why it is the case, and (c) suggest ways in which journalists might change their behavior so as to do a better job of meeting their ethical obligations.

DOCUMENTING THE PROBLEM

Let us begin by considering how the mainstream media cover censorship of the press when it is practiced in foreign countries. Since freedom of the press is obviously a value of great importance to journalists and to news organizations, and since press censorship presumably is "newsworthy," and of interest to readers and viewers of journalism, one would expect the press to be ever ready to focus on it. Obviously, this is not to say that it would be reasonable to expect the press to cover all, or even most, instances of censorship—there are too many such instances, and there is a finite amount of space in newspapers and time in news broadcasts available for such coverage. Thus, we might well expect even the most responsible of news media to ignore instances of censorship which are small in scale, minor in effect, or which occur in places that are otherwise of little current interest to their readers or viewers. But we would not expect a *responsible* press to highlight censorship activities of our "enemies," as defined by those who wield political power in our country, while ignoring much more serious instances of censorship perpetrated by those officially designated our "friends."

One good test of the responsibility of mainstream US journalism in its coverage of freedom of the press, then, would be to compare its coverage of censorship as practiced in the 1980s by the governments of Nicaragua and El Salvador. These two countries are geographically proximate to each other and to the US, and were in the 1980s of interest to the US news audience. (Or at least, there was at that time a great deal of news coverage of these two countries, in comparison to most foreign nations.) Thus, to the extent that the US press is unbiased and non-partisan, we should expect its relative coverage of censorship in the two countries to vary in accordance with such factors as the relative scale and severity of effects of the censorship in the two nations. On the other hand, since El Salvador was officially our "friend" and a "fledgling democracy," while Nicaragua under the Sandinistas was officially our "enemy" and a "totalitarian dungeon," we should expect a more partisan press, a less responsible one, to play up censorship in Nicaragua while ignoring it as much as possible in El Salvador. What, then, do we find?

Censorship in Nicaragua did indeed receive extensive coverage during the period in question. For example, one study of 104 articles from the *Boston Globe*, *New York Times*, and *Washington Post* dealing with the 1984 Nicaraguan elections, found that 65 mentioned press censorship.[2] Another study, conducted in 1988, found 263 references in the *New York Times* to the difficulties of the Nicaraguan newspaper *La Prensa* over a period of four years.[3]

Coverage of censorship in El Salvador, on the other hand, was so scanty that I cannot assume my readers to know of the existence of such censorship, let alone be familiar with its details. Thus,

I quote the following from the September 1985 Americas Watch Report on El Salvador:

Any discussion of press freedom in El Salvador must begin by pointing out the elimination of the country's two main opposition newspapers. *La Crónica del Pueblo* was closed in 1980 when members of the security forces raided a San Salvador coffee shop where the paper's editor and one of its photographers were meeting. Editor Jaime Suarez, a 31-year-old prize-winning poet, and Cesar Najarro, were disemboweled by machete and then shot. In 1981 *El Independiente* was closed when army tanks surrounded its offices. This was the culmination of a long series of attacks, which included the machine gunning of a 14-year-old newsboy, bombing and assassination attempts against editor Jorge Pinto. The Archdiocese's radio station, WMAX, spent several years out of commission after its offices were repeatedly bombed. Since 1981 the Salvadoran press has either supported the government or criticized it from a right-wing perspective. Daily newspapers do not publish criticism ... from a leftist perspective, nor do they print stories critical of government forces from a human rights standpoint.[4]

In contrast to the extensive coverage in the *New York Times* of censorship in Nicaragua, these far more serious abuses of press freedoms in El Salvador have gone unmentioned in that publication. The newspaper which claims to publish "all the news that's fit to print" has not seen fit to report the use of terrorism by the government of El Salvador against the press of that nation.[5] The story (or lack thereof) is very much the same when we turn to abuses of press freedoms in other "pro-US" nations. Thus, when security forces of the Guatemalan government in June 1988 succeeded in "persuading" the editor of *La Epoca* to shut down that weekly newspaper by firebombing its offices, stealing its valuable equipment, kidnapping its night watchman, and threatening to murder its "traitor journalists"—not a threat to be taken lightly in view of the fact that dozens of journalists in Guatemala already had been murdered in recent years—no report of these events was to be found in the *New York Times* or *Washington Post*.[6] Two months prior to these events, and one month following them, there were many articles in those two newspapers about lesser abuses of the press in Nicaragua.

In September 1988 Israeli security forces raided the offices of *Al-Fajr*, a leading daily newspaper in Jerusalem, arrested its managing editor, Hatem Abdel-Qader, and jailed him for six months without trial on unspecified grounds. This story was not covered in the *New York Times* or *Washington Post*.[7] In this non-coverage the two papers followed the precedent which they had set in 1986 when, during the height of their coverage of the suspension of publication of *La Prensa* in Nicaragua, they failed to inform their readers that the government of Israel had closed two newspapers, *Al-Mithaq* and *Al-Ahd*, on the grounds that their publication was "harmful to the state of Israel."[8]

An appropriately skeptical reader might object at this point that perhaps my examples are unfair. Of course it is easy, such a reader might argue, to find examples in which the US mass media irresponsibly ignores press censorship and other human rights abuses perpetrated by nations regarded as "friendly" by US political elites, while simultaneously, and hypocritically, trumpeting comparable or much lesser abuses carried out by "our enemies." The problem, to conclude my imaginary reader's argument, is that there may be other cases in which the media exhibit the opposite bias, or even no bias at all, in which case I would be guilty of making my case by means of a highly selective presentation of evidence.

My response to this objection is that there is no need to be selective in marshalling the evidence for the simple reason that there is *no* counterevidence. To be sure, one can find a different "slant" in non-mainstream journals of opinion, such as *The Nation*, *Z Magazine*, or *The Progressive*, and an occasional isolated article of this sort occasionally finds its way into mass media publications as well. But one can never find a case in which, on balance, the *New York Times*, the *Washington Post*, *Time Magazine*, *Newsweek*, or ABC, CBS, or NBC news deals even-handedly with the transgressions of "our friends" and "our enemies." Rather, these media always adopt the perspective of the US government, and never—literally never—develop an alternative, independent framework of their own.

Readers with a little time, energy, access to a good library, and eagerness to understand the world in which they live can easily verify this for themselves. Let me suggest one way of doing so. Many highly respected organizations are devoted to the task of investigating and documenting human rights abuses around the world. Their diversity is suggested by the following partial list: Amnesty International, Americas Watch, the International Association of Democratic Lawyers, the International Federation of Human Rights, the International League for the Rights of Man, the International Commission of Jurists, Writers and Scholars International, and the International Red Cross. I suggest that you pick any human rights issue that interests you—the use of torture, the imprisonment of political dissidents, press censorship, the staging of fraudulent elections, you name it. Now go through the reports of these organizations and find examples of comparable abuses carried out by two nations, one of which establishes policies and practices conducive to the financial interests of large US-based corporations (and which receives lots of US aid, both in terms of cash and weapons), and the other of which is readily condemned by US governmental officials as an enemy (or "communist" or "terrorist") state. Obviously, it is in the US corporate and governmental interest to play down the abuses in the former nation and to play up the ones occurring in the latter nation. And, in every case, that is how the US mass media, on balance, plays it.[9] You, dear reader, can refute me by finding a single counterexample. Good luck![10] …

SUGGESTIONS FOR IMPROVEMENT

If the analysis presented above is cogent, there are at least five steps that journalists might take that would immediately enable them to do a much better job of meeting their fundamental ethical responsibilities.

First, journalists should engage in much more investigative reporting and rely much less on handouts from authority figures, since, in addition to the defects of such reliance noted above, "in the nature of public relations most authority figures issue a high quotient of imprecise and self-serving declarations."[11] To be sure, such a change might harm the media outfit's bottom line, but if journalism is correct in viewing itself as a genuinely honorable profession, it cannot allow its concern for profit to overwhelm its ethical responsibilities.

Secondly, insofar as it is necessary for journalists to rely on others to gather evidence for them, they should dramatically enlarge the pool of authorities from which they draw their information. Thus, with regard to international affairs, journalists would do well to engage in some library research, consulting the reports of the major human rights organizations mentioned above, as well as taking advantage of the findings of academics and foreign journalists. Similarly they might take advantage of the information that is readily available at such "beats" as the United Nations and the World Court. Finally, in consulting all of these alternative sources, there should be a concerted effort to find and to present to news audiences perspectives other than those of US corporate and governmental elites, so that these audiences might be better equipped to evaluate critically both mainstream perspectives and their competitors.

Thirdly, journalists should not allow US corporate and governmental spokespersons to "set the agenda" for media coverage of international affairs. Rather, the media should assert their own independence in this regard, as part of their professional responsibility. Thus, rather than remaining content to report the mainstream elite consensus, handed to reporters, that country A's elections are fraudulent because of factor X, while country B's are legitimate because of factor Y, the media would better serve us by drawing up a comprehensive list of the factors that tend to push an election in the direction of legitimacy or illegitimacy, and then check, preferably by direct investigation, but alternatively by a scrupulous assessment of a variety of independent sources, how different countries fare with regard to these factors.

Fourthly, journalists should abandon the confused and irresponsible doctrine of objectivity that currently guides the profession, and replace it with a more scientific or scholarly conception of objectivity. The difference between the two is this. While the former requires the (impossible) avoidance of opinions, conclusions, and theories, the latter allows, indeed insists upon, these, while demanding that they be well grounded in evidence, logic, and reasoning, and that they hold up under the pressure of counterargument and counterevidence. Objectivity in this scholarly sense is not undermined by taking a strong position, displaying emotion, or anything of that sort. To the contrary, a strong position might be warranted, or even required, by a scrupulous examination of the relevant facts and arguments, and strong feelings might be utterly fitting and appropriate. Moreover, to think that objectivity requires a "balanced," "play it down the middle" result is just a confusion. To be committed to drawing conclusions based solely on the evidence is to be committed to letting the conclusions fall where they may. Thus, the fact that a person arrives at a "one-sided" conclusion is no more evidence of a lack of objectivity on his or her part than would the fact that a referee in a basketball game called thirty fouls on one team and only twelve on another. Perhaps the one team simply committed way more fouls. Indeed, for all we know, the referee might have been biased the other way, so that a more appropriate job of officiating would have resulted in a margin of forty fouls to two.

Fifthly, journalists should also abandon the "both sides" approach to the presentation of opinion. To be sure, there is something to be said for airing more than one view when considering difficult or controversial issues, but no special magic should be accorded to the number two. On many issues, several different perspectives, as opposed to merely two, are worthy of consideration. Moreover, when multiple perspectives are aired, there is less chance that fundamental convictions held in common by the two sides usually heard from will go unchallenged. On the other hand, some issues, such as the question of whether or not cigarette smoking is harmful to health, are sufficiently well established as to make it a waste of time to consider "the other side." Such an insistence on always presenting "both sides" even when the currently available evidence is adequate to show that one is correct has the unfortunate consequence of suggesting that no issues ever are decidable on the basis of evidence, and that all issues are ultimately "subjective." Thus, journalists would be well advised to be guided by evidence in determining which views to include, as opposed to insisting on precisely two views (and two mainstream ones sharing most of the important contestable principles in common, at that)....

NOTES

1   Often this is put in more general terms, and it is not explicitly spelled out that the "power" which journalism is to confront in its zeal to unearth the truth is that of the government. Still, if power itself is what needs watching, one wonders why journalists do not see it as their duty to provide a counterweight to corporate power, given its enormous, and steadily increasing, dominance in American culture. I trust my readers will not regard me as overly cynical if I suggest that the answer lies in the fact that American mass media outlets, without exception, either are owned by giant corporations or else are such entities themselves.

2   Jack Spence, "The US Media: Covering (Over) Nicaragua," in Thomas W. Walker, ed., *Reagan versus the Sandinistas* (Boulder: Westview Press, 1987), 192.

3   Francisco Goldman, "Sad Tales of La Libertad de Prensa," *Harper's Magazine* (August 1988), cited in Noam Chomsky, *Necessary Illusions* (Boston: South End Press, 1989), 42.

4   Americas Watch, *The Continuing Terror: Seventh Supplement to the Report on Human Rights in El Salvador* (September 1985), cited in Spence, "The US Media," 192.

5   Spence, "The US Media," 192; Chomsky, *Necessary Illusions*, 41.

6   Chomsky, *Necessary Illusions*, 125, and sources cited in that work, 378, note 46.

7   Chomsky, *Necessary Illusions*, 125; *Boston Globe*, Sept. 5 1988.

8   Chomsky, *Necessary Illusions*, 127–28; *Al-Hamishmar*, July 25 1986 and August 13 1986; *Jerusalem Post*, Aug. 12 and Aug. 24 1986.

9   I should note one other protocol for this experiment. To make the comparison between the two nations fair, some care should be taken to note the overall amount of coverage, as well as the favorable coverage, they each receive. Otherwise, one might claim to refute me by, for example, noting that the US pays more attention to political corruption in Canada than in some tiny "hostile" African nation of little interest to US political elites. Such a claim would be absurd, since US audiences are obviously much more interested in Canadian affairs than in those of this African nation, so that the greater attention to corruption in the former nation is clearly to be attributed to this rather than an anti-Canadian bias, a point that is also indicated by the comparatively vastly greater favorable coverage Canada receives.

10 Edward S. Herman and Noam Chomsky have made extensive and excellent use of this "matched pair" method, and it is a pleasure to acknowledge my great debt to their works. See especially their *Manufacturing Consent* (New York: Pantheon, 1988), Herman's *The Real Terror Network* (Boston: South End Press, 1982); and Chomsky's *Necessary Illusions*.

11 Ben H. Bagdikian, *The Media Monopoly*, 4th ed. (Boston: Beacon, 1992), 180.

—73—

THE MILITARY

A Profession Like No Other

Patricia Cook

WHAT DISTINGUISHES THE MILITARY PROFESSION as a profession? All professions use intellectual achievement and learning, and all professions render service. The profession of arms is the ultimate in each of these respects, involving academic learning in several disciplines, and the dedication of both body and soul in service to the public. The profession is unique in that the aspiration toward its most salient activity, killing, would disqualify the aspirant from membership in it. All professions have a code of conduct, but the military has, in addition, a complex, in some ways convoluted, moral arena that its members must navigate. These are the points that will be developed in this chapter....

II. THE MORAL CODE OF THE PROFESSION OF ARMS

Professionals have traditionally sworn an oath that commits them to upholding the moral standards of their guild.[1] These standards are themselves a hallmark of the autonomy and self-regulation of the professions, though they tend to be derived from the sacred trust to serve primarily the client's good (or the public good) interpreted through the specialized knowledge of best practices. There is no question that the military is oriented to the public good: after all, military duty can include "the ultimate sacrifice." But it is important to note that the profession of arms has intricate architectonic principles for effectively putting the public

good ahead of its own: discrimination and proportionality. These standards are deceptively simple to state, but, in practice, they can be bewilderingly complex. Their application involves one more species of the specialized expertise required of the military professional.

Consider the principle of discrimination: the military professional discriminates between those who are enemy combatants and those who are noncombatants. I do not know if there was ever a time in history when this task was straightforward, but it certainly is no longer with guerrillas, insurgents, and nonstate terrorists in the battle space. The duty of the military officer is to take upon himself any danger the conflict introduces to noncombatants—"to assume that danger himself," as Michael Walzer puts it.[2] This is, of course, what makes the profession of arms a noble one. There are other dangerous occupations—driving a racing car is a dangerous occupation, but it is not for that reason noble. What is noble is the warrior's deliberately taking any peril to innocents upon himself. The confrontation in Afghanistan of SEAL Team 10 with the local goat herders illustrates the radical jeopardy this ethos involves.[3] Much notice has been taken of the newest "remote control" technologies that distance the warrior from the battlefield and thus insulate him from personal risk. But we should remember, on the other hand, the unprecedented kinds of risk to which the tactics of counterinsurgency (and other kinds of irregular warfare) expose the warrior.[4]

When noncombatant casualties are foreseeable but unavoidable, the principle of proportionality requires that this damage be weighed against the military advantage being sought. The military professional is never allowed to inflict collateral damage for his own convenience, and he cannot cause harm or destruction simply to enhance his own safety. Proportionality assessments are accordingly complex and non-formulaic. Judgments have to be made by a competent military authority on a case-by-case basis. Even the law defers to the military professional in a command position to make these interrelated strategic, tactical, and moral judgments. Here, by the way, is a cardinal example of the autonomous professional expertise that is constantly being exercised in the military. This also exemplifies a specialized virtue, or excellence, that must be part of the moral outfit of the military professional. Call it "astuteness in sizing up proportionality": this is a special kind of prudence or practical wisdom, and it cannot be cultivated outside of the military profession. So, like other professions, the military has proprietary virtues, excellences that can only be expressed, and only be developed, within the context of the profession itself....

IV. PROFESSIONAL PARADOXES

So the military profession is unique in this way. Its moral purpose is to defend the innocent and to safeguard rights and justice, but its main activity, on the pre-reflective or instinctual level, is abhorrent. One of the tasks of this singular profession is to regulate, and reconcile, this stark tension. I would argue that the tension has to be addressed philosophically, since it apparently defies common sense. I often hear the quip (from civilians with no close ties to the military) that "military ethics" is an oxymoron. The idea seems to be that, in resorting to war, we give up on ethics and rely strictly on power. This idea, though profoundly mistaken, sometimes crops up even among people who have seen firsthand what scruples restrain us in a just war.

I have been teaching philosophy to military officers—most of them naval aviators—for six years. They have varying levels of awareness of military ethics and the just war tradition, and often do not have a ready answer to the question of how their service in Iraq and Afghanistan squares with morality. I ask them if the principles of morality change during wartime. Obviously, the "rules" change: it is not normally permissible to break things and kill people. Is this a suspension of morality? Is there a "wartime morality" that is different from ordinary morality?

Some officers have an "us or them" kind of response.[5] The use of force in wartime is necessitated by the showdown. There is often some version of the Augustinian/Thomistic idea that violence is wielded as a last resort to thwart the triumph of evil. Many make the point that they do not want to kill people. Pilots, in particular, report that they joined the military because they loved flying and wanted "to serve their country." They honed their aviation skills, only to find themselves flying aircraft that carry ordinance during wartime. This is, in one sense, the highest achievement: these are elite aviators flying the most technically sophisticated aircraft, and, by this reckoning, they are in a coveted position. On the other hand, being the bearer of the bomb was never part of anyone's aspiration. No one grew up wanting to drop the bombs that kill people. These young aviators have to struggle to overcome their abhorrence of killing people—perfect strangers—on the ground. Even if these are uniformed combatants, even if the target is cleared in accordance with rules of engagement, even if the mission is in close support of allied troops on the ground, these pilots do not want to kill, maim, and destroy.

One student—an F/A18 pilot—described how his conscious ambition had been to be a fighter pilot, not a killer. He recounted how the full realization seemed to unfold for him during Survival, Evasion, Resistance, and Escape (SERE) School. The "captors" at SERE school "would beat us and demand [to be told] why we were killing their children." As a student-captive, this aviator found that he did not know. His youthful aspiration of becoming a pilot had nothing to do with combat:

> I only wanted to be a pilot and did not realize that I might have to kill people, and I really had no idea what the United States' policies were on world issues. First, becoming a pilot is certainly a difficult endeavor. The training is very intense and trying. Flight students have very little control on what platform they will eventually fly. Ethical quandaries typically do not arise since it is out of our control. There is also no specific training on the perils of killing people whether intentional or unintentional as a result of us conducting our mission....[6]

Thus, although we might think it should be obvious that being a military aviator will involve violent combat and mortal danger, there is, at least in some cases, a disjunction between aspiration and reality. Rectifying this disjunction—forging the psychological and moral connections behind it—is a distinctive task for this profession....

V. A SINGULAR PROFESSION

My conclusions from all of this sound a chord with the conclusions of other authors in this section. First, the military officer is indeed in the situation of the traditional professional. I have been suggesting that the profession of arms may in fact be the most demanding of the professions in precisely the respects by which professionalism is delineated: knowledge, ethos, and public service. The military professional's activities require knowledge, skill, and discernment, which can only be acquired through sustained study and apprenticeship. And the military professional's need for knowledge, skill, and discernment seems to be expanding: the indispensable level of mastery, while obviously greatest for those at the highest echelons of command, is estimable for even the junior officer. Alasdair MacIntyre's example of Colonel MacFarland illustrates how, in contemporary war, the officer on the ground can be

proxy for executive authority and political power.[7] Deep knowledge of history, cultural anthropology, political theory, religion, and philosophy—in addition to knowledge of military strategy—would not be wasted in such circumstances. Those in lower ranks are also exercising discretion in ways their predecessors were not. Here is how one of my students puts it:

> Prior to the recent conflicts the option to "refuse dropping a bomb" was not a moral decision typically placed in the hands of aircrew. If a soldier on the ground wanted a bomb, the pilot's job was to provide it. The best telltale of this shift in mindset is in previous wars aircrew received medals for dropping bombs. In Afghanistan I know of pilots who received medals for not dropping when legally capable of it. The asymmetric warfare confronting aircrew and soldiers today has pushed ethics into the cockpit. A squadron commanding officer used to say "one bomb will not win this war but one bomb may lose it." (Anonymous military ethics course attendee)[8]

This young lieutenant is referring, obviously, to counterinsurgency doctrine, and he was happy to report that his command recognized, and tried to provide, something far beyond mere technical training.[9] The individual warfighter, with advanced communications systems and sensitive equipment, has astonishing information and control at his disposal, and he is being asked to exercise his own judgment in a way that is unprecedented. A corresponding level of expertise—and virtue—is accordingly being called upon. The pedagogical implications are clear. Real education—not just "training"—is *sine qua non*. People can be trained to externally comply with certain rules, but education at a theoretical level is necessary to develop the discretion and autonomy that sets a profession apart from a job within a bureaucracy. Unfortunately, education is neither quick nor easy. In an earlier era, all gentlemen who became officers were very well educated. That is no longer the case. Universities mainly do technical training these days—which is appropriate, because technology is complex today, and it requires sustained study. However, that has preempted John Paul Jones-style liberal education. Most officers these days are technical experts in some field, but may not come to the profession with the depth of education of their predecessors. The military, as an organization, is well served to the extent that it esteems and emphasizes such learning.

Consider now the ethos of the military profession. Again, like traditional professions, the military has a distinctive code that is inculcated and enforced within the profession itself. A particular set of virtues, or excellences of character, pertain to it. Other chapters in this section enumerate the specific virtues of character that the military exalts. I have tried to point out others that, from the vantage of an outsider, I see being practiced, even if they do not have well-known names. To a certain extent, the specifics of the military ethos emerge from the practice of the profession itself, but the ethos is also informed from the outside by treaties and conventions, plus the political will of the public it serves. I want to reiterate, in this connection, the unparalleled burden on the military as a profession. Today's military operates with a backdrop of never-again resolutions from the twentieth century (trench warfare, carpet bombing, Vietnam). They have to develop tactics for new kinds of warfare, and figure out how they can fight terrorism without becoming terrorists themselves. In recent counterinsurgency efforts, they have had to embody law and order among the local populace, to incarnate goodness itself. These may be signposts for a conceptual crisis, or paradigm shift, that Professor MacIntyre suggests may be upon us. Following MacIntyre's thesis, new warfare invites the military to rethink the profession, reassess its cardinal virtues, and add conceptually new ones to the ideal officer's outfit (such as political prudence).[10] In any case, we are seeing the old martial virtues—which were already difficult achievements—being put to rigorous new tests. Imagine responding only to "accurate fire" (as the Petraeus manual decrees), not pulling the trigger when every instinct you have is sensing danger. Imagine a rule of engagement (ROE) that allows a response to fire only where the shooter can be identified. The excellence of character that would enable a soldier to function in such a situation seems to be different from—and perhaps more than—the time-honored virtue of courage.

One thing is clear: nothing that goes by the name of "training" could prepare members of the military to handle such circumstances. Obedience (which might be equated with the good soldier on the bureaucratic, chain-of-command model of the military) would be a rather minor virtue in the picture I am sketching. There is certainly no rulebook or formalized code that can simply be applied in service of any of these ends. It is the task of any profession—including the profession of arms—to identify the relevant virtues, and to underwrite the excellences of character that will allow practitioners to achieve its ends. My own view is that this task requires considerable erudition, and calls upon learning in sociology, history, philosophy, and more. The profession of arms has to be, in other words, a learned profession....

NOTES

1   The oaths taken by military officers vary from country to country, but the moral code of any military professional includes discrimination and some version of proportionality and restraint. See Shannon French, *Code of the Warrior: Examining Warrior Values Past and Present* (Lanham, MD: Rowman & Littlefield, 2003).

2   Michael Walzer, "On proportionality," *The New Republic* (January 8, 2009): www.newrepublic.com/article/politics/proportionality. See also "Responsibility and proportionality in state and nonstate wars," *Parameters* (Spring 2009): 51, where Walzer suggests that proportionality arguments must be accompanied by responsibility arguments: "What risks have [the soldiers] accepted in an effort to minimize the risks imposed on civilians?"

3   Marcus Luttrell and Patrick Robinson, *Lone Survivor: The Eyewitness Account of Operation Redwing and the Lost Heroes of SEAL Team 10* (New York: Little, Brown & Company, 2007).

4   See Department of the Army, *Tactics in Counterinsurgency* (2006): "Thus military personnel will need to accept greater physical risks to achieve military objectives than they would in conventional conflicts" (see vignette in FM 3–24/7–13) and "This risk-taking is an essential part of the Warrior-Ethos" (7–21).

5   See section IV of Don Snider's chapter ("American military professions and their ethics" in [the *Routledge Handbook of Military Ethics*, ed. George Lucas, Routledge: London & New York, 2015], quoting Dr. James Toner: "even when soldiers are not dying they must be preparing to die."

6   This is from a paper for a class called "Ethics and moral development" at the Naval Postgraduate School. The author, name withheld, was a Navy lieutenant.

7   See Alasdair MacIntyre's chapter, "Military ethics: A discipline in crisis," in [the *Routledge Handbook of Military Ethics*]. MacIntyre also cites Emile Simpson in connection with the thesis that officers in the field now make both military and political decisions.

8   This is from a paper for a class called "Ethics and moral development" at the Naval Postgraduate School. The author, name withheld, was a Navy lieutenant.

9   Here is how he described the educational exercise: "I was fortunate to participate in a few of these discussions prior to my last deployment. Our [carrier wing's l]eadership designed case studies and implemented them through a Socratic template to help aircrew articulate and self-criticize their answer to a very important question in combat, 'Under what circumstances will you refuse to drop a bomb at the request of a soldier on the ground?' The complexity of that moral question is difficult to confine to the limits of this paper. It requires a comprehensive understanding of tactical doctrine, standard operating procedures (SOP), and rules of engagement (ROE). What is easy to understand is that it calls upon interwoven beliefs, norms, and universal moral certainties to arrive at that decision."

10   See Alasdair MacIntyre's chapter, "Military ethics: A discipline in crisis," in [the *Routledge Handbook of Military Ethics*] for his discussion of political prudence.

REFERENCES

Brough, M.W. (2007). "Dehumanization of the enemy and the moral equality of soldiers." In M.W. Brough, J.W. Lango, & H. van der Linden (Eds.), *Rethinking the Just War Tradition* (pp. 149–170). Albany, NY: State University of New York Press.

Case Western Reserve University (2013). "Exploring the brain." *Think: The Online News Source for Case Western Reserve University*, Fall/Winter. Available at: http://case.edu/think/fallwinter2013/discover/ dehumanizing-the-enemy.html#.U_N2Fvk8Ar5.

Collins, T. (2003). "UK troops told: Be just and strong." *BBC News*, March 20. Available at: http://news.bbc.co.uk/2/hi/uk_news/2866581.stm.

Department of the Army (2006). *Tactics in Counterinsurgency (FM3–24)*. Boulder, CO: Paladin Press.

French, S. (2003). *Code of the Warrior: Examining Warrior Values Past and Present*. Lanham, MD: Rowman & Littlefield.

Grossman, D. (2009). *On Killing: The Psychological Cost of Learning to Kill in War and Society*. New York: Little, Brown & Company.

Jackson, J.A. (1970). "Professions and professionalization: Editorial introduction." In *Profession and Professionalization Volume 3: Sociological Studies* (pp. 1–16). New York: Cambridge University Press.

Keen, S. (1986). *Faces of the Enemy: Reflections of the Hostile Imagination: The Psychology of Enmity*. New York: Harper & Row.

Krause, E.A. (1996). *Death of the Guilds*. New Haven, CT, & London: Yale University Press.

Lucas, G. (2004). *Ethics and the Military Profession: The Moral Foundations of Leadership*. Upper Saddle River, NJ: Pearson.

Lucas, G.R., Jr. (2011). "New rules for new wars: International law and just war doctrine for irregular war." *Case Western Reserve Journal of International Law*, 43(3), 677–705.

Luttrell, M, & Robinson, P. (2007). *Lone Survivor: The Eyewitness Account of Operation Redwing and the Lost Heroes of SEAL Team 10*. New York: Little, Brown & Company.

MacIntyre, A. (2015). "Military Ethics: A Discipline in Crisis." *Routledge Handbook of Military Ethics*. George Lucas, Editor. New York: Taylor Francis and Group.

Mayhood, K. (2013). "A way of thinking that may enable battle but prevent war crimes." *Think: The Online News Source for Case Western University*, June 6. Available at: http://blog.case.edu/think/2013/06/06/a_way_of_thinking_may_enable_battle_but_prevent_war_crimes.

Plato (1979). *The Republic* (trans. R. Larson). New York: Blackwell, Croft Classics.

Puckle, B.M. (1926). *Funeral Customs (Chapter IV)*. Available at: www.sacred-texts.com/etc/fcod/fcod07. htm.

Reichberg, G., Syse, H., & Begby, E. (Eds.) (2006). *The Ethics of War: Classical and Contemporary Readings*. Oxford: Blackwell.

Walzer, M. (1977). *Just and Unjust Wars*. New York: Basic Books.

Walzer, M. (2009). "On proportionality." *The New Republic*, January 8. Available at: www.newrepublic.com/article/politics/proportionality.

Walzer, M. (2009). "Responsibility and proportionality in state and nonstate wars." *Parameters*, 39, Spring, 40–52.

Zimbardo, P. (2007). *The Lucifer Effect: How Good People Turn Evil*. New York: Random House.

—74—

LEADERSHIP ETHICS

Mapping the Territory

Joanne B. Ciulla

WE LIVE IN A WORLD WHERE LEADERS ARE OFTEN morally disappointing. Even the greats of the past, such as Martin Luther King, Jr., and George Washington are diminished by probing biographers who document their ethical shortcomings. It's hard to have heroes in a world where every wart and wrinkle of a person's life is public. Ironically, the increase in information that we have about leaders has increased the confusion over the ethics of leadership. The more defective our leaders are, the greater our longing to have highly ethical leaders. The ethical issues of leadership are found not only in public debates, but they lie embedded below the surface of the existing leadership literature....

Throughout the paper I will use the term *leadership ethics* to refer to the study of the ethical issues related to leadership and the ethics of leadership. The study of ethics generally consists of the examination of right, wrong, good, evil, virtue, duty, obligation, rights, justice, fairness, etc. in human relationships with each other and other living things. Leadership studies, either directly or indirectly, tries to understand what leadership is and how and why the leader/follower relationship works (i.e. What is a leader and what does it mean to exercise leadership?, How do leaders lead?, What do leaders do? and Why do people follow?).[1] Since leadership entails very distinctive kinds of human relationships with distinctive sets of moral problems, I thought it appropriate to refer to the subject as *leadership ethics*; however, my main reason for using the term is that it is less awkward than using expressions like *leadership and ethics*....

II. LOCATING ETHICS

What Do the Definitions Really Tell Us?

Leadership scholars have spent a large amount of time and trouble worrying about the definition of leadership. Rost analyzes 221 definitions to make his point that there is not a common definition of leadership. What Rost does not make clear is what he means by a definition. Sometimes he sounds as if a definition supplies necessary and sufficient conditions for identifying leadership. He says, "neither scholars nor the practitioners have been able to define leadership with precision, accuracy, and conciseness so that people are able to label it correctly when they see it happening or when they engage in it."[2] He goes on to say that the various publications and the media all use leadership to mean different things that have little to do with what leadership really is.[3] In places Rost uses the word definition as if it were a theory or perhaps a paradigm. He says that a shared definition implies that there is a "school" of leadership. When the definition changes, there is a "paradigm shift."[4]

Rost's claim that what leadership studies needs is a common definition of leadership is off the mark for two reasons. One would be hard-pressed to find a group of sociologists or historians who shared the exact same definition of sociology or history. It is also not clear that the various definitions that Rost examines are that different in terms of what they denote. I selected the following definitions from Rost's book on the basis of what Rost says are definitions most representative of each particular era. We need to look at these definitions and ask the following questions: Are these definitions so different that there is no family resemblance between them, i.e. would researchers be talking about different things?[5] Lastly, I will look at what these definitions tell us about the place of ethics in leadership studies.

1. 1920s [Leadership is] the ability to impress the will of the leader on those led and induce obedience, respect loyalty and cooperation.[6]

2. 1930s Leadership is a process in which the activities of many are organized to move in a specific direction by one.[7]

3. 1940s Leadership is the result of an ability to persuade or direct men, apart from the prestige or power that comes from office or external circumstance.[8]

4. 1950s [Leadership is what leaders do in groups.] The leader's authority is spontaneously accorded him by his fellow group members.[9]

5. 1960s [Leadership is] acts by a person which influence other persons in a shared direction.[10]

6. 1970s Leadership is defined in terms of discretionary influence. Discretionary influence refers to those leader behaviors under control of the leader which he may vary from individual to individual.[11]

7. 1980s Regardless of the complexities involved in the study of leadership, its meaning is relatively simple. Leadership means to inspire others to undertake some form of purposeful action as determined by the leader.[12]

8. 1990s Leadership is an influence relationship between leaders and followers who intend real changes that reflect their mutual purposes.[13]

If we look at the sample of definitions from different periods, we see that the problem of definition is not that scholars have radically different meanings of leadership. Leadership does not denote radically different things for different scholars. One can detect a family resemblance between the different definitions. All of them talk about leadership as some kind of process, act, or influence that in some way gets people to do something. A roomful of people, each holding one of these definitions, would understand each other.

Where the definitions differ is in their connotation, particularly in terms of their implications for the leader/follower relationship. In other words, *how* leaders get people to do things (impress, organize, persuade, influence, and inspire) and *how* what is to be done is decided (obedience, voluntary consent, determined by the leader and reflection of mutual purposes) have normative implications. So perhaps what Rost is really talking about is not definitions, but theories about how people lead (or how people should lead) and the relationship of leaders and those who are led. His critique of particular definitions is really a critique of the way they do or don't describe the underlying moral commitments of the leader/follower relationship.[14]

If the above definitions imply that leadership is some sort of relationship between leaders and followers in which something happens or gets done, then the next question is, How do we describe this relationship? For people who believe in the values of a democratic society such as freedom and equality, the most morally unattractive definitions are those that appear to be coercive, manipulative and disregard the input of followers. Rost clearly dislikes the theories from the 20s, 70s and 80s, not because they are inaccurate, but because he rejects the authoritarian values inherent in them.[15] Nonetheless, theories such as the ones from the 20s, 70s and 80s, may be quite accurate if we were to observe the way some corporate and world leaders behave.

The most morally attractive definitions hail from the 40s, 50s, 60s and Rost's own definition of the 90s. They imply a non-coercive participatory and democratic relationship between leaders and followers. There are two morally attractive elements of these theories. First, rather than *induce*, these leaders *influence*, which implies that leaders recognize the autonomy of followers. Rost's definition uses the word influence, which carries an implication that there is some degree of voluntary compliance on the part of followers. In Rost's chapter on ethics he says, "The leadership process is ethical if the people in the relationship (the leaders and followers) freely agree that the intended changes fairly reflect their mutual purposes."[16] For Rost consensus is an important part of what makes leadership leadership and it does so because free choice is morally pleasing. The second morally attractive part of these definitions is they imply recognition of the beliefs, values and needs of the followers. Followers are the leader's partner in shaping the goals and purposes of a group or organization....

III. THE NORMATIVE THEORIES

Transforming Leadership

So far we have located the place of leadership ethics in definitions and in some of the empirical research on leadership. Now we will look at two normative leadership theories.

James MacGregor Burns' theory of transforming leadership is compelling because it rests on a set of moral assumptions about the relationship between leaders and followers.[17] Burns' theory is clearly a prescriptive one about the nature of morally good leadership. Drawing from Abraham Maslow's work on needs, Milton Rokeach's research on values development and research on moral development from Lawrence Kohlberg, Jean Piaget, Erik Erickson and Alfred Adler, Burns argues that leaders have to operate at higher need and value levels than those of followers.[18] A leader's role is to exploit tension and conflict within people's value systems and play the role of raising people's consciousness.[19]

On Burns' account, transforming leaders have very strong values. They do not water down their values and moral ideals by consensus, but rather they elevate people by using conflict to engage followers and help them reassess their own values and needs. This is an area where Burns is very different from Rost. Burns writes that "despite his [Rost's] intense and impressive concern about the role of values, ethics and morality in transforming leadership, he underestimates the crucial importance of these variables." Burns goes on to say, "Rost leans towards, or at least is tempted by, consensus procedures and goals that I believe erode such leadership."[20]

The moral questions that drive Burns' theory of transforming leadership come from his work as a biographer and a historian.[21] When biographers or historians study a leader, they struggle with the question of how to judge or keep from judging their subject. Throughout his book, Burns uses examples of a number of incidents where questionable means, such as lying and deception are used to achieve honorable ends or where the private life of a politician is morally questionable.[22] If you analyze the numerous historical examples in Burns' book you find two pressing moral questions shape his leadership theory. The first is the morality of means and ends (and this also includes the moral use of power) and the second is the tension between the public and private morality of a leader. His theory of transforming leadership is an attempt to characterize good leadership by accounting for both of these questions.

Burns' distinction between transforming and transactional leadership and modal and end-values offers a way to think about the question "What is a good leader?" in terms of the relationship to followers and the means and ends of actions. Transactional leadership rests on the values found in the means of an act. These are called modal values which are things like responsibility, fairness, honesty and promise-keeping. Transactional leadership helps leaders and followers reach their own goals by supplying lower level wants and needs so that they can move up to higher needs. Transforming leadership is concerned with end-values, such as liberty, justice and equality. Transforming leaders raise their followers up through various stages of morality and need.[23] They turn their followers into leaders and the leader becomes a moral agent.

As a historian, Burns is very concerned with the ends of actions and the change that they initiate. In terms of his ethical theory, at times he appears to be a consequentialist, despite, his acknowledgment that, "insufficient attention to means can corrupt the ends."[24] However, because Burns does not really offer a systematic theory of ethics in the way that a philosopher might, he is difficult to categorize. Consider for example, Burns' two answers to the Hitler question. In the first part of the book, he says quite simply that once Hitler gained power and crushed all opposition, he was no longer a leader. He was a tyrant.[25] Later in the book, he offers three criteria for judging how Hitler would fare before "the bar of history." Burns says that Hitler would probably argue that he was a transforming leader who spoke for the true values of the German people and elevated them to a higher destiny. First, he would be tested by modal values of honor and integrity or the extent to which he advanced or thwarted the standards of good conduct in mankind. Second, he would be judged by the end values of equality and justice. Lastly, he would be judged on the impact that he had on the well-being of the people that he touched.[26] According to Burns, Hitler would fail all three tests. Burns doesn't consider Hitler a leader or a transforming leader, because of the means that he used, the ends that he achieved, and the impact of Hitler as a moral agent on his followers during the process of his leadership.[27]

By looking at leadership as a process and not a set of individual acts, Burns' theory of good leadership is difficult to pigeon hole into one ethical theory and warrants closer analysis. The most attractive part of Burns' theory is the idea that a leader elevates his or her followers and makes them leaders. Near the end of his book, he reintroduces this idea with an anecdote about why President Johnson did not run in 1968. Burns tells us, "Perhaps he did not comprehend that the people he had led—as a part of the impact of his leadership—have created their own fresh leadership, which was now outrunning his." All of the people that Johnson helped[,] the sick, the blacks and the poor[,] now had their own leadership. Burns says, "Leadership begat leadership and hardly recognized its offspring." …

Servant Leadership

The second example of a normative theory of leadership is servant leadership. Robert K. Greenleaf's book *Servant Leadership: A Journey into the Nature of Legitimate Power and Greatness* presents a view of how leaders ought to be, however, the best way to understand servant leadership, one needs to read *Journey to the East*, by Hermann Hesse.[28] Hesse's story is about a spiritual journey to the East. On the journey a servant named Leo carries the bags and does the travelers' chores. There is something special about Leo. He keeps the group together with his presence and songs. When Leo mysteriously disappears the group loses their way. Later in the book the main character HH discovers that the servant Leo was actually the leader. The simple, but radical shift in emphasis is from followers serving leaders to leaders serving followers.

Servant leadership has not gotten as much attention as transformational leadership in the literature, but students and business people often find this a compelling characterization of leadership.[29] According to Greenleaf, the servant leader leads because he or she wants to serve others. People follow servant leaders freely because they trust them. Like the transforming leader, the servant leader elevates people. Greenleaf says a servant leader must pass this test: "Do those served grow as persons? Do they *while being served* become healthier, wiser, freer, more autonomous, more likely themselves to become servants?" He goes on and adds a Rawlsian proviso, "*And*, what is the effect on the least privileged in society?"[30] As normative theories of leadership both servant leadership and transforming leadership are areas of leadership ethics that are open to ethical analysis and provide a rich foundation of ideas for developing future normative theories of leadership....

In conclusion, the territory of ethics lies at the heart of leadership studies and has veins in leadership research. Ethics also extends to territories waiting to be explored. As an area of applied ethics, leadership ethics needs to take into account research on leadership, and it should be responsive to the pressing ethical concerns of society. Today the most important and most confusing public debate is over what ethical issues are relevant in judging whether a person *should* lead and whether a person is capable of leadership. Research into leadership ethics would not only help us with questions like, "What sort of person should lead?" and "What are the moral responsibilities of leadership?", it should give us a better understanding of the nature of leadership.

NOTES

1   Many areas of leadership literature from psychology focus on different types of relationships. For example contingency theories focus on the relationship of the leader and the group in a given situation. See: Fred Feidler, *A Theory of Leadership Effectiveness* (New York: McGraw-Hill, 1967) and Victor H. Vroom and Paul W. Yetton, *Leadership and Decision-Making* (Pittsburgh: University of Pittsburgh Press, 1973). The vertical dyad linkage model focuses on dyads such as the relationship between leaders and managers. See: Fred Dansereau, Jr., George Graen, and William J. Haga, "Vertical Dyad Linkage Approach to Leadership within Formal Organizations: A Longitudinal Investigation of the Role Making Process," *Organizational Behavior and Human Performance*, 13 (1975, pp. 46–78).

2   [Joseph Rost, *Leadership for the Twenty-First Century* (New York: Praeger, 1991)], p.6

3   *Ibid.*

4   *Ibid.*, p. 99.

5   The theory of meaning that I have in mind is from Ludwig Wittgenstein, *Philosophical Investigations*, tr. G.E.M. Anscombe 3rd ed. (New York: Macmillan 1968) pp. 18–20 and p. 241.

6   Rost, p. 47 from B.V. Moore, "The May Conference on Leadership," *Personnel Journal*, Vol. 6, 1927, p. 124.

7   *Ibid.*, p. 47 from: E.S. Bogardus, *Leaders and Leadership* (New York: Appelton-Century, 1934), p. 5.

8   *Ibid.*, p. 48 from Reuter 1941 p. 133.

9   P. 50 The bracket part is Rost's summary of the definition from C.A. Gibb, "Leadership," in G. Lindzey (ed.) *Handbook of Social Psychology*, Vol. 2, 1954, pp. 877–920.

10 P. 53. From: M. Seeman, *Social Status and Leadership* (Columbus: Ohio State University Bureau of Educational Research, 1960), p. 127.

11 P. 59, R.N. Osborn & J.G. Hunt, "An Adaptive Reactive Theory of Leadership," in J.G. Hunt & L.L. Larson (eds.), *Leadership Frontiers* (Kent, OH: Kent State University Press, 1975), p. 28.

12 P. 72. From S.C. Sarkesian, "A Personal Perspective," in R.S. Ruch & L.J. Korb (eds.) *Military Leadership* (Beverly Hills, CA: Sage, 1979), p. 243.

13 P. 102.

14 Burns criticizes leadership studies for bifurcating literature on leadership and followership. He says that the leadership literature is elitist, projecting heroic leaders against the drab mass of powerless followers. The followership literature, according to Burns, tends to be populist in its approach, linking the masses with small overlapping circles of politicians, military officers and business people. [See Burns, James MacGregor, Leadership (New York: Harper & Row, 1979, p. 3)]

15 One's choice of a definition can be aesthetic and/or moral and/or political (if you control the definitions, you control the research agenda).

16 Rost, p. 161.

17 Burns uses the terms *transforming* and *transformational* in his book. However, he prefers to refer to this theory as *transforming* leadership.

18 I think that Burns is sometimes overly sanguine about the universal truth of these theories of human development.

19 [James MacGregor Burns, *Leadership* (New York: Harper Torchbooks, 1978)], pp. 42–43.

20 Rost, 1991, p. xii.

21 I am very grateful to Professor Burns for the discussions that we have had on the ethics of leadership. Burns' reflections on his work as a biographer have lead me to this conclusion.

22 For example, see Burns' discussion of Roosevelt's treatment of Joe Kennedy, pp. 32–33.

23 One of the problems with using the values approach to ethics is that it requires a very complicated taxonomy of values. The word *value* is also problematic because it encompasses so many different kinds of things. The values approach requires arguments for some sort of hierarchy of values that would serve to resolve conflicts of values. In order to make values something that people do rather than just have, Milton Rokeach offers a very awkward discussion of the ought character of values. "A person phenomenologicaly experiences 'oughtness' to be objectively required by society in somewhat the same way that he perceives an incomplete circle as objectively requiring closure." See Milton Rokeach, *The Nature of Human Values* (New York: The Free Press, 1973) p. 9.

24 *Ibid.*, p. 426.

25 *Ibid.*, p. 3.

26 P. 426.

27 The third test has an Aristotelian twist to it. The relationship of leaders and followers and the ends of that relationship must rest on eudaimonia or happiness that is understood as human flourishing or as Aristotle says "living well and faring well with being happy." Aristotle, *Nicomachean Ethics*, Book I (1095a19) from *The Complete Works of Aristotle Vol. II*, edited by Jonathan Barnes (Princeton: Princeton University Press, 1984) p. 1730.

28 Greenleaf takes his theory from Hesse. See Greenleaf, Robert K., *Servant Leadership* (New York: Paulist Press, 1977). Hesse, Hermann, *The Journey to the East* (New York: Farrar, Straus and Giroux, 1991).

29 The Robert K. Greenleaf Center in Indianapolis works with companies to implement this idea of leadership in organizations. The Robert K. Greenleaf Center, 1100 W. 42nd St., suite 321, Indianapolis, IN 46208.

30 Greenleaf, 1977, pp. 13–14.

—75—

PROFESSIONAL ETHICS FOR POLICE

Seumas Miller

THE TERM "POLICE ETHICS" TYPICALLY REFERS TO an area of academic inquiry within philosophical ethics concerned with ethical issues that arise for police officers and police organizations (Heffernan and Stroup 1985; Delattre 1994; Kleinig 1996a; Miller and Blackler 2005). Let me describe some of the main ethical or moral (I use these terms interchangeably here, to avoid unnecessary complication) issues that arise in policing.

As with other socially important institutions and occupations ... the role of police officers and police organizations raises various foundational normative questions pertaining to their nature and to the moral purposes they serve or ought to serve. In response to these questions, a number of normative theories of policing have been developed, notably a social contract theory ... (Cohen and Feldberg 1991; Kleinig 1996a) and a teleological rights-based theory ... (Miller and Blackler 2005: ch. 1; Miller and Gordon 2014: ch. 1). Moreover, there are various descriptive theories of policing proffered by theoretical criminologists, for example that of Egon Bittner, who defines policing in terms of the use of coercive force ... (Bittner 1980).

The social contract theory will be familiar to students of political philosophy, since it is a version of that propounded by Hobbes, Locke, Rousseau, and the like. Roughly speaking, persons in a highly insecure state of nature make an agreement or contract to provide themselves with security by giving up at least some of the rights that they enjoy in the state of nature to a government with a monopoly on the use of force (the police service).

On the teleological rights-based theory of policing, the protection of moral rights is the central and most important moral purpose of police work, albeit an end whose pursuit ought to be constrained by the law ... (Miller and Blackler 2005: ch. 1; Miller and Gordon 2014: ch. 1). So, while police institutions have other important purposes that might not directly involve the protection of moral rights—such as to enforce traffic laws or to enforce the adjudications of courts in relation to disputes between citizens, or indeed themselves to settle disputes between citizens on the streets or to ensure good order more generally—these turn out to be purposes derived from the more fundamental purpose of protecting moral rights; in other words they turn out to be (nonderivative) secondary purposes. Thus laws against speeding derive in part from the moral right to life, and the restoring of order at a football match ultimately derives in large part from moral rights to the protection of persons and of property.

If the central and most important end of policing is the protection of moral rights, what about the means to it? The achievement of this fundamental end requires specialized skills, knowledge, and individual judgment.... However, there is a further defining feature of policing that is crucial, namely the routine and inescapable use of harmful methods..., including coercive force, deception, and the infringement of privacy. Some of these methods might not be regarded as harmful, for example surveillance of people who are unaware that they are being surveilled and therefore are to that extent unharmed (Kleinig 1996a: ch. 7; Miller and Gordon 2014: ch. 10). However, the methods in question, even if not directly and immediately harmful, infringe moral rights, for example the right to privacy ... or are otherwise in breach of moral principles. Moreover, one way or another, these methods typically cause harm to someone, for example when surveillance tapes are produced as evidence. Naturally, sometimes causing minor harm to those who commit serious offences is unavoidable, if they are to be brought to justice; in such cases there is a clear moral justification. Matters are less clear-cut when the harm done is substantial or when the suspect turns out to be innocent. Indeed, in some cases the rights of persons known by the police to be entirely innocent are foreseeably infringed, for example through intrusive surveillance of a criminal who frequently interacts with family members who are not criminals. This combination of good ends and morally problematic means is a distinctive feature of policing, and one that gives rise to acute moral dilemmas.

In the context of the rise of extremist jihadist terrorist groups, such as Al Qaeda and the Islamic State ... electronic intelligence gathering, surveillance of suspects, and the like by police have increased, albeit the advent of strong encryption methods has provided an obstacle to intelligence agencies.... Moreover, the lines between police intelligence collection and analysis on the one hand and military intelligence collection and analysis on the other have been blurred, giving rise to privacy versus security issues in a particularly acute form. The controversy that has arisen from the disclosures made by Edward Snowden regarding the electronic data collection and analysis processes of United States' National Security Agency ... graphically illustrate the problem (Miller and Gordon 2014: ch. 10).

There are a number of ethical problems that arise in relation to both the individual authority of police officers and the independence or sphere of authority of police organizations vis-à-vis government in particular.... Issues include the problematic concept of operational autonomy and its importance, for example in relation to the need for investigatory independence of the police from the government (a case in point here is the independence of the FBI from Congress and from the presidency in its investigation of a possible collusion between President Trump's campaign managers and Russian security agencies during the US presidential election campaign), and the concept of the original authority attached to the office of constable in the United Kingdom and Australia. Moreover, there is the related and much discussed concept of police discretion (Davis 1975; Doyle 1985; Kleinig 1996b).

The law has to be interpreted and applied in concrete circumstances.... There is a need for the exercise of discretion by police in the interpretation and application of the law. And the law does not exhaustively prescribe. Accordingly, a number of police responses might be possible in a given situation, and all of them might be consistent with the law. Further, upholding and enforcing the law is only one of the ends of policing; others are the maintenance of social calm and the preservation of life. When these various ends come into conflict, there is a need for the exercise of police discretion, and in particular a need for the exercise of discretionary ethical judgment. The judgments in question are typically ethical judgments, since they involve a conflict between ethical or moral ends, or between such ends and harmful means.... For example, deciding to arrest a youth in a volatile ghetto area who is committing an offence may be the wrong decision if such an attempt would lead to a situation of uncontainable public disorder. There is a clear moral duty to arrest offenders. But there is also a clear moral duty not to cause public disorder....

The unavoidability of the exercise of discretionary ethical judgment in policing means that it will never be sufficient for police simply to learn the legally enshrined ethical principles that govern the use of harmful methods and to act in accordance with them.

Police culture is another much discussed phenomenon in the literature on police ethics and, indeed, in academic and other literature more generally (Skolnick 1975). Police culture is characterized by a high degree of solidarity among police officers. This is in part due to the trust that individual police officers need to be able to place in one another, given the dangers they face in their work.

The morally problematic features of police culture have often been noted, for example feelings of loyalty on the part of fellow officers that protect criminal actions of the police (Kleinig 2004; Miller 2016a: ch. 5). However, loyalty and other elements of police culture also serve to further legitimate purposes, for example by ensuring that fellow officers cooperate effectively in stressful and even life-threatening situations.

Historically, corruption has been a feature of police organizations in many, if not most jurisdictions … (Sherman 1974; Prenzler 2009; Miller 2016a). Corruption takes many forms in policing, including theft, bribe-taking, 'testilying', and fabricating or withholding evidence. Notoriously, the use of coercive force by police is, on occasion, not only morally unjustified—indeed a violation of the rights of suspects; it is also an act of corruption—it corrupts morally and legally legitimate processes and purposes. Consider in this connection the use of the so-called "third degree" to extract a confession from suspects. Here it is important to distinguish common or garden-variety corruption, for example greedy police officers helping themselves to drug money, from so-called noble-cause corruption, for example fabricating evidence against a heroin dealer. The latter is corruption in the service of a good end and is typically believed to be morally justified by those engaged in it (Klockars 1980; Delattre 1994; Miller 2016a: ch. 3).

There are a number of factors that contribute to the moral vulnerability of police officers and, as a consequence, to police corruption. These include (1) the necessity, at times, for police officers to deploy harmful methods, such as coercion and deception, which are normally regarded as immoral; (2) the high levels of discretionary authority and power ... exercised by police officers in circumstances in which close supervision is not possible; (3) the fact that police officers have ongoing interaction with corrupt persons who have an interest in compromising and corrupting police; (4) the fact that police confront morally ambiguous or lose situations, which call for discretionary ethical judgments; (5) the circumstance that, in contemporary times, police officers operate in an environment in which there is widespread use of illegal drugs, large amounts of drug money, and little evidence that the drugs problem is being adequately addressed.

The term "integrity system" has recently come into vogue in relation to the problem of corruption, whether it be in organizations, in occupational groups, or indeed in whole polities and communities (Alexandra and Miller 2010; Prenzler 2009; Miller 2016a: ch. 4). However, integrity systems are not simply concerned with corruption; rather they are focussed more generally on the problem of promoting ethical behaviour and eliminating or reducing unethical behaviour. Nevertheless, corruption reduction is a key priority.

Here the term "system" is somewhat misleading in that it implies a clear and distinct set of integrated institutional mechanisms that operate in unison and in accordance with determinate mechanical—or at least quasi-mechanical—principles. In practice, however, integrity systems are a messy assemblage of formal and informal devices and processes and operate in often indeterminate and unpredictable ways.

Integrity systems for police organizations can and do vary; however, such systems ought to have at least the following components or aspects:

- an effective, streamlined complaints and discipline system;
- a comprehensive suite of stringent vetting and induction processes reflective of the different levels of risk in different areas of the organization;
- a basic code of ethics and a specialized codes of practice, for example in relation to the use of firearms, supported by an ethics education in recruitment training and by ongoing professional development programs;
- adequate welfare support systems, for example in relation to drug and alcohol abuse and psychological injury;
- intelligence gathering, risk management, and early warning systems for at-risk officers, for example officers with high levels of complaints;
- internal investigations, that is, the police organization should take a high degree of responsibility for its own unethical officers;
- proactive anticorruption intervention systems, for example through the integrity-testing of officers suspected of corruption (by setting traps for them);
- ethical leadership, for example police leaders who give priority to collective ends definitive of the organization rather than to their own career ambitions should be the ones promoted;
- external oversight by an independent, well-resourced body with investigative powers.

Naturally, the use of coercive and especially of lethal force is a very important ethical issue in police work ... (Waddington 1991; Kleinig 2014). There are a number of justifications offered for police use of deadly force, including those available to ordinary citizens, namely self-defense and defense of the rights of others.... These justifications presuppose compliance with the principles of necessity and proportionality. If containment and negotiation are a viable option in relation to an armed offender, then they should be preferred to the use of deadly force; it is not necessary to use deadly force. Fleeing pickpockets should not be shot dead by police, since deadly force is a disproportionate response to minor theft.

In addition to self-defense and defense of the rights of others, there is a justification for police use of deadly force that is normally not available to ordinary citizens, namely the use of deadly force to enforce the law. Arguably, this justification is not simply a special case of one of the other two justifications (Miller 2016b: ch. 4).

Consider the possible moral justifications for the use of deadly force in cases in which police confront a choice of either letting an offender go free or shooting him/her. In these sorts of case, the police are not necessarily engaged in self-defense. In many of these cases, the best thing for police officers—if they were interested in self-defense—would be for them to get back into their patrol cars and return to the police station. Nor are these necessarily cases of killing in defense of others. The lives of ordinary citizens might not be at risk. For example, an offender—say, an armed burglar—might simply want to be left alone to spend his ill-gotten gains....

REFERENCES

Alexandra, Andrew, and Seumas Miller 2010. *Integrity Systems for Occupations*. Aldershot: Ashgate.

Bittner, Egon 1980. "The Capacity to Use Coercive Force as the Core of the Police Role," in Egon Bittner, *The Functions of the Police in Modern Society*. Cambridge, MA: Oelgeschlager, Gunn & Hain, pp. 36–47.

Cohen, Howard, and Michael Feldberg 1991. "A Social Contract Perspective on the Police Role," in Howard Cohen and Michael Feldberg, *Power and Restraint: The Moral Dimension of Policework*. New York: Praeger, pp. 23–38.

Davis, K.C. 1975. "The Pervasive False Pretense of Full Enforcement," in K.C. Davis, *Police Discretion*. St. Paul, MN: West Publishing Company, pp. 52–77.

Delattre, E.J. 1994. "Tragedy and 'Noble Cause' Corruption," in E.J. Delattre, *Character and Cops*. Washington, DC: AEI Press, pp. 190–214.

Doyle, James F. 1985. "Police Discretion, Legality and Morality," in W.C. Heffernan and T. Stroup (eds.), *Police Ethics: Hard Choices for Law Enforcement*. New York: John Jay, pp. 47–68.

Heffernan, William C., and Timothy Stroup (eds.) 1985. *Police Ethics: Hard Choices for Law Enforcement*. New York: John Jay.

Kleinig, John 1996a. *The Ethics of Policing*. New York: Cambridge University Press.

Kleinig, John (ed.) 1996b. *Handled with Discretion*. Lanham, MD: Rowman & Littlefield.

Kleinig, John 2004. "The Problematic Virtue of Loyalty," in Peter Villiers and Robert Adlam (eds.), *Policing a Safe, Just and Tolerant Society*. Winchester: Waterside Press, pp. 78–87.

Kleinig, John 2014. "Legitimate and Illegitimate Uses of Police Force," *Criminal Justice Ethics*, vol. 33, no. 2, pp. 83–103.

Klockars, Karl 1980. "The Dirty Harry Problem," *Annals of the American Academy of Political and Social Science*, vol. 451, pp. 33–47.

Miller, Seumas 2016a. *Corruption and Anti-Corruption in Policing: Philosophical and Ethical Issues*. Dordrecht: Springer.

Miller, Seumas 2016b. *Shooting to Kill: The Ethics of Police and Military Use of Lethal Force*. Oxford: Oxford University Press.

Miller, Seumas, and John Blackler 2005. *Ethical Issues in Policing*. London: Routledge.

Miller, Seumas and Ian Gordon 2014. *Investigative Ethics: Ethics for Police Detectives and Criminal Investigators*. Oxford: Wiley Blackwell.

Prenzler, Tim 2009. *Police Corruption: Preventing Misconduct and Maintaining Integrity*. London: CRC Press.

Sherman, Lawrence 1974. "Becoming Bent," in Lawrence Sherman, *Police Corruption: A Sociological Perspective*. New York: Anchor Books/Doubleday, pp. 191–208.

Skolnick, Jerome 1975. "A Sketch of the Policeman's 'Working Personality,'" in Jerome Skolnick, *Justice without Trial*, 2nd edn. New York: John Wiley & Sons, pp. 42–70.

Waddington, P.A. 1991. "Deadly Force," in P.A. Waddington, *The Strong Arm of the Law*. Oxford: Clarendon, pp. 75–120.

76

THE CERTIFIED CLINICAL ETHICS CONSULTANT

Kenneth Kipnis

CLINICAL ETHICS CONSULTANTS HAVE BECOME A presence in American medical centers. Despite the importance of their work, it is not currently possible for hospitals to evaluate candidates for positions, as they assess doctors' qualifications in their "credentialing" procedures. This paper analyzes how the certification of clinical ethics consultants and the accreditation of CEC degree programs—key steps toward professionalization—might emerge for practitioners within this field. [Except where ambiguity would result, the abbreviation "CEC" will be used to refer both to the field—clinical ethics consultation—and the practitioner—the consultant.]

SKETCHING THE PROBLEM

Given medicine's well-publicized dilemmas, it is no longer a surprise to encounter CECs in American hospitals. Coming from a variety of academic backgrounds—including medicine, nursing, philosophy, religion and social science—these men and women characteristically circulate freely in hospitals; consult with clinicians, patients and families; enter notes in medical charts; mediate disagreements; and often contribute to an atmosphere in which health care is delivered with due respect to salient social values. The increasing presence of these "strangers at the bedside" has been described, critiqued, analyzed and condemned by a parade of scholars and commentators

(Baylis, 1994; Scofield, 2008; Bosk, 2008]; Andre, 2002; Rothman, 1991; Jonsen, 2003).

The emerging role of the CEC can be an occasion for wonder. Where might we be going with this? While this paper conceives an answer to this question, it is primarily intended as a road map for future inquiry, a survey of the terrain that might have to be traversed. Though the ultimate destination need not be reached in order to secure pertinent goods, the end-in-view that has provoked the present inquiry is the professionalization of clinical ethics consultation. How might CEC proceed in that direction?

Let me, at the outset, register a few limitations on this study. First, its focus is on individuals designated by hospitals as on-the-floor ethics consultants. While hospitals use in-house ethics committees for related purposes and while clinical ethics consultations are often assigned to a team, I will not be addressing certification procedures for groups. Second, this paper has very little to say about the field of bioethics, as distinguished from clinical ethics consultation. The former is a scholarly enterprise, aimed at publication and dissemination of research results. The second, though drawing heavily on bioethics, is a practical activity carried out within the clinical setting. Finally, I will say nothing about the character traits that CEC should evidence. In part, this emerges from doubts about whether it is possible to teach the requisite virtues and test for their presence.

Despite the doubts registered by the critics, it cannot be denied that the work that CECs do can be of considerable moment. Whether there is perplexity about an end-of-life decision, disagreement about the appropriateness of aggressive care for a severely compromised newborn, or distress about the refusal of treatment by a curable patient, the practices of clinical ethics consultants can make the difference between a patient's living and dying. Working shoulder-to-shoulder with doctors, nurses, social workers and the panoply of credentialed specialists that make up the "health care team," one might reasonably assume that these new clinicians—like their colleagues—have earned academic degrees that attest to their preparation for their distinctive responsibilities. One might reasonably assume that, as with nursing, social work and so on, the academic programs that turn out those hired as clinical ethics consultants have been accredited by pertinent associations and boards. One might reasonably assume that hospitals seeking qualified personnel to carry out or oversee ethics consultation can easily confirm a candidate's qualifications for the job.

However it can come as a surprise—often a shocking one—to learn that none of these assumptions are correct. Although there are graduate-level programs in bioethics and medical humanities, and although a few of these, as a part of what they do, independently undertake to prepare their graduates for careers as clinical ethics consultants, there are neither agreed-upon standards for a minimally acceptable curriculum nor checks on whether graduates have achieved the requisite masteries. The degrees offered by these programs cannot authoritatively certify that their recipients are qualified to do clinical ethics consultation.

The reality is that far too many health care facilities rely on untrained or inadequately trained staff to provide ethics consultation services. A 2007 survey reported that only 1 in 20 ethics consultants had completed a fellowship or a graduate degree program in bioethics, and fewer than half had had formal, direct supervision by an experienced ethics consultant as a part of their preparation (Fox, Meyers & Pearlman, 2007).

It is arguably a scandal that those who hold themselves out as clinical ethics consultants are wholly lacking in credentials that would authoritatively establish their competency to offer guidance regarding the ethical problems that arise in the practices of health care. In the field of accounting, for example, novices have to complete required coursework, pass a standardized examination, and undergo a properly supervised internship before they can offer independent assistance as *certified* public accountants. It is not that today's clinical ethics consultants are falsely claiming to be certified as such. Nor is the complaint that there are no certificates: those who attend week-long "intensives" and the like will usually receive an informal "certificate" attesting to their participation. The problem is, rather, that there are no *authoritative* certificates as there are in nursing, medicine, accounting, and the like.

When a hospital grants medical privileges, hospital personnel will consider, among other things, the applicant's medical degree and board certifications. Other doctors, intimately familiar with medical expertise, will be a part of the review process. But, absent standardized certificates, absent staff with comparable expertise, any judgments about a candidate's clinical ethics consultant's "professional qualifications" must be made by hospital personnel without the backgrounds necessary to warrant a responsible assessment.

In many fields, the layman's inability to assess professional qualifications is a major reason for requiring key practitioners to be objectively certified as having the requisite knowledge and skills: electricians, architects, lawyers, nurses and airplane pilots for example. Even job-seeking college instructors will generally have graduate-level degrees, as will others involved in their hiring.

Given the importance of the CEC's role, it may be useful to imagine a future in which hospital personnel can summon a *certified* specialist in clinical ethics, just as they do for orthopedic surgeons, psychiatrists and pharmacists. This paper is intended as the beginning of a systematic conversation, an outline of some of the questions that must be addressed if the field is to advance to a more "professionalized" status. In addition to arraying the questions, I will suggest some tentative answers. These have been arrived at without the collective deliberation that must precede responsible judgment, but in the hope that any needed corrections will be forthcoming....

SALIENT TASKS, CORE COMPETENCIES AND CORE VALUES

Although clinical ethics consultation characteristically deals with ethical difficulties arising in connection with active cases in hospitals and comparable settings, non-case consultation can focus on other types of problems: e.g., doing a post-mortem on a case that is no longer active, or participating in deliberations about cases that are anticipated. In theory, CECs are specialists whose job is helping to sort out conflicts and ambiguities involving the values and norms that are implicated in health care decision-making. The CEC's work can be especially challenging when a patient's well being is on the line and when there is limited time to resolve the issue.[1]

The distinctive "difficulties" that give rise to a need for clinical ethics consultation can occur at three levels.

Level 1. At the first level we have the simplest and most characteristic case: someone is uncertain about an ethical question arising in the care of some patient. A clinician may, for example, wish to know how medical treatment decisions should be made for a patient lacking a surrogate, or whether the terms of an advance directive should be followed when the family insists on setting aside an incapacitated patient's instructions. Here a CEC must be teacher, a knowledge-broker, combining pedagogical skill with a broad and deep understanding of the relevant subject matter. He or she must be prepared to draw on the debates of bioethics, setting out and assessing the reasons given for various positions, reviewing the history of the

arguments, all in the service of bringing responsible clarity to a vexed clinician (or other stakeholder) who is unlikely to have been following the relevant literature, who will not know the current state of the field as regards the issue at hand, and who will not understand how the field got to where it is. CEC expertise can be helpful. What does the vexed stakeholder need to know? Sometimes there will be several acceptable approaches that are plainly within the standard of practice. Sometimes there is only one that has weathered criticism well enough to be called a consensus position. Sometimes the ethical problem is one that the field has not seen before: a "case of first impression" as the lawyers say. And sometimes the literature is too scanty to discern a consensus, or the published judgments are seriously divided.

In addition to subject matter knowledge, the CEC must also have mastered the skills needed to tease out hidden agendas and concealed complications. What a clinician asks for may not be what is needed. For level one problem presentations, the needed competencies would include subject matter knowledge and teaching skills, including the ability to listen.

Level 2. For cases at the second level, a lack of collective clarity is complicated by disagreement between two or more parties. A dispute is a prominent feature of the situation. In these cases, in addition to the teacher's knowledge and skill, the CEC needs to have a mastery of mediation and conflict resolution. Assuming that the options on the table are professionally permissible, the CEC may need to explore the values and reasoning of the parties to the dispute, reframing questions as needed, and working toward a conceptualization within which disagreement ceases to be center stage.

Level 3. Finally, cases at the third level highlight a serious or a recurrent problem that may evidence shortcomings within the structure of the health care setting itself. Here the CEC may need to be an agent of organizational change: laboring with key administrators, designing and implementing educational programs, drafting corrective policies, negotiating a path within a rigid and complicated bureaucratic structure. All of these and more may be called for in reconfiguring a hospital's generic response to problematic cases. In some cases, the effort to effect change will have to draw on resources beyond the organization's boundaries. State agencies, the courts, the legislature, professional associations all may have roles to play. Though I can think of some desiderata—diplomatic sophistication, a knowledge of organizational structures, skill in policy formulation—I am less confident about the competencies for diagnosing and managing problems presenting at this third, organizational level, nor am I confident that the field is ready to take these on as a part of its responsibility. Perhaps these difficulties call for the attentions of a CEC specialist.

Without arguing for it, it would seem that specialized knowledge and skill are called for in the responsible management of all three types of problem, and that it can be hazardous to hand these difficulties off to personnel who may not be equipped to manage them. If the field of clinical ethics consultation chooses to appropriate responsibility for any of these distinctive tasks, then the field, collectively, needs to organize itself to be able to manage them. However, if these difficulties are ones that CECs do not want to take on as its distinctive responsibilities, then hospitals will have to find some other way of managing those problems. CEC will not be a part of the solution....

CERTIFICATION AND ACCREDITATION: A PROCESS

If the reader has not objected to points made in the preceding paragraphs, he or she will likely be upset by the many questions I have sidestepped or ignored. Sometimes it may serve progress to make new mistakes, leaving it to critics to identify errors and propose better questions. But if the preceding analysis was sketchy, what follows fails even to reach that level.

So let us suppose we have reached consensus on the salient tasks of CEC, on the values and practice standards that should inform our work,

and on the knowledge and skill that would have to be mastered before taking on responsibilities as a CEC. How do we move from that foundation to the certification of CECs and the accreditation of graduate programs that might prepare novices for the work?

One caveat before we proceed. We can distinguish between two types of desiderata: competencies that are "good to have" and competencies that are essential. While we might agree that it would be desirable if CECs had, for example, familiarity with the history of professional codes, we might not regard such knowledge as so essential that the needed mastery would have to be built into curricula and systematically assessed prior to certification. On the other hand, familiarity with the futility debate might be deemed essential. The boundary line between the two categories would likely be contested and unstable over time. Certification and accreditation would need to focus primarily on "key" competencies rather than desirable ones.

Let us begin then by noting two categories of person who would be candidates for certification: those who have been doing clinical ethics consultation for some time and those completing a graduate program devised to equip novices with the requisite knowledge and skill. Differences between the two groups highlight two approaches to certification: the examination and the degree program. Examinations are arguably more open to everyone, not requiring completion of a course of study. Degree programs, especially when they meet standards for accreditation, can require months or years of invested time and effort. But if hospitals with job openings come to favor those who have earned pertinent degrees, it may become essential to complete a graduate-level education.

Certainly both approaches can be used together. Indeed, a standardized examination of degree recipients can be an element of the accreditation process. Programs whose graduates too often fail to display the requisite mastery may need to remedy shortcomings in either instruction or admission criteria. As regards practicing CECs who are not graduates of CEC-accredited bioethics programs (all present-day CECs fall into this category), a certifying examination could be used to identify deficiencies. These might be remedied by completing an accredited narrowly focused educational program and subsequently passing a standardized examination in the area where the deficiency was identified.

Assuming we could achieve consensus on the salient tasks of the CEC and on the requisite competencies and normative commitments, we would still need to reach agreement on how to assess these masteries in candidate CECs, and how to accredit graduate programs that would want to prepare CECs for clinical work....

NOTE

1   Here and elsewhere I owe much to the Core Competencies Report compiled by the Society for Health and Human Values—Society for Bioethics Consultation, Task Force on Standards for Bioethics Consultation, 1998. I have also benefited from reviewing preliminary drafts of the unpublished revised version....

REFERENCES

Andre, J. (2002). *Bioethics as practice*. Chapel Hill: University of North Carolina Press.

Baylis, F.E. (ed.) (1994). *The health care ethics consultant*. Totowa: Humana Press.

Bosk, C.L. (2008). *What would you do?* Chicago: University of Chicago Press.

Fox, E., Myers, S. & Pearlman, R.A. (2007). Ethics consultation in United States hospitals: a national survey. *American Journal of Bioethics* 7(2), 13–25.

Jonsen, A. (2003). *The birth of bioethics*. New York: Oxford University Press.

Rothman, D. (1991). *Strangers at the bedside*. New York: Basic Books.

Scofield, G. (2008). What is medical ethics consultation? *Journal of Law Medicine and Ethics* 36(1), 95–118.

Society for Health and Human Values—Society for Bioethics Consultation, Task Force on Standards for Bioethics Consultation (1998). *Core competencies for health care ethics consultation: the report of the American Society for Bioethics and Humanities*. Glenview: American Society for Bioethics and Humanities.

77

CLERGY ETHICS AND THE PROFESSIONAL ETHICS MODEL

Paul F. Camenisch

... IN ORDER TO ASSESS THE PROFESSIONAL ETHICS model as a tool for "doing" clergy ethics, we will first have to establish what we mean by "profession," whether the clergy is indeed a profession, and what the professional ethics model is. We will then have to weigh the considerations that support and those that challenge the application of that model to clergy ethics.

There are at least two distinguishable but finally inseparable ways to approach our first two questions. One is predominantly historical and descriptive; the other is predominantly contemporary and analytical. The first looks at the development and interaction of the two realities that concern us—the clergy and the concept of a profession—over a period of time, to see how they were linked by observers and by the clergy themselves. Given that across time the two entities will vary, a clear and unequivocal verdict about their relation is hardly to be expected from history. At the same time, the greater complexity of history and its ambiguous answer are crucial checks on the possible abstractness of the second approach.

The second approach is contemporary in that it examines the clergy in its current form and situation. It is analytical in that it begins its examination of the question of the professional standing of the clergy by stating as precisely as possible what we mean by "profession."

One question any critical historical approach must be aware of is whether the concept of the profession to be applied to the changing forms of the clergy is to be the understanding of "profession" that prevailed during the period being studied, or whether it is a contemporary understanding of profession being projected back into an earlier time. Both approaches have their uses. The major mistake would not be to choose the wrong approach, but to be unaware of the differences between the two approaches and between the kinds of information they yield.

In the following brief historical sketch, I will assume a contemporary and rather general understanding of "profession" that I believe to be widely, although not universally, shared. Although this understanding of profession will be elaborated later in the contemporary/analytical section, for the moment it can be summarized as follows: a profession is an organized group (a) whose members possess specialized skills and knowledge widely believed to be useful, even crucial, in the pursuit of highly valued conditions or states of affairs such as justice, health, and spiritual well-being; (b) who have certain kinds of control over their professional work; and (c) who usually claim to be, and are expected to be, motivated in their professional activities by more than personal gain.

THE HISTORICAL APPROACH

It is clear not only that the clergy in America have not always conformed to the professional model, but that other models have also helped shape it. Martin Marty suggests:

> Three broad, chronologically sequential yet overlapping and not displacing forms of the clergy profession ... emerged in the United States. First, from 1492 to the 1830s, the ministry can be seen chiefly as a *public* role in a congregational-territorial context, its soil being that of church establishment. The second period remembers the public dimension but produces a new professional context, the *congregational-denominational*. It remains strong and institutionally it even dominates, but cultural shifts have worked to produce a third model. This one took shape during the rise of other professions in America, and builds on the congregational-denominational. The emergent accent for the past century at least has been toward the *private clientele* setting and expression.

(Marty, 1988, 76–77)

The current professional model was least influential in the early centuries of America's history, with significant changes becoming evident in the early 1800s. For this early period, our best evidence comes from Donald M. Scott's study of "the New England-based and derived Congregational-Presbyterian ministry" (Scott 1978, xiii). Scott acknowledges that the image or model on which he focuses, that of "clerical public guardianship," was most fully developed among Congregational ministers during the period of establishment (xiii). No such limited group can adequately represent the great variety of American clergy from the 1700s to the present. However, the importance of New England in the nation's early history and of Congregationalism in its early religious history suggest that this group's experience may well reveal dynamics crucial to the clergy of other denominations and faiths, of other regions and times.

During this early period, the Congregational minister of New England was not just a religious leader serving a congregation of believing, practicing Christians. Because of the establishment of the Congregational church and because of the role of religion and theology in the total life of the community, he was as much the holder of a public office as the church in which he preached was a public building for nonreligious as well as for religious assembly....

But whatever seeds of the future professionalization of the clergy can be found in those early stages of American ecclesiastical history, and whatever dynamics were at work there to bring those seeds to maturity, the church—including both lay people and clergy—was also part of the larger society and subject to the forces shaping its evolution. Burton J. Bledsuasius has persuasively argued that a number of such forces at work in American culture from early on led predictably, perhaps almost inevitably, to the professionalization of practically everybody. At work here were simple and immediate human drives such as the desire to better one's situation in a social hierarchy strikingly flattened and open compared with that of Europe. Professional training and the subsequent rise in status were the most accessible ways of achieving this, which accounts for the humble origins of many early ministers.

But also at work here, according the Bledstein, were deeper, more complex drives: "Mid-Victorians would structure life, its space, its words, its time, and its activities. And professionalism with its cultural rituals, ceremonies and symbols satisfied this need" (Bledstein 1976, 105). This national trend toward professionalization can be seen in a number of developments but probably most indicative of what happened during the 1800s to theology, law, medicine, dentistry, pharmacy, and veterinary medicine is the growth in the number of professional schools. During the period of 1801–1825 there were thirty-five such schools, with eighteen of them being theological and twelve being medical. During the following three-quarters of a century, the total number moved up so that by 1900 it had reached 283. Although divinity, or theology, had led the way in numbers until 1875, by 1900 it was only 47 of the total 283, being exceeded by medicine (86) and law (50), and equaled by dentistry (Bledstein 1976, 84).

Although such general trends were evident in the larger society and by no means left the clergy untouched, there were also developments peculiar to the clergy that pushed it closer to the professional model as currently understood. One of these was the shifting, we might even say the declining, role of religion and church in the society itself, which tended to diminish the role of the minister as public officer. But there were also more positive developments that pulled the clergy toward the professional model. These had to do primarily with the emergence of causes or campaigns to which the clergy felt called, but which clearly transcended the local parishes from which they had hitherto drawn their standing and authority. The two major such causes in the experience of the New England clergy studied by Scott were the abolition of slavery and the evangelization of the country (Scott 1978, chaps. 4, 5). Once ministers began seeing their calling in terms of such translocal movements, and seeing themselves as having responsibilities and audiences larger than their local parishes, they predictably thought increasingly in terms of their connections with professional colleagues with whom they took up these new and larger battles. Some such coming together of increasingly "professional" colleagues happened in emerging denominational structures, and some through the various voluntary associations founded to further those larger causes now competing for clerical attention....

THE ANALYTICAL APPROACH

The second approach to our question of the professional status of the clergy is the analytical and contemporary one, which begins with the attempt to state as clearly as possible what we mean by "profession." In the absence of a universally accepted definition of a profession, I suggest that full-fledged professions are distinguished by four characteristics (Camenisch 1983, chap. 2).

The question of how many of these characteristics an occupational group must exhibit to be a profession, and whether they must be exhibited in precisely the form specified here, seeks a precision that current usage will not sustain.

1. Members of a profession are distinguished by the possession of *specialized skills and knowledge* not possessed by the population at large. These skills and knowledge currently are almost invariably acquired by extended formal education and rest on a theoretical base also known to the professional. Knowledge of the theory enables the professional to apply such skills and knowledge in novel situations.

2. A profession and its member enjoy *professional autonomy*, which encompasses both self-governance, or regulation, and liberty of professional action. Such autonomy is seen in (a) the profession's general insulation from assessment of its professional performance by any but members of that profession (that is, insulation from lay assessment); (b) the profession's control over the preparation and admission to the profession of new members; (c) the profession's power, whether exercised or not, of continuing oversight of its members and their professional activities; and (d) the right to admit to and expel from membership. This autonomy is established and protected by the larger society through legal statute, usually in the form of licensure or certification laws, and sometimes results in a legally enforced monopoly in some areas of professional activity.

3. A profession pursues with and on behalf of its clients and/or the larger society *a distinctive goal* that may involve the use of products and which includes services, but that is essentially a state of affairs (health, justice, knowledge, spiritual health) generally highly valued by the client and by the larger society and is widely seen as linked to our fullest well-being as human beings. This state of affairs often needs to be established or protected in crisis situations and is such that the client is usually unable, or at best is questionably able, to attain alone.

4. Finally, professions and professionals have traditionally exhibited, and at their best are still expected to exhibit, in their professional activity an *atypical moral commitment* to the interests and well-being of the client, and possibly to those of the larger society as those interests relate to the distinctive goal of that profession, a commitment that we do not normally expect of other economic agents and that may on occasion be in tension with the professional's own self-interest.

Status, power, and income level have not been mentioned because these are derivative and are not essential to what it means to be a professional....

This brings us to the question of whether the clergy constitutes a profession as defined (Camenisch 1985). Our brief historical excursion above has already given us some sketchy data on this matter. But given that we now wish to address the question head-on, it will be most helpful to approach it on the basis of the above characteristics. Clearly, many clergy do have specialized skills and knowledge acquired during extended formal education, which do rest on a kind of theoretical base that the well-prepared clergyperson has mastered.

However, three qualifications must be added: Although some specialized skills and knowledge can often rightfully be claimed, many clergy, especially those holding a congregational charge alone, find they are expected to be a jack-of-all-trades, including properly clerical, but also administrative, counseling, financial, managerial, and other more general kinds of tasks. This situation breaks down the rather sharp focus professional activity usually aspires to and can undercut the clergy's sense of being practitioners in a specialized, professional field....

This brings us to the question of distinctive and highly valued goal of professional activity that distinguishes other professions and that helps determine the content of each profession's distinctive ethos and ethics. Can the clergy lay claim to such a goal? Often the purpose of the clergy is presented as identical to that of the religious community it serves. For our present purposes I will let that equation stand. I assume that the religious community and its leaders, the clergy, can indeed claim to have such a goal, even if it is not universally recognized or valued....

PROFESSIONAL STANDING OF CLERGY

The above observations lead to no clear, easy verdict concerning the professional standing of the clergy nor to the related question of the appropriateness of the professional ethics model for doing clergy ethics. A brief summary of the relation of the clergy to the suggested professional model will lay the groundwork for addressing this second question. Counting against professional standing for the clergy are (a) the variation—among different religious traditions and the denominations within them—in requirements for admission to the clergy; (b) the resulting absence of a comprehensive and reasonably homogeneous professional community bridging these lines between traditions and denominations to establish and enforce professional standards for clergy; and (c) membership in the clergy being granted by a number of discrete limited communities and not by the larger society. Complicating the clergy's professional standing by at least making it a distinctive profession is the clergy's claim to be in the service of some transcendent reality or set of norms, which may on occasion rightly claim precedence over all other claims upon the clergy, including any deriving from professional considerations.

It is increasingly clear that we cannot answer the question of the professional standing of the clergy definitionally, that is, by a careful examination of the definition of "profession" followed by an equally careful examination of the characteristics of the clergy to see if they qualify. This approach is defeated by the imprecision and variety of definitions of "profession" and by the variety of the clergy themselves....

CONCLUSION

What can we conclude about the appropriateness and helpfulness of the professional ethics model for use in clergy ethics? There is no simple answer. I have suggested that both the concept of "profession," or "professional," and the derivative idea of professional ethics are constellations of factors. There are enough similarities between the clergy as generally perceived and the professions as defined above, that to some extent the clergy can usefully be seen as a profession. On the other hand, there are enough divergences between the two to caution us against subsuming the clergy completely under that model. The similarities are seen in that the clergy generally claim to have and are expected to have skills and knowledge not possessed by most laypersons; that they do aim in their professional activity at a distinctive sort of goal for clients or the society as a whole (or at least the community of faith) that is seen by many as essential to human well-being; and that they claim to have an atypical moral commitment to those they serve. Needless to say, they probably fall short of the ideal performance on all these matters with roughly the same frequency as do other professions. But that is not the question here....

REFERENCES

Bledstein, Burton J. 1976. *The Culture of Professionalism: The Middle Class and the Development of Higher Education in America*. New York: W.W. Norton.

——. 1985. "Are Pastors Professionals?" *The Christian Ministry* 16, no. 4 (July): 12–13.

Camenisch, Paul F. 1983. *Grounding Professional Ethics in a Pluralistic Society*. New York: Haven Publications.

Marty, Martin E. 1988. "The Clergy." In *The Professions in America*, edited by Nathan O. Hatch. Notre Dame, Ind.: University of Notre Dame Press.

Scott, Donald M. 1978. *From Office to Profession: The New England Ministry 1750–1850*. Philadelphia: University of Pennsylvania Press.

MY LAI MASSACRE

Just Following Orders

T.J. Broy

1. BACKGROUND

ON MARCH 16, 1968 US ARMY CAPTAIN ERNEST Medina led his infantry company to the Vietnamese hamlet of My Lai as part of an operation to find and destroy a Vietcong battalion operating in the area. When the company arrived at My Lai, they did not find any Vietcong, instead they found a village full of women, children, and the elderly. When the soldiers began sweeping the area, they killed everyone they came across. By the end of the day, between 347 and 504 Vietnamese civilians had been killed.[1] Of these, 50 were younger than 3 years old and 210 were younger than 12. The killing only stopped when Warrant Officer Hugh Thompson landed his helicopter between the American soldiers and the Vietnamese civilians and warned the Americans that his helicopter's gunner would open fire if they threatened any more civilians.[2]

The story of the My Lai massacre begins before any soldiers had entered the village. Captain Medina's briefing to the company before the mission left many soldiers believing their orders were to kill everyone in the village. One private, Dennis Bunning, reported that Captain Medina had explicitly ordered the men to kill everyone while another, James Bergthold, reported that while Medina had not ordered the company to kill everyone in the village, many soldiers came away from the briefing with that belief. The company had faced heavy losses in the weeks before the massacre. On March 15 a memorial service was held

for a sergeant who had died from a Vietcong booby trap. Captain Medina explained during his briefing that the company had to be aggressive in defeating the Vietcong in order to avoid future casualties. This mission was an opportunity "to avenge their fallen comrades."[3]

Central to the events of the massacre was Lieutenant William Calley who commanded the company's first platoon. Upon entering the village, Calley found two privates guarding civilians whom they had detained. Calley ordered the privates to "take care of them." When Calley found other members of the company at a drainage ditch guarding more than 50 civilians, he ordered his men to shoot the Vietnamese civilians. When Warrant Officer Thompson landed his helicopter and stopped the killing, it was Lieutenant Calley whom he confronted.

After the massacre, Thompson reported the events to his superiors. Captain Medina and others lied about the events that took place at My Lai and attempted to cover up the massacre. The general in charge of the division never insisted on an accurate count of civilian deaths at My Lai. It wasn't until a year and a half later that a whistleblower named Ronald Ridenhour wrote letters to the White House, Pentagon, State Department, and members of Congress, which included details of the massacre, that an Army investigation was launched. The public became aware of the events months later when journalist Seymour Hersh wrote an article detailing the events.[4] Lieutenant Calley was the only person involved with the massacre who was convicted. He served three years under house arrest and was released in 1975. In 2009, when speaking about his actions, Calley said, "If you are asking why I did not stand up to them when I was given the orders, I will have to say that I was a second lieutenant getting orders from my commander and I followed them—foolishly, I guess."[5]

2. ANALYSIS

When offering an ethical analysis of the My Lai massacre, we are faced with a different set of questions than we might be faced with when analyzing other cases. Rather than trying to determine how one ought to act in a given case or who was in the wrong in a given case, the most pressing questions in the My Lai case regard who is to blame for what went wrong and how the relationship between professionals and the institutions in which they serve impacts our moral judgments.

Given that soldiers operate within the structure of the army, one might think blame can be mitigated by appeal to the chain of command. If it is true that soldiers were "just following orders," that might make a soldier less responsible for his conduct. Because of the strict control superiors have over those under their command, there is a special tension when orders are given that might be morally blameworthy to follow. Furthermore, when orders are not clear it can lead to misunderstanding, with terrible results. Reports of the briefing before the mission to My Lai disagree as to how explicit Captain Medina's orders were. If the massacre were the result of miscommunication, this would provide for a particularly institutional dimension of the tragedy.

A further dimension of analysis follows from trying to determine the ways in which institutional structures influenced the events at My Lai. Many of the officers serving in the company were inexperienced. More experienced officers did not deploy to Vietnam with the company because of army regulations regarding how long a soldier must wait between deployments. The hierarchical structure of the army put special pressure on officers to hide the massacre. Because superior officers were trying to gain promotion and did not want to be seen as complicit in a tragedy like that at My Lai, they were happy to be complicit in the cover up that followed it. The general in command of the division made sure to emphasize the rules of engagement, but did nothing to follow up on reports of the massacre, thereby allowing the officers in charge of the mission to perpetrate the cover up.

NOTES

1   Christopher J. Levesque, "The Truth Behind My Lai," *The New York Times*, 16 March 2018, https://www.nytimes.com/2018/03/16/opinion/the-truth-behind-my-lai.html.

2   Jon Wiener, "A Forgotten Hero Stopped the My Lai Massacre 50 Years Ago Today," *Los Angeles Times*, 16 March 2018, https://www.latimes.com/opinion/op-ed/la-oe-wiener-my-lai-hugh-thompson-20180316-story.html.

3   Levesque, "The Truth Behind My Lai."

4   Ian Shapira, "'It was insanity': At My Lai, U.S. Soldiers Slaughtered Hundreds of Vietnamese Women and Kids," *The Washington Post*, 16 March 2018, https://www.washingtonpost.com/news/retropolis/wp/2018/03/16/it-was-insanity-at-my-lai-u-s-soldiers-slaughtered-hundreds-of-vietnamese-women-and-kids.

5   Associated Press, "Calley Apologizes for Role in My Lai Massacre," last updated 21 August 2009, http://www.nbcnews.com/id/32514139/ns/us_news-military/t/calley-apologizes-role-my-lai-massacre#.XCpfyVVKiUk.

DISCUSSION QUESTIONS

1. How should blame for the My Lai massacre be apportioned? Is the general commanding the division more responsible than the privates firing the weapons?

2. How might institutional structures have been different to avoid something like the My Lai massacre taking place?

3. Are soldiers who commit immoral acts under orders from their superiors less blameworthy because they were ordered to do it? When should a soldier refuse such an order?

4. Is the institution of the army more blameworthy because a cover up took place? Would the institution still be to blame if the soldiers who carried out the massacre were immediately held accountable?

CHURCH SEX ABUSE

T.J. Broy

1. BACKGROUND

THOUSANDS OF CASES FROM ACROSS THE WORLD have come to light since, in 2002, reporters at *The Boston Globe* published their reports of sexual abuse of children by priests in Boston-area churches. Recently, thousands of more cases have come to light in Pennsylvania after a report by the state attorney general was made public. Of particular concern is the institutional nature of the abuse.

As the Pennsylvania attorney general's report shows, the institution of the Church was heavily involved in these abuse cases. More than 1,000 children were abused by more than 300 priests over the course of the past 70 years in six Pennsylvania dioceses. Priests who abused children were frequently shuffled from one parish to another in order to avoid detection. This was done without alerting parishioners or civil authorities.[1] Catholic officials have also been slow to identify priests with credible allegations against them. A recent report by the Illinois attorney general found that only 185 of the 690 priests subject to credible allegations had been publicly identified by the Catholic Church.[2]

Most of the sexual abuse cases involving priests that have been investigated have been investigated by the Catholic Church itself. Commissions and committees have been formed at various levels of the Catholic hierarchy in order to investigate allegations of abuse. That the Catholic Church has investigated most of these cases internally has left many victims without legal recourse. Because many of these cases did not come to light for decades following the abuse, the statute of limitations has ensured priests will not face prosecution for their crimes. The Church has been slow to institute reforms; for example, a 2015 proposal to form a tribunal to oversee bishops was unsuccessful. What reforms have been instituted have been enforced unequally across dioceses.

2. ANALYSIS

That adults abuse children is a terrible fact about the world. It adds to the horror of these situations when adults in positions of power and trust use their positions to victimize children. This is made even worse when the institutions responsible for putting these adults in positions of power and trust are complicit in the abuse. Rather than protecting the children who had been entrusted to the Catholic Church's care, Church authorities protected their abusers and facilitated the abuse of more children. By moving abusive priests to new parishes without any word to civil authorities or the parishioners, the Church empowered those priests to continue their abuse of children.

There are at least two areas of analysis that stem directly from the institutional nature of the abuse. First, we can ask what the role of the institution was in perpetrating the harms. Relevant considerations here include how Church authorities moved priests between parishes along with how the Church handled the aftermath of the abuse. By only using internal investigations in response to the abuse allegations, the Church did further harm to victims by allowing the statute of limitations to expire. This means that abusive priests cannot be tried for their crimes and, in some cases, victims cannot sue to recover damages against the priest who abused them.

Second, we can ask how the involvement of the institution impacts available responses to the abuse. For example, many are critical of the internal investigators that the Church employed, because they had loyalties to the institution of the Church, putting them in a compromised position. The Church's investigators were pressured to downplay or dismiss both the existence and severity of abuse. This conflict of interest makes it difficult for a reputable investigation to be carried out from within the institution of the Church.

Matters are further complicated by considerations of guilt and punishment. An individual who commits sexual assault can be held accountable by being held criminally liable. How can an institution be held accountable? Where an abusive priest can be fined or imprisoned, there are not similar mechanisms for holding the Church responsible. The Catholic Church is too large for any fine to be punitive and the institutional nature of the harm makes it so that there is no one person to be imprisoned for the institutional harms inflicted on the victims.

NOTES

1   Daniel Burke, "'How Could This Happen Again?' Why This Catholic Abuse Scandal Seems Worse than 2002," 20 August 2018, https://www.cnn. com/2018/08/19/us/catholic-sex-abuse-outrage/index.html.

2   Elvia Malagon, "More Than 500 Priests Accused of Sexual Abuse Not yet Publicly Identified by Catholic Church, Illinois Attorney General Finds," *Chicago Tribune*, 20 December 2018, https://www.chicagotribune.com/news/local/breaking/ct-met-illinois-attorney-general-catholic-priest-abuse-20181219-story.html.

DISCUSSION QUESTIONS

1. How should blame be apportioned for cases of abuse by Catholic priests? Is the Church itself responsible? Why or why not?

2. What remedies are there for the harm done to the abuse victims? How might we hold the institution accountable for the harm it inflicts?

3. Does the institutional nature of the crime affect the severity of the wrong? Is it worse that a priest within the Catholic Church commits abuse than that an individual commits the same crime? Why or why not?

4. How should institutions like the Catholic Church be reformed so as to prevent these sorts of abuses from happening in the future? What is the role of an institution like the Church in instituting these reforms? Should the Church be allowed to reform itself or should reform be imposed by government authorities?

PERMISSIONS ACKNOWLEDGMENTS

Adler, Jonathan E. From "Lying, Deceiving, or Falsely Implicating," *Journal of Philosophy* 94.9 (1997): 435–52. Reproduced with permission.

Allhoff, Fritz, and Jonathan Milgrim. Adapted from "Conflicts of Interest, Emoluments, and the Presidency," *International Journal of Applied Philosophy* 31.1 (2017): 45–67. DOI: 10.5840/ijap201771082. Reproduced with permission.

Allhoff, Hans. "Willful Ignorance and the Limits of Advocacy." Reproduced with permission.

Anderson, John. From "Sophie's Choice," *Southern Journal of Philosophy* 35.4 (1997): 439–50. Republished with permission of John Wiley and Sons, Inc. Permission conveyed through Copyright Clearance Center, Inc.

Armstrong, Mary Beth. From "Confidentiality: A Comparison across the Professions of Medicine, Engineering and Accounting," *Professional Ethics: A Multidisciplinary Journal* 3.1 (1994): 71–88. DOI: 10.5840/profethics1994314. Reproduced with permission.

Audi, Robert. From the Introduction to "Some Approaches to Determining Ethical Obligations," in *Honest Work: A Business Ethics Reader*, 3rd ed., edited by Joanne B. Ciulla et al. Oxford University Press, 2013. Reproduced with permission of the Licensor through PLSclear.

Bayles, Michael D. From *Professional Ethics*, 2nd ed. Copyright © 1989 South-Western, a part of Cengage, Inc. www.cengage.com/permissions.

Bok, Sissela. From *Secrets: On the Ethics of Concealment and Revelation*. Copyright © 1982 by Sissela Bok. Used by permission of Pantheon Books, an imprint of the Knopf Doubleday Publishing Group, a division of Penguin Random House LLC. All rights reserved.

Boon, Andrew, and John Flood. From "Globalization of Professional Ethics? The Significance of Lawyers' International Codes of Conduct," *Legal Ethics* 2.1 (1999): 29–57. Adapted by permission of the authors.

Brecher, Bob. From "Against Professional Ethics," *Philosophy of Management* 4.2 (2004): 3–8. Copyright © 2004, Springer International Publishing AG. Reprinted by permission of Springer Nature Customer Service Centre GmbH.

Brinkman, Bo. From "An Analysis of Student Privacy Rights in the Use of Plagiarism Detection Systems," *Science and Engineering Ethics* 19.3 (2013): 1255–66. Copyright © 2012, Springer Science Business Media B.V. Reprinted by permission from Springer Nature Customer Service Centre GmbH.

Caminsch, Paul F. From "Clergy Ethics and the Professional Ethics Model," in *Clergy Ethics in a Changing Society*, edited by James P. Wind. Westminster John Knox Press, 1991, 114–34. Reproduced with permission.

Cath, Yuri. From "Reflective Equilibrium," in *The Oxford Handbook of Philosophical Methodology*, edited by Herman Cappelen et al. Oxford University Press, 2016. Copyright © 2016 Yuri Cath. Reproduced with permission of the Licensor through PLSclear.

Chesley, G.R., and Bruce Anderson. From "Are University Professors Qualified to Teach Ethics?" *Journal of Academic Ethics* 1.2 (2003): 217–19. Copyright © 2003, Kluwer Academic Publishers. Reprinted by permission of Springer Nature Customer Service Centre GmbH.

Ciulla, Joanne B. From "Leadership Ethics: Mapping the Territory," *Business Ethics Quarterly* 5.1 (1995): 5–28. Copyright © Society for Business Ethics 1995. Adapted by permission of the author.

Clements, Curtis E.,et al. From "The Impact of Cultural Differences on the Convergence of International Accounting Codes of Ethics," *Journal of Business Ethics* 90.3 Supplement (2009): 383–91. Copyright © 2010, Springer Science Business Media B.V. Reprinted by permission of Springer Nature Customer Service Centre GmbH.

Coleman, Stephen. From "Conflict of Interest and Police: An Unavoidable Problem," *Criminal Justice Ethics* 3 (Summer/Fall 2005): 3–11. Copyright © John Jay College of Criminal Justice of The City University of New York. Reprinted by permission of Informa UK Limited, trading as Taylor & Francis Group, www.tandfonline.com on behalf of John Jay College of Criminal Justice of The City University of New York.

Cook, Patricia. From "A Profession Like No Other" in *Routledge Handbook of Military Ethics*, edited by George Lucas. Copyright © 2015 Patricia Cook. Republished with permission of Routledge/Taylor and Francis, a division of Informa PLC. Permission conveyed through Copyright Clearance Center, Inc.

Corvino, John. From "Under God's Authority: Professional Responsibility, Religious Accommodations, and the Culture Wars," in *Ethics Across the Professions*, 2nd ed., edited by Clancy Martin et al. Oxford University Press, 2017. Copyright © 2017 by John Corvino. Reprinted with the permission of the author.

Davis, Michael. From "Conflict of Interest Revisited," *Business and Professional Ethics Journal* 12.4 (1993): 21–41. DOI: 10.5840/bpej19931243. Reproduced with permission. From "Professional Responsibility: Just Following the Rules?" *Business and Professional Ethics Journal* 18.1 (1999): 65–87. DOI: 10.5840/bpej19991811. Reproduced with permission. From "Is There a Profession of Engineering?" *Science and Engineering Ethics* 3.4 (1997): 407–28. Copyright © 1997, Opragen Publications. Reprinted by permission from Springer Nature Customer Service Centre GmbH.

Detmer, David. From "The Ethical Responsibilities of Journalists." Copyright © David Detmer. Reproduced with permission.

Donaldson, Thomas. From "Values in Tension: Ethics Away from Home," *Harvard Business Review* 74.5 (1996): 48–58. Reproduced with permission.

Dworkin, Ronald. From "Why Bakke Has No Case," in *The New York Review of Books*. Copyright © 1977 by Ronald Dworkin. Reproduced with permission.

Eriksen, Andreas. From "What Is Professional Integrity?" *Etikk i praksis (Nordic Journal of Applied Ethics)* 9.2 (2015): 3–17. Copyright © 2015 Andreas Eriksen. https://doi.org/10.5324/eip.v9i2.1836.

Fisher, Josie. From "Social Responsibility and Ethics: Clarifying the Concepts," *Journal of Business Ethics* 52.4 (2004): 391–400. Copyright © 2004, Kluwer Academic Publishers. Reprinted by permission from Springer Nature Customer Service Centre GmbH.

Fitzpatrick, Kathy, and Candace Gauthier. From "Toward a Professional Responsibility Theory of Public Relations Ethics," *Journal of Mass Media Ethics* 16.2/3 (2001): 193–212. Copyright © 2001, Lawrence Erlbaum Associates, Inc. Reprinted by permission of Taylor & Francis Ltd., http://www.tandfonline.com.

Flanagan, Caitlyn. "The Problem with HR," *The Atlantic*, July 2019. Copyright © 2019, The Atlantic Monthly Group, LLC. All rights reserved. Used under license.

Fourie, Carina, et al. From "The Nature and Distinctiveness of Social Equity: An Introduction," in *Social Equality: On What It Means to Be Equals*, edited by Carina Fourie et al. Copyright © Oxford University Press, 2015. Reproduced with permission of the Licensor through PLSclear.

Frankfurt, Harry. From "On Truth, Lies, and Bullshit," in *The Philosophy of Deception*, edited by Clancy Martin. Copyright © 2009 by Oxford University Press, Inc. Reproduced with permission of the Licensor through PLSclear.

Geronemus, David. From "Lies, Damn Lies, and Unethical Lies: How to Negotiate Ethically and Effectively," *Business Law Today* 6.5 (1997): 10–17. Reproduced with permission.

Glasser, Theodore L. From "Objectivity Precludes Responsibility," *The Quill* (February 1984): 13–16. Reproduced with permission.

Gowthorpe, Catherine, and Oriol Amat. From "Creative Accounting: Some Ethical Issues of Macro- and Micro-Manipulation," *Journal of Business Ethics* 57.1 (2005): 55–64. Copyright © 2005, Springer. Reprinted by permission from Springer Nature Customer Service Centre GmbH.

Grace, Pamela. From "Nursing as a Profession," in *Nursing Ethics and Professional Responsibility in Advanced Practice*, 3rd ed. Jones and Bartlett

Learning, 2018. Copyright © 2018 John Wiley & Sons Ltd. Adapted by permission of the publisher.

Greenwood, Ernest. From "Attributes of a Profession," *Social Work* 2.3 (July 1957): 45–55. Copyright © 1957, Oxford University Press. Adapted by permission of Oxford University Press.

Held, Virginia. From "The Ethics of Care as a Moral Theory," in *The Ethics of Care: Personal, Political, and Global.* Copyright © 2006, Oxford University Press, Inc. Reproduced with permission of the Licensor through PLSclear.

Hemphill, Thomas A., and Waheeda Lillevik. From "U.S. Pharmacists, Pharmacies, and Emergency Contraception: Walking the Business Ethics Tightrope," *Business and Professional Ethics Journal* 25.1/4 (2006): 39–66. DOI: 10.5840/ bpej2006251/43. Reproduced with permission.

Irmak, Nurbay. From "Professional Ethics in Extreme Circumstances: Responsibilities of Attending Physicians and Healthcare Providers in Hunger Strikes," *Theoretical Medicine and Bioethics* 36.4 (2015): 249–63. Copyright © 2015, Springer Science Business Media Dordrecht. Reprinted by permission from Springer Nature Customer Service Centre GmbH.

Kipnis, Kenneth. From "Ethics and the Professional Responsibility of Lawyers," *Journal of Business Ethics* 10.8 (1991): 569–76. Copyright © 1991, Kluwer Academic Publishers. Reprinted by permission from Springer Nature Customer Service Centre GmbH. From "A Defense of Unqualified Medical Confidentiality," in *Economic Justice: Private Rights and Public Responsibilities.* Rowman and Allanheld, 1985. From "The Certified Clinical Ethics Consultant," *HEC Forum* 21.3 (2009): 249–61. Copyright © 2009, Springer Science Business Media B.V. Reprinted by permission from Springer Nature Customer Service Centre GmbH.

Koehn, Daryl. From "What Can Eastern Philosophy Teach Us about Business Ethics?" *Journal of Business Ethics* 19.1 (1999): 71–79. Copyright © 1999, Kluwer Academic Publishers. Reprinted by permission from Springer Nature Customer Service Centre GmbH.

Kolers, Avery. From "Am I My Professions Keeper?" *Bioethics* 28.1 (2014): 1–7. Copyright © 2013 John Wiley & Sons Ltd. Adapted by permission of John Wiley & Sons Inc.

Landesman, Bruce M. From "Confidentiality and the Lawyer-Client Relationship," *Utah Law Review* 4 (1980): 765–86. Reproduced with permission.

Lau, Joanne. "The West Gate Bridge: Who Was Responsible?" Reproduced with permission.

Lichtenberg, Judith. From "Truth, Neutrality, and Conflict of Interest," *Business and Professional Ethics Journal* 9.1/2 (1990): 65–78. DOI: 10.5840/ bpej199091/29. Reproduced with permission.

Luebke, Neil R. From "Conflict of Interest as a Moral Category," *Business and Professional Ethics Journal* 6.1 (1987): 66–81. DOI: 10.5840/bpej1987617. Reproduced with permission. From "Conflict of Interest in Engineering," in *Conflict of Interest in the Professions*, edited by Michael Davis and Andrew Stark. Copyright © 2001 by Oxford University Press. Reproduced with permission of the Licensor through PLSclear.

Lurie, Yotam, and Shlomo Mark. From "Professional Ethics of Software Engineers: An Ethical Framework," *Science and Engineering Ethics* 22.2 (2016): 417–34. Copyright © 2015, Springer Science Business Media Dordrecht. Reprinted by permission from Springer Nature Customer Service Centre GmbH.

McCoy, Bowen H. From "The Parable of the Sadhu," *Harvard Business Review* (1997): 1–7. Reproduced with permission.

Melé, Domènec. From "Ethical Education in Accounting: Integrating Rules, Values, and Virtues," *Journal of Business Ethics* 57.1 (2005): 97–109. Copyright © 2005, Springer. Reprinted by permission from Springer Nature Customer Service Centre GmbH.

Merry, Michael S. From "Should Educators Accommodate Intolerance? Mark Halstead, Homosexuality, and the Islamic Case," *Journal of Moral Education* 34.1 (2005): 19–36. Copyright © Journal of Moral Education Ltd. Reprinted by permission of Informa UK Limited, trading as

Taylor & Francis Group, www.tandfonline.com, on behalf of Journal of Moral Education Ltd.

Metz, Thaddeus. From "Toward an African Moral Theory," *Journal of Political Philosophy* 15.3 (2007): 321–41. Republished with the permission of John Wiley and Sons, Inc. Permission conveyed through Copyright Clearance Center, Inc.

Miller, Seumas. From "Police Ethics," in *International Encyclopedia of Ethics*, 2nd ed., edited by Hugh LaFollette. Copyright © 2019 John Wiley & Sons, Ltd. Reproduced with permission.

Moore, Adam D. From "Privacy: Its Meaning and Value," *American Philosophical Quarterly* 40.3 (2003): 215–27. Reproduced with permission.

Mungai, Ndugia wa, Gidraph G. Wairire, and Emma Rush. From "The Challenges of Maintaining Social Work in Kenya," *Ethics and Social Welfare* 8.2 (2014): 170–86. Adapted by permission of the authors.

Nathan, Christopher. From "Liability to Deception and Manipulation," *Journal of Applied Philosophy* 34.3 (2017): 370–88. Copyright © 2017 Christopher Nathan. *Journal of Applied Philosophy* published by John Wiley & Sons Ltd. on behalf of Society for Applied Philosophy. Licensed under the terms of the Creative Commons Attribution License.

Pellegrino, Edmund D. From "The Virtuous Physician and the Ethics of Medicine," in *Virtue and Medicine: Explorations in the Character of Medicine*, edited by Earl Shelp. Copyright © D. Reidel Publishing Company 1985. Used with permission of Springer Nature. Permission conveyed through Copyright Clearance Center, Inc.

Perkins, Michael. From "International Law and the Search for Universal Principles in Journalism Ethics," *Journal of Mass Media Ethics* 17.3 (2002): 193–208. Adapted by permission of Donnette Perkins.

Pizzimenti, Lee A. From "Informing Clients about Limits to Confidentiality," *Business and Professional Ethics Journal* 9.1/2 (1990): 207–22. DOI: 10.5840/bpej199091/24. Reproduced with permission.

Pritchard, Michael. From "Responsible Engineering: The Importance of Character and Imagination,"

Science and Engineering Ethics 7.3 (2001): 391–402. Copyright © 2001, Opragen Publications. Reprinted by permission of Springer Nature Customer Service Centre GmbH.

Quinn, Aaron. "Breaking a Promise to Prevent a Lie," in the Australian Computer Society's 'Computers and Philosophy 2003', *Conferences in Research and Practice in Information Technology*, Volume 37. Reproduced with permission.

Reamer, Fredric G. From "Social Work and Ethics: An Overview," in *Social Work Values and Ethics*, 4th ed. Copyright © 2013 Fredric G. Reamer. Reproduced with permission of Columbia University Press.

Resnik, David B. From "What Is Ethics in Research and Why Is It Important?" in *National Institute of Health*, Research, December 2015. https://www.niehs.nih.gov/research/resources/bioethics/whatis/index.cfm.

Robertson, Lori. From "Ethically Challenged: Plagiarism in Journalism," *American Journalism Review* 23.2 (March 2001): 20–29. Reproduced with permission.

Robinson, Simon. From "The Nature of Responsibility in a Professional Setting," *Journal of Business Ethics* 88.1 (2009): 11–19. Copyright © 2009, Springer Science Business Media B.V. Reprinted by permission of Springer Nature Customer Service Centre GmbH.

Rubinstein, Ira S., and Nathaniel Good. From "Privacy by Design: A Counterfactual Analysis of Google and Facebook Privacy Incidents," *Berkeley Technology Law Journal* 28.2 (2013): 1333–1413. Copyright © 2013 Ira S. Rubinstein & Nathaniel Good. Reproduced with permission of Nathaniel Good.

Sanders, John T. From "Honor among Thieves: Some Reflections on Professional Codes of Ethics," *Professional Ethics* 2.3/4 (1993): 83–103. DOI: 10.5840/profethics199323/411. Reproduced with permission.

Siewert, Wally. "The Schiavo Case and End-of-Life Decisions." Reproduced with permission.

Stark, Andrew. From "Comparing Conflict of Interest across the Professions," in *Conflict of Interest in the Professions*, edited by Michael Davis and Andrew

Stark. Copyright © 2001 by Oxford University Press. Reproduced with permission of the Licensor through PLSclear.

Superson, Anita M. From "A Feminist Definition of Sexual Harassment," *Journal of Social Philosophy* 24.1 (1993): 46–64. Copyright © Wiley Periodicals, Inc. Adapted by permission of John Wiley & Sons, Inc.

Thomasma, David C. From "Telling the Truth to Patients: A Clinical Ethics Exploration," *Cambridge Quarterly of Healthcare Ethics* 3 (Summer 1994): 375–82. Adapted by permission of Doris Thomasma.

Thompson, Dennis F. From "Privacy, Politics, and the Press," *The Harvard International Journal of Press/ Politics* 3.4 (Fall 1998): 103–13. Copyright © 1998, © SAGE Publications. Reprinted by permission of SAGE Publications, Inc.

Weil, Vivian. From "Professional Standards: Can They Shape Practice in an International Context?" *Science and Engineering Ethics* 4.3 (1998): 303–14. Copyright © 1998, Opragen Publications. Reprinted by permission of Springer Nature Customer Service Centre GmbH.

Welch, Don. From "Just Another Day at the Office: The Ordinariness of Professional Ethics," *Professional Ethics* 2.3/4 (1993): 3–14. DOI: 10.5840/ profethics199323/413. Reproduced with permission.

Werhane, Patricia H. From "The Ethics of Insider Trading," *Journal of Business Ethics* 8.11 (1989): 841–45. Copyright © 1989, Kluwer Academic Publishers. Reprinted by permission from Springer Nature Customer Service Centre GmbH.

Wirth, Daniel J. "Earnings and Ethics: Thinking about Enron."

Zhang, Hengli, and Michael Davis. From "Engineering Ethics in China: A Century of Discussion, Organization, and Codes," *Business and Professional Ethics Journal* 37.1 (2018): 105–35. DOI: 10.5840/bpej201821967. Reproduced with permission.

The publisher has made every attempt to locate all copyright holders of the articles and illustrations published in this text and would be grateful for information that would allow correction of any errors or omissions in subsequent editions of the work.

From the Publisher

A name never says it all, but the word "Broadview" expresses
a good deal of the philosophy behind our company. We are
open to a broad range of academic approaches and political
viewpoints. We pay attention to the broad impact book
publishing and book printing has in the wider world; for
some years now we have used 100% recycled paper for most
titles. Our publishing program is internationally oriented and
broad-ranging. Our individual titles often appeal to a broad
readership too; many are of interest as much to general readers
as to academics and students.

Founded in 1985, Broadview remains a fully independent
company owned by its shareholders—not an imprint or
subsidiary of a larger multinational.

For the most accurate information on our books (including
information on pricing, editions, and formats) please visit our
website at www.broadviewpress.com. Our print books and
ebooks are also available for sale on our site.

broadview press

www.broadviewpress.com

This book is made of paper from well-managed FSC® - certified
forests, recycled materials, and other controlled sources.